INDIAN POLITICAL THOUGHT

Urmila Sharma
S. K. Sharma

ATLANTIC
PUBLISHERS & DISTRIBUTORS (P) LTD

ATLANTIC
PUBLISHERS & DISTRIBUTORS (P) LTD
7/22, Ansari Road, Darya Ganj, New Delhi
Tel.: +91-11-4077 5252, 2327 3880
E-mail: orders@atlanticbooks.com
Web: www.atlanticbooks.com

Reprinted in 2026, 2024, 2022, 2020, 2019, 2018, 2011, 2001

Published by Atlantic Publishers & Distributors (P) Ltd.

Printed & bound in India by Atlantic Print Services

Preface

National polity of a country is rooted in its philosophy and culture. Indian Political Thought started from Hindu Polity and gradually developed in the contemporary times by the influence of Western political thought. However, continuing the ancient tradition, Contemporary Indian Political Thought is based upon Neo-Vedanta, a modern version of ancient Vedanta Philosophy. This is not to say that no Indian political thinker developed ideas based on Western political thought. Subhash Chandra Bose, J. L. Nehru and M. N. Roy, to mention only a few, presented political thought based upon a critical analysis of modern Western polity. However, as has been already said, from Manu to Kautilya and M. K. Gandhi the main current of Indian political thought has been based on Neo-Vedanta, characterised by monism, spiritualism, decentralisation, welfare of all, spiritual democracy and world brotherhood.

This book on Indian Political Thought covers University syllabi in Political Science in the papers : Hindu Polity, Indian Political Thought, Modern Indian Political Thought etc. Divided into three parts : The ancient, the modern and contemporary, this book analyses Indian political thought since Manu to M. N. Roy. In order to keep it brief and precise only selected thinkers have been included while those of only historical importance have been left out. The method followed is construction through criticism so that besides knowing the thought of eminent Indian political thinkers, the reader may develop an insight into political processes, their causes and consequences. While matter has been drawn from authentic sources, it has been narrated in simple language. A balanced holistic approach has been maintained in controversial matters.

Thus, the authors have left no stones unturned to make this book an ideal text book for students and reference book for teachers. However, suggestions for improvement will be thankfully acknowledged.

URMILA SHARMA
S. K. SHARMA

Contents

PART I
ANCIENT INDIAN POLITICAL THOUGHT

1
Historical Review

In the history of political thought, Indian political thought represents the East. While China, Japan, Iran and South-East Asian countries have developed rudimentary political thought, India, like ancient Greece, developed a political thought in ancient times which may still be favourably compared with some of the most developed political thoughts in the world. Therefore, the study of Indian political thought is a necessary prelude to understanding Indian political problems. This is particularly important for students and researchers working in Indian society. The researchers from the West and the Indian researchers, looking through the spectacles of the Western political thought, have more than often missed the real spirit of Indian political concepts. It is patently wrong to compare Machiavelli to Chanakya to understand the Indian political philosophy. The current Western concepts cannot be directly applied in the analysis of Indian polity. Indian political thinkers developed their own tools and concepts to understand the political fabric. It is, therefore, necessary to have a background of Indian political thought to understand Indian society and social institutions.

Ancient Indian Political Thought

Ancient Indian political thought has been significantly represented by the Vedas, the Upanishads, and the Bhagwadgita. The political thought found in the great Epics, the Mahabharata and the Ramayana, is more complex and comprehensive. The Manusmriti, along with other Smritis, dealt with every political institution and the entire panorama of human life vertically and horizontally. The vertical perspective led to the concept of the state. The horizontal perspective led to the concept of Dharma. Both these concepts together form the backbone of Indian political thought. Both these concepts were supported equally by philosophy and science. Therefore, it is no wonder that the contemporary Indian political thinkers have unanimously appreciated Raja Dharma as the sound basis of polity.

POLITICAL PHILOSOPHY OF BHAGWAD GITA

The Bhagwad Gita is often referred to as the essence of the Upanishads because the fundamental thought of the latter has been presented in practical and easily communicable form in the Gita. In the Mahabharata, the teaching of the Gita occurs at a significantly humanistic occasion because Arjuna had become puzzled by a conflict of loyalties. In the 18 chapters of the Gita, Sri Krishna advanced various kinds of arguments to convince Arjuna of his duties in accordance with his status in society, and to urge him to fulfil them with detachment towards the result. In order to give forceful justification to his humanistic advice, Sri Krishna indulged in a detailed analysis of man, Nature and God. This analysis is, in essence, rooted in the spiritualism of the Upanishads. Thus, in the Gita also, as in the Upanishads, the relationship of unitariness existing between man, Nature and God has been pronounced. According to the Gita, Man's highest objective is realization of God or consolidation of society. This is a humanistic ideal, and by placing it along with realization of God in the Gita, the highest significance has been attached to it. This ideal is attainable through knowledge, devotion or action. The Gita provides a detailed consideration of each of these paths, as a result of which further commentators concentrated on one or the other and thereby produced independent analyses or critiques of the Gita. But Sri Krishna himself believed that these three paths were identical because they relate to the three aspects of the human personality — cognitive, conative and affective. All the three occupy an equally significant place in human life. In the Gita, the ideal individual is called 'sthitapragya'. His thoughts and actions are described in details in the Gita. This makes it explicit that the Gita supports the integral personality, and that it provides a harmonious blend of hedonism and stoicism, external action and internal peace, activism and renunciation, involvement and detachment, knowledge and devotion, individual freedom and social solidarity.

The concept of social harmony in the Vedas, the Upanishads and the Bhagwad Gita has a metaphysical, a sociological and a psychological aspect. While the metaphysical aspect believes in the unity of man, Nature and God, the sociological aspect is the Varna systems and the psychological aspect is the Ashram system and the ideal of Purusharthas. These three aspects are in fact one, even identical and cannot be separated from one another. Indian philosophy does not differentiate between the metaphysical, the sociological and the psychological aspects of Reality. Its approach is total and integral. The aspects have been distinguished to help the understanding of them. The theory of Karma and rebirth is an elaboration of the Varna system since duties are not confined to human world but form a part of total cosmic fabric and divine purpose.

The Metaphysical Aspect of Society

Like the Vedas and the Upanishads the Gita maintains identity between man, Nature and God. This identity in the form of Brahman is the basis of harmony, integrality and justice in the individual, society and humanity. Jiva is an eternal part of God. Therefore, God realisation is self-realisation. Prakriti is the manifestation of God. He guides Prakriti. The Prakriti of God has two aspects — *Para* and *apara. Apara* or lower Prakrtii includes life, water, air, ether, mind and intellect. These are the material, the physical, the vital and the psychological worlds. The Para Prakriti or higher Nature sustains the limited, embodied soul. The *Apara* Prakriti is unconscious, while the *Para* Prakriti is conscious. Both are God's powers. Hence, ultimately God is the material as well as the efficient cause of the universe. Both man and Nature aim at realisation of divine values. God himself helps man in the realisation of the ideal of harmony. Harmony must win in the end. Social harmony is bound to achieve its aim. The destiny of the individual, however, lies in becoming a successful instrument of this divine purpose.

Varna System as Social Stratification

The Gita has preached the Varnashram Dhrama but the fulfilment of this Dharma becomes a duty only because it has been ordained by God. Krishna, the author of Gita himself asserts, "The four strata of society *(viz.,* the Brahman, the Kshatriya, the Vaisya and the Sudra) were created by Me classifying them according to their prenatal qualities and apportioning corresponding duties to them; though as the author of this creation, know Me the immortal Lord, to be a non-doer." Every man has some native determined duties. He may achieve his personal and social ultimate end by performing these determined actions. The distinctions of traits and actions have been utilized for the stratification of society into four Varnas, *viz.*, Brahman, Kshatriya, Vaisya and Sudra. Sattva abounds in the Brahmanas while rajas overpowers tamas and the reverse is the case with the Sudras. Clarifying the duties of different Varnas the author of Gita say, "Arjuna, the duties of Brahmans, Kshatriya and Vaisyas, as well as of Sudras, are classified according to the qualities born of their respective natures. Control of mind, control of the senses, undergoing hardship for the sake of duty, purity (both internal and external), forgiveness, straightness of mind and body, belief in God, the scriptures and the other world, knowledge of the sacred lore and knowledge of God based on direct experience — these are the Brahman's duties, born of his own nature. Prowess, majesty, Firmness, bravery, ingenuity, not running away from battle, generosity, rulership — these are the Kshatriya's duties, born of his own nature. Cultivation, protection of cows and trade are the Vaisya's duties, born of his own nature. Service of all the three varnas is the Sudra's duty, born of his own nature." Accordingly, the Gita's ethics resembles that of F. H. Bradly in the idea of every person having a particular station to fulfil in society. The only point where they differ is that while Bradley treats self-realisation to be the motivating cause, the Gita considers the aim to be the attainment of God or consolidation of society.

The single most important teaching of Gita is the devotion to one's duties in society. Consolidation in society is a divine purpose. It is the same as God realisation. However, performance of social service and observing one's social duties is better than mere knowledge and devotion. Laying emphasis upon performance of duty or realisation of individual and social harmony, the author of the Gita says, "He from whom is the emanation of all beings, by whom all this prevaded, — by worshipping Him through the performance of his own duty, man attains perfection." Since the Varna Dharma has been prescribed by Divine, no one has a right to swap his duties. According to Gita "Better is one's own duty, thought devoid of merit, than the duty of another well-executed. He, who performs the duty-enjoined by his own nature, does not incur sin."

Ashram System and Purusharthas

As has been already pointed out, Gita believes in Varna Ashram Dharma originated in the Vedas. Besides the Varna system mentioned above, Gita accepts the Vedic Ashram system. The author of the Gita distinguishes between different types of duties peculiar to the Varna, the Ashram, the human nature and the daily cycle of activities. All these duties have to be performed without fail. The Purusharthas have been referred to in the words, "And the firmness by which the man, who seeks the fruit of actions, catches with extreme foundness the first three objects of life, *viz.*, Dharma (Virtue), Artha (Prosperity) and Kama (Pleasure), that firmness, son of Kunti, is Rajasic." Thus, the Gita recommends not only the first three Purusharthas but also the fourth. In fact, the fourth is the aim of the first three. However, the first three are not neglected. What has to be renounced is not action but the attachment to their fruits. In the words of the Gita, "He who neither hates action, which does not lead to happiness, nor is attached to action, which is conducive to good, that person, imbued with the quality of goodness, has attained freedom from doubts : he is wise and a man of true renunciation."

According to Gita the divine order itself fixes the process of time, the destiny, the social duties, the duties of different Varnas and the duties of the individual in day and night and at different occasions. All these duties have been elaborately prescribed by the scriptures. The Gita lays emphasis upon following the scriptures, not because they have been socially approved or sanctioned by the state but because they embody the divine injunctions to men, having faith that whenever the cause of morality suffers, the divine power itself helps the man to maintain the balance. Thus, ultimately, the establishment of social harmony is a must, the man has only to follow it without attachment. It is on this basis that the author of Gita asks Arjuna to follow his duties.

POLITICAL PHILOSOPHY OF MAHABHARATA

Value of Danda

In addition to the Vedas, the Upanishads, the Aranyakas and Brahman texts, the great epics can also be treated as ancient Indian political literature. The two main epics are the Mahabharata and the Ramayana. The Bhagwad Gita is a part of the Mahabharata. In fact, the philosophy of the Mahabharata is crystalized in the Gita. The political philosophy of the Gita is humanist. In the Mahabharata the most important part, from the political viewpoint, is the Shantiparva, in which a theory of punishment is advanced as a political theory or the science of government. In general, Indian thinkers have regarded the power of punishment (Danda) as the chief characteristic of the state, although they have consistently stressed the use of punishment exclusively for public welfare. Temporally, punishment originated earlier than the state. This important realization proves that punishment was universal, that the state was not created to implement it, nor was punishment evolved to make the state functional. This makes it clear that long before the emergence of the state, punishment existed for the purpose of maintaining social organization.

State as Means

According to the Shantiparva in Mahabharata, Vishnu first created a monumental text on life and administration, and then established a king, government and a state. This implies that power should not be used as a means by the state; instead, the state should be considered a means whereby power is concretized so as to help in the maintenance of social organization. In this way, from very ancient times to the present day, the state has always been a means to public welfare in India. Vishnu's text on political science mentioned in the Mahabharata, gives an account not merely of the rules pertaining to governance by the state but also of rules governing relations between states. A study of these rules clarifies the fact that they are inspired by humanist sentiment. Tolerance has been given special significance. According to the Mahabharata, administration is a part of the normal social organization. The duty of the state is to establish the varna-ashrama system. The state should create such an organisation in which every individual should be able to perform the duties appropriate to his status and stage of life. By this time, the brahmins had begun to be treated with special respect within the varna system. Consequently, there were special provisions for the punishment of a person murdering a Brahmin. However, on this subject, discrimination between individuals on varna basis was avoided.

Theory of Origin of the State

In the Vana Parva of the Mahabharata, it has been shown that in the ancient period, the life of people was exceptionally happy and contented. The Shanti Parva also provides a glowing description of the life of the period. However, there came a gradual deterioration in human relations as a result of which the gods felt profound grief, which compelled them to approach the God Vishnu. Vishnu did not want to give supreme authority to any individual. So, with his own power, he brought into existence a king whom he called Virjas. But in the dynasty of Virjas, a corrupt ruler named Vena came to be born. Divine again intervened and took away Vena's power and handed it over to his son who was eager to use the administration for the public weal. The Shanti Parva provides a detailed account of the advice given to Vena's son by gods and seers. In this way, the Mahabharata theory concerning the origin of the state postulates the concept that not merely men but even the gods consider it the king's divine duty to promote the welfare of the populace. If the king fails in this duty, not only men but even the gods consider it necessary to depose him and to replace him with one who is devoted to his fundamental duty.

Harmony in Political Organisation

In the Mahabharata, the greatest importance has been given everywhere to the state, and the people have been directed to show patriotism to the state. The proper functioning of the state and the administration required the mutual cooperation of the brahmins and the kshatriyas. But equally important was the creation of harmonious relations between these two classes on the one hand and the vaisyas and the shudras on the other. In this way, as is the case with the Vedas and the Upanishads, in the Mahabharata, too, harmony or synthesis have been considered important for political organization. All of them support the theory of a welfare state, because its objective is security and happiness. In all these texts, the king's duty is assumed to be the establishment of social harmony, without which he cannot administer the state. The state must create conditions which are conducive to the achievement of the values of dharma, artha and kama.

Decentralisation of Power

The Mahabharata consistently supports the decentralized state. The decentralization of the state's power is a humanist concept which has characterized Indian political thought from ancient times to the present day. In the same way, the humanist principle governed the relations between states also. Although, the thought of gaining victory over other states frequently appears in these texts, the ancient wars were considered normal wars which were characterized by the observance of certain moral rules.

Democracy in Practice

In this way, although the Mahabharata supports autocracy or kingship in the sphere of political thought, in practice this autocracy was not inferior to a democratic organization. In the Shanti Parva, Bhishma has hinted at the various difficulties implicit in a democracy, which indicates that it was because of these difficulties that democracy did not find support. However, harmony between the various organs of the state was considered as the basis of politics, even in a theoretic system, though it is seen often as a characteristic of democracy.

POLITICAL PHILOSOPHY OF RAMAYANA

The Ramayana, like the Mahabharata, provides important insights into social and political thought but these are not as comprehensive as in the case with the Mahabharata. In fact, the vision of an ideal state presented in the Ramayana has been an important aspect of Indian political thinking from ancient times till today, so much so that Mahatma Gandhi, a modern political thinker, used the term 'Ram Rajya' for his conception of the ideal state. The ideal organization of the Ram Rajya has been providing constant inspiration to Indian political thought from the period of the Ramayana till the present day. Valmiki refuted the idea of anarchism and supported order. God is not an anarchist. Even in modern India political thinking, not a single thinker supports anarchism. Hence, Indian political thought has consistently supported the state, but the ideals of the king stated in the Ramayana are democratic ideals, which is made clear from the fact that Rama banished Sita on the basis of the allegations made by a simple washerman. Hence, the advocacy of kingship in the Ramayana is ultimately based on democratic postulates. The state was a means to public welfare, which was the purpose for which it was created, and since human welfare was impossible in a state of anarchy, the political state was considered essential. However, since the basic objective was public welfare, the Ramayana also, like the Mahabharata, evinces the humanist viewpoint in its political thought.

POLITICAL THOUGHT IN THE MANUSMRITI

In the history of Indian political thought, the period succeeding the epic period is the period of the Smritis. In this period, the ancient harmony gradually declined. Social and political laws became more rigid. The Smritis are a collection of these laws. Whereas equality was a feature of the various Varnas in society during the ancient period, in the period of the Smritis, the Brahmins and the Kshatriyas were given greater importance. The most important among these Smritis is the Manusmriti. Its importance from the humanist viewpoint is established by the fact that it is called Manava Dharma Shastra. It provides a detailed analysis of almost every aspect of human life. In addition to psychology, ethics and philosophy, it provides valuable concepts on political science, justice, law and education. The characteristics of dharma elaborated in the second chapter of Manusmriti are the features of varna dharma. The third chapter elaborates the ashrama system. The fourth chapter gives a detailed picture of grihastha ashrama, or the period of domestic life. From the viewpoint of political science, the fifth, sixth, seventh, and eighth chapters are the most important, and even among these, the last two are of special significance.

Duties of the King

In the seventh chapter, Manu indulges in a subtle analysis of the various aspects of the state. First of all, the duties of the king are elaborately discussed. The just king has been praised and the unjust king criticized. According to Manu, the king has been created to protect the varnashrama system. Hence, he has considered in detail the functions as well as the non-functions of the king, along with his qualities and shortcomings. In addition to the king, such other organs of the state as ministers, diplomats or ambassadors, heads of villages, etc., have been considered in detail. The principles underlying the appointment of ministers, and the justice of such considerations have been explained. In addition, the duties of the army generals have also been clarified.

Decentralisation of Power

Manu's elaboration of the duties of the head of a village indicate that he supported decentralization. Each village had a state functionary whose activities were supervised by the ministers.

Ruler of Statecraft

Corrupt officials were subject to severe penalties. There were provisions for collecting taxes from traders and others. Heavy taxation of sculptors was prohibited. The Manusmriti explains the importance of safeguarding the public. The characteristics of a friend, an enemy and an alienated person have been described. The methods and occasions for treaties and wars have been analysed. Detailed rules have been suggested for war. The duties of the king subsequent upon a war have also been considered. Rules concerning the king's diet, his mode of life, etc., have been made explicit. In this way, Manu has provided a very detailed picture of the various aspects of a king's life and duties.

System of Justice

The eighth chapter of Manusmriti provides a detailed analysis of the system of justice. Manu has laid down different forms of punishment for different kinds of criminals belonging to different varnas. He makes provision for judgement on criminal action by the Brahmins in the absence of the king. The duty of the state towards immoral women has been specified. A detailed system of punishment has been made explicit for such crimes as theft, looting, rape, cheating in trade, etc. There is provision for different forms of punishment for person of different castes committing the same crimes because according to Manu's system, the duties of a person in society correspond to his rights. The greater the rights, the greater the duties. In this way, Manusmriti makes mention of a human religion, and assuming politics to be a prominent aspect of human life, its principles have been made explicit.

Humanism in spite of Brahmanism

The evaluation of the Manusmriti clarifies the humanist attitude of Manu but the brahmanism that pervades it indicates that the humanism characterising the political thought of the ancient period came to fall below the level of humanity during the period of the smritis. The importance attached to first two varnas in the varna system later on gave birth to casteism, which has been severely criticized by all modern Indian political thinkers. Despite this, Manusmriti reflects all the characteristics of the humanist attitude of Indian political thought, apart from its brahmanism. It assumes the existence of unity in diversity in the universe and believes that man's ideal is the expression of his spirituality. It talks of basing society on duties.

Lower Status of Women

Apart from brahmanism, another feature of Manusmriti, which militates against its humanism, is the inferior position allotted to women. In the field of education, too, the principle of equal rights for all was abolished.

Divine Right of the King

By assuming the king to be invested with divine power, every action of the king was regarded as sanctified and therefore important. According to the eighth couplet of chapter seven, the child king should not be insulted by regarding him as merely human because in the king's form there existed a great divine power. By assuming the king to be divinely inspired, Manusmriti helped in establishing autocracy and the infinite supremacy of the king. According to the thirteenth couplet, the system propounded by the king should not be violated even by its opponents, which implies that it is wrong to violate any law of the state in any circumstance. It is clear that such a view supports the institutionalization of kingship. Despite this, Manusmriti upholds the just king and denigrates the unjust, and believes that humility and denial of sensual pleasures are important for the king. Hence, it would be wrong to argue that Manusmriti is not basically humanist, though it can certainly be argued that at this stage, the humanism of traditional Indian political thought had lost most of its vigour.

POLITICAL PHILOSOPHY OF ARTHASHASTRA

An even greater decline in humanist thought than in the Manusmriti is evident in Kautilya's Arthashastra although many Indian and Western scholars regard Kautilya's treatise as the most significant text on Indian political thought. As far as the question of scientific and systematic cognization is concerned, Kautilya's treatise provides detailed and subtle analysis of every aspect of a welfare state. In simple terms, the view propounded in the Arthashastra of Kautilya is that the state creates circumstances in society which favour the achievement of the ideals of fulfilment of duty, material wealth and satisfaction (dharma, artha and kama). To this extent, the Arthashastra is as much a supporter of the welfare state as the Manusmriti is. As a part of the ancient Indian tradition, Arthashastra also regards dharma as the foundation stone of the state as well as of relations between states. But from the humanist viewpoint, the ideas concerning diplomacy expressed in Arthashastra cannot be regarded as humanistic because it sanctified every means for the achievement of goals, irrespective of their moral propriety. Though Kautilya has supported the divine theory of the origin of the state, he has laid greater emphasis upon a king's duties rather than his rights, but unlike the preceding Indian thinkers, he does not give importance to decentralization, though he does give considerable authority to smaller groups within the state.

Though in comparison to ancient Indian political thought, the political views of Manu and Kautilya possessed minimal humanistic leanings, they still exhibited all those features which characterize Indian political thought, such as basing society on dharma, visualizing a welfare state, emphasizing social justice, adopting a harmonious attitude towards human life, etc. The Dharma sutras, the Dharmashastras and the commentaries written on them subsequent to Manusmriti and Arthashastra provide a detailed analysis of political laws but they did not have as much influence as the Manusmriti and the Arthashastra.

EVOLUTION FROM PURANAS TO NITISHASTRAS

After the Dharma Shastras, that is, between 5 and 10 A. D., political ideas are to be found in the eighteen puranas which evolved gradually. From the political viewpoint, the puranas which have special significance are Agni Purana, Vayu Purana, Markandeya Purana, Matsya Purana, Vrahnardiya Purana, Padma Purana, Varaha Purana, Narsingha Purana, Koorma Purana, and Srimad Bhagvada.

Buddhist and Jain Texts

In addition to the Hindu socio-political literature, during the medieval period, Buddhist and Jain thinkers meditated upon social institutions, though their thoughts differed markedly from the Brahmanic tradition. However, even their thinking exhibits clearly the notable features of Indian political thought. The stupas, columns and caves which bear the inscriptions inspired by Ashoka are coloured by the humanist sentiment. Even more than the Brahmanic thinkers, the Jain and Buddhist scholars preached the equality of man in human society. In fact, it would be appropriate to say that when the harmony of the Varna system collapsed during the period of the Smritis, and excessive importance came to be given to brahmins, Buddhist and Jain thinkers revolted against this discrimination and taught the principle of human equality. The Jataka stories of the Buddhists reflect primarily this humanist tendency. The characterization of Buddha Ashvaghosa, reflects the importance of a welfare state established on the basis of religion. Another text, the Sutralankara, provides a detailed account of the skills which a prince must necessarily possess. According to Suchi, happiness, misery, love, insight, modes of behaviour, death, fear and life are common characteristics of all men and therefore they should not be distinguished on the basis of Varna. Like the Buddhist philosophers, the Jain thinkers also opposed the discrimination between men on the basis of Varna.

Nitishastras

After Arthashastra, Dharmashastra, Purana, Up-purana and the Buddhist and Jain texts, political ideas are to be found in the texts called Nitishastras. Among these, the Nitishastra of Kamandaka deserves special mention but in general, it provides the same ideas as Kautilya's Arthashastra. In addition to this text, detailed analysis of the various organs of political philosophy is to be found in the 'Shukraniti' also. Apart from these, the remaining Nitishastras have, in the main, merely repeated the ideas of Arthashastra.

2
Fundamental Concepts

Rajdharma was said to be the root of or the quintessence of all Dharma by Dharmashastras. However, separate treatises dealing with Rajdharma alone came into existence in very early times. These were unknown as Arthashastras of which the Arthashastras of Kautilya is the most important. *The Mahabharata* has described in details the duties of the king particularly in Santiparva. The word *Rajashastra* meaning the systematic discussion of the kingly duties was first employed by the *Mahabharata.* The science of Government was called Dandaniti and the chief duty of the king was to wield Danda. The science of government was also known as a *nitishastra* or *Rajnitishastra.* These words were used by Mahabharata. Rajnitishastra was part and parcel of Dharmashastra. Rajdharma was a very important subject of Dharmashastra. Even Arthashastra was properly speaking, a part of Dharmashastra.

RAJDHARMA

Though the duties of a king, as described by the *Mahabharata* and the *Arthasastras,* are very important, we will confine our discussion here to Dharmashastras alone. According to Dharmashastra a king has to dispense justice, being free from anger and avarice and in accordance with Dharmashastra. Therefore, when a suit comes before a king he must decide it according to law, even though be may lose the friendship of person if his decision goes against the latter. According to *Manusmriti,* the king, protecting his subject and meting out punishment to those who deserve it, performs every day sacrifices in which the fees are one hundred thousand cows.[1] Yajnavalkya also supports this view. Pointing out the duties of a king, Manu maintains that the king, when protecting his subjects against invasion, should not run away from the battle. The kings who die fighting in battle go to heaven.[2]

Thus, the primary duty of the king was the protection of his subjects from internal and external dangers.

---

1. *Manusmriti,* IX. 306.
2. *Ibid.,* VII, 87-89.

Positive Duties of the King

However, the duties of the king were less negative and more positive. According to Dharmashastras the duty of the king is not only to protect but also to support his subjects. In the words of P. V. Kane, "The functions of Government were not supposed to end with the maintenance of peace and order, but the Government must be an instrument of the diffusion of culture.[1] Thus, the king was called upon to support helpless and aged people, the blind, the cripple, lunatics, widows, orphans, those suffering from diseases and calamities, pregnant women by giving them medicines, lodging, food and clothing according to their requirements. Madhatithi states that when a king supports his subjects in famine distributing food from his treasury no question of his being in mourning would come in the way.[2]

These provisions for the old, the blind, the widows, orphans and helpless persons and for the relief of unemployed kshatriyas, vaisya and shudras strike one as rather modern in tone. It has been rightly remarked by P.V. Kane, "In ancient India, though there were naturally no acts of Parliament guaranteeing the above services to the subjects, public opinion, the views of eminent writers and the practice of the best kings created an atmosphere in which it was thought that it was imperative for the king representing the State and its resources to encourage learning, to care for the blind, the decrepit, the old and the widowed and to give employment to those who were unemployed.[3] Manu advised the king, on rising from his bed every day, to wait upon Brahmins learned in the three *Vedas* and endowed with wisdom and to abide by their directions.[4] The Dharmashastras have described in details the responsibilities of the king, his daily duties, his high ideals, grades of sovereignty, conditions for different titles, types of conquerers, conquerer's duties, procedure of coronation, safeguards against enemies, hereditary monarchy, republics and oligarchies, Janapadas, checks on king, his legislative powers and limited scope for royal edicts. Of these we will mention here only those which are relevant from the point of view of the provision of social justice in state by the king.

Checks and Limitations on the King

The king was the pivot of the whole state. Therefore, some dangers were naturally possible to him. The Dharmashastras have given detailed instruction about his safety. In spite of all his importance, the Dharmashastras have laid down several checks and limitations upon the king. Exhortations addressed to the king himself exercised a restraining influence. According to *Manusmriti Danda,* personified as a Deity, strikes down a bad king. Therefore, the king was not to act as he pleased but to regard his high office as a sacred trust. He

1. Kane, P. V., *History of Dharmashastra,* Vol. III, p. 59.
2. *Madhatithi of Manu,* V. 94.
3. Kane, P. V., *History of Dharmashastras,* Vol. III, p. 60.
4. *Manusmriti,* VII. 37.

was to rule according to the dictates of the Dharmashastras. He had to seek advice from his ministers and purohits. The shastras have even allowed the subjects to abandon a worthless king or even to kill a misguided tyrant. Manu lays down that since the king has in him the glory of all deities, whatever rule, as regards desirable matters, the king establishes and whatever action he declares as undesirable among those actions that are harmful, should not be transgressed by any one.[1]

Functions of the King

The king's functions were both religious and secular. The first required him to do certain acts for propitiating gods and unseen powers and removing dangers therefrom with the help of the purohits and sacrificial priests and he had to guard dharma. His secular functions included those that led to prosperity, that helped the people in famine and similar calamities, dealing even-handed justice, guarding persons and property from thieves and trespassers and against invasion.

DUTIES OF THE GOVERNMENT AND THE SUBJECTS

The state is constituted not only by the king but also by the *amatya, janpada, durga, kosa, danda* and *mitra.* Of these seven *angas* of the state the question of functions arises concerning the *svamin,* the *amatya* and the *mitra,* the rest being material constituents. Thus, while the king has duties towards the subjects, the subjects have also duties towards the king. Again, the king's duties are not solitary. He is not the sole ruler. He is helped by his ministers and a whole retinue of state officers. He can rule according to justice provided all these equally follow justice. It is insufficient for the king to follow his own duties, he has also to ensure that other officers follow their duties. Thus, the king along with his officers, together fulfils the duties of the government. On the other side the subjects too have to fulfil their duties. Though this fulfilment must be voluntary yet sometimes it is also imposed by the state. In fact, both the government and the subjects should watch each other's performance since their interests are inter-related. While each has to fulfil his duties, it has also to see and insist that the other part of the state also performs its duties. It is not only the state which punishes the defaulter subject. The authors of dharmashastras have not only given a right but considered it a duty of the subjects to punish the government which does not fulfil its duty. Thus, the duties of the government and the subjects were interdependent, inter-related, complementary and integral to each other.

Duties of Ministers

According to Kamandaka, it is the duty of the ministers to prevent a king from pursuing an evil course. Sukra asks, "How can the kingdom be brought

---

1. *Ibid.*, 13.

to prosperity by those ministers whom the king is not afraid to offend? They are no better than ladies who are to be decked with ornaments and fine clothes. What is the use of those ministers, whose advice does not tend to the advancement of the kingdom, the people, the army, the treasury, good government and to the destruction of enemies?"[1] It was difficult for the ministers sometimes to please the king and also to placate the subjects. However, normally the minister was supposed to do both while in cases of conflict he was praised for doing the welfare of the people even at the cost of his post.

The main duty of the ministers was to provide *mantra, i.e.*, the line of policy to be adopted by the State. This mantra was panchanga (five-fold) *viz.*, means of carrying out actions or works, plenty of men and materials, proper allotment of time and place, remedies against pitfalls, the happiness of the kingdom or people that will result from the accomplishment of the course decided upon.[2] Different ministers used to be incharge of different portfolios and so differed their duties. Each was required to provide advice to the king in his own field. Of these the most important were the chief ministers, the commander-in-chief, the purohita and the treasurer. Each minister was also responsible for ensuring the fulfilment of the duties of the officers under him. The *Sukranitisar* lays down that each minister should be allowed portfolio according to his ability and there should be a change of portfolios among the ministers from time to time, since otherwise there is a danger of their being intoxicated with power.[3]

Duties of the Officers

The Dharmashastras have described in very minute details the duties of the officers of the State. It is impossible to enumerate all these details here. However, it will be relevant to summarise the most important duties of some of the big officers of the state. This summary is as follows:

1. **Yuvaraja** Yuvaraja or crown prince had to assist the king and the ministers in whatever matters he was asked to do so. He, however, got full powers of the king after the latter's death. Before that he used to perform duties firstly, on unimportant offices and gradually on the important ones.
2. **Purohita** The duties of purohita were mainly concerned with Dharma, religious rights and education. He was required to know all types of rituals. He was also consulted by the king for the auspicious moments in peace and war. According to Yajnavalkya the rise and fall of kings depend on the aspects or influences of planets and therefore it is the most important duty of the purohits to advise the king in these matters.

1. *Sukranitisar*, II. 82-83.
2. *Arthasastra*, X. 15.
3. *Sukranitisar*, II. 107-113.

3. **Senapati** The duties of senapati or the commander-in-chief were generally concerned with maintaining internal peace and external security.
4. **Duta** The chief duties of the duta, the ambassador or the messenger, were concerned with foreign affairs. He had to follow the policy of his state and achieve the welfare of his nation in foreign affairs. Kamandaka briefly set out the following duties of the duta: determining those who are inimical to the king to whom he is sent, winning over to his side the friends and relatives of the enemy king, finding out the number and equipment of forts, the economic resources and military strength of the enemy king, collection of news as to what the enemy intends to do, of enemy country, collecting knowledge about the places of the enemy where battles can be waged by the king or whence he can pass away swiftly.[1]

Besides the above senior officers the king used to appoint superintendents in different departments of the state. The duties of these officers have been described by the Dharmashastras in details. The state was divided into several sections, each section into sub-sections and each sub-section into mandals of 8 to 10 villages. These categories have been named differently by different Dharmashastras. Each sub-division was prescribed over by the officer whose duties has been specified by the Dharmashastras. Thus, the Dharmashastras have described the duties of not only the government officers but also of the officers of local self-government. A vast literature has been created by so many Indian and Western scholars about the institution of Republic in India which could be favourably compared with any contemporary local self-government in the West. The Dharmashastras have also described in details the duties of the officers concerning constituents of the states such as Durga (fort of capital), Kosa (treasury of finance), Bala (the Army) etc. Besides, much has been written about the duties towards allies or friends. Thus, the Dharmashastras have propounded sound principles of international affairs, the principles concerning war, peace and treaties, etc.

CRITICAL EVALUATION

1. **Religious Colouring** The entire political structure together with political ethics exhibits a religious colouring which underlies all theories and ideals.
2. **Moral basis** The duties of the king and other constituents of the state were based upon high moral ideals. This ensured the provision of political justice as well as social justice.
3. **Highest Status to the King** Highest status was given to the king in society. He was sometimes considered equal to gods. He was given privileges and exceptions in so many matters. Monarchy has been the only form of government in India before and even after the Christian

[1] *Kamandaka,* XII. 22-23.

era. The king was almost synonymous with the government and the state though at some places the Dharmasastras have prescribed revolt and even killing of a tyrant king by the subjects. However, in practice the king enjoyed all the rights, though of course, tyrants were exceptions.

4. **Support of the *status quo*** The Dharmashastras generally insisted upon following the prescribed rules in every sphere of life by each member of society rigidly and without change. Exceptions were condemned. This in its term served to maintain the *status quo* which suited to both the Brahmins and the Kshatriyas, the two dominant social classes.
5. **Insistence upon confirmation** Thus, the Dharmashastras insisted upon confirmation of the established rules. P.V. Kane rightly laments, "Besides, once the main outlines of the theory of the State were established by the first writers on polity, for about two thousand years succeeding generations of authors were content to follow in the old grooves and hardly ever made any fresh approach to the problems of government or started any rival conceptions of theories.[1]
6. **Total absence of discussion on other forms of government** One finds a total absence of discussion on other forms of government such as oligarchy or democracy in Dharmashastras. Their central theme has been the monarchy.
7. **Lack of national outlook** Pointing out this defect P.V. Kane has written, "The old thinkers spun the same old webs of theories that have been there for centuries, they did not formulate new theories nor did they take steps to infuse into the common people a sense of solidarity and unity as Indians and did not inculcate deep and abiding sentiments of partriotism similar to those we find in Western countries for the last two or three hundred years.[2]
8. **Low estimate of human nature** The Dharmashastras had a very low estimate of human nature. They believed that ordinarily men were depraved. Therefore, they recommended that men should be kept in the straight path by the fear of punishment. According to Yajnavalkya Smriti the king should punish and bring to the proper path caste and guilds when they swerve from their Dharma.[3] Similar passages may be found in *Manu Smriti*. This shows that the Dharamashastras do not rely on the natural moral impulses of man and on his will to do the right thing. From the point of view of social ethics this state of affairs is not satisfactory whatever may have been its use in actual life. At least such a lack of faith in the moral fibre of man is against the contemporary moral principles.

---

1. Kane, P.V., *History of Dharmashastra*, Vol. III, p. 235.
2. *Ibid.*, p. 236.
3. *Yajnavalkya Smriti*, I. 363.

9. **Insistence on swadharma** Of the above characteristics, while the first two are favourable, the remaining six are unfavourable from the point of view of ethics. However, the most important concept in Hindu political ethics having everlasting value is the concept of *swadharma.* As has been already pointed out, Indian social thinkers unanimously accepted Dharma as the highest ideal of the individual and society. Thus, *rajadharma* was the goal of the state. In the fulfilment of *rajadharma* each constituent of the state was required to fulfil his own *swadharma.* The king was primarily required to protect varnasaram Dharma. Every citizen of the state was required to fulfil *swadharma* according to varnasrama. It is undeniable as P.V. Kane and others have pointed out, that undue emphasis on the confirmation to the written injunctions concerning varnasrama dharma, led to *status quo.* However, the Indian thinkers also held that ultimately *swadharma* must be reinterpreted according to times and climes, and also according to the individual moral reason of the person concerned.
10. **Extra-terrestrial goal** Moksha has been considered to be the goal of life by the Indian philosophers. The same was the goal of the state. Though generally the values were considered four-fold, as is clear in the concept of purusarthas, in practice most of the Dharmashastras have laid exclusive emphasis upon moksha. This undue emphasis upon moksha made the goal extra-terrestrial.

However, the most valuable characteristic of Hindu polity was to consider state as the means and not the end, of social life. The Dharmashastras considered Dharma as the supreme power, above both the king and the state. The state was only an instrument to realise the goal of Dharma. Therefore, it was prescribed that if the state is anti-Dharma it should be opposed and changed.

The above critical evaluation shows that in spite of some grave defects in the prescriptions of the Dharmashastras concerning political ethics these can be favourably compared with similar scriptures in any other country of the world of that time. The ideal of basing political institutions upon Dharma fulfils the requirement of ethics. Thus, theoretically the system has all the possibility of delivering justice. In practice, however, if it supported vested interests and *status quo* it could be changed by others. It will be wrong to see a conspiracy of the Brahmins and the Kshatriyas in the prescriptions of the Dharmashastras.

PURUSHARTHAS

Since Ancient times the Indian ideal of four Purusharthas *i.e.*, Dharma, Artha, Kama and Moksha has presented an integral view of life. Some maintain that the ideals of renunciation and liberation in Indian thinking exhibit other-worldliness and escapism. Admitted that in some philosophical schools the ideal of liberation has been presented in a way which has no consistency with the terrestrial aims of life, it is however, necessary to go deeper into the meanings of these values before arriving at any final conclusion. In spite of Buddha's ideal of Nirvan, his characteristic sympathy for human beings makes it difficult to admit that his philosophy should be called other-worldly. In Hindu social philosophy the concept of Varna again, shows the same integral approach. While Samkara has emphasised the value of liberation in human life, the sage Vatsyayana has laid emphasis upon the ideal of Kama in his famous treatise *Kamasutra*. In the history of man, wherever any culture too much emphasised some one particular aspect of human personality or life and left the other aspects unfulfilled, it led to cultural degeneration and the birth of opposite reactions. The conflict observed everywhere among man and man, man and society, nation and nation, and even the conflict within the individual himself only exhibits Nature's attempt everywhere to achieve harmony, synthesis, balance and integrality. This tendency is found not in human society alone but even in the animal and plant life. In man it becomes only more conscious. This is proved by the fact that man cannot rest peaceful unless he solves his problems and removes his tensions. The integral philosophy of life shows the limitations of every need and value, gives it a sufficient place, leaves none, since the warp and woof of human life has been knitted by all these and however one may wish he cannot remove any element of human personality and life, though by suppressing it one may make his life one-sided, frustrated and full of tensions.

The idea of Purusharthas is a fundamental principle of Indian ethics. According to it, the aim of every person in the world is to attain the four Purusharthas — Dharma, Artha, Kama and Moksha. Kama is a natural tendency in every person. Wealth is the means of fulfilment of kama and other needs and the life system of society. Dharma implies the laws or principles on which society is based. According to the Vaisesika philosophy, Dharma is that which leads to improvement in this world and to moksha in the next. Dharma or duty, wealth and kama relate to objects of this world. These are, in brief, called the Trivarga. Duty, wealth and sex indicate respectively ethical ideals, physical means and physical, mental and vital desires of man. In this way it is man's duty to fulfil all the three. Besides trivargas, moksha is just as important in human life. At one time the Hindus interpreted trivarga as a means to moksha but generally all the four purusharthas have been stressed. Vatsyayan writes, "A man in hundred years of age should gain knowledge in childhood, sex satisfaction in youth and attend to duty and moksha in old age."[1] Manu states clearly, "Some people attribute more importance to duty, some to wealth and some to sex. Actually, all three are equally important and creditable."[2] Manu has gone to the extent of saying that man should try for moksha only after he has passed through the three ashrams to fulfil duty,

1. Vatsyayan, *Kamasutra*, II.
2. Manu, *Dharmashastra*, III.

attain wealth and enjoy sex, and has rid himself of the three *rinas* because a person not doing so will find himself in trouble.

DHARMA

Dharma as Cosmic Principle

Like all other fundamental references in Indian social philosophy the first references to the universal nature of Dharma have been made in the Vedas. The Vedic term Rta, as has been pointed out earlier, stands for the cosmic principle of Dharma. Varnashrama Dharma, the basis of Vedic social organisation, was the main form of Dharma. The Vedic ethics was based upon Dharma. Thus, Dharma was the cosmic principle expressing as Rta in cosmos and Varnasrama Dharma among human beings. In fact the Indian social philosophers never distinguish between cosmic, natural, social and individual. All these, according to them, are essentially one and the same. This was known as Brahman in Upanisads. By the identity of Atman and Brahman it was maintained that what is individual is cosmic and *vice-versa*. Thus, individual justice can be achieved only by achieving social justice. Social justice, in its turn, can be achieved by following natural law which is only an aspect of universal law.

This cosmic nature of Dharma however, is more explicit in Upanisads. The Upanisads identify Dharma (Righteousness) with Satya (Truth). The Brahadaranyakopanisad declares, "Verily, that which is righteousness is truth. Therefore, they say of a man who speaks the truth, he speaks righteousness, or of a man who speaks righteousness that he speaks the truth. Verily, both these are the same thing."[1] This Dharma leads to Brahman realisation which is impossible without moral uplift. Hence, Taittiriya Upanisad says, "Having taught the Veda, a teacher further instructs a pupil: Speak the Truth (Satyam Vada), practice virtue (Dharmam Chara)....' One should not be negligent of truth. One should not be negligent of virtue. One should not be negligent of welfare. One should not be negligent of prosperity."[2] According the Chandogya Upanishad, Dharma is Yajna or sacrifice. It is soul force. It is the spiritual energy in the universe. Besides the Upanisads, the Geeta also treated Dharma as the cosmic principle. Continuing this tradition the Dharmasastras also insisted upon the universal form of Dharma. In the words of P. V. Kane, "The writers on dharmasastra meant by dharma not a creed or religion but a mode of life or a code of conduct, which regulated a man's work and activities as a member of society and as an individual and was intended to bring about the gradual development of a man and to enable him to reach what was deemed to be the goal of human existence."[3] This goal of human existence

---

1. *Brih*, II. 5, 11.
2. *Taittiriya Upanisad*, I.
3. Kane, P.V., *History of Dharmasastra*, Vol. II, Part I. Bhandarkar Oriental Research Institute, Pune, 1941, p. 2.

was liberation. Liberation has been defined as realisation of Brahman. The Upanisadic Mahavakya, "Tattavamasi", "Ayamatma Brahman", "Atmacha Brahman", "Sarvam khalvidam Brahman", express the universal nature of Brahman which is the same as Dharma.

One of the noblest prayers in all literature occurs in the Brihadaranyaka Upanisad, "Lead me from falsehood unto truth, from darkness lead me unto light, from death lead me unto immortality."[1] This is the universal form of Dharma. Dharma has been further described in terms of universal virtues. Its identity with truth has been already pointed out. Dharmasutras have included almost all the moral virtues in it. The Gautama Dharmasutra holds that daya (compassion or love for all beings), ksanti (forebearance), anasuya (freedom from envy), saucha (purity of body, speech and thought), anayasa (absence of painful efforts or ambitions), mangala (doing what is commended), akarpanya (not demeaning oneself before others), asprha (not hankering after sensual pleasures or the possessions of others)[2] are the qualities of the soul. Vasistha says that avoiding backbiting, jealousy, pride, egoism, unbelief, crookedness, self-praise, abuse of others, deceit, covetousness, delusion, anger and envy is the dharma of all ashrams and further he delivers a fine exhortation 'practise dharma (righteousness) and not adharma; speak the truth and not untruth; look far ahead, not near: look at what is highest, not at what is not highest."[3] The reason for the cultivation of the above mentioned virtues and abstention from the opposite vices is based upon the philosophical principle that there is one universal essence underlying everyone. Thus, the ideal of dharma combines morality and metaphysics. Like Kant, Daksa declares, "One who desires happiness should look upon another just as he looks upon himself."[4] In the words of Devala, "The quintessence of dharma is that one should not do to others what would be disliked by one's self."[5] As a universal principle dharma stands higher than Artha and Kama. The Mahabharata says: "A wise man tries to secure all three, but if all three cannot be attained, he secures dharma and artha or only dharma if he has a choice of only one from among the three. A man of middling discipline prefers artha to the other two; dharma is the source of both artha and kama."[6] In the words of Gautama, "One should not allow the morning, midday and evening to remain fruitless so far as dharma, artha and kama are concerned. But among these three one should attach most importance to dharma."[7] According to Yajnavalkya also dharma is the highest among Purusarthas.

Since the moral qualities prescribed for the following of Dharma were common to all, they express the universal nature of Dharma. According to

---

1. *Brih,* 1. 3, 28.
2. *Gautama Dharma Sutra,* VIII, 24-26.
3. *Vasistha Dharma Sutra,* X, 30.
4. *Daksa,* III. 22.
5. Devala, quoted in *Kratyaratanakar,* p. 17.
6. *Mahabharata,* Uddyogaparva, 124, 34-38.
7. *Gautama Dharma Sutra,* IX. 46-47.

Sankhasmriti, "forbearance, truthfulness, self-restraint and purity are common to all varnas."[1] According to Mahabharata, "Three are the best qualities among all beings *viz.*, absence of enmity, truthfulness and freedom from anger."[2] Vasistha says that "truthfulness, freedom from anger, generosity, ahimsa (non-injury) and procreation of offspring are the common dharma of all varnas."[3] According to Gautama, "Even the Shudra has to submit himself to the dharma of truthfulness, freedom from anger and purity of body and mind." Manu says that "ahimsa, truthfulness, no wrongful taking of another's possessions, purity and restraint of senses are in brief the common dharmas of all varnas."[4]

General Characteristics of Dharma

From the above discussion concerning the nature of dharma as cosmic principle some general characteristics can be deduced. The most important among these are as follows:

1. **Three active modes** According to Chandogya Upanishad there are three active modes of dharma: yajna, adhyayana and dana (sacrifice, study and dedication).[5] Yajna or sacrifice is qualified as tapas. The meaning of tapas is soul-force. It refers to the spiritual energy which is generated by bringing one's physical nature under the control of his rational will. The second mode of dharma is adhyayana or study. Related to the study of scriptures is the exposition of the scriptures or pravachana. The third mode of dharma is dana. Commenting on these three modes of dharma, Prof G. Mukhopadhyaya summarises the inter-relatedness and ethical intentionality of the ideas expressed above: "By yajna or sacrifice one is linked with the world of the gods, through study or adhyayana one is joined with the supreme sphere of Sabda-Brahman, and lastly through dana, self-giving or gift of things one gets connected with the human world. Dharma thus covers all the spheres of life and is not an isolated state of things.[6]
2. **Social Principle** In the words of S. Cromwell Crawford, "The key to understanding Brahmanical society is found in the first purusartha, namely, dharma. It is a development of the earlier Rg-Vedic idea of Rta which, as we have been, represented cosmic law operating in all phenomena — natural, religious and moral. In the smriti period this law permeating the whole universe was called dharma. Within the social order dharma was explicitly defined in terms of certain duties and obligations which were codified in the great Law Books."[7]

1. *Sankhasmriti*, I. 5.
2. *Vasisthasmriti*, IV, 4.
3. *Manusmriti*, X, 63 and I. 62.
4. *Gautamadharma Sutra*, X, 52.
5. *Manusmriti*, IV, 175.
6. G. Mukhopadhyaya, *Studies in the Upanisads*, Calcutta, Oriental Press, 1960, p. 157.
7. S. Cromwell Crawford, *Evolution of Hindu Ethical Ideals*, p. 80.

3. **Criteria of Duty** While, Advaita Vedanta has developed dharma as a metaphysical principle, the Mimamsa philosophers develop the concept of dharma as duty. Jaimini starts his sutras with an enquiry regarding the nature of dharma *i.e.*, the nature of Vedic duties, relevant proofs, means of the production of dharma and its fruits.[1] Whatever is enjoined by Vedic injunctions is dharma or duty (yascondanalaksanah sa dharmah), provided it is not intended to produce any injury to other persons. There are certain sacrifices, such as syena-yaya, which are performed for injuring one's enemy; though there are injunctions regarding such sacrifices, nevertheless, since they produce injury for others, they are not to be regarded as dharma. Dharma cannot be known by any of the other pramanas such as perception, inference or implication; the only way of knowing it is by the Vedic injunction. Dharma is thus, according to the Mimamsa not a quality of the understanding of the self, but is of the nature of the Vedic sacrifices. It means only such prescribed sacrifices of the Vedas as have not been associated with any harmful effects. Dharmas are either enjoined by the Vedas or directed towards beneficial ends. In the words of Surama Das Gupta, "When it is said that Vedic injunctions or prohibitions define the nature of dharma or adharma, the idea is that whether any sacrificial action will produce advantage or disadvantage cannot be known by any other means but the injunction or the prohibition of the Vedas."[2]
4. **Practical Principle** Summing up the practical nature of the concept of dharma in Dharmasastras, P. V. Kane writes, "The foregoing discussion establishes that all dharmasastra writers attached the highest importance to moral qualities and enjoined them upon all with all the emphasis they could command; but as their main purpose was a practical one, *viz.*, to guide people to right acts in everyday life, they dealt more elaborately with the acts, rites and ceremonies that each person had to do with reference to his station in society."[3]
5. **The Principle of Good** The concept of Dharma seems to be closely associated with that of punya or the good. The Brihadaranyak upanisad defines Dharma as sreyah (good). There is nothing greater than Dharma. In Kathopanisad Dharma has been defined as mystic self-knowledge. Thus the upanisads define Dharma in the sense of good. Adharma therefore means the opposite of good or evil. This has been also elaborated in the Nyaya Vaisesika concept of good. The Nyaya Vaisesika philosophers define Dharma as merit and Adharma as demerit. Therefore, in order to achieve liberation one must follow Dharma.

---

1. Jaimini, *Sastradipika*, I, 1.1.
2. Das Gupta, S., *Development of Moral Philosophy in India*, p. 79.
3. Kane, P. V., *History of Dharmasastra*, p. 11.

6. **Differentia of Men** According to Indian thinkers it is Dharma which distinguishes between man and animal. It is so since it represents the moral law in human society, which is a part of universal divine principle. Dharma, therefore, is the basis of all values. It is the substratum of Purusarthas. It is the regulative principle. In the words of K. N. Upadhyaya, "The persistence and intensity with which the inquiry into dharma has been pursued in India is mainly on account of the firm conviction of the Indian people that dharma constitutes the differentia of man, whereby he is distinguished from brutes, just as in the West, following Aristotle, rationality is regarded as the distinguishing mark of man. This approach at once reveals....that what is most vital to man's life is not his mental, but his moral and spiritual nature."[1]
7. **The Principle of Statecraft** But the most important characteristic of dharma is that it is the principle of statecraft. In Hindu polity the king was entrusted the responsibility of upholding dharma. According to Manu, government is an extension of the eternal divine order of society, and the king is responsible for upholding dharma.[2] Thus, dharma is the principle of state-craft. It is the basis of law and order in the state. Prof. Basham reminds us that in ancient and classical India, government, no matter what its shape, was not an end in itself. "The Hegelian concept of the state as an organism of supernatural size and power, transcending all other entities upon earth and mystically linking man with the Absolute, is completely foreign to anything ever thought of in India."[3] The state as protector of dharma comes closer to the Thomistic doctrine of government as the means for promoting salvation.
8. **Principle of Law and Order** Therefore, Dharma sastras consider dharma as the principle of law and order. Legislation and the theory of punishment in ancient Indian states was based upon the principle of Dharma. The country observing law and order was known as Dharmarajya. According to Mahabharat, kingship was imposed by Divine upon mankind, designed to help people live by the laws of Dharma.[4] Manusmriti regards the king as the repository of all Dharma and responsible for maintaining the order of law. Kamandaka describes the king as the preserver and the maintainer of the duties of varnas and Asramas who should himself also be entirely obedient to the laws relating to them.[5] Thus, the rule according to Dharma not only included legal justice but also social justice.

1. Upadhyaya, K.N., *Dharma as a Regulative Principle*, p. 1.
2. *Manu*, VII, 35.
3. A.L. Basham, *Aspects of Ancient Indian Culture* (New York), Asia Publishing House (1970), p. 5.
4. *Manu*, VIII. 307-316.
5. *Mahabharata*, XII, 59.

9. **Integral approach** The most important characteristic of Dharma from the point of view of culture, is the integral standpoint. The principle of following *swadharma* is the basis of unity in diversity in society. Integral approach has been characteristic to Indian culture. Indian philosophy has emphasised one ultimate element underlying the multiplicity of the phenomenal world. Leaving aside exceptional philosophies as that of Charvaka, from the philosophers of the ancient Vedas down to the contemporary Indian thinkers including Rabindranath Tagore, Sri Aurobindo, Swamy Vivekananda, Mahatma Gandhi and others, one finds an integral approach in philosophy. Dharmasastras advocated a multisided integral progress as the ideal. Since ancient times the Indian ideal of four Purusharthas *i.e.,* Dharma, Artha, Kama and Moksha has presented an integral view of life.[1] 'The integral viewpoint does not negate the distinctions but shows unity in diversity and neither emphasises unity nor diversity exclusively but harmonises both in a more integral vision.[2]
10. **Characteristics of Indian Culture** One of the meaning of the term Dharma is culture. Therefore, all the characteristics of Indian culture are the characteristics of Dharma in India. The fundamental characteristics of Indian Culture are: religious orientation, spirituality, religious tolerance, synthetic spirit, adaptability, freedom of thought, integral approach and most of all, unity in diversity. All these characteristics are equally the characteristics of Dharma. Dharma is cultural organisation and spirituality. It has been equated with self-knowledge. According to Sri Aurobindo, spirituality is the key to the Indian mind.[3] We can say that spirituality is the key to understand Dharma. Spirituality is spontaneity. It is totality. It is synthesis. It is integrality. It is dynamism and comprehensiveness. It is natural principle. All these characterise Dharma.
11. **Humanism** Another significant characteristic of Dharma is humanism. Humanism is the philosophy in which man occupies the central place. Dharma, the universal principle is basically a moral principle which is essentially human. We have already referred to the humanist interpretation of Atman, Brahman and their identity in chapter III in the conceptions of Upanisads and Bhagwad Geeta. Humanism propounds unity in diversity, in individual, national and international affairs. The same has been propounded by Dharma. Each country and each human being in a particular time and place has some specific 'Dharma' and the sole aim of his life is to realize it. Similarly, humanity too has a 'Dharma' and that is the maximum and most comprehensive realisation of human values.

---

1. Kamandaka, *Nitisara,* Second Sarga, Verse 35.
2. Sharma, R.N., *Indian Society and Social Institutions,* Munshiram Manoharlal, 1981, New Delhi, pp. 31-32.
3. Sri Aurobindo, *The Foundations of Indian Culture,* p. 5.

12. **Dynamic approach** The followers of Dharmasastras have generally followed the letter in place of spirit and have been too much conservative. Dharma, on the other hand, has the characteristic of a dynamic principle. Defining Dharma as the dynamic human property Prasastapada has maintained, "It brings about to the agent happiness, means of happiness and final deliverance, it is supersensuous; it is destructible by the experiencing of the last item of happiness; it is produced by the contact of the man with the internal organ, by means of pure thoughts and determinations; and with regard to the different castes and conditions of men there are distinct means of accomplishing it."[1] In the words of S. Cromwell Crawford, "Hindus call their religion Sanatana Dharma which literally means "Eternal Law". The name should in no wise suggest that the ethical ideals connected with this religion are eternal in the sense of being fixed, static, unchanging substances. To the contrary, Hindu ethics, like the river Ganges, has been in a state of ceaseless flow down the ages, constantly changing its course and currents relative to the hard, intervening realities of Indian history. All of its fundamental presuppositions — karman, samsara, dharma — have evolved from streams of thought originating in earliest times. These elements have survived to the present day, not in spite of change, but because of change. Thus, under the rubric of eternal universal law, Hindu ethics combines continuity with dynamic diversity."[2]

It should be remembered here that the description of the characteristics of Dharma in the Vedas, the Upanisads, the Bhagvadgita, the Dharmasutras, the Dharmasastras, the Six systems and even in the writings of contemporary Indian philosophers is only different in emphasis but same in essentials. Therefore, the above description of the characteristics of Dharama is equally applicable in case of Dharmasastras as in all other cases. The above characteristics however, do not exhaust the list. In fact the list cannot be easily exhausted.

CONCEPT OF JUSTICE

The 8th chapter of Manusmirti describes the system of dispensation of justice. Besides Manusmriti, Yajnavalkyasmriti and other Dharmashastras describe various aspects of Justice.

Vyavahara

The dispensation of justice was known as Vyavahara. This word has been defined by several smritis and commentators. V.K. Apte has quoted several Dharmashastras while defining the term vyavahara in these words, "The

---

1. Prasastapada, *Padarthadharmasamgraha*, Tr. G. Jha, Allahabad, E. J. Lazarus and Co., 1916, VI, 133.
2. S. Cromwell Crawford, *Evolution of Indian Ethical Ideals*, Introduction, p. xi.

(upasarga) vi is employed in the sense of various, ava, in the sense of doubt, hara means removing, vyavahara is so called because of its removing various doubts.'[1] P.V. Kane has defined vyavahara as law and administration of justice."[2]

Vyavahar Pad

The topic or subject matter of litigation of dispute was known as vyavahara pad. Kautilya called it vivadpad. According to Manusmriti pad means athana.[3]

In the words of Yajnavalkyasmriti, "If a person, who is set at naught by others in a manner that it opposed to the rules of smriti and to good usage or conventions, inform the king (or his judge), that is a vyavaharapada."[4] Thus, justice was not a personal retribution but the restoration of the rules of Dharmashastras. Clearly, the sole avowed purpose of jural ethics according to Dharmashastras, was the provision of social justice as the authors of Dharmashastras conceived it. This will be further clarified by our discussion of the functions of various agencies providing legal justice in which the sole concern was to decide according to the Dharmashastras. From very ancient time vyavaharapadas were enumerated 18. In other words most of the disputes among human beings are classified under 18 heads. According to Manusmriti, this enumeration was a matter of convenient arrangement. The number 18 did not embrace all the disputes but only the largest number and the most important of them. There is some difference about the number and nomenclature of the vyavaharpadas among Manusmriti and other Dharmashastras. According to Yajnavalkya Smriti vyavaharapada includes only those disputes that are started and brought before the court at the instance of the parties.[5] According to Manusmriti neither the king nor his officers should start a legal dispute nor should he hush up a matter which has been brought before him by a party.

MACHINERY OF JUSTICE DISPENSATION

The function of dispensation of justice was chiefly the responsibility of the king. The king had to decide dispute according to the prescriptions of the Dharmashastras. According to Manusmriti the king should also take into consideration the duties and usages of the several varnas and the 18 low castes.[6] The king fully dressed and with an undisturbed mind after taking his seat in the Hall of Justice, should perform obeisance to the gods the guardians of the eight quarters (Indra and others).[7] Then he should commence the work

1. Apte, V.M., p. 283, *Manu,* VIII, 1.
2. Kane. P.V., *History of Dharmashastra,* Vol. III, p. 242.
3. *Manusmriti,* VIII, p. 8.
4. *Yajnavalkyasmriti,* II. 5.
5. *Ibid., 23.*
6. *Manusmriti.*
7. *Ibid.,* VIII, 1-2.

of looking into the legal business. The transaction of legal business has four stages from the king's or judge's point of view *viz.*, first receiving information from a person then finding out under what title of law of vyavaharapada the information falls, then consideration of the pleadings of the parties and the evidence led by them and lastly the decision. When a litigant comes before the court a proper time *i.e.*, when the court is sitting and makes his bow, he, the king or judge, should address him as follows: What is your business? What is the injury done to you? Don't be afraid, speak out, man. By whom, when, where and why was the injury caused? When thus asked whatever he replies should be considered by the judge with the sabhyas and brahmins and if the matter be legally entertainable he, the judge, should deliver the sealed order to the plaintiff or order the bailiff to summon the defendant."[1] Very elaborate rules are led down about the summoning of the defendant or accused by some *Dharmashastras.*

The Dharmashastras have given an elaborate description of the machinery of dispensation of justice. According to *Manusmriti* the king, desirous of looking into the disputes of people, should enter the sabha, the hall of justice accompanied by brahmins, ministers and should there decide every day the causes of litigants.[2] The Mit. on Yaj., says that protecting the subjects is the highest duty of a king and that duty cannot be discharged without eradicating and punishing the wicked, when latter requires that the king should administer justice vyavahara-darsana.[3] Medhatithi on Manu also says that protection consists in the removal of troubles, secular and spiritual adrsta.[4]

The Dharmashastras have equated dispensation of justice with provision of Dharma. The judge was considered a personification of Dharma itself. His sole duty was to give a verdict according to Dharma. In other words his job was to restore the order of Dharma. According to Manusmriti the administrator of justice is Dharma incarnate who represents that when justice is administered the dart of adharma or falsehood by which dharma is pierced is taken out from the body of Dharma.[5] According to Yajnavalkyasmriti the impartial administration of justice yields the same reward as solemn Vedic sacrifices do.[6] In this way, administration of justice was held to be a very sacred duty. Manu declares that a king who punishes those that do not deserve to be punished and who does not punish those that deserve punishment incurs great obloguy and goes to hell.[7] In keeping with this line of thinking the king's court of justice was called dharmasthara, dharmasara[8] or dharmadhikarana.

1. *Narada,* I. 36; KAI, 86-88.
2. *Manusmriti,* VIII, 1-3.
3. *The Mit. on Yaj.*, II, 1.
4. *Methatithi on Manu,* VIII, 1.
5. *Manusmriti,* VIII, 12-14.
6. *Yajnavalkyasmriti,* I, 359-360.
7. *Manusmriti,* VIII, 128.
8. *Manu,* VIII.

Original Court and Appellate Tribunal

Thus, the king was the original court as well as the appellate tribunal. However, it was insisted by the Dharmashastras that the king cannot dispense justice by himself alone. He must do so with the help and guidance of others. It was prescribed that the king wearing no guard dress or ornaments is to enter the sabha, the Hall of Justice, for looking into the causes of litigants, accompanied by learned Brahmins and ministers proficient in statecraft, is to be free from hot temper and greed and decide according to the law laid down in dharmashastras.[1] As has been pointed out earlier, the king or judge was required to decide according to the rules of Dharmashastras. In the absence of clear verdict of the Dharmashastras the king should decide in accordance with the recognized custom of the country. If owing to the pressure of other weighty business the king cannot attend to work of administering justice, he should appoint a learned Brahmin together with three sabbyas to decide the dispute of people.[2] Manusmriti calls the judge *Dharmaprevaktur*[3]. Others have called him Dharmadhyaksaha and Dharmadhikarine etc.

The Chief Justice and his Associates

The chief justice, according to the Dharmashastras, must be a learned Brahmin.[4] According to Manusmriti the king may prefer a Brahmin who is not learned and maintains himself by the mere fact of his caste, but should never have a shudra as the expounder of dharma and that the country whose king has a shudra as judge to expound dharma comes to ruin as a cow sinks in mud.[5] According to Dharmashastras the king should appoint at least three sabhyas (judges or members of the court of justice) to associate with the Chief Justice in the disposal of suits.[6] Three was the minimum number of the sabhyas to be appointed. Appreciating such a court of justice Manu has said, "When in a sabha three Brahmins, learned in the Vedas sit along with the chief judge appointed by the king that is like the sabha of Brahma or it is like a sacrifice."[7] The Dharmashastras have laid down the following qualifications for the sabhyas: they should be endowed with the study of the Vedas, should know dharmashastras, should speak the truth, should be impartial to friend or foe, should be steady, devoted to their work intelligent, hereditary, proficient in arthasastra.[8] Thus, all and sundry were not to meddle in the trials before the court, but only those were learned in Dharmashastra were allowed to express their opinions. Again, the chief judge and the sabhyas

1. *Manu,* VIII, 1-2 and Yaj., II, 1.
2. *Manusmriti,* 9-10, Yaj., II-3.
3. *Manusmriti,* VIII, 20.
4. *Ibid.,* VIII, 9, Yaj., II, 3.
5. *Manusmriti,* VII, 20.
6. *Ibid.,* 10-11, Yaj., II. 3.
7. *Manusmriti,* VIII. 11.
8. *Yajnavalkavasmriti,* II. 2.

were not to hold conversation in private with anyone of the litigant while the suit was pending and if they did so they were liable to be fined.

Control over Judges

Thus, the judges were subject to files and even corporal punishment for violating the rules of justice. It is difficult to find such a high standard of fairness in dispensation of justice anywhere in the world. If the sabhyas give a decision which is opposed to smriti and usages through friendship, greed or fear, each was liable to be fined twice as much as the fine to be paid by the defeated party.[1] Some of the scriptures, however, have not been so strict in this matter. Others have prescribed fines and removal from office for corrupt practice and bribery. The injustice done by the judges was sought to be rectified by the king. Some of the texts prescribed employment of spies in various disguises to test the honesty of the judges or the magistrates. Some kings are reported to be following the practice by personally investigating into this matter.

Kinds of Court of Justice

A court of justice was of four kinds, *viz.,* one established *(pratisthita)* in a fixed place such as a town, *apratisthita* not fixed in one place, but moving from place to place as on a circuit, *mudrita* or the court of a judge appointed by the king, who is authorized to use the royal seal, *sasita* or *sastrita,* or the court in which the king himself presides. The Court of justice in the capital was to be to the east of the palace. The court house should be decorated with flowers, statues, paintings, idols of gods and should be furnished with incense, throne or seat for the king or judge, seeds, fire and water. The time for holding the court is the morning.[2] There were holidays on which courts were closed *i.e.,* on 8th and 14th *tithis,* full Moon day and the amavasya of every month.

Constituents of the Court

The court is said to have ten angas *viz.,* the king, the chief judge appointed by him, the sabhyas, smriti, *ganaka* or accountant, *lekhaka* the scribe, gold, fire, water and svapurusa a bailiff, otherwise called *sadhyapala.* The chief judge declared the law, the king awarded punishment, the sabhyas examined the dispute, smriti (dharmashastra) laid down the rule of decision, the success (of one party or the other) and the punishment; gold and fire were required for taking oaths; the water was for man when they feel thirsty, the *ganaka* counted the wealth or subject matter of dispute, the scribe wrote down the pleadings, depositions and the decision, the purusa summoned the sabhyas, the defendant, the witnesses and he guarded the complainant and the defendant when they had furnished no surety (for appearance). The

1. *Ibid.,* II. 4.
2. *Manusmriti,* VII. 145, Yaj., I. 327.

ten angas enumerated above (*viz.*, king etc.) are respectively identified with the head, the mouth, the arms, the hands, the thighs (*ganaka* and *lekhaka*), the two eyes (gold and water), the heart, feet. In the Hall of Justice the king faces the east, the sabhyas, the accountant and the scribe respectively face the north, the west and the south. Omitting the king and the chief judge the sabha is said to have eight angas in certain works. The chief justice, the sabhyas and the learned brahmins were probably elderly people. Besides the above mentioned court of the king or the chief justice which was the highest court, the Dharmashastras also recognized other tribunals and courts.

Division of Judicial Powers

According to Yajnavalkya law-suits may be decided by village councils (kulanj), corporations (sreni), assemblies (puga in *yaj.*, ganga in Nar.), the judges appointed by the king and the king himself, each later one being superior to each preceding one.[1] The first three were practically arbitration tribunals like the modern panchayats. The kulas, srenis and ganas that are well-known to the king may decide the disputes of litigants except those that fall under *sahasa* and that it was only the king who could carry out the order for fines or corporal punishments. The arbitration courts could only decide disputes not involving *sahasa* and they had no power to execute their decrees about fines and corporal punishments, but that their decisions had to be filled with the king, who, if he did not disapprove of them, put them into execution. A dispute decided in a village may be taken to the city and one examined in the city (court) to the king; a dispute decided by the king whether correctly or incorrectly cannot be reviewed. The sabhyas are superior to the kulas and the rest, the chief justice is superior to sabhyas and the king is superior to all. According to P.V. Kane, "The foregoing gradations of tribunal did not exist at all times in ancient and medieval India. One thing is, however, quite clear. There was always a court of the Chief Justice appointed by the ruling power and final appeal lay to the ruler himself."[2]

Decision in Disputed Matters

According to the prescription of the Dharmashastras, in disputes between residents of the same country, the same city or the same hamlet of cowherds of the same capital or village, the decision should be according to their own conventional usages, but in disputes between these and others (who are not residents of those respective places) the decision must be in accordance with the sacred texts. Secondly, when there is an apparent conflict between two smritis, reasoning is to decide in ordinary life what should be followed or reasoning based on the actions of the aged and the experienced is to decide what text to follow and the business of the interpreter consists in holding that one of the smritis contains a general rule and that other an exception

1. *Yajnavalkyasmriti*, I. 30, *Narad*, 1-7.
2. Kane, P.V., *History of Dharmashastra*, Vol. III, p. 285.

or that the two apply to different sets of circumstances (*visayavyavastha*) or that an option may be intended.[1] Again, in the administration of justice dharmasastras rules were considered to be superior to those of arthasastras. Further, in certain cases the court was to call in outsiders to help in deciding disputes. For example, it was prescribed that in disputes about the boundaries of villages and about field in a village, four, eight or ten neighbours were to settle the boundaries.[2] In complicated cases the jury system was to be resorted to for settling them. There is nothing to show that there was any class of lawyers or persons whose profession was pleading for or against a case in exchange of money. However, persons well versed in Dharmashastras and the procedure of the courts were appointed to represent a party and place his case before the court. The Dharmashastras have given detailed instructions concerning plaints, court fees, adjournments, defective plaints, rules of pleading, grounds of defeat, means of proof, documentation, classification of documents, proof or document, forgeries and almost all the important matters concerning dispensation of justice.

DISTINCTIONS AMONG VARNAS

According to *Oxford Concise Dictionary* the term distinction means making different, discrimination, being different, thing that differentiates, mark, name, title: showing of special consideration, mark of honour, distinguished character, etc. The Dharmashastras have generally maintained a distinction in dispensation of justice among varnas. This is understandable since while the Brahmins prescribed rules of justice, the Kshartriyas put them into practice, so that these two varnas were given more privileged status as against the remaining two, particularly the shudras. This is explicit specially in the prescription of punishments for different varnas. In discussing punishments for various offences, Manu has treated Brahmins as a class apart. In the administration of justice and in being a witness, Brahmins have been given special treatment. There are separate rules for the appearance as a witness of a Brahmin. A person speaking ill for a Brahmin is to be punished. A Brahmin accepting charity from a Chief is also to be punished. The sexual intercourse with a Brahmin woman attracts severe penalty. A Shudra having sexual relation with a twice born women was to receive heavier punishment than if he had done the same with a Shudra woman. Whereas death sentence for other varnas means actual death, for a Brahmin the same end was supposed to be achieved if his head was shaved clean. Thus, a Brahmin was in no circumstances to be punished by death. He could not die no matter what his offence may be. According to shloka 380 of chapter VIII, "A king should under no circumstances kill a Brahmin even if he is guilty of all kinds of offences. He can be exiled after being given sufficient money and goods." It is written in the shloka 381 that there is nothing more sinful than killing of a Brahmin. Therefore, a king should not even conceive of such an idea.

1. *Yajnavalkyasmriti*, II. 21.
2. *Manusmriti*, VIII, 258, *Yaj.*, II. 150-152.

A Brahmin enjoying women of a lower varna is to get less penalty than a non-Brahmin. The king is enjoined to respect Brahmin duly. Brahmin was also economically privileged. The teaching was the sole prerogative of the Brahmin.

Brahmanism Pointing out to this undue distinction in favour of the Brahmins, S. Cromwell Crawford has pointed out to four evil influences of caste system (varna vyavashtha): First, the caste system has the effect of attributing greater moral depravity to the non-Brahmin. A Brahmin violating a Shudra's wife was considered less guilty than a Shudra ravishing the wife of Brahmin.

Second, the criterion for being a good Brahmin was often more biological than ethical. The law stated that it was better to give alms to a Brahmin, unworthy though he be, than to a non-Brahmin possessed of merit. In the same vein, when making offerings to the gods, one must "not inquire into the qualities or descent of a Brahmin whom he means to invite." Apparently, his being a Brahmin by birth was a sufficient qualification of merit. Third, notwithstanding the ideal calling for humanity in respect of birth, there was the arrogant claim: "A Brahmin though ten years old, and a member of the kingly caste though a hundred years old, must be considered as a father and son" and of these two, the Brahmin was the father. With equal arrogance it is stated that should a Brahmin and Kshatriya cross paths, the Brahmin assumes the right of way. The real height of contempt and exorbitant self-importance is reached in the law which ordinarily forbid a Brahmin to give left over to non-Brahmins, but this law is waived, provided the Brahmin shall clean his teeth and give the food after having placed in it the dirt from his teeth. Fourth, despite the ideal that privilege entails responsibility a great deal of the caste legislation was aimed at securing all kinds of preferential treatment for the Brahmins. These privileges included preferential treatment in respect to sacrifice, marriage, means of livelihood, offerings, property and judicial treatment. The last mentioned privilege became the breeding ground for flagrant injustices. All of these discriminatory laws were enforced by invoking rewards and punishments.[1]

Besides the Brahmins and Kshatriyas the other two varnas were discriminated against in penal laws. For instance a vaishya guest was to be treated on par with a Shudra in respect of all items of hospitality. The humiliation of the Shudras has been already referred to earlier. Similarly, one also finds discrimination against women concerning particularly the social and the economic rights in which they were very much unequal to men.

CONCEPT OF EVIDENCE

Like all developed systems of justice the Dharmashastras prescribed a system which provided proper ethics of evidence. According to the Dharmashastras when the two persons litigate and there is a doubt or discrepancy between the

1. Cromwell Crowford., *Evolution of Hindu Ethical Ideals,* p. 83-84.

two the determination of the truth in the dispute is due to witness *(saksinah)*. It was provided that a proper witness is one who has himself either seen or heard or experienced the matter in dispute. The word *saksin* occurs in the Svetasvataropanisad where it is applied to the one immanent Spirit of the universe as All seeing.[1] Panini explains the words *saksin* as meaning one who has directly seen.[2] Emphasizing the importance of direct witness as against hearsay Medhatithi says that hearsay evidence occurs when a person who hears from another (that has himself heard something from another) comes forward as a witnessed and that hearsay is no legal evidence.[3] Manu prescribed that even though a man may not have been expressly asked or appointed by the parties he is a proper witness when asked as to many matter in dispute that he has himself seen or heard.[4] The only exception to hearsay evidence was that when a person that is appointed as a witnessed is dead or gone abroad those who have heard what he said may give evidence. The evidence was examined by the king or the judge. It was prescribed that the king or the chief judge should himself examine the witnesses that are present in court and should consider along with the sabhyas the statements made by witnesses and that, where it is doubtful who the witnesses on a disputed matter are, time should be given for producing the witnesses in order to ascertain the proper means of proof but that where it is clear who the witnesses may be should make the hearing of the case proceed at once. When it is impossible to bring witnesses because they reside in foreign country evidence taken in writing before a man learned in the three Vedas and sent by him should be read in deciding the cause. This corresponds to the modern rule of taking evidence on commission as provided for in Order 26 rules 4 and 5 of the Indian Civil Procedure of 1908. According to the Dharmashastras ordinarily there should be at least three witnesses in a cause.[5] However, according to Yajnavalkyasmriti along with some others one man alone may be a witness in a cause if he is endowed with the regular performance of his religious duties, and is accepted as a witness by both sides.[6]

Manusmriti also allows a single witness to furnish valid proof if he is a dutaka (messenger), an accountant one who has accidentally witnessed the transaction or if he is the king or the chief justice.[7]

Qualifications of Witnesses

The Dharmashastras lay down the qualifications of witnesses to be examined in a law suit.[8] The principle qualifications of a good family, should have lived

1. *Svetasvataropanisad*, VI. 11.
2. *Panini*, V. 2. 91.
3. *Manusmriti*, VIII. 74, *Medhatithi on Manu*, VIII. 74.
4. *Ibid.*, VIII. 76.
5. *Ibid.*, VIII. 60. Yaj., II. 69.
6. *Yajnavalkyasmriti*, II. 74.
7. *Manusmriti*, VIII. 77.
8. *Ibid.*, VIII. 62-63, Yaj., II. 68.

from birth in the country, should be householders having a son or sons, should be well-to-do and men of character, should be trustworthy, should know dharma and act up to it, should not be covetous and should have been cited by the parties as witnesses. Dharmashastras including Manusmriti and others provide that ordinarily witnesses should be of the same varnas or caste as the parties, that women should be witnesses in disputes between women, that men of the lowest castes (*antyajas*) should be witnesses for litigants of those castes and that a litigant of a lower caste should not try to prove his case by citing witnesses of a higher caste or a Brahmin (unless the latter is an attesting witness on a deed).[1] But most of the dharmashastras give an option and say that persons of all castes (even sutras) may be witnesses for all.[2]

Incompetent Witnesses

The Dharmashastras have given a long list of persons who may be regarded as incompetent for the purpose of evidence.[3] According to Manusmriti the general grounds why oral evidence tends to be false are covetousness, infatuation, fear, desire of pleasures, anger, friendship, ignorance, minority.[4] The king cannot be cited as a witness except possibly to prove the plea of *res-judicata* or to prove what transpired before him when a litigation was going on.[5] This may be compared with Taylor's contention about the sovereign giving evidence on oath; his considered opinion being that the sovereign, if so pleased, may be examined as a witness in any case, civil or criminal but not without being sworn.[6] Most of the Dharmashastras expressly point out that strict examination of the character of witnesses should be entered upon in disputes about debts and the like which are of a fixed nature (of a civil nature), but that in complaints about all kinds of *sahasa* (heinous crime), in robbery, adultery or the two kinds of parusya *viz.,* defamation and assault, there should be no (strict) inquiry into the character of witnesses that is, all can be witnesses in such cases and that even those like slaves and fault-finders who have been enumerated among incompetent witnesses can become witnesses in grave matters.[7] The idea is that in such cases the witnesses need not be strictly examined as to their possessing the good qualities ordinarily required in witnesses. But this does not authorize the examination of such persons as lunatics or idiots as witnesses, because they have not the power to understand things.

1. *Manusmriti,* VIII. 68.
2. *Ibid.,* VIII. 69, Yaj. II. 69.
3. *Ibid.,* VIII. 64-67, Yaj. II. 70-71.
4. *Ibid.,* VIII. 118.
5. *Ibid.,* VIII. 65.
6. Law of Evidence, XII, Ed. Vol. II, p. 872, para 1381.
7. *Manusmriti,* VIII. 72. *Yaj.,* II. 72.

Women as Witnesses

According to Manusmriti even a single male, if he is free from greed, may be sufficient as a witness, but not women of good character, even though they be many, since the feminine intellect is apt to be unsteady.[1] But even Manu had to concede that a woman or a minor or a very old person or a pupil, relative, slave or a hired servant may be a competent witness, if it is impossible to find another witness in matters that occurred inside a house or in crimes where life is lost.[2] There was no total disqualification of women as witnesses, since Manu quoted above allows them to be witnesses, in disputes between women and in cases where it is not possible to have other witnesses. Medhatithi holds that women are disqualified as witnesses only where the plaintiff and defendent are both males but that where there is a litigation between a man and woman or between women alone, a woman may be a competent witness.[3] This may be compared with the condition in so many other countries of the world in ancient as well as modern times. According to Best, ancient Roman Law and the Medieval laws of several countries of Europe more or less excluded the testimony of women, and some states in the U.S.A. excluded the testimony of Negroes and persons of coloured blood.[4] According to Taylor the Canon Law gave more credit to male than female witnesses.[5]

Cross Examination

According to Dharmashastras, before a witness for a party begins to depose, it is the duty of opposite party to point out the ground or grounds, if any, of the incompetence of the witness put forward for examination. A detailed procedure has been given for giving evidence and the cross examination. According to Manusmriti the judge should in a conciliatory manner exhort all witnesses assembled inside the court in the presence of the plaintiff and defendants as follows: "Whatever acts of these two (litigants) between themselves you know as regards this matter in (in dispute) narrate theme all truthfully, since you are the witnesses in this case.[6] According to Yajnavalkyasmriti witnesses should be made to depose in the presence of the parties.[7] The Dharmashastras contain very long exhortations addressed by the judge to the witnesses relating to the importance and high worth of truth, stating how the conscience of a man pricks him, what rewards await the truthful witness here and in the next world and what sin and terrible torments in Hell are the lot of an untruthful witness, what evil befalls even the deceased ancestors of an untruthful witness and how

1. *Ibid.*, VIII. 77.
2. *Ibid.*, VIII. 70.
3. *Medhatithi on Manu*, VIII. 68.
4. Best, *Evidence*, XII, Ed., 1992, p. 53-56.
5. Taylor, *Law of Evidence*, 1848, p. 655.
6. *Manusmriti*, VIII. 79-80.
7. *Yajnavalkyasmriti*, II. 73.

he is liable to be punished by the king.[1] Distinctions have been made among different varnas in this connection. According to Manusmriti a Brahmin witness is to be addressed by the judge as to speak and to be exhorted to swear by his veracity, a kshatriya one was to be addressed as to speak the truth and to be sworn by the animal he rides and his weapons which he is to touch, a vaisya is to be sworn by his kin, grain and gold and a shudra is to be sworn by implacating on his head all grave sins.[2] The Dharmasastras insist that it is the duty of the witnesses to attend the call of the court. According to Manusmriti and others if a witness knowing all facts and not prevented from coming by disease or similar causes refuses to come as a witness he incurs the sin of false witness, has to pay the amount in disputes and ten per cent thereof as fine to the king.[3] This is in accordance with the principle enforced in modern times that it is the duty of a citizen to appear before a court of justice when summoned. Punishment was prescribed for violating this rule.

Rules About Evidence

When there were many witnesses who differed in their statements the Dharmashastras prescribed rules for evidence. For example, it was prescribed that the statement of the majority of witnesses should be accepted, but if they are equally divided then the statement of those who are more pure (in character or more disinterested) should be accepted and if the meritorious are divided equally then those who are the best among them should be accepted as true.[4] The Mit. On Yaj. adds that if there is a conflict of testimony between the statements of a few but eminently qualified witnesses on the one hand and those of a larger number of ordinary witnesses, then the former should be accepted.[5] In answer to the important question as to how much has to be proved by the party calling witnesses, the Dharmashastras state the general rule that party whose averments are supported in their entirety as true by the witnesses become successful, while that litigant whose claim is declared by them to be false certainly loses.[6] Further, there are rules about the late production of evidence. According to Yajnavalkyasmriti if a witness having promised with other witnesses to depose to a state of things, denies at the time of his examination that he saw the matter in dispute, he should be fined eight times the amount that a defeated litigant would have to pay and a Brahmin witness similarly guilty if unable to pay may be banished or his house should be raised to the ground.[7]

---

1. *Manusmriti,* VIII. 107, *Yaj.,* II. 77.
2. *Ibid.,* VIII. 88-113.
3. *Manusmriti,* VIII. 107, Yaj, II. 77.
4. *Manu,* VIII. 73, *Yaj.,* II. 78.
5. *Mit.* on *Yaj.,* II. 78.
6. *Yajnavalkyasmriti,* II. 79.
7. *Ibid.,* II. 82.

RULES ABOUT PERJURY

After the witnesses have deposed, the chief justice and sabhyas have to consider the depositions of witnesses. According to Manusmriti depose falsely through covetousness, wrong ideas, fear, friendship, sexual passion, wrath, ignorance and minority and Manu prescribes varying fines for perjury arising from these several causes.[1] Yajnavalkayasmriti prescribed that the litigant who procures perjured evidence and the witnesses guilty of perjury should each be separately fined double the amount of the fine prescribed for defeat in various disputes and a Brahmin guilty of doing the same should be banished from the country but not fined.[2] But when a person of any of the three castes other than Brahmin is frequently guilty of perjury he should be fined and given physical punishment as cutting the tongue or death and a similarly guilty Brahmin should be fined and banished or degraded by being carried naked through the streets or deprived of his house. The Dharmashastras prescribe that a witness may depose falsely in a cause when, if he were to speak the truth, a person of the four varnas is liable to suffer the sentence of death.[3] It was prescribed that as a penance for the falsehood a witness of the three higher speech (Sarasvati) or he may offer into fire clarified butter with the mantras called Kusmanda.[4]

The Dharmashastras have also discussed in detail, what is known as circumstantial evidence. According to Manusmriti the just kind should not condemn to death one accused to theft unless his guilt is proved as certain by proof that the accused had in his possession the articles stolen and tools for theft for house-breaking.[5] Similar prescriptions were given about other types of crime. According to Yajnavalkyasmriti adultery may be inferred from the man and woman being caught in the act of dalliance with hair or from the signs left such as marks of nails or teeth on the lips, cheek etc. after carnal enjoyment or from the admission of the woman concerned or of both. However, it has been admitted that circumstantial evidence leads to conclusions that are false in several instances. Therefore, the dangers of circumstantial evidence were discussed by Dharmashastras.

If the circumstantial evidences do not enable the court to arrive at a decision, it may take resort to other methods such as divine proof known as daivikikriya and special caths etc. Manu gives the admonition that a wise man should not make a false oath, because by so doing he incurs loss of reputation here and after death by falling into Hell.[6] According to Yajnavalkya a fine of 100 panas may be given for one who takes an improper or profane

1. *Manusmriti,* VIII. 118. 120-122.
2. *Yajnavalkyasmriti,* II. 81.
3. *Manusmriti,* VIII. 104, *Yaj,* II. 83.
4. *Manu,* VIII. 105-106, *Yaj,* II. 83.
5. *Manusmriti,* IX. 270.
6. *Ibid.,* VIII. 111.

oath.[1] It was also prescribed that the benefit of doubt is to be given to the accused. Thus, several centuries before Christ the authors of Dharmashastras recognized the rule of benefit of doubt of the modern administration of justice.

THEORIES OF PUNISHMENT

The authors of Dharmashastras have given several theories and detailed rules on the subject of punishment. They were aware of the several purposes served by punishment for crime. However, they did not develop a regular science of penology. Some Western authors have praised the discussion of penology in Dharmashastras and pointed out the comparatively humane treatment of criminals in Ancient India as compared with the horrible and revolting methods for punishing criminals employed in the West.[2]

1. **Retributive Theory** The most ancient theory of punishment is retributive theory. According to the retributive theory the purpose of punishment is to underscore revenge. It is the theory described in the old Testament as an eye for an eye and a tooth for a tooth. According to the German philosopher Kant, the offender should not be punished for the reason that it is the means to his or another's benefit but for the simple reason that he has committed a crime. A court of law repays to one only that which he has acquired. He has done crime and it is logical that the reward of his crime, the equivalent of his destructive value, be given to him. The punishment which the society confers upon him, does not deprive him of his right but gives to him that which he has earned and deserves. According to Hegel and Aristotle, punishment is the negative reward of the criminal, who acquires it by infringing the moral law. It is his award which he must receive. For this reason, when some offenders escape with lighter punishment than the severity of their crimes, they try to reap the reward of their misdeeds by penance. Pointing out to this theory known as the *lex talionis* (the law of retaliation *viz.*, an eye for an eye, a tooth for tooth), the Dharmashastras prescribe that with whatever limb a man of low caste offends against a Brahmin, that very limb of his shall be cut off.[3] It may be noted here that similar retribution was not prescribed when a Brahmin offends against a Shudra.
2. **Preventive Theory** Another most important theory of punishment is known as deterrent or preventive theory. According to the preventive theory the aim behind punishment is to set an example to other and to prevent them from criminal tendencies. In this way, the object of punishment is prevention. The theory is expressed by the judge's formula, "You are not punished for stealing sheep, but in order that

---

1. *Yajnavalkyasmriti,* II. 236.
2. Barnes, Harry Elmer, *The Study of Punishment,* 1930, New York.
3. *Manu,* VIII. 280. *Yaj.,* II. 215.

sheep may not be stolen." This theory does not invalidate even capital punishment because though there is no question of improvement in the criminal, other people derive a lesson not to indulge in homicide. This aspect of punishment has been dealt by the Dharmashastras in their discussion of Rajdharma. This aimed to protect the society and secure its happiness. With this purpose in view the punishments were sufficiently mild, particularly from the times of Yajnavalkyasmriti. As Fa Hein (399-400 A.D.) noted, "The king governs without decapitation or other corporal punishments. Criminals are simply fined, lightly or heavily, according to the circumstances. Even in circumstances of repeated attempts at wicked rebellion they only have their right hands cut off."[1] This May be contrasted with the condition during the earlier times, particularly under Maurya Empire. Thus 700 years before Fa Hein, Magasthenes noted, "A person bearing false witness suffers multiplication of his extremities. He who means anyone not only suffers loss of the same limb but his hand also is cut off. If he causes an artisan to lose his hand and eye he is put to death."[2]

3. **Reformative Theory** The most advanced theory of punishment is known as the reformative theory. According to the reformative theory, the aim of punishment is the improvement of the offender himself. Modern age seems generally to favour and apply this theory. In this theory, the behaviour directed at the criminal shows him the consideration due to an individual and not conduct analogous to treatment of objects and means. An offender is punished for his own benefit. This theory finds mention in the Dharmashastras in the form of redemption of the evil doer. The punishment was deemed to be a part of expiation which purged the man of sinful promptings and reformed his character. Manu states that men who are guilty of crimes and have been punished by the king go to heaven becoming pure like those who perform meritorious deeds.[3] Manu drew distinction between Dharma and Adharma, righteousness and unrighteousness. By Dharma was meant an act which was according to law and by Adharma the act against or violative of the law. The lawful was contributory to the social interest and welfare and the unlawful was that which is harmful to the social welfare and subversive of social order and organization.

METHODS OF PUNISHMENT

The Dharmashastras speak of four methods of punishment (danda) *viz.* by gentle admonition, by severe reproof by fine and by corporal punishment and declare that these punishments may be inflicted separately or together

1. Fa Hein, *Legge,* 1886 p. 43.
2. *Magasthenes, Fragment,* XXVII, p. 71.
3. *Manusmriti,* VIII. 318.

according to the nature of the offences.[1] The emphasis upon reformative theory of punishment is clear by the fact that in so many cases verbal condemnation was considered sufficient punishment. One reason why some of the works on Dharmashastras prescribed mild punishments is the doctrine of *karmavipaka,* according to which a man committing certain sins is born in the next life afflicted with certain diseases or bodily deficiencies or is born as a low or filthy beast or bird.[2]

In modern times there are controversies among several schools of criminology. Some hold that every man has freedom to act criminally or not or to act in the way he does and that each man has complete moral responsibility for his own acts. On the other hand there are some who go to the other extreme and propound that a so-called criminal act is mostly due to biological, physiological, pathological or sociological conditions, to the upbringing and environment of the person charged with crime. They favour determinism. The ancient Indian writers do not enter into these speculations. But when they said that regard must be paid to time and place and other considerations they were conscious of or were groping towards the ideas of the 2nd school.

Laws for Punishment

In Manusmriti the laws were divided into two classes. The first class of law dealt with the general behaviour and conduct. In this were laws regarding borrowing and lending, partnership, sale, promises, conflicts about animals, division of wealth, land and boundary disputes, marital relations etc. The main concern of criminal laws related to contempt, attack, gambling, rape, theft and loot.

Authority for Punishment

According to Manusmriti punishment could be given by a competent authority only. The judges should be learned, impartial, selfless and free from greed and bigotry. Only man of high academic attainments, pure of morals and heart and lovers of truth, justice and fair play should be appointed judges.

TYPES OF PUNISHMENT

According to Manusmriti, an official found guilty of graft should be exiled out of the country and all his property and belongings should be attached. Before delivering judgments all the circumstances of the case must be duly considered and the extenuating circumstances of the crime must be given due weightage. Besides, in delivering judgement, the judge must not only consider the crime and the situation of the crime but the nature and character of the criminal should also be considered and given due weightage. There was a separate penal code for the men of high ability and attainments.

1. *Manu,* VIII. 129. *Yaj.,* I. 367.
2. *Manu,* XI. 49-52, *Yaj.,* III. 207-216.

Accordingly, a man of high talents was let off with mere warning for his crime. If his crime is serious and more reprimand would not meet the ends of justice then he may be fined. But if the talented persons abuse this privilege and keep committing crimes in the hope of being easily let off, they must not be allowed to carry this impression. If a crime is committed fourth time or the criminal commits four crimes in succession he should be flogged and for serious crime even hanged. Theft was the most commonly committed crime. The king was allowed wide power to penalize the thieves. He could get their limbs, for example, hands, arms, legs etc., chopped. A person who stole a drinking utensil from a public well had to compensate for it by giving 2 grammes of gold. If the costly ornaments and clothes were stolen, the thief could be given death sentence. Adulteration was a crime, Adulterators were severely dealt with. A person who took away the property of others by deceit was to be flogged. Perjury was a serious crime and a man who gave false witness was to be exiled. Adultery was a serious crime. A man who defiled the wives of others was to be exiled after piercing holes in his lips and ears. A sexually excited women who attracted others for sexual intercourse was considered a devilish soul. She was thrown before hungry dogs. A women who drunk and danced obscenely in public was also punished. Gambling was declared a crime and the gamblers were also punished. A forgerer who falsely produced the documents of the state which could be accepted as the degree of king was a serious criminal. He was given death sentence. A person who stole from the government treasury attracted the punishment of chopping of hands and tongue. Similarly, a burglar's hands were chopped. A goldsmith must not steal from the gold given to him for ornaments. If any goldsmith was found guilty of misappropriation of gold given to him for ornaments, he was chopped into pieces. The stealing of agriculture implements was also a crime. Besides stealing, it was also a crime to give shelter to the criminals. It was regarded a serious crime and such person was to be beheaded.

Favour of Reformative Theory

According to the Concise Oxford Dictionary the term dispensation means distributing, ordering, arrangement made by Nature or providence, special dealing of providence with community or person, religious system regarded as divinely ordained for a nation or period.[1] This definition of dispensation of justice is particularly applicable in the case of the Dharmashastras. As has been already pointed out, though the Dharmashastras mention different theories of punishment, yet they generally favour the reformative theory. That is one reason why capital punishment has been prescribed by the Dharmashastras in very few cases. While in 19th century England more than a hundred offences were punishable by death.[2] This number, in the case of Dharmashatras extended only by few dozens. The basic aim of penology,

1. *The Concise Oxford Dictionary*, 1976. p. 197.
2. Dr. Hart, *Way of Justice*, p. 94.

according to the Dharmashastras, was the restoration of Dharma, the social order, the natural order and the order of Divine. If in a certain crime it was considered that the criminal will achieve his negative reward in the next birth, he was given only lighter punishment, particularly if he felt sorry for his offence and was prepared to undergo prescribed expiations.

Affective and Constructive

Thus, in keeping with the general purpose of a sound penology, Indian penology, as developed by the Dharmashastras, sought to formulate effective and constructive technique to keep and maintain social peace and security. The dispensation in this context was not due to providence or Nature but to Divine order or Rta. which, according to Indian philosophy, is the cosmic order.

Sound Procedure

Along with the aim, the Indian penology had a sound procedure of dispensation of justice. Justice was not the sole responsibility of the king. Judiciary function was decentralized among so many persons and tribunals. This was a check against despotism or suppression of justice, by the despot. The machinery of dispensation of justice again, was on par even with the modern system, with the provision of evidence, the jury, the advocate for and against with a knowledge of Dharmashastras, and the decision purely on the basis of prescription of the Dharmashastras. The most important qualification for the function of the judge was the knowledge of Dharmashastras. However, sufficient value was attributed to the local customs in dispensation of justice. Along with the knowledge of Dharmashastras, the judge was required to have a sound knowledge of the local customs and traditions so that his judgement may not violate either. The Dharmashastras rightly honoured the direct witness, and prescribed for the benefit of doubt in its absence. Thus, it is clear that penology, as prescribed by the Dharmashastras, amply met the purpose of social justice. This is more so in comparison with the contemporary conditions in Western countries as reported by so many contemporary scholars.

Favour of High Castes

However, one great slur on Indian penology is the favoritism of the higher castes and lack of justice towards the lower castes. Different types of punishment were prescribed for the same offences. According to Manusmriti, a kshatriya or a vaisya or shudra abusing or defaming a Brahmin was to be respectively punished with the fine of 100 panas, 150 panas and with corporal punishment (cutting off the tongue) while a Brahmin defaming a kshatriya, vaisya or shudra was to be fined 50, 25 or 20 panas respectively or nothing in the last case.[1] Yajnavalkya prescribed the highest punishment for adultory with a woman of the same caste, the middling one when the paramour was of a higher caste, but if the male be of a lower caste than the women, the male offender was sentenced to death and the women had her ears cut off.[2] Similar prescriptions can be found in so many other cases. In so many offences while the other three varnas met punishment, the Brahmin was only banished from the country. For example, Manu provides that punishment may fall upon any one or more often places in the case of the three higher castes, *viz.,* the private parts, the belly, the tongue either whole or half; the hands, the feet, the eyes, the nose, the ears and the whole body; but a Brahmin shall depart, unhurt from the country, he is to be only banished.[3] These prescriptions are clearly violations of the ideal of jural ethics and therefore must be condemned. The condemnation, however, will be softened by a perusal of those statements where punishment was prescribed in inverse order according to social responsibility which was maximum upon the Brahmin and moderate upon the other two varnas while nil upon the shudras. Thus, Manu prescribed that a vaisya, a kshatriya and a Brahmin should respectively be fined twice, four times and eight times of the fine to be imposed upon a shudras for a theft, since each of these is deemed more and more aware of the heinousness of the crime.[4]

1. *Manusmriti,* VIII. 267-268, *Yaj.,* II. 206-207.
2. *Yajnavalkyasmriti,* II. 286.
3. *Manusmriti,* VIII. 125.
4. *Ibid.,* VIII. 338-39.

3
Political Ideas of Manu

Like Plato the author of *Manusmriti* sought to maintain a balance and harmony between different parts of society. Thus, the aim was social progress and the provision of social justice. From the metaphysical point of view the work believed in a single element behind the diversity of creation. Everywhere in the universe there is manifestation of one universal being, one supreme consciousness. The soul and matter are not fundamentally diverse and incompatible. The material being is permeated by consciousness in a latent form. In the living creatures the consciousness dominates over material being. The ascendancy of consciousness over matter accounts for the creation of life. The motive power behind all activity in the universe is provided by intelligence. The evolution is not blind development; it is purposeful and goal-seeking. The intelligence is manifestation of consciousness and not matter. Manu has explained the universe in terms of soul. The *terminus ad quem* (the destination) and the *terminus ad quo* (the starting point) of the universe is the state of consciousness and Bliss and Intelligence. The purpose of the entire creation is the achievement of a state of non-duality. Lastly, Manu has described the place of matter, life, etc., in the social structure. The social values are not the products of experience. They are not dependent upon man. They are the values of the Universal Being.

THE CONCEPT OF VARNA

The social structure and organization delineated by Manu should be understood in the context of the above philosophical background. In line with the ancient Indian tradition Manu distinguished between various human beings on the basis of their basic tendencies and inclinations. The element of desire, action and knowledge was found among persons varying according to the proportion of three *gunas* of *Rajas*, *Tamas* and *Sattvik* in them. The human beings were classified on the basis of the preponderance of a particular *guna*. Thus in Brahmin, the *sattvik* guna preponderates; in Kshatriya the *Rajas* preponderates and the *tamas* preponderates in the Vaishyas and Shudras. In ancient texts the four varnas were compared with the limbs of human body. Thus, brahmin was represented by mouth; the kshatriya by arms; the vaishya by navel and the shudra by feet. This is why brahmins got the top status. They used to teach, preach and advise, that is, the functions of higher intellect were their prerogative. The kshatriyas were the protectors of dharma, while vaishyas performed trade and agriculture. The shudras used to serve the higher varnas. Though the possession of quality and not the accident of birth was said to determine one's varna; but in actual fact this salutary advice was followed more in breach than in observance. Therefore, it is not surprising that many thinkers have held that Manusmriti is partial to brahmins.

CENTRAL PRINCIPLE OF SOCIAL ORGANIZATION

In *Manusmriti* dharma has been considered to be central to social organization. Indeed Manu says that *dharma* sustains and preserves the society. Therefore, each person should follow his respective dharma. The *Vedas* are the authority on what is dharma or adharma of a particular man or class. All twice-born persons, that is, Brahmin, Kshatriya and Vaishya are entitled to study the Vedas. By Varna dharma is meant the duties which become enjoined by virtue of his belonging to a particular Varna. In Manusmriti the specific dharmas of each Varna are given in detail. Those duties which become necessary to man by virtue of being of a particular class and in a particular stage of life are *varnashrama dharma.*

CONTENTS OF MANUSMRITI

In the first chapter Manu has tried to answer to sages the question regarding the nature of duty. Discussing the creation of the universe, the water and Brahman, it described how mind, matter and ego came into being; also as to how the heaven and hell were made. The Karmas of the each class of this phenomenal world were created separately. Manu discusses the cycle of various ages and the preponderance of Dharma in *Satya Yuga* and its gradual decline in the *dvapara* and *treta* ages. Manu has discussed in detail the entire gamut of creation ranging from mind to space. He has discussed how earth was formed out of water, the consequences of time gaps between the creation of Manus. He has also prescribed the duties of Brahmin and other castes. The superiority of the Brahmin is greatly emphasized. The prerogatives of Brahmin are also described. He is the Lord of all wealth and all sorts of enjoyments are permitted to Brahmin. After giving the description of creation, the aim and purpose of Manusmriti is discussed next. Brahmins have the prerogative to study this book and the good consequent upon its reading is discussed. The duties, virtues and vices are the topics of this book. In the tenth chapter the relations between different varnas are discussed. First of all the importance of Brahmin in society is emphasized. The difference between high and low classes is explained. The superiority of class is discussed. The behaviour and its rules in reference to relation between varnas are given.

Context of Manusmriti

From the above discussion regarding the contents of *Manusmriti,* it is clear that in it we find detailed description of duties, injunctions and disinjunctions of various varnas based upon the material and social conditions obtaining at the time of the composition of this *Dharma Shastra.* Some thinkers overlook this historic background in their discussion of *Manusmriti* and try to evaluate its subject-matter in the current context. Though there are many things in *Manusmriti* which have universal application and are not altered by spatio-temporal conditions; but, on the whole, it will be wrong to overlook the context in which it was written. By a deep consideration of duties of a man and also the nature of true politics, economy, penology, justice, social organization and division of labour in society, Manu has rendered the task of an average man easy in knowing what is his duty. But duties cannot be absolute; these are bound to change as the material and social conditions change. The Indian thinkers have always conceded that eternal truths must be viewed afresh in every era. Therefore, if we find certain matters in *Manusmriti* which are not acceptable to the modern mind, its importance, on that count, does not become less.

BRAHMANISM IN MANUSMRITI

It is written in *Manusmriti* that inasmuch as Brahmin was born from the mouth of Brahma and prior to the other three varnas and insofar as he was first to conceive of *Vedas,* Brahmin is the lord of all creation. In order to feed gods and ancestors, Brahma, after a long period of austerities, created the Brahmin. The gods partake of *havya* from the mouth of the Brahmin and the ancestors eat *kavya* likewise. The 96th shloka of 1st chapter of *Manusmriti* says. "Among earth and five elements, living being is superior; amongst living learned is superior; and amongst the learned Brahmin is supreme."

Qualities of Brahmin

A person born of Brahmin parentage does not *ipso facto* become a Brahmin, because as Manu states in the shloka 97th, "Amongst Brahmins also learned is superior; even amongst learned a man well-versed in Vedic injunctions and rituals is learned and even amongst these pandits, *Brahmagyani* is the supreme." Thus, it is obvious that *Manusmriti* considers Brahmin superior because he has the intuitive knowledge of Brahman. Brahmin is created for the performance of religious duties and is assured of moksha. As he is the protector of religion, he is a supreme person in the land. All created things are in his custody; he is their Lord. Therefore, whatever he partakes, the alms he accepts are indeed his own. The other varnas are able to feed themselves only by the kindness and altruism of Brahmin.

Functions of Brahmin

The *Manusmriti* charges the Brahmin with the duty to teach Manava *Dharma Shastra* to other varnas. The persons belonging to other varnas are not entitled to teach *Dharma Shastra*. But amongst Brahmins also only learned and competent can take up the task of teaching. Thus, it is obvious that while emphasizing the importance of Brahmin, Manu has laid stress upon their special qualifications. Being a knower of Reality, Brahmin is worthy of reverence. By daily practice in teaching *Dharma Shastra*, Brahmin becomes free from mental, vocal and bodily defects. The study of *Dharma Shastra* ensures *moksha*. But a corrupt Brahmin is denied the fruits of *Vedic studies*; only a virtuous Brahmin will receive the beneficial fruits of *Vedic study* and teaching. Being a teacher, Brahmin has the paramountcy in social order; he is the first and most respectable member of the society. The Brahmin must lead a life of utmost purity. The various impieties to be eschewed by Brahmin are also discussed in detail. According to shloka 88 of chapter I, "Brahmin was created for the purpose of vedic study, performance of yajnas and the receipt and gift of charities." In the 7th chapter the king has been enjoined to protect *dharma*. In the varna system of Manu, each varna has been enjoined duties peculiar to it. The learned Brahmins were to act as advisers to the kings and the kings were supposed to trust them deeply. The Brahmins were to be looked after well by the king. It was his duty. Brahmins were provided brides, household artifacts and money by the kings. The charities given to deserving Brahmins are highly acclaimed by Manu.

Paramountcy of Brahmins

In chapter VII, shloka 14, Manu says that the food, etc., thrown into sacrificial fire during havana may spoil, may miss the target; but the alms given to Brahmin are never split nor do these ever dry up. The alms given to undeserving Brahmin bring only two-fold reward but those given to learned or Brahmagyani Brahmins bring forth rewards which are infinite. The alms given to persons of other varnas are not considered very meritorious; only those given to Brahmin have the real potency to multiply infinitely in fruits.

Causes of Brahmin's Paramountcy

The paramountcy of Brahmin is to be accounted for by the very creation of the world. According to tradition the universe came out of Brahma. From the mouth of Brahma, the Brahmin took birth. Therefore, it is obvious that the Brahmin should have a place of pride in creation. However, the importance of Brahmin was not due merely to contingency of birth but on account of his qualities and abilities. Brahmin was a man of pure conduct; he was deeply learned. He was valuable to society because he possessed the knowledge of the *Vedas* and therefore was a knower of Reality. Thus, the importance and value accorded to the Brahmin in society was indeed on account of the high value attached to learning in ancient India.

Three Professions of Brahmins

According to Manu, Brahmin performs three functions in society: firstly, he was a teacher; secondly, he was a preacher and thirdly, he was an adviser to the king. Thus, there were three classes among Brahmins. All of them, however, had to perform the role of guide in some area of social life. Manu has described in detail the qualities of the three classes of Brahmins. The teacher should be self-disciplined, interested in learning, and observe austerities. He should live a life of purity and eat only clean and wholesome food. He should possess knowledge of various disciplines and impart knowledge to various varnas according to their needs and merits. The teacher should also be well-versed in *Dharma Shastras.*

The preacher should have adequate knowledge of prayers and yajnas. He should be well versed in the knowledge of scriptures. A Brahmin who does not possess these qualifications is condemned by Manu.

The advisers to kings must be well-versed in all aspects of statecraft. He should be upright and righteous in conduct; only then can he administer justice. He should not confer any privilege on any body merely by virtue of the accident of birth. He should also be above flattery and corruption. He should keep secret the name of his ancestors, class and clan. When offered salutation he should know how to respond. A Brahmin who does not respond to the salutations offered is not worthy of respect.

It is written in the shloka 155 of chapter II that the Brahmin is great by virtue of his learning, the Kshatriya by virtue of his valour, Vaishya by virtue of wealth and Shudra by virtue of service. Thus, Manu clearly recognizes that nobody is a born Brahmin or Kshatriya but that the varnas are due to the qualities and abilities of men. The Brahmin is great by virtue of his mental abilities and learning but he should not crave fame and honour. A Brahmin should not only not crave honour but should be forgiving even if insulted. While Manusmriti is full of praises for the learned and righteous Brahmin, it has not spared criticism of foolish and vicious Brahmin. Therefore, it will be wrong to label Manusmriti as unnecessarily partial to Brahmins.

Consequences of Brahmanism

From the above discussion of the role of Brahmin in society it is clear that Brahmin enjoyed a place of pride in the social organization as conceived by Manu. Brahmin was first to be created among various varnas; he had exclusive prerogative of teaching, preaching and acting as a guide to the king. The Brahmin alone had the authority to interpret scripture and administer justice. But from all these privileges and rights accorded to Brahmin, it will not be justified to interpret Manu as being partial to Brahmins. The Brahmins occupied top status in society because they possessed the ability and capacity for it and not by virtue of birth. A fool, even if Brahmin, was not to be shown respect. But it cannot be denied that there are certain rights which are exclusive to Brahmin.

But the most important reason for the Brahmanism of *Manusmriti* is historical. As K.P. Jayaswal points out about the Code of Manu, "His Code is the mirror reflecting the national sentiment of the time. His absurd claims for Brahmanism were admitted at the time, for they were based on the facts of the time. The Brahmin, in fact, was 'the lord of everything' at the moment."[1] At the time Buddhism when Buddhist State stood discredited, Saketa, Mathura and Panchala were lost to the viciously valiant Greeks. Pataliputra itself was in danger and the whole country in consternation. The astronomer Garga summed up the sentiment of the time in his characterisation of the last Maurya emperor as "Talking of dharma that anti-dharma king, the fool." At this time the Brahmin king Pushyamitra took up the sword and saved the Dharma and also rehabilitated it. He liberated the whole country and completely destroyed the power which had threatened confusion in the holy land of Aryans. The contempt for the Shudra was due to the treacherous behaviour of the Shudra rulers before whose very eyes the kingdom was sinking like a cow in the mire. Thus, the Brahminical prejudice of Manava Code was not religious but political and social. As K.P. Jayaswal rightly pointed out, "The Dharma Code of the militant Brahmin was the Code of the Manava Dharma Sastra, and the Manava Dharma Sastra is militant throughout.[2]

FATHER OF INDIAN POLITY

Manu is the author of Manu Smriti, which is one of the most authoritative book on Indian Polity. Manu has dealt with every aspect of political life and administration with clarity. He has discussed pros and cons of every political problem. In this book he has not only posed problems but suggested solutions too. He has called the King divine but still placed him subservient to judiciary and suggested twice more punishment than an ordinary if found guilty. He has laid the standards of life and administration. As the standards laid down by him are still true he is called the father of Indian Polity:

1. Manu Smriti is the most reliable and important book on polity.
2. Manu Smriti forms the foundation of the social order of Vedic times.
3. Manu Smriti deals with different aspects of the life and administration.
4. According to Manu because in primitive period there was anarchy, God created King to restore welfare to the people.
5. Manu has clearly mentioned the qualities of King, Ministers and judges.
6. According to Manu the guilty who defy or disturb land must be punished.
7. According to Manu the king must bring welfare to the people, respect learned people, have council of the ministers and act according to the advice of ministers.

---

1. *op. cit.*, p. 43.
2. *Ibid.*, p. 52.

8. Manu has laid stress on the division of power and distribution of functions.
9. Manu Smriti deals with judicial administration, the evidence, the procedure of Court, different types of Courts etc.
10. Manu deals with the appointment of ambassadors, their qualities and qualifications.
11. In Manu Smriti the system of taxation has been dealt with in detail, but the taxes should not be heavy.
12. Manu lays emphasis upon the importance of the boundaries of village.
13. Manu has given importance to the maintenance of the international relations between different states.

Thus Manu, as the real father of the ancient Indian polity, has very aptly dealt with all aspects of administration.

4
Political Ideas of Shukracharya

Though the Historians admit that the Shukra Niti was written by Shukracharya but, there is a difference of opinion about who was Shukracharya and when this book was written. Widely divergent views are held about the date of Shukracharya's Niti. Some place it even in the pre-Christian period. Dr. U. N. Ghoshal thinks that the book was written between 1200 and 1600 A. D. The view of R. L. Misra is similar. The work was composed and re-touched down to the fourteenth century. Its greater part, however, may be ascribed to the eleventh or the twelfth century A. D. There is a great unanimity of views that the work of writing Shukra Niti commenced in the eleventh or twelfth century A. D. This has been deduced from — (i) The statement that the Mlechhas resided in the north-west of India. (ii) The reference to the samantas as both feudatories and officials. (iii) The information that the price of gold was sixteen times of silver as stated by Bhaskracharya. (iv) The inclusion of Deshbhasas (vernaculars) as topics of study. (v) The reference to the vedanta doctrine of Shankara that peace should even be made with Anarya, because otherwise he may uproot the kingdom. (vi) The enunciation of the principle that the treasury should have reserve equal to twenty years revenue, which was obviously followed by Hindu kings of the eleventh century as shown by the coins of plunderers obtained from their treasuries by Muslim conquerors. All these tend to show that the book belongs to the period between 900 and 1200 A. D. However, the verses dealing with fire-arms and gun powder may have been added by the end of fourteenth century when gun powder is known to have been used by the Army of Vijay Nagar.

Shukra Niti was not written at a stretch, or written in a period of years, but it was continued to be written for a very long period. It appears that additions were continued to be made as considered necessary but the bulk of the book must have been written at a time.

SHUKRACHARYA

According to ancient Indian thinkers, Shukracharya was not an individual. It was seat of learning which was occupied by his disciples. This view is corroborated by the fact that Shukracharya has been mentioned in Rigveda, Atharvaveda and also in Ushna Kavya, Bhargava Kavi, Dataya Guru etc.

There is also its mention in Mahabharata. It can safely be assumed that Shukracharya was the designation of the head of the educational institutions since the age of Mahabharata.

SCOPE OF SHUKRA NITI

(i) *Monarchy.* Shukra Niti deals with monarchical system of Government.

(ii) *Society.* It has also dealt with different aspects of society.

(iii) *Divine Origin and Organic Theory.* Shukra Niti believes in divine origin as well as organic theory of State. Here there is some contradiction. On the one hand, State is of divine origin and on the other hand it has been compared to divine organisms. It has been said that the king is the head, the ministers eyes, friends of king ears, etc. State has also been compared with a tree callint, king as root of tree, the ministers as trunk, army chief branches etc. It has also been stated that the king is the representative of various gods such as Vayu, Surya, Agni, Varun, Chandra, Kuber and Yama. It has been emphasised that the king has an element of divinity in him.

The functions of King, Ministers, Officials, Judiciary, Treasury, Army and Law, Civil and Military administration have been described and specified.

The welfare state should remove the sufferings of people. Emphasis has been laid on awarding suitable punishment to evil doers, law breakers and enemies of the State. The nature of punishment for each sort of crime has been mentioned in Shukra Niti.

CHARACTERISTICS OF SHUKRA NITI

As a writer on Hindu Polity Shukracharya has a high status. His book Shukra Niti is a very important book dealing with all aspects of administration.

1. **Ways of Administration** It has suggested practical ways of administering a State.
2. **Organs of Administration** It deals with monarchy and the different organs of its administration.
3. **Subjects of State Administration** It gives description about different subjects pertaining to state administration.
4. **Theocracy** According to Shukracharya, king was the creation of God to watch and ensure welfare of the people.
5. **Qualifications of the King** The following qualifications for the king has been laid down in Shukra Niti: (i) Intelligent; (ii) Capable of arriving at proper decision; (iii) Having control over his senses; and (iv) Free from allurement etc.
6. **Theories of Succession** The following theories for succession to throne or privileges and rights of the king are laid down in Shukra Niti: (i) Hereditary theory (ii) Succession on the basis of seniority. (iii) On the basis of physical fitness or capacity. (iv) Superiority or character. (v) Theory of consent of people.

7. **Functions of the State** The following are the functions of State: (i) protection of the people, (ii) destruction of evil doers.
8. **Force and Punishment** A great stress has been laid on the use of force or punishment of the evil doers after thorough investigation and proof.
9. **Procedures for Appointment** Procedure for appointment of ministers and other officials is laid down in detail.
10. **Council of Ministers** King will act in consultation with the Ministers. Stress has been laid for the appointment of Council of Ministers which is inevitable for the smooth functioning of State.
11. **Qualifications of the Ministers** In Shukra Niti following qualifications have been laid for the ministers: (i) They should be the nationals of country. (ii) They should be men of strong and high character. (iii) They should be loyal to the king and the state. (iv) They should belong to noble family.
12. **Checks on Govt** Several ways and means have been suggested for the proper check about the functioning of Government and working of ministers and other officials.
13. **Army** Shukracharya has laid great stress on maintaining efficient army.
14. **Resources of the State** Several ways have been suggested for increasing the resources of Government by means of levy of various taxes. Shukracharya has cautioned that taxes should not be heavy and beyond the capacity of people.
15. **Judiciary and Penology** Shukracharya has dealt in detail the judicial system. He has prescribed different punishment for different crimes. He has laid down a scientific theory of crime and punishment.
16. **Checks on the King** Definite checks have been prescribed over the functioning of king so that he may not become tyrant, injust and inefficient.

PURPOSE OF SHUKRA NITI

The main purpose of Shukra Niti was to advise the king about the proper administration of the state as an organisation for the welfare of the subjects. It is a book, not of a theoretical discourse but a book of practical knowledge and also contains several contemporary ideological trends. Of course, we find that while writing about other views Shukracharya had described one particular theme and without completing it disgressed towards another subject.

Monarchy

Its polity is of course monarchical, republics having disappeared long before the date of work. Besides discussing the duties of king and the functioning of his ministers and officers the work describes the problems of foreign policy and methods of warfare. Civil administration has been described in detail and we get a vivid picture of judicial administration.

Contribution to Hindu Polity

Though the theories laid in the book are out of date now but it has certainly contributed a lot and it represents Hindu Polity of the time when this was written.

5
Political Ideas of Kautilya

In his translation of Kautilya's *Arthashastra*, Vachaspati Geraula has aptly observed that the supremely eminent personality of Acharya Kautilya gets merged in the unparalleled fame of Maurya empire. As a political thinker on the other hand, he has left his indelible impress upon Sanskrit literature on account of the high literary merit of his *magnum opus*. To Acharya Kautilya belongs the honour of being the lone scholar of eminence on political thought in the Indian history. Thus, Kautilya has the merit of being both a political thinker and an economist of highest excellence. In the history of Indian political theory Kautilya occupies the place of highest thinker on all aspects of secular knowledge. In politics he exhibits an unusual insight. His *Arthashastra* has come to be known as the imperial Gazetter of Mauryan epoch. In this book the fine points of statecraft and social welfare are discussed in depth. In the introduction of Shri Shyam Shastri's edition of *Arthashastra,* Dr. J. F. Fleet has observed correctly: 'Kautilya was not only a king maker but also the greatest Indian exponent of the art of government, the duties of the kings, ministers and officials and methods of diplomacy.'

HISTORICITY OF KAUTILYA

The real name of Kautilya was Vishnugupta. A reference to Kautilya is found in Acharya Kamandak's *Niti Sara* which was written in 400 A. D. Being a son of Chanak, he was known as Chanakya and being a shrewd politician he was known as Kautilya. In Kamandak's *Niti Sara* it is said that Vishnu Gupta had written *Arthashastra.* This is a strong evidence in favour of Kautilya being the writer of *Arthashastra.* In the conclusion of *Arthashastra* it is simultaneously the art of warfare, literature and the kingdom ruled by Raja Nanda. This observation also proves that Kautilya was the author of *Arthashastra.*

TRADITION REGARDING ARTHASHASTRA

Kautilya's *Arthashastra* had wide influence on Sanskrit literature. Ranging From 100 B. C. to 700 A. D. we find the influence of Kautilya on Sanskrit literature. Those influenced by him include the great poet Kalidasa, Yajnavalkya, Vishnu Sharma and Vishakhadatta. The eminent dramatist Bana was also influenced by him besides many others. Arthashastra has an old tradition. The tradition of Arthashastra dates from 500 B. C. In the beginning is the reference to statecraft and penal system. After Kautilya we find reference to social welfare in Arthashastra. The scope of political economy is made clear by the definition of the word artha given by Kautilya. In explaining the meaning of artha Kautilya says, "By artha we understand the land inhabited by the people". The Arthashastra is that science in which the possession and upkeep of state is discussed.

In the sixth century B. C. when Greeks were making experiment on the art of Government, the Aryans, after a long period of experimentation in the statecraft, had developed the democratic form of government. They had discovered that democracy was the best way to govern the people. In this connection, Sri Aurobindo has written "Republican states were already long established and in vigorous functioning in sixth century before Christ, contemporary therefore with the brilliant but ephemeral and troubled Greek city commonwealths but this form of political liberty in India long outlasted the period of Greek republican freedom."

SOCIAL CONDITIONS IN KAUTILYA'S TIME

Alexander invaded India in the 4th century B. C. It was the time of Magadha empire. This empire was established by Nanda dynasty and at that time a king named Mahapadam Nanda or Mahananda used to rule. Mahapadam Nanda was a despot who perpetrated atrocities on his subjects. In his kingdom the political and social conditions were extremely bad. The people were badly oppressed and prayed for relief from despotism of the king. Regarding the end of Nanda dynasty by Kautilya, it is written in Vishnupuran: "Mahananda and his nine sons will rule for one hundred years. Then, long last, a Brahmin by name of Kautilya will destroy this empire. After the destruction of Nanda dynasty's empire, the emperor Chandragupta of Maurya Empire will be crowned by Kautilya." It is clear from these lines that Chanakya destroyed the Nanda empire and established the Mauryan empire. Mahanand was son of Bimbsara by a Sudra women and he established the Nanda dynasty. Mahapadam Nanda was the first glorious king of Nanda dynasty. He ruled for 78 years and his heir ruled for another 22 years. Afterwards, Chandragupta, with the help of Chanakya, succeeded in uprooting the Nanda dynasty.

Kautilya was a man of simple habits and dress: pride had not touched him. He did not ignite revolution against Nanda dynasty merely because of personal affront. The real reason behind this was his sense of patriotism and deep insight. Alexander's invasion was stoutly opposed everywhere: still Alexander kept his advance. Chanakya and Chandragupta deeply pondered over the reasons which had weakened the country. As a result of his thinking, Chanakya concluded that the division of country into small kingdoms was the main cause of his weakening. India needed to be united and become a single empire.

Chandra Gupta was a small officer in the army of Nanda, but the spirit of extreme valour, fortitude and patriotism had percolated to every fibre of his person. Several times Nanda was angered by his activities and tried to get him killed, but did not succeed. Chanakya sent an invitation to Chandragupta through his disciple Shilabhadra and enquired of Chandragupta as to what did he think was the reason behind Alexander's military advance. Impressed by the self-confidence of Chandragupta, Chanakya decided that he will help in making Chandragupta the new king. But before taking this step he visited the court of Raja Nanda and warned him that if Magadha failed to check the advance of Alexander the whole country will be in peril. In return Chanakya was insulted and abused. Now Chanakya and Chandragupta started the process of merging the small kingdoms and uniting them. Chandragupta enthused and inspired patriotism and evoked Raja Parvataka to take up arms. The princes of Panch Nada also started giving trouble to Alexander's army. Chanakya was mightily pleased by the efforts of Chandra Gupta. He went to Sindha and Makran and encouraged the kings of that area to oppose Alexander and not to let him return alive to his homeland. They succeeded to a large extent in their plans. By the time Alexander returned from India the bulk of his army had been destroyed and he himself died in Babylonia. Later on Chanakya and Chandragupta hatched a conspiracy against Raja Nanda. The besiege of Kusumpur by Chandra Gupta resulted in the fall of Nanda dynasty and the establishment of Mauryan empire. There is some evidence for the fact that Chanakya had sent Chandra Gupta to meet Alexander in order to elicit his help against Nanda empire. Initially, Alexander was reluctant but later on he agreed to help on the condition that he would have the same rights over Pataliputra as he had over the kingdom of Porus. But Chandra Gupta was not ready to surrender Pataliputra to Alexander. He threatened to take the Magadha empire by force. To this the reply of Chandra Gupta was that he will meet stiff resistance. Angered by this reply Alexander ordered that Chandra Gupta be taken a prisoner. This was against all diplomatic norms. However, Chandra Gupta succeeded in escaping. Later on Chanakya and Chandra Gupta drew up a plan to throw Alexander out of India.

How Chanakya tried to stabilize the unsettled conditions of India in his times is clear from the above historical review, Kautilya was the most astute political thinker of ancient India. These facts also go to show why *Arthashastra* is regarded as the best treatise on diplomacy and political economy. The appreciation and praise of Chanakya is to be found in the entire range of Indian literature. Praising Chanakya in his *Niti Sara*. Acharya Kamandaka writes, "I heartily salute the great scholar Vishnugupta who uprooted the rock like solid empire of Nanda dynasty, who crowned Chandra Gupta and who composed the great book *Arthashastra*."

MEANING AND VALUES OF ARTHA

Purusartha has been given an important place in Indian Culture. Kautilya has defined Artha, in his Arthasastra as, "The livelihood of human beings is the Artha." Thus Artha is the use of Earth for the means of livelihood in human lives. Vatsyayan, in his *Kamasutra* has defind Artha as including knowledge, land, animals, friends and earned money etc., following one's own Dharma and increasing it.[1] Thus, Artha includes the primary needs of men. As has been pointed out by different Dharmasastras, it was essential for the householder to Pursue Artha. According to *Kamasutra.* "A person who did not achieve learning in the first stage, did not earn the money in the second nor did observe penance in the third cannot do anything in the fourth." Thus, it was obligatory on the part of every person to work for Artha. The stage of the householder has been given a central place in Hindu Ashram system. The main aim of this stage was the achievement of Artha, not only for himself but for so many others in society. It was said that even the fulfilment of Dharma and Kama are based on Artha. According to Vatsyayana every householder must pursue Artha. Arjuna said in Mahabharata, "Whatever is considered Dharma in the world is completely based upon wealth... all the religious activities, all the pleasures, even the heaven can be achieved by means of wealth." In Arthasastra, Kautilya has pointed out that among Dharma, Artha and Kama, Artha is the highest since it is the means for the achievement of Dharma and Kama.[2] This has been also supported by Panchtantra and Hitopadesha. However, the Indian thinkers seldom considered Artha without Dharma as desirable. While wealth was many a times considered the highest value, it was insisted that it must be based upon Dharma.

Another extreme is the negation of Artha. Some Indian thinkers have supported fatalism and did not include Artha among Purusarthas. They have insisted that wealth is achieved by fate and does not depend upon efforts. This vein of thinking can be observed in the sayings of so many saints in India including Malukadas, Kabirdasa, Dadu etc. However, this has not been given much importance by most of the thinkers. Hitting hard at the supporters of fate, Vatsyayan, in his *Kamasutra*, pointed out that success is impossible without efforts since Purusartha is the root cause and substratum of all activities. Even necessary things do not happen without it. Therefore one should make sustained efforts to attain Artha, without it is useless to expect pleasure or welfare. According to a famous Sanskrit verse, Lakshmi, the goddess of wealth smiles on the brave and persevering. Similar quotations can be found, in so many Sanskrit works.

As Dharma was systematically and elaboratory discussed by Dharmashastras, India has a tradition of Arthasastras as systematic and detailed works upon the subject of Artha. Kautilya has considered Artha

---

1. Vatsyayan, *Kamasutra,* 1.2.9.
2. Kautilya, *Arthashastra,* 1.2.6.

as the main among trivarga. According to him, in Trivarga Artha is the most important, since both Dharma and Kama depend upon it. According to Vatsyayana one should constantly make efforts to increase his learning, land, gold, animals, wealth, clothes, ornaments and friends. The Arthasastras present a scientific analysis for the achievement of Artha. Among Arthasastras, the Arthasastra of Kautilya is the most important. It includes a summary of earlier Arthasastras. These earlier Arthasastras, however, have not been available. The Arthasastra of Kautilya is not only the first available but also the most important work concerning Artha.

Defining the scope of Artha, Kautilya has pointed out in Arthasastra that Artha means the habitat of human beings or the region in which human beings are established. Arthasastra is the science which discusses the establishment of the state and the rules of its preservation. Kautilya has discussed the subject in great details. His work is considered as one of the most important works not only upon Indian Economics and Hindu Polity but among the most important works on this subject in the world. According to Kautilya the state is the root of Artha. Therefore, a society can achieve Artha only under favourable state. Since the state aims at Artha, the king should have a tendency in its favour. The king is central in the state and therefore for him Artha should be more important than even Dharma and Kama. It is only when the king leads in this matter that others may follow it. Thus, Kautilya has insisted that the king should present ideal conduct and character in the achievement of Artha and should maintain conditions in which the citizens may achieve Artha. Thus, Indian thinking was socialistic and humanistic. No one can achieve Artha alone or acting against the society. Artha should be achieved collectively. According to Gita all land belongs to God. It has been clearly maintained by Kautilya that the king who fails to do his duties concerning Artha he may be removed.

ARTHASHASTRA

The most outstanding characteristic of Kautilaya's *Arthashastra* is that in it every aspect of the welfare state has been discussed minutely from a practical and realistic point of view. All aspects of state — administration, economy, justice, law and order, war and peace and system of penalties for various crimes — are found elaborately dealt with in this book. In his work Kautilya has tried to edit successfully the views of his predecessors on political economy and therefore developed his own characteristic views.

Subject Matter of Arthashastra

The following subjects are found discussed and described in Arthashastra:

1. **Concerning discipline** The topics described in the first chapter include educational policy; association with the aged; restraint of the organs of sense; the creation of ministers; the creation of councillors and priests; ascertaining by temptations, purity or impurity in the character of

ministers, the institution of spies, protection of parties for or against one's owm cause in an enemy's state; the business of council meeting; the mission of envoys; protection of princes; the conduct of princes kept under restraint, treatment of a prince kept under restraint; the duties of a king; duty towards the harem; personal safety.

2. **The duties of government servants** The topics included in the second chapter include formation of village; division of land; construction of forts; the duty of chamberlain; the business of collection of revenue by the collector general, the business of keeping up accounts in the office of accountants, detection of what is embedded by government servants out of revenue, examination of the conduct of government servants, the procedure of forming royal writs, the superintendent of treasury, examination of gems that are to be entered into treasury, conducting mining operations and manufacture, the superintendent of commerce, the superintendent of forest produce; the superintendent of armoury, the superintendent of weights and measures, measurement of space and time, the superintendent of tolls, the superintendent of weaving, the superintendent of agriculture; the superintendent of slaughter-house, the superintendent of prostitutes, the superintendent of ships, the superintendent of cows, the superintendent of horses, the superintendent of elephants, the superintendent of chariots, the superintendent of infantry, the superintendent of pasture lands, the duty of revenue collectors, spies in the guise of householders, merchants and ascetics, the duty of city superintendent etc.
3. **Concerning laws** The chapter III includes determination of form of agreements, the determination of legal disputes concerning marriage, division of inheritance, building, non-performance of agreements, recovery of debts; rules concerning deposits; rules regarding slaves and labourers; cooperative undertaking, revision of purchase and sale; resumption of gifts, and sale without ownership; robbery; defamation; assault, gambling and betting and miscellaneous.
4. **Removal of thorns** In chapter IV the topics discussed include protection of artisans; protection of merchants; remedies against national calamities; suppression of the wicked living by foul means; detection of youths of criminal tendency by ascetic spies, seizure of criminals on suspicion or in the very act; examination of sudden death; trial and torture to elicit confession; protection of all kinds of government departments; fines in lieu of mutilation for limbs; death without torture: sexual intercourse with immature girls, time serving consolidation of the kingdom and absolute sovereignty.
5. **Conduct of courtiers** The fifth chapter includes topics like concerning the awards of punishment, replenishment of the treasury; concerning

subsistence to government servants; the conduct of a courtier; time serving; consolidation of the kingdom and absolute sovereignty.

6. **The source of sovereign states** This includes the elements of sovereignty; concerning peace and taxation.
7. **The ends of six-fold policy** The sixth chapter includes the six-fold policy; determination of deterioration, stagnation and progress, the nature of alliance; the character of equal, inferior and superior kings; forms of agreement made by an inferior and superior kings, forms of agreement made by an inferior king; neutrality after proclaiming war or after concluding a treaty of peace; marching after making war or proclaiming peace; the march of combined powers; consideration about marching against an unassailable enemy and a strong enemy; causes leading to the dwindling, combination of greed and disloyalty of the army; consideration about of powers; march of combined powers: agreement of peace with or without definite terms, and peace with renegades, peace with and war by adopting the double policy; the attitude of an assailable enemy; friends that deserve help; agreement for the acquisition of gold; agreement for undertaking work; recruitment of house power; measures conducive to peace with a strength and provoking peace, the conduct of Madhyama king, of a neutral king and a circle of states.
8. **Concerning Vices and Calamities** The topics dealt in the VIIIth chapter include the aggregate of the calamities of the elements of sovereignty, consideration about the troubles of the king and his kingdom; the aggregate of the troubles of men; the group of molestations; the group of obstructions; the group of financial troubles; the group of troubles of the army; and the group of troubles of a friend.
9. **The Work of an Invader** This chapter includes topics like the knowledge of power, place, time, strength and weakness; the form of equipment; the work of arraying a rival force; considerations of annoyance in the rear; remedies against internal and external troubles; consideration about loss of men, wealth and profit, internal and external dangers, persons associated with traitors and enemies; doubts about wealth and harems; the success to be obtained by the employment of alternative strategic means.
10. **Relating to War** In the 10th chapter are dealt with the topics like encampment, march of the camps, protection of the army in times of distress and attack, form of treacherous fights, encouragement to one's own army, the fight between one's own and enemy's armies, battle-fields, the work of infantry, cavalry, chariots and elephants, distinctive array of troops in respect of wings, flanks and fronts, distraction between strong and weak troops, battles with infantry, cavalry, chariots and elephants, the array of army like a staff, a snake, a circle or in detached order, the array of the army against that of an enemy.

11. **The Conduct of Punishment** The XIth chapter includes causes of dissension and secret punishment.
12. **Concerning a Powerful Enemy** In XIIth chapter, Kautilya deals with the duties of a messenger, battle of intrigue, slaving the Commander-in-chief, the inciting a disaffection of states, spies with weapons, fire and poison, destruction of supply of stores, and of granaries, capture of the enemy by means of secret contrivances or by means of the army, and complete victory.
13. **Strategic Means to Capture a Fortress** In the XIIIth chapter the topics include sowing the seeds of dissension, enticement of kings by secret contrivances, the work of spies in a siege, the operation of a siege, restoration of peace in a conquered country.
14. **Secret Means** In the XIVth chapter the topics included are means to injure an enemy, wonderful and delusive contrivances, remedies against the injuries of one's own army.
15. **The Plan of Treatise** The Shastra, bereft of undue enlargement, and easy of grasp and transparent to understand, has been composed by Kautilya in words, the meaning of which, has been definitely settled.

Salient Features of Arthashastra

Kautilya's Arthashastra is widely recognized as a complete treatise on statecraft. In order to appreciate it we need to discuss the salient features of this work. These briefly are:

1. **Conception of trinity of values** In place of the ancient quartile of values, namely, righteousness, wealth, sex and liberation, Kautilya has emphasized the importance of first three and rather disregarded moksha or liberation. He condemns the views of both hedonists and ascetics. He formulates the golden principle: 'extremes must everywhere be avoided'.
2. **Realist political philosophy** Kautilaya was opposed to hedonism and self-indulgence; but he was equally critical of asceticism in life. His political philosophy is realistic and has suggested all kinds of means to achieve common welfare.
3. **Scepticism** Kautilya's thinking was highly practical and he was not swayed by idealist sentiments. He advises the king to be sceptical about the motives of others and not to rely upon anyone.
4. **Rationalism** Kautilya's philosophy is rationalist. He wants that the king should be a person of intellectual discriminations. He must use his intelligence in dealing with the problems of statecraft.
5. **Harmony between wordly and transcendental** While Kautilya has accepted the role of transcendental elements in the affairs of men, he considers them to be of secondary importance and exhorted human being to rely on the efficacy of their own actions.

6. **Promotion of good and suppression of evil** Being a realist, Kautilya recognises that there are both good and evil forces present in every state. Accordingly, while there are good elements like righteousness, prosperity and procreation instinct in the world, there also exist side by side evil elements like wickedness, poverty and grief. The ability of a statesman depends upon the promotion of good and suppression of evil.
7. **Stress upon discipline** Kautilya advocates the observance of discipline both in individual and social life. According to him indiscipline leads to backwardness and disintegration.
8. **Stress on civility** Kautilya has laid great stress upon the polite manners and behaviour in human life. The aim of both physical and intellectual discipline is the promotion of politeness and good manners.
9. **Harmony between secular and spiritual knowledge** According to Kautilya, a balance between secular and spiritual knowledge is essential. Therefore, a king should be well-versed both in secular and spiritual matters.
10. **Qualities of the king** According to Kautilya, a king should be well versed in various disciplines in order to be a successful ruler. These include political economy, religion and statecraft. Kautilya considers the knowledge of logical reasoning most essential. He should also have knowledge of trade, commerce and animal husbandry. The king should also have mastery over penology. Without the system of penalties and the fact that any violation of law would attract the penalty no king can rule effectively. Regarding the origin of the state Kautilya favours the divine origin of the state. But his divine theory of the state is different from the similar theory of Western thinkers, because Kautilya has emphasized more the duties of the king than his rights. Regarding the state of society prior to the emergence of the state Kautilya is silent. Kautilya did not believe in the division of sovereignty though he recognized the rights of minority in the state.
11. **Administration** In chapter II of Arthashastra, Kautilya has described the appointment of various heads of the departments who are to supervise the works in various spheres. In doing so Kautilya has presented a conception of welfare state. In the third chapter Kautilya has described the various types of crimes and the penalties in respect of each of these.
12. **External relations** In dealing with foreign relations, Kautilya has emphasized that the king must jealously guard the interests of his subjects and do everything in his power to promote their welfare. Kautilya has also described in detail the foreign relations — how and when to maintain peace and also how and when to declare war.
13. **War and peace** The ancient states were often involved in war. Kautilya has described in detail the duties of king in peace and war. In the

9th chapter the various aspects of invasion like military formation, financial involvement, the good and evil of attack are discussed. In the 10th chapter, we find discussion of matters like encampment, march of army, forms of treacherous fight, encouragement of one's own army and sowing seeds of dissension in enemy's army, battle with infantry, cavalary, chariots and elephants etc., are discussed. In 12th chapter are discussed matters like duties of messenger, battle of intrigues, slaying the commander-in-chief and inciting a circle of states, spies with weapons, capture of enemy by secret means or battle etc. In the 13th chapter are discussed matters like sowing seeds of dissension, enticement of kings by secret contrivances, the work of spies in a siege and restoration of peace in the conquered army. In the 14th chapter are discussed matters like means to injure an enemy, wonderful and delusive contrivances, the application of medicines and matters and the remedies against the injuries of one's own army. Thus, we find in Arthashastra a detailed description about the conduct of war and the administration in time of peace.

ETHICS AND POLITICS IN INTER-STATE RELATIONS

The organization of the Hindu State was determined by its geographic and economic environment. The extensive plains favoured the growth of large states, but the difficulties of transport and communication were so formidable that the Central Government could not usually make its power felt at the circumference. So began that interplay of centripetal and centrifugal forces around which a good deal of the history of India, as of every other country, seems to revolve. Every State tended to encroach upon its neighbours. It was not long before opinion and philosophy held up to admiration the ideal of the "the big kingdom", "the kingdom extending upto the sea", "the universal dominion". On the other hand, such an empire could not last long. The outlaying regions were constantly tempted to cut adrift from the main body, to start on an absolutely independent career and, in their turn, to make a bid for supremacy.

Federalism and Feudalism

Normally, a compromise was struck in the interests of peace and harmony. A kingdom or empire came to mean a fusion of two features which, for want of perfectly suitable terms, may be designated federalism and feudalism. There was a king or emperor at the centre claiming suzerainty over a number of princes who offered allegiance to him, subordinated their foregoing policies to his diplomatic moves, usually served him in war and offered him tribute, but who retained their foreign policies to his diplomatic moves, usually served him in war and offered him tribute, but who retained their autonomy in internal administration. These princes in their turn might have feudatories who stood towards them more or less in the same relation in which they stood towards their suzerain. So there might be a third, a fourth, and even further layers in the political hierarchy.

Four Instruments of State Policy

The game of power-politics naturally lowered the tone of statecraft and imparted to it a Machiavellian tinge. For instance, all the writers enumerate the four instruments of policy, *viz.* Sama or conciliation, Dama or gift, Danda or chastisement, and Bheda or sowing dissensions. Kautilya recognised deceitfulness and secret punishment among the legitimate means of statecraft. There were, however, a few writers who repudiated the whole doctrine of reason of State. Thus, Arya Deva declared that morality, *i.e.* righteousness, must everywhere be supreme, in public as well as in private life.

It was a natural consequence of this state of things that there should grow up conventions and rules on relations between suzerains and vassals as well as between independent sovereigns. There is accordingly a regular network of doctrines and maxims on what may be based foreign affairs or inter-state relations.

Six-fold Policy

The most comprehensive account of this is given in Kautilya's Arthashastra. It enumerates the following Six-fold policy determining the relations of States with one another:

1. Sandhi (Treaty of peace or alliance):
2. Vigrha (War);
3. Asana (Neutrality);
4. Yana (Making preparation for attack without actually declaring war);
5. Samsharaya (Seeking the protection of another);
6. Dvadhibhava (Making peace with one and waging war with another).

Aim of the State

Kautilya points out in detail the most important conditions that should influence the decision of a ruler in the matter of adopting one or other of the above policies. This discussion shows a penetrating insight into the affairs of State. The sole guiding principle in making the choice is also material welfare of the State. "A wise king," says Kautilya, "shall observe that form of policy which, in his opinion, enables him to build forts, to construct buildings and commercial roads, to open new plantations and villages, to exploit mines and timber and elephant forests, and at the same time to harass similar works of his enemy."

No Spirit of Chivalry

Kautilya is not guided by any spirit of chivalry when it is not conducive to the material interest of a State. Thus, when a weak king is attacked by a powerful king, he should seek the protection of a powerful king, combine with a number of his equals or even inferior kings, or shut himself up in an impregnable fort. Failing all these means, he should, according to one school of writers, rush against the enemy like a moth against a flame, with a view to secure death or victory. But Kautilya is definitely against this. According to him, the weak king should rather accept the most humiliating terms, biding his opportunity to free himself from this servitude. The details given by Kautilya about these terms indicate the extent of a suzerain king's authority over his vassal. Without the permission of the former the latter could not undertake, among other things, to construct forts, celebrate marriages of sons or daughters, hold the installation ceremony of his heir-apparent, purchase horses, capture elephants, perform sacrifices, march against for or even to go out on excursions for amusements. He was not free even in his dealings with his officers and subjects. Even on occasions of worshipping the gods and making prayers he should invoke the blessings of God on the suzerain king. He should help the protector as much as he can, and always proclaim his readiness to place himself at the disposal of his suzerain.

No Moral Considerations

One school of political writers thought that mere honesty and oath were not sufficient, but hostages were necessary for the due fulfilment of the treaty. Kautilya differs from this, though he enunciates the principle that "whoever is rising in power may break the agreement of peace". In general, moral considerations have no place in Kautilya's statecraft, its sole guiding principle being the welfare of the state.

No Humanitarian Rules of Warfare

It is difficult to say whether there was any definite body of rules regulating the relation between the different States, such as we have, for example, in the international law of the present day. Some such usage as the inviolability of ambassadors, or the personal safety guaranteed to cultivators even in times of war, may be regarded as coming under this category. The humane rules of warfare laid down by Manu might be regarded as generally recognised by States. These forbid the use of weapons, which are concealed, poisoned or barbed, or the points of which are blazed with fire, and also striking down an enemy who is wounded, engaged to flight, broken his weapon or lost his coat of mail. But the elaborate directions of military campaigns laid down in Kautilya's Arthashastra do not take into account these humanitarian rules of warfare. He recommends, without scruple, and means, fair or foul, that may bring success against the enemy.

Kautilya, however, agrees generally with Manu in recommending mild and beneficent measures to be adopted towards a conquered country. The conqueror should "follow the friends and leaders of the people", and "adopt the same mode of life, the same dress, language and customs as those of the people. He should follow the people in their faith with which they celebrated their national religious and congregational festivals or amusements." Manu, however, further recommends that a relative of the vanquished ruler, approved by the people, should be put on the throne on stipulated conditions.

NATURE AND FUNCTIONS OF THE GOVERNMENT

Monarchy

The normal form of government in India was monarchical, but it was different from that which flourished in Europe during the Roman Empire, for the most part during the Middle Ages, and in the modern period upto the outbreak of the French Revolution. The Hindu State rarely presented that high degree of centralization which is associated with the Roman Empire and the modern nation-State.

The King

But it had a centre whose main features demand attention. This was the king usually hereditary in accordance with the rule of primogeniture, living in high style and a blaze of glory, in enjoyment of an immense revenue from private and public property. Political theory which usually, though not uniformly, approached political questions from the ethical standpoint, expected the king to lead a blameless life, disciplined to ceaseless administrative labour and consecrated to the public good. It laid heavy responsibilities, temporal and spiritual, on him, promised him lasting bliss in heaven or threatened him with all the tortures of hell in accordance with his success or failure in the great moral and political venture. In practice, doubtless, the absence of constitutional, as distinct form conventional, checks left many a crowned head comparatively free to indulge in luxury and vice, caprice and injustice. But it is only fair to remember that all despotic authority was tempered by rebellion or assassinations. So long as he was on the throne, the king presided over the executive and judicial departments of government and was expected to take the lead on the field of battle.

Executive Machinery

The machinery for executive administration was well organized. It was the special care of the king assisted by ministers and a number of high officials. Below the great functionaries stood a host of minor officials, military officers, diplomats and spies, secretaries, clerks, technical employees and so forth.

No Separation of Powers

There was no separation of the executive and judicial functions. But in practice there were a number of men whose primary function was adjudication and who were assisted by a set of minor functionaries. Hindu theory laid the highest emphasis on justice. In theory and practice alike judicature was one of the most important aspects of governance.

Centre-State Relations

Such was the machinery outlined that normally worked at the centre. But it was difficult to ensure its extension to the provinces, districts and towns or villages. It was necessary to devise means for reconciling central with local government and administration. Three lines were struck by political theory:

(i) *Federalism.* A great deal of autonomy was left to feudatories and sub-feudatories.

(ii) *Feudalism.* The King or feudatory organized a regular system of provincial and district administration.

(iii) *Autonomy.* A great deal of autonomy was left to villages, more in the Deccan than in the North, and most of all in the South.

Parallel Organisations

Thus, territorial organization contained elements of federalism, feudalism and local autonomy. But it did not exhaust the whole subject of social regulation. There existed parallel organizations, on the basis of function, in the form of village communities, kinship associations, and guilds of manufacturers, merchants, bankers or others. They enjoyed considerable autonomy, in the management of their affairs. Their customs or rules were recognised by the state and upheld by the law-givers. It will be observed that in India the principle of function dovetailed into that of kingship and was, therefore, often vested with greater significance than in medieval Europe. In any case, it was the basis of an important part of the machinery of social control.

Horizontal and Vertical Government

Thus, organization was both horizontal and vertical, and comprised a number of local and functional jurisdictions and intermediate associations standing in various, more or less ill-defined, relations with the State. Incidentally, the vocational association often cut across the lines of caste and locality. For instance, Shreni or a guild consisted of persons following the same craft though belonging to different castes, while the Nigama formed a guild of traders belonging to various towns.

PART II
MODERN INDIAN POLITICAL THOUGHT

6
Indian Nationalist Movement (1828 — 1947)

A nation may be defined as a human group occupying a country with definite boundaries, sharing common traditions, aspirations and bound by common sentiments. It should possess aims and goals which bind up community by a unifying thread. Among the constituent elements of nation the sentiment of nationalism is the most important. The sentiment of nationalism is a communal feeling that binds a group into a homogeneous whole. The sentiment of nationalism received maximum fillip during the British rule. In the development of nationalism the elite has to play a crucial role. The spread of English education has given rise to educated group which is fully conscious of the value of freedom and has drawn inspiration from the West. By the study of Western history, the Indian elite became aware of the value of nationalism. This is of course not to suggest that the glory of Indian history did not inspire the Indian elite. But the current wave of nationalism is the product of English education.

SOCIAL BACKGROUND

The Indian nationalism is a fact of modern history. The interaction of a number of subjective and objective forces during the British rule and the pressure of numerous international forces were responsible for the rise of nationalism in India. The study of nationalism is important from many viewpoints. The rise of nationalism in India has been very complex and many-sided. Before the onset of British rule, the social structure of Indian society was unique. It was very different from the situation and socio-economic structure prevalent in pre-medieval European society. India is a multi-lingual, multi-religious society of teeming millions. From the social point of view, the Hindu society which forms the largest chunk of Indian society has been divided into numerous castes and sub-castes. In itself the Hindu religion is not a homogeneous entity, having a particular set of rituals and a uniform method of worship. Indeed Hindu religion is very heterogenous comprising of diverse forms of worship and rituals. Thus, Hindu society is divided into many social and religious segments. On account of vast social, economic and political structures the growth of nationalism was slow, but though India is a vastly diverse country there is a fundamental thread of unity underlying the whole fabric of diversities. An important feature of Indian nationalism is that by and large it is a product of British rule. The British made wide ranging changes in the Indian economic structure, developed a strong centre, introduced modern education and means of communication, in order to subserve their interests. This led to the emergence of an elite which promoted Indian nationalism and new social forces came into existence and these gave challenge to the British imperialism. Thus, the social background of the development of Indian nationalism is complex and multi-sided.

Pre-British Background

In order to understand the Indian nationalism, it is necessary to understand its pre-British background. Before the arrival of British there were self-reliant rural communes in India. They were small democratic units which were self-sufficient. Thus, the Indian feudalism was quite different from the European feudalism. Before the British rule, the Indian rural society was based upon agriculture and cottage industry. It was so for centuries. The agriculture also was quite backward from the technical viewpoint. In the social realm, family, caste panchayat and rural panchayat exercised social control. In the urban areas some cities were important from religious, some from commercial and others from political viewpoint. The capitals of various states were cities. In cities there were cottage industries. These industries were helped by the government. There was little cultural exchange between various cities because the means of communication were poor. Therefore, the political upheavals made little impact upon rural India. Because of lack of communication among persons living in different regions the national spirit could not develop. The only sense of unity among the Indian people was religious and ideological. In order to go on pilgrimage people used to visit the four corners of India. The rural India, however, remained untouched by the political and social changes. The Indian culture has primarily been religious. The economic and political values did not occupy the place and importance which they do in the modern culture. It is religious and spiritual, it lacks the spirit of nationalism.

IMPACT OF BRITISH RULE

1. **Change in Agriculture System** Consequent upon the British rule there were wide ranging changes in India. The reason of the

establishment of British supremacy was the decline of Mughal empire and division of the country into small units. The pre-British administrative machinery was quite different from the post-British administrative machinery. Compared to Indian people the sentiments of nationalism, discipline, cooperation and patriotism are found in much more intense form in the English persons. These qualities of the British impressed the Indian elite and they tried to imbibe them. The British rule has had far-reaching consequences on the Indian economic system. This gave a blow to the Asian values and helped to establish a Westernized society. This led to political unification. This in turn gave rise to national movement. It also helped to bring about a fundamental change in the agriculture. During the British rule the land ceased to be the communal property; it became the property of the individuals. Thus, in certain parts the landlords and in the other tillers became the owners of the land. During the viceroyality of Lord Carnwalis a class of landlords came into existence in Bengal, Bihar and Orissa. This led to far reaching changes in the rural economy. By the ryotwari system the tillers were granted ownership rights. In 1820, Sir Thomas, the Governor of Madras, started the system of ryotwari. This produced wide ranging social, cultural and economic impact. The landlord and the tiller began paying the revenue direct to government. The agriculture became a trade and the traditional rural society underwent disintegration. The fragmentation of land-holdings had adverse impact upon economy. This led to impoverishment and economy was shattered. The rural indebtedness increased. The tillers were forced to part with their holdings. The tillers became farm labourers.

2. **Spread of Education** The British spread the education of English in order to recruit volunteers for their administration. In the pre-British days the education was given in Pathashalas and Madarsas. The Christians helped to spread modern education. Their main aim was to swell the number of Christians; but this helped the processes of secularization and democratization. The British not only encouraged academic education but also opened many institutes for technical education and professional training. The Western education helped the emergence of an elite class which drew attention to national problems. This class fully appreciated the value of education. The notables among those who concentrated their attention to the problems of education were Messers Maganbhai Karamchand Karve, Tilak, Gokhale, Malaviya and Mahatma Gandhi. The Brahmo Samaj, Arya Samaj, Ram Krishan Mission and Aligarh movements helped the progress of education. Banaras Hindu University and Aligarh Muslim University came into being. The D. A. V. colleges sprang up all over the country. The spread of education threw up two types of people — ones

who were Indian by birth only but were English in all respects and the others who were educated into the Western style but were equally proud of the past tradition. The persons proud of Indian past and tradition made a beginning of nationalist movement. Whatever may be said against the English education, it must be conceded that without English education there could have been no nationalist movement. But the Indian nationalism is not a product of English education alone, it was a reaction against British imperialism and exploitation of Indians by foreigners. The modern education did of course help in this process.

3. **Impact of English Education** The English education helped to spread the cultural values like democracy and rational and scientific thinking. On reading English literature, the educated Indians began to dislike the actionary institutions and revolted against them. The knowledge of world culture helped to broaden the thinking and outlook of Indians. Under the influence of English education Indians reviewed their past and critically evaluated the merits and demerits of their ancient heritage. A critical evaluation of the traditions showed that the laws of development were universal and operated uniformly all over. The changed political and economic atmosphere threw up the problems in a new light for the elite. The economists like Ranade, Gokhle, and K. T. Shah reviewed the Indian economy. They discovered that the economic problems of India could not be resolved by the theories of Chanakya but by the theories of Adam Smith, Ricardo, or Karl Marx. The educated persons having benefited by the scientific ideas tried to disseminate them among the masses. The Western literature was translated into Indian languages. Thus, outstanding literature on science, art, culture and politics became available in the Indian languages. Besides translations, Indians wrote original works on these subjects. Both translation and original literature helped people to become well versed with modern ideas. The English language became a link language and it brought the intellectuals from all over the country on one platform. This helped the formation of many all India level societies. The fact that the English language helped in the rise of national movement can be gauged from this very fact that the leaders of these movements were English knowing persons.

4. **Role of Political Elite** The concept of elite generally covers the intellectuals, but the intellectuals alone do not constitute the elite. Among the elite are also included the upper classes, the persons who either financially or socially or both ways occupy a higher status in the society. Thus, in the class of elite are included the intellectuals and the persons belonging to upper strata of the society. This elitist class is responsible for all the progressive movements. This class provides leadership and is responsible for the prosperity of the country. These persons usher in the political, economic, cultural and religious

progress. Without this class no country can make any progress and the wonderful progress made anywhere in the world is due to elite group. In ancient India also the elite group was responsible for all progress. During the middle ages the elite group became very weak. In modern times the nationalist and freedom movements were led by this class. Now we shall study the various groups which constitute the elite class.

(i) *Role of Intelligentsia.* As we have referred to earlier, the class of intellectuals is the most important class of the elite group. In the modern times, under the impact of Western culture, a new class of intellectuals has emerged imbibing the values of rationalism, democracy, positivism etc. The Brahmo Samaj, established by Rajarammohan Rai, did the pioneering work. In the first decade of the 19th century, the number of educated Indians was very small. Gradually schools, colleges and universities were set up and by the middle of the 19th Century the number of educated Indians was formidable. This intellectual class made a significant contribution towards the development of modern Indian nationalism. They started numerous progressive and reformist movements. All the political parties were launched by the intellectuals and they were the leaders. These persons spread the message of freedom and nationalism through education. They also produced a vast amount of patriotic and nationalist literature in the various regional languages. Among this group there were eminent scientists, poets, historians, philosophers, economists and social thinkers. These persons studied the western culture, the western society and western ideology and applied the conclusions of their research to the solution of our national problems. Between 1851 and 1884, a number of intellectual associations were set up and they demanded the mechanization of the government services. After 1857, a number of universities were set up and this swelled the ranks of highly literate Indians. In 1885, an all-India political organization named *Indian National Congress* came into existence. The proceedings of the Congress used to be in English because all its leaders were English educated. Posterior to the establishment of Indian National Congress, the history of Indian national movement is the history of Indian National Congress. Gradually, the movement of I. N. C. spread to middle and lower classes but the leadership remained in the hands of the intellectuals. The leaders of both moderate and extremist groups in the Congress were intellectuals. After 1918, there was a rapid progress of the national movement and its leadership came in the hands of M.K. Gandhi, C.R. Das, Motilal Nehru, Vitthalbhai Patel, C. Rajgopalachari, Rajendra Prasad, Jawaharlal Nehru, Subhash Chandra Bose and others.

Besides Indian National Congress, there were political parties representing other communities and their leadership was also in the hands of intellectuals. For example, Dr. B.R. Ambedkar was the leader of the backward classes. The future of the country depends upon the intellectuals.

(ii) *Role of Capitalist Class.* Besides the intellectuals, the capitalist class constitutes another elite group. These persons are leaders in the trade and commerce. They control the economic power. In India this group came into existence with the development of trade and commerce.

(iii) *Contribution of Press.* In modern India press has made a significant contribution in the development of nationalism. In all countries the nationalist movements have been spread and pushed up through propaganda carried on by the press. The intellectuals in France took the help of press to propagate their ideals. In England, Germany, Italy and other European countries the press made a significant contribution. In the pre-British India, in the absence of press, it was difficult to propagate one's views. During the British rule there was growth of press and this promoted nationalist awakening. Raja Rammohan Rai was the founder of the nationalist press. In political movement the newspapers made significant contribution. Many national leaders set up their own magazines and newsletters to disseminate their views. M.K. Gandhi propagated his views through the news magazine *Young India,* and B.G. Tilak did so through *'Kesri'* and *'Maratha'*. Thus, the various political parties adopted press for propagation of their views. Besides political parties, the elite group also issued newspapers etc. Some news magazines were issued by students. With the spread of nationalist movement the demand for the freedom of press was also voiced. Gradually, new laws were enforced which helped the freedom of press. Undoubtedly, the nationalist press has been an effective instrument in the growth of nationalist movement.

5. **Anti-Caste Movement** With the growth of nationalism and extension of English education the educated persons began a review of the social institutions. The caste system was criticized and a campaign for its eradication was launched. The new proprietary rights, the growth of cities, new legal and new social system, beginning of class conflict and the impact of modern education gave a blow to the caste system. The political movements also worked for its eradication though the politicization of society has given encouragement to this system, too. The Indian caste system is a great obstacle in the democratization of the Indian society. Therefore all eminent leaders have pleaded for its eradication. Among these leaders the names of Raja Rammohan

Rai, D.N. Thakur, K.C. Sen, Swami Dayananda, Mahadev Govind Ranade etc., are noteworthy. On the other hand, some caste based organizations also sprang up. An attempt to provide special protection to low castes has also encouraged the caste system.

6. **Campaign Against Untouchability** Along with the campaign against caste system, a campaign against untouchability was also launched. A number of reform movements were started in this connection. The history of these reform movements is hoary and the names of Lord Buddha, Ramanuja, Ramananda, Chaitanya Mahaprabhu, Sant Tukaram etc. are notable. Arya Samaj, under the stewardship of Swami Dayananda, played a significant role in this connection. M.K. Gandhi made the removal of untouchability a mission of his life. B.R. Ambedkar made a valiant attempt to uplift the condition of backward classes and infuse in them a sense of honour. In 1932, M.K. Gandhi established an All-India Harijan Sewak Sangh. The new economic forces, modern education, national movement, urbanization and industrialization also helped in this matter.
7. **Religious Reform Movements** The nationalist movement in India has also shown itself in the form of religious reform movements. Most of the religious movements desired to promote the democratic values. Brahmo Samaj, Prarthana Samaj and Arya Samaj were such religious movements. Besides Hindus there were religious movements among Muslims also. Many political leaders also participated in these religious movements. Among these persons the names of Sri Aurobindo, B.G. Tilak and M.K. Gandhi are notable. Most of the political leaders in India were religious-minded. Very few political leaders in India were materialist. That is why the Indian politics was dominated by religion. The dominance of M.K. Gandhi on the Indian politics was due to this factor. But after 1930, rationalist and materialist movements gained momentum. With the establishment of the communist party the philosophy of Marxism became popular in India. In Muslims, Ahmediya and Aligarh movements were reformist movements. Among the Muslim reformists, the names of Shah Abdul Aziz of Delhi, Syed Ahmed of Bareilly, Sheikh Karamat Ali of Jaunpur, Kazi Shariatulla of Faridpur and Sir Mohd. Iqbal are notable. Sheikh Abdul Halil Sharar of Uttar Pradesh and Tayabji of Bombay also participated in the reform movement.

The religious reform movements have both helped and hindered the nationalist movement. For example, some of the Muslim religious reform movements were responsible for encouraging the feeling of communalism and the mystical teachings of religious reformers encouraged life-negating philosophy. These factors have militated against purposeful social reconstruction.

CAUSES OF UNREST

The political movements in India were an expression of the nationalist sentiments. Modern nationalism emerged as a reaction to the foreign domination, because the British rulers were exploiting Indians for their own ends. The first expression of Indian nationalism manifested itself for the first time in 1828 in the form of Brahmo Samaj. In 1851, various political groups organized themselves under the banner of British India Society. In 1857, the entire country rose in rebellion against the exploitation by the British. The struggle of 1857 cannot be strictly termed as freedom struggle because various individuals had personal motives in this matter. But this has to be recognized that the ultimate aim of these rebels was the freedom from the foreign domination. Therefore, this movement inspired a sense of patriotism among people. It also proved that the Hindus and Muslims can fight unitedly against the foreign domination. This encouraged the concept of one nation, embracing both communities. They became aware of the serious implications of this for them and they even tried to sow the seeds of dissension among the two. They adopted the policy of divide and rule. It was this policy which ultimately lead to the partition of the country. In 1871, British suppressed the 'Wahabi' movement. During this period agricultural economy was very unsound. Between 1867 and 1880 India faced a number of famines. Of these the famine of 1877 was most acute. This affected about 6 millions. The agricultural economy was completely ruined and at places there were Kissan rebellions. When arrangements of the Imperial Court for Queen Victoria in Delhi in 1877 were made, this added insult to the injury. People were infuriated. The Vernacular Act of 1878 and the Arms Act of 1879 fomented further the seeds of disaffection. In 1882 government reduced the levies on imported Lancashire textiles in order to encourage the industry in Britain. This also annoyed people. People were now convinced that the Britishers were exploiting them.

All this encouraged disaffection among the educated. The study of the freedom movements in other countries and an acquaintance with the writings of liberal thinkers inspired a new wave of enthusiasm in the Indian intellectuals. By 1883 the disaffection had become explosive.

INDIAN NATIONAL CONGRESS

From 1885 to 1905, the leadership of the Indian National Movement was in the hands of moderates. Among them W. C. Banerjee, Anandmohan Bose, Lalmohan Ghosh S. B. Banerjee from Bengal, Dadabhai Naroji, Feroze Shah Mehta, Badruddin Tayabji, Apte, Aagarkar, Telang, Ranade, Gokhale, Dinshawacha from Bombay and K. P. R. Naidu, Subramanya Aiyer, Anand Charlu, Virraghavchariyar from Madras are the notables. Besides these Kesha Pillai, Madan Mohan Malaviya and among Englishmen A. O. Hume, Wederburn and Henry Cotton are worth mentioning. In the Indian National Congress the movement was spearheaded and carried on by the intellectuals and certain capitalist elite. Thus, the leadership of the Indian National Movement remained with the elite.

PROGRESS OF POLITICAL MOVEMENT

Under the moderate leadership, the Indian National Congress was more or less a resolution passing body without having a mass base. It used to pass resolutions, listing bill of demands which included among other things Indianization of services, reform of Indian economy and a cut in the military budget. A demand to encourage the cottage industry was also made. Uptil 1918, only few of these demands were met. On the contrary, the Britishers were making a concerted effort to suppress the nationalist movement. A few ordinances were issued to curb the freedom. This acted as an eye opener and the faith of the moderates in the fairplay and sense of justice of the British was rudely shaken. This policy of repression adopted by the British encouraged extremism. In 1905, the extremists tried to assert themselves in the conference of I.N.C. Lala Lajpat Rai and Lokmanya Tilak raised the slogan of Swadeshi and boycott of foreign goods. In 1906, Muslim League came into existence to define and protect the interest of Muslims. Outside Congress a number of revolutionaries carried on their violent protest. The partition of Bengal further kindled the flames of protest and a demand for boycotting foreign goods, and establishing national education and autonomy was raised. A protest movement was launched. In Bengal, Punjab and Maharashtra the revolutionary fervour picked up the momentum. In 1907, in the Surat conference of INC, the signs of split between extremists and moderates became visible. After 1908, Sri Aurobindo was tried in the court of law. In the same year Lokamanya B. G. Tilak was imprisoned for six years and sent to Mandlay prison. In Punjab Lala Lajpat Rai and Sardar Ajit Singh were exiled from Punjab. In 1918, the moderates walked out of INC and set up Liberal Federation. After this nationalism grew intense in the Congress, and the revolutionary movement spread all over the country and abroad. Among the revolutionaries the names of Madal Lal Dhingra, V. D. Sarvarkar, Sri Aurobindo, Lala Hardayal, Rashbihari Bose, Amir Chand, Bhagat Singh and Chandra Sekhar Azad are noteworthy. On April 13, 1920, Jalianwala Bagh tragedy occurred and this produced deep and wide impact all over the country and abroad.

After this the leadership of Congress passed into the hands of M. K. Gandhi and under his stewardship India got her independence. Under his leadership there was a multi-sided development of the nationalist movement. He made valiant efforts to purge the Indian society of the evils of casteism, communalism and untouchability. He also worked for the education of women and spread of swadeshi. In 1920 he launched a non-cooperation movement. In 1923, Swarajya party was formed and by 1925 it became very powerful. Along with these movements the philosophies of Socialism and Marxism also found roots here. In 1928, Simon Commission was bycotted.

On Dec. 23, 1929, M. K. Gandhi, T. B. Sapru, M.A. Jinnah and Motilal Nehru met the Viceroy and put up the demand for Dominion Status. On Jan. 26, 1930, a resolution demanding full freedom was passed by I. N. C. in Lahore. The same year civil disobedience movement started and a bonfire was made of foreign goods. Within Congress a socialist group was formed. In 1937, Congress agreed to form government in various states. In 1939, a conflict between the rightists and leftists came to the fore and a Forward Bloc was established to represent the view of the leftists.

Along with nationalist movement, Mohd. Ali Jinnah led the Muslims and demanded a separate state for them. Ultimately in 1947, India was given freedom but was partitioned.

Stages of Nationalist Movement

(i) *Before 1885.* Before 1885, Rajarammohan Rai and other enlightened Indians worked for the freedom of press and certain administrative reforms.

(ii) *1885 to 1905.* During this period moderates led the nationalist movement. Among them were educated and rich people. These persons worked for the Indianization of services and economy.

(iii) *1905 to 1918.* During this period the leadership passed into the hands of extremists. Because some persons had tried to base the movement on Hindu philosophy, in reaction the Muslim communalism grew and Muslim League was established.

(iv) *1918 to 1934.* During this period the nationalist movement spread to masses. This was a period of mass awakening when people were infused by the spirit of patriotism. After the World War the faith of people in the British justice and fairplay was rudely shaken. A number of international events helped the growth of nationalism. The industrialist and capitalists also supported nationalist movement, because Swadeshi and boycott of foreign goods were in their interest. M. K. Gandhi's call of class cooperation in place of class conflict also drew the support of capitalists. In the same period, however, the philosophy of Marxism became popular in India. Between 1930 and 1934, M. K. Gandhi launched civil disobedience movement and young men and women participated in it on a large scale.

(v) *1934 to 1939.* During this period Subhash Chandra Bose established a new party, named *Forward Bloc.* The power and influence of Muslim League increased. Among the students, Kissans and industrial labourers, communism became popular. A number of new organizations of students, Kissans and labourers emerged and these supported the Congress.

(vii) *1939 to 1947.* During this period there was multi-pronged growth of nationalism in India and on August 15, 1947, the country became free.

After this one could observe a contradiction in the national life. While, on the one hand, there was development of nationalist tendencies, on the other hand parochialism has been receiving boost. This had given rise to many disintegrating forces in the national life. The present state of affairs is far from satisfactory. Politicization in India is increasing. On the one hand, democratization is going on, on the other the tendencies of fascism and communism are raising head. What will be the future shape of things cannot be predicted in view of the complex and contradictory forces operating in the society at the moment. But this much is certain that the elite will play a crucial role in shaping the future.

7
Liberalism in India (1885 — 1917)

After the downfall of Mughal Empire, India was politically disunited. There was no central authority. There were small princely states warring with each other and having mutual jealousies with practically no sense of patriotism or nationalism. These princely states had no sense of political unity. The princes were enjoying in their own palaces mostly without caring for the suffering masses. However, there were a few enlightened princes working with the idea of promoting patriotism in their narrow sphere of activity in which on the whole patriotism was virtually missing. It is at this stage that the Britishers penetrated deep into India and took full advantage of India's political disintegration and disunity. The superiority of British armed strength was established. Most of the Indian Princes bowed before the mighty armed strength of the Britishers one after the other. Their sway increased and the British empire extended day by day. In 1857 an attempt was made by the Indian nationals to check this growth of British power by waging an armed revolt. This national struggle met with a failure and the armed revolt was crushed. For about three decades India remained virtually where it was. However, the idea of an armed revolt was always a nightmare for the Britishers. In 1858 when Indian administration passed from company to crown, high promises were made to the people of India assuring them equality of opportunity, justice and legal equality without caring for caste, creed and religion. These promises however, remained on paper.

Indian National Congress

It was under these circumstances that in 1885, Hume founded Indian National Congress. The fundamental task before the Congress was to make the people of England realise the need and necessity of giving political advancement to the Indians and also redress their legitimate and reasonable grievances However, there was a controversy whether the task before the Congress was to be accomplished by showing armed strength or by touching the conscience of the rulers till they felt quality in themselves and decided to give constitutional advancement to India. It was under these circumstances that the founders of the National Congress had to work. They had before them the experiences of 1857 and the consequences which followed from that armed revolt. They also had before them the strength and weaknesses of Indian masses and a fair idea of their military strength.

LIBERALISM

Indian National Congress was founded in 1885. For two decades it remained completely under the control of the moderates who were rather liberals and very much influenced by liberalism in England. All these liberals used to praise British rule in India. They felt that it was an act of providence that Britishers were ruling over India. They were also under the influence of Western culture and civilisation. They were the product of English education. Most of them had been brought up and developed under the English educational system with a Western cultural background. They loved British political and social institutions. These people believed in the constitutional methods of struggle. They were vehemently opposed to violence or any other method except that of making petitions and prayers. They had faith in British sense of justice and fair play. In their opinion if at any stage the Britishers acted in an un-British manner that was an isolated misdeed rather than a reflection on their national character and outlook. These moderates remained in absolute power and authority till they were challenged by the extremists like Lokmanya Bal Gangadhar Tilak, Lala Lajpat Rai, Bipin Chandra Pal and Aurobindo Ghosh. After the death of last great liberal leader, Gopal Krishna Gokhale, the extremists then held the ground till Mahatma Gandhi came on the political scene. Liberals failure was primarily because during their stay their leaders could not make Congress a mass organisation but made it an organisation of the classes. Moreover, at that time in Congress there were few leaders and followers. Congress sessions of those time have rightly been described as big assembles which met once in a year to pass certain resolutions to take their own care and the situation was reviewed only next year. With all love for their country and the noble task which they took on their shoulders the fact remained that most of liberal leaders were idealists. Many a time they were devoid of hard realities of life.

FUNDAMENTALS OF LIBERALISM

The liberals controlled national affairs through Indian National Congress for over two decades. They introduced many brilliant sons of India to the Indian political life. They had their own method of working and approach to the political problems which faced the nation at that time. Some of the significant political ideas and features of liberal thinkers were as under:

1. **Scholars** The liberals of India were great scholars. They had a clear approach to political problems. For them, religion was no hindrance or bar to solving national problems. According to them the people of various communities without any caste, colour of creed could meet at a platform for getting concessions from the Government. In liberal's

view, India was a vast nation in which the people belonging to all communities were living and suffering. They told Indians that it was in their common interest that they should improve their lot and should also try to develop and prosper without any distinction whatsoever. They pleaded that the people of all communities in India should use Congress forum and platform for their national struggle against British imperialism.

2. **Faith in Representative Institutions** The liberals were very much inspired by the British representative institutions and parliamentary form of Government. They had deep love for such institutions. They wanted to introduce them in India. In their view the only feasible solution to Indian political problems lied in increasing share of Indians in the Legislatures. Elected representatives should have increasingly more and more powers, so that they could plead for the people.
3. **Opposed to Violence** The liberals were absolutely opposed to violence or force for solving their political problems. They had faith in non-violence and the technique of making prayers and representations. In their opinion the vast majority of Britishers were not aware of India's problems. In case Indians could enlighten and educate the British masses and authorities, there was every possibility of India's having more and more rights. Liberals had faith in British sense of justices and fair play. They believed that delegations should go to England to enlighten British public opinion. As K. P. Karunakaran put it, "The moderate method of resistance was verbal only, prayers, petitions and protests were methods of their struggle." They believed that Indians should put their demands before the British Government and ask them to solve their difficulties. A moderate like Gokhale felt that our demands should be of two types. Firstly, those which required immediate attention and solution, such as reforms of Legislative Councils, appointment of Indians to the judicial and other services, reduction in military expenses and extension of primary education etc. Secondly, there were the demands regarding extension of educational facilities both technical and non-technical and so on. The liberals believed that if at times the Britishers acted in an un-British manner that was due to bureaucracy in India and not a reflection on British national character.
4. **Supported the Continuance of British Rule** The liberals did not wish to severe Indian connections with the Britishers. They wanted to have Swaraj by stages and by remaining within the British Empire. Even such an extremist as Tilak, did not openly say that India wanted to severe connections with the British Empire all at once. In the words of M. A. Buch, "The British connection meant slow but sure emancipation of the Indian mind form its blind attachment to an unmeasuring past. They wanted the whole men in India to be Westernised, not merely

in form but in spirit; and they saw the salvation of India in complete assimilation of best Western ideals. They pined for the ideal of a free man in a free state, a free Church in a free state, a free woman in a free society."

5. **Opposed to the *Laissez Faire* Theory** The liberals knew that India was industrially backward. They felt that the theory of *laissez faire* will ruin industry and increase poverty. They understood that this theory was useful for the people of England which was an industrially advanced country and could compete in the world. On the other hand Indian industry was in its infant stage. It required state protection. Therefore, the liberals stood for the protection of industries by the state. They desired that Indian industries should be subsidised so that they could come up to market standard. Most of the liberals came to the conclusion that Indian poverty was due to drainage of the Indian economic resources and also because of the deliberate policy of the Government to keep India industrially backward. Under the circumstances the liberals thought it futile to think that the theory of *laissez faire* could help in eradicating India's poverty.
6. **Ideal of National Unity** Liberals were great nationalists and patriots. They stood for the Indian national unity. For them India was one great country inhabited by the people representing various shades and opinions. Most of the Indian liberals travelled throughout the country and saw themselves India's unity in her diversity. They came to the conclusion that the poverty was the bane of India and the rulers were deliberately trying to divide India into various castes and creeds. Sir Pherozeshah Mehta said in 1890, "To my mind a Parsi is a better and truer Parsi, as a Mohammedan or a Hindu is better and truer Mohammedan or Hindu, the more he is attached to the land that gave him birth, the more he is bound in brotherly relations and affection to all the children of the soil; the more he recognises fraternity of all the native communities in the country, and the immutable bond which unites them together in the pursuit of a common aim, and objectives under a common Government. It is impossible to imagine that Dadabhai, for instance, a true Parsi that he is, is anything but an Indian, living and working all his life for India, with a true and tender loyalty of a son."
7. **No demand for Fundamental Rights** The liberals understood that rights could be demanded by a nation which was powerful and strong enough to get them if otherwise denied. Indians could demand constitutional development not as a matter of right but as a privilege or concession. According to liberals politically Indians have been so much degenerated that they have now fallen on the mercy of the British rulers. They can get a share in administration only after touching the conscience of those in authority. Therefore, in liberals opinion there

was no sense in demanding reforms as a matter of right. It was only after the fall of liberalism and the advent of Tilak into power that he declared that Swarajya was India's birth right and they shall have it. This philosophy of rights developed by the extremists was not acceptable to the liberals who controlled Indian politics for about 3 decades.

8. **Relationship between Ethics and Politics** One of the most important problems of the time was as to what should be the relation of ethics with politics. The question was whether religion and politics should be separated from each other or they should be combined to go hand in hand. Ethics should save politics from degradation and from being barren and devoid of hard realities of life. Very many liberals, were religious men. Gokhale was an orthodox Brahman who wanted to spiritualise politics. Similar was the case with Surendra Nath Banerjee. According to liberals, in politics one should not be hesitant to accept the mistakes which one had committed during the course of experimentation. Thus, the politicians should be morally able to confess their wrongs. Raja Ram Mohan Roy and M. G. Ranade were religious people but true politicians of their times. These politicians wanted to spiritualise politics and to establish close affinity between the two.
9. **Social Reforms** The liberals knew that India had fallen down socially and the social reformers had absolutely failed to save Indian society from further degradation. They knew that without social advancement India could not dream of political advancement. It was in a healthy and socially developed society that the sermons of freedom and Swaraj could be listened to by millions of Indians. Therefore, the liberals realised the need and necessity of social and political developments going hand in hand. To the complex problem of state intervention in social set up, the liberals saw no objection in it to check social degradation. According to liberals, the aid and assistance of state was in national advantage, if sought to check this social backwardness. Raja Ram Mohan Roy invited state to legally ban social evils of Sati and child marriage. Most of the liberals supported Consent Age Bill which was a social subject. It was however bitterly opposed by Tilak on the ground that the State had no right to interfere in the social set up.
10. **Criticism of Government** Liberals fearlessly and frankly criticised the Government for its acts of omission and commission. They felt that the nation had an inherent right of criticising the Government. They demanded rights which were being deliberately denied to the people and for which the nation was ready after putting in long and arduous labour. Dadabhai Naoroji, one of the foremost liberals of India, criticised the Government, both in India and England, both as a member of House of Commons and the President of Indian National Congress. Pherozeshah Mehta and Gopal Krishna Gokhale criticised

the policies of the Government in the Imperial Legislative Council as well as from the forum of Indian National Congress. Thus, the liberals did not spare any opportunity to criticise the Government. What they pleaded was that after having been criticised the Government should not be discarded or boycotted or left alone but should be extended the hand of co-operation and goodwill. In their opinion such an attitude alone could help India in getting some positive results.

11. **Indianisation of Administration** Liberals believed that the services should be gradually Indianised and Indians should he associated with bureaucracy. In their opinion an increasing share in both civil and military administration was advantageous to Indians as well as the Britishers. In the absence of such a gradual policy of Indianisation the Government shall not for a very long time be in a position to give the benefit of their advancement to the people of India. Liberals demanded that Indianisation was the only solution to many problems because history was a witness that only those nations had succeeded which governed India from within and associated the people of this land with their administration. Liberals did not fail to tell the Government that their present policy of dissociating Indians from Indian administration was not based on very wise and sound principles.

CAUSES OF DECAY OF LIBERALISM

Liberalism developed and flourished in India for about three decades. Under the leadership of these enlightened and patriotic liberals, the nation was in a position to awaken the British conscience. It successfully advanced the demands for Indian welfare. They made Indian National Congress a national organisation where the people from various parts of India could come and discuss the problems of the nation as a whole without any consideration of religion or provincialism. Liberals had among them very brilliant persons of all India reputation and fame such as Raja Ram Mohan Roy, Gopal Krishna Gokhale, Dadabhai Nauroji, Sir Pherozeshah Mehta, Surindra Nath Banerjee and M. G. Ranade. However, liberalism in India could not resist the severe blow given to it by the extremists under the leadership of Bal Gangadhar Tilak and his close contemporaries and associates like Lajpat Rai, Bipin Chandra Pal and Aurobindo Ghosh. There were certain serious causes for such a decay. These were as follows:

1. **Love for British Rule** Liberals felt that British rule in India was an act of providence and that it was in the interest of the Indians that the Britishers should continue to stay in this country. For quite some time, this concept continued to be accepted and the blessings of British rule in India received more propaganda than the evils of this rule. For quite some time these liberals continued to tell the people of India that due to British stay in this country people could get an atmosphere of peace and a concept of United India. British system of justice and administration

and the advanced means of transportation and communication were a matter of praise by these liberals. However, as the time passed, these liberals could not convince the people about the continued blessings of British rule. The evils of this rule began to come to the forefront. Increasing poverty, lowering standards of evils, constant and regular drainage of the Indian financial and material resources, deliberate policy of non-industrialisation along with that of sacrificing Indian interests for British interests and the denial of superior posts to Indians shocked most of the educated and enlightened Indian people who began to feel that continued stay of Britishers in India was bound to affect Indian social, economic and political life adversely. It was due to this contradiction in ideology between the liberal leaders and the enlightened public opinion that liberalism got a great set-back.

2. **No contacts with the masses** Unfortunately the liberals could not maintain any healthy contacts with the masses. They were intellectuals and patriots and also had deep affection for India but at the same time they were leaders without followers. Under them Congress remained an organisation of the classes and not of the masses. Congress sessions were a big show where these people assembled together once in a year to pass resolutions to highlight the activities of the Government and demand some rights for the people of India and leave all these decisions to take their own care till they again assembled next year. Delegations were sent to England with a mission of arousing their conscience but with no real achievement. Some of the liberal leaders did contact the masses by touring the country and seeing things for themselves. But on the whole these liberals remained out of touch with the masses. Such an organisation which is not in touch with the masses cannot claim to be a national organisation, the Congress remained only a class organisation leading to failure of liberals in India.
3. **Influence of Western culture and civilisation** India had a rich past. She taught the whole universe the lessons of spiritualism. In art and architecture, dance and drama, India was the leader of the whole world. Even some Western thinkers described India as Guru of the whole universe. But the liberals however, could not appreciate the significance of Indian culture and civilisation. Most of them were under the influence of Western culture and civilisation. They saw the evils of Indian society, such as child marriage, caste system, denial of widow re-marriage and superstitions. These appeared to them quite unscientific. On the contrary, they saw how high a place the women enjoyed in England with all opportunities given to them to develop their faculties. Educational rights were enjoyed by the women of England as against the women of India who were denied higher education and in some cases even the elementary education. Untouchability, which was widespread in India, was unknown to the people of England. From

these facts the liberals concluded that India had nothing good whereas England had everything noble. They came to the conclusion that if India was to be saved from its present degradation and degeneration only the West could help in the matter. This approach was unhealthy and unacceptable to the people of India. As the people awakened they began to appreciate their past and the natural reaction was that they discarded these liberals in India. For them now, India was much superior than Britain in so far as our social customs were concerned. They realised that it was the duty of our reformers to reform Indian society and to save it from degradation. It was none of the business of the Western people to reform Indian society.

4. **Secularism** Indians are traditionally a religious people. The people of India are Godfearing. They have faith in the religion to which they belong. In Indian social and economic systems religion has a significant and permanent place. In India a movement could be a success if it appreciated the religious values of the people and accepted religion as its creed. It was through religion that the masses could easily be approached. The liberals failed to exploit this important point of Indian national life. They did not exploit religion nor did they try to interpret it in their own way. They feared that if religion was brought to the forefront they might not be in a position to impose Western ways of living and thinking which they considered to be superior. Hence, the liberals could not touch the minds of the people. When subsequently, religious reformers like Swami Dayananda Saraswati, Swarni Vivekananda, Swami Ram Tirath and Sri Aurobindo Ghosh and Lala Lajpat Rai came to the front, their views had a mass appeal. People were more attracted by them than by the liberals.
5. **Absence of political philosophy** India had the privilege of producing great liberals such as Dadabhai Naoroji, M. G. Ranade, Gopal Krishna Gokhale, Surindra Nath Banerjee and Pherozeshah Mehta. Unfortunately, none of these liberals had any philosophy of his own. They did not have any concept of nationalism nor that of nation or nationhood. Most of them accepted the philosophy of Western political thinkers since it suited their convenience. Each liberal tried to develop the ideas in the way he liked with the basic principle that British stay in India should be supported and Western culture and civilization should be imitated by the people of India. To quoit S. N. Dubey, "Their starting point was Government of the people, not Government by the people; good Government and not democracy. Faith in the rationality of the man and superiority of collective wisdom over individual wisdom, the theory of natural rights of man, belief and self-expression as the basis of human happiness, constitute the essence of democratic philosophy but did not appeal to the early Congress leaders. At the same time they could not give to the nation in very concrete and clear

terms what they liked. For full three decades these liberals remained the masters of political movement in India but they were a miserable failure in producing a philosopher of any calibre or a philosophy of any standing. It has perhaps rightly been said that India had no political philosophers. We had only political thinkers."

6. **Method of petitions and representations** Liberals felt that India could get rights by making petitions and representations. They did not hesitate to condemn violent actions. History is however, a witness to the fact that freedom never comes by representations and prayers of delegations to the rulers convincing them about the desirability of granting additional constitutional reforms. Freedom never comes as a gift. It requires sacrifices and toil by the millions of a nation. Liberals forgot this fundamental principle. Constitutional advancement is given by the rulers to a subject country only to the extent to which it suited their own convenience. Unless the people are willing to make sacrifices the freedom could not be achieved. Most of the liberals were not willing to go behind the bars or to sacrifice their everything for the sake of nation. Their method of petitions and representations proved to be a failure. During their long stay on the political scene of India they could get a few constitutional reforms here and there even which were not exclusively due to their efforts.
7. **Policy of British Government** However, a death-blow to liberal political thought in India was struck by the policy of the British Government. Congress as a forum came into being to express the grievances of the people and make them known to the Government. The founders of the Congress thought that the Government would be willing to oblige them by listening to their prayers and petitions and accepting them. But as the time passed it became clear that the Government accepted only those demands that suited its convenience and left the other parts of the resolutions untouched. Regardless of the resolutions and opinions expressed by the forum, the Government continued to act in the way it liked. The bureaucracy remained as rigid as it used to be. Various Acts were passed without caring for the sentiments and feelings of liberals and even against the wishes of Indian public. The Government of Lord Curzon was particularly autocratic and rigid and devoid of respect for public opinion in India. The partition of Bengal was the most clear example of utter disregard for Indian public opinion. These acts of the Government proved the futility of liberal methods. It became very clear to the people of India that the liberals can not be in a position to deliver the goods and that some alternative methods will have to be found out to obtain national freedom.

INFLUENCE OF WESTERN LIBERALISM

1. **Political field** During the 19th century there was a wave of liberalism throughout Europe. Hence, in many parts of the world the people began to assert themselves. They demanded more and more share in their administration. The problem of individual *vs.* State prominently came to the forefront. Gradually, the individual began to get prominence over the State. The individual began to be considered as an end in itself. The people were given more and more rights and an increasing share in their administration. In 1832, England was obliged to pass the Bill of Rights. So was the case in France where the writings of Rousseau and other national scholars glorified the individual. Rousseau's slogans of liberty, equality and fraternity became the watch-words of French Revolution. Representative institutions began to get more and more respect from the masses. The elected representatives of the people began to command the faith of their citizens. The people began to actively participate in the national legislation. The idea of no taxation without authority of the Legislature more or less became a creed of the day. More and more people demanded the right to exercise franchise and the right of contesting the election. Even the women were also given this privilege since now they were considered as equal partners in national social, economic and political development. The liberals in Europe had so much faith in representative institutions that in their philosophy there was no place and no scope for violence. All were considered to be law abiding citizens honouring their legal and constitutional institutions.
2. **Economic field** Under the influence of Adam Smith in the economic field in Europe came the theory of *laissez faire* or free trade. It was based on the political idea of liberalism or what is called as political *laissez faire*. The basic assumption of the theory was that there should be free competition all over the world and that artificial barriers imposed by the State were disadvantageous to ordinary consumer. If there were free trade with no imposition of duties the consumer shall get best goods at cheapest rate. This sort of free trade will promote healthy competition among various industries. Those lagging behind shall try to come up to compete with advanced industries and those which failed shall be eliminated from the market. In other words, both in political and economic field survival of the fittest became the creed of the day. Under the influence of Adam Smith many European countries accepted this theory of *laissez faire* in practice.
3. **Social life** The trend of European liberalism did not end in economic and political fields. It also touched the social life of Europe. Gradually, it began to be considered that the grip of the State over the society should be loosened. There should be more and more social reforms so that a healthy society emerged and social degradation effectively

plugged. Many intellectuals tried to point out to the evils of the society demanding to make it more progressive and receptive to political and economic advancement.

4. **Influence on Indian liberation** Such a trend was bound to influence Indian liberals who were developed and brought up in Western culture and civilization. Most of the liberals were students of English literature. They had all praise and appreciation for the superiority of Western civilisation. Indian liberals accepted basic principles of Western liberalism more particularly in the political field. In accordance with the liberal trends of Europe, Indian liberals also developed a faith in representations and prayers. None of the liberals ever preached the use of violence even in extreme circumstances. Like the liberals of Europe they wanted to fight their national struggle by constitutional methods though in India there was no Constitution in technical sense of the term. They also stood to demand more and more rights for the people of India and their increasing share in legislatures. They had faith in parliamentary institutions and associations. They wanted to have expansion of Legislature so that more and more Indians may be given the right of franchise. Under the influence of these Western liberals, these people wanted to have reforms in social field and most of them tried to root out social evils of our society. They invited the intervention of Government in checking these social evils.

LIBERALISM IN ENGLAND AND INDIA

In spite of all this, there were certain basic differences between liberalism in England and in India. Some such differences were as under:

1. ***Laissez faire*** The essential difference between the two was their ideas about *laissez faire.* The liberals in England had all faith in the theory of liberalism and that was quite logical and natural to them. England was industrially advanced and could compete with any other industrially advanced or developing country. For India quite contrary was the case. Due to political conditions, India remained industrially backward and the indigenous industries got a serious set-back, with the result that they required state protection and could only develop if subsidised by the State. Therefore, India could never think of free competition. In the face of cheap and better foreign goods Indian industries were completely ruined. Therefore, as against *laissez faire,* Indian liberals stood for protection of industry by the State.
2. **Political Philosophy** Indian liberals had no political thinkers and in fact had no political philosophy of their own. They set forth their ideas according to their convenience and the need of the time. Neither Raja Ram Mohan Roy, or M.G. Ranade nor any other liberal leader of India was a political philosopher. On the contrary, English liberals produced many political philosophers including J. S. Mill and T. H. Green who

are even today shining examples of British liberal political philosophy. Thus, while English liberals had their own political philosophy, the Indian liberals had no such philosophy to their credit.

3. **Individual *Vs.* State** According to British liberals the individual was end and the state only means to an end. The only object of the State was to look after collective interests of the individuals and to see that each citizen receives fullest development of his hidden faculties without any hindrance. In fact British liberalism was an outcome of renaissance which gripped Europe as a reaction to the evils of industrial revolution. The Indian liberals, on the contrary, had more faith in the State. Instead of individual they laid more and more stress on the State. M. G. Ranade once said, "The state in its collective capacity represents the power, the wisdom, the mercy, the charity of its best citizens." In England liberalism developed as a challenge to the State authority which had gripped all the power and was not willing to part with that. On the contrary, in India liberalism grew with the idea that the State should be given all the rights and it should be left to its discretion to give to the people what it liked so that there was no serious dislocation in political and social life. Indian liberals wanted State intervention even in social affairs.
4. **Political conditions** This difference was also due to different political conditions prevailing in England and in India. Whereas England was a politically advanced and independent country, its citizens thought in quite different terms. The questions of poverty, exploitation and non-industrialisation were not there whereas these were the main problems in India. Most of the Indian leaders drew the attention of the Government towards their policy of non-industrialisation and growing poverty of India. One also finds difference due to the size and population of the two countries. As compared with England India is a very vast country. She has diversity and in that no sense of unity. It has always been a problem for Indians to maintain essential unity in diversity. But for the people of small Island of England there was no such problem. Therefore, the liberals of England had to work in quite different atmosphere than those of Indian.

The libeals of England had faith in parliamentary institutions and parliamentary democracy. For them, the constitution was supreme and they themselves were constitution makers. On the contrary, being a subject nation India had to depend on British sense of justice and fair play. India had to accept that the Britishers had given her peace and unity though at the cost of exploitation and increasing poverty. Thus, the liberals of India and England had to work under quite different circumstances. Hence, their approach as well as reaction to problems was bound to be different. However, essentially Indian liberals were influenced by the Britishers and believed in their basic principles and ideologies.

ROLE OF INDIAN LIBERALISM

There has been much controversy about the role of liberals in Indian national movement. Some of the critical thinkers have said that the liberals were great nationalists but their methods and approach to the problem were of no great use and utility to Indians. They have said that the reforms which were introduced in India from 1885 to 1905 were not due to the efforts of liberals but were bound to come with the passage of time. It is a natural phenomenon of history that with the passage of time, certain changes do come in all fields of life. Hence, slow, unsatisfactory political reforms given by the Acts of 1892 and 1909 were bound to come in accordance with this process. These changes were introduced as these suited the convenience of our British masters without caring for the demands of the liberals or sentiments of the Indian masses. They also highlighted the failure of the liberals in making Indian National Congress a mass organisation. As such their demands had no moral support. They were taken in that spirit by the Government. In fact the liberals were treated as friends of the British Government. They were an agency for knowing the views of Indian masses so that the story of 1857 may not be repeated. However, all this criticism may not be very true. Before critically analysing the situation it is necessary to study the needs of the time, the contemporary circumstances and the approach which could be adopted.

1. **Contemporary circumstances** The liberals in India were working at a time when the philosophy of liberalism was developing throughout the Western world. The significance of representative institutions was being increasingly stressed. There was no central political authority in India. There was economic, social and political degeneration. Therefore, it was necessary to convince the Britishers to reform society, to raise its living standard and to grant it constitutional reforms. By that time it was well established that India could not throw away the Britishers with the aid of any armed strength. Under these circumstances it was essential that the liberals should adopt constitutional means and methods for getting their demands accepted. Some critics have underestimated the significance of the liberals. They have said that these people were the product of Western culture and civilization. They had love for Western way of life. They have been charged for maintaining connections with the Britishers and remaining within the British empire agreeing to accept only dominion status. However, in defence of these liberals it may be said that their was no way out or alternative. They stood for constitutional agitation and the method of petitions and representations, since the nation was not ready for rising in armed revolt. Hardly 30 years earlier a national armed revolt had failed and chances of another armed revolt were remote. The importance of liberals may be judged from the fact that even an extremist like Lokmanya Tilak declared that his aim was never to have an armed revolt in India. He only wanted to change British

bureaucracy and not dethrone the King Emperor. Even an extremist like Sri Aurobindo Ghosh, in 1907, felt that India was not ready for an armed revolt. She was not prepared to launch an effective campaign of non-payment of taxes to the Government.

2. **No possibility of natural right** If liberals had not demanded right by petitions and prayers they could base their demands on the theory of natural rights. That too was not practicable in India. Firstly, a subject nation has no natural rights. Secondly, England was not accustomed to such a theory. The English people based their rights and demands not on any such theory but derived their rights from the Parliament which they considered as supreme and sovereign authority on the land. To put a theory of natural rights before such a nation was bound to result in failure. Therefore, this method too could not be adopted.
3. **Preparing the nation** Again, all of a sudden the liberals could not place their demands before the rulers. It required preparing the nation and making it conscious for it. Unfortunately the people were not conscious for their rights in India due to various reasons. Firstly, The Britishers had tried to portrary India as a backward nation. Secondly, The Britishers developed superiority complex for themselves and that of inferiority for their subjected nation. They tried to convince that Indians were uncivilized and uncultured. They maintained that it was one of the missions of their rule in India that the millions of Indians should become cultured and civilized.
4. **Poverty and Illiteracy** The majority of Indians were suffering from poverty and finding it difficult to make their both ends meet. Hence, they could not devote time for understanding their political problems. Illiteracy was widespread. An illiterate nation was bound to be indifferent to political problems.
5. **Love for Western culture** It was a tragedy that the educated Indians had begun to love Western culture and civilization. They did not take pride in their own cultural heritage. Under these circumstances, it was difficult for the liberals to unite the people of India and to bring before them the image of one united nation ready to struggle for getting their political rights. No demand could be effective unless that climate was created. Judged in this background, the plea that the liberals could not put forward an exhaustive list of political rights, gives an answer in itself.

CONTRIBUTION OF THE LIBERALS

In spite of the above mentioned difficulties, the achievements of the liberals in India were notable. These were as follows:

1. **United nation** Due to the efforts of the liberals the image of a united India was portrayed and a forum was provided where the people from all over the country belonging to different provinces, castes and

religions could come together and put their heads together in solving India's political problems. One may very well imagine the fate of this national platform, if the extremists had captured it rather than the liberals. In that position the Government certainly would have been hostile and even this platform would not have been available to Indians.

2. **National forum** Thus, the liberals helped the nation in providing a national forum. Its significance in no way can be underestimated.
3. **Social service** Liberals created a sense of public service in the minds of Indian people. No doubt they have been criticised by saying that they made Indian National Congress a very big source of entertainment where the people met once in a year to pass resolutions which subsequently took their own care. It has also been said that these people were not willing to make sacrifices but only preached nationalism and patriotism to the extent to which it did not involve their personal sacrifices. However, these prominent leaders created a sense and spirit of public service. Many of Indian young educated people were inspired for serving the nation and to devote their time and energies for the public service. Thus, due credit may be given to these liberals for creating favourable climate in India whereby the demands could be put before the Government for political advancement. Earlier, there was no such national forum and organisation for demanding rights and as such the people could not draw the attention of the British Government.
4. **Political consciousness** The liberals created a sense of political consciousness among the millions of Indians who were politically backward. It was most obligatory for Indians to demand political rights. Therefore, the liberals could not come upto the expectations of the extremists. However, that should be no consideration in judging their significance in creating climate for demanding political rights. One should also be grateful to the liberals that they drew attention of the Government to the poverty of teeming millions of India toiling and working under most unfavourable and difficult circumstances. It was due to the labour of the liberals that the educated masses came to know that Indian poverty was due to a deliberate attempt of the Britishers by not industrialising India and putting heavy drainage on Indian economic and financial resources. It was also due to the efforts of the liberals that a sense or consciousness came whereby the people began to feel that the richness of the Britishers was only at the cost of increasing poverty of the Indian people. No liberal failed to draw the attention of the Government in this regard. No one ever hesitated to criticise the Government. The liberals stood to reform Indian legislatures by demanding more and more rights for the masses of India. They demanded enlargement of legislatures. They pleaded for the extension of franchise to the largest possible number of people in India.

8

Raja Ram Mohan Roy (1772 — 1833)

The present upheaval in Indian social and political thought may be traced to the eighth decade of 17th Century when Raja Ram Mohan Roy was born in 1772. Almost for a whole century there was no other illustrious social or political thinker in India besides Ram Mohan. Ram Mohan was the first awakening of the Indian consciousness from the slumbers of last several centuries due to long slavery, in the form of a critical revaluation of the contemporary down-trodden condition of Indian masses. It was in the consciousness of Ram Mohan that the Indian elite, impressed by the concepts of social liberty and equality in the West, felt that the same liberty and equality should be created in Indian society. Ram Mohan, therefore, raised his voice against the exploitation of the backward classes particularly the women and the untouchables. He worked hard to abolish their disabilities and bring out not only social reforms but also political reforms through the enactment of new social legislations.

After Ram Mohan another wave of social and political reforms in the country was visible in 18th century. Among the notable contributors to this movements were Keshab Chandra Sen, Dayananda, Annie Besant and Ramkrishna Paramhansa. These were active in the second half of the 18th century right upto the beginning of the 19th century.

SOCIO-POLITICAL CAUSES OF RENAISSANCE

The following were the most important socio-political causes of Indian renaissance movement:

1. **Western Education** Almost all the important Renaissance thinkers including Bhandarkar, Ranadey, Chiploonkar, Tilak, Agarkar, Gokhale, to name only a few, had high academic degrees in Western education. Though Macaulay aimed at creating a class of civil servants by introducing English education in India, the same education created revolutionary thinkers like Raja Ram Mohan Roy, Keshab Chandra Sen, Mahadev Govind Ranadey and Vivekananda. The most important characteristics of Western education were: intellectual bias, rationalism, individualism, critical attitude to scriptures, synthetic

approach to religion, secularism, cosmopolitanism and humanism. All these characteristics were imbibed by the intelligentsia through the growth of Western education in India. Thus, the spread of education by the Britishers in India was undoubtedly the most important social factor responsible for the new awakening and reconstruction of Indian thought.

2. **Establishment of new associations and societies** Western education and a more intimate contact with the Western society led to an intense urge for social and political reforms in India. This led to the establishment of dozens of associations and societies. Jatirao Fule established Satya Shodhak Samaj with the purpose of reforms in Maharashtra. Prarthana Samaj was another important institution of social reforms in Maharashtra. In Bengal Brahmo Samaj was established by Raja Ram Mohan Roy mainly for intellectual awakening but also for social and political reform. Another important association was Ramakrishna Mission founded by Vivekananda in the name of his master Ramakrishna. Swami Dayananda established Arya Samaj which rapidly spread throughout the northern India and carried out reforms in almost all the directions. Besides, theosophical society established by Annie Besant was an important society for religious reforms in India. All these new associations and societies encouraged new thinking and reconstruction of social institutions on the pattern of ancient Indian specimen.
3. **Indian approach to the economic problems** An important part of the revivalist tendency of the Renaissance period was an Indian approach to the economic problems. Eminent economic thinkers pointed out that India cannot solve its economic problems by an uncritical application of the doctrines of Smith, Ricardo and Mill. They, on the other hand, pointed out that solutions can be found in the procedures adopted by ancient Indian village republics. M.G. Ranadey, in *The Essays on Indian Economics* pleaded for an Indian approach to economic problems. This emphasis is the background of the economic programmes of reconstruction found in the thought of Rabindranath Tagore and M.K. Gandhi in 20th century.
4. **Rise of nationalism** The Renaissance period witnessed a rise of nationalism in almost all the slave countries of the world including India. Illustrious poets and thinkers wrote works expressing intense sentiments of patriotism. Vishnu Krishna Chiploonkar was a powerful writer of Bengal. Bankim Chandra Chatterjee founded the *Banga-Darshan* in 1872 and published his famous patriotic novel Ananda Matha. This novel was highly acclaimed by Sri Aurobindo who was another great patriotic writer that India produced. Swami Dayananda also strongly advocated nationalism in most of his writings. The most important leader of the rise of nationalism in India, however, was

B. G. Tilak, who, through his two famous weeklies, *The Kesari* and *The Maharashtra* took the leading part in spreading patriotic sentiments in the country. Vishnu Shastry Chiploonkar was another great patriotic writer of Maharashtra. Other poets and writers praised national heroes in their writings and aroused national sentiments in the nation. Ram Das and Shivaji, Maharana Pratap and Guru Govind Singh were praised by these poets and writers. All this created a wave of nationalism and patriotism very much explicit in the writings of contemporary Indian political thinkers including Vivekananda, Tagore and Gandhi.

5. **The growth of Hindi literature** An important social factor in the new awakening and reconstruction of Indian thought was the growth of Hindi language and literature. This is so since the rise of a nation is very much dependent on the growth of a national language. Hindi was propagated as the national language of India and as a popular vehicle for the communication of national and patriotic sentiments. Among the noteworthy writings of this period were *Premsagar* of Lallulal, *Nasiketopakhyana* of Sadal Misra and *Bharat Durdasha* of Bharatendu Harischandra. Swami Dayananda Saraswati wrote his famous Satyartha Prakash in Hindi. Most of the prose and poetry works of his period expressed patriotic and nationalistic sentiments.
6. **Establishment of Western political institutions** The most important political factor responsible for new awakening and reconstruction of Indian thought was the introduction in India of Western political institutions such as executive council, the law member, the Law Commission and the Supreme Court etc. These political institutions aroused nationalism in Indian political thought and Indian nationalists started demanding more and more political rights and equality before law. There was a growing demand for the introduction of British type representative political bodies in the country by Raja Ram Mohan Roy, Dadabhai Nauroji, Surendranath Banerji, Gopal Krishna Gokhale and other Indian political leaders.
7. **Establishment of Indian National Congress** The most momentous event in the history of Indian nationalism was the establishment of Indian National Congress by A. O. Hume in 1885. Though Hume established Indian National Congress with the purpose of creating a class of thinkers who could advise the British to introduce necessary reforms in India, gradually Indian National Congress became a platform for the demand of complete freedom from the British rule. The most important contribution in this direction was made by B. G. Tilak, Lala Lajpatrai and Vipin Chandra Pal. After the extremists were separated from the main organisation they carried on their activities separately. In 1920 the same Indian National Congress which was a beginning of political activity in Renaissance period became the herald of Indian Nationalism under the leadership of M. K. Gandhi who

demanded *Purna Swarajya.* Along with presenting political demands before the Britishers, leaders of Indian National Congress were active in social and political reforms activities. Each one of them intensely thought over the social and political problems of the country and tried to find out solutions on the basis of suggestions from the West and inspirations from the ancient Indian literature.

8. **Rise of new economic class** No country can progress in thought or in practice without the indigenous economic support. The British rule in India gradually encouraged Indian people to carry on trade and commerce on capitalistic basis. This led to the rise of a new economic class which gradually became the economic base of social and nationalistic movements. It was this class which contributed generously to the funds of Brahmo Samaj, the Arya Samaj and the Indian National Congress. It can be said without exaggeration that without the economic support of this class modern Renaissance could not get a momentum in the country.
9. **Western political literature** Besides the introduction of Western political institutions, the Britishers introduced Western political literature in India. While some of the literature was imported from the West such as the works of Karl Marx, Lenin, Mussolini, Hitler, Spencer, Mill, Tolstoy and Ruskin etc., literature was produced by Indian writers also introducing the life and works of the leaders of Western society to the Indian people. The important among these writers were Surendranath Banerji, Lala Lajpatrai and V. D. Savarkar. Among the later writers were Iqbal and Sri Aurobindo and the celebrated Nobel prize-winner Rabindranath Tagore.
10. **Social legislations** All the above factors led to an increase in intellectual awakening and a demand for social legislation in different fields. Almost all the Renaissance thinkers were pained at the condition of women and low-caste people in India. Raja Ram Mohan Roy, Keshab Chandra Sen, Swami Dayananda, Ishwar Chandra Vidyasagar, M. G. Ranadey and Telang demanded social legislation in every field of social life. They demanded the abolition of Sati custom, the emancipation of women and elimination of all the drawbacks of the down-trodden elements in the society. Before this demand the Britishers were almost cool to social reform in India. But the demands raised by these eminent leaders gradually resulted in social legislation in different fields leading to social and political emancipation of the backward class.

NEW AWAKENING

The above socio-political factors created a new awakening in the country. This awakening resulted in several social and political reform movements. Of these the most representative movements of the period were Adi Brahmo Samaj of Rammohan Roy, Brahmo Samaj of Keshab Chandra Sen, Ramkrishna Mission of Vivekananda, Theosophical Society of Madame Blavatsky and Colonel Olcott and last though not the least the Arya Samaj of Swami Dayananda. A brief reference to some of these representative movements will present the background of the social thought of contemporary Indian thinkers, the main theme of this book. This will point out how the Renaissance thinkers led to a reorientation of the ancient Indian thought and worked out social implications of ancient ideals and principles.

RAM MOHAN ROY

The first Indian religious reformer of the nineteenth century was Raja Ram Mohan Roy whose efforts in his chosen field left a deep impression upon contemporary social, political and religious thinking. Ram Mohan Roy was born in a small village named Radhanagar in Bengal in the year 1772. He belonged to a family of Brahmins. He was a linguist who had mastered Sanskrit, English, Hindi, Persian, Hebrew, Greek and Latin. He made use of his knowledge to study the religious books in each of these languages and thereby he became quite knowledgeable on the subject of religion. He realized that if Hindu religion was to retain its life and strength it must undergo some modification, and it was with this end in view that the Brahmo Samaj was established in 1822. The principles of this society avoided all rigidity, stressing the importance of universal brotherhood and equality and the existence of a single God. In the social sphere Ram Mohan Roy opposed all inequality, child marriage, sati, bigamy, caste discrimination and the rest of problems that beset Hindu society. In the field of religion he could not and did not support the practice of priestly hypocrisy, worship of stone idols, the elaborate rituals, human and other sacrifices made as part of yagya, etc. He pointed out the need for widow remarriage and the education of women. He did not oppose the Western style of education since he was aware that the gulf of scientific learning that existed in Indian society could be filled only by this form of education. He exerted himself for the improvement and advancement of Indian literature and culture. He wanted the people to restrict themselves to constitutional methods in fighting for their freedom.

Brahmo Samaj

Brahmo Samaj achieved wide popularity among the Bengalis, and after Ram Mohan Roy it was further propagated by such great figures as Rabindranath Tagore and Keshab Chandra Sen. After some time the Samaj broke up into two groups on account of differences on basic principles, resulting in the formation of the Adi Brahmo Samaj led by Tagore and the Brahmo Samaj headed by Keshab Chandra Sen. Later on, the latter became prominent and progressive when such eminent persons as Jagdish Chandra Basu, Bipin Chandra Pal, C.R. Das and Aurobindo Ghosh joined it.

The main teaching of the Brahmo Samaj can be summed up as enunciated by Devendranath Thakur as follows:

1. In the beginning there was naught. The one Supreme alone existed. He created the whole universe.
2. He alone is the God of Truth, Infinite wisdom, Goodness and Power, Eternal and All-pervading, the one without a second (*Ekamevadvitiyam*).
3. In his worship lies our salvation in this world and in the next.
4. Loving Him and doing that which He loveth constitute His worship.

The philosophy of Brahmo Samaj can be summed up in the following words of Devendranath, "He who desireth the good of mankind must look on others as he looks on himself. It behoves thee to love thy neighbour, since it pleases thee to be loved by him; and to avoid giving pain by hatred, since it causes thee pain to be hated by another. Thus, in all things shalt thou deal with others by comparing them with thyself; for as pleasure and pain affect thee, so do they affect all creatures. Such conduct alone is the means of attaining well-being. He who adores God and loves man, is a saint. Such a man never rejoices in finding fault with men, for man is beloved of him. He is pained by the sight of a fault in others, and lovingly does he labour for its correction. He loves man as man; and owing to that love, is pleased by the sight of good, and grieved by the sight of evil in man. Therefore, he is unable to proclaim the faults of others with rejoicing. The satisfaction of the inner spirit, or, in other words, a good conscience, is the unfailing fruit of the practice of righteousness. In this approval of conscience is felt the approval of Good. If the inner spirit is satisfied, all sufferings cease. Without the practice of righteousness, the inner spirit is never satisfied. The mind may find enjoyment in the pleasure of the world, but if the conscience is diseased then even the height of worldly bliss becomes valueless. Therefore, by the practice of rigorousness, ye shall preserve a clear conscience, and ye shall abandon all things whereby the satisfaction of the spirit may be marred.

The renaissance thinkers advocated a synthetic approach to religion which was followed by our modern Indian social thinkers. This tendency was most eloquent in the sayings of Ramakrishna. It was circulated by his able disciple Vivekananda. The same tendency was again expressed in Gandhi's evening prayer where he used to recite Koran and Bible along with Gita. Among the Renaissance thinkers Ram Mohan Roy was almost the first to start this synthetic approach to religion. He was equally impressed by Bible, Koran, Upanishads and Gita. He believed in monotheism and monism though he failed to distinguish between the two. He was bitterly against sectarianism, superstition and idolatory but he did not repudiate Vedic religion. Like Benedict Spinoza he accepted substance as the ultimate reality, but unlike him he considered attributes as much necessary as the substance. Here he was more impressed by Ramanuj and Vaishnav Saints.

LIBERALISM AND INTERNATIONALISM

Ram Mohan Roy is known not only by Brahmo Samaj but more by his untiring efforts for social and political reform in India. Therefore, social and political ideas are even more important than metaphysical concepts in his social thought. The following are the important principles he enunciated:

1. **Personal and political freedom** An important characteristic of Renaissance thinkers and then of modern Indian thinkers, was emphasis on personal and political freedom started by Ram Mohan Roy. Pointing out his insistence in this direction Bipin Chandra Pal wrote, "the Raja was the first to deliver the message of political freedom to India. He so keenly felt the loss of this freedom by his people, that even as a boy yet within his teens he left his country and travelled to Tibet, because he found it difficult to tolerate the domination of his country by another nation, though, subsequently, with close acquaintance with the culture and character of the British people, who seemed to him to have been 'more intelligent, more steady and moderate in their conduct', the Raja became inclined in their favour, feeling persuaded that their rule, though a foreign yoke, would lead more speedily and surely to the amelioration of the native inhabitants. But he never believed or found it possible to tolerate the idea that India's unending subjection to the British rule was at all necessary for the amelioration of the Indian people."

   In spite of his insistence for political freedom Ram Mohan Roy recognised British rule as a blessing to India. This tendency starting from Roy and followed by Keshab Chandra Sen and others can be seen right upto M. K. Gandhi who declared that our struggle is against the foreign rule and not against the British people. Hailing the British rule in India Ram Mohan Roy wrote, "Among other objects, in our solemn devotion, we frequently offer up our humble thanks to God, for the blessings of British rule in India and sincerely pray, that it may continue in its beneficent operation for centuries to come."
2. **Freedom of the Press** Along with Dwarkanath Tagore, Harchandra Ghosh, Gauri Charan Banerjee, Prasanna Kumar Tagore and Chandra Kumar Tagore, Ram Mohan Roy drafted a petition for freedom of the press in India and addressed it to the Supreme Court. When the petition was rejected an appeal was made to the king-in-council. Ram Mohan Roy made a fervent appeal which proved his immense love for freedom of the press.
3. **Reform of Judiciary** Summing up Raja's insistence on judicial and administrative reforms in India, J. C. Ghosh wrote, "At the request of the Board of Control he submitted in writing his famous evidence to the Select Committee of the Commons, upon the working of the judicial and revenue systems of India, and the general character and condition of its native inhabitants, and upon various important matters connected with India. He published it in a pamphlet form with the title *An Exposition of the Revenue and Judicial Systems of India*. It embraces some of the most important questions relating to the administration

of India, such as, the reform of courts, the jurisdiction of the courts of the country over Europeans, the jury system, the separation of the executive and judicial offices, the confiscation of laws, the consulting of the people in legislation, the establishment of a native militia, the larger employment of natives, the age and education of civil servants, the amelioration of the condition of the ryots and the making of laws for their protection, and the permanent settlement..."

4. **Humanism and universal religion** Another important characteristic of the Renaissance thinkers followed by modern Indian political philosophers was started by Ram Mohan Roy in his emphasis on humanism and universal religion. He was a great champion of human rights and believed in cooperation, toleration and fellowship. He was a cosmopolitan and stood for liberty and fraternity. His study in the field of religion was deep and wide which convinced him that God is one though different religions worship Him in different forms. Thus, he carried the spiritual tradition of Kabir, Nanak, Dadu and Tukaram in social and political fields. This tendency started from Roy continued upto M. K. Gandhi.
5. **Welcome to English education** However they may have struggled against the British, Indian leaders generally always praised the English education in India. Roy, among others, considered it to be a boon for India. He wrote, "If it had been intended to keep the British nation in ignorance of real knowledge, the Baconian philosophy would not have been allowed to displace the system of the schoolmen which was the best calculated to perpetuate ignorance. In the same manner the Sanskrit system of education would be the best calculated to keep this country in darkness if such had been the policy of the British legislature. But as the improvement of the native population is the object of the Government, it will consequently promote a more liberal and enlightened system of instruction, embracing Mathematics, Natural Philosophy, Chemistry, Anatomy, with other useful sciences."
6. **Cultural synthesis** Like other Renaissance thinkers after him and later on like the modern Indian political thinkers, Roy wanted a cultural synthesis of East and West. He was so much impressed by the Western knowledge and Christian religion that he adopted many activities which were rebuked in Orthodox circles. He was a feminist and championed the rights of women. Throughout his life he fought like a hero against the exploitation of backward classes. Thus, it can be said that Roy was the pioneer of almost all the important tendencies witnessed in our time.

CONTEMPORARY DEGENERATION

Raja Ram Mohan Roy was living at a time when there was all-round political, economic and social degeneration.

(1) **Political degeneration** After the fall of Mughal Empire, India was disintegrated. There was virtually no sovereign authority to command respect of united India. East India Company was gradually extending its sway. It was penetrating deep into Indian soil. Gradually its authority was being established. There was no one in India to check this advancement of East India Company.

(2) **Social degeneration** There was a considerable social degeneration. During the Mughal regime there existed a social chasm between Hindus and Muslims. The latter who were the favourite sons of the Mughal Government no longer enjoyed that position. Hindu society was suffering from banes of Hindu religion and society. There were evil customs of idol worship and caste system. Polygamy was another evil of this time. Women were considered as inferior and denied their due status in society. They were denied education and their due share in the ancestral property. Hindu culture and civilisation was under great strain. Christian missionaries were doing their best to underestimate the significance and importance of Hindu cultural heritage. There was an attempt to expose weakness of Hindu culture. It was a time when the question was practically of survival of India's religious institutions. It was the foremost problem of Indian social life.

(3) **Economic degeneration** The conditions in India were not very satisfactory economically. Agriculture was the main profession. People had to depend on land which was not yielding much. The landlords usually arbitrarily enhanced the land rates. This put the peasants to great inconvenience. Sometimes the tenants were not in a position to pay the enhanced rates. Living standard of the Indian people was not very high.

(4) **Other evils** Indians were considered superstitious multitudes. The image of India with the Britishers was gloomy. There was none to wipe out this impression. An Indian was supposed to study only Hindi, Urdu and Sanskrit. No other language was studied, with the result that Indians could not get what was best in the literature of other languages.

Under these circumstances, the task of Raja Ram Mohan Roy, who was Hindu by heart yet influenced by the Western civilization, a man who wanted to be a patriot yet liked that the Europeans should settle in India and give us the benefit of their civilization, a man who was through and through a patriot and yet was required to adjust his ideas with the philosophy that stay of Britishers in India was desirable, was stupendous. This was, not only difficult but required great spirit and courage. It goes to his credit that he boldly solved these problems and gave his ideas. His ideas, if properly appreciated, in the background of his times, are bound to leave an impression that he was the pioneer thinker of modern Indian liberalism and renaissance.

CONTRIBUTION OF RAJA RAM MOHAN ROY

Taking into consideration the above mentioned times and conditions no one can deny that the magnitude of India's problems was very grave. It required not only a genius but a bold personality who could solve the problems. Raja Ram Mohan Roy had a mind not only to tackle political but also social and economic problems of his times. It goes to his credit that he successfully solved all those problems. He has been called the pioneer of liberalism and renaissance in India.

1. **Abolition of Sati custom** Ram Mohan Roy was the man who boldly challenged evils like the Sati and caste systems. It goes to his credit that he proposed to the Government of his times to legally abolish Sati which was a curse on the fair name of Hindu society.
2. **Religious reforms** Raja Ram Mohan Roy paved the path for liberalism. He pleaded for humanism and liberty. In an age of intolerance he stood for religious toleration. He successfully challenged idol worship which the Brahmins and others of his times were so vigorously pleading. He established a society by the name of Brahmo Samaj which was to preach the worship of one Supreme God above everything else. He was moved with a passionate love for country. He realised that in the present conditions when the Indians are disunited and disintegrated they could not challenge British supremacy. He understood his times very rightly and pleaded that the Britishers should be persuaded to carry out reforms. He earnestly believed in the British sense of justice. He was so much patriotic that for the sake of his country he would even allow the Christian missionaries to come and stay in India thereby giving the masses of India the benefit of their knowledge and wisdom.
3. **Freedom of press** Raja Ram Mohan Roy pleaded for the rule of law which was practically denied to the people of India since ages. It was a very bold demand and yet he made it very forcefully. He raised a voice against every step which denied freedom of press and stressed on the rules that their policy of denial of freedom of press might lead to revolution. At the same time he knew well that it was only through the freedom of press that the people of India could express their feelings and grievances to their rulers. He went to the extent of suggesting that freedom of press was in the interest of rulers themselves and for the stability of their empire in India.
4. **Synthetic approach** Raja Ram Mohan Roy was a man who loved Western culture and very thoroughly studied Western literature. He was loved by British liberals. Even his Majesty the King gave him audience. However, he upheld the great flag of Indian culture and civilization which he felt was the noblest. He did not borrow his ideas blindly from Western political philosophers. Nor did he try to establish the supremacy of Western over Indian culture. He simply and clearly

drew his inspiration from Indian religious books thereby establishing the values and worth of Indian spiritualism.

5. **Regeneration of women** Raja Ram Mohan Roy felt that the treatment which was being given to the women in India was unjustified. Not only did he plead for women's share in the ancestral property but he wholly supported many of their other causes. He stood for female education and also widow remarriage. In order to give the women their rightful place in the society he stood against polygamy and also for inter-caste marriages. He was a symbol of Indian spirituality and had deep faith in that. He studied Indian religion in proper sense of the term. He believed that the ancient Indian religion in its true sense stood for religious toleration, universal brotherhood, humanism and liberalism. He very boldly said that untouchability or caste system or idol worship were only such institutions which were subsequently introduced in religion by the selfish people and thus not part of original and pure Hindu religion.
6. **Assessment of Raja Ram Mohan Roy** Raja Ram Mohan Roy has been assessed very highly by different people. Those who came in his contact were greatly influenced by him. As a liberal he paved way for Gokhale, Dadabhai Naoroji and many others who followed him. Ranadey also very much borrowed from him. V. N. Naik writes about him that the Raja, "himself a devout worshipper at the shrine of liberty, realised even so for as 1820 that liberty to be properly enjoyed must be regulated liberty, that freedom has its own restraints as much as order. In the field of social and religious reform no less than in journalism and in politics his one endeavour was to awaken his countrymen not only to their rights as free men, but also to their obligation to society." Dr. Brajendranath Seal writes, "He went on to link them up with representative Government, trial by jury and freedom of press and he corrected and pleaded the Hindu personal law of marriage inheritance, religious worship, woman's status; Stri Dhana and Varnashrama Dharma by introducing the most liberal principles of justice and equity for which he found sanction also in the Law Codes, thus working out a synthesis between Eastern and Western social values and postulates against the common background of Universal Humanity." The great British liberal Bentham wrote about him, "Your works are well-known to me by a book in which I read a style which but for the name of a Hindu, I should certainly have ascribed to the pen of superiorly educated and instructed English man."
7. **Modernity** The teachings and ideas of Raja Ram Mohan Roy hold good even in a modern society. Sati today stands condemned. Exploitation of man by man has been condemned both at national as well as international levels. If we account for his liberal ideas through which he justified foreign rule in India, there is perhaps nothing ancient in

him but everything modern and up-to-date even today. One cannot deny that his basic principles of liberalism and toleration were adopted subsequently for quite a long time by Indian National Congress in its formative stages and upto the end in its national struggle. He was the man who rightly kept his hand on the nerves of the Indian masses of his times and his approach to the problem was the approach of a genius and a well brought up and developed man.

9
Gopal Krishna Gokhale (1866 — 1915)

When Gopal Krishna Gokhale died in 1915 Gandhiji walked barefoot for one year to mourn the death of this political Guru. This was how he registered his acknowledgement of Gokhale's greatness. Gokhale combined rare qualities of intelligence with courage, patriotism with honesty, statesmanship with liberal outlook, political shrewdness with clear foresight of future. He rose to extraordinary eminence in national and international life due to his personal character and ability, hard labour and public spirit.

BIOGRAPHY

Nine years after the first war of Indian independence Gokhale was born on 9 May, 1866 in a little village of Kotluk in the district of Ratnagiri of then Bombay Presidency. His parents were poor and had only a small unprofitable plot of land. His father Krishna Rao lived with meagre earnings as a low paid clerk and later on as Sub-Inspector of Police. However, his only ambition was to give modern education to his two sons, Govind and Gopal. Consequently after initial education in the village both the brothers were sent to a High School at Kolhapur in 1876. They lost their father in 1879. The elder brother Govind was eighteen years old and already married. In order to support the family he left his studies and took up a job. He made up his mind to fulfil the desire of his father in educating Gopal in spite of hardships.

Gokhale passed his Matriculation in the year 1881. He thought of leaving studies to help his brother in supporting the family, but his brother did not agree. Thus, Gokhale joined the Raja Ram College at Kolhapur. Later on he shifted to the Deccan College, Poona for graduation. For the final year of the degree course he joined Elphinstone College, Bombay. During those days of his study Gokhale had to manage with Rs. 8 per month for all his expenses. He would often go without meals to save mess expenses and read under the street lamp whenever he had no money to buy kerosene. Poverty brought him nearer to the poor whose cause he pleaded throughout his life. As a student he had keen competitive spirit and always tried to excel others. With extraordinary memory he would often memorise chapters or even the entire books. In 1884 he graduated with Mathematics. Due to stiff competition his desire to become an engineer could not materialise. His desire to join the Indian Civil Service could not be fulfilled due to poverty. The plan of taking up the legal profession, could not succeed as he did not go beyond passing of the first Law examination. Thus, there was something else in store for him than mere taking up a profession to lead a peaceful life. "My ambition," confessed Gokhale to his friend Hari Narayan Apte while as a student in the Deccan College, "is to become a Cabinet Minister so as to be able to serve my country." He took up the job of teaching in the New English School in Poona in January, 1885. The extraordinary progress of the School attracted attention of all people and won admiration from even influential English men. Gokhale gradually strengthened his relations with the public life of Poona by joining the Deccan Education Society and later on Fergusson College as Lecturer. During these formative years he came in contact with M.G. Ranade and became his life-long disciple. Ranade brought Gokhale in association with Poona Sarvajanik Sabha. Due to Ranade again he joined the Indian National Congress in 1889 and rose rapidly in public life of the country as political leader and social reformer. His intelligence, dedication to duty and transparent sincerity helped him in winning appreciation from all those who came in his contact.

For ten long years Gokhale associated with the Poona Sarvajanik Sabha as its honorary secretary from 1885 to 1895. The politics of the Sabha was national, secular and progressive. After joining the Indian National Congress, Gokhale entered the wider political field. The Congress enabled India to breathe as one nation creating an opportunity for men of different opinions to work for a common cause, Gokhale seized the opportunity offered by the new situation. He was already famous as a teacher in the Fergusson College. He was elected to the Bombay Legislative Council in 1899 where he raised issues based on rights and justice and tried to behave as a sincere public servant. With the blessings of Sir Pherozeshah Mehta, he became a member of the Imperial Legislative Council in 1901.

Gopal Krishna Gokhale inherited the historical legacy left by A.O. Hume, William Wedderburn, Charles Bradlaugh, M.G. Ranade, Pherozeshah Mehta and Dadabhai Naoroji. Influenced by their ideas Gokhale was cast in the liberal mould. He looked upon the British rule as an opportunity to prepare the people of India for social, political and economic freedom.

POLITICAL ACTIVITIES

In his political views Gokhale grew to be a moderate, liberal and constitutionalist. He was a realist or practical idealist stressing on the possible, desirable and attainable. He transformed the field of practical politics into one of political ethics. He was against fruitless political agitation. Though loyal to the British government, he wanted it to work for the welfare of the people in India. He told Britishers, "It is not wrong to love one's country." He visited England seven times in different capacities and pleaded the cause of India in most impressive manner. During his first visit in 1897 he said at a public meeting, "Indian people were living under a despotic and perfectly irresponsible government." In 1905 he demanded self-government and replacement of the Britishers by Indians to manage their own affairs. He advocated constitutional methods for the realisation of his goal which included passive resistance and other democratic procedures. In all his visits to England he carried the voice of Indian nationalism to the people of that country. He was a humanist and did not subscribe to the myth of European hegemony and superiority. He denounced the privileges conferred on English men in the name of race. He transformed the Congress into a forum recognised by the government and supported by people. He gave a direction and a vision to the Congress and helped it in overcoming many crisis. Paying tribute to him Lord Curzon once said, "I have never met a man of any nationality more gifted with what one could describe in this country as Parliamentary capacities, than was Mr. Gokhale." In 1915 Lord Willingdon, the Governor of Bombay requested Gokhale to suggest constitutional reforms. Gokhale suggested autonomy for provinces. He wanted Indians to take over the control of the country by peaceful and constitutional methods against radical approach. On this issue he was opposed by some of his friends like Tilak and Lajpat Rai.

SOCIAL PHILOSOPHY

Though Gokhale had no ambition to enlist himself as a social reformer like Rammohan Roy, he developed a definite social philosophy and gave free expression to his views. At the Dharwar social conference in 1903 he called upon the young men of India to follow the ancient tradition of dedication to the service of man and God. He asked his audience, "Cannot a few men, five per cent, four per cent, three or two or even one per cent of hundred's and hundred's of graduates that the university turns out every year, take it upon themselves to dedicate their lives to this sacred work of the elevation of low classes." In all social matters Gokhale stood for reform of the society. He could not tolerate injustice. He was deeply concerned for women, oppressed and the weaker section of the society he voiced his feelings in the Imperial Legislative Council. While he fought for political rights, he was deeply worried about effects of the caste system.

HUMANISM

Gokhale's concern to alleviate the condition and status of Indians not only in India but everywhere else was the proof of this intrinsic humanism. On Gandhiji's request Gokhale came forward to help him in his struggle for just rights of Indians. In 1903 at a public meeting in Bombay's Town Hall he moved a resolution calling upon the British government to prevent injustice and ill-treatment of Indians in South Africa. Through his efforts, a ban on recruitment of indentured labour for Natal and other overseas colonies was imposed. His visit to South Africa in 1912 was a great moral booster for Gandhiji and other Asians living there. The British government could not treat Gokhale lightly due to his political stature at that time. Gokhale condemned racial discrimination as inhuman and immoral.

Gokhale raised his voice against the evil of caste system, ill-treatment of women and the poor. He said, "If you want to stand where you were a thousand years ago, the system of caste need not be modified in any material degree. If, however, you want to emerge out of the slough in which you have long remained sunk, it will not do for you to insist on a rigid adherence to caste, the larger humanity of these days requires that we should acknowledge its claims by seeking the amelioration of the helpless condition of our downtrodden countryman." Gokhale believed that India could not progress with large a number of people living in poverty, ignorance and the life of segregation.

SERVANTS OF INDIA SOCIETY

Gokhale called upon the people to realise the blessings and boons of cooperation and discipline to minimise differences and to strengthen public spirit. He thought of building up a band of selfless public servants dedicated to the welfare of the people and service of the country. He set up the Servants of India Society for regeneration of Indian society based on political faith of common nationality. According to him the Servants of India Society was being established "to train men prepared to devote their lives to the cause of the country in a religious spirit, for the work of political education and agitation and will seek to promote by all constitutional means, the national interest of the Indian people." The Society was formally founded on 12 June, 1905. The six maxim charter of work and duties for the members of the Society consisted of creating love of the motherland, education of people, assisting educational activities, helping in industrial development and elevation of depressed classes. The Society was to grow as a politico-social organisation of workers without religious bonds. In the political field the Society cooperated with the Indian National Congress in the national movement. Its branches were established in some important cities of the country.

SECULARISM : HINDU-MUSLIM UNITY

Gokhale had prepared the constitution of the Society himself. The promotion of the cordial goodwill and cooperation among the different communities living in India was embodied as the ideal of the Society. Every member of the Society was supposed to regard all Indians as brothers without any distinction of caste and creed. Gokhale was a great advocate of Hindu-Muslim unity. For himself he said, "I am by birth a Hindu but for many years it has been the earnest aspiration of my life to work for the advancement of this country only as an Indian." Gokhale was secular-minded and worked to promote goodwill between different communities, particularly Hindus and

Muslims. He said there was no future for India if the two great communities did not live together in peace and harmony. He worked for the one-nation idea. Even the foremost advocate of the two-nation theory Mr. M.A. Jinnah paid meaningful tribute to Gokhale when he said, "it was his one ambition to become the Muslim Gokhale."

Gokhale faithfully adhered to the Catholic line of his master, M.G. Ranade. He affirmed, "The India of the future could not now be only a Hindu India or a Mohammedan India, it must be compounded of all the elements which existed in India." Due to his broad-based tolerance Gokhle could easily get on with Muslim leaders of his times. He welcomed the formation of the Indian Muslim League in 1906. During his tour of U.P. and Punjab in 1907, he received warm affection from the Muslim community. He addressed a conference of Muslims at Lahore on Hindu-Muslim relations. Hindu-Muslim conference was arranged at Allahabad in January 1, 1911. It was agreed to appoint a committee of sixteen members, eight drawn from each community to examine controversial issues. After the committee was announced the Muslims demanded the inclusion of Gokhale in the committee. Gokhale protested that he was a Hindu. But the audience shouted, "You are a friend of us; all we wish you should be on the committee." Gokhale worked to bridge the gulf between Hindus and Muslims and moved Muslims of U P. and Punjab to work for national unity. He asked Hindu leaders to appreciate the genuine fear of Muslim community, being in minority, and work for removal of that fear by responsible behaviour. He also warned Muslims to be on guard against divisive forces in the country and work for national freedom without reservation. Muslim response to his call delighted him when out of enthusiasm his carriage was pulled by the students of Aligarh Muslim University shouting, Gokhale Zindabad." But in the following years partition of Bengal and demand for separate electorate created antagonism between Hindus and Muslims.

SUPPORT TO EDUCATION

V.S. Srinivasa Sastri, a disciple and great admirer of Gokhale, has remarked that "Mr. Gokhale has made in his life two renunciations, a lesser and a greater. The lesser renunciation he made in his nineteenth year when for little than a subsistence he undertook to devote his great talents and youthful energy to the education of his poor countrymen. The greater renunciation he made when after twenty years of strenuous labour in education he dedicated his life, still full of vigour and promise, to the political regeneration of his country." Gokhale considered education of the people as the necessary precondition of social and political freedom. As a political thinker and leader he fought for the removal of widespread illiteracy and ignorance among the Indian masses.

Like other social reformers Gokhale felt that widespread illiteracy was at the root of all social evils. No measures of social reform could bring about necessary social change and progress when the ignorant millions could not distinguish between the good and bad in society. Gokhale saw in the expansion of education, an important and effective medium for the welfare of the masses. In his budget speech in the Imperial Legislative Council on March 26, 1902, he said, "Nine children out of every ten are growing up in ignorance and darkness, and four villages out of every five are without a school, whereas in England every child of school-going age must attend a school." Highlighting the injustice done to the people Gokhale went on to say, "There are altogether about five lakh fifty thousand villages in British India, out of which it has been calculated four-fifths are at present without a school, the residents of these villages pay the local cesses just like other villagers, and yet the necessary educational facilities for education of their children are denied to them." In 1906 Gokhale pleaded for compulsory free primary education. He moved a bill in the Imperial Legislative Council on March 16, 1911 when received made support from all sections. The government was forced to set up a separate department of education under Sir Harcourt Butler. Through his speeches and writings Gokhale stressed the need for bringing millions and millions of children under the humanizing influence of education. He asked Indians to take up the cause of education and not to depend only on government initiative.

POLITICAL GOALS

1. **Constructive Statesmanship** Gokhale believed in constructive programmes. As a statesman, his political philosophy contained both idealism and realism. He was called idealistic because of his lofty ideals of nationalism and purity of life. He was a realist because he never wandered about abstract idealism. He believed that attainment of self-government was only possible under the framework of the British kingdom, hence he believed in the policy of gradual achievement of self-government.
2. **Moderation** Gokhale advocated for the British rule in India. He marked British as guardians of India and hence pursued a policy of loyal cooperation. He liked the British Liberalism and had faith in British conscience to get justice and fairplay.
3. **Political justice** Gokhale was of the opinion that English politicians would do justice to India. In his budget Speech in Indian Legislative Council in the year 1902 he said: "What is needed is that we should be enabled to feel that we have a government, national in spirit though foreign in personal, a government which subordinates all other considerations to the welfare of the Indian people, which resents the indignities offered to Indians abroad as though they were offered to Englishmen, and which endeavours by all means in its power to further the moral and material interest of the people in India and outside India. The statesman who evokes such a feeling among the Indian people will render a great and glorious service to this country and will secure for

himself an abiding place in the hearts of our people. Nay he will do more service to his own country in a true spirit of imperialism, not the narrower imperialism which regards the world as though it was made for one race only and looks upon subject races as if they were intended to be mere footstools of that race — but that nobler imperialism which would enable all who are included in the Empire to share equally in its blessings and honours."

POLITICAL TECHNIQUES

1. **Faith in constitutional methods** In political techniques, Gokhale was moderate *par excellence.* For acquiring the Indian demands he advocated constitutional methods. He advocated constitutional agitation and discarded extreme measures and outbursts of popular frenzy. As he said, "Constitutional agitation is agitation by methods which we are entitled to adopt to bring about the changes we desired through the action of constituted authorities."
2. **Moral pressure** The only way to attain what we desire is to bring moral pressure on the ruler. He said again, "Redress must be obtained, through the constituted authorities, ... the idea we should leave the authorities, severely alone and seek to attain our goal independently of them is inadmissible and absurd." In fact, Gokhale was a middleman between the government and the people. He interpreted popular aspirations to the Viceroy and the governments' difficulties to the Congress. At times he was not liked by both the wings. His fellow-workers complained of his being mild. On the other hand, at times government held him to be too radical. Dr. Pattabhi Sitaramayya spoke of him, "Gokhale had a knack of saying the hardest things in the gentlest language. Gokhale used soft word, with clear meanings."
3. **Search for self-government** Being disappointed, Gokhale changed the words as seen for the repressive policies adopted by Lord Curzon. This shook him for British sincerity. In his unusual words he used to utter, "Then, all I can say is, good bye to all hopes of cooperating in any way with the bureaucracy in the interest of the people." Disappointed at the end of his life he said: "The bureaucracy was becoming frankly selfish and openly hostile to national aspirations." Hence, during (Congress Session of 1905, he said that self-government goal is a last resort, boycott was to be used. In the words of Pandit Moti Lal Nehru he was the great Apostle of self-government. About the partition of Bengal, he said it to be bureaucracy's gross irresponsibility and extreme indifference to the public will.
4. **Mutual cooperation** Gokhale had faith in mutual cooperation of both India and England. He planned for the moral and material advance of the country. He asked the British that Indians should be given more places in the government.

5. **Spreading western education** To free Indians of the old ideas based on blind faith, superstitions and dogmas, Gokhale gave importance to Western education to generate a greater responsiveness to the appreciation of freedom and value of free institutions.
6. **Patriotism and nationalism** Gokhale gave importance to Ranade's view that "British Empire in India was in the scheme of diviner dispensation and was meant to be of immense benefit to India". Secondly, strong nationalism could be created through hard work and sacrifices. According to him nationalism was a kind of self devotion to a higher cause. Without suffering and friendship and simplicity of life nationalism could become a living force. Gokhale said, "The real moral interest of a struggle, such as we are engaged in lies not so much in the particular readjustment of present institutions which we may succeed in securing as in the strength that the conflict brings to be a permanent part of ourselves. The whole life of a people, which is broader and deeper than what is touched by purely political institutions is enriched by failures, provided the effort has been all that it should be."
7. **No confrontation with the Government** Gokhale maintained that he was a peacemaker and confrontation with government will bring chaos, and peace and order will be disturbed. According to him, slow and gradual transfer of power to Indians was possible only through Dominion Status. When Tilak criticised his idea of peaceful transfer of power, through history, he said "It may be that the history of the world does not furnish an instance where a subject race had become free without violent agitation. If so, we shall supply that example for the first time. The history of the world had not yet come to an end, there are more chapters yet to be added."
8. **Training of political workers** Servants of Indian Society was started by Gokhale to train the political workers with full interest. It pleaded for the loyalty to the British Empire and pledged to work for the motherland.
9. **Primacy of means over ends** According to Gokhale in order to bring good ends the means should also be good. He never believed that ends justify means. He believed that politics and morality should go together. Hence, he spoke of self government as the end for all nationalists in India but the means to achieve it must be noble. If unfair means were adopted for that end, the aim could not be achieved. If India was to become free by foul means, such freedom will not be a freedom at all. For Swarajya, we must deserve it.
10. **Swadeshi movement** Gokhale was an advocate of Swadeshi Movement. It was not an economic weapon to beat the foreign government. The use of Swadeshi would regularly remind us for our being Indian first. In Benaras Congress Session 1905, as President, he said "The true Swadeshi Movement is both a patriotic and an economic movement.

The idea of Swadeshi or one's own country is one of the noblest conceptions that have ever stirred the heart of humanity.... The devotion to mother land, which is enshrined in the highest Swadeshi, is an influence so profound and so passionate that its very thought thrills and its actual touch lifts one out of itself. The Swadeshi Movement, as is ordinarily understood, present one part of this gospel to the mass of our people, in a form which brings it within their comprehension. It turns their thoughts to their country, accustoms them to the idea of voluntarily making some sacrifice for her sake, enables them to take an intelligent interest in her economic development and teaches them the important lesson of cooperating with one another for a national end. But the movement on its material side is an economic one, and though self-denying ordinance, extensively entered into, must serve available economic purpose namely, to ensure a ready consumption of such articles as are produced in the country and to furnish a perpetual stimulus to production of keeping the demand for indigenous things largely in excess of the supply, the difficulties that surround the question economically are so great that they require the cooperation of every available agency to surmount them."

11. **Legislative and administrative reforms** At the Benaras Congress Session Gokhale put nine demands: (i) Reforms in Legislative Councils by raising the number of elected members to one-half and budgets be passed by the council; (ii) Three Indians be appointed to the India Council; (iii) Countryside creation of District Advisory Boards and District Magistrate should compulsorily consult them in matters of administration; (iv) Judicial branch should consist of legal professionists for Indian Civil Service; (v) Judicial and executive administration should be separated; (vi) Military expenses should be reduced; (vii) Primary education should be expanded; (viii) Industrial and Technical education should be expanded; and (ix) Rural indebtedness should be avoided.
12. **Hindu-Muslim Unity** Gokhale was a champion of Hindu-Muslim unity. He avoided the controversy between the two communities, so that their relations may not become ambittered. He told Hindus to protect Muslim minority and remove an inferiority complex in them. He tried to avoid the festivals held by Tilak during Ganeshotsava and Shivaji anniversary and thus avoided communal consciousness.
13. **Decentralization of Powers** Gokhale championed the cause of decentralization of powers. He advocated checks on the bureaucracy. Legislatures in provinces should be given more powers to discuss the budget. Recommendation of Advisory boards of district councils was his gift. While giving evidence before Hobhouse Decentralization Commission he advocated the necessity of (i) Village Panchayats at

the village level; (ii) District councils at the intermediate level; and (iii) Reformed Legislative Councils at the top level.

14. **Tests for judging the Government** With the spread of the Western education new problems sprang up. This spread the response for liberty and free institutions. He aimed at forwarding some tests for judging the ability and the progressive policies of the Government. During the year 1911 he said, "I suggest four tests to judge whether the Government is progressive and further whether it is continuously progressive. First test, I would apply is what measures it adopts for the moral and material improvement of the mass of the people and under these measures I do not include those applied in this country because they were appliances necessary for its very existence, though they have benefited the people such as the construction of the Railways, the introduction of Posts and Telegraphs and the things of that kind. By measures for the moral and material improvement of the people, I mean what the Government does for education, what the Government does for sanitation, what the Government does for agricultural development and so forth. That is my first test. The second test that I would apply is what steps the Government takes to give us large shares in the administration of local affairs that is in municipalities and local bodies. My third test is what voice the Government gives us in its councils in those deliberative assemblies where policies are considered. And lastly, we must consider how far Indians are admitted into the ranks of Public Services.

15. **Constitutional advance** In consultation with Ferozeshah Mehta and Aga Khan he formed a plan for India's constitutional advance. This was designed on the basis of federalism. During 1914-15, he accepted the powers of intervention of the Governor-General. His schemes recognized separate but direct representation of the Muslims and other minorities.

10
Bal Gangadhar Tilak (1856—1920)

Bal Gangadhar Tilak was born at Ratnagiri in Bombay Presidency on 23 July, 1856. The political atmosphere of India was charged with deep dislike for the new rulers and exactly after one year it found expression through armed struggle to free the country. His father Gangadhar Pant though gifted with rare qualities of character and learning, started as a teacher and could not rise beyond the post of Deputy Education Inspector. But he decided to give the best possible education to his only son Bal. After initial education at home, Tilak was sent to school before he was 11. As a student he proved to be extraordinary in Mathematics and Sanskrit. He did his Matriculation in 1872. He solved problems of Mathematics orally. Once his teacher asked him "where is your method", Tilak replied, "It is here," pointing to his head. Tilak pursued his further studies in the Deccan College and did his B.A. with first class in 1876 and his LL.B in 1879.

After passing the LL.B examination there were alluring prospects before Tilak of becoming a High Court Judge and a comfortable life. But, he was moved by three events, first, the trial of Malhar Rao Gaekwar by a special commission for alleged attempt to poison his resident Col. Phayre, second, an abortive attempt to overturn the British government in 1876 made by a band of fanatics under the leadership of Wasudeo Balwant Phadke, a clerk in the government service and lastly, the terrible famine of 1877-78 with its toll of 50 lakhs of lives. Moved by these events Tilak decided to lead a life of total dedication to the cause of poor people and service to the country.

EFFORT IN EDUCATIONAL FIELD

Tilak felt that to be useful education must be in the hands of the nation's chosen leaders. With these ideas and a strong desire to initiate a movement for national education, in cooperation with his friend and fellow student of Deccan College, Gopal Ganesh Agarkar, Tilak developed an ambition to establish a network of schools by their initiative to enlighten the masses about the condition of their country. They took the help of some more people and started the New English School at Poona in January 1880 with 19 students on the role. Tilak and his colleagues took up the work of teaching at a nominal pay. The School made remarkable success as a centre of education. Tilak thought of setting up a college so that young graduates from the college would help in spreading education through more schools. The Deccan Education Society was formed in 1884 to initiate the opening of a college. In 1885 the Fergusson College was established and Tilak worked till 1890 as a specialist in Mathematics and Sanskrit. He was the guiding spirit of the institution and did the work of organisation and collection of funds. Due to his loyalty to the original ideals of dedication and service Tilak developed differences with members of the Deccan Education Society in 1887 and severed his connection in 1890. He thought of giving more time and attention to the two weekly papers *Kesari* (Marathi) and *Mahratha* (English) as the editor.

RADICAL POLITICAL ACTIVITIES

Tilak joined the Indian National Congress in 1889. The Congress was dominated by moderate leadership full of praise and admiration for the Britishers. The Congress leaders believed in the method of petitions and prayers for securing genuine rights of the people. But the Indian Council Act of 1892 did not satisfy the aspirations of even moderates. Introducing a new thinking Tilak said, "Political rights will have to be fought for." Having no faith in the constitutional methods he said, "protests are of no avail. Mere protests not backed by self-reliance will not help the people. Days of protests and prayers are gone." He asked nationalists to rely on the character and capacities of the Indian people. He asked people to build their own future through self-effort. He asked the Congress leaders to change their attitude towards the government and educate people about their rights. He said, "We must give the best political education possible, to the ignorant villagers. We must meet them on terms of equality, teach them their rights and show how to fight constitutionally. Then only the government will realise that to despise the Congress is to despise the Indian nation." Tilak remained very active during the epidemic of plague which took a toll of one crore lives. He worked to keep suffering humanity and started a plague hospital to serve poor people. In utter disregard of his services and cooperation with the government, Tilak was put on trial after the plague was controlled. He was sentenced to 18 months' imprisonment for sedition. He spent his term of imprisonment in Yervada Jail doing research work on the Vedas.

When Tilak was released from the prison he decided to infuse vigour into the public mind. For this he organised Ganapati and Shivaji festivals and gradually converted these into a social and national force. Tilak thought of gathering patriotic and national forces round the personality of Shivaji. But unfortunately he could not convince the moderate leadership of the Congress about the validity of his actions. Between 1898 to 1904 Tilak remained preoccupied with litigation. In 1905 Lord Curzon declared partition of Bengal. Tilak, Sri Aurobindo, B.C. Pal, Lajpat Rai and some other Congressmen voiced their opposition to the policy of Congress leaders and threatened open revolt. Tilak emerged as an uncompromising champion of

Swaraj. He asked the nation to get prepared for decisive struggle for freedom and reminded people that "the path of duty is never sprinkled with rose water nor do roses grow on it." Forging alliance with all radicals of the Congress, Tilak made a whirlwind tour of the country and asked people to support the extremists for liberation. In 1907 an open clash took place between the moderates and the extremists at the Surat session of the Congress. With the spirit of cooperation and for the sake of higher ideals Tilak offered to compromise if the Congress agreed to work for Swaraj, Swadeshi, boycott and national education. However, due to the obstinacy of the moderates the break of Congress could not be averted.

In 1908, Tilak was put to trial by the Bombay High Court for writing an article alleged to be seditious. He was sentenced to six years transportation to Mandalay Jail where he was kept in a solitary room. The moderate leaders including Gokhale did not utter even a word of protest. They were careful about not offending the government while doing "good" for the country. But when Gokhale died, Tilak motored down to Poona and in his funeral oration said, "This diamond of India, this jewel of Maharashtra, this prince of workers is laid to eternal rest on the funeral ground. Look at him and try to emulate him."

DEMAND OF HOME RULE

On his return from Burma after completing the term of imprisonment Tilak thought of organising people to demand Home Rule. As he was out of the Congress, he also thought over the question of re-entry of extremists into the Congress. The year 1916 was important in the political career of Tilak for two reasons: Firstly, he joined his old comrades at the Lucknow session of the Congress, and secondly, he formed the Indian Home Rule League with the object of attaining self-government for Indian people within the British Empire by constitutional means. Tilak undertook an extensive tour of the country propagating in favour of Home Rule. By 1917 the extremists took complete control of the Indian National Congress. Tilak went to England in 1918 to represent the country demanding Home Rule. He made a great impact on English public opinion through his writings and speeches. In a letter to an English man Tilak wrote, "It is necessary for me to dwell upon the imperative importance of solving the Indian question for purposes of ensuring the future peace of the world and the progress of the people of India." The Home Rule movement launched by Tilak was the natural culmination of the nationalist movement. The call for swadeshi and the movement for swaraj had been gathering force since the partition of Bengal in 1905. The Home Rule movement marked a new important phase in the struggle for independence. During 1916-17 Tilak was admired by the whole country for his sincerity, unbending patriotism and fearlessness. The mass movement which he initiated worked a miracle in the hands of Gandhi after the death of Tilak in 1920.

THE FIRST MASS LEADER

Pattabhi Sitaramayya in the book on the *History of Congress* rightly said "Lokmanya was the first nationalist who took the movement for freedom struggle to the common man". Before the entry of Tilak to the Congress, the association was cornered by moderate educated persons who were ignored by the Britishers. They were cautious in their actions. They only liked to have certain concessions to the educated class from the English rulers. Tilak advocated a strong fight against the unjust foreign government. Tilak had to work under the unfavourable state as opposed by moderates. But he emerged as a national leader. On the other hand, in those days, the economic condition of the country was rather depressing. Economic resources were utilised for their own good. The credit of being a first mass leader goes to Tilak. In the words of Pandit Jawahar Lal Nehru, "The early founders of Congress were great men. But they rather made the intellectual foundation in the early stages of the freedom movement. I don't think that it is unfair to them to say that they were not mass leaders in the sense that some subsequent state leaders became. I think the first great mass leader of this new state of our revolutionary movement was Lokmanya Tilak."

THE POLITICAL GOAL OF SWARAJ

Tilak was of the opinion that reliance on the constitutional methods of struggle was without foundation as India had not its own Constitution. Moderates gave importance to administration and its improvement and tried to win over the foreign government through love, goodwill and sympathy. Tilak, on the other hand, relied upon non-cooperation, obstruction and passive resistance. Politicians of Pre-Tilak period depended on alien government's benevolence, sense of equity, justice and fairplay. Tilak, on the other hand, trusted self-sacrifice, suffering and service of the people. Other leaders appealed to elite class while Tilak appealed to the masses in millions. The moderates wanted to voice their resentments and feelings through the Council Chambers. Tilak used village Mandaps as platform for voicing his feelings. While other leaders used English as their medium of expression, Tilak used Indian dialects. Other leaders winded to participate in the administration step by step, while Tilak declared 'Swaraj is my birth-right and I will have it'. He thought of freedom to be never achieved by charity but to be demanded as a right. Freedom was necessary for social, political and economic uplift of the public. It was a political and spiritual necessity of the people. By it they can remove their misery, starvation and degradation. Tilak knew Indian National Congress not to be a body for mass movement against the British Government. He demanded that Congress meetings should be held more frequently and not once in a year. The message of Swaraj should reach everywhere in India through towns, cities and villages. Because of these reasons English rulers called Tilak the father of 'Indian Unrest'.

Meaning of Swaraj

By Swaraj Tilak meant a Dharma Rajya. It was not only a transfer of political power but beyond that. It was required to build a superstructure on Indian culture and civilization. It was a status in which every Indian would get all the rights natural to man. He also recommended federal structure for the country so that all races, languages, religion and culture could be accommodated. This could not be done under British Emperor, it would lead to an independent existence.

1. **Self-rule** Swaraj meant the operation and management of domestic affairs of India by Indians. According to Tilak, "Swaraja is possessing these rights which the native princes had in the Indian States with this difference that instead of hereditary chiefs under Swaraja there would be an elected president." Foreign policy was to remain in English hands. British King Emperor was not to be replaced. According to Tilak "The ideas of Swaraj is an old one. Of course, when Swaraj is spoken of, there is some kind of rule opposed to 'Swa' *(i.e.* our) and this idea arises at that time. Thus, when such a condition arises it begins to be thought that there should be Swaraj and even make efforts for that purpose." Again, "The question of Swaraj really means in whose hands should be vested the control of our affairs. I have said that we do not wish to change the immutable government or the King but what we demand is that the management of our affairs should not be, as it now is, in the hands of invisible government, the bureaucracy, but should be transferred to our hands."
2. **National necessity** According to Tilak, Swaraja was a necessity. By Swaraj he meant a federal type of political set up. Like the American Congress, the Government of India should have power and the same powers be used through the Imperial Council. He accepted the possibilities of linguistic provinces. He said "India is a big country. Divide it if you want, according to the language."

POLITICAL TECHNIQUES

1. **Swadeshi** According to Tilak, to attain in Swaraj, many sufferings and sacrifices are required but not the prayers and petitions. He proposed Swadeshi and Boycott movements as effective methods. For Swadeshi movement he said once, "We send our boys to schools completely aloof from the national movement. On the other hand, our object is that they should get an education that will inspire them with patriotism."
2. **Boycott** In the words of Karmarkar, "Tilak attached a great importance to boycott as a means of exercising pressure on Britishers to compel them to grant Indians legitimate rights." Tilak said, "We have neither the strength nor the desire to rise in arms against our rulers, but should it not be possible for us to stop the drain of crores of rupees which we

are giving to the British merchants, labourers by purchasing British goods."

3. **Passive resistance** Tilak said that people should not obey those laws that go against justice and morality. "Passive resistance was the means to an end but was not the goal in itself. Public has to see its merits and demerits. The demerits should be fought but not by violence or anarchism."
4. **No constitutional methods** Tilak had no faith in constitutional methods. Constitutional agitation was out of question as there was no Constitution of India. He said, "There is no Constitution in India. The Government in India is irresponsible and non-constitutional. Constituted authorities in India are irresponsible and we have to take our rights from them. The legality of our action may be illegal according to their point of view, but we should not worry whether our agitation is legal or illegal. We must see whether justice, morality and historical traditions are in our favour or not, and if our actions are correct, according to these standards, we should not care whether they come within the law or not because the power making of law is in the hands of foreigners."
5. **Propaganda and agitation in England** Tilak gave birth to Home Rule League in 1916 with Mrs. Annie Besant's collaboration. During April 1916 he started this movement which aimed at Home Rule under British Empire. He pointed out that the British Parliament can do this by introducing a Bill to this effect. Therefore, Tilak maintained that propaganda and agitation was required to be started in England also.
6. **Condemnation of moderate method** Tilak condemned the method already adopted by the moderates who were dominating the Indian National Congress at that time. Their method depended on prayers, petitions and memoranda. Independence could not be got by these methods in charity. English people were selfish. They were bent upon unkind torture and economic exploitation of the Indians. They tried to exploit the toils of Indians to the benefit of their home country. Tilak had no faith in justice from them. Hence, he put forward his methods for conducting struggle such as swadeshi, boycott, national education and passive resistance. This would stop the British goods consumption and their earnings would be reduced.
7. **National education** Tilak supported the impartation of national education. He criticised the British system of education prevalent at that time as it only produced clerks to work for British administration in India. National education would bring the growth of patriotism and nationalism.
8. **Condemnation of British Bureaucracy** The English breacuracy in India was corrupt and misused the authority. Hence, Tilak accused the British officials engaged in India for maladministration and said, "To

deport national leaders without trial, to prohibit peaceful meetings... to sentence editors of newspapers like criminals...to keep respectable people under trial for months together and such like actions being taken in India are similar to autocratic policy adopted by Czars of Russia. This repressive policy is likely to result in consequences similar to those of Russia."

9. **Propagation of Indian culture** Tilak aimed at the political freedom of India. So he brought forward the Indian heritage and coupled it with the nationalist and democratic ideas of the West. He believed in the Indian philosophy of Vedanta according to which the soul was supreme. All were entitled to spiritual freedom. In *Gita Rahasya* Tilak gave the concept of freedom like this: "Divine instinct of freedom never aged.... Freedom is the very life of the individual and which Vedanta declares to be not separate from God but identical with Him. Thus, freedom was a principle that could never perish, Swaraja was not only a right but a Dharma. Politically Swaraj meant home rule. Spiritually, it meant realization of inner freedom. Morally, Swaraj aimed at perfect self-control so very essential for performance of one's duties (Swadharma)."

   In this way Swaraj, in Tilak's opinion, presented an essential ingredient of good life. He emphasized that without Swaraj people would suffer in life on earth as well as in future life.

10. **Nationalism** According to Tilak, nationalism is a psychological and spiritual means. It is the modern version of old patriotism in tribal form. Now it covers the whole nation. Moreover, nationalism flourished with common language, decent, religion, habitation and territory. All these lead to unity of nation. These factors are objective. At the same time subjective psychological factor is created by heritage of historical traditions. From immemorable past this has helped to build India.

    This spiritual side of nationalism was spread by the sages like Vivekananda, Tilak, Aurobindo Ghosh, Bipin Chandra Pal and Mahatma Gandhi. Secularism was spread by Dada Bhai Naoroji, Feroze Shah and Gokhale. Tilak said "Festivals are symbolical adjuncts of nationalism. The festivals meant for unity of participators can be utilized by leaders for national purposes." Ganapati and Shivaji festivals, started by Tilak, led to nationalism and unity. Ganapati festivals were celebrated from the past by the donations received from chiefs. Tilak gave it a public character and this helped to foster nationalism in the masses. Shivaji festivals were started through the initiative of English rulers in 1895. Samadhi of Shivaji was reconstructed at Rajgarh. Tilak called him 'Vibhuti' of Gita. Vibhuti was said to have all creative powers of divine nature. After Tilak's release in 1900 a grand celebration was held at Rajgarh. This festival spread upto Bengal and Japan in the beginning of 20th century.

In *Kesari* dated 8th April, 1901, Tilak spoke of Congress movement for getting some rights. Shivaji festival worked as a tonic. Tilak said: "Nationalism is not a visible and concrete entity but is a kind of symbolism, an idea and in generating this idea, the historic memories of the great figures of the country play a significant past. Indian nationalism should come from the heart of public and not by the Western writers." So Tilak thought that the memories of Shivaji would foster the national sentiments among the public. Shivaji gave the symbol for resistance against the oppressors.

Advaitism taught the supremacy of the concept of freedom. Tilak said: "Freedom was the soul of the Home Rule movement. The divine instinct of freedom never aged, freedom is the very life of the individual soul and which Vedanta declares to be not separate from God but identical with Him. The freedom was a principle that could never perish." Hence, according to Tilak, freedom was a divine attribute. Tilak based his nationalism on Western theories of national independence and self-determination. In his historical trial speech of 1905 he quoted J. S. Mill's view about nationalism. In 1919 he accepted Wilson's idea of self-determination and applied it to India. Hence, his philosophy of nationalism was a mixture of Western and Eastern thoughts, he gave the word 'Swaraj' which was used by Shivaji also in his Maratha policy.

It was because of his spiritual approach and outlook that Tilak regarded nationalism as right as well as Dharma. He gave Swaraj a moral as well as spiritual interpretation. According to him politically it meant Home Rule while morally it meant attainment of the perfection of self-control which was required for the performance of Swadharma (one's duty). Spiritually, Swaraj meant the attainment of inner freedom and delight. In the words of Tilak, "It is a life centred in self and dependent upon self. There is Swaraj in this world as well as in the world hereafter. The Rishis who laid down the law of duty took themselves to forests because the people were already enjoying Swaraj or people's dominion which was administered and defended in the first instance by Kshatriya Kings. It is my conviction; it is my thesis that Swaraj in the life to come cannot be the reward of the people who have not enjoyed in this world." Hence, Tilak asked for political and spiritual freedom.

By nationalism, Tilak meant psychological and spiritual requirements. It was a tribal instinct to control the vast population in a single nation, some conditions are required such as unity of race, religion, language and geography. Common history and culture also promoted the cause of unity of India in the past.

11. **Revivalism** Tilak wanted to revive the past. Thus, he advocated revivalism. He reminded of the Vedic culture which caused to know

the spiritual Reality and revive moral enthusiasm among the people. Tilak said, "A true nationalist desires to build an old foundations. Reform based on utter disrespect for the old does not appeal to him as constructive work. We do not want to anglicise our institutions and so denationalize them in the name of social and political reforms." Hence, Tilak revived the festivals of Ganpati and Shivaji. He termed those festivals to look timely and move with historical traditions. Thus, Tilak was a revivalist. Some call him a Hindu nationalist as he loved Hindu culture but he never opposed Muslims. Zakaria in his book 'India — A Restatement' spoke of him as an anti-Muslim retaliation. Palme Dutt said of him as raising Hindu revivalism which cut off Muslim masses from National movement. However, prominent Muslim personalities like M. A. Jinnah, M. A. Ansari and Hasan Imam had admired him. On his advice Lucknow Pact was done in 1916. Shaukat Ali and Hasrat Mohani regarded him as their political Guru. Shaukat Ali said, "I would like to mention again for the hundred times that both Mohammed Ali and myself belonged and still belong to Lokmanya's political party." Hasrat Mohani wrote, "I even at that early chose the Lokmanya as the ideal leader for me — during that period I had ample opportunities of appreciating the thought and abilities of almost all political leaders and basing my remarks on that close personal study, I can state without the least fear of contradiction that I found the Lokmanya the greater and superior to every other leader in every respect. When I declare that all through Tilak's life I was both intellectually and practically a blind follower of his, any one can well judge thereby of the love that I cherished towards him."

Though Tilak advocated national movement through strong cultural and religious revival still he acceded the economic reasons of Dada Bhai Naoroji. In an article written by Tilak in June 1887, he, said Indian art and industries were suffering and declining under English reign. Foreign investment has created a setback to the Indians and poverty is the ultimate result. In 1907 an interview with Newinson pointed out the economic drain of India. The same year, Allahabad speech of Tilak asked for protection of Indian trade and boycott of the English goods. He pleaded for Swadeshi, boycott and national education. In his commentary on Gita he wrote of his love of mother country. For him the whole world was one big family. This proves Tilak's love of internationalism.

VIEWS ON REFORMS ACT 1919

Tilak's views on Representation under Reforms Act 1919 or Monteford Reforms of 1919 started a great controversy among the Indian political thinkers. Even the moderates thought it unwise to act according to it and take part in legislative bodies. Tilak had no belief in representation to such bodies. However, he thought that it should act as a check to the bad laws and hence elections should be fought to take initiative under the law-making of the nation.

Tilak did not believe in representations. He sent a memorandum to Peace Conference in Paris. However, as he could not attend it due to cancellation of the passport, he asked the conference to extend the principle of self-determination to India for which English people had fought the war. He asked right share in the family of nations. He said, "It is necessary for me to dwell upon the imperative importance of solving Indian question for the purpose of ensuring the future peace of the world and the provess of the people of India. India is self-contained, it harbours no design against the integrity of other states, and had no ambition outside. With the vast area, enormous resources, prodigious population, she could, therefore, be a powerful steward of the League of Nations in the East for maintaining the peace of the world and the stability of the British Empire against all aggressors and disturbers of peace whether in Asia or elsewhere." Tilak maintained that Indian problems could only be solved by Indians. Indian fitness had been recognised by Nottingham Conference to make two pronouncements: (1) India would be accorded all the rights of representation in the League of Nations which have been given to British self-governing colonies. (2) It should be declared that Indians are fit for carrying on their government and the principle of self-determination should be applied to India so that Indians could establish a democratic form of government. Tilak maintained that such a pronouncement would generate sentiments of enthusiasm in the hearts of Indians. Reacting to the opposition stand of the moderates Tilak founded Congress Democratic Party to fight the elections.

CONCEPT OF RIGHTS

Tilak maintained that Indians should claim rights. Demand of rights was not an act of sedition. It was a sacred duty of Indians to claim it and those who fail to claim did disservice to the nation. According to Tilak rights were essential for the healthy life of the nation. He said, "What do we ask for? Do we say, Drive away the English Government but I ask what is it to the Emperor? Does the Emperor lose anything? Whether the administration is carried on by the Civil Servants or by our Delhi Sahibs? The rule still remains, the Emperor still remains. The difference will be that the white servants who were with them would here be replaced by black servants. From whom does this opposition come? This opposition comes from those people who are in power. It does not come from the Emperor. From the Emperor's point of view there is neither anarchy nor want of loyalty nor sedition in this. What does sedition means, hatred of the king. Does king mean a police society." Thus, Tilak asked for the demand of rights and maintained that it should not dislocate the political set-up.

WAS TILAK A REVOLUTIONARY ?

Historians of the Indian National Movement held different opinions about Tilak. Revolutionary is one who brings revolution in the socio-economic system in the country. Tilak was neither socialist nor a communist. His aim was to get the Home Rule. By Home Rule he meant attainment of Indianization of the existing civil and military administration under the British Emperor. The unrest in India was the outcome of the political and social conditions mixed with economical circumstances which were all brought about by the foreign rule. In his book. *'Indian Unrest'* Chirol wrote, 'Tilak had been the first to create the atmosphere which breeds murders." John S. Hoyland said, "Tilak had been coquetting with the doctrine of physical force." The Advocate General in 1908, Branson, while conducting Tilak's case said, "Tilak's articles contained a covert threat of mutiny and he was preaching Swaraj and Bombs." Dr. P. S. Khankhoje, a prominent revolutionary of Nagpur, maintained Tilak's being a revolutionary in the articles under *Kesari* during August 1953 and February 1954. He spoke of Tilak as "a teacher and preceptor of the revolutionary youth of India."

As compared to moderates of his time, Tilak was an extremist in his views. He was fearless in his attack on bureaucracy. He called petitions and prayers as useless. Though he advocated passive resistance still he returned while the force was to be used. It was known that he had established an arms factory in Nepal in 1903. He was more advanced than his times. Only Tilak could dare to oppose the Government. He was not a believer of Ahimsa. He was in touch with the revolutionaries of the calibre of Shyamji Krishna Verma and V.D. Savarkar. He accepted that today's extremist might be a moderate of tomorrow. He never tried to murder anybody nor did he incite anybody to murder. He adopted the legal methods of political organisations and agitation. He said, "From begging to open rebellion choose any one according to your ability and do it but remember the supremacy of Swadharma." He maintained that Gita gave the theory of righteous violence for doing an act. A revolution means a fundamental change in the socio-political field. Tilak wanted only the management of one's own affairs by Indians themselves favouring the retention of King Emperor. He only wanted to replace British bureaucracy by Indian civil service. He said, "I may say once for all that we were trying in India as the Irish Home Rulers have been doing in Ireland for the reforms of a system of administration and not for the overthrow of government and I have no hesitation in saying that the acts of violence which have been committed in different parts of India are not only repugnant to me but have, in my opinion, actually, unfortunately retarded to a great extent, the cause of our political progress." Tilak's activities were mainly bound to Maharashtra. His only aim was emancipation of India from foreign domination. Through his paper *Kesari,* he preached political liberty, natural rights and justice.

TILAK AND GOKHALE

Tilak and Gokhale were great men of Modern India. Tilak was the leader to the people's movement in Maharashtra. He was of the extremist views. His opinions and methods of working were different from that of the moderates who were quite ineffective in their efforts. He was convicted several times and paid penalties for that. For his free spokesmanship Tilak underwent many trials and tribulations. Thus, he was quite different from the moderates like Gokhale and Gandhi.

Similarities between Gokhale and Tilak

Gopal Krishna Gokhale and Bal Gangadhar Tilak were both prominent personalities of the modern India. Both were the sons of Maharashtra. Both belonged to the same family of Chittapawan Brahmins. Both were pioneers of Indian struggle for emanicipation. Poona was the centre of activity of both of them. After completing their education both worked for the Deccan Education Society for some years. Both started as teachers at the Fergusson College, Poona. Both were the life members of the Deccan Education Society. Both were leaders at the national level. Both were top ranking patriots and worked ceaselessly for India's freedom. Both were great leaders in their own ways. Both were imbued with the spirit of sincere patriotism. Both made great sacrifices for the sake of the country in and through the Indian National Congress. Both joined and worked in the National Congress but belonged to different groups in the Congress and to different schools of thoughts.

Contrast of Gokhale and Tilak

Pattabhi Sitaramayya, a great political historian of national struggle, brought out the contrast between the two stalwarts of freedom struggle as follows:

1. **Leaders of different sections** Gokhale was the leader of moderate school of thought in the Indian National Congress whereas Tilak was the leader of extremist section of the same organization.
2. **Different techniques** Along with other moderates, Gokhale believed in the British sense of justice, equity and fairplay. He, therefore, appealed to the Britisher's sense of reason through petitions, prayers and memoranda. He believed in what the moderates called constitutional methods for achievement of their goal. Tilak, on the other hand, was a typical Maharashtrian full of valiant spirit of struggle. Along with Aurobindo Ghosh, Lala Lajpat Rai, Bipin Chandra Pal, Tilak did not believe in any sense or reason in the Britishers who ruled over India with a clear and simple intention of exploiting the economic resources of India to the benefit of their mother country. He ridiculed the idea of constitutional methods on the ground that India had no constitution as such. He believed that political freedom could never be achieved

through an appeal to mercy. No nation, however good it may be, would grant freedom to any occupied nation just for asking. Freedom is something which had to be won from unwilling hands. Therefore, Tilak mobilized the Indian masses for attainment of freedom. Instead of trying to win favours from British bureaucracy he believed in putting up a fight. He believed in self-help, self-reliance, self-sacrifice and self-suffering.

3. **Difference in attitude towards British** Gokhale and other moderates were admirers of British people and English rule. They believed that it was a blessing in disguise and that India made tremendous progress under benevolence of British rule. On the other hand, Tilak regarded British rule as the greatest curse to India and maintained that the sooner the people got rid of the same the better it would be.
4. **Improvement *Vs.* replacement of Government** Gokhale believed in improving the British administration while Tilak wanted to replace it by Indian government.
5. **Cooperation *Vs.* conflict** Gokhale believed in offering cooperation to the British bureaucracy, Tilak wanted to fight it out.
6. **Not only reforms** While Gokhale was mostly concerned with administration and its reforms, Tilak's concern was the nation and her uplift.
7. **Love *Vs.* suffering and sacrifice** Gokhale believed in love and sweet reasonableness. Tilak believed in suffering and sacrifices.
8. **Classes *Vs.* masses** While Gokhale looked to the classes, Tilak looked to the masses. Gokhale and his moderate associates tried to mobilize the intelligentsia and win concessions and favours for them. Tilak, on the other hand, made a direct approach to the masses, generated political consciousness amongst them and prepared them for a great struggle for national liberation.
9. **Different platforms** Gokhale's field was the Council Halls, Tilak used village mandaps as platforms for expression of his opinions.
10. **Different dialects** Gokhale delivered his speeches in English while Tilak mostly expressed himself in vernacular.
11. **Different political goals** Gokhale wanted to bring about reforms in British administration in India step by step, Tilak announced Swaraj as his political goal. He would not be satisfied with anything less than that.
12. **Difference in mobilization** While Gokhale aimed at the mobilization of the educated classes in India and England, Tilak believed in mobilization of world public opinion against the British rule in India. Hence, Tilak visited England and presented the Indian case to the labour and liberal leaders of the country in an attempt to win over their support.
13. **Gokhale's loyalty to the British** Gokhale admired British rule and relations. This can be judged from his reply to Lord Harding's question,

"How would you like if I were to tell you that all British officials and British troops would leave India within a month?" Gokhale replied, "I would be very pleased to hear the news but before you had all reached Aden, we would be telegraphing to you to come back. "In this way, Gokhale regarded the British as guardians of the Indian public and advocated a policy of loyal cooperation. In his budget speech in 1902 in the Indian Legislative Council he said about the expectation of justice from Britishers, "What is needed is that we shall be enabled to feel that we had a government national in spirit though foreign in personnel — a government which subordinates all other consideration to the welfare of the Indian people."

On the other hand, Tilak thought that constitutional methods were no solution to nation's problems. He said, "There is as such no Constitution in India. The government of India is irresponsible and non-constitutional. Constituted authorities in India are irresponsible and we have to take our rights from them. The legality of our actions is decided by this government. Our actions may be illegal according to their point of view, but we should not worry whether our agitation is legal or illegal. We must see that the justice, morality and historical traditions are in our favour or not and our actions are correct according to these standards. We should not care as to whether they came within the law or not, because the power of making law is in the hands of foreigners. Of course, it is true that the infringement of law will result in punishment but if law is repressive it will be resisted by suffering such punishment, there is no other way. This is bound to happen when law and morality are in conflict with each other." At the same time Tilak advocated the self-reliant way for the achievement of one's end. He asserted "Swaraj is my birth right. I shall have it." About the method of moderates Tilak said "Political rights have to be fought for. The moderates are wrong to think that these can be won by persuasion." He suffered imprisonment thrice and won for himself the crown of martyrdom.

In his book *'Story of my experiments with truth'* Mahatma Gandhi compared "Tilak to the ocean and Gokhale to the Ganga."

Mutual Regards of Gokhale and Tilak

Tilak had great regard for Gokhale. He said about him, "It requires a great self-restraint, it requires a great will, to turn out one's back on the temptation of the life, with prospect of sure happiness especially when one is confident of more than normal achievements, and to devote oneself ceaselessly to national work and to find life's fulfilment in such work, with a perfect willingness to suffer, in the face of all adversities that may come." Though Tilak and Gokhle both differed in political ideals still they were great friends and paid respect to one another. Tilak received Gokhale heartily when he returned from England after giving Indian opinion in 1905. He even recommended Gandhiji to see Gokhale when he met him after return from South Africa. Tilak had deep regard for Gokhale. Tilak commented at the funeral pyre of

Gokhale, "This is not the time of cheers, this is the time for shedding tears. This diamond of India, the gem of Maharashtra, this prince of workers is laid to eternal rest in the funeral ground. Look at him and try to emulate him."

TILAK AND M.K. GANDHI

Similarities

Bal Gangadhar Tilak and Mohandas Karmachand Gandhi were two remarkable leaders and brave sons of India. They did great sacrifices for Swaraj sake. Both believed in the attainment of Swaraj from the British Government. Both thought it in terms of political and spiritual attainments. Both tried to bring ethics in politics. Both believed in ancient Indian culture. Both loved India and Indian ways of living and thinking. Both worked in Congress but differed at times in approach and programme. Both thought Swadeshi and Boycott as instruments of politics. Both believed in conditions of India not favourable for revolution. Both appealed to masses and not classes. Both believed that only mass movement could bring the desired object. Both were clear that by the sufferings of the Indian people and selfless sacrifice, Britishers would give independence.

Tilak could not live long to see his long cherished goal while Gandhi lived for a short time after independence. Both believed in the non-cooperation with the British rulers. Both thought that politics thrived on spirituality and morality. Both condemned the Western civilization and culture as it depended on materialism.

Mantle of Tilak on Gandhiji

There is a truth in the statement that the mantle of Tilak fell on Gandhi since the latter used all those methods which were advocated by the former. Gandhiji adopted the methods of non-violence, non-cooperation as means for the achievement of the freedom. Passive resistance, Swadeshi, Boycott and National education were also adopted by Gandhiji. Gandhi himself said, "I cannot claim the honour of being a follower of the late Lokmanya. I, admire him like millions of his countrymen for his indomitable will, his vast learning, his love of country and above all, the purity of his private life and great sacrifice. Of all the modern men of his time he captivated the imagination of the people. He breathed into us the spirit of Swaraj. No one perhaps realised the evils of the existing system as Tilak did. And in all humility I claim to deliver his message to the country as truly as the best of his disciples. But I am conscious that my method is not his method."

Thus, while Gandhi praised Tilak he did not follow him. He was more near to Gokhale than to Tilak.

Differences between Tilak and Gandhiji

1. **Difference in political ethics** While Tilak believed in democratic realism Gandhiji believed in ethical realism. Tilak derived his

inspiration from Mahabharat, Gita and Upanishads for politics and action. Gandhiji was influenced by Tolstoy, Thoreau, Ruskin, Narsi Mahta and Raichand Bhai. Tilak thought of Ahimsa for political expediency while Gandhi had absolute faith in it. However, Tilak would not use force and diplomacy in dealing with the opponent till the opponent is not mischievous. At Shivaji Festival, Tilak said, "Let us even assume that Shivaji first planned and then executed the murder of Afzal Khan. Was this act of Maharaj good or bad? This question which has to be considered should not be viewed from the standpoint of Indian Penal Code or even Smritis of Manu or even the principle of morality laid down in the Western or Eastern ethical systems. The laws which bind society are for common man like yourself and myself... Great men are above the common principle or morality. Did Shivaji commit a sin in killing Afzal Khan. The answer to this question can be found in Mahabharat itself: Krishna's advice to Arjuna to kill his Guru and Kinsmen for the sake of the conquest of Dharma over the evil. No blame attaches to any person if he is doing deeds without being actuated by a desire to reap the fruits of his deeds. Shivaji did nothing with a view to fill the small void of his own belly from interested motives. With benevolent intentions, he murdered Afzal Khan for the good of others. If thieves enter our house as we have no sufficient strength in our wrist to drive them out, we should, without hesitation, shut them up and burn them alive. Do not circumscribe your vision like a frog in a well, get out of the penal code, enter into the extremely high atmosphere of the Bhagwad Gita and then consider the actions of the great men."

Tilak never believed in ethical aspect of non-violence. The policy of forgiveness and meekness cannot be practised in this world which is full of sins. Tilak was a realist and not an idealist. He once wrote to Gandhiji that politics was not the game of Sadhus and Sanyasis, it was a game of worldly people. Tilak would like Gandhiji to follow Krishna than to follow Buddha, Krishna gave priority to the practicality of the situation and would destroy evil and restore Dharma. Buddha would return evil with goodness. Gandhiji followed the latter and regarded violence for good or evil as unethical.

2. **Difference in methods** Both Tilak and Gandhi used different methods for the achievement of their goal. Tilak was a lawyer first and so he preferred legal methods though he ridiculed constitutional methods and spoke of India having no constitution at all except the Indian Penal Code. Mahatma Gandhi spoke of sacred rights to resist bad laws. In South Africa he asked Indians to have the basic civil rights. And as such he started Satyagrah in India to revoke such laws. Thus he gave Civil Disobedience as the weapon.

3. **Difference in faith** Tilak was an orthodox sanatan Hindu by faith. While Gandhi was a holist in religious thoughts and praised whatever looked good in world religions.
4. **Legal *Vs.* Moral Democracy** Tilak believed in representative democracy while Gandhi believed in moral sovereignty. Gandhi gave moral supremacy of a single man superiority over big parliament.
5. **Realism *Vs.* Idealism** Realism of Tilak and ethical idealism of Gandhi were clear as to their approaches to the Reforms Act of 1919. While Gandhi was against contesting elections, Tilak condemned the reforms but advocated contesting of elections for assemblies. He wanted more and more of the rights for which he aimed to work both inside and outside. He agreed to non-cooperation, but did not agree to boycott the councils.

Mutual Admiration

There is no doubt that Tilak and Gandhi differed in their view yet they were the torch bearers of the Indian struggle for Independence. Tilak appreciated the programme of non-cooperation. Before his death, he spoke to Gandhi at Sardar Griha Hotel Bombay in 1920 "I like the programme well enough but I have my doubts as to the country being with us in the self-denying ordinance which non-cooperation presents to the people. I will do nothing to hinder progress of the movement. I wish you every success and if you gain the popular ear, you will find in me an enthusiastic supporter." About entering the legislative councils Tilak told to Gandhi, "I personally believe that it will be better to go to the councils and to obstruct, when it was necessary and to cooperate also, when it was necessary." According to some political historians Gandhi was a follower of Tilak and completed the remaining task left by him. Gandhi wrote about this in *Young India,* dated 23rd July, 1921. He said, "I cannot claim the honour of being the follower of the late Lokamanya. I admire him like millions of his countrymen for his indomitable will, his vast learning, his love of country and above all the purity of his private life and great sacrifice. Of all the men in modern times he captivated most of the imagination of his people. He breathed into us the spirit of Swaraj. No one perhaps realized that evil of the existing system of government as Mr. Tilak did. In all humility I claim to deliver his message to the country as truly as the best of his disciples. But I am conscious that my method is not Mr. Tilak's method, that is why I have still difficulty with some of the Maharashtra leaders. But I sincerely think that Mr. Tilak did not disbelieve in my method, I enjoyed the privilege of his confidence. And his last word to me in presence of the several friends was just a fortnight before his death, that mine was an excellent method, if people could be persuaded to have it. But he said he had doubts."

11
Lala Lajpat Rai (1865 — 1928)

Lala Lajpat Rai, known as Sher-e-Punjab, is remembered as the foremost national leader and hero of the freedom movement in Punjab. He was one of the three extremists of the earliest period of the nationalist movement, the other two being Bal Gangadhar Tilak and B.C. Pal. He was not a philosopher or a political theorist, a social reformer or a crusader of a new religion. His was a composite personality which contained traits of a great thinker and emancipator of the human race. He was one of the builders of modern India.

BIOGRAPHY

Early Life

Born in 1865, Lala Lajpat Rai belonged to an Aggrawal family of Jagraon village in the district of Ludhiana, in Punjab. Though traditionally a shopkeeper, his father Lala Radhakrishan became an Urdu and Persian teacher after some education. Under the influence of a Muslim teacher of his Persian School Radhakrishan grew to be a great admirer of Islam and developed a deep dislike for Hinduism and Hindu religion. Short of formal conversion to Islamic faith he accepted everything of Muslim religion. He recited namaz and observed fast during Ramzan. It is difficult to say what prevented him from conversion to Mohammadanism, but the pious Hindu character of his wife must have been a factor in his way. Due to meagre income of Lala Radhakrishan the family lived in limited means.

Education

Lajpat Rai had his early education at Ropar in Ambala district. When Lajpat Rai shifted to Lahore in the year 1881, he came in contact with people who changed the course of his life. These were Pandit Gurudatt and Lala Hansraj. Due to illness and the desire to dedicate his life in the service of people he could not acquire a graduate degree. However, he passed two examinations of law, qualified himself to be a lawyer and started practice at Hissar. In the meantime, he first came in contact with the social reform movement of Brahmo Samaj founded by Raja Rammohan Roy and later on joined the Arya Samaj. During his stay at Lahore he was a front-rank worker of the Arya Samaj and actively participated in its educational and reformatory activities.

In Congress

In 1885 the All India National Congress was formed to voice public grievances through constitutional methods. Lajpat Rai took interest in its working and attended the fourth and fifth annual conference as a delegate from the Punjab. He expressed his disagreement on the question of separate Muslim respresentation in the legislative councils. Consequently for the next fourteen years he did not take part in the Congress activities as the Congress had no programme for dealing with the political, social and economic problems of the country. As against the Congress, the Arya Samaj appeared to him a much more important forum for work. He started the practice of law and very shortly earned distinction as a lawyer and also as a public figure in Panjab.

In Arya Samaj

In 1882 Lajpat Rai was attracted to Arya Samaj for its nationalistic outlook and social reform programme. Lajpat Rai felt that the "social life in India must be reconstructed on a scientific basis. The struggle will be long and tiresome but it must be faced by those who realise the importance of the issue." He wanted social reform to become a national movement.

Relief Work

During 1896-97 an unprecedented famine broke out in U.P. and in 1899-1900 in Rajputana and in 1907-08 in Bihar. With a band of dedicated workers of Arya Samaj, Lala Lajpat Rai organised relief work for the poor and needy people. In 1905 Kangra valley experienced a most horrible earthquake involving the lives of lakhs of people including the whole family of Lala Hans Raj's sister. Lajpat Rai came forward with a large number of workers belonging to the Arya Samaj for relief work.

SOCIAL REFORMER

Lajpat Rai condemned social distinctions based on caste, creed and colour. Calling upon people to rise above petty personal interests and work for social justice, he said, "We are individually wanting in that sense of social responsibility which requires each and every member of the organism (social) to place the interest of the community of the nation over and above those of his own." Lajpat Rai reminded people that "national decline has its origin in oppression upon others, and if we Indians desire to achieve national self-respect and dignity, we should open our arms to our unfortunate brothers of the depressed classes and help to build up in them the vital spirit of human dignity." Lajpat Rai raised his voice against the evil of untouchability and set up a new organisation named the All India Achhut Uddhar Sabha. Appealing to the sense of humanity, justice and fair play, he asked people to work for raising the depressed people to the life of dignity. He advocated broad outlook on human affairs and realisation of social responsibility by the educated section of the society. He said that the condition of untouchables and depressed as "a disgrace to our humanity or our sense of justice, and our feeling of social affinity. It is useless to hope for any solidarity so long as the depressed classes continue to be so low in the social scale as they are." He wanted to make social reform a national movement. Lajpat Rai said, "The cause of the depressed classes combines in it the best of religion, the best of humanity and the best of nationalism."

Lajpat Rai was a great socio-economic as well as a liberator of Hindu society. Under the influence of the Arya Samaj, he raised his voice for the liberation of women. He condemned child marriage as the greatest crime against humanity and asked people to desist from it. Laying great stress on the necessity of educating women Lalaji suggested establishment of national Vidya Pithas for girls throughout the country.

NATIONAL LEADER

Lajpat Rai was a national leader. He always thought in terms of the country and all people regardless of caste, creed and sex. He accepted the concept of composite nationality. In 1914 he said that India was not exclusively for Hindus. India's future lay in reconciliation of Hinduism with Indian nationalism. In 1924 he wrote a series of articles on the Hindu-Muslim unity. He called for purging politics of religion. He advocates rational approach in religious matters to avoid conflict. He opposed the separate electorate for Muslims as it gave the impression of communal interests of two communities. He wrote, "In my judgement the cry of a Hindu Raj or a Muslim Raj is purely mischievous and ought to be discouraged. The correct thing for us to do is to strive for a democratic Raj in which the Hindus, Muslims and other communities may participate as Indian and not as followers of any particular religion."

SERVANTS OF PEOPLE'S SOCIETY

Though initiated to public life by his friends of the Arya Samaj Lajpat Rai got inspiration from the ideas of Tilak and Gokhale. The Servants of India Society founded by Gokhale attracted his attention and he established a society as Servants of Poeple's Society. Mahatma Gandhi inaugurated the Society on 9 November, 1921. The aim of the Society was to enlist and train national missionaries for the service of the motherland. Its members were entrusted with the work of educational cultural, economic and political advancement of the country. Under his leadership the Society worked in close collaboration with the Indian Congress. It rendered very valuable service in the various fields of social life. It worked to bring about cordial relations between different communities. The Society produced many social and political leaders in the country.

EDUCATIONIST

Lajpat Rai began his life as a lawyer, but he developed great interest in education of the people. Not even a graduate, he rose to be a great educationist and original thinker on educational problems of the country. He wrote. "The study of educational institutions, educational ideals and educational methods has been one of the passions of my life." He declared that, "Education is the most vital question for us. It is most important of all our problems. In a way it is the fundamental problem. We cannot afford to have loose and confused ideas about education, the aim and ends of education, and the methods of education. Our whole future hangs on it."

Lajpat Rai's association with various educational institutions conducted by the Arya Samaj in Punjab provided him an opportunity to have an insight into the educational system. He felt that education should be directed to the all round progress of children. He was one of the founders of D.A.V. College at Lahore and actively supported the College with finances. He also established the Tilak School of Politics. In 1911 he founded an educational trust and opened a High School in his native village Jagraon in the memory of his father. He was a pioneer of the scheme of national education. His book *The Problem of National Education of India* contains his educational philosophy. His scheme of national education included Swadeshi and teaching of modern languages. He wanted students to grow in the atmosphere of frankness, freedom and mental confidence. Education must become an effective instrument of social progress and must contribute to social efficiency. Due to his efforts national institutions were established at different places in India. He believed that education must create consciousness about social obligations.

NATIONAL EDUCATION

In his draft of the policy of national education Lajpat Rai laid down that education must be controlled, administered and financed by the state with the aim of promoting social welfare. Education must ensure physical and mental development. Production of literate skilled labour with a sense of citizenship should be the basic aim of educational policy. Patriotism and nationalism must form part of national education. Children at primary level should be taught to love their motherland and all the inhabitants of the country regardless of caste and creed. The scheme of national education consisted of two parts, one devoted to language and the other devoted to subjects. Lajpat Rai advocated of Hindustani as the national language. He favoured provincial languages as medium of instructions. He said that a teacher should be more worried about mental and physical development of children than examination. "The broad aim of education", he said, "is to help man to become a thinking being."

As early as in 1919 Lajpat Rai wrote, "We should come to a clear understanding of what our national ideals are. Do we want to be an integral part of the civilized world, making our contribution to its progress, by thought and action, or do we want to be an isolated national unit, happy in our retirement and liberty, economic independence, social solidarity and religious freedom, but for what ends? If so, what is that end?" After considerable thinking on the problem of national education Lajpat Rai said, "Let the boys and girls be surrounded by the conditions of life in which they have to move and in which they have to meet in after life. To let the boys and girls grow in isolation, ignorant of the conditions of actual life... with no experience of the sudden demands and emergencies of group life is to deprive them of the most valuable element in their education." The real education must prepare the youth of the country to face the battle of life. Education must be useful for practical purposes of life based on a full knowledge of the different phases of social life. Fully alive to the future needs of the country and the ideal of social efficiency Lajpat Rai said, "Education being a social function must fit its recipient to increase his productive capacity, thereby adding to his own usefulness as well as to that of the society of which he is a member. The first requisite of an efficient system of national education is that it enables every citizen to live better and to help others in living better." There should be proper coordination between the theoretical and practical training.

The most advanced point of view of education which Lajpat Rai put forward won appreciation from great national leaders like Mahatma Gandhi and Zakir Hussain. Zakir Hussain wrote, "Lajpat Rai's insistence that education should develop children into thinking and acting persons, that it should be vocational, that it should enable every citizen to live in a clear anticipation of the principles underlying basic education and his proposal to establish vocational institutes is something on which we have started working now."

MILITANT POLITICAL LEADER

Lala Lajpat Rai started taking interest in national politics and formally joined the Congress in 1888 at the fourth session of the Congress held at Allahabad. He was then twenty-four years old. From that day he remained associated with the organisation for forty years in different capacities. In the ninth session of the Congress held at Lahore in 1893 Lajpat Rai took active part and met B.G. Tilak for the first time. They became intimate friends. Lajpat Rai moved a resolution on education and industry which was passed. As a militant nationalist he condemned the attitude of Congress leaders approaching the government for their rights. He demanded militancy in the political programme. In 1905 he was chosen to represent India in England along with Gokhale.

Lajpat Rai was a great patriot, nationalist and humanist. He worked for unity between different sections of the Congress. He made a strong plea for Hindu-Muslim unity. He opposed separate representation to Muslims on communal basis as it was against nationalism. Lajpat Rai came out with a strong criticism of the Congress for accepting the Morley-Minto Reforms Act. Hindus and Muslims should live together and work together for the common welfare and common nationality. Lajpat Rai broke with the Swaraj Party in August 1926 for its policy of cooperation with the government. He was of the view that "British rule in India would be an impossibility without the cooperation of Indians." He favoured a clear-cut policy for achieving the goal of freedom by peaceful methods. Though he admired the courage of young revolutionaries, yet he never advocated violence.

SWADESHI

Besides political freedom, Lajpat Rai wanted social and economic emancipation of the country. He came out to support the Swadeshi movement. The Swadeshi could lead to self-reliance and self-help, an essential condition for political freedom. He said, "For me Swadeshi and patriotism are synonymous. It has importance because it is the remedy of the sufferings of our country, it is the salvation of this country. Its aim is to make us self-dependent, self-respecting and self-supporting. In my opinion Swadeshi ought to become the common religion of united India."

SOCIALIST

Lajpat Rai was the first socialist leader of India. He wanted India to evolve as a classless society. His social and economic outlook was unique among the leaders of his generation. "True socialism", he said, "emphasises cooperation as against competition — we want equal opportunity and equal justice for all." During his visits abroad Lajpat Rai came in contact with some prominent leaders of the socialist movement. He looked at the dawn of an era of equal opportunities and equal justice for all. He offered his support for any scheme or policy which would open a way for equal and just distribution of wealth and land, which would ensure an equal share and rightful place to all workers and farmers in the country. Though he refused to accept the Marxist dialectics but he favoured equality and justice as a humanitarian socialist and not a scientific socialist in the Marxist sense. India had to evolve into an ideal socialist society through the gradual process of greater participation of people in nation-building.

While presiding over a meeting held to welcome Lalaji on February 20, 1920 at Shantaram Chauk, Bombay. Mr. M.A. Jinnah described Lala Lajpat Rai as one of the greatest sons of India. He was a true representative of India's culture and social heritage. He played a very important part in the movement of religious and social renaissance of India. As a political thinker and leader he contributed his best for the nation up to the end when he received lathi blows from the police while opposing the Simon Commission in 1928 and succumbed to it.

12

Subhash Chandra Bose (1897 — 1945)

Subhash Chandra Bose was born on 23rd January, 1897 at Codolia village in 24-Parganas District of West Bengal. His father, Janki Nath, was a lawyer in Orissa. His family was well educated and cultured. Subhash received his early education in a Missionary school at Cuttack from where he passed his High School examination. After this he joined Presidency College, Calcutta from where he passed his F. A. in first division. In 1919 he joined the local Scottish Church College from where he Passed B.A. Examination and stood first in philosophy in the university. When he was studying in M.A. he left India for U.K. to appear in I.C.S. Examination in order to respect the sentiments of his father. It was there that he passed his I.C.S. examination and stood 4th among the successful candidates. In 1921 he plunged in the national movement then being organised by C. R. Das. In December of the same year he went behind the bars. In 1927 he was again imprisoned in Burma on account of his nationalist attitude and activities. In 1938 he was elected as the President of Indian National Congress at Haripura, which brought him great fame and respect. In 1939 he was again elected as the President of the Congress defeating Dr. Pattabhi Sitaramayya, a nominee of Gandhiji. This election was significant in the sense that it was an election of ideologies. Pattabhi represented the right wing of the Congress, whereas Subhash Bose represented the leftists who were extremists. As a result of this election differences between the Congress organisation grew so deep that many members of the Working Committee, who were opposed to Subhash Bose, resigned from the organisation. As a matter of protest Subhash also resigned and founded his independent party with the name Forward Bloc. In 1940 Subhash prsided over Anti-Compromise Conference at Ramgarh. In December of the same year he managed to escape from India. In March, 1941 he reached Berlin by air from Kabul. In 1942 he started propaganda from Berlin against British Imperialism. In 1943 he founded Indian National Army with the ideal of liberating India by exerting pressure from outside and creating discontentment among the Indian armed personnel captivated and deserted during war. He successfully managed the show for 2 years and the Indian National Army reached Burma and Kohima. It is said that in 1945 while he was travelling in an aeroplane he met with a fatal accident.

However, it is yet a controversial issue as to whether he met his tragedy or is still alive, Whereas a committee, subsequently set up by the Government of India which went to Japan, is of the view that Netaji died in the air crash, the unofficial version, especially that of Forward Bloc, is that he is still alive awaiting an opportunity to come to India. Mostly however, it is believed that he is no more.

Influences

Netaji Subhash Bose was under the influence of the writings and teachings of Swami Vivekananda. He was very much inspired by him. He learnt from him not only broadness in outlook but also the glory that India had in the past. It was from him that Subhash got the idea that India had a mission of spreading civilisation in the world which free India alone could do. Among others who influenced Subhash was Aurobindo Ghosh, an extremist of Indian national movement. Though Aurobindo's stay in Indian politics was short, Subhash Bose was so much inspired by his ideas that he also became an extremist and began to significantly value his ideas and philosophies. While in England he was also influenced by persons like Lenin, Mussolini and Kamal Pasha. He studied their life, career and methods of working. Their patriotism, devotion to duty and sincerity of purpose very highly influenced his future course of action. He found in them qualities of patriots and made them his ideal heroes for his subsequent struggle.

Writings

Subhash Chandra Bose did not write much nor did he speak much. His ideas and thoughts are available to us in his *'Indian National Army — INA'* (1920 to 1934) which is a specimen of his patriotism and inspiring career. It is also a torch light for freedom fighters. It is evident from the fact that it was banned by the Britishers and could be published only in 1948.

POLITICAL IDEAS

Subhash Chandra Bose was working at a time when the Indian National Congress was on the cross-roads. It was required to decide between the Gandhian right wing views and Subhash Chandra's left wing philosophy. The death of C.R. Das and Moti Lal Nehru very much cleared the way for Gandhiji to dominate the political scene yet Subhash Bose continued to struggle. He was the leader of the youth and the extremists. He was elected to the Presidentship of the Indian National Congress in 1939, though Gandhiji had very clearly sided with Dr. Pattabhi Sitaramayya. The political ideas of Subhash Chandra Bose can be summed as under:

1. **About Gandhism** Subhash Bose was not very much in agreement with Gandhian philosophy. However, he appreciated Gandhiji for his devotion to the cause of national freedom. He praised Gandhi for high qualities of his character. He also loved Gandhi for his humanitarian

approach to the problem and also for his love for the poor and down-trodden. Not only that but he very much appreciated Gandhiji for giving a national outlook to India's freedom struggle. But Gandhian philosophy and method of working did not very much appeal to Subhash. According to him Gandhian ethical approach was no solution to our problems. Subhash felt that Gandhiji was trying to play a double role by being a spiritual leader as well as a political thinker. He believed that it was very difficult that he would succeed. He charged Gandhiji by saying, "The logic of the Mahatma is not the logic which appeals to John Bull. He has failed because his policy of putting all his cards on the table will not do. We have to render Caesar what is unto Caesars; and in a political fight, the art of diplomacy cannot be dispensed with. He has failed because he has not made use of the international weapon. If we desire to win our freedom through non-violence, diplomacy and international propaganda are essential." Subhash Bose also felt that Gandhiji had no method of judging and understanding the psychology of his opponents who were far more clever than Indian masses whom Gandhiji knew and understood. Indian agitation was not a struggle of Indians against Indians but a struggle of natives against the aliens who behaved in quite a different way and had different values and attitudes towards the problems of life. He also criticised Gandhiji on account of institutional foundations of Gandhian method of trying to combine divergent interests, *e.g.*, those of the labourers and the factory owners, tenants and the landowners or the peasants and the landlords. He said, "We are clearly of the opinion that Mr. Gandhi, as a political leader, has failed. The time has therefore come for a radical reorganisation of the Congress on a new principle with a new method for which a new leader is essential as it is unfair to expect Mr. Gandhi to work the programme inconsistent with his life-long principles." Subhash also criticised Gandhiji saying that Gandhian philosophy was exploiting the weaker elements of the society whereas the stronger elements did not very much care for his philosophy. He was therefore, opposed to Gandhian methods and basic principles of his philosophy. He was very much sure that non-violence, truth and satyagraha could not bring independence to India. According to him, if India was to win her cherished goal of freedom and national independence, it was very essential that some effective and useful methods should be adopted. He opined that it was a great mistake of Gandhi to have not spoken boldly at the Round Table Conference or not to have left the conference during the proceedings when he was sure that no tangible and concrete results were to come out. For Subhash, it was a diplomatic failure not to have exposed the wickedness of British diplomacy before the whole world and thus to have won the universal moral sympathy. He, therefore, laid stress on adopting a different course than was suggested and followed by Gandhi.

2. **About Communism** Subhash Chandra Bose was very critical of communist philosophy. He was a leftist in the Congress but his interpretation of leftist philosophy was different from what it was commonly understood by the communists. According to him, the leftists in the Congress could not compromise with imperialism. According to him, leftists were the supporters of socialism and aimed at wiping out poverty and illiteracy from India. He stood for the abolition of zamindari system. He wanted to relieve the agriculturists from their indebtedness He felt that there should be no system of landlordism. According to him one of the methods of achieving the aim was cooperative cultivation and introduction of cooperative system in our major walks of life. As a leftist he also wanted to give more and more recognition to the rights an interests of the working classes. However, his interest in the working classes and his leanings towards leftism should not leave an impression that he was a communist or he had praise for Marxian philosophy in any way. According to him, Communism was not suited to Indian conditions and as such it was out-dated for India. He pointed out that the Indians, who are tradition-ridden and religious, will not emotionally accept Communism which was for all purposes anti-religious. According to him, the people of India believe more in evolution and as such they would not accept Communist revolutionary concepts which might bring serious political and social dislocations. Communism was a success in Russia because conditions prevailing there at that time, were very conducive but such were not the conditions in India, felt Subhash.
3. **Indian History** According to Subhash Chandra Bose India's past was very glorious. Indian nation could rightly take pleasure which not only changed with the passage of time but also adjusted very conveniently in the circumstances. Decay, however, came when Indian dynamic instinct was replaced by stagnancy and the nation became inactive. Modern times were brining back an outlook introducing action in life but Subhash felt that such like preachings, as fate and ahimsa were the causes of decline of Indian nation. He was, in this regard, close to Swamy Vivekananda. He rightly said, "After all, what has brought about India's downfall in material and political sphere. It is her inordinate belief in fate and in the supernatural her indifference to modern scientific development — her backwardness in the science of modern warfare, the peaceful contentment engendered by her later day philosophy and adherence to ahimsa carried to the masses to absurd length."
4. **Fascism** Subhash Bose was very much influenced by the fascist method of struggle and their determination and will power. He was fully convinced that Indian nation will have to show determination and get ready to struggle hard for attaining freedom. He said, "The

logic of history will therefore, follow its inevitable course. The political struggle and social struggle will have to be conducted simultaneously. The party that will win social and economic freedom for India will also be the party that will win social and economic freedom for the masses." Subhash was also inspired by the onslaught which the fascist leaders made on the social, economic and political institutions of their time in order to rid the society of its evils. Subhash was also willing to some extent to sacrifice individual freedom in order to strengthen the State and enable Government to have full grip of the situation and have control over it. In spite of all that he did not allow Communism. He could not appreciate the absence of moral and spiritual values from politics. He also could not go to the extent to which the fascists went in subordinating the individual under the control of the Government of the party leaders. Subhash Bose could not adjust himself to fascist's philosophy under which the interests of working classes were not protected to the extent which he wanted to protect. In other words, he was close to fascism only to the extent to which their leaders promoted action and spearheaded their activities in eradicating the evils of their society and Government.

FORWARD BLOC

In 1939 Subhash Bose was elected President of the Indian National Congress defeating Gandhi's candidate Dr. Pattabhi Sitaramayya. This victory was the symbol of Subhash Bose's popularity. However, some of the members of Congress Working Committee could not adjust themselves to Subhash Bose's ideas and uncompromising attitude and his proposition to British rule in India. They also could not adjust themselves to the criticism which Subhash made against Gandhi's philosophy of Ahimsa and non-violence. The result was that there was friction in the Congress organisation and Subhash Bose left and founded a new organisation known as Forward Bloc. Its aims and objects were to make an attempt to bring Congressmen closer to the new Bloc. It aimed at complete national independence and bring about unity among the leftists of the country. The Bloc was to continue its struggle for freedom. It was to make India a thoroughly modern and socialist State and believed in large-scale production for economic regeneration of the country. It also stood for social ownership and control of both means of production and distribution. The party also aimed at freedom for the individual in the matters of religious worship. It gave equal rights for every individual. It sanctioned linguistic and cultural autonomy for all sections of Indian community. It advocated the principle of equality and social justice in building up the new order in the Free India. In his famous book *The Indian Struggle* Subhash Bose has given the aims and objects of Forward Bloc in the following words:

"1. The party will stand for the interests of the masses, *i.e.*, of peasants, workers etc., and not for the vested interests.

2. It will stand complete political and economic liberation of Indian people.
3. It will believe in a sound system of State planning for the reorganising of the agricultural and industrial life of the country.
4. It will seek to build up a new social structure on the basis of village communities of the past.
5. It will seek to abolish landlordism and introduce a uniform land tenure system for the whole of India.
6. It will not stand for a democracy of the mid-Victorian sense of the term but will believe in Government by a strong party bound together by military discipline as the only means of holding India together and preventing chaos.
7. It will not restrict itself to a campaign inside India but will resort to international propaganda."

Thus Subhash Bose was one of the top ranking nationalists and pattriots of India. The very fact that he left the land of his birth to organize his struggle of liberating Mother India from a foreign soil is in itself a sufficient proof of his patriotism. The vigour and energy with which he could manage the political affairs both in Japan dnd Germany and his capability with which he organised Indian National Army are in themselves proof of his administrative capability and presence of mind. It would not be an exaggeration to say that it was due to his efforts that British Government realised the magnitude of Indian National Struggle for freedom and also the brewing discontentment among the Indian armed personnel. It was also due to his untiring efforts that Indian national struggle for freedom got world-wide publicity and propaganda and to a great extent the British Government was obliged to bow before Indian nationalism. Subhash was one of the few Indian leaders who vigorously pleaded that social and political reforms must go hand in hand and one could not be separated from the other. Subhash was a patriot of the first order. He lived and died while struggling for the freedom of Mother India.

13
Swami Dayanand Saraswati
(1824 — 1883)

Born in a deeply religious family in 1824, Dayanand was led to embrace the whole humanity. The religious orthodoxy of his father Karsanji Lalji Triwari and the tender humanitarian outlook of his mother made the young Dayanand a true devotee of the existing religion. At the early age of thirteen, he had a unique experience on the day of Sivaratri fast. In the temple of the Lord Siva he saw a mice moving over the idol of Shiva. In order to remove his doubt about idol worship, he made enquiries from his father and came to know that the idol was only the symbol of the Lord Siva and not the god himself. This was the turning point of his life. Dayanand, felt that he must know the truth. Like the Buddha, he was also shaken by the phenomenon of death.[1] Thus, three ideas settled in his mind which later on shaped his personality and philosophy of religion; disrespect for idol worship; detachment from the world; and disbelief in ritual ceremonies. Thinking that he must prepare himself for knowing the truth and for the service of mankind, Davanand left his home in the month of May, 1846.

During his stay in Mathura at the feet of the renowned saint Swami Virjanand, Dayanand was shaped into a real *mahatma,* a sage and a prophet. The Guru explained to him the burden of sin and suffering beneath which the mother Earth was groaning. He got a promise from Dayanand to spread the Vedic message to the whole of mankind. With determination and confidence in himself, Dayanand set out to fulfil his promise to his Guru. He did not take rest during his life-time and fought single-handed against all kinds of onslaughts till he sacrificed himself in 1876. To quote M.R. Jigyasu, "Dayanand's profound scholarship, his magnetic powers of persuasion, his powers of bombardment of an impregnable orthodox position with bombs carefully selected from the armoury of *sastric* learning, his fiery eloquence inspired by righteous indignation and a heart aglow with unselfish love of humanity which transfused his words and made them scalding and

---

1. Dayanand was shocked by the sudden death of his sister whom he loved very much.

scorching, and above all his infinite pity for his suffering fellowmen carried all before them."[1]

ADVOCATE OF VEDIC CULTURE

Swami Dayanand showed that the Vedic culture was universal in its outlook for it catered to the essential needs of man as a spiritual being. Vedic culture was the civilisation of mankind for the good of the entire human community. The Vedic civilisation was ideal. The Aryans had a society in which every man and woman enjoyed material and spiritual goods to their satisfaction. Through his book *Satyartha Prakash,* Dayanand tried to show that the Vedas presented a scheme of life for the acceptance of mankind. In the words of Tarachand, his biographer, "The Rishi holds out a promise that through the Veda the world's good shall be promoted. Through the teachings of the Veda peace shall come on earth and happiness rule every home. Through the Veda shall be hastened the advent of the Golden Age, the age of which the poets have sung. The philosophers dreamt and to which the prophets have pointed."[2]

SATYARTHA PRAKASH

Among the contemporary Indian philosophers Swami Dayananda may be called to be the greatest rationalist. While on the one hand he was a great supporter of *Vedas* and other holy texts, his approach everywhere was that of a rationalist. He never accepted anything without meditating upon its advantages and disadvantages. His magnum opus *Satyartha Prakash* is an eloquent testimony to his rationalism. Pointing out the object of this great work Dayananda wrote, "... there is not the remotest idea to hurt the feelings of any person either directly or indirectly, but on the contrary, the book proposes that men should distinguish truth from falsehood. Thus, alone can the human race steadily advance on the path of happiness, since none but the practising of truth is the cause of the improvement of the human family." These words express both his rationalism and humanism. It should be remembered that modern humanism is rationalism. Its sole aim is human welfare and that too on this earth here and now. As is clear by the above object of the chief work of Dayananda, like a true humanist, he aimed at the progress of humanity on the path of happiness. Thus, it was in keeping with this aim that Dayananda presented his political ideas.

CONCEPT OF VEDIC SWARAJ

Meaning of Vedic Swaraj

Swami Dayananda believed in Vedic Swaraja. Therefore, he has quoted from the Vedas about the science of government. In accordance with ancient

1. Munshi Ram Jigyasu, *The Arya Samaj and its Detractors,* Hardwar, Gurukala, 1910, p. 6.
2. Tarachand Deumal, *The Life of Swami Dayanand Saraswati,* p. 162, Lahore, Punjab Printing Works, 1915.

Indian traditional polity Dayananda advocated politics based on ethics. He propounds close relationship in Ethics and Politics. In the XI chapter of his famous work *Satyartha Prakash,* Dayananda states about Raj a Dharma by quoting Manu. The Great Manu says to the Rishis, 'After discoursing on the duties of the four classes and the four orders, we shall now describe Raja Dharma or the duties and qualifications, etc., of rulers. In other words, we shall discuss as to who is fit to be a king, how he is to be selected, and how he can attain the highest bliss-salvation. Let a Kshatriya, whose knowledge, culture and piety are as perfect as those of Brahmin, govern the country with perfect justice.' According to Rig Veda, "Let there be for the benefit of the rulers and the ruled three Assemblies — 1. Religious, 2. Legislative 3. Educational. Let each discuss and decide subjects that concern it, and adorn all men with knowledge, culture, righteousness independence, and wealth and thereby make them happy." In the words of Atharva Veda, "Let the three Assemblies, Military, Councils, and the Army harmoniously work together to carry on the government of a country."

To quote Atharva Veda, again 'A king should address the Assembly thus. 'Let the leader of the Assembly abide by the just laws passed by the Assembly, and let other members do the same.'

It means that no single individual should be invested with absolute power. The king, who is the president of the Assembly, and the Assembly itself should be inter-dependent on each other. Both should be controlled by the people, who in their turn should be governed by the Assembly.

Shatpatha Brahman points out if this system be not followed and the king be independent of the people and have absolute power, "He would impoverish the people being despotic and hence arrogant and oppress them, aye, even eat them up, just as a tiger or any other carnivorous animal pounces upon a robust animal and eats it up. A despotic ruler does not let any one else grow in power, robs the rich, usurps their property by unjust punishment, and accomplishes his selfish end. One man should, therefore, never be given despotic power."

In the words of Atharva Veda, 'O men, let the man alone among you be made a king the President of the Assembly — who is a very powerful conqueror of foes, is never beaten by them, has the capacity to become the paramount sovereign, is most enlightened, is worthy of being made a President, who possesses most noble qualities, accomplishments, character and disposition, who is thoroughly worthy of the homage, trust and respect of all.'

In the words of Yajur Veda, 'O ye learned men, proclaim that man with one voice your king the President and Head of the State — who is just, impartial, well-educated, cultured and friend of all. In this way alone shall ye attain universal sovereignty, be greater than all, manage the affairs of the State, obtain political eminence, acquire wealth, and rid the world of its enemies.'

God teaches in the Rig Veda, 'Rulers, your implements of warfare (such as guns, rifles, bows, arrows, etc.), and war-materials (such as gunpowder) be worthy of praise, strong and durable to people and conquer your enemies. Let your army be a glorious one, so that you may always be victorious. But the aforesaid things shall not be attainable to the contemptible the despicable, and the unjust.' In other words, it is only as long as men remain honourable, just and virtuous that they are politically great. When they become wicked and unjust, they are absolutely ruined. From the above, Swami Dayananda inferred what he later called Vedic Swaraj.

Characteristics of Vedic Swaraj

1. **Head and administrators of state** Let a nation, therefore, elect the most learned men, as members of the Educational Assembly, the most devout men, as members of the Religious Assembly and men of the most praiseworthy character, as members of the Legislative Assembly; and let that great man in it, who possesses most excellent qualities, is highly accomplished, and bears most honourable character, be made the Head or President of the Political Assembly.
2. **Three assemblies** Let the three assemblies harmoniously work together, and make good laws, and let all abide by those laws. Let them all be of one mind in affairs that promote the happiness of all. All men should subordinate themselves to the laws that are calculated to promote general well-being; they should be free in matters relating to individual well-being.
3. **Rate of taxes** Swami Dayananda quotes Manu's words, 'Let the king take from trades-people and artisans one-fiftieth part of their profits in silver and gold, and one-sixth, one-eighth or one-twelfth of agricultural produce such as rice: If he takes it in cash instead of in kind, then to let him take it in such a way that the farmers and others would not suffer from poverty or from want of necessaries of life such as, food, drink and so on. Because when the people are rich, healthy and have abundance of necessaries of life, the king flourishes. Let him therefore make his subject happy as he would his own children, and let the people regard the king, his ministers and other officials as their natural protectors, since it is a fact that the farmers and other wealth producers are the real source of kingly power. The king is their guardian. If there were no subjects whose king would he be? Or on the other, if there were no king whose subjects will they be called? Let both — the rulers and the ruled — be independent of each other in the performance of their respective duties, but let them subordinate themselves to each other in all those matters that require natural harmony and co-operation. Let not the rulers go against the voice of the people, nor let the people and ministers do anything against the wish of the sovereign.

   The political duties of kings have thus been briefly described. Let those that want to study this subject in detail consult the four Vedas, The Manu Smriti, the Shukraniti, the Mahabharat and other books. The method of administering justice may be studied from the eighth and ninth chapters of Manu.

4. **The administration of justice** Swami Dayananda quotes Manu approvingly. 'Let the King, the Court and the Judges daily decide justly law suits — which are classified under eighteen heads — according to the laws of the land and the teachings of the Dharma Shastra. To the question who shall punish the king or the Queen, the Lord Chief Justice or his wife, if any one of them commits such wicked crimes as adultery, Dayananda replied, The Assembly (or the court of justice). They should be punished even more severely than other people. According to the Roman Law which holds way in the Occident at the present time 'The king can do no wrong' and no court is competent to try a sovereign, for all the courts derive their authority from him. The ancient Aryan Judges derived their authority from God because they had to administer justice according to principles sanctioned by the Veda-Divine Law. The king, therefore, like his meanest subject, was subject to judicial trials. Unlike modern states the ancient Indian state had means of legal redress against the sovereign, now the only redress is rebellion. In this as in so many other respects, the ancient Aryan sage was ahead of the modern jurist.

   To the question why will the king and other high personages suffer the Assembly (or the court of justice) to punish them, Dayananda answered what is a king but a man endowed with virtue and favoured by fortune. Why would he to go unpunished and why would others obey the law? Besides, if the people and other persons in authority and the Assembly would deem it just and necessary to punish the king, how can he single-handed refuse to suffer punishment? Where king and other high personages go free, the king, ministers, and other men of influence and power would simply set justice and righteousness at naught, sink into the depths of injustice and ruin the people as well as themselves.

   Remember ye the teaching of the Vedic text that says 'Verily the just law alone is the true king, yet, the just law is the true religion.' Whosoever violates it is lowest of the low.'

5. **Penology and Rigorous Punishment** To the question, how can it be right to inflict such severe punishments, since man has no power to make a limb or bring the dead to life again, Swami Dayananda replied: whosoever calls it severe punishment is ignorant of the true principles of Right Government. Infliction of a heavy punishment on one man prevents others from committing similar crimes, and tends to keep them steadfast in righteousness. Truly speaking, this so-called heavy punishment is no heavier than the weight of a mustard seed when distributed among all the members of a community, whilst so-called light punishment, by its failure to check crime, is really a thousand

times heavier than the first, as it is multiplied a thousand times by the proportional increase of crime. Now take for an illustration, a community of one thousand persons whilst if one man in this community of one thousand persons be punished, say, one hundred pounds and should that punishment succeed in preventing the repetition of similar crimes, the total punishment will not be more than a hundred pounds, which is ten times less than one thousand pounds. Thus, the seemingly light punishment in the long run turns out to be the heavier one.

6. **Tax** Manu said 'Let the king impose toll on all the ships and boats passing up and down sea-canals (or bays) and rivers — big and small — proportionate to the length of the country that they traverse; at sea to settle duty can be imposed, hence let him do what best suits the occasion. Let him in such cases make laws that may prove beneficial both to the state and the proprietors of ships. Let him always protect his subjects who go to different foreign lands by means of these ships, wherever they are. Let them never suffer in any way.'
7. **King's duties** 'Let the king daily watch the results of various measures (adopted for the good of the state, etc.), inspect elephants, horses and other conveyances, inquire into his income and expenditure, inspect his mines of precious gems, and his treasury. A king who discharges all these duties most faithfully is freed from all taint of sin, and shall attain to the Supreme State.'
8. **Perfect Government** To the question — is the ancient Aryan system of Government perfect or imperfect, Swami Dayananda replied — Perfect; because all other systems of Government, that prevail at present or shall prevail, have and will have for their basis the Aryan system of Government. The laws that have not been declared expressly have been provided for by the text. To quote Manu 'Let the Parliament composed of scholars, frame such laws as are just and beneficial to the rulers and the ruled.'

VEDIC SYSTEM OF GOVERNMENT

Dayananda maintained that the king as well as his advisers should bear in mind that early marriage must not be allowed, nor the marriage of grown up people without mutual consent. Let the king encourage the practice of Brahmacharya; let him put a stop to prostitution and the custom of plurality of wives (as polygamy, etc.) so that both body and soul may attain perfect strength and power. For if only mental powers and knowledge be developed, but not physical strength, one man of great physical strength may vanquish hundreds of scholars. On the other hand, if physical strength alone be sought after and not mental, the high duties of government can never be rightly discharged. Without proper training and requisite knowledge and without the proper discharge of these duties, there can be no harmony. All will be discord, division, mutual disputes, quarrels and feuds that ultimately ruin all. Let, therefore, both mind and body be developed. There is nothing more prejudicial to the growth of physical and mental powers than prostitution and excessive sexual indulgence. Kshatriyas should, in particular, be physically strong and possess well developed bodies, because if they be lascivious, the government of the country is irrevocably ruined. The proverb 'As is the king, so shall the people be' should never be lost sight of. It, therefore, behoves the king and other high personages never to misconduct themselves. Instead, let them always set a good example to others in the matter of just and righteous living.

Thus, have the duties of rulers been briefly described. Those, who went to study them in detail, are referred to the Vedas, the seventh, eighth and ninth chapters of Manusmriti, the Shukraniti, Vidur-prajagar; Rajadharma, and Apadadharma chapters of Shanti parva of the Mahabharata. They should perfectly master the science and art of government, and rule one country or Empire of the whole earth. Let all understand in the words of Yajur Veda, "We are the subjects of the Lord of the Universe, the king of kings. He is true king and we are all his humble servants. May we in this world, through His mercy, be privileged to occupy kingly and other high offices and may He make us the means of advancing His Eternal Justice."

POLITICAL IDEAS OF DAYANANDA

1. **Swaraja** It was Swami Dayananda Saraswati who for the first time raised a voice and inspired a feeling among Indian multitudes that they should struggle neither for dominion status nor for remaining in British Empire but for trying to get their own national government. In this way he was much against the liberals who all along preached that British rule in India was to the advantage of both the Indians and Britishers. Dayananda argued that such a rule might be in the interest of the rulers but it can never be in the interest of the ruled.
2. **Relationship between religion and politics** According to Swami Dayananda there was close relationship between religion and politics and in fact all other religious institutions must have close working relationship with political institutions. According to him both must go hand in hand. Along with persons like Gopal Krishna Gokhale, Ranade and Dadabhai Naoroji, Dayananda believed that politics devoid of religion was no politics at all and could never produce any lasting results.
3. **Faith in enlightened monarchy** Dayananda laid stress on enlightened monarchy. He believed that monarchy was the only institution which could lead the nation on the path of development and progress. According to him, the king should be a person who was accepted by the society as a superior being and all should be most willing to give their obedience to him. That could only be when the king was

elected by the assembly of people as being considered to be the most superior person by the wise people constituting the assembly set up for his election. According to Dayananda a monarch should always remain enlightened and ready to give benefits of his ability to the people. He should maintain peace. He should be regularly controlled by the spiritual leaders. Spiritual leaders and the king must maintain close cooperation with each other. The seer should see that the king maintains a high moral character and sets examples for others in wisdom, morality and intelligence.

4. **Faith in swadeshi** Swami Dayananda was a strong and staunch devotee of swadeshi in the sense in which M.K. Gandhi subsequently preached that concept. Surinder Nath Banarjee said that swadeshi means adopting foreign goods to suit our national convenience. On the other hand, Swami Dayananda pleaded that swadeshi means using what was produced in our country and to make the nation struggle for self-sufficiency in what was insufficient in our country.
5. **Faith in democracy** From his studies of the Vedas and Manusmriti, Dayananda had come to the conclusion that in our olden days when India was at the height of its glory, the only and widely acceptable institution was that of democracy. Dayananda had many instances before him where the kings were elected and remained in power only as long as the people wanted them. He came to the conclusion that the most suitable institution from India at present is the democratic set up. He, therefore pleaded that democratic institutions should be introduced in our social and political set up. Dayananda, in this regard, was not only theoretical but more practical. Arya Samaj, which was his creation, was organised only on democratic principles and all its office-bearers were supposed to be elected. Dayananda wanted to introduce this system even in governmental institutions. In his *Satyarth Prakash* he says, "It means that no single individual should be invested with absolute power. The king who is president of the assembly and the assembly itself should be interdependent on each other."
6. **Love for education** Dayananda maintained that education was not social but a political problem because without proper literacy political institutions could not properly develop. He, therefore, argued that there should be free compulsory primary education which should be arranged by the government. He had no objection if voluntary associations and institutions also came forward but education should mainly be the responsibility of the government and not of voluntary institutions. Education should aim at producing good citizens who were useful to the nation. In other words, according to Dayananda, education should be national in character. Dayananda's system of education was based on the Gurukul system of education in which there was provision for educating both the boys and girls.

7. **Decentralisation of authority** Democratic decentralisation implies that there should be transfer of power from the centre to local self-government institutions. This system is also known as the system of decentralisation of authority. Gokhale preached this very system when he said that there should be District Councils for advising district administration and Panchayats for running village administration. Dayananda was also in favour of a system of decentralisation of authority. Taking into consideration the Indian political set up, he came forward with the idea that the village should be the most important and integral part of our administration. He did not agree to the idea that administration should follow from above to down below. He believed that the administration should run from below and go upward.
8. **Functions of the state** Dayananda's concept of state was very enlightened. According to him the State should not only perform the police functions of maintaining law and order and collecting taxes, it should rather be a welfare state. It was the duty of state to see that economic conditions of the people were improved. State should provide opportunities for employment as could prosper the masses. There should be increase in wealth. The state should aim at moral development of its citizens. According to Dayananda, the state should also see to it that the people were safe from outside aggression and no foreign power violated India's territorial boundaries.
9. **Ahimsa** In modern times Mahatma Gandhi is considered as the greatest apostle of Ahimsa both in letter and spirit. This concept is generally considered as an idea in which none is to be harmed or injured in any way. Swami Dayananda also believed this concept. He had, however, a different interpretation. According to him, normally, Ahimsa should be practised because violence created counter-violence and hatred counter-hatred. But there were certain occasions when Ahimsa could not be practised or its practising could possibly lead to unhealthy results. Dayananda, therefore, did not object to use of force while checking the activities of criminals, anti-social elements and those who transgressed social limitations established by a healthy society. In other words, his concept was that of relative Ahimsa rather than absolute Ahimsa.
10. **Government authority** Dayananda has very clearly stated as to who should control the government and society. According to him the government and the society should be controlled by three organs, namely, Rajya Sabha, Dharma and Vidya Sabha.
    (i) *Rajya Sabha.* Rajya Sabha was to act as the legislature. It should consist of persons who possessed high qualities of character and were responsible for improving the living standard and character of the people. This Sabha should enact laws for the people and also see that decisions were properly implemented.

(ii) *Dharma Sabha*. This should consist of wise Brahmins who had established themselves as spiritual leaders of the society. Brahmins included only those persons who were leading a life of real renunciation and followed and understood Dharma in its true sense. Dharma Sabha was to control Rajya Sabha because according to Dayananda religious people should always control the political people.

(iii) *Vidya Sabha*. This should be responsible for promoting education. It should see that in educational field there was no superiority or inferiority. The students think in the terms of mutual love. Both the teachers and the taught should promote a spirit of nationalism and brotherhood. According to Dayananda that could best be achieved when there were no public schools. In other words, he believed in the concept of neighbourhood schools rather than public schools which is even appreciated today.

11. **Chakravarty ruler** At many places Dayananda has made a reference to India's having a Chakravarty ruler. Some writers have interpreted it by saying that he was an imperialist who believed in expansion. This, however, does not appear to be a very correct interpretation of what has been said about him. By Chakravarty rule Dayananda meant a world governmental system based on Vedic teachings. He desired that there should be a world empire based on spiritualism. It should promote moral development of the people. He believed in the concept of universal brotherhood and made it clear both in his writings and speeches. He, however, did not conceal his wish that there should be a Vedic universalism and no corner of the world should remain in darkness without the light of the teachings of Vedas.

Critical Evaluation

Thus, Dayananda was the person who initiated renaissance in India. He gave quite a new outlook to Indian political philosophy. He denounced the idea that India's miserable conditions could be improved in any way by Britishers. When liberals in the Congress were speaking in praise of British rule Dayananda gave the idea that self-government in its worst form was better than the foreign government in its best form. To quote Jayaswal, "The Sanyasi Dayananda gave freedom to the soul of the Hindus, as Luther did unto the Europeans." Similarly Jawahar Lal Nehru said about Arya Samaj "The Arya Samaj was a reaction to the influence of Islam and Christianity more especially to the former."

SOCIAL IDEAS OF DAYANANDA

Swami Dayananda was born at a time when Hindu Society was suffering from many social evils and in fact had completely degenerated itself. Religion was being wrongly interpreted and in fact many of those who claimed to know religion did not know as to what religion essentially meant. The society was also suffering from such evils as caste system, child marriage etc. Therefore, swami Dayananda came forward to challenge the social evils and to interpret religion in its true form. Before coming to the forefront lie meditated and sat at the feet of a great religious and devoted Guru Virjanand whose only mission in life was to rid the Hindu society of its evils.

Before Dayananda such like institutions as Brahmo Samaj founded by Raja Ram Mohan Roy were quite popular. Christian missionaries were spreading their religion and leaving no stone unturned to expose the evils of Hindu society and to tell the people the bright side of their religion. The down-trodden and depressed who had been condemned by Hindu society were gladly embracing Christianity which presented them a very bright future. The plight of the women was shocking. Doors of knowledge had been closed on them. There was no provision by the social laws, whereby they could attend schools and colleges. They had a lower status than men in the Hindu Society. The great teaching of Hindu religion that all were equal without distinction of sex, had been ignored. It was under these circumstances that Swami Dayananda came to the forefront to challenge the orthodoxy of time with all his might without caring for the pleasure and displeasure of the orthodox sections of society. He knew the magnitude of the task before him but before he left his Guru he had given him a solemn promise that he would endeavour his best to realise the society of this great burden. Some of his social ideas were as under:

1. **Stress on education** A society cannot underestimate the necessity of educating its members. A healthy society must provide for the education of all without any distinction of sex. It should also have a cheap system of education with stress on producing educated young patriots. In India during the period of Dayananda, the situation was quite different. It was a time when society had ignored one complete section, *i.e.* the women. They were not allowed to get education and to attend schools and colleges. The British education which was being given to the Indian citizens was more on the pattern of Western system of education which was not suited to Indian conditions. Therefore, Dayananda provided for a system of education commonly known as Gurukul system of education. In this system of education each student was required to remain in the Gurukul to study upto the age of 25. Here he was to be taught not only arithmetic and science but also ancient Indian culture, civilization and religion contained in books like Vedas and Upanishads. It was here that he was to be taught about nationalism and his duties towards the country in which he was born and developing. Vedic system of education provided for both men and women without any distinction whatsoever. Dayananda pleaded for co-education. According to him there was no distinction

between the talents of men and women. Education should create a sense of oneness and as such while getting education there should be a common dress. Every effort should be made to see that there was no apparent distinction between a rich student and a poor one. Dayananda provided for a Vidya Sabha, which was to be exclusively held responsible for the propagation of education and to formulate national educational policies and programmes.

2. **Condemnation of untouchability** Swami Dayananda was very much pained to see the caste system as it was prevailing at that time. He openly condemned the system saying that it was not with the sanction of any religion but it was a subsequent arrangement brought about by certain selfish people to suit the convenience. Therefore, he suggested that caste system should only be based on the functions which one actually performed in his life rather than on birth as presently was the case. He believed in the inherent right of every individual to the choice of his profession. What pained him was that in caste it was not the profession but birth which was coming to the forefront.
3. **Plea for widow re-marriage** As a social reformer Swamy Dayananda raised his voice in favour of the widows. The society had put an unnecessary bar on widow re-marriage. It had made the life of thousands of Indian women quite miserable. This restriction was promoting moral degeneration. The society was rapidly becoming corrupt. Therefore, Dayananda pleaded that there should be widow re-marriage because a woman was widowed not because of her fault but because what lay in store for her.
4. **Plea for status of Hindu women** Swami Dayananda very emphatically believed that the women of India were not only brave but highly intelligent and wise. He pointed out that history is a witness that in the past the women, when they were free to act, acted in a fashion which could give glory to the nation. Instances were not wanting when women guided the destiny of the nation. Therefore, Dayananda was surprised to see that women were being ignored and given a lower status in Hindu society. He raised his voice against this age old tradition. He said that women should be given their due and rightful place in the society. It was an intentional and wicked action on the part of the men to have subordinated the women and also to have refused them status of equality. Therefore, Dayananda desired that all social bondages which were to the disadvantage of women should forthwith be removed. He asked that women should be properly educated. There was no harm in mixing of girls and boys in a healthy atmosphere. The women should be given their due place socially, economically and politically.
5. **Propagation of national language** Unfortunately, even today India is not in a position to decide as to what should be our language policy.

Whether India should accept two-language or three-language formula is a matter yet to be decided. Swami Dayananda realised that English could never be a medium through which the people of India would at any stage express themselves so clearly as in Hindi. Therefore, he very strongly advocated the cause of Hindi as the medium of common expression. It was with this end in view that he himself wrote all his works in Hindi though he himself was a Gujarati and could better express himself in that language.

6. **Interpretation of history** Swami Dayananda was never a student of History in the present sense of the term. He had never studied Western culture and civilization. In fact, he was never a student of any other literature for that matter. He knew only one religion and one literature and that was Hindu religion and Vedic literature. He carried out deep researches in this literature which he said was as vast as the oceans full of diamonds to pick them up. From his study of Vedic literature he concluded that in ancient times India was so rich in culture and civilisation that the West could not dream of that even today. Therefore, Dayananda pleaded that history should not be ignored as merely a thing of the past but it had close bearing on the present. Without regeneration of our national glory we could not go ahead on the path of progress. History was a great lesson which could be taken in those terms and to which due importance must be attached. It was through this history alone that India could attain that unity which was badly wanted by it. According to Dayananda, if the people of India came to know of their past history there shall be a social revolution and every one shall be filled with great energy. He, therefore, asked that let each and every Indian study the history of India with attention and care.
7. **Close relation of ethics and politics** Swami Dayananda believed that a healthy society was one which was morally healthy and in which the moral character of the people was exemplary, he laid great stress on moral character and nation building activities. He pointed out that if the people had low moral character and did not care for national morality, that nation must end itself. That was the main reason as to why India had completely degenerated itself. It is the morally strong people who raise the nation high in the estimation of the world. Therefore, for Dayananda ethics was very important. He wanted that this ethics should have its influence on politics. Ethics and politics must go hand in hand, otherwise one without the other was just barren and devoid of religious life. Therefore, Dayananda said that politics must be spiritualised. It was in an ethically advanced nation that fearlessness could develop and nourish. The more frank and fearless a nation is the more progressive and economically well that must be.

To conclude, there is no aspect of society which Dayananda left untouched. In his zeal to reform the society, he criticised a few religions which were damaging Hindu society. He, however, did not condemn them but did it only for the sake of providing a comparative study of these religions with the Hindu religion which was most dear to him. Some have tried to characterise him as a narrow-minded person who wanted only one religion to prosper and others to perish but that assumption appears to be without any solid support. His object was only to provide a comparative study of various religions and in that process some or the other religion came under his criticism that should be taken in that spirit. Dayananda was a person who tried to seal the flow of Christianity into India and to revive Hinduism in its true sense. He sought for a healthy society and for that he could make every sacrifice.

THE ARYA SAMAJ

India's Conditions During 19th Century

1. **Social degeneration** When Swami Dayananda came forward to find for himself answers to his problems, Indian society had completely degenerated itself. India had practically defaced herself politically, economically and socially. The influence of Christian missionaries and others had considerably increased. There was large scale conversion from Hinduism to many other religions with the result that there was danger of Hindu society being completely demoralised. The problem of the day was to save the society from its degeneration.
2. **Liberal politics** In the political field, the liberals in the Congress, had practically full control over this organisation which had assumed more or less a national character. The liberal leaders usually believed that British Government in India was in the interest of the Indians. They pleaded that one should welcome this stay as it was an act of providence and essential for Indian advancement. They also believed that political advancement of India was closely associated with Indian association with the Britishers. Thus, these patriots wanted to prolong Britishers' stay in India without any limit to this foreign rule.
3. **Police state** The character of the British Government in India was more or less that of a police state. The state confined itself only to collection of taxes and revenues without caring much for the welfare of the people. It had no obligation to provide employment to the people or arrange for their higher education. In religious and social affairs the British Government had more or less adopted the policy of *laissez faire.*
4. **Poverty** Equally alarming were the conditions in the economic field in India. The British trade and commercial policy had squeezed the blood of Indians. India's poverty was writ large on each individual Indian. The government did not take the help of active steps to improve this situation.

5. **Religion** In the religious field the conditions were still more alarming. Even a person like Swami Dayananda could not find a suitable Guru for himself for years with the result that he had to wander from place to place in search of a teacher. The religion was superstition ridden. Religion was a hoax and in its name many were being cheated.
6. **Education** Education was not bringing out patriots. Indian educated masses were closer to Western culture and civilization than Indian system of living, thinking and behaving.

Need of the time

It was under the above mentioned circumstances that Swami Dayananda came forward. He wanted that the Indians should have a platform from where Indian economic, social and political problems could be solved. He sought to overhaul and reorganise the system drastically changing the present set-up so that the society could move forward from its stagnancy. The new organisation should be most dynamic. It should have scientific approach to problems. It should shed away all orthodoxy. Its members should have receptive minds to accept change which the society needed. Such a platform should also produce patriots and people who had unshakable faith in Indian culture and civilization with a determination to spread that wherever they went. These people should have high moral character and exemplary living with devotion to duty and an inspiring personality. One should expect a regeneration of the society only in such an atmosphere. Dayananda had also before him the message of his Guru Virjanand who wanted that Vedic philosophy should be spread throughout the world. With these objects in view Swami Dayananda founded his Arya Samaj in 1875 at Bombay. Two years later Arya Samaj was founded at Lahore.

BASIC PRINCIPLES

Swami Dayanand founded Arya Samaj with the following objects in mind:

(i) God is one and Supreme and there are no gods and goddesses.

(ii) Vedas are the foundation of all knowledge and it is the duty of all Aryans to read and spread the teachings of Vedas.

(iii) Every action should be motivated and guided by what is true.

(iv) It is the duty of each member of Arya Samaj to look after the physical, social and religious welfare of all.

(v) Every person should be treated in the way he behaves and get what he deserves.

(vi) Education should be widespread and illiteracy should be wiped out.

(vii) No one should be satisfied only with his own development but in the collective development one should think of his own development also.

(viii) Each individual is free to think in terms of his personal welfare but in collective welfare all are bound to each other.

Such was and continues to be the philosophy of Arya Samaj. Dayananda wanted that these ideals should be followed most honestly and vigorously by all Arya Samajists.

Programmes of Arya Samaj

(i) *Education.* Dayananda wanted to revive the knowledge of Sanskrit literature. He made it the responsibility of Arya Samaj to run Gurukulas where the Indian young minds should be educated in terms of Indian culture and civilization. These young men should be taught the value of high moral character. They should be nourished, brought up and developed in an atmosphere where patriotism was above everything else. Gurukulas should be centres of Vedic study and research. The Arya Samaj should raise a voice against social evils. These should be fought boldly without caring for the orthodoxy.

(ii) *Social Reforms.* Dayananda felt that orthodoxy was bound to oppose such regeneration in Hindu society. He made it obligatory on the part of Arya Samajists to stand for widow re-marriage and to oppose child marriage or caste system and other evils or similar institutions vehemently which had corrupted the Hindu society. Keeping in view the trend of the time, Dayananda asked the Arya Samajists to expose what was unwanted in the religious doctrines and books of other religions so that missionaries were demoralised and they hesitated from condemning and criticising Hindu religious teachings and philosophy. Dayananda propagated *shuddhi* by which he meant that those who wanted to willingly remembrance Hindu religion should not be forbidden to do so.

(iii) *Democratic Constitution.* Dayananda introduced elective system in the constitution of Arya Samaj which was then unknown to the religious institutions of those days. He laid down that Arya Samaj should be organised on democratic lines. Arya Samajists were obliged to see that their office-bearers are elected by their members and that there are no hereditary or nominated members.

(iv) *Political Reforms.* In the political field Dayananda asked the Arya Samajists that it was obligatory on them to preach and propagate the use of swadeshi and also to demand self-government. There should be decentralisation of authority and a desire on the part of Government to place individual above everything else.

Contemporary Influence

Arya Samaj was responsible for political, social and economic resurgence in India. It had deep influence on many contemporaries. Most of the national leaders closely studied the doctrines of Arya Samaj. Lala Lajpat Rai said, "In short, I learnt my lessons in public life from and in the Arya Samaj. It was there that I saw models of purity in public life, and there that I met my dearest friends. I am under enormously heavy debt to Arya Samaj and even if I sacrifice the last hair of my body for the name of Samaj I would not be able to pay back what I owe" The influence of Arya Samaj is evident from the fact that among those who were influenced by it were persons like Lala Har Dayal, Har Krishan Lal, Krishan Lal. Krishan Verma, Gopal Krishna Gokhale and Mahatma Gandhi and Rabindra Nath Tagore. Mahatma Gandhi was so much influenced by Dayananda, that he called him his political Guru and so did Rabindra Nath Tagore. In the north-west India the influence of Arya Samaj was felt even in the very early stages of its development. It was due to the work and contribution of Arya Samaj that ancient Indian glory was revived and a network of Gurukulas set up for educating young men and women of India. It was under the influence of Arya Samaj that social evils were checked and the influence of Christianity on Hindu society considerably lessened. The contribution of Arya Samaj in the resurgence of our political life may be summed up in the words of Lala Lajpat Rai who said, "It was the Arya Samaj that taught me to love the Vedic religion and to feel proud of Aryan greatness. It was the Arya Samaj that linked me with ancient Aryans and made me their admirer and devotee. It was Arya Samaj that instilled into me the spirit of truth, of Dharma and liberty. My organising capacity too I owe to the Arya Samaj. It was the Samaj again that taught me that society, dharma and country command our worship and that those shall inherit the kingdom of heaven who make sacrifices to serve these."

14
Ramkrishna Paramhansa (1835 — 1897)

Ramkrishna Paramhansa, born on 18th Feb. 1835 influenced almost all the great men of 19th century in India. He was not at all an academic philosopher, still less a social reformer or a politician, but his great religious status and power of magnetic spiritual force influenced national leaders far and wide. In the tradition of ancient Indian philosophy and religion he preached monism. According to him reality is one though it manifests in different ways at different places. Through the help of small stories he explained to his audience that ultimately the essence of everything is the same. The ancient Indian *Mahavakyas of Aham Brahmasmi and Tatvamasi* were the main bases of his religious teachings. He, however, synthesised Advaita Vedanta with Vaishnava cult of Bhakti. On the other hand, he had equal respect for other great religions of the world including Islam, Christianity and Buddhism. He preached that the essentials of all these religions are the same and there is hardly any occasion to fight on this issue. God realisation is the aim of life and Ramkrishna could realise God not only in inner consciousness but sometimes even in his physical body. His contact so much impressed Vivekananda that the latter immediately became his disciple and toured the entire world to preach the teaching of Ramkrishna. As Socrate's ideas are known through the dialogues of Plato, similarly the teachings of Ramkrishna are better known through the speeches of Vivekananda.

IDEAS AND IDEALS

The chief aim of spiritual practice according to Ramkrishna is the realization of God. He preached discarding desire for material prosperity and lure for women and gold. This, however, does not require escape from the worldly life but a constant meditation upon God. Ramkrishna believed that passions can be eliminated by their re-direction towards God. He explained this idea by several parables such as:

"As an unchaste woman, busily engaged in household affairs, is all the while thinking of her secret lover, even so, though man of the world, do thy round of worldly duties; but fix thy heart always on the Lord."

"As a wet nurse in a rich family brings up the child of her master, loving the baby as if it were her own, but knows well that she has no claim upon it; so think ye also that you are but trustees and guardians of your children whose real father is the Lord God in Heaven."

The life of Ramkrishna was a laboratory for the synthesis of great religions. He believed that all the religions of the world were true and any one may lead to salvation. He experienced that the spiritual practices in any religion were equally effective. Every religion leads to the path of salvation. He was asked how God could be both immanent and transcendent, to which he said, "Exactly as water can exist in a liquid, solid and invisible form." Again, "As water is called by different names in different languages, so different religions call God by different names like Hari, Siva, Allah, Christ, etc., but all denote the same God."

He was further asked that "if the God of every religion is the same, why is it then that the God is painted differently by different religionists? He answered: God is one but His aspects are different: as one master of the house is father to one, brother to another, and husband to a third, and is called by these different names by those different persons, so one God is described and called in various ways according to the particular aspect in which He appears to his particular worshippers." This spirit of catholicity and tolerance is the essence of the teachings of Ramkrishna and therefore of Vivekananda. Admitting his debt to Ramkrishna, Vivekananda, while delivering an address at the Shakespeare Club of Pasadona, California, on January 27, 1900 said: "Now all the ideas that I preach are only an attempt to echo His ideas. Nothing is mine originally except the wicked ones. But every word that I have ever uttered which is true and good, is simply an attempt to echo his voice."

AIMS AND IDEALS OF RAMKRISHNA MISSION

On May 5, 1897 a meeting of the disciples of Ramkrishna under the leadership of Swami Vivekananda unanimously adopted the following aims and ideals of Ramkrishna Mission:

1. The Association (Sangha) shall be known as the Ramkrishna Mission.
2. (a) This new Mission is to preach the truths which Sri Ramkrishna has, for the good of humanity, preached and demonstrated by practical application in his own life, and to help others to put these truths into practice in their temporal, mental and spiritual advancement;

   (b) To conduct the activities of the movements for the establishment of fellowship among the followers of different religions, knowing them all to be so many forms only of one underlying Eternal Religion.

3. Its methods of action are:
   (a) To train men so as to make them competent to teach such knowledge or sciences as are conducive to the material and spiritual welfare of the masses;
   (b) To promote and encourage arts and industries; and
   (c) To introduce and spread among the people in general Vedantic and other religious ideas in the way in which they are elucidated in the life of Sri Ramkrishna.
4. It should have two branches of action:
   (a) Indian Work Department, and
   (b) Foreign Department.
   (a) The activities of the Indian Department should be directed to the establishment of Mathas and Ashrams in different parts of India for the training of Sannyasins and such of the householders as may be willing to devote their lives to the teaching of others;
   (b) Whereas its work in the Foreign Department should be to send trained members of the Order to countries outside India to start centres there for the preaching of Vedanta in order to bring about a close relation and better understanding between India and foreign countries.
5. The aims and the objects of the Mission being purely spiritual and humanitarian, it shall have no connection with politics.
6. Anyone who believes in the Mission of Sri Ramakrishna, or who sympathizes or is willing to cooperate with the above mentioned aims and objects of the Association, is eligible for the membership."

Under the able presidentship of Vivekananda Ramkrishna Mission did very important work in the field of social and religious reform. Its branches were spread throughout the country and even outside India. After Vivekananda the illustrious followers of the Mission such as Yogananda and Swami Brahmananda carried out the work of the Mission.

PART III
CONTEMPORARY INDIAN POLITICAL THOUGHT

15
Vivekananda (1863 — 1902)

On 12th January 1863 a child was born in the house of Vishvanath Datt, resident of Gormohan Mukerjee Street in North Calcutta in Bengal, who was known to the world as Vivekananda. The child was named Narendra Nath. Ramkrishna, the teacher of Vivekananda called him by this name. Bhuvaneshwari Devi, the mother of Narendra Nath was a very intelligent and religious lady. She used to recite Ramayana and Mahabharata and performed her house-hold chores with a calm mind. Thus, like M.K. Gandhi, Vivekananda owed some of his religiosity to the influence of his mother.

The early education of Narendra Nath was given through Bengali and English. His mother used to tell him the stories of Ramayana and Mahabharata. The child showed special interest in Ramayana and particularly in the character of Rama. Wherever the story of Rama was recited the child Narendra Nath used to hear it with rapt attention forgetting all childhood plays. Once he meditated in a room of his house with so much rapt attention that the door of the room had to be broken to awaken him. Thus, Yogic consciousness was evident in Vivekananda from the very beginning. He used to have peculiar experiences while sleeping. In these experiences he used to feel light between the eye-brows which gradually spread throughout his body. This experience proved the spiritual power of Narendra Nath. On the other hand, the child used to commit so much childhish pranks that his mother used to say that she asked for a son to Shiva but he sent a demon to him. Narendra Nath was particularly intimate with the domestic servants.

At the age of 6, Narendra Nath started going to school. Here within a year he memorized Muktibodha. He also memorized most of the portions of Ramayana and Mahabharata. After a year he was admitted to the educational institution of Ishwar Chandra Vidyasagar. His teachers here were very much impressed by his intelligence and genius and used to praise him very much. Narendra Nath was not only a good student but also a good player. He possessed sound health. In Entrance class Narendra Nath had sufficient knowledge of English and Bangla literature and Indian history. His understanding was deep and memory sharp. He could follow a writer by only reading some of the lines written by him. He could understand the subject of a book by merely reading some portions of it. He passed Entrance examination in first division. After it he entered Presidency College. Here also he very much impressed his teachers. His principal W.W. Hasti used to say that he never saw a genius like Narendra Nath. Narendra Nath had a multisided genius. At the college stage he had achieved an intimate knowledge of English literature, European history, philosophy, science, art, music and medicine.

During this period, Brahmo Samaj was very popular in Bengal. The leaders of Brahmo Samaj had wide influence over the Bengali youth. Narendra Nath was also influenced by Brahmo Samaj and became a member of it. This influence was particularly due to his intellectual outlook. He never agreed to admit a thing without understanding it. He was vehemently against superstitions. He was a staunch supporter of social reform. He had a keen desire to participate in the progress of his country. All these tendencies took him to Brahmo Samaj. However, gradually he became dissatisfied. Once he asked Devendranath Thakur, the greatest leader of Brahmo Samaj, "Sir, Have you seen God." He did not receive any satisfactory answer.

During this time Ramakrishna, the priest of the Kali temple of Dakshneshwar had a name in Calcutta. He was a devotee of a high order and it is said that he realised Kali directly. He used to believe in the value of all the religions. He preached that all religions are essentially similar. The principal of the college of Narendra Nath told him about Ramakrishna. Narendra Nath went to Ramakrishna. Ramakrishna identified the spiritual powers of Narendra Nath at the very first sight. He exclaimed that here is an incarnation of Narayan who is born to remove the sufferings of mankind. On the other hand, Narendra Nath felt that Ramakrishna was a bit abnormal. However, he asked the old question. "Sir, Have you seen God?" The reply which he received was never expected. Ramakrishna told him, "Yes, I see him just as I see you here." Narendra Nath was deeply impressed but not completely satisfied. He continued to meet Ramakrishna more often and gradually came under his influence.

In 1884 the father of Narendra Nath passed away due to heart attack. At this time Narendra Nath was only a graduate and studying law. But now the entire financial responsibility of the family came upon his head. His relatives used to tease his family. He did not get any job. He could not repay the debts he owed to many persons. Under these hard circumstances Narendra Nath had crisis of faith. However, the adversities, sufferings and troubles subdued his ego and evoked his faith. Like Gautama, the Buddha, he experienced that everywhere there is suffering in this world. This led him to the resolve to remove sufferings of his countrymen. This also increased his faith in Ramakrishna.

Narendra Nath received his initiation in Vedanta from Ramakrishna. Ramakrishna had extraordinary yogic powers. In 1885 he gave Narendra Nath the experience of attributeless Samadhi by his mere touch and ordered him that his first duty is to fulfil the mission of Ramakrishna. Narendra Nath was the leader of the association of the young followers of Ramakrishna. This association was founded with the purpose of spirituality and welfare of humanity. As the leader of this association, called Ramakrishna Mission, Narendra Nath propagated the views of Ramakrishna everywhere. Beloor near Howrah was made the head office of Ramakrishna Mission and the centre of its activities. Narendra Nath was now known as Vivekananda. He extensively toured the country and tried to understand and solve its problems.

In 1888 Vivekananda left Calcutta alone. He went to Varanasi, Ayodhya, Lucknow, Agra, Vrindavan and Hathras. At Hathras he was accompanied by his disciple Sadanand. Both of them now toured Himalayas. In Himalayas Vivekananda had a vision of the soul of India. After a year Vivekananda again toured several places within the country including Gazipur and Varanasi. In February 1891 he went to Rajasthan, Bombay and Rameshwaram. From Rameshwaram he went to Kanyakumari. There he sat on a rock in the sea and had his realisation of the great unity of India. At present there is on this rock the world famous Vivekananda Memorial.

In 1883 Vivekananda heard that a Parliament of Religions was being organised in Chigago in U.S.A. He decided to participate in this parliament in order to give his message to the World. He was very much pained by the poverty of India and wanted to draw the attention of the West towards this problem. This was one of the important purpose of his visit of U.S.A. Before going to U.S.A. he went to Khetri, the king of this state was his disciple. It was this princely disciple who suggested the name of Swami Vivekananda which was adopted by Narendra Nath.

On May 31, 1893 Swami Vivekananda left Bombay for U.S.A. In the way he went to Ceylon, Penong, Singapore, Hong Kong, Kentan and Nagasaki. Seeing the influence of Indian culture and Sanskrit language at all these places he realised the spiritual unity of Asia. He reached Chicago in mid-July. Seeing the spectacular progress of knowledge and science at U.S.A., he was highly impressed. After twelve days he reached the information office of the proposed Parliament of Religions. He was told that the parliament will be held in the first week of September and his name cannot be included in the list of delegates until it is recommended by someone in U.S.A. or elsewhere. Vivekananda sent a telegram to his friends to Madras for recommendation but got no success. However, the genius like Vivekananda hardly needed any introduction. His personality was his best certificate. While travelling in the train at Boston Swami Vivekananda met a rich lady of Messachusetts. She called him at her residence and introduced him to Professor J.H. Wright of the department of Greek studies at the Harward University. Wright was very much impressed by Vivekanand and introduced him to Dr. Bros, the chairman of the selection committee of the delegates by writing, "Here is a person who is a greater scholar than all our scholar professors added together." He insisted that Vivekananda should be admitted as the representative of Hinduism at the Parliament of Religions. He also gave Vivekananda rail ticket to Chicago and a letter of recommendation of lodging and boarding. Unfortunately Vivekananda lost these papers during the journey. However, these were received by a lady G.W. Hale who contacted Vivekananda and took him to the Parliament, where he was respectfully admitted as a delegate and arrangements of his stay were made alongwith other representatives from the East.

The Parliament of Religions was inaugurated on 11th September 1883 at Columbus Hall. Religious leaders of the world had gathered there to hear Swami Vivekananda in the evening of the first day. They welcomed by prolonged clapping the first words of Vivekananda, "American brothers and sisters." Leaving all formalities of the Parliament Swami Vivekananda presented his ideas in such a direct and clear language that the Parliament was very much impressed. After it he delivered a dozen lectures in U.S.A. which made him famous in the West. *New York Herald* proclaimed him as the greatest person at the Parliament of Religions and wrote that after hearing him we feel that how much foolish it is to send religious missionaries to the nation of such a great scholar. During his lectures Swami Vivekananda repeatedly drew the attention of the West to the problems of India. On the invitation of Bureau he visited several places in U.S.A. and delivered lectures which had wide influence over American intelligentsia. He was offered the headship of department of Eastern philosophy at Harvard University and Sanskrit language at Columbia University which he declined saying that he was a Sanyasin.

On 7th August, 1895 Swami Vivekananda left U.S.A. for England. The British newspapers compared him to Raja Ram Mohan Roy, Keshabchandra Sen and even Gautama the Buddha. He was welcomed by heads of various churches and he delivered several lectures in England. It is here that Miss Margaret E. Nobel, the later Sister Nivedita met his teacher Vivekananda for the first time. His lectures on Jnanayoga in London particularly became famous.

On 6th December, 1895 Swami Vivekananda reached New York from England. Here he delivered lectures on Karmayoga and Bhaktiyoga at the residence of Miss S.E. Waldo who later on became his disciple known as Hari Dasi. Vivekananda delivered lectures in a very informal but influential style. Gradually, the number of his American disciples increased. In Februaiy 1896 he laid the foundation of the famous Vedanta Society of New York. He also delivered lectures on Vedanta philosophy in the philosophy department of Harward University. His lecture here on 25th March, 1896 was so impressive that he was offered the chair of Eastern philosophy. Swami Vivekananda had no financial difficulty as he was receiving overwhelming cooperation from all sides.

In April 1896 Swami Vivekananda left America for England and in the month of May delivered 5 lectures per week on Vedanta. He delivered three lectures, at Royal Institute of Painters, Picaddelli. He also spoke at Princess Hall, Annie Besant Lodge and other well known Clubs and Educational institutions. Max Muller invited him to his residence at Oxford and was very much influenced by him. From England Swami Vivekananda went to Switzerland on the persuasion of some of his friends. In August 1896 he was invited by Professor Paul Deussen of Kiel University of Germany. Deussen was very much impressed by Vivekananda and accompanied him on his return journey to London. Vivekananda stayed in London for next few months and then left for India with two of his disciples Mr. and Mrs. Sevier.

When Vivekananda reached India he was given a tumultous welcome. A meeting of the disciples of Ramakrishna was called on 1st May, 1897 at Bagh Bazar in Calcutta at the residence of Mr. Balram Bose. Vivekananda explained the problems of the country before this gathering and pleaded for their remedies. The meeting accepted his proposals and Ramakrishna Mission was established on May 5, 1897 with the express mission of serving humanity through the service of followers of various religions. It aimed at trainee missionaries who could propagate Vedanta everywhere. The programme of the mission was entrusted to two departments, Indian and Western. Swami Vivekananda was elected president of the mission and Swami Yoganand and Swami Brahmanand were elected Vice-President and President of Calcutta Branch of the Mission respectively.

As president of Ramakrishna Mission Swami Vivekananda toured the whole of the country. He went to historical places in North India, Punjab, Kashmir and Rajasthan. Everywhere he propagated the preachings of the Mission and clarified the problems of the country asking for remedies. His ideas were a combination of Vedanta and science, East and West, ancient and modern, idealism and realism. He discussed the plan of establishment of a branch of mission at Kashmir with the King of Kashmir. On 30th March, 1898 he reached Darjeeling but left for Calcutta in April to serve the people suffering from plague epidemic. The service rendered by followers of Ramakrishna Mission to the suffering people of Calcutta was a rare example. However, some members of Ramakrishna Mission did not agree with the precept of Swami Vivekananda about public service. Some of them even remarked that Vivekananda did not go to America for propagation of preachings of Ramakrishna but for his own propaganda. These and other instances shocked Swami Vivekananda.

In order to provide a centre in the Himalayas for practising Vedanta Philosophy by his disciples from East and West, Vivekananda established Advaita Ashram at Mayavati, 50 miles away from Almora on 19th March, 1899. It was at this centre that the chief organ of Ramakrishna Mission came out under the title *Prabudha Bharata*. Besides Advaita Ashram Swami Vivekananda established several other centres of public service in various parts of the country.

On 20th June 1899 Swami Vivekananda again left for West with his disciples Sister Nivedita and Swami Turiyanand. During the course of his journey he established centres at San Francisco, Aukland and Alamada. He saw symptoms of destruction of humanity in the technological advance of the West which he discussed later on in his various lectures. He returned to Beloor in India on 24th January, 1901, and went to Mayavati Ashram. He also toured other centres of the country. This herculean labour for the propagation of his preachings gradually adversely affected his physical health. He suffered from diabetes and lung diseases. Gradually his condition worsened. On the insistence of his several disciples, he stayed at Beloor for 7 months and transferred all his responsibilities to his disciples. But his keen desire to serve humanity did not allow him rest. Therefore, he went to Bodh Gaya on the insistence of Japanese Artist Okakura. From there he went to Varanasi and established a centre of Ramakrishna Mission there. All this tour adversely affected his health. He used to say, "I will not live for seeing 40." This happened. On 4th July, 1902 Swami Vivekananda left for his heavenly abode at the early age of 39 years.

CONTEMPORARY PROBLEMS

The problems of the time of Vivekananda were partly economic, partly social and political. Vivekananda was not a revivalist or obscurantist. He was fully aware of the various problems of his time both Indian and Western. He was particularly concerned about the low level of living of Indians, ill-health, diseases, malnutrition, illiteracy, factionism, casteism, poverty etc. He was also troubled by the political problems such as slavery, collectivism, stale repression etc.

1. **Lack of Synthesis of East and West** Due to low economic condition, Indians had an inferiority complex wherever they met Western people. Swami Vivekananda exhorted his countrymen not to imitate West because Western civilization is too young. He tried to infuse patriotism and love for the country. He demanded that India must be understood in the background of its spiritual achievement. "He made them see that India's culture was incomparable, being developed through thousands of years of trial and experimentation till it had attained the highest standard ever reached by humanity, and consequently possessed an unshakable stability and strength. He made them see the 'why' of every Indian custom."[1] On the other hand, he criticized those Indians who

[1] Eastern and Western Disciples, *Life of Swami Vivekananda*, Vol. I, Mayavati Advaita Ashrama, pp. 553-54.

were against material advancement. He said, "We talk foolishly against material civilization. The grapes are sour."[1]

Thus, the chief problem of attitude in his time was the lack of synthesis of East and West. Vivekananda pleaded for such a synthesis in his lectures.

2. **Backwardness** Vivekananda very much realised the economic and social difficulties of the poor classes in India. They were poor, illiterate, without sufficient nutrition and suffering from various types of diseases. Decrying this situation Vivekananda asked, "Who constitutes society? The missions or you, I or a few others of the upper classes."[2] He pointed out that majority is more important. He remarked, "For the luxury of a handful of the rich, let millions of men and women remain submerged in the hell of want and abysmal depth of ignorance, for if they get wealth and education, society will be upset."[3] Thus Vivekananda pleaded for freedom and growth of all the Indian people.
3. **Political Ignorance** The most important political problem of the time of Vivekananda was the complete ignorance of majority of Indian people about the political developments elsewhere. In the words of Vivekananda, "Not one of them had heard of what is meant by a socialism and anarchism." [4] But political awakening is not possible by hungry people. Food and cloth are the first needs of life. Laying his finger on the priorities, Vivekananda said, "First make the people of the country stand on their legs, by rousing their inner power, first let them learn to have good food and clothes and plenty of enjoyment then tell them how to be free from this bounding of enjoyment."[5]
4. **Low Status of Women** An important problem of the time of Vivekananda was the low social status of Indian women. He exclaimed, "It is very difficult to understand why in this country (India) so much difference is made between men and women, whereas the Vedanta declares that one and the same conscious Self is present in all beings."[6] He pointed out, "In the highest reality of the Parabrahman, there is no distinction of sex. We only notice this on the relative plane."[7] He suggested, "Women must be put in a position to solve their own problems in their own way. No one can or ought to do this for them. And our Indian women are as capable of doing it as any in the world."[8] Illiteracy was the main cause of the low status of women, according to Vivekananda. His disciple sister Nivedita organised women's education

---

1. Vivekananda, *The Complete Works*, Vol. IV (1966), Advaita Ashrama, Calcutta-14, p. 368.
2. *Ibid.*, Vol. 5th (1964), p. 145.
3. *Ibid.*
4. *Ibid.*, Vol. III, 1964, p. 204.
5. *Ibid.*, Vol. VII (1964), p. 182.
6. *Ibid.*, Vol. III, p. 214.
7. *Ibid.*, p. 219.
8. *Ibid*, Vol. V (1964), pp. 229-30.

in India. She established a Math for this purpose. Thus, Math observed all the rules of male missionaries and provided education for character. Vivekananda even prescribed physical training to women since he pointed out, "In the present day it has become necessary for them also to learn self-defence."[1] The education of women was considered a remedy for problems concerning marriage and family. Vivekananda pointed out the evil of senseless growth of population.

5. **Child Marriage** Another problem of the times of Vivekananda was child marriage. Expressing his feeling in this connection, Vivekananda said, "I have a strong hatred for child marriage... I would hate myself if I had such a diabolical custom directly or indirectly."[2] Explaining this problem Vivekananda said, "Oh, how, sweet is child-marriage... Can there be anything but love between husband and wife in such a marriage, such is the whine going round nowadays...The truth is that, in this country, parents and relatives can ruthlessly sacrifice the best interests of their children and others for their own selfish ends, to save themselves by compromise to society."[3] Education of women was suggested as one of the remedies for this state of affairs.
6. **Restriction of Inter-caste marriage** During this period strict restrictions were imposed upon inter-caste marriages. Pointing out to this problem Vivekananda said, "Reform we should have in many ways; who will be so foolish as to deny it? There is, for example, a good reason for inter-marriage in India, in the absence of which the race is becoming physically weaker day by day."[4] Vivekananda emphatically declared, "It is the inter-marriage between people of the same religion that I advocate."[5] He also pointed out the need of inter-provincial marriages. He said, "The time is yet very long in coming when marriages of that kind will be widely possible. Besides, it is not judicious now to go in for that all of sudden."[6] Referring to and condemning the evil of forbidding inter-caste marriage Vivekananda said, "Don't you see how in our society, marriage, being restricted for several hundred of years within the same sub-divisions of each caste, has come to such a pass nowadays as virtually to mean marital alliance between cousins and near relations; and how, for this very reason, the race is getting deteriorated physically, and consequently all sorts of diseases and other evils are finding a ready entrance into it?"[7] Suggesting remedies Vivekananda said, "It is only by widening the circle of marriage that we

1. *Ibid.*, Vol. V (1964), p. 342.
2. *Ibid.*. Vol. VIII (1964), p 365.
3. *Ibid.*, Vol. IV, p. 491.
4. *Ibid.*, Vol. V (1964), p. 334.
5. *Ibid.*, p. 340.
6. *Ibid.*
7. *Ibid*, Vol. V (1964), pp. 340-41.

can infuse a new and a different kind of blood into our progeny, so that they may be saved from...consequent evils."[1]

7. **Low Status of Backward Classes** Besides the low status of women, the Indian society during Vivekananda's period suffered with the evil of low status of the poor and down-trodden masses. Pointing out their disabilities Vivekananda said, "They have no chance, no escape, no way to climb up.... They sink lower every day; they feel the blows showered upon them by a cruel society and they do not know whence the blow comes. They have forgotten that they too are men."[2] Pointing out their importance in social fabric, Vivekananda said, "Whether the leadership of society be in the hands of those who monopolize learning or wield the power of riches or arms, the source of its power is always the subject masses. They are the backbone of the country, because they produce all wealth and food. They will certainly want the satisfaction of their material needs, less work, no oppression, no war, more food. The present system of distribution of wealth makes the poor poorer and the rich richer."[3] Vivekananda warned the rich and high caste people that the down-trodden will no more tolerate exploitation. He said, "Very soon they will get above you in position... You have so long oppressed these forebearing masses: now is the time for their retribution."[4] He pointed out, "The lower classes are gradually awakening to this fact making a united front. Masses of Europe and America have been the first to awaken and have already begun the fight. Signs of this awakening have shown themselves in India, too, as is evident from the number of strikes among the lower classes now-a-days. The upper classes will no longer be able to repress the lower, try they ever so much."[5] According to the historical insight of Vivekananda, the down-trodden class will give rise to many great men so that the backward may come up.
8. **Poverty** The most important social problem according to Vivekananda, however, was the utter poverty of Indian masses. While touring the Western countries he compared their standard of living with the standard of living of Indian masses and felt that life in India was generally sub-human. He realised that no spiritual uplift is possible without first solving the problem of poverty. He asked, "In all India, there are, say, a hundred thousand really spiritual men and women, who for the spiritualization of these three hundred millions be sunk in savagery and starvation.?"[6] He pointed out, "Empty stomach and religion go ill together. It was mockery to offer religion to a starving man."[7]

---

1. *Ibid.*, p. 341.
2. *Ibid.*, Vol. IV, p. 468.
3. *Ibid.*, Vol. V (1964). p. 45.
4. *Ibid.*, Vol. VII (1964), p. 148.
5. *Ibid.*, p. 149.
6. *Ibid.*, Vol. IV (1966), p. 368.
7. *Ibid.*

9. **Crisis of Character** But the basic cause behind poverty, according to Swami Vivekananda, was not economic as it was for Karl Marx, but moral. Most of the problems, according to him, show the crisis of character. It is hence that his education aimed at man-making or character building. Holding the rich people responsible for the poverty of the masses Vivekananda said, "You, the upper classes of India, do you think you are alive? It is among those whom your ancestors despised as 'walking carrion', that the little of vitality there is still in India is to be found; and it is you who are the real 'walking corpses'...You merge yourselves in the void and disappear, and let 'New India' arise in your place. Let her arise out of the peasant's cottage, grasping the plough... Let her spring from the grocer's shop, from beside the oven of the fritter seller. Let her emanate from the factory, from marts, and from markets. Let her emerge from groves and forests from hills and mountains."[1] Like Karl Marx Vivekananda realised that the backbone of the nation is not the rich class but the so-called down-trodden people. Pointing out their importance he said, "The Indian social order is but the reflex of the infinite Universal Motherhood... the lower classes, the ignorant, the poor, the illiterate, the cobbler; the sweeper are its flesh and blood."[2] On the other hand, "Rich men... are merely the ornaments, the decorations of the country. It is the millions of poor lower class people who are its life."[3] Therefore, Vivekananda concluded, "The only hope of India is from the masses. The upper classes are physically and morally dead."[4] These words are no less prophetic than that of Karl Marx. Vivekananda was the Karl Marx of India, the vedantin version of the great Western revolutionary. He sounded the death-knell of capitalism in India on the basis of his practical Vedanta. He exhorted the leaders to rebuild Indian society upon the ancient principle of Swadharma, allotting each person a social role according to his capacities. He said, "If the Brahmin has more aptitude for learning on the ground of heredity than the Pariah, spend no more money on the Brahmin's education, but spend all on the Pariah. Give to the weak, for there all the gift is needed...Our poor people, these down-trodden masses of India, therefore, require to hear and to know what they really are."[5] Thus, Vivekananda sought to build up a new social order in India, real socialissm, real democracy, a society free from exploitation. His motto was elevation of the masses without hindering their religion. It is here that he differs from Karl Marx. His solution of social evils was basically spiritual and not material. He asked, "Can you give them

---

1. *Ibid.*, Vol. V(1964), p. 45.
2. *Ibid.*, Vol. IV (1966), p. 480.
3. *Ibid.*, Vol. VII, p. 354.
4. *Ibid.*, Vol. V (1964), p. 81.
5. *Ibid.*, Vol. III (1964), p. 193.

(the masses) their lost individuality without making them loose their innate spiritual nature."[1] This phenomena of the rise of down-trodden, according to Vivekananda, was universal. By his wide tour of the West, Vivekananda developed cosmopolitan vision of the rise of humanity. In spite of being a staunch nationalist he was equally a humanist and internationalist. He solved the Indian problems in a wider perspective involving the problems of total humanity. As he said, "The rising of the Shudras will take place first in Russia, and then in China, India will rise next and will play a vital role in shaping the future world."[2] He also professed, "Europe, the centre of the manifestation of material energy, will crumble into dust within fifteen years, if she is not mindful to change her position, to shift her ground and make spirituality the basis of her life."[3] Thus, while admitting with Karl Marx the ideal of creation of a society without exploitation, Vivekananda did not agree with Karl Marx concerning the means of revolution. Marxist concept of class struggle and expropriation of expropriators was, according to Vivekananda, a levelling down of the moral fabric of the society. He, on the other hand, sought to raise the moral level of society, "not by bringing down the higher, but by raising the lower up to the level of the higher."[4] This makes for the fundamental difference between Indian and Western thinking on moral issues. This again makes for the distinction of Indian brand of socialism which Vivekananda used to preach.

METAPHYSICAL BACKGROUND

Metaphysics of Vivekananda is based upon the philosophy of Vedanta. According to Vedanta philosophy Brahman is the ultimate reality, the world is a *Maya* and the ultimate end of the jiva is to attain salvation by being one with Ishwar or Brahman. The Vedanta philosophy is expressed through the *Mahavakyas — Aham Brahma Asmi, Tat Twam Asi, Sarvam Khalvidam Brahma* etc. These Mahavakyas form the basis of the message of Vivekananda.

The Ultimate Reality

The central idea in the philosophy of Vivekananda, as it is in that of the Vedanta, is the Brahman, the Sacchidanand. Expressing his Central teaching about the ultimate reality Vivekananda said, "In the Advaita philosophy the whole universe is one in the self which is called 'Brahman'. That self when it appears behind this little universe, the body, is the soul ... Universal self which is beyond the universal modification of 'Prakriti' is what is called 'Isvara', the Supreme Ruler, God."[4] 'Isvara' alone is the creator, sustainer and

1. *Ibid.*, Vol. V, p. 29.
2. Datta, B.N. Vivekananda *Patriot-Prophet*, Nav Bharat Press, Calcutta, 1954, p. 335.
3. Vivekananda, S., *India and Her Problems*, p. 39.
4. Vivekananda, S., *Complete Works*, Vol. III, p. 194.

destroyer of the world and its destiny. "But, the Vedantic Brahman accepted by Vivekananda is neither the concrete Absolute of Hegel nor the 'Sunya' of the Madhyamikas nor the 'Alayavijnana' of the Yogacaras. It resembles to some extent the 'Tathata' of Asvaghosa but the difference is that the latter (Asvaghosa) is not very emphatic on the mystical perception of the 'Tathata.'"[1] Drawing the social implications of this metaphysical idea Vivekananda said, "Thus, there is a great opening for the Vedanta to do beneficial work both here and elsewhere. This wonderful idea of the sameness and omnipresence of the Supreme Soul has to be preached for the amelioration and elevation of the human race, here and elsewhere. Wherever there is evil and wherever there is ignorance and want of knowledge, I have found out by experience that all evil comes, as our scripture says, relying upon differences, and that all good comes from faith in equality, in the underlying sameness and oneness of things. This is the great Vedantic ideal...I base my teachings on the great Vedantic truth of the sameness and omnipresence of the Soul of the Universe."[2] Vivekananda maintained that there is a harmony between the concepts of Vedanta and Science. Brahman is the Absolute, Ishwar is primal creative energy, Prana is force and Akash is the matter.

The absolute of metaphysics is the God of religion. From the religious point of view, Brahman has been called Isvara. Jiva is the Atman in material and mental bondage. This bondage is due to karma which determines the birth.

Maya

Though Vivekananda called his philosophy practical Vedanta yet he accepted the philosophy of Maya. His position here is far from being consistent as on the one hand he accepts the word as Maya in the terms of Advaita, while on the other hand he equally emphasizes the role of karma and activity in the world. Like his predecessors of Advaita Vedanta he admits, "The very question why the Infinite became the finite is an impossible one, for it is self-contradictory. This is far from being an explanation of the world." Sri Aurobindo, on the other hand, has very well explained the world by the concept of Lila and condemned the concept of Maya.

Immortality

The concept of immortality is the postulate of the ideal of freedom, since if man is immortal by nature his goal of life is freedom. The freedom in the ultimate sense, is liberation. Man, according to Indian philosophy, is not subservient to anything, the state, the community, the economic factors, even his body and intellect. Delivering his famous lecture to Americans Vivekananda called them, "children of immortal bliss." Explaining the implication of the immortality of man he further said, "Children of immortal bliss — what a sweet, what a hopeful name! Allow me to call you, brethren, by that sweet name — heirs

1. Verma, *V.P., Modern Indian Political Thought*, Laxmi Narain Agarwal, Agra, 1971, p. 86.
2. Vivekananda, S., *Collected Works*, Vol. III, p. 194.

of immortal bliss — yea, the Hindu refuses to call you sinners. Ye are the Children of God, the sharers of immortal Bliss, holy and perfect beings. Ye divinities on earth — sinners! It is a sin to call a man so; it is a standing libel on human nature. Come up, O lions! and shake off the delusion that you are sheep; you are not matter, ye are not bodies; matter is your servant, not you the servant of matter."[1] This is the spiritual psychology, the basis of spiritual axiology supported by all the contemporary Indian philosophers. This again is the spiritual, political and social philosophy advocated by them. In the words of Sri Aurobindo, "The individual does not owe his ultimate allegiance either to the state which is a machine or to the community which is a part of life and not the whole of life: his allegiance must be to the truth, the self, the spirit, the divine which is in him and in all; not to subordinate or lose himself in the mass, but to find and express that truth of being in himself, and help the community and humanity in its seeking for its own truth and fulness of being must be his real object of existence."[2]

The nature of immortality, according to Indian philosophy, is an ontological truth. It is a law of nature and a law of Divine. It is the inner principle of evolution. It is the meaning of the cycle of transmigration. It is the secret of human existence In the words of Vivekananda, "The whole of nature is that book which the soul is reading. Each life, as it were, is one page of that book; and that read, it is turned over, and so on and on, until the whole of the book is finished, and the soul becomes perfect, having got all the experiences of nature, yet at the same time it never moved, nor came nor went; it was only gathering experiences."[3] The entire cycle of birth and rebirth is meant to give the self various types of experiences so that it may understand its real nature and become free. As for the ancient Vedanta so for Vivekananda, "The soul is the unchangeable One, the immortal, the pure, the ever-blessed One."[4] This immortality, as is clear to everyone in this life, is not the nature of mundane life. The fact of that is too potent to be contradicted by anyone. There is however no place for despair, since the journey of self lies beyond mundane life. As Vivekananda pointed out, "Immortal life is contradiction in terms, for life, being a compound, cannot be immortal. True Being is undifferentiated and eternal."[5]

Immortality and Freedom

The concepts of freedom and immortality are interdependent. Not only freedom follows from immortality but immortality also follows freedom. Man's immortality is a direct corrolary of his essential freedom. The drama of the present life is not the last act in the journey of man. He had a prehuman past and has a post-human future. The process of evolution is not linear

1. Vivekananda S., *The Complete Works*, Advaita Ashrama, Almora, 1946, p. 9.
2. Sri Aurobindo, *The Life Divine*, American Edition, p. 930.
3. Vivekananda, S., *The Complete Works*. Vol. VI, 1947.
4. *Ibid.*, p. 22.
5. *Ibid.*, p. 42.

but spiral but the process goes on till the self achieved freedom. Explaining the close connection between freedom and immortality, Vivekananda said, "Freedom is inseparably connected with immortality. To be free one must be above the laws of nature. Law exists so long as we are ignorant. When knowledge comes, then we find that law is nothing but freedom in ourselves. The will can never be free, because it is the slave of cause and effect. But the "I" behind the will is free, and this is the Self. "I am free" — that is the basis on which to build and live. And freedom means immortality."[1]

The Concept of Freedom

The Western philosophers have failed to understand the self due to their limitation to the rational method. Agnosticism in metaphysics is the logical conclusion of rational psychology and rational metaphysics. The final verdict in this field has been rightly given by the German philosopher Immanual Kant. Indian philosophy however, considers realisation as a method above reason. To know is to be. Realisation succeeds where reason fails. Therefore, while appreciating Kant's agnosticism in rational philosophy, Vivekananda does not accept it as man's destiny. To quote his words, "Kant has proved beyond all doubt that we cannot penetrate beyond the tremendous dead wall called reason. But that is the very first idea upon which all Indian thought takes its stand, and dares to seek and succeed in finding something higher than reason, where alone the explanation of the present state is to be found."[2] Agnosticism logically leads to scepticism. In spite of Kant's Herculian efforts to answer Hume, the destiny of philosophy, as Hume predicted, remains undefended. If reason is the only method, philosophy is bound to end in contradictions. For Indians, however, philosophy is not a rational knowledge. The search of *Darshan* is nothing less than complete realisation. If philosophy fails to satisfy man the only alternative is *Darshan*. Vivekananda rightly pointed out, "If a man is agnostic of everything but money, fame and name, he is only a fraud."[3] And man is not a fraud nor is he destined to an evolutionary failure. Since the ancient Vedanta to this day Indian philosophers have been always optimistic about the spiritual destiny of man and humanity. Whatever may be the gloomy prediction of the contemporary Western futurist thinkers, Indian philosophers have firmly believed that man will overcome the present rational *impasse*. This dogmatic optimism is based upon the realisation that where reason fails, intuition helps. According to the Indian philosophers self cannot be known by senses, the intellect or the reason, but it can be known through direct identity. If the reality of self is not accepted, Vivekananda asks, "Why are we going through this circle all the time; what reason can explain the world."[4] Secondly, "What reason is there," asks Vivekananda, "to believe

1. *Ibid.*, p. 50.
2. *Ibid.*, Vol. I. 1965, p 199.
3. *Ibid.*
4. *Ibid.*

in the testimony of the senses? If reason is all in all it leaves us no place to stand on this side of nihilism."[1]

Liberation is identity with God, the infinite. In the words of Vivekananda, "Each soul is potentially divine. The goal is to manifest this divine within, by controlling nature, external and internal. Do this either by work, or worship, or psychic control, or philosophy, by one, or more, or all of these — and be free. This is the whole of religion. Doctrines, or dogmas, or rituals, or books, or temples, or forms, are but secondary details."[2] Elsewhere he puts it more clearly when he says, "hear ye children of Immortality, Hear ye Devas who live in higher spheres, I have found out a ray beyond all darkness, beyond all doubt. I have found the Ancient One. The way to this is contained in the Upanishads. On earth we die. In heaven we die. In the highest heaven we die. It is only when we reach God that we attain life and become immortal."[3] This God, according to Upanishads, is not extra-terrestrial. He interpenetrates the universe. He is human and in everything. Thus, it is clear that Moksha cannot be called an individualistic or extra-terrestrial goal. Sri Aurobindo, particularly, has interpreted it in the light of the consciousness of the modern man. Even the most recent exponents of Indian Yoga such as Rajneesh, Mahesha and others have given an interpretation of Moksha which is acceptable even to the Western men and women. The popularity which Yoga is receiving these days in the West shows that in it Indian culture has offered something which is valuable in all times and climes.

In the end liberation can be best defined as freedom. In the words of Vivekananda, "The idea of freedom is the only true idea of salvation — freedom from everything, the senses, whether of pleasure or pain, from good as well as evil."[4]

Liberation, according to Vivekananda, can be achieved by all the three traditional paths of Jnana Yoga, Karma Yoga and Bhakti Yoga. In his own circumstances, however, Karma Yoga was the best way to realise liberation. Explaining liberation through Karma Yoga he said, "But the life of God is infinite. Who can live a moment, breathe a moment, if this all powerful One does not will it? He is the ever active Providence. All power is His and within His command. Through His command the winds blow, the sun shines, the earth lives, and death stalks upon the earth. He is the all in all; He is all and in all. We can only worship Him. Give up all fruits of work; do good for its own sake; then alone will come perfect non-attachment. The bonds of the heart will thus break, and we shall reap perfect freedom. This freedom is indeed the goal of Karma Yoga."[5] Those who think that Indian philosophy docs not find a suitable place for ethics forget that Indian philosophers considered ethics

1. *Ibid.*
2. *Ibid.*, Vol. I, 1946, p. 119.
3. *Ibid.*, Vol. VI, 1947, p. 53.
4. *Ibid.*, p. 59.
5. *Ibid.*, Vol. I, 1946, p. 105.

as a part of spiritual goal. Ethics in India did not stop only at the rational limit, it trascended to supra-rational, the spiritual. Thus freedom is both an ontological as well as moral ideal. As Vivekananda rightly pointed out, "The greatest goodness is the highest freedom. Our aim should be to allow the individual to move towards this freedom."[1]

Freedom is best expressed in the freedom of will since on the terrestrial plane, freedom of will is the expression of essential freedom. Clarifying the concept of freedom of will Vivekananda said, "Freedom of the will — it is as you feel you are here to act. But this freedom is a species of necessity. There is one infinite link before, after and between the thought and the action, but the latter takes the name of freedom — like a bird flitting through a bright room. We feel the freedom and feel that it has no other cause. We cannot go beyond consciousness, therefore we feel we are free. We can trace it no further than consciousness. God alone feels the real freedom. Mahapurushas (saints) feel themselves identified with God; hence they also feel the real freedom."[2]

Among the systems of Indian philosophy liberation has been interpreted both positively and negatively. But the most significant interpretation of liberation is neutral. Neutral interpretation may be found in Samkhya and Yoga philosophy. According to Samkhya Moksha means complete elimination from the three types of pains and a status of absolute detachment of the self. Yoga aimed at the attainment of a consciousness absolutely detached and free from all impulses. The tradition of Yoga started in the Vedas and it has been constantly developed and practised by Indian philosophers to our own time. It has been the most significant contribution of Indian culture to the world. It gives what is known as liberation while living, which has been accepted as possible, not only by the orthodox schools of Indian philosophy but also by hetrodox schools of philosophy — the Jainism and Buddhism. Explaining this ideal Vivekananda said, "Thus we realise that all these phenomena are but the reflections, bifurcated or manifolded of the One existence. Truth-bliss-unity-my real Self and the reality of everything else. Then and then only is it possible to do good without evil, for such a soul has known and got the control of the material of which both good and evil are manufactured, and he alone can manifest one or the other as he likes, and we know he manifests only good. This is the Jivan-mukta — the living free — the goal of the Vedanta as of all other philosophies."[3]

Spirituality

This is the spiritual life, the whole, of which moral life is the part. The nature of this spirituality has been explained by Sri Aurobindo in these words, "Spirituality is in its essence an awakening to the inner reality of our being, to a spirit, self and soul which is other than our mind, life and body, an inner aspiration to know, to feel, to be That, to enter into contact with the greater Reality beyond and pervading the universe which inhabits our own being also,

1. *Ibid.*, Vol. VI, 1947. p. 66.
2. *Ibid.*, p. 83.
3. *Ibid.*, *p.* 342.

to be in communion with It and union with It, and a turning, a conversion, a transformation of our whole being as a result of the aspiration, the contact, the union, a growth or waking into a new nature."[1] Thus, spirituality is a dynamics of a higher luminous and infinite consciousness. It is the breaking of the lid, the tearing of covering or the opening of a door to Divine, which alone can fulfil the end sought by all science, ethics, religion and philosophy. It is truly realised in yoga. According to Upanishads, ignorance is the cause of bondage and liberation is the result of knowledge. In the ignorance there is no distinction of the eternal and ephemeral. In it there is dualism, egoism and plurality. It is the intellectual knowledge having the distinction of the subject and object. Liberation is the freedom from such a knowledge which is in fact ignorance. Liberation, according to Indian thinking, is not rational but a suprarational status. This suprarational status determines the *summum bonum* in ethics as well. According to Vivekananda, morality is not an end in itself; mukti is its end, it is only a means for the achievement of liberation. From Vedas to Sri Aurobindo, Indian thinkers have always considered moksha as the aim of life. It is however, wrong to consider liberation as the sole ideal of human life. Indian thinkers aimed at a four-fold scheme of values in which each was valuable. Moksha was the last but not the only value. In the realisation of other values however, man ultimately aims at the final value liberation. As Vivekananda, puts it, "There is unconscious struggle of the human with the spiritual, of the lower with the higher mind... to preserve one's 'individuality'... we are born rebels... No law for us. As long as we obey the laws we are like machines, and on goes the universe, and we cannot break it.. Freedom is the song of the soul."[2] The same idea has been differently expressed when Vivekananda says, "With every movement, man asserts his freedom... From highest thinker to the most ignorant man, everyone knows that he is free... (but) his will is as rigorously bound by the laws of causation as the growth of any little plant or the falling of a stone, and, yet, through all this bondage runs the indestructible idea of freedom."[3]

REAL FREEDOM

Explaining the importance of freedom and its variety Vivekananda said, "Freedom is the one goal of all nature, sentient or insentient and consciously or unconsciously, everything is struggling towards that goal. The freedom which the saint seeks is very different from that which the robber seeks. The freedom loved by the saint leads him to the enjoyment of infinite, unspeakable bliss, while that on which the robber has set his heart only forges other bonds for his soul."[4] Thus, freedom to enjoy the objects of senses is not the real freedom. Defining real freedom, Vivekananda said, "Blessedness,

1. Quoted by Sharma, R.N., *The Philosophy of Sri Aurobindo*, IIIrd Edition, 1977, Kedar Nath Ram Nath, Meerut, p. 164.
2. Vivekananda, S., *The Complete Works*, Vol. I,1965, pp. 334-35.
3. *Ibid*, Vol. II, pp. 382-83.
4. *Ibid*, Vol. I, 1965, pp. 108-9.

eternal peace arising from perfect freedom, is the highest concept of religion, underlying all the ideas of God in Vedanta, absolutely free Existence, not bound by anything, no change, no nature, nothing that can produce a change in Him. This same freedom is in you and in me and is the only real freedom."[1]

Indian philosophy has interpreted everything in terms of spirituality. Hence, everybody has been enjoined to follow Dharma. Freedom has also been interpreted in the spiritual sense. It is not absence of restraint or self-control or the liberty to do whatever one likes. It requires renunciation and not indulgence. As Vivekananda points out, "He is free, he is great, who turns his back upon the world, who has renounced everything, who has controlled his passion, and who thirsts for peace. One may gain political and social independence, but if he is a slave to his passions and desires, he cannot feel the pure joy of real freedom."[2] Vivekananda is against any slavery to mechanical civilization. Man, according to him, as according to ancient Vedanta, is essentially spiritual. Therefore, instead of subordinating ourselves to material commodities, we should seek freedom from matter. It is so since the self is free from material laws. Vivekananda is against man's subordination to the nature. Man, on the other hand, should conquer physical nature As Vivekananda puts it, "The goal of each soul is freedom, mastery-freedom from the slavery of matter and thought, mastery of external and internal nature."[3] This is not only the goal of the individual but also the collectivity. Both the self and the Nature aspire after it. To quote Vivekananda, "Consciously or unconsciously the whole universe is going towards that goal."[4] "... Our earth is trying to fly away from the sun, and the moon from the earth. Everything has a tendency to infinite dispersion."[5]

Thus, the concept of freedom in the philosophy of Vivekananda synthesises materialism and idealism. Man has a body which is governed by natural laws. Real freedom is not possible for the body. Whoever is born he must die. But his death is the characteristic of the body. The self is neither bound nor subject to death. It is free as well as immortal. Thus, man is a combination of both bondage and freedom. The individual is "free and not free at the same time: never free on the earthly plane, but ever free on the spiritual."[6] Freedom is characteristic to man. Nature becomes self-conscious in man. Therefore man aspires to be free from nature. Vivekananda regarded man as "the highest being in creation because he alone attains to freedom."[7] Man is not a sinner. While Christianity makes too much of evil in the life of man, Hinduism insists upon bliss as the essence of life. Vivekananda does

1. *Ibid*, Vol. I, 1946, p. 336.
2. *Ibid.*, Vol. VI, 1947, p. 124.
3. *Ibid.*, Vol. I, 1965, p. 172.
4. *Ibid.*, p. 421.
5. *Ibid.*, p. 108.
6. *Ibid.*, Vol. VII, 1964, p. 32.
7. *Ibid.*, Vol. II, p. 258.

not agree with the deterministic explanations of human nature. He rejects the Marxist economic determinism in the individual as well as collective life. All determinism is foreign to human nature. In the words of Vivekananda, "Now, on one hand, this denial of freedom as an illusion is no explanation: on the other hand, why not say that the idea of necessity or bondage or causation is an illusion of the ignorant... Therefore, the only way left to us is to admit that the body is not free, neither is the will but that there must be something beyond both the mind and body which is free."[1]

Freedom is beyond both the subject and object. Indian philosophy aims at an ideal beyond both good and evil. As Vivekananda points out, "A golden chain is as much a chain as an iron one. There is a thorn in my finger, and I use another to take the first one out; and when I have taken it out, I throw both of them aside. I have no necessity for keeping the second thorn, because both are thorns after all." Thus Vivekananda emphasises that "the ultimate freedom means freedom from both good and evil tendencies."[2] Freedom from good and evil requires making spirituality as the basis of life. Ignorance is not bliss. It is rather bondage and death. Indian philosophers have always considered ignorance to be bondage. Misery is also a form of ignorance. As against the Buddhist doctrine that everything is misery, Hindu philosophers maintained Ananda (bliss) as the essence of life. As Vivekananda points out, "Life is of very little value, if it is a life in the dark groping through ignorance and misery."[3] "Ignorance is the mother of all the evil and all the misety we see."[4] This ignorance can be removed by spiritual knowledge or rather spiritual realisation. Therefore, Vivekananda said, "We may convert every house in the country into a charity asylum, we may fill the land with hospitals, but the misery of man will still continue to exist until man's character changes."[5] He further writes, "If a man's wants can be removed for an hour, it is helping him indeed; if his wants can be removed for a year, it will be more help to him; but if his wants can be removed for ever, it is surely the greatest help that can be given to him; spiritual knowledge is the only thing that can destroy our miseries for ever; any other knowledge satisfies wants only for a time."[6]

Freedom and Equality

Freedom is linked with equality. Laying emphasis upon the value of equality Vivekananda points out, "I have found out by experience that all evil comes, as our scripture says, relying upon differences, and that all good comes from faith in equality, in the underlying sameness and oneness of things. This is the great Vedantic ideal... I base my teachings on the great Vedantic truth

1. *Ibid.*, pp. 282-83.
2. *Selections from Swami Vivekananda* (1963), Advaita Ashrama, p. 43.
3. Vivekananda S., *The Complete Works*, Vol. I, 1965, p. 52.
4. *Ibid.*, p. 53.
5. *Ibid.*
6. *Ibid.*, p. 52.

of the sameness and omnipresence of the soul of the Universe."[1] Freedom is meaningless without equality. Equality, on the other hand, is not equality of endowment but equality of opportunity. In this sense equality is the "way to freedom; inequality, the way to bondage. No man and no nation can attempt to gain physical freedom without physical equality, nor mental freedom without mental equality."[2]

The Method To Achieve Freedom

Contemporary Indian philosophers agree with the ancient Indian thinking that Yoga is the best way to achieve liberation. This yoga however, is neither Raja Yoga nor Karma Yoga or Bhakti Yoga alone. It is a synthesis of the three. Agreeing with Bhagwadgita that yoga is essentially a balance in body and mind, Vivekananda says, "A Yogi must avoid the two extremes of luxury and austerity. He must not fast, nor torture his flesh. He who does so, says the Gita, cannot be a Yogi: He who fasts, he who keeps awake, he who sleeps much, he who works too much, he who does no work, none of these can be a Yogi."[3]

The Message of Vivekananda

Thus the message of Vivekananda to the world is the message of freedom from all types of bondage. It is a message to shed all fears since man is essentially divine. It is a message to be one with the cosmos and the eternity. To quote a couplet from the great Master:

> From dreams awake, from bonds be free.
> Be not afraid. This mystery,
> My shadow, cannot frighten me,
> Know once for all that I am He.[4]

PHILOSOPHY OF HISTORY

The philosophy of history of Swami Vivekananda was very much similar to that of Hegel. Like Hegel he believed that the world is the march of the Absolute. Here his interpretation is opposed to the economic interpretation of history advanced by Karl Marx because the Absolute according to Vivekananda is not Matter but the Spirit. He pointed out different periods in the history of Philosophy, Religion and Society. He emphasised the role of dialectical process in social progress. He accepted the role of great individuals in social progress. He pointed out the importance of each of the Varna in social history and maintained that each will rule one after the other. He proclaimed the downfall of European culture and civilization like other contemporary philosophers of history. He could visualise that the down-trodden class of

1. *Ibid.*, Vol. III, p. 194.
2. *Ibid.*, Vol. IV, 1966, p. 328.
3. *Ibid.*, Vol. I, 1946 p. 136.
4. *Ibid.*, Vol. VI, 1947, p. 150.

Sudras will rise everywhere in world and rule for some time. Explaining his vision of the future course of history, Vivekananda said, "Yes: the Sudras of the world will rise. And that is the dictate of social dynamics that is 'Shivam'. It is as clear as day-light that the entire Orient will have resurrection or build anew a human world. Lo! the future greatness of China, and in the wake of it, of all the Asiatic nations. I can see, through the veil, the shadow of coming events of the world."[1] His vision of history has come out true not only in the case of China and Russia but also in the case of other countries. He maintained that the future course of history requires a meeting of the East and West for mutual good. In 1895 he wrote, "Europe is on the edge of a volcano. If the fire is not extinguished by a flood of spirituality, it will erupt."[2] This warning came true in the form of the First World War after 19 years.

SOCIAL PHILOSOPHY

Society and Social Institutions

Society, according to Vivekananda, is not a human creation but created by God himself. He said, "Love, Renunciation, Unselfishness — three great manifestations of spirituality — from these alone can rise any society, and stand. Neither physical prowess, nor economic superiority, nor practical dexterity can form such a basis."[3] Thus, against the Western idea of society advanced by Hobbes and others, Vivekananda believed love and sacrifice to be the basis of society. This emphasis is characteristic of Indian culture. In the tradition of Indian philosophy, Vivekananda believed that there is an organic relationship between the individual and the society and therefore the good of either depends upon the other. Explaining this intimate relationship Vivekananda said, "The aggregate of many individuals is called Samashti (the whole), and each individual is called Vyashti (a part). You and I — each is Vyashti, society is Samashti. You, I, an animal, a bird, a worm, an insect, a tree, a creeper, the earth, a planet, a star — each is Vyashti, while this Universe is Samasthi."[4] Thus society is the same as the Absolute. It is a divine creation. It is an aggregate of numerous individuals whose self-sacrifice is required for its welfare. The individual starting from individuality should gradually transcend to the stage of identity with society where collective happiness becomes his own happiness. Religion is the backbone of this structure. It is *Dharma* as maintained by the ancient Indian thinkers. In the tradition of ancient Indian concept of *Purusharthas* Vivekananda maintained that *Dharma* or religion is the keynote of the social solidarity. Explaining this idea he said, "The sole, the whole force, the whole sanction, the whole cementing power behind society is one and only one... *viz.* Religion, Spiritualism, Other-worldliness. Society

1. Swami Vivekananda, *Patriot and Prophet*, pp. 334-5.
2. Vivekananda, S., *A Biography*, pp. 163-4.
3. *Centenary Volume*, p. 359.
4. *Ibid.*, p. 488.

must, of course, provide for economic well-being and physical comforts. But the final aim, as everywhere else, is the development and perfection of the soul — whatever it may mean."[1] This religion was the Vedanta, the revelation through the Vedas, the spiritual heritage of the Hindus. According to Vivekananda this religion is not only the basis of society but the central binding force of the national life. As opposed to the idea of a secular nation or a national life without religion Vivekananda said, "In India religious life forms the centre, the keynote of the whole music of national life; and if any nation attempts to throw off its national vitality, the direction which has become its own through the transmission of centuries, that nation dies, if it succeeds in the attempt. And, therefore, if you succeed in the attempt to throw off your religion and take up either politics or society, or any other thing as your centre, as the vitality of your national life, the result will be that you will become extinct. To prevent this you must make all and everything work through that vitality of your religion."[2]

Social Stratification : The Varna System

In contrast to the Western system of economic classes, Vivekananda believed that the ancient Indian system of social stratification based upon varna is still the most scientific system. Calling it a kind of social communism he said, "In India, we have social communism, with the light of Advaita — that is, spiritual individualism — playing on and around it; in Europe, you are socially individualists, but your thought is dualistic, which is spiritual communism. Thus, the one consists of social institutions, hedged in by individualistic thought while the other is made up of individualist institutions, within the hedge of communistic thought. While Manu laid emphasis on the superiority of Brahmins, Vivekananda condemned the doctrine of *Adhikarvad.* He on the other hand, championed the concept of spiritual equality in the Varna system. He was, however, not against giving the highest place to the learned and the scholars called Brahmins. He was rather proud of the fact that Varna system assigns highest place to the Brahmins. He pointed out that "Spiritual intellect is the central fact of Indian civilisation, all throughout the ages. And all the social customs, even political injunctions, invariably reflect it as natural. Hence, the head of Indian society is not the warrior, but the scholar, the intellectually high and the spiritually sublime wise man — the Brahmin, literally meaning, one whose refuge is Brahman, the Absolue."[3] Pointing out the difference between the Western society and India concerning social stratification Vivekananda said, "In every other country, the highest honour belongs to the Kshatriya — the man of the sword. In India the highest honour belongs to the man of peace — the 'Shramana' or the 'Brahmin', the man of God."[4]

---

1. *Ibid.*, p. 354.
2. Vivekananda, S., *The Complete Works*, Vol. III, p. 220.
3. *Centenary Memorial Volume*, p. 365.
4. *Complete Works,* Vol. IV, p. 243.

Thus, the social thought of Vivekananda can be termed as socialistic. In his own words, "Thus Western man is born individualistic, the Hindu is socialistic, entirely socialistic."[1] This is Neo-vedanta socialism which we shall explain in sequence.

Criticism of Caste-system

In spite of his immense praise for Varna system, Vivekananda was well aware of the fact that the present degeneration of that ancient idea into a rigid caste system is the cause of the degeneration of the nation. He condemned the present caste system in very clear words. He said, "In spite of all the ravings of the priests, caste is simply a crystallised social institution which after doing its service is now filling the atmosphere of India with its stench, and it can only be removed by giving back to the people their lost social individuality."[2] He rebuked those who considered following of the caste restrictions necessary for religion. Distinguishing between religion and caste system he said, "In religion there is no caste. A man from the highest caste and a man from the lowest may become a monk in India and the two castes become equal. The caste system is opposed to the religion of Vedanta. "[3] Thus Vivekananda, in tradition with the social reformers of the Renaissance period, strongly advocated the abolition of inequalities based upon caste system. He wrote, "Caste is a social custom and all our great preachers have tried to break it down. Buddhism downwards, every sect has preached against caste, and every time it has only riveted the chains. Beginning from Buddha down to Rammohan Roy, everyone made the mistake of holding caste to be a religious institution and tried to pull down religion and caste all together, and failed."[4]

In spite of the above-mentioned severe criticism of caste system Vivekananda realized that this stratification cannot be uprooted unless some better substitute is available. Comparing even the present caste system with the Western class system of social stratification, Vivekananda found it better. Since no society can exist without some sort of social stratification, Vivekananda advised that the present caste system may be maintained only if we could eliminate casteism. He said, "What caste really is not one in a million understands. There is no country in the world without caste. In India from caste we reach to the point where there is no caste. Caste is based throughout on that principle. The plan in India is to make everybody Brahmin, the Brahmin being the ideal of humanity. If you read the history of India you will find that the attempts have always been made to raise the lower classes. Many are the classes that have been raised. Many more will follow till the whole world will become Brahmin. That is the plan. We have only to raise them without bringing down anybody. And this has mostly to be done by Brahmins themselves, because it

1. Vivekananda, S., *Women of India*, p. 20.
2. Vivekananda, S., *The Complete Works*, Vol. V, p. 23.
3. *Ibid.*, Vol. III, p. 1.
4. *Ibid.*, Vol. V, pp. 22-3.

is the duty of every aristocracy to dig its own grave; and the sooner it does so, the better for all. No time should be lost. Indian caste is better than the caste which prevails in Europe or America."[1] Thus, the idea underlying the caste system, according to Vivekananda, is to evolve every individual of the society to the level of Brahmin, the supreme and best human individual. Thus, caste as a social institution has been given by God to India. Therefore, there is hardly any question of abolishing the caste system. Suggesting re-adjustment of the ancient system according to contemporary needs, Vivekananda said, "From the time of Upanishads down to the present day, nearly all our great teachers have wanted to break through the barriers of caste, *i.e.,* caste in its degenerated state, not the original system, what little good you see in the present caste clings to it from the original caste, which was the most glorious social institution."[2] It should be noted here that similar ideas can be traced to our Renaissance thinkers as well as the contemporary Indian social philosophers.

Some sort of social grouping or stratification is necessary for a social life. Social stratification requires social differentiation. Differentiation, however, need not lead to privileges. It should be accepted only as a natural order. Condemning the provision of special privileges for the higher caste in Hindu social system Vivekananda said, "Caste is good: That is the only natural way of evolving life. Men must form themselves into groups, and you cannot get rid of that. Wherever you go there will be caste. But that does not mean that there should be these privileges. They should be knocked on the head. If you teach Vedanta to the fisherman he will say, "I am as good a man as you, I am a fisherman, you are a philosopher, but I have the same God in me, as you have in you. And that is what we want, no privilege for anyone, equal chances for all, let everyone be taught that the divine is within, and everyone will work his own salvation."[3]

Condemnation of Untouchability

The chief evil of casteism is untouchability. It is this evil that is at the basis of all the condemnation of casteism. Like other social thinkers before him Swami Vivekananda severely condemned untouchability. He called it don't-touchism. Explaining this evil and its consequence he lamented about the present degeneration and said, "The paths of knowledge, devotion and yoga — all have gone, and now there remains only that of don't-touchism — don't touch me: don't touch me : The whole world is impure and I alone am pure. Lucid Brahmajnana : Bravo! Great God: Now-a-days Brahman is neither in the recesses of the heart, nor in he highest heaven, nor in all beings — now he is in the cooking pot. Formerly the characteristic of a noble minded was to please the whole universe by one's numerous acts of service, "But now it is — I am pure and the whole world is impure..."[4]

1. *Ibid.,* p. 214.
2. *Ibid.,* Vol. V, p. 198.
3. *Ibid.,* Vol. III, pp. 245-6.
4. *Ibid.,* Vol. VII, p. 276.

Vivekananda's objections against untouchability were not only social but also philosophical and religious. Untouchability is against the essential spirit of Vedanta which preaches equality of all selves. It is against the socialist idea. Vivekananda has elaborately described in his writings his painful experiences of the disabilities suffered by the untouchable castes. He appealed to Hindus to rise above this petty mentality and to develop love and selflessness for selfishness and narrowness is death while expansion and selflessness is life. He was against everything that narrows, restricts or separates one man from another. Therefore, he pleaded against untouchability and casteism. He not only analysed the malady of untouchability but also suggested possible reforms. The aim of his reform movement was based on the idea of evolving the lower groups of society to the spiritual level of the higher group.

Vivekananda presented three steps as suggestions for raising the level of the untouchables to that of Brahmins. Firstly, he laid emphasis upon circulating spiritual information among all. He said, "My idea is first of all to bring out the gems of spirituality that are stored up in our books and in the possession of few only, hidden as it were, in monasteries and in forests... In one word I want to make it popular. I want to bring out these ideas and let them be the common property of all, of every man in India."[1] Secondly, Sanskrit must be taught to all of them since that is the language of the scriptures which are the sources of Indian spiritual knowledge.

Advancing his argument in favour of mass teaching of Sanskrit Vivekananda said, "The attempts of the great Ramanuja and Chaitanya and of Kabir to raise the lower classes of India show that marvellous results were attained during the life-time of those great prophets; yet the later failures have to be explained, and causes shown why the effect of their teachings stopped almost within a century of the passing away of these Masters. The secret is here. They raised the lower classes; they had all the wishes that these should come up, but they did not apply their energies to the spreading of the Sanskrit language among the masses. Even the great Buddha made one false step when he stopped the Sanskrit language from being studied by the masses."[2] Thirdly, the diffusion of Brahmanic culture in the whole society is also essential. All the privileges and honours attached to Brahmins must be diffused to every member of society and should be available to every one.

Thus, in short, though Vivekananda considered the Varna system as the ideal form of social stratification and pleaded for the maintenance of caste system in a proper form he upheld the democratic principle of equality and fraternity above all. This will be more clear in our discussion of his Neo-vedanta socialism and his support of democracy. Finally, his criticism and evaluation of the forms of social stratification is based upon humanistic tendency. Like his great master Ramakrishna he was a great humanist and the essence of his Vedanta teaching may be summed up as man-making.

---

1. *Ibid.*, Vol. III, p. 290.
2. *Ibid.*, p. 290-1.

Regeneration of the Masses

Thus, Vivekananda waged a movement for regeneration of Indian masses, particularly the backward classes including untouchables and women. He placed the responsibility upon the higher and privileged classes to realise this uplift. According to him the cause of this downfall is not religion but rather the absence of it. He did not hold Hinduism responsible for this lower status of Hindu society. He said, "Religion is not at fault, but it is the Pharisees and the Sadducees in Hinduism, hypocrites, who invent all sorts of engines of tyranny."[1] Hinduism teaches equality as it is based on Vedanta philosophy according to which there is one essence underlying everyone.

Religion and Society

As has been already pointed out, Vivekananda considered religion as the keynote of social and national life. This religion was the Vedic religion or the religion preached in Bhagwadgita. Being in tune with modern science and socialist thought, it lays emphasis upon the reality of this world. Neo-Vedanta of Vivekananda was different from Advaita Vedanta of Shankar in laying emphasis upon the reality of the world. He did not negate the objective world but rather considered it as much real as Brahman. He not only praised Sanyas but considered Grahastha to be equally involved. Clarifying his teaching he said, "You can have your wife; it does not mean that you are to abandon her, but that you are to see God in the wife. So also you are to see God in your children. So in everything. In life and in death, in happiness and in misery, the Lord is equally present. The whole world is full of the Lord. Open your eyes and see Him. This is what the Vedanta teaches."[2]

PRACTICAL VEDANTA

Thus, Vivekananda called his Vedanta teaching, a practical Vedanta. In making Vedanta practical philosophy for life he particularly laid emphasis upon the following teaching of Vedanta:

1. **Oneness** The idea of unity or oneness in the cosmos is the central idea of Vedanta philosophy. This oneness in not only in the multiplicity but also in the facts and ideals, present and future. In the words of Vivekananda, "The actual should be reconciled to the ideal; the present life should be made to coincide with the life eternal."[3]
2. **Faith in ourselves** In the practical Vedanta of Vivekananda faith is above everything else. He realised that the main cause of the present degeneration of Indians is the lack of faith in themselves. This was the

1. *Swami Vivekananda on India and her Problems*, p. 67.
2. *Centenary Volume*, pp. 269-270.
3. Swami Vivekananda, *Practical Vedanta*, p. 11.

result of hundreds of years of slavery under the foreign yoke. Realising this fact Vivekananda urged in most of his lectures in very inspiring words to the Indians to have faith in themselves, in their heritage, their philosophy, their language, their literature and their physical, mental and spiritual strength. This faith is essentially as an Atman, a part of the Brahman, the universal force present everywhere. In the words of Vivekananda, "You are that Satchitananda, not the small, miserable being that you ignorantly think yourself to be. Your self is the universal self that is one with all things and beings, that shines in the sun, the moon and the stars and illuminates them all. You are first to hear about this self and then constantly meditate on it. Think of yourself as the birthless, the deathless, the blissful, the omniscient, the omnipotent, the very glorious soul. Think on it day and night till the thought enters into your flesh and blood, and you have a vision of the Atman as Brahman. Here you realise your real self as none other than Brahman itself. With this realisation there comes a total transformation of your life and your activities. You live the Vedantic ideal, it becomes a matter of your practical life."[1]

3. **God realisation** God realisation in oneself and in society is the teaching of Vedanta. This will result not only in the individual evolution but also in uplift of the masses. Laying emphasis upon this practical teaching of Vedanta Vivekananda said, "He who sees Shiva in the poor, in the weak, and in the diseased, really worships Shiva, and if he sees Shiva only in the image, his worship is but preliminary."[2]
4. **Toleration of other religions** In the tradition of the teachings of his Master Ramakrishna, Vivekananda preached for the toleration towards all the religions of the world. This is particularly required in India since it is the home of the followers of almost all the great religions of the world.
5. **Synthesis between the East and the West** Vivekananda was against blind imitation of the West. He urged every nation to follow its own Swadharma. Pointing out the fruitlessness of social Westernisation in India he said, "Vain is the attempt to imitate the lines of action that foreign societies have engrafted upon us. It is impossible. Glory unto God, that it is impossible, that we cannot be twisted and tortured into the shape of other nations. I do not condemn the institutions of other races; they are good for them, but not for us. With other sciences, other institutions, and other traditions behind them, they have got their present system. We, with our traditions, with thousands of years of 'Karma' behind us, naturally can only follow our own bent, run in our

1. *Centenary Memorial Volume*, pp. 279-80.
2. *Thus Spoke Vivekananda*, p. 42.

own grooves, and that we shall have to do."[1]

In his synthetic outlook Vivekananda considered both East and West as mutually complementary though apparently contradictory. Laying emphasis upon the need of their synthesis he said, "The West is groaning under the tyranny of the Shylocks, and the East is groaning under the tyranny of the priests; each must keep the other in the check. Do not think that one alone is to help the world."[2] The advantages of the contact with the West have been elaborated by so many thinkers including those of Renaissance and modern period in India. But no one raised his voice so high as did Vivekananda, in pointing out the advantages to the West of coming in the contact of India. Warning that without the spiritual contact with the East, the West cannot live, he said, "Europe, the centre of the manifestation of material energy, will crumble into dust within fifty years, if she is not mindful to change her position, to shift her ground and make spirituality the basis of her life. And what will save Europe is the religion of the Upanishads."[3]

MESSIAH OF DOWN-TRODDEN

A Messiah of the down-trodden, no less than Karl Marx, Vivekananda preached elimination of all exploitation as the highest and eternal morality. Explaining his ethics in most clear terms he said, "Men will be born differentiated; some will have more power than others. We cannot stop that ... but that on account of this power to acquire wealth they should tyrannise and ride roughshod over those, who cannot acquire so much wealth, is not a part of the law, and the fight has been against that. The enjoyment of advantage over another is privilege, and throughout ages the aim of morality has been its destruction."[4] Thus, the task of ethics is to teach the established moral principles such as enjoyment of happiness and elimination of superiority and privileges. All moral philosophy is based upon equality of self in everyone. The teachings of Neo-Vedanta here are very much similar to the democratic ethics.

ENDS AND MEANS

Karl Marx believed that the means justify the end. According to Vivekananda, however, the ends justify the means. This close connection between ends and means, emphasised by Vivekananda, was followed by M.K. Gandhi and popularised in Indian politics after him. Pointing out the inseparable relation between the ends and means, Vivekananda said, "One of the greatest lessons I have learned in my life is to pay as much attention to the means as to its end. He was a great man from whom I learned it, and his own life was a practical demonstration of this great principle. I have been always learning

1. Vivekananda, S., *The Complete Works*, Vol. III, pp. 219-22.
2. *Ibid.*, Vol. III, p. 158.
3. *Ibid.*, p. 159.
4. *Ibid.*, pp. 434-35.

great lessons from that one principle, and it appears to me that all the secret of success is there : to pay as much attention to the means as to the end."[1] In tune with the teachings of Bhagwadgita on this issue Vivekananda pointed out that man has a right over the means and never on the achievement of the end. The end is determined not only by our own efforts but by so many other circumstances which are beyond our control. Therefore, it is necessary that we concentrate all our attention upon the means. In the words of Vivekananda, "But whenever failure comes, if we analyse it critically, in ninety-nine per cent of cases we shall find that it was because we did not pay attention to the means, proper attention to the finishing, strengthening, of the means, is what we need. With the means, all right, the end must come. We forget that it is the cause that produces the effect : the effect cannot come by itself; and unless the causes are exact, proper and powerful, the effect will not be produced. Once the ideal is chosen and the means determined, we may almost let go the ideal, because we are sure it will bc there, when the means are perfected. When the cause is there, there is no more difficulty about the effect, the effect is bound to come. If we take care of the cause, the effect will take care of itself. The realisation of the ideal is the effect. The means are the cause: attention to the means, therefore is the great secret of life."[2]

EMANCIPATION OF WOMEN

Besides casteism and untouchability the main evil in Indian society, as diagnosed by Vivekananda is the lower status of women. In Vedic age the status of Indian women was no less than that of men. But after it one witnesses a gradual decline in the status of women in India. After the invasion by foreigners their status became lower and lower so much so that in the time of Vivekananda it was no better than the status of the untouchables. Therefore, Vivekananda wrote, "In India there are two great evils, trampling on the women and grinding the poor through caste restrictions."[3] Hence, uplift of the women, the awakening of the masses must come first, and then only can any real good come about for the country."[4] "If the women are raised, then their children will by their noble actions glorify the name of the country — then will culture, knowledge, power and devotion awaken in the country. All nations have attained greatness by paying proper respect to the women. That country and that nation which do not respect the women have never become great, nor will ever be in future."[5] Vivekananda, however, warned that Indian women cannot raise their status by blindly imitating the Western women. He held Sita as an ideal woman and urged Indian women to follow her. Women education, according to him, was no less important than the education of

---

1. *Ibid.*, Vol. II, p. 11.
2. *Ibid.*
3. *Ibid.*, Vol. VI, p. 303.
4. *Centenary Volume*, p. 400.
5. Swami Vivekananda on *India and her Problems*, p. 95.

men. Emphasising the education of women in India Vivekananda wrote, "With...education women will solve their own problems, servile dependence on others, and so they are good only to weep at the slightest approach of a mishap or danger. Along with other things they should acquire the spirit of valour and heroism. In the present day it has become necessary for them also to learn self-defence. See how grand was the Queen of Jhansi."[1]

POLITICAL PHILOSOPHY

Patriotism

Vivekananda was one of the great patriot sons of India of his time, and even of all times to come. In spite of being very catholic and tolerant and widely travelled he was proud of India and her great culture. He had great faith in the future role of India in the world. Praising the greatness of his country he said, "If there is any land on this earth that can lay claim to be the blessed Punya Bhumi, to be the land to which all souls on this earth must come to account for Karma...the land where humanity has attained its highest towards gentleness, towards generosity, towards purity, towards calmness, above all, the land of introspection and of spirituality, it is India."[2] As an argument to support his faith in the greatness of Indian culture, he pointed out that dozens of great cultures were born in this world, lived for centuries, but today Indian culture is the only ancient culture which is not only alive but which may guide the world in future. He said, "There have been other nations equally glorious that have come and gone, living a few hours of exaltant and of exuberant dominance, and of a wicked national life, and then vanishing like ripples on the face of the waters . . . but we live, and if 'Manu' come back today he would not be bewildered, and would not find himself in a foreign land. The same laws are here, laws adjucated and thought out through thousands and thousands of years; customs the outcome of the acumen of ages and the experience of centuries, that seem to be eternal, and as the days go by, as blow after blow of misfortune has been delivered upon them, they seem to have served one purpose only, that of making them stronger and more constant."[3] Spirituality is the characteristic of Indian culture that is her gift to the world. Besides spirituality the world has to learn sympathy, toleration and other human virtues from this great country. While praising India, Vivekananda used such sentimental language and inspiring words that he was known as the very embodiment of emotional patriotism.

It was because of his patriotism that Vivekananda so many times pleaded for political liberation of the country, otherwise he was not a politician. He said, "I am no politician or political agitator. 1 care only for the Spirit...So you must warn the people that no political significance be ever attached falsely

1. *Centenary Volume*, p. 405.
2. Swami Vivekananda : *To the Youth of India*, Advaita Ashrama, Almora (1963), p. 1.
3. *Ibid.*, pp. 3-4.

to any of my writings or sayings... I have said a few harsh words in honest criticism of Christian Governments in general, but that does not mean that I care for, or have any connection with politics."[1] His demand for political liberation, presented in most inspiring and strong language, influenced almost all the political leaders of his time. During his tour in 1901 at Dacca he said, "Read Bankim Chandra and emulate his 'deshbhakti' (patriotism) and 'Sanatan Dharma'. "Abolish the multiplicity of nations for the unity of the world. He said, "Each nation has its own peculiar method of work. Some work through politics, some through social reforms, some through other lines. With us religion is the only ground along which we can move. The Englishman can understand religion even through politics. Perhaps the American can understand religion even through social reforms. But the Hindu can understand even politics when it is given through religion; sociology must come through religion, everything must come through religion. For that is the theme, the rest are the variations in the national life music."[2] Thus, according to Vivekananda, each nation has its national character and in Indian character religion is the dominant element.

Explaining the constituents of a nations Vivekananda said, "Race, religion, language, Government — all these together make a nation."[3] Considering all these elements India is a nation, a nation of the Aryans, Vedic religion, Sanskrit language and its own cultural heritage. What is however required to make it a complete nation is sovereignty. It is therefore that Vivekananda worked for awakening of the masses, the development of their physical and moral strength and creating in them a consciousness of the pride in the ancient glory and greatness of India. It is hence that he was hailed as one of the great architect of modern nationalism in India. Urging the Indian masses to regain their individuality and to rise on the occasion he said, "We as a nation have lost our individuality, and that is the cause of all mischief in India. We have to give back to the nation its lost individuality and raise the masses. The Hindu, the Mohammedan, the Christian, all have trampled them under foot. Again, the force to raise them must come from inside, that is, from the orthodox Hindus. In every country evil exists not with, but against religion. Religion, therefore, is not to blame, but men."[4] Explaining his Neo-vedanta religion required for the mass-uplift in India, Vivekananda declared, "The essence of my religion is strength. The religion that does not infuse strength into the heart, is no religion to me, be it of the Upanishads, the Gita, or the Bhagvatam. Strength is greater than religion and nothing is greater than strength."[5] The chief source of this strength, according to Vivekananda, is proper education of the masses. He said, "We

1. *Eastern and Western Disciples,* Complete Works, Vol, III, p. 407.
2. Vivekananda, S., *The Complete Works,* Vol. IV, p. 104.
3. *Ibid,* pp. 471-2.
4. *The Life of Swami Vivekananda,* Vol. I, pp. 306-07.
5. *Ibid.,* Vol. II, p. 699.

have to give them secular education. We have to follow the plan laid down by our ancestors, that is, to bring all the ideals slowly down among the masses. Raise them slowly up, raise them to equality. Impart ... secular knowledge through religion."[1]

Internationalism

In spite of being a great patriot and a staunch nationalist, Vivekananda was no less an internationalist. Though he wanted his nation to maintain its individuality, he was against exclusiveness in national life. He said, "I am thoroughly convinced that no individual or nation can live by holding itself apart from the community of others, and wherever such an attempt has been made under false ideas of greatness, policy or holiness — the result has always been disastrous to the secluding one. The fact of our isolation from all the other nations of the world is the cause of our degeneration and its only remedy is getting back into the current of the rest of the world. Motion is the sign of life."[2] Laying emphasis upon the need of international cooperation in political, economic and social field, Vivekananda said, "In politics and sociology, problems that were only national twenty years ago can no more be solved on national grounds only. They are assuming huge proportions, gigantic shapes. They can only be solved when looked at in the broader light of international grounds. International organisation, international combinations, international laws are the cry of the day. That shows the solidarity."[3]

Neo-Vedanta Socialism

During his tour of the West, Vivekananda had occasions to study intimately, socialism, communism and their practical application. He had also occasions to discuss these political philosophies with renouned people. Defining socialism he said, "The doctrine which demands the sacrifice of individual freedom to social supremacy is called socialism, while that which advocates the cause of the individual is called individualism."[4] Knowing the advantages and limitations of socialism Vivekananda proclaimed, "I am a socialist not because I think it is a perfect system, but half a loaf is better than no bread." He prophesied about India that the fiiture of socialism is bright in this country. He investigated the cause of social and political decline of India and lamented that the privileged classes have everywhere tried to exploit the lower classes.

Thus, with the socialist and communist thinkers of his time, Vivekananda was convinced that the labour class has the potentiality of creating a social, economic and political revolution in the country. The inner processes in this

---

1. Swami Vivekananda on *India and her Problems*, p. 71.
2. Quoted in : *The Political Philosophy of B.R. Ambedkar* by Dr. D.R. Jatava, 1965, p. 59.
3. Vivekananda, S., *To the Youth of India*, pp. 89-90.
4. *Ibid.*, Vol. IV, 1966, p. 488.

revolution have been however very differently explained by Vivekananda. As against the role of economic and material forces in future revolution, Vivekananda considered the revolution to be possible only through the spiritual forces. His socialism therefore, is different from the materialist socialism of the West.

In spite of his emphasis on spirituality Vivekananda admitted the value of material possessions in life. He said, "In material civilization — nay, even luxury is necessary to create work for the poor. Bread ! Bread ! I do not believe in a God who cannot give me bread here, giving me eternal bliss in heaven ! ..." [1] And yet he condemned the materialist philosophy of levelling down and maintained the Vedanta philosophy of levelling up. The higher varnas, in revolution, have not to come down to the level of the lower varnas, but the lower varnas have to rise higher to the level of the higher varnas. In this way the revolution imagined by Vivekananda is almost opposed to that of Karl Marx. In his own words, "In the beginning of the Satya-Yuga (Golden age) there was one caste, the Brahmins, and then by difference of occupations they went on dividing themselves into different castes ... And in the coming Satya-yuga all the other castes will have to go back to the same condition."[2] Therefore, the revolution need not be violent or through class hatred, on the other hand it will be through democratic techniques and spiritual methods. Thus, socialism, according to Vivekananda, is not an end in itself, it is a mere means, one of the best means to achieve a spiritual democratic society. In fact, though Vivekananda praised socialism here and there, his social ideal was spiritual democracy and not a socialist society. This ideal is very much in keeping with the ancient Indian traditional social philosophy.

SPIRITUAL DEMOCRACY

Spiritual Liberty

Democracy is based upon the three fundamental values of liberty, equality and fraternity. While praising these triune principles Vivekananda interpreted them in spiritual sense. Explaining his idea of spiritual freedom he said, "To advance towards freedom, physical, mental and spiritual, and help others to do so is the supreme prize of man. These social rules which stand in the way of the unfoldment of this freedom are injurious, and steps should be taken to destroy them speedily. Those institutions should be encouraged by which men advance in the path of freedom..."[3] Pointing out the value of liberty as a natural right he said, "Liberty does not certainly mean the absence of obstacles in the path of misappropriation of wealth, etc., by you and me, but it is our natural right to be allowed to use our own body, intelligence or wealth according to our will, without doing any harm to others; and all the

1. *Ibid.*, Vol. IV, p. 313.
2. Swami Vivekananda, *Caste, Culture and Socialism* (1970), p. vii.
3. *The Life of Swami Vivekananda*, Vol. II, p. 753.

members of society ought to have the same opportunity for obtaining wealth, education, or knowledge."[1]

In tradition with the Renaissance thinkers Vivekananda considered the individual as the centre of society. A nation is great because of the greatness of its individuals. Therefore, Vivekananda asked Indians to develop self-reliance and self-confidence. Real freedom, according to him, is the spiritual freedom which includes individual as well as social freedom. In fact it is a gradual progress towards liberation. This freedom can be attained by the individual through constant unceasing effort to help others and love others, through worship in prayer, praise and meditation and through the knowledge following meditation. Thus, liberty is complimentary to action.

Essential Equality

Besides liberty equality is also necessary to realize a democratic society. Equality is the way to freedom while inequality is the way to bondage. Pointing out the value of equality for liberty Vivekananda said, "No man and no nation can attempt to gain physical freedom without physical equality, nor mental freedom without mental equality."[2] Absolute equality, however, is impossible. It is against the law of nature. Though all beings are equally manifestations of God, yet difference is the basis of manifestation. This, however, does not eliminate the spiritual equality, which can be seen everywhere. Explaining this spiritual equality as a fundamental principle of Vedanta, Vivekananda said, "The idea that one man is born superior to another has no meaning in Vedanta; that between two nations one is superior and other inferior has no meaning whatsover. Put them in the same circumstances, and see whether the same intelligence comes out or not. Before that you have no right to say that one nation is superior to another. And as to spirituality, no privilege should be claimed there ... There are no special messengers of God, never were, and never can be. All beings great or small, are equally manifestations of God, the difference is only in the manifestations."[3]

Spiritual Fraternity

Liberty and equality are incomplete without fraternity. This fraternity again, according to Vivekananda, should be spiritual fraternity. Explaining this idea he said. "That is a grand idea we ought to remember. In every man, in every animal, however weak or wicked, great or small, resides the same omnipresent, omniscient soul. The difference is not in the soul, but as a principle he is the same as I am, he is my brother, he has the same soul as I have."[4]

1. *Ibid.*, p. 752.
2. Vivekananda, S., *Complete Works*, Vol. IV., p. 328.
3. *Ibid.*, p. 114.
4. *Ibid.*, Vol. III, p. 126.

Ancient Democratic Ideal

Thus, Vivekananda considered democracy as the best form of government. He was against monarchy though it has been praised in ancient Indian literature. He also condemned aristocracy as the tyranny of a minority. Though he was very much aware of the defects of democratic forms of government in different countries of his own time, he praised it as the only type of government in which a spiritual society may be possible. Explaining his idea of democracy in the tradition of ancient Indian thought he said that, "the voice of the ruled in the government of their land — which is the watchword of the modern Western world, and of which the last expression has been echoed with a thundering voice in the Declaration of the American Government, in the words, 'That the government of the people of this country must be by the people and for the good of the people' — cannot however be said to have been totally unrecognised in Ancient India. "[1]

Self-Government

Thus, the ideal government is self-government. *Swadharma* is the principle of life everywhere, individual, social, economic or political. This self-government is possible only through acting upon the teaching of Upanishads. In the words of Vivekananda, "When the government of a country is guided by codes of laws, enjoined by Shastras which are the outcome of knowledge inspired by the divine genius of great sages, such a government must lead to the unbroken welfare of the rich and the poor, the wise and the ignorant, the king and the subjects alike."[2]

---

1. *Ibid.*, Vol. IV, p. 442.
2. *Ibid.*, p. 441-2.

16
Annie Besant (1847 — 1933)

Early Experiences

Born in a conventional Christian family in London, Annie Besant started her life like any average woman but her restless spirit could not brook stagnation. Compelled by Truth, she broke her family ties with her husband. With indomitable spirit of brotherhood and compassion, she decided to espouse the cause of the poor, the oppressed and the helpless. From her very early life she had a tendency to oppose dogmas and superstitions in order to uphold the dignity of man. Her work for the sake of human welfare started with certain experiments like a support to the Knowlton case,[1] active part in the strike by the Match Girls, for higher wages and work under the Free Thought Movement. From these early experiments she got tremendous impetus and strengh to enter into the wider field of human activity. She came into contact with persons, dedicated to the cause of humanism, Charles Bradlaugh, Charles Voysey and W.T. Stead, made her a valiant fighter against common hatred and oppression of humanity.

Influence of Hinduism

Annie Besant was greatly influenced by the Hindu religious scriptures, especially the Bhagavadgita, the Ramayana, the Mahabharata, and the Upanishads. She translated the Bhagavadgita into English with the help of her close friend Dr. Bhagwan Dass. In its preface she wrote that since the teachings of the Gita lift man from the lower levels to the loftier heights where desires are dead, it could become a practical guide to actions.[2] She used the message of the Gita to curb rivalries among various religions. In her lectures on religions of the world, she quoted freely from the Hindu scriptures. Long before she came to India, she had discovered in the Vedas

1. In 1935, an American physician Dr. Charles Knowlton published a pamphlet in favour of planned family system. Annie Besant with the help of Charles Bradlaugh republished it in 1877.
2. Annie Besant, *The Bhagavadgita*, Madras, T.P.H., 1957, p. 11-12.

and the Upanishads, the most complete expression of Theosophy. She openly called herself a Hindu of the ancient Aryan type.

Love for India

Annie Besant first set foot on Indian soil on November 16, 1893. She had repeatedly stated her belief that in her previous lives she was again and again born in India. She attributed her Western birth to the purpose of supplementing her Indian character with something of the Western influence for doing better work in India. To quote Sri Prakasa, "She loved India with a fervour and devotion all her own. Our country's philosophy, our history or legends, our spiritual heritage, our achievements in the past, our sorrows in the present, our aspirations for the future, were part and parcel of Mrs. Besant's own life."[1] Through the Young Men's Association, Mrs. Besant placed before the Indians the idea of a united India. She showed how men of different religions could fraternise without being untrue, to their different faiths. At Mrs. Besant's instance Mr. Jinnah and Mr. Savarker could meet together in her presence. Like Gandhi, she was an ardent follower of truth. Annie Besant settled down at Banaras and built her house there. She adopted the orthodox Hindu way of living in spite of much criticism from her fellow theosophists.

The Upanishadic view of human spirit as identical with the Absolute Reality found agreement with her metaphysical beliefs. The spirit as the Universal Element in man is the principle of unity. She was so much impressed by this that she proclaimed that Indians formed the last hope of the spiritual upliftment of men. If India yielded to the exclusive material advancement and power, then humanity is doomed and mankind shall find its grave. In the words of Dr. Iqbal Narain Gurtu. "Till the end of her earthly life, she kept on reminding us that if India could be regenerated, purified and re-spiritualised, she would become the priest-people of humanity."[2]

Atheism

Annie Besant was greatly influenced by Charles Voysey who used to preach the principles of Christianity. She came to understand that the traditional belief in religion and its concepts was based on dogmas and false understanding of God. She refused to accept the Christian notion of God and declared herself to be an atheist. She believed that the ideal humanity for the Christian was the humanity of slaves — poor, humble, submissive and oppressed; the ideal humanity of the atheist was the humanity of the free man — who relies on his own powers and who makes his neighbours' cause his own.[3] In one of her essays, she writes, "My heart revolts against the spectre of Almighty indifferent to the pain of sentient being. My conscience rebels

1. *The Annie Besant Centenary Book*, Madras, the Besant Centenary Celebrations Committee, 1947, p. 51.
2. *Ibid.*, p. 72.
3. Annie Besant, *Gospel of Atheism*, London, 1876.

against the injustice, the cruelty, the inequality that surrounds me on every side. But believe in man; in man's redeeming power; in man's remoulding energy; in man's approaching triumph through knowledge, love and work."[1]

POSITIVISM AND HUMANISM

Annie Besant denied the traditional view of religion in order to affirm the reality of man and his life on earth. Those whom people generally call atheists refuse to look beyond to the other world in order to improve conditions of life on the earth, they ignore God in their zeal for man. With the deep urge to relieve humanity from its suffering, Annie Besant attempted a fresh interpretation of religion based on humanism. All religions are based on the same principles of love and service of man. The true business of a religious man, according to her, was to help his race in its march on the right path and fight the evil in all its forms. Man is the symbol of what we call divine. She said, "To know man is to know God."[2] In her interpretation of religion there was no room for dogmas and superstitions which usually divide religions.

IMPACT OF THEOSOPHICAL SOCIETY

Annie Besant's thoughts on religion became much more clear after joining the Theosophical Society. It was in the year 1888 that she suggested to her friend W.T. Stead the need to establish a new Church for teaching social duty, for upholding righteousness and building up of a true commonwealth. She felt the necessity of forming a new brotherhood on the basis of doing good to all. In May 1889, she first came into contact with Madam H P. Blavatsky, the founder of the Theosophical Society. She was so much influenced by her work, *The Secret Doctrine* that she joined the society. She had three main aims in joining the society: first, to propagate her ideas on religion; second, to establish a universal brotherhood without distinction of race or creed; and third, to investigate unexplained laws of nature and the physical powers latent in man. The theosophical movement was very much strengthened by her. Through her writings and lectures, she tried to draw the attention of people towards a new theology based on the brotherhood in which service of man becomes the service of God. Her passage from Free Thought Movement in which she was active during the earlier years, to Theosophy was mostly on humanistic grounds.

Sanatan Dharma

As a Theosophist, Annie Besant developed unlimited faith in religion as the supreme basis of every form of human activity. She was never tired of proclaiming that such a comprehensive religious basis had been provided only by India through her 'Sanatana Dharma'. Delivering the Kamala lectures

1. Last words of her essay — "Why I do not believe in God" — published 1887, quoted by her in the Autobiography, Madras, Theosophical House, 1939, *op. cit.*, 243.
2. Annie Besant, *The Self and its Sheaths,* London, Theosophical House, 1894, p. 1.

in 1925, she said, "Religion is essentially, the search for, the cry of spirit by fragment; that is, the spirit in man for the whole spirit by fragment; that is, the spirit in man for the whole spirit, the unsatisfied craving of the part for completeness, the pressure against the limitations of Time and Space of the Eternal and Spaceless."[1] It was her belief that mankind could be helped in realising the majesty of God and its own greatness. Religion, leads to the discovery that there is no validity in the artificial divisions imposed by race, customs or creed. Religion is the uniting rather than the dividing factor.

Idea of God

Annie Besant taught that God is one, that he dwells in every man, is the inmost self of all the *antryamin* of the Upanishads.[2] In all the multiplicity of living beings around us we form but one body, and as, with a physical body, no one part can be injured without the whole body suffering, so is it with the Great Being — Humanity,[3] "To her man was God in making and his essentially divine nature must be allowed to express itself more and more fully through his mental, emotional and physical activities."[4] Inclined towards the Vaishnavite view of all-inclusive God she felt the possibility of a personal relation between God and man. She found God in man as 'the crown of creation'. She was confident that God dwelt in all men and there was only one spirit to which we were all rooted. She writes, "The recognition of the one self dwelling equally in all is the one sure foundation of Brotherhood."[5]

Religion is the foundation of all that is good in life. Man is the final image of the Supreme on earth. Therefore, a true religion must be rooted in man instead of God. She regarded God as one reality outside which nothing can exist, the one life on which all lives depend and from which all existence is drawn.[6] Speaking to her London audience in 1905, Annie Besant said that nothing was outside the conception of universal religion or theosophy which tended to serve, to uplift and ennoble humanity. It could help in understanding the harmonious relation among the apparent dividing factors and in realising the divinity of man.[7]

Meaning of Religion

According to Annie Besant religion must permeate the whole life of man. Religion must be considered the basis of morality. It must not be separated

1. Annie Besant, "Indian Ideals in Education, Philosophy and Art" (Kamala Lectures, Calcutta), Calcutta University Press, 1925, p. 37.
2. *Kathopanishad*, 2, 5, 6; *Manduk Upanishad*, 2, 8.
3. *The Universal Textbooks of Religions and Morals*, Part II, edited by Annie Besant, p. 4.
4. Iqbal Narain Gurtu on Besant in *The Annie Besant Centenary Book*, 1947, p. 71.
5. Annie Besant, *The Ancient Wisdom*, Madras, T.P.H., 1959, p. 189-90.
6. Annie Besant, *Theosophy*, Madras, T.P.H., 1952, p. 19.
7. Annie Besant's inaugural address on the occasion of opening ceremony of art exhibition at Queen's Hall, London on July 7, 1905 — Col. Olcott's biographical notes — *Autobiography*, Madras, T.P.H., 1939, p. 507.

from our usual activities of life. To quote Besant, "You are religious in temple, you must be religious in the market place. You are religious in the Puja-room, you must be religious in the court, as Vakil pleading : as judge giving judgement; as doctor healing; as soldier fighting; as merchant trading."[1]

Concept of Man

The influence of ancient Indian philosophy helped Annie Besant in evolving a conception of man as a symbol of latent powers. By man, she meant the living, conscious, thinking self, the individual by bodies, the various casings in which the self is enclosed, each enabling the self to function in some way. To quote her words, "Man is not body : the body is but the garment that he wears; and man can never be understood, when you leave out of his pedigree, the spirit that makes him eternal."[2] At another place she writes. "Man is a spiritual intelligence, a fragment of Divinity clothed in matter."[3] Man is the highest spirit and the lowest matter joined together by intelligence, thus a true manifestation of God. Man realises himself and forms contact with the world through his three aspects of knowledge (*jnanam*). Because of his divine nature, man has power to make what progress he chooses. The real nature of man cannot be understood without the spirit, that constitutes his eternal character. In man there is a warfare between spirit and matter, each striving for supremacy. The recognition of the supremacy of spirit over physical body may pave the way for the spiritual progress of man.

Seven Principles of Man

Following the theosophical teachings Annie Besant described man as a seven-fold being. Man may be studied from seven different points of view; he is composed of seven principles. These seven principles refer to his evolving character. These seven principles are — dense physical body, etheric double, life or *prana*, the desire body or *kamarupa*, the mind or *manas* the intellect of *buddhi*, and the spirit or *atman*. The first, three principles constitute man's physical nature, the fourth his sensuous and emotional nature, the fifth his thinking aspect and the last two his spiritual nature.

In her book *Seven Principles of Man*, Annie Besant defines the seven aspects of human nature and gives their vivid explanation and mutual relationship. The dense physical body is the organism with the senses and nervous system. The death of the body means the withdrawal of its controlling life energy. The etheric double is the vitality, the vehicle of the life principle. "It is the state of physical matter which is just beyond our solid, liquid and gas which forms the dense portion of the physical plane."[4] It attaches man to

---

1. Annie Besant's address at the Annual Theosophical Convention in December, 1916, at Madras.
2. Annie Besant, *The Pedigree of Man*, Madras, T.P.H. 1908, p. 2.
3. Annie Besant, *Man's Life in Three Worlds*, T.P.H., 1952, p. 2.
4. Annie Besant, *Seven Principles of Man*, Madras, T.P.H., 1956, p. 9.

life. Life or *prana* is the principle through which the universe manifests itself. In the ocean of life each individual contains its own breath of life — this is *prana* in Theosophy. The desire body includes the whole body of appetites, desires, passions and emotions. All animal needs of man come under this principle. This is the most material aspect of man which binds him fast to the earthly life. The mind is the thinker in man. It is the immortal individual, the real 'I' that clothes itself over and over again and endures forever. The last two are the spiritual aspects. Annie Besant defines intellect as "the faculty of cognising, the channel through which divine knowledge reaches the Ego, the discernment of good and evil, also divine conscience, the spiritual soul which is the vehicle of the spirit or Atman."[1] The spirit of *atman* means the most abstract part of man's nature the breath which needs a body for its manifestation.

Human Evolution

According to Annie Besant, the evolution of man during the present cycle of human development takes place on five out of seven aspects. The two higher aspects will not be reached by him in the present cycle except in most exceptional cases. Annie Besant's discussion on the process of evolution through different stages, from the physical to the spiritual is in line with the Hindu conception of evolution from *annamaya to anandamaya kosa.* Hindu philosophy describes five kosas of man's spiritual progress. These are — *annamaya, pranamaya, manomaya, vijnanamaya* and *anandamaya.* Following the central doctrine of the Theosophy or the brotherhood of man, Annie Besant expressed confidence in spiritual growth of mankind. The real aim of the spiritual progress is to unfold the Divine life which is man. Born in the material world and engrossed in the senses, an average man finds it difficult to realise his true being, his kinship with the Divine force. Annie Besant held that the unfolding of the spiritual element in man does not depend upon external conditions. She did not agree with the common belief that the man could not lead a spiritual life so long as he lived in the material world. The worldly life is the channel through which the spirit can find expression. All useful activities are forms of divine activity. Annie Besant gave a call to mankind, "wherever you may be, in whatever workshop of this world, you may find yourself at labour, keep over in your heart the ideal that you fain would realise. Feel the presence of the imprisoned Divinity that you have the mighty privilege, and you alone, of liberating; and take in hand your tools, cut away the worthless stone, liberate the splendid statue and then you will know yourself self-consciously as that which you really are man in the image of God."[2]

1. *Ibid.*, p. 73.
2. Annie Besant, *Spiritual Life of the Man of the World,* Madras, T.P.H., 1953, p. 19-20.

Humanism

In her explanation of man and his relation with the Supreme Spirit, Annie Besant refuted the general Christian belief that man is created by God as a helpless creature looking at the mercy of God. According to her, being divine himself man is capable of making progress in whatever direction he likes. The humanistic principle of universal brotherhood is based on the belief that God is one and dwells in all men in the form of spirit or self. Recognition of this supreme truth itself is sufficient to eradicate the artificial divisions among men. In the establishment of this truth the task of Annie Besant as a humanist was largely fulfilled.[1]

Annie Besan't philosophy is based on her tremendous faith in humanity. She was confident that it was neither creed, nor machinery, nor even organisation that would save the world but the realisation of the oneness of life, the unity of great human family. Conscious of the duties of Theosophy towards humanity, in 1909 Annie Besant announced the formation of another new organisation, The Theosophical Order of Service. It was based on the Hindu tradition of ascetic devotees who renounce all worldly possessions in order to work for the spiritual improvement of mankind. Annie Besant not only preached this ideal but worked throughout her life with an altruistic motive.

ON EDUCATION

According to Annie Besant, the ideals of Theosophy could not be achieved without the right type of education. From the very beginning of her public life she evolved a definite philosophy of education. She thought it necessary to provide proper training to the children in accordance with the attitudes which are required to be developed in them. Hence, she took a strong stand against the teaching of sectarian and one-sided religious doctrines to children. Education must be a process of wholesome development outlook. Children must be made to realise that they constitute a fragment of the vast evolutionary process. According to Annie Besant 'do good, be good must be the law impressed on our children." She said, "cearly, the theosophical ideal of education is that each child who comes into the world should receive an education suited to develop his particular faculties, and also such an education as will make him useful in his future life to his community and to his country."[2] The real aim of education must be to make boys and girls good citizens of a free and spiritual commonwealth of humanity.[3] With these ideals Annie Besant set up to revolutionise the Indian educational system when she came to India.

---

1. Annie Besant, *The Ancient Wisdom,* Madras, T.P.H., 1959, pp. 189-191.
2. Annie Besant, *The Ideal of Theosophy,* Madras, T.P.H., 1912, p. 36.
3. Annie Besant, *India : Bond or Free,* London, Theosophical Publishing Society, 1926.

Theosophical Education

Annie Besant contributed to the birth of a truly Indian system of education. From 1898 upto almost the end of her career, she directed and inspired theosophical education in India. She shaped its policy, and energised it as true education for humanity. She stressed the importance of culture and refinement of thought, emotion and will building a strong and noble character. Education must inspire high ideals and inculcate a real human culture. Annie Besant considered the Indian ideals of education to be in agreement with Theosophy. Therefore, in her educational plan for India, she attempted to restore what her fellow countrymen took away. In her letter to Mr. Hirendra Nath Datta in September 1905, she wrote, "The needs of India are, among others, the development of a national spirit, and an education founded on Indian ideals and enriched, not dominated by the thought and culture of the West."[1] With these ideas Mrs. Annie Besant thought of some kind of marriage between Western education and Indian religion under the control of Indians. Thus, students could acquire the best of both the cultures without losing touch with the Indian way of living.

National Education

Annie Besant's plan of theosophical education in India aimed to establish a national system of education. Her scheme of National Education started with village education supplying the needs of the village and from there ascending tier upon tier through the town and the metropolis and regional universities until it culminated in the National University, serving all the technical and commercial needs of the country. Annie Besant organised the Theosophical Educational Trust under the supervision of her associate, Ernest Wood in order to give a practical shape to her plans. Work in this direction started with the opening of certain institutions like Central Hindu College and Vasantashrama Girls School at Banaras, Anglo-Sanskrit High School at Bankipur, Sanatana Dharma High School at Bhavanagar, and Theosophical High School at Kanpur. Through these institutions Annie Besant taught reverence for all and universal brotherhood. In founding Central Hindu College at Banaras, Annie Besant wanted to bring men of all religions together under the ideal of brotherhood in order to promote Indian cultural values and to remove ill-will among the different sections of the Indian population. She wanted to relieve young Indians from the slave mentality and revive in them a true understanding of Hinduism and citizenship.

Another means of advancing her mission of Theosophy was the establishment of an organisation called, the Sons and Daughters of India in 1911. The principle of this organisation was one act of service every day. Besides this organisation, Annie Besant organised the Scout movement in India for inculcating in young boys the real spirit of service to their fellowmen

1. Col. Olcott, Biographical Notes —*Autobiography of Annie Besant,* Madras, T.P.H., 1939, p. 508.

and women. Robert Baden Powell, founder of the International Scout organisation refused to recognise it. Annie Besant began a campaign for it through her writings in *New India* on 13 October, 1916 under the title "Why Not Indian Scouts". She organised the first troop of scouts at Theosophical High School in Madras. This was Indian Boy Scout Association which later on merged with the international organisation. In this Annie Besant got help from many young Indians, including Mr. V.K. Krishna Menon and his cousin, Mr. Shankara Menon.

SOCIAL REFORM MOVEMENT

In the words of Sidney A. Cook, "Dr. Besant was a rebel reformer."[1] She opposed all kinds of oppression and exploitation of mankind, she was against any and every form of prejudice and cruelty that limited human happiness and progress. As a reformer she worked for improvement of living conditions of the less fortunate of mankind. She was against the continuation of ugly and harmful effects of inhuman relations between exploiters and the exploited workers. Throughout her life she remained a valiant fighter for mass human welfare. She worked with selfless love for mankind in removing ignorance suffering and unbrotherliness among men of different religions, castes and social status. In the field of social activity, she emphasised the importance of 'Dharma' or duty above everything, duty towards a larger self, the organised society, the state and the whole humanity.

In her ideas on desirability of social change Annie Besant was much influenced by Charles Bradlaugh, Bernard Shaw, Sidney Webb and many others. She made a thorough study of the social conditions of her time and analysed the causes. In her autobiography she wrote : "I believe that the poverty is the result of ignorance and of bad social arrangements, and that therefore it may be eradicated by knowledge and by social change."[2] She thought that an important test of human progress was progressive social change, which meant increasing happiness and equality among different sections of people. Annie Besant declared herself to be a socialist in favour of radical change in social and economic conditions. As early as 1877, she favoured planned family system and supported Charles Knowlton's theory of scientific check on population growth. From 1884 to 1888, she led labour movements for better wages and working conditions; she did not recognise any distinction between the 'haves and have nots', the higher and the lower. Her theory was that all were partners in the same game of life and would work in the spirit of brotherhood for creating a worthy of human beings.

AMELIORATION OF WOMEN STATUS

Annie Bcsant was particularly concerned for women, who were subjected to live and work in inhuman conditions without any political privileges. She

1. Sidney A. Cook, *On Dr. Annie Besant.*
2. Annie Besant, *Autobiography*, Madras, Theosophical Publishing House, 1939, p. 408.

denounced the belief that women were inferior to men. As early as 1874, when she was only 27 years old. she started her campaign for the political rights of women.[1] She wanted recognition of the fact that men and women were equally important for the progress of any society. She said, "The man shall bring his greater strength and more sustained determination, the woman her quicker judgement and purer heart, till man shall grow tenderer, and woman stronger, man more pure and woman more brave and free. Till at last, generations hence, the race shall develop into a strength and beauty at present unimagined, and men and women shall walk this fair earth hand in hand, diverse, yet truly one, set each to each as perfect music unto noble words."[2] She worked throughout her life for improving the condition of women and for eradicating evil practices subjecting women to suffering and humiliation.

Annie Besant reminded Indians of their ancient culture when women were treated as equals in all walks of life; she rebuked them for their inhuman treatment of their mothers and sisters. She sad, "Indian greatness will not return until Indian womanhood obtains a large, a freer and a fuller life, for largely in the hands of Indian women must lie the redemption of India."[3] To Annie Besant the movement for the emancipation of women was a human movement because men and women constituted one humanity. In a series of lectures delivered at Banaras in 1900 she outlined changes required to restore Indian women to their rightful place in Indian society. She became instrumental in the passing of a resolution for women's suffrage by the Indian National Congress in 1917. In the same year she organised Women's India Association for spreading education among women for abolition of child marriage and for the restoration of equal rights for them in social and political fields. Her work ultimately led to the establishment of equality among men and women in India.

ERADICATION OF CASTE SYSTEM

Annie Besant was irked by inhuman effects of the caste system. She denounced the social division and friction resulting from the divisions and sub-division of the caste system leading to rivalries in the place of co-operation for the general good. According to her the caste system had fallen into decay under the most disintegrating forces like pride, bigotry, hatred, selfishness, etc. She was confident that most of the social problems could be solved if the abuses interwoven with the caste system could be eliminated.[4]

---

1. Annie Besant's first public speech on : "The Political Status of Women" was published in the London paper *The National Reformer* of 20 August, 1874.
2. Annie Besant, *The Political Status of Women*, London, T.P.S., 1885, p. 14.
3. Annie Besant, *The Education of Indian Girls*, London, T.P.S., p. 10.
4. Annie Besant, *Hinduism*, Madras, T.P.H., 1915, p. 79-81.

POLITICAL IDEAS

In the field of politics Annie Besant's humanistic stand for lofty principles, such as freedom and brotherhood, nationalism and sectarianism were prominent. She was convinced that there is no other way to world peace. There was hardly any political and social movement of her time to which she did not actively take part. On her joining the Theosophical Society, she made it clear that religion and politics could not be divorced. The ideal of Theosophy or universal brotherhood could not be realised unless men were politically treated equal. She was a brilliant orator who could rouse thousands to go out and work for the social and political salvation of mankind.

Demand For Home Rule

When Annie Besant came to India, she promised not to enter into politics of this country. After some time she felt that she could no longer tolerate political discrimination against Indians in their own land. She had already condemned the mis-government of India in her book, *England, India and Afghanistan* in 1878. In 1914, Annie Besant finally decided to join Indian politics intent on seeking Home Rule for India. Her educational scheme was already motivated for inculcating a truly national spirit among the growing generation. She concluded that India could never grow to her full stature unless her soul found expression in every detail of her life. She drew up a charter of Indian liberties listing : individual freedom; self-government; freedom of making or breaking government; internal army; internal financial system and budget; freedom of education; soveregnty; and internal currency system.

Constitutional Methods

Annie Besant never left the path of truth. In her campaign for freedom and political equality for Indians she never ignored the constitutional methods. She repudiated violent methods, leading to breaking of law and subsequent bloodshed. At the Lahore session of the Indian National Congress in 1920, she opposed the resolution of civil disobedience movement of Gandhi. It was her attitude which earned her tributes even from her opponents like Gandhi, who once said, "Annie Besant within a few years brought Home Rule within the consciousness of every Indian village, let alone the town and cities. As had no other Indian worker, she embodied Swaraj (self-rule for India) within the whole of her being."

Annie Besant worked for the constitutional attainment of equality in basic human rights and opportunities. In the words of Jamshedjee Nusserwanjee. "One of the greatest contributions of Dr. Besant to the world was her impersonality. Her actions, attitudes, aims and emotions, all of these were impersonal...She looked upon herself as debtor to every created being.

She came across and acted as if she had to pay up such debts to all and as early as possible."[1] Annie Besant considered herself a servant of humanity and advised others to work in that spirit. In her birthday message on 1 October. 1924 she exhorted her followers by uttering the following words: "Think of the one who is dearest to you on earth; one for whom sacrifice is joy. Then lift up your eyes to the ideal and remember that such debt, limitless love, such joy full of sacrifice are what we each owe to all human brothers."[2]

1. *The Annie Besant Centenary Book,* Madras, The Besant Centenary Celebrations Committee 1957, p. 140.
2. Olcott, Col. H.S., Biographical Notes, *op. cit.*, p. 615.

17
Rabindranath Tagore (1861 — 1941)

Born in 1861 in a rich family in which Upanishads were highly valued. Rabindranath himself could not get high education. In 1893 he raised a voice against the passing of Sedition Act. In 1918 he became the Nobel Prize winner due to his *Gitanjali* and was subsequently given the title of Knight. In 1919 he gave up the title as a protest against the high-handedness and cruelties of British Government in Jallianwala Bagh. In 1941 he died but till his last he continued to work and write.

Born and brought up as an aristocrat and a lover of beauty, Rabindranath Tagore became conscious of his higher mission of bringing men closer to each other. With eyes fixed on the future of mankind, he explored political, social and religious areas of human relationship. His philosophy of man is largely based on perception: "In the vessel of man's affection I taste His divine nectar."[1] He voiced the ancient wisdom of India.

Contemporary Circumstances

In his speech in China in 1924, Tagore is reported to have pointed out that at the time he was born, three distinct movements had met in the life of his country. The first was the religio-intellectual movement led by Rammohan Roy which restored confidence in Indians about their religion and culture. The second was the literary movement whose greatest representative was Bankim Chandra Chatterjee. The third was the national movement for the political, economic and social relief of the country. For twenty-three years of his early youth, Tagore wrote poetry and looked at life as a visionary inspired by his father Maharishi Devendranath Tagore. In 1883, Tagore published his poem "The Awakening of the Waterfall", which marked his entry into the wide world. The "Waterfall" suggested the life-force and symbolished the enlargement of the individual's and his entry into the universal life of humanity.

Influence of Upanishads

With the onset of the twentieth century Tagore's ideas turned from the praise and contemplation of beauty to that of the Lord of life. Under the influence

1. Tagore, *Arogya*, p. 29.

of the liberal tradition of his family and the philosophy of the Upanishads, he developed a positive view of life and love of humanity. He carried India's message of love and universal brotherhood to all parts of the world and thus tried to bring East and West together on the pure and lofty platform of human relationship. He abhorred all conflicts between man and man, between nation and nation. He could easily understand the demands of the new age and warned. "From now onward any nation which takes an isolated view of its own country will run counter to the spirit of the New Age, and know no peace. From now onward the anxiety that each country has for its own safety must embrace the welfare of the world."[1]

Influence of Buddhism

Rabindranath was deeply influenced by the humanist tradition of the Buddha, and the Buddhist way of life appealed to him most. Tagore stressed that man must come out of the shell of his individual self in order to enter into the larger self of humanity. So long as he remained confined within the walls of his individuality, his selfishness, his own material longings, joys and sorrows, he could not realise the universal man, neither could he get relief from the misery of the world. Tagore said, "To live in perfect goodness is to realise one's life in the infinite. This is the most comprehensive view of life which we can have by our inherent power of the moral vision of the wholeness of life. And the teaching of Buddha is to cultivate this moral power to the highest extent, know that our field of activities is not found to the plane of our narrow self."[2]

Influence of Medieval Indian Spiritualism

Rabindranath was deeply influenced by the medieval Indian religious and social philosophy. In the spirit of the medieval saints and poets he talked of the divinity of Man. Like Rajjab, a poet-saint of medieval India, he considered man as God-man (*Nara-narayana*). Like Ravidas, another saint, he called man Divine Man (*Narhari*). Like Chandidas, he said that the truth of man was the highest truth. All this proves that Tagore perceived humanity as an objective truth.

Influence of Kabir

Kabir's attempt to reconcile Mohammedan mysticism with the traditional theology of Brahmanism in the interest of harmony left an abiding impression on Tagore. Kabir's direct apprehension of God as the supreme object, of love as a comrade, which finds passionate expression in his poems captivated Tagore's imagination and coloured his religious outlook. Tagore translated

---

1. W. Norman Brown, "Some Ethical Concepts for the Modern World from Hindu and Indian Buddhist Tradition" (Article in *Centenary Volume of Rabindranath Tagore*), Delhi, Sahitya Academy, 1961, p. 395.
2. Tagore, *Sadhana*, London, Macmillan and Co., 1954, p. 57.

one hundred poems of Kabir into English. He may be considered as the most sympathetic interpreter of Kabir's vision and thought.

Like Kabir, Rabindranath considered the universe as the manifestation of God. This finds expression in his poetry, especially in *Gitanjali.* For example, at one place he wrote:

Thou art the sky, and thou art
the nest as well.[1]

This idea of divine manifestation in Kabir's poems[2] was interpreted by Tagore in the light of his own belief in the reality of both God and Nature. Kabir's large-heartedness, his love for all mankind irrespective of caste, creed and sex, his relentless campaign against all kinds of dogmas and superstitions of Hinduism, and lastly, his attitude towards life in the world largely moulded Tagore's philosophy of life.

Product of Composite Culture

Rabindranath Tagore has been aptly described as a product of a composite culture. The best of Indian culture was preserved in the traditions of his family. At the same time it also borrowed liberally the virtues of the European culture. Early in his youth, Tagore was influenced by humanism of the West, especially love of freedom and the large hearted radicalism of the British people. He accepted the Western definition of humanism that man was the dominant and ultimate reality. If there is a God, He must be interpreted in human terms. Rejecting the traditionalism and orthodoxy of Hinduism, Tagore adapted to the spirituality of Western humanism.

Humanism

Tagore felt that it was only on the basis of humanism that the wide gulf between the East and the West could be bridged, a synthetic culture could be evolved. His imagination was roused and the desire of creating a new civilisation from the synthesis of East and West began very early in his life, and throughout his life he worked for the fulfilment of his noble ideal. Tagore carried the humanistic message of India and the nationalism of the East for the universal brotherhood, peace and prosperity of all mankind irrespective of nationality, religion and colour.

Cosmopolitanism

Appreciating the variety of cultures of the different nations, their development in different ways, Tagore considered it essential that all nations meet at a point of benefit to each other. "It is best for the commerce of the spirit that people differently situated should bring their different products into the market of humanity each of which is complementary and necessary to the other."[3] As

1. Tagore, *Gitanjali-67,* London, Macmillan and Co., 1953 (English).
2. Kabir, *Tu surat main nihat — Kabir's poems*, Calcutta, Macmillan and Co., 1929, LXXVI, 1929.
3. Tagore, *Sadhana*, London, Macmillan and Co., 1954, p. 12.

a realist, Tagore was of the opinion that national differences were essential for the smooth and harmonious development of humanity. Such differences should only create a desire for greater understanding of each other's point of view and each other's merits. In 1917 Tagore said, "The monsoon clouds generated on the banks of the Nile fertilise the far distant shores of the Ganges — ideas may have to cross from the East to the Western shores to find a welcome in men's hearts and fulfil their promise. East is East and West is West — God forbid that it should be otherwise, but the twain must meet in unity, peace and mutual understanding."[1] Thus Tagore was better fitted than anybody else to call for a real appraisal of the spirit of East and West and their reconciliation.

Rationalism and Humanitarianism

As a rationalist and humanitarian in his attitude towards the whole problem of East and West relationship Rabindranath was disgusted by the artificial divisions in men on the basis of castes and creeds and rebuked Indians for being dogmatic and superstitious. He was pained by the materialistic basis of Western civilisation. He wanted a compromise between Western science and Indian spiritualism in order to guide the human race, in order to evolve a common culture and uniform ethical standards. He was aware that the mechanical character of occidental civilisation had turned human beings into mere slaves, killed their freedom and initiative, to act in a natural way. But he also discovered that there was an organised effort in the West toward physical and intellectual perfection. Tagore wanted it to come forward with its science and culture to the aid of the weak and helpless nations. Thus, could it justify itself in the eyes of humanity.

Opposition to Colonialism

At times he was disturbed with the attitude of the British imperialists in their exploitation of the various Asian colonies including India. Reminding the Westerners, Tagore said, "You must know that red tape can never be a common human bond; that official sealing-wax can never provide means of mutual attachment."[2] On the occasion of his eighteenth birthday at Santiniketan, Tagore said. "It is no longer possible for us to retain any respect for that mockery of civilization which believes in ruling by force and has no faith in freedom at all."[3]

East and West

Distinguishing the attitude of the East and the West, Tagore pointed out that the West did not believe that the universe had a soul, it only believed in the

1. Tagore, *Lectures on Nationalism*, Macmillan and Co., London, 1917.
2. Tagore, *Creative Unity*, London, Macmillan and Co., 1926, p. 109.
3. Sasadhar Sinha, *Social Thinking of Rabindranath Tagore*, p. 143, N. Delhi, Asia Publishing House, 1962.

soul of man. On the other hand the whole mental contribution of the East to mankind is filled with the idea of universal soul. Both must cooperate with each other, give each other whatever they can offer in order to fulfil their aspirations. No one can deny the scientific achievements of the West. At the same time India could supply a corrective to the misuse of science through her contribution to religion and philosophy. The unity between East and West would mean the unity of spiritual and scientific knowledge.

Ideal of One World : Vishwa-Bharati

Rabindranath wanted to realise the ideal of one world on the basis of intellectual cooperation between the East and the West. In order to provide a common platform to the men of different cultures, Tagore planned to establish an international university. The synthesis of the East and West, as for their religious and cultural values, he thought could help in realising lasting peace and happiness for mankind. The idea of such a university included the thought of a conference of East and West, a common fellowship of learning and common spiritual striving for the unity of the human race. Tagore said, "Being strongly impressed with the need and responsibility, which every individual must realise according to his power, I have formed the nucleus of an international university in India as one of the best means of promoting mutual understanding between the East and West."[1] Thus, Visva-Bharti became the centre of world culture to promote goodwill among people of different nations and religions. The ultimate aim before Tagore was to promote international amity and understanding and fulfil the highest mission of the present age, the unification of mankind. The motto he selected for his university is *'yatra visvam bhavti ekanidam'* — where the universe becomes a single nest.

Tagore knew that in spite of efforts from various directions the East and West were not showing any real sign of meeting. He felt that, "the reason is because the West has not sent out its humanity to meet the man in the East, but only its machine."[2] The political civilization which has sprung up from Europe has overrun the weak nations of the world. Instead of helping the weak nations in their progress, it has gone everywhere with hungry jaws and bloody teeth.

With his strongest faith in man, Tagore, could never accept the idea of non-cooperation with the West. He always advised his countrymen to have a wide outlook and meet vice with good, hatred with love. At the same time, he considered it essential for the East to learn from the West with an open mind. The true greatness of the West consisted in its spirit of service devoted to the welfare of man.

A few weeks before his death Tagore wrote, "I had one time believed that the springs of civilization would issue out of the heat of Europe. But today,

1. Tagore, *Creative Unity*, London, Macmillan and Co., 1926, pp. 172-73.
2. *Ibid.*, p. 109, 1926.

when I am about to quit the world, the faith has gone bankrupt altogether."[1] Tagore advised all nations to take up the responsibility in future to build a new society devoid of hatred and selfishness. He was of the view that only a humanitarian approach could resolve mutual conflict. In the words of Dr. S. Radhakrishnan, "Rabindranath puts forward a plea for mankind by advocating the ideal of a family of nations to which every member will bring his unique gift. This ideal of international unity and national independence will break down barriers of nations and make for sweet harmony."[2]

NEO-VEDANTA

Rabindranath Tagore imbibed Vedantic orientation from his early childhood. The family had a mixed environment. He was very much impressed by his father, "The Maharishi". Upanishads too appealed to him most. He was a lover of nature from the very beginning. The seclusion of the child made a positive contribution towards drawing him more and more to nature. It made him think for long about the secrets of nature. The young mind would think not only over the creation but the creator also.

Upanishad's impact on Tagore's mind is evident from his lines: "To me the verses of the Upanishads and the teachings of Buddha have ever been things of the spirit, and therefore endowed with boundless vital growth; and I have used them, both in my own life and in my preachings as being instinct with individual meaning for me, as for others, and awaiting for their confirmation, my own special testimony, which must have its value because of its individuality."[3]

PHILOSOPHY OF RELIGION

Tagore thought and worked in Indian tradition. His entire thought is based on personal observation or 'Anubhava'. He was a visionary who reached conclusions by deducting generalities from observation. This method of his holds good for his religion also. He admits "my religion is a poet's religion; all that I feel about it is from vision and not from knowledge. I frankly say that I cannot satisfactorily answer your question about evil, or what happens after death. And yet I am sure that there have been some moments when my soul has touched the Infinite and has become intensely conscious of it through the illuminations of joy."[4]

For Tagore religion is an effort of man to attain the ultimate truth. He says, "It consists in the endeavour of man to cultivate and express those

---

1. Tagore, *Towards Universal Man*, p. 356. Bombay, Asia Publishing House, 1962.
2. S. Radhakrishnan, *Philosophy of Rabindranath Tagore*, p. 285. London, Macmillan and Co., 1918.
3. Tagore, R.N., *Sadhana*, Preface. D. VIII
4. Soarej, Anthony, *Lectures and Addresses of Rabindranath*, pp. 16-17.

qualities which are in him. If those qualities were absolutely natural in individual, religion could have no purpose."[1]

For Tagore religion is a means to higher values in man. "Man in his religion cultivates the vision of a being who exceeds him in truth and with whom also he has his kinship. These religions differ in details and often in their moral significance, but they have a common tendency. In them men seek their own supreme value in some personality, anthropomorphic in character. The mind which is abnormally scientific, stops at this; but it should know that religion is not essentially cosmic or even abstract; it finds itself, when it touches the Brahman in man; otherwise it has no justification to exist."[2]

Tagore has assigned a definite constructive purpose to religion. He opines "Religion has its function in reconciling the contradiction by subordinating the brute nature to what we consider as the truth of man... Religion concentrates itself on humanity, which illumines our reason, inspires our wisdom, stimulates our love, claims our intelligent service."[3]

Opposed to Ritualism

In order to translate their preachings into action religious leaders develop some organization. Tagore feared that with the coming up of the organization the natural growth of the religion is hampered. He points out, "Where religion has to make way for religious organization it is like the river being dominated by its sandbed; the current stagnates and its higher aspects become desert-like."[4]

The ritualistic aspect of religion presupposes some deity or set of deities, places of worship, rituals and dogmas. This aspect is as essential as the ideational one. Tagore is opposed to this aspect of religion. He maintained that unintelligible rituals and dogmas are at best only cohesive principles that hold together individuals of a particular community marking them off from individuals of other groups. Rabindranath has no sympathy for these. Man tends to separate one individual from another, or one group from another, tends in effect to deny the humanity of man and is as such anti-religious, unless, of course, religion is something totally divorced from the essential spirit in man, *viz.*, reason, morality and love. This, in a netshell, is Rabindranath's reaction against rituals and dogmas."[5]

Opposed to Orthodoxy

Due to his humanistic orientation towards religion Tagore was opposed to fanaticism. He opines that "orthodoxy is not necessarily narrow-mindedness.

1. Tagore, R. N., *The Religion of Man*, p. 144.
2. *Ibid.*, p. 63.
3. *Ibid.*, p. 144.
4. *Modern Review*, p. 325.
5. Bhattacharya, K., *Homage from Visva-Bharati* (1962), p. 32.

What matters seriously is whether these orthodox people are fanatics or not. Fanaticism is definitely anti-religious, and when Rabindranath condemns unintelligible rituals and dogmas, this is only because the line between fanaticism and orthodoxy is very thin."[1]

Opposed to Idolatory

As a result of this rational outlook towards religion, Rabindranath opposed Idolatory. "Rabindranath is against Idolatory, not so much because idolators circumscribe God but primarily because they hypostatise as a person or entity what is really a living function; and he would equally speak against those who, even knowing that he is a functional unity, yet personify him. If God is a person, He is ever dynamic, ever dissolving Himself, as the indwelling spirit of all individuals."[2]

Votary of Golden Mean

Tagore always believed in the theory of golden mean. He was a synthesiser and as such "he had never been an orthodox puritan and had no sympathy for the iconoclasts of his time, and yet he never shook hands with the orthodox."[3]

Unity of Mankind

The main end of religion for Rabindranath was the unity of mankind. He believed that this unity could come through spirituality alone. Though Tagore had great faith in the spirituality of the East yet he did not contribute to the opinion that it was the monopoly of the East. He was convinced that the material advancement of the West could not occur in the absence of spirituality.

> Tagore's God lives at humble places in the company of humble people. "Here is thy footstool and there rest thy feet where live the poorest, and lowliest and lost...
> My heart can never find its way where thou keepest company with the companionless among the poorest, and the lowliest and the lost."[4]
> The God is there "Where the tiller is tilling the hard ground and where the path maker is breaking the stones, He is with them in sun and shower, and His garment is covered with dust. Put off thy holy mantle and even like Him come down on the dusty soil."[5]

PHILOSOPHY OF HISTORY

Philosophy is in a certain sense based upon interpretation of history, since history is not merely an anthology of the deeds of some individuals

1. *Ibid.*, p. 33.
2. *Ibid.*, p. 42.
3. *Ibid.*, p. 44.
4. Tagore, R.N., *Gitanjali,* Song 10.
5. *Ibid.*, Song 11.

but a record of the pace of humanity in its various stages and directions, it gives a peep into the future of man. Tagore was a keen student of history. This is explicit from his article "Itihas Katha". Written in 1905 this article is an important document about Tagore's interpretation of history. He laid emphasis upon the importance of knowledge of history. He said, "If you think closely, we shall see that the greatest disparity in knowledge between the educated and uneducated in our country lies in the knowledge of history...It is a most lamentable ignorance for man not to know what man has done or can do in this world."[1]

Histoiy acquaints people with their country. It is the record of the glory and weaknesses of the race. Therefore, the historians owe a great responsibility towards the people. Indian history so far, however, has been rather royal biography. Therefore, Tagore pleaded for re-writing of Indian history. Explaining his idea of history he said, "History is a manifestation of the dialectical process, of the play of opposing forces and the attempt to establish a balance between them. Indian history presents a clear picture of this historical dialectics and the attempt to strike a balance, which should be duly stressed by historians."[2]

He also criticised teaching of history in India which was mainly based upon cramming of instances. He, on the other hand, emphasised critical examination and authenticity. In the words of H.B. Mukherjee, "Tagore attached considerable importance to the collection of original and authentic historical material by the students from direct sources through 'region study' and independent researches as also excursions and tours to places of historical interest in order to have a vivid and realistic impression of the historical significance of the places visited and the objects seen at first hand."[3]

Interpretation of Indian History

In the words of Tagore, "Man's history is the history of his journey to the unknown in the quest of the realization of his immortal self — of his soul. Through the rise and fall of empires, through the building up of gigantic piles of wealth and the ruthless scattering of them upon the dust; through the creation of vast bodies of symbols that give shape to his drama and aspirations, and the casting of them away like the playthings of an outworn infancy, through the forging of his magic keys with which to unlock the mysteries of creation, and through his throwing away of this labour of ages to go back to his worship and work afresh in some new form! yes: through it all man is marching from epoch towards the fullest realization of his soul, — the soul which is greater than the things man accumulates, the deeds he accomplishes, he themes he builds, the soul whose onward course is never checked by death or dissolution."[4]

1. *Rabindra Rachnawali,* Vol. XII, Visva-Bharati, 1939-48, p. 520.
2. *The Vishvabharti Ideal,* Vishvabharti, Natesan, pp. 13-14.
3. Mukherjee, H.B., *Education for Fulness,* Asia Publishing House, 1965, p. 401.
4. Tagore, R. N., *A Message,* p. 78.

Indian history is a record of the stages, progress, the ideals of Indian people. It records the social life and spiritual attainments of India. According to Tagore Indian history however needs to be re-written. It has been a process of constant adjustment between different sections of people. Explaining the goal of history Tagore pointed out, "Neither the colourless vagueness of cosmopolitanism, nor the fierce self-idolatoly of national worship, is the goal of history. And India has been trying to accomplish her task through social regulation of differences on the one hand, and the spiritual recognition of unity on the other. She has made grave errors in setting up the boundary walls too rigidly between races, in perpetuating in her classifications the results of inferiority, often she has crippled her children's minds and narrowed their lives in order to fit them into her social forms, but for centuries new experiments have been made and adjustments carried out."[1]

In his analysis of Indian history Tagore found the keynote in the principle of unity in diversity. This has been supported by other historians as well. Even the *Mahabharata* and the *Ramayana* mainly portray attempts at synthesis and adjustment between good and evil, different classes, various races and ideologies. In his pamphlet entitled, *A Vision of India's History,* Tagore showed a deep insight into the processes of Indian history when he said, "The history of India has been the history of the struggle between the constructive spirit of the machine, which seeks the decadence of order and conformity in social organisation, and the creative spirit of man, which seeks freedom and love for its self-expression. We have to watch and see that the latter is still living in India; and also whether the former offers its service and hospitability to life, through which its system can be vitalized."[2]

Thus, Tagore maintained that the history of India is a history of social evolution. In his interpretation of the two great epics the *Ramayana* and the *Mahabharata,* Tagore has shown them as records of two great social revolutions. *Mahabharata* and *Ramayana* both depict the conflict between Aryans and the Dravidians and finally a synthesis between the two. In his interpretation and explanation of both these epics Tagore has laid special emphasis on their spiritual nature. He has taken special pains to explain the mythology found in these epics. He has accepted Rama and Krishna as Avataras, who came on the earth for some special purposes. According to Tagore both the epics depict cultural assimilation between Aryans and Dravidians. In his opinion Indian culture is a product of cross-fertilization between these two great cultures. To quote his words, "Dravidians might not be introspective or metaphysical, but they were artists, and they could sing, design and construct. The transcendental thought of the Aryans by its marriage with the emotional and creative art of the Dravidians gave birth to an offspring which was neither fully Aryan, nor Dravidian, but Hindu."[3]

---

1. Tagore, R.N., *Nationalism,* Macmillan, London, 1960. p. 5.
2. Tagore, R.N., *A Vision of India's History,* Visva-Bharati, 1960. p. 90.
3. *Ibid.,* p. 31.

Besides these two cultures, India has been the scene of the synthesis of several other cultures of the people who invaded the country from the West. Tagore was against dividing Indian history into periods based upon the rule of particular people of the country such as Moghal period and Pathan period etc. This, according to him, is an unwarranted division of a continued history of the country. About the Moghal and Pathan periods he points out that they were invaders and not part of the nation. Therefore their rule should not be particularly emphasized. Similarly, British rule in India was a great misfortune and therefore it should not be emphasized in the teaching of history. As compared to earlier invaders the Britishers had some novelty which was realised by Tagore though he did not mince words in condemning the rule of British people over India. Thus, according to Tagore, Indian history was yet to be written in its true spirit. In his own words, "The real history of India was yet to be written by Indian writers, who were in a better position to undertake the task from a more accurate perspective than foreign writers nursed in different historical traditions. Though the Indian historians are likely to interpret Indian history from a viewpoint entirely opposed to foreign historians, and to be equally blameworthy for partisanship and lack of dispassionate historical objectivity, the two opposite extremes would help a third party to approach the task with considerable impartiality and objectivity."[1]

IDEAL OF PROGRESS

Interpretation of history very much depends upon the ideal of progress. Progress is interpreted in terms of movement towards a goal. Different thinkers have laid emphasis upon different goals of life, thereby presenting different concepts of progress. Tagore's ideal of progress is religion-oriented. The ideal of man, according to him, is perfection. This requires spiritual progress. For the attainment of this aim man has to conquer the weaknesses of his flesh. The real progress, however, is not only the progress of the individual, it is the progress of the Nation and ultimately of the Humanity.

According to Radhakrishnan, "To him progress and reform consist in conserving the ancient ideas and building upon them. Preserving the soul of the Indian style, we may adopt whatever is good and noble in the West."[2] Thus, Tagore synthesized the Eastern and Western concepts of progress. Progress, according to him, lies in harmony. Harmony has been the central principle of Indian culture. Disharmony, on the other hand, is detrimental to progress. In Indian society the agricultural pattern has to be synthesised with the industrial order. Science has to be harmonised with the spirituality. The knowledge of the West should be synthesised with the wisdom of the East. It is accepted that India is more spiritual while West is more material.

1. Tagore, R.N., *Itihas Katha*, p. 118.
2. Radhakrishnan, S., *The Philosophy of Rabindranath Tagore*, Macmillan, London, 1919, p. 197.

A solution for their ideal progress requires a synthesis of both. Criticising the materialistic ideal of progress Tagore said, "What is called progress is the progress in mechanical contrivances; it is in fact an indefinite extension of our physical limbs and organs, which, owing to the enormous material advantage that it brings to us, has tempted the modern man away from his inner realm of spiritual values."[1]

Thus, Tagore wanted a synthesis of spiritual and material values for real progress of mankind. This is very explicit in his ideas concerning Indian society and its problems and remedies which we will now discuss in sequence.

PHILOSOPHY OF SOCIETY

Social philosophy is philosophy of society. Society is a web of social relationships. It includes social relations between different sections of society. These social relations involve processes of social control and social change. The social relationships are regularised through social institutions. In his philosophy of society, Tagore analysed the structure of Hindu society of his time, pointed out its evils, and suggested remedies.

Evils of Hindu Society

As an enlightened and intellectual leader of his time, Tagore was very much conscious of the evils of the society around him. As a poet he was most sensitive to the atrocities of the strong over the weak. He revolted against the prevalent evil customs of Hindu society. Since he was basically a devout Hindu, his analysis is mainly concerned with Hindu society. His ideal everywhere has been humanistic and synthetic. The bases of Hindu society are philosophical. Varnashram system is the backbone of Hindu social structure. Pointing out to this system, Tagore said, "The Indian mind has ever been oriented towards that transcendentalism which does not hold religion to be ultimate but rather to be a means to a farther end. This end consists in the perfect liberation of the individual in the universal spirit across the furthest limits of humanity itself."[2]

Thus, the sages of Hindus established a uniform social order throughout the country. In this social order people were categorised in different varnas and life was understood as a sequence through four stages known as Ashramas. Tagore was a great admirer of this system though he condemned the narrow use of the term *dwija* for Brahmins. According to him this term should be used for all the people and therefore no one should be barred from any Hindu Sanskar. Praising the social system and its uniformity in India Tagore said, "In India, the whole mind of the people spread itself over the entire country even to the remotest villages, in thought and deed and joy. This explains why the successive onslaughts of various foreign powers in different

1. Tagore, R.N., *Boundless Sky*, Visva-Bharti, 1964, p. 297.
2. Tagore, R N., *The Religion of Man*, George Allen & Unwin, 1932, p. 191.

periods of her history have not been fatal to her. Not a village was without its institution for elementary education, located in the 'Chandimandap' of the local magnate. For every four or five villages there was at least one learned Pundit freely giving his store of learning to those who sought it. On such men rested the responsibility of maintaining the purity of the traditional social ideal. The enjoyment of wealth in those days was not narrowly personal. From each main current of wealth branched out a number of irrigation canals on every side. Similarly, intellectual treasures of the wise were freely open to all. Teachers, far from demanding fees, did not look to the students for their maintenance. Thus, did the multifarious life force permeate each village. That was why there was then no scarcity of food or water, and the spirit of man had not to starve."[1] Pointing out the evils of Hindu society Tagore particularly condemned the following:

1. **Super Naturalism** In Indian social thought the duties have been determined by some supernatural power or God. Therefore, there is no option to doing one's own duties allotted by the Caste in which he is born. Indian society is duty-oriented, this has suppressed rights of a section of people. Condemning this irrational situation of basing everything on supernatural powers and the scriptures which record the dictates of these supernatural powers Tagore said, "Reason and judgement have no place in our social customs either; it is simply not the form to ask why we do, or how to do, this or that. In the entire universe India alone is exempt from the law of cause and effect, her courses are latent in the scriptures. It is the scriptures that must determine whether sea voyages are good or bad, and the Pundits must decide whether the entry of a person in your room would contaminate the water in your Hookah. Why it should be transgression to drink water touched by a low caste hand but not milk, date, juice or treacle; why one should lose caste if one eats rice prepared by a non-Hindu but not if it is wine — you ask these questions and you will be forced into silence by threats of social ostracism."[2]
2. **Casteism** Almost all the contemporary Indian social philosophers have maintained that casteism is the main evil of the present Hindu society. All these have condemned this evil and Tagore was no exception. Pointing out to this evil of Hindu society in his characteristic poetic expression, Tagore said, "In her caste regulations India recognized difference but not the mutuality which is the law of life. She accepted nature where it produces diversity, but ignored it where it used that diversity, for its world-games of infinite permutations and combinations. She treated life in all truth where it is manifold, but insulted it where it is moving. Therefore, life departed from her social system and in its place she

1. *Ibid.*, p. 20.
2. *Ibid.*, pp. 150-151.

is worshipping with all ceremony the magnificent cage of countless compartments that she has manufactured."[1]

Thus, Tagore, "was a severe critic of caste system."[2] He believed and repeatedly declared that the caste system and its attendant practice of untouchability were among the darkest blots of Indian society."[3]

3. **Untouchability** Vivekananda, Gandhi, Tagore and other contemporary Indian social philosophers have also condemned untouchability along with casteism practised in Hindu society. While Gandhi was the architect of the anti-untouchability reform movement in India, Tagore as a writer and poet analysed the malady in all its details. His dance drama *Chandalika* and his novel *Gora* analysed in details the feelings of the untouchables, their disabilities and suggested remedy. He not only condemned the practice of untouchability but made solid efforts for its removal. He organised a scouting team named 'Brati Balak' for fighting untouchability. He organised Hindu Mela as a social get-together of all the sections of Hindu society. The purpose of this get-together was the development of a general community consciousness among Hindus. In his novel *Gora* Tagore has given a vivid description of the social evils found in rural India. To quote his own words, "Gora saw the image of his country 's weakness, naked and unashamed, in the midst of the lethargy of village life where the blows from outside could not work so readily. He could see nowhere any trace of that religion which through service, love, compassion, self-respect for humanity as a whole, gives power and life and happiness to all. The tradition which merely divided men into classes and separated class from class, driving to a distance even love itself, did not want to carry its effect that results of man's intelligent thinking, and only put obstacles at every step in the way of man's coming and going."[4]

Paresh Babu in *Gora* explains the wrath of untouchability in these words, "There is no harm in a cat sitting by and eating right besides you. But if certain men so much as enter the room, the food has to be thrown away. How can one not condemn the caste system which has resulted in this contempt and insult of man by man? If that is not unrighteous, I do not know what is, those who can despise their fellow-men so terribly can never rise to greatness; for them in turn, shall be reserved the contempt of others."[5] The heartfelt sorrow of this old man is depicted in these words: "What I actually see before me is

1. Tagore, R.N., *Nationalism,* Macmillan, London, 1960, p. 116.
2. Sinha, S., *Social Thinking of Rabindranath Tagore,* Asia Publishing House, 1962, p. 7.
3. Kabir, H., *Social and Political Ideas of Tagore,* p. 146.
4. Tagore, R N., *Gora,* Macmillan, London, 1963, p. 368.
5. *Ibid.,* p. 120.

the intolerable aversion of man for man in our country and how it is dividing and sub-dividing our people."[1]

The different characters in this novel have condemned the practice of untouchability in strongest words. They maintain that unless the society can give them social justice it has no claims upon the individuals. The relation of the individual and society, according to Tagore, is mutual and interdependent. A true Indian, according to him, should not be against any religion because Hinduism does not preach hatred. In his vision of Indian society Tagore was not limited to Hinduism alone. He wanted the society in which the distinctions of caste, untouchability and religions should go. In the words of Gora, Tagore said, "Today give me mantram of that deity who belongs to all, Hindu, Mussulman, Christian and Brahmo alike — the doors of whose temple are never closed to any person of any caste, whatever, He who is not merely the God of the Hindus but who is the God of India herself."[2]

4. **Joint family** In rural India the family has been joint for centuries. The joint family system had its own advantages, but under the present changed circumstances these advantages have almost dwindled. The disadvantages of the joint family system, on the other hand, are very conspicuous. Therefore, most of the contemporary Indian social thinkers are in favour of abolition of joint family. This is so also because of the fact that joint family is connected with caste.

   Tagore pointed out that joint family system is particularly injurious for marital adjustment of the newly wedded couples. Neglect of children and lack of privacy for the couple are the two banes of joint family which have led to its present disintegration. In one of his letters to his wife Tagore wrote, "I have come to the conclusion that at least for a short period immediately after marriage a girl should keep away from her parents and give herself unrestricted opportunity for being with her husband. The presence of her parents in the midst of this union interferes with it because the habits and tastes of her husband's family are not the same as those of her own, and there are bound to be differences of opinion. With her parents near at hand a girl cannot forget her old ways and identify herself wholly with her husband."[3]

5. **Lower status of women** As a poet and a novelist Tagore was naturally sensitive towards the difficulties of women in our society. In his different literary works he has vividly described the evils of child marriage, the Purdah system and the custom of Sati practised in Indian society. He has deplored the Hindu concept of superiority of men over women and called it a relic of the barbaric age. He has praised the women for their qualities of chastity, modesty, devotion, power of self-

1. *Ibid.*
2. *Ibid.*, p. 407.
3. Chakravarti, A., *A Tagore Reader*, Macmillan, New York, 1961, p. 18.

sacrifice, grace and sweetness, stability, rhythm, reciprocity and other human qualities. He maintained that in the present cultural crisis of Hindu society women can play an important role for which they should be given equality of status. Without such equality the family institution cannot work because according to Tagore balance of power is the central core of family. In his own words, "Balance of power, however, between man and woman was in a measure established when home wielded a strong enough attraction to make men accept its obligation."[1] While emphasising equality for women Tagore warned her that freedom is not frivolity. He was against overlapping roles of the male and the female. He emphasised different roles for males and females which are complementary to each other. He pointed out that without the regeneration of women, our society cannot progress. He said, "Women can bring her fresh mind and all her power of sympathy to this new task of building up a spiritual civilization, if she will be conscious of her responsibilities. Of course, she can be frivolous or very narrow in her outlook, and then, she will miss her great mission. And just because woman has been insulted, has been living in a sort of obscurity behind man, I think she will have her compensation in the civilization which is waiting to come."[2]

From the above discussion it is clear that Tagore wanted to give equal status to women in society. He regarded family as an institution based upon balance of power, a balance between the wife and husband, the parents and the children. In this balance both the parts of a relationship were complementary. Thus, Tagore visualized a society based on perfect harmony, cooperation and absolute absence of exploitation. In his novels Tagore has often commented upon the mercilessness of society. He has condemned evil customs concerning marriage and family such as bride price, dowry and domination of male over female etc. He was a vehement critic of Purdah system.

POLITICAL THOUGHT

Society and Individual

The most important concept in social philosophy is the relation between the individual and society. Here, as everywhere, Tagore has maintained that harmony is the basis of all relationships. It is the aim of all attempts at social reconstruction. Tagore believed in the functional and organic concept of society. In his own words, "Society as such has no ulterior purpose. It is an end in itself. It is a spontaneous self-expression of man as a social being. It is a natural regulation of human relationships, so that men can develop ideals

---

1. Tagore, R.N., *Creative Unity*, Macmillan, London, 1926, p. 160.
2. Tagore, R.N., *Personality*, Macmillan, London, 1954, p. 183.

of life in cooperation with one another."[1] Like Sri Aurobindo, Tagore believed that society is the expression of the divine. Both individuals and society are equally expressions of the divine force.

Tagore has analysed human nature with the insight of a poet and novelist. About human nature he said, "Man has two sides — the individual and the social. One is unreal without the other. When man in a sudden impulse rushes headlong in the direction and losing balance causes all manner of trouble, the counsellor wanting to cut short the crisis advises chopping of one side altogether. When individualism turns into downright selfishness and runs foul of society, the lopping off of "self" at one stroke from self-interest is the proposed remedy for all trouble. Trouble may thereby be lessened but it is not improbable that society will cease to move altogether."[2] Thus, man is by nature individual as well as social and the real problem is to create a harmony between these two sides of men. Pointing out the importance of the concept of society in the social philosophy of Tagore, Bhattacharjee has written, "Samaj or society is the key concept in his social philosophy. He visualized it as a living organism, the basic institution necessary to ensure the material, cultural, moral and spiritual fulfilment of the individuals composing it. The goal of the samaj is to advance the 'civilization' of the people."[3] This goal can be achieved by giving perfect spiritual freedom to the individuals and creating in them a strong sense of social trust and responsibility.

The State and the Individual

While on the one hand Tagore was an admirer of the Russian system of communist society, on the other hand as a poet he was against the dominance of the state. He wanted the state to function as a subordinate institution for the maintenance of law and order. He was not an anarchist but he believed in individual freedom. Though he was against domination of the state he did not think that the state functions are only negative. Like his contemporary philosophers he believed in a welfare state. Pointing out the relation between his social and political philosophy, Sachin Sen has rightly said, "Tagore's social and political philosophy are integrally linked with each other. That is why he could never think of political freedom and growth in isolation from social freedom and integral development. Nay, he went much further and also included in the content of freedom, economic independence, and emancipation of the individual in every respect."[4] Freedom, according to Tagore, has a comprehensive meaning. It is not only social but also economic, political and finally spiritual freedom. It is hence that Tagore was equally against social evils, poverty and political exploitation. Explaining the real meaning of the term freedom in his social philosophy Tagore points

---

1. Tagore, R.N., *Nationalism*, p. 9.
2. Tagore, R.N., *The Religion of Man*, George Allen & Unwin, 1932, p. 143.
3. Bhattacharjee, J.P., *Homage from Visva-Bharati*, Visva Bharti, Santiniketan, 1962, p. 204.
4. Sen, Sachin, *Political Ideal of Rabindra Nath Tagore*, V.B.Q. Vol. 24, Nos. 3 & 4, p. 155.

out, "Real freedom is of the mind and spirit; it can never come to us from outside. He only has freedom who ideally loves freedom himself and is glad to extend it to others. He who cares to have slaves must chain himself to them; he who builds walls to create exclusion for others builds walls across his own freedom; he who distrusts freedom in others looses his moral right to it. Sooner or later he is lured into the meshes of physical and moral servility."[1] This emphasis on human freedom is the basis of Tagore's Religion of Man, Humanism, Cosmopolitanism and his faith in democracy. He was opposed to Totalitarianism. He had firm faith in democratic values. Like his contemporary philosophers he opposed British Rule in India. He was a great patriot who loved his country with all his heart. He was proud of his country and his people. He has praised Indian people in his novels. He took very active part in struggle for independence against the British. Whenever there was an occasion he raised his voice against the Government. In his political views he was not an extremist but in the political programme of Indian National Congress he was not with the moderates. Pointing out his position in this matter K. Kripalani has written, "Tagore has no sympathy with the moderates of the Congress Party whose political faith is symbolized by the mid-victorian catchwords of Rationalism and Enlightenment, progress and liberty, and whose method is the peaceful constitutional agitation through the press and the platform...He thinks that the moderates have developed mendicancy in politics into a fine art. The followers of this "Begging Method" do not know what paths lead to success, and even if they know, have not the courage to pursue them. The extremists are not the bomb-throwers and the train wreckers but the advocates of independence of action."[2]

Having no sympathy with the moderates, Tagore was very critical of Gandhi's idea of non-cooperation and spinning. He did not accept Charkha as a solution of Indian poverty. He ridiculed the programme of boycott of foreign goods. Though he admitted Gandhi as a religious man he did not accept him as an economist. Clarifying his views about boycott of foreign goods Tagore said, "We have been ordered to burn foreign cloth. I, for one, am unable to obey. First, because I believe it to be my duty to fight the habit of blind obedience, secondly, I feel that the cloth to be burnt is not mine. It belongs to people who are sorely in need of it. He who seems to be doing an act of sacrifice through this incendiarism has other sources of supply; but those who are really hit cannot stir out of doors because of their nakedness."[3] Tagore's opposition had its scientific basis. Like Gandhi he was against machine and mechanization but he also maintained that we cannot absolutely do away with science and technology. He wanted to go deeper into the economic and political evils. He wanted a real Swaraj which is thus described in his own words: "Swaraj for the whole of India would

1. *Idem.*
2. Krishan Kriplani, *Tagore : A Life*, p. 143.
3. Tagore, R.N., *The Call for Truth*, 1921.

begin in the village where the people have formed themselves into a united community set on improving its health and education, its economic life and amusements no less. That Swaraj would then advance by its own power, its propulsion inherent in the organic process of its own living growth, and not in the mechanical solution of the spinning wheel."[1] To achieve this political goal Tagore wanted to give a positive programme to the country. He wanted to teach them lesson of self-discipline. He planned for Rural leadership, abolition of Zamindari, cooperative movement and consolidation of land. He laid down criteria for the assessment of political achievement of Indian National Congress. He laid down the following points as guidelines for National reconstruction:

(i) Unless we can move with the times, we are lost.
(ii) The watch-word of the day is organization.
(iii) Our national consciousness does not yet fully and uniformally pervade our organization.
(iv) The many points of artificial differences that separate the sophisticated classes from the masses are so many bars to the proper growth and spread of (National) consciousness.
(v) Internecine conflict among the cultured classes cannot but retard the consummation."[2]

ECONOMIC RECONSTRUCTION

As a religious man Tagore believed in the Christ's saying that blessed are the poor since they will be rewarded. Like all religious persons including Gandhi and Vivekananda, Tagore believed in service of men as the best means of service of God. He rightly called his religion 'Religion of Man'. Of the God of masses he said, "He is there when the tiller is tilling the hard ground and where the path maker is breaking the stones. He is with them in sun and in shower, and His garment is covered with dust. Put off thy holy mantle and even like him come down to the dusty soil."[3]

In his different writings Tagore has given a vivid description of poverty in Indian villages. He was in direct and personal touch with the rural people. He observed their conditions, understood their problems and pondered for remedies. His solutions everywhere emphasized the principles of harmony and synthesis. This principle is visible in his discussion of the relationship of the landlord and the tenant, the village and city, the rich and poor. He believed in the principle of the Golden mean. While on the one hand he appreciated maintenance of Indian culture and rural society he was also in favour of the progress of science and technology, industrialization and urbanization. Pointing out the equal importance of the village and the city in a society,

---

1. Tagore, R.N., *The Striving for Swaraj*, 1925.
2. Tagore, R. N., *The One National Party*, 1908.
3. Tagore, R. N., *Gitanjali, Song* 11, Macmillan, London, 1962.

Tagore said, "In the natural state, that is, when the community does not incline too much to one side, the village and the town have harmonious interactions. From the one flow food and health and fellow feeling. From the other return gift of wealth, knowledge and energy. A civilisation which comprises mainly village life cannot advance very far. There the individual is unimportant, the community predominant. On the other hand, where the town predominates, the individual is all powerful, the community negligible."[1]

Since ancient time Indian society had been a rural and agricultural society. Gradually, there was an impact of the system of large scale organization of production which led to the growth of cities and centres. The industrial economic system laid stress upon profit and cut throat competition which resulted in class conflicts. Due to the ruthlessness of the British rule in India, society lost its self-propulsion. In ancient time, economic achievement was subservient to the attainment of social virtue, but now economic achievement has become the supreme God. Tagore criticized this economic approach to life. The poet in him revolted against the artificial and mechanical urban life. His play *Red Orleanders* was a protest against the machine age. He was very much conscious of the evils of mechanization though he considered it necessary for the progress of the country. Thus, he was not against industrialization and urbanization but he pleaded for decentralization of power. He wrote, "Be it science or its outcome the machine, the power they give should not be monopolized by a few."[2]

Like Gandhi, Tagore was very much pained by the widening of the gulf between the rich and the poor in India. Like Gandhi again, he suggested the principle of social and economic trusteeship as the solution of the problem. Pointing out to the causes of the weakening of the principle of trusteeship in Indian society, Tagore said, "Once Indian society was mainly rural. In this intimate environment there was harmony between personal and communal property. Public opinion was so strong that the rich man was ashamed of enjoying his wealth alone. He felt honoured when society accepted favours from him; in short, in this relationship there was nothing of what is called charity in English. The wealthy took his place by the side of the destitute. To maintain his status in society he had to contribute very liberally in many indirect ways. Pure water, medical aid and education, temples, entertainments and village roads were provided out of private means flowing into several channels and not out of royal revenue. Here individual and communal will could cooperate. It was spiritually creative because its basis was voluntary and not a political agency, in other words, it implied not merely the external success of law but personal improvement as well. The latter element, indeed, is the lasting living refuge of human welfare."[3]

Besides decentralization of economic power and the operation of the principle of trusteeship of the rich over the poor, Tagore emphasized the

---

1. Tagore, R. N., *City and Village*, 1928.
2. *Ibid.*, Tagore, R.N., V.B. Bulletin No. 10, 1928.
3. Tagore, R.N., *Letters from Russia*, pp. 118-119.

importance of consolidation of holdings for the success of mechanized cultivation. He laid emphasis upon cooperative movement in agriculture. In his opinion the evils of industrialization can be checked by cooperation. He said. "If the farmers in a village or, better still in a community unit, combined and engaged in a joint cultivation of their land on a cooperative basis, they could all profit by the use of these modern machines, which would reduce cost and help produce large yields."[1]

Besides encouragement to cottage industries Tagore made special efforts to encourage agriculture in his villages. He sent one of his sons and a nephew to U.S.A. to learn mechanized cultivation. He reorganized his zamindari so that maximum social and economic reconstruction may be possible. He arranged for banks and agricultural implements. He introduced controlled mechanized cultivation. He tried to arrive at a synthesis between agricultural and industrial economies. He made all efforts to improve farming on cooperative basis. Summing up Tagore's efforts at rural reconstruction in his area, it has been written in his centenary volume, "The pargana of Kaligram, with its headquarters at Potisar, consisted of 150000 bighas (roughly 70 square miles). There were 6 to 7 thousand people living in 125 villages. The development of such an area was quite a large undertaking even when compared with the national Extension Blocks of the present day. For efficient management, he divided the Estate into three zones, each with a self-governing organization but federated to a central administrative body called the Hitaishi Sabha. Each village had an elected headman. Then such headmen elected a pradhan. These pradhans again elected five headmen from amongst themselves to represent the total population of the Estate and they were called the panch pradhan. The Hitaishi Sabha met once a year to scrutinize and pass the year's accounts, draw up a budget for the next year, assign to the vibhagas the grants they would each receive from the sadharan (general) fund, forward any complaints with regard to the management of the Estate, to the zamindar and to discuss the general policy to be followed in improving the condition of the village."[2]

Soon after the Hitaishi Sabha was organized and met for the first time at Potisar, the members proposed that a compulsory levy of three pice for every rupee paid as rent by them should be imposed for carrying out the work undertaken by the sabha. This proposal had the full support of the entire population. Later on the sabha increased the amount of this self-imposed betterment tax to fifteen pice per rupee. The state made a substantial contribution to the fund which had come to be known as the sadharan (general) fund. The money was spent through the vibhag organization in establishing and maintaining schools and dispensaries, constructing roads, filling of stagnant polls, re-excavating tanks, and in general, carrying out public welfare projects.

1. Tagore, R.N., *The City and Village*, 1928.

2. *Centenary Volume*, pp. 53-54.

Thus, Tagore's scheme of rural upliftment included eradication of casteism and untouchability, modification of joint family system, emancipation of women, cooperative farming, consolidation of holdings, encouragement to self-government through elected leaders, encouragement to dignity of labour and finally a proper relationship of the village with the city. Like other notable thinkers, Tagore realized that the progress of this country very much depends on re-generation of the village society. He not only thought over this problem but also made actual experiments in his villages. Pointing out the value of rural reconstruction in the social philosophy of Tagore, it has been rightly said, "Gurudev Rabindra Nath Tagore's work on or approach to agrarian reform followed firmly from his social philosophy and his particular analysis of the process of the historical evolution of the Indian society and of the structure and role of village communal life in her ancient civilization."[1]

NATIONALISM

As has been already pointed out, Tagore believed in democratic political institutions. He not only accepted democracy as the only form of Government which can provide freedom to the individual but also practised it as the philosophy of his life in dealing with people all around him. He was a great patriot and a nationalist but at the same time he was an internationalist and humanist. His political philosophy may be described as cosmopolitan universal humanism. The highest aim of all political activity, according to Tagore, should be to create national unity. He desired that our political programme should be dominated by the constructive ideas of spiritual freedom. Tagore's political philosophy is the climax of his social philosophy. In his philosophy the higher includes and integrates the lower though also transcends it. Thus, he was a nationalist and a patriot though his nationalism and patriotism were subordinated to internationalism.

Expressing his love for his motherland Tagore said, "The basis and the foundation of the great India lies in the recovery of her soul and the regaining of a fresh confidence in her own national life. If India recovers her strength of soul and grip of spirituality, which is the secret spring of life, then no power on earth can stand against her newly acquired energy of spirit."[2] And yet he did not accept nationalism as the highest sentiment in man. Defining the nation he said, "A nation in the sense of the political and economic union of people, is that aspect which a whole population assumes when organized for a mechanical purpose."[3]

In fact Tagore's conception of nationalism was based upon his observation of this phenomena in Europe where different nations continued to conflict with each other and each tried to gain ascendency over the other

1. Mukherjee, K., *Tagore's Thoughts and Work on Agrarian Reform, Homage from Visva-Bharati*, V.B.O. 1962, p. 220.
2. Radhakrishnan, S., *Philosophy of Rabindra Nath Tagore*, Macmillan, London, 1919, p. 201.
3. Tagore, R.N., *Nationalism*, p. 9.

by hook or by crook. It was with this type of nationalism in mind that Tagore exclaimed, "When this organization of politics and commerce, whose other name is the nation, becomes all powerful at the cost of harmony of the higher social life, then it is an evil day for humanity."[1]

Tagore however, was conscious of the fact that in the progress of collective consciousness of man nationalism was a necessary step from individualism but wanted to limit it so that it may not lead to conflict with other nations. Hence, he maintained, "Ideally speaking, the nationalism which stands for the expression of the collective self-interest of a people, need not be ashamed of itself if it maintains its true limitations."[2] Without this self-limitation nationalism becomes a profession. It is a profession of training people for a narrow idea. It is not a creative idea but a destructive one. It creates a monotonous organization of society.

Criticising this type of nationalism as dangerous to man Tagore said, "But what we see in practice is, that every nation which has prepared has, done so through its career of aggressive selfishness either in commercial adventures or in foreign possessions or in both,..as for a nation, selfishness is a necessity and therefore a virtue. It is the emphasis laid in Europe upon the idea of the Nation's constant increase of power, which is becoming the greatest danger to man, both in its direct activity and its power of infection."[3] Therefore Tagore concluded that increases in national sentiment is a danger to human civilization itself. He was led to this judgement also because of the examples of extreme nationalism presented by Germany, Italy, England and other nations in Europe, who tried to expand their empire everywhere to achieve their own selfish interests. Thus, Tagore rightly asserted that, "With the unchecked growth of nationalism the moral foundation of man's civilization is unconsciously undergoing a change. The ideal of the social man is unselfishness, but the ideal of the nation, like that of the professional man, is selfishness. This is why selfishness in the individual is condemned, while in the nation it is extolled, which leads to hopeless moral blindness confusing the religion of the people with the religion of the nation."[4]

INTERNATIONALISM

Similar ideas have been expressed by Sri Aurobindo in his book *The Ideal of Human Unity.* Sri Aurobindo however, has been more clear about the nature of true nationalism as spiritual subjective nationalism which he distinguished from false nationalism or narrow objective nationalism. What the man has to avoid is the latter form of nationalism while the former form of nationalism leads him ultimately to humanism. Here Sri Aurobindo's views about nationalism are more balanced than that of Tagore. D P. Mukherjee has lightly pointed out, "Tagore was critical of the sentiment of nationalism, but he did

1. *Ibid.*
2. Tagore R.N., *The Creative Unity,* p. 150.
3. *Ibid.*
4. *Ibid.,* pp. 148-149.

not fully realize (1) that nationalism in Europe was that particular phase of socio-development in which the vested interests had come home to roost, (2) that nationalism in India was an uprise of those indigenous interests which had been openly backed by imperialism of their divine right to exploit, and (3) that these two were inerconnected even as contradictions."[1] However, it can be said in favour of Tagore's view that the growth of nationalism so far has only confirmed his doubts and suspicions. In Germany nationalism has expressed the worst form of racism. In fact racism in our time is a product of nationalism, hence to do justice to Tagore's view we may conclude with D.P. Mukherjee, "Rabindra Nath's foresight about the future of a power civilization was prophetic, but it was more intuitive than analytic, more scientific than just poetic. He has not only made a prophetic assertion but frequently has proved what he has said by concrete facts. We find today that nation and nationalism without certain limitations can do no good to people. Those limitations may be taken as theoretically possible, but practically once when these cults are given ground they go unchecked."[2]

Therefore in place of nationalism Tagore pleaded for internationalism. He was convinced that cooperation and friendship between nations is absolutely necessary for the progress of mankind. Here his views have been supported by almost all the notable thinkers of the world. It has been generally accepted that no nation can solve its problems unless the problems of humanity have been solved. In the progress of humanity, according to Tagore, each nation will use its special gifts for the good of mankind and spirituality will be the contribution of India as she has been the meeting place of different nations since ancient times. This is possible in spite of our material properties. Pointing out to internationalism as the need of our time, Tagore maintained that for its own safety each nation should now work for universal welfare. It was to meet this end that Tagore established Vishwa Bharti. The international aim of this reputed institution was explicit from the three-fold programme including consolidation of Indian culture, consolidation of Asian culture, and finally cultivation of international contract in the fields of learning and culture.

Thus, Tagore was one of the greatest humanist of our time. In the words of professor Humayun Kabir, "Rabindra Nath Tagore was one of the greatest humanists the world has known. The keynote of his life was resistance to tyranny in all forms. He struggled against economic exploitation, political subjugation, social inertia and injustice and religious intolerance and insensitiveness."[3] Tagore's humanism is expressed through his literature. He gave man a central place in his social philosophy, in his religion, politics and his educational and economic thoughts. In his struggle against British rule in India he maintained a deep love and great respect for British people and

1. Mukherjee, D.P., *Tagore : A Study*, Padma Publication, Bombay, 1963, pp. 46-47.
2. *Ibid*, p. 47.
3. Verma, R., *Rabindra Nath Tagore : Prophet against Totalitarianism*, Foreword, Asia Publishing House, 1962.

English literature. Summing up the message of humanism given by Tagore it has been rightly said, "Humanity is the very epitome of the wide and varied universe. To know it properly is to realize the highest manifestation of Brahma, since in all its world-wide aspects humanity is permeated with the spirit of God. This universal greatness of humanity has truly found its triumphant poetic expression in our age in the literature of Rabindra Nath.[1]

1. Sen, Kshitismohan, *The Genius of Rabindra Nath : Its Character and Lineage*, V.B.O. No. 3 and 4, Tagore Centenary, Vol. V, 33.

18
Sri Aurobindo (1872 — 1950)

Born in a Bengali Hindu family in Calcutta on August 15, 1872, Sri Aurobindo grew up in an European atmosphere. His father Dr. K.D. Ghose had adopted the English way of life. He wanted to keep all his children ignorant of Indian languages, religion and way of life. Sri Aurobindo received education through the medium of English in India at different schools. In England he acquired proficiency in the Classics, and the English language. He also mastered languages like French and Latin. His extraordinary brilliance in studies led him to obtain distinction in the first part of the Tripos at King's College and finally in the open competition for the Indian Civil Service. He did not care to pass the final test for becoming an I.C.S.

Stay in England

In spite of a European upbringing and ignorance of the Indian language and culture, Sri Aurobindo was influenced by the attitudes of his parents. His mother was wholly Indian although unassertive. His father was every inch an Englishman but cherished noble ideals of patriotism and service of the poor. A true lover of his country Dr. Krishnadhan believed that the salvation of India would come about through the importation of the Western methods and ways of life. At times he protested strongly against the injustices of the British Government in India and conveyed his reactions to his sons in England. Thus, Sri Aurobindo got the first lessons in patriotism from his father.

Aurobindo's fourteen years of stay in England was the formative period of his life, both as a period of his intellectual growth and preparation for the life to come in India. It was in England that his desire to serve his motherland became explicit. His association with the Indian Majlis, a students association, and a secret group of revolutionary Indians known as the "Lotus and Dagger" gave him ample opportunity to foster his patriotism. Some of his statements given in England against British imperialism could easily be characterised as revolutionary. This revolutionary fervour of Sri Aurobindo, came out openly when he returned to India in 1893.

Return to India

The deep desire to serve his motherland which Sri Aurobindo cherished since the age of fifteen, found expression and fulfilment during the periods between 1893 to 1910, and then at Pondicherry after 1910 till his death. His purpose of taking active part in a revolutionary movement was two-fold. He wanted to relieve India from the chains of foreign domination. In the freedom of India he saw the hope of the freedom of the entire world. As early as 1907 he said, "India awakes not for herself but for humanity." He wanted to raise politics to the plane of spirituality. He interpreted political freedom in terms of spiritual perfection. "It is the spirit alone that saves and only by becoming great and free in heart that we can become politically great and free."[1] That is why he remained faithful to the high ideals of truth and universal love even as a leader of the revolutionary movement in India.

Spiritual Quest : Three Insanities

As a professor of English and French in Baroda State Service and as the Principal of the National College at Calcutta, Sri Aurobindo always felt an urge to do something more effective and lasting for the good of mankind. In 1904, he started the practice of Yoga as he felt that it could be the only cure for his own deep-rooted sorrow and for the manifold ills of humanity. It was also the time when he felt that attachment to the world for the sake of personal comforts was one great obstacle in the way of attaining high ideals. To his wife Mrinalini he wrote in 1905, "Our quest for happiness in this world reveals to us sorrow in the very midst of happiness. This holds good not merely in the case of attachment to our children but it is applicable to all our desires for worldly things."[2] He became conscious of his peculiar and extraordinary ambitions in life described as his three insanities. The first consisted of his faith that all things belonged to God and therefore man had no right to work for his own personal ends. The second consisted of the determination to see God face to face. For this personal perfection through Yoga became essential. His third madness consisted of his love for the motherland. He thought that if he could not do anything for the elevation of his brethren in the country, he could do nothing for the rest of humanity. But Sri Aurobindo had faith in his own self and said, "I am confident that I have the strength in me to bring salvation to these our fallen people."[3]

He resisted the inner call to devote himself heart and soul to the salvation of the human race owing to preoccupation with tense political activities till his arrest and trial under the Alipore bomb and Conspiracy case in 1908. This event gave him an opportunity to meditate about his future plan of action. In the jail he had a profound spiritual experience and underwent

1. Sri Aurobindo, *Essays in the Karmayogin*, 1909.
2. Sri Aurobindo's letter to his wife dated August 30, 1905 — quoted by R.R. Diwakar in his book *Mahayogi Sri Aurobindo*, p. 139, Bombay, Bhartiya Vidya Bhawan, 1967.
3. R.R. Diwakar, *Mahayogi Sri Aurobindo*, p. 147, Bombay, Bharatiya Vidya Bhawan 1967.

a transformation which found expression in his Uttarpara speech after his release. He said, "God seemed to whisper: The bonds you had not the strength to break I have broken for you, because it was not my will nor was it ever my intention that should continue. I have had another thing for you to do and it is for that I have brought you here, to teach you what you could not learn for yourself and to train you for my work". Besides, the changed political condition in India with most of his associates in jails had also a deep effect on him and led him to renounce politics for ever. In *Bande Mataram* he wrote, "We must first ourselves be free in heart before our country is free."[1] Thus, he decided to abandon active politics in order to seek spiritual development and the ultimate reconciliation of India and mankind during the rest of his forty years of life.

PHILOSOPHY OF HISTORY

According to Sri Aurobindo, "The law for humanity is to pursue its upward evolution towards the finding and expression of the Divine in the type of mankind, taking full advantage of the free development and gains of all individuals and nations and groupings of men, to work towards the day when mankind may be really and not only ideally one divine family, but even then, when it has succeeded in unifying itself, to respect, aid and be aided by the free growth and activity of its individuals and constituent aggregates." Sri Aurobindo presents a psychological interpretation of history. In his Philosophy of History, his vision is firmly centred on the integral principle, working through all the stages of the cycle of social development, as it is that integral principle which the social philosopher seeks to grasp, know and utilize for the regeneration of mankind.

Stages in the Cycle of Social Development

Like Lamprecht of Germany, Sri Aurobindo finds symbolic, typal, conventional, individualist and subjective stages in the cycle of social development. The process of evolution, according to him, however, is not linear, as it was for the nineteenth century philosophers of history, but spiral. He borrows the names suggested by Lamprecht. But there the similarity ends, as he always keeps a keen eye on the multiple and complex nature of man and society. As he says, "A constant rediscovery and new formulation and larger synthesis in the mind, a mighty remoulding in its deeper parts because of a greater enlarging Truth not discovered or not well fixed before, is that Spirit's way with our past achievement when he moves to the greatness of the future."[2]

---

1. *Bande Mataram,* Weekly edited by Aurobindo, April 12, 1908.
2. Sri Aurobindo, *The Human Cycle,* American Edition, p. 298.

The Symbolic Age

The earliest stage in the primitive beginning of human society, Sri Aurobindo calls, Symbolic. This stage is always imaginatively religious. It is what Freud and other psychologists and the philosophers of religion call the totemistic stage. They have taken the totem in its external form. According to Sri Aurobindo, on the other hand, the totem was merely a symbol for the power which man sensed behind the forces of Nature.

The Vedic Symbolism

Thus, Sri Aurobindo has presented a deeper and more intuitive interpretation of the Vedic symbolism. The Vedic Age and also the Pre-Vedic is full of symbols which represent the forces working behind them. Thus, the Surya, the Vayu, Indra, etc., are not the celestial objects but the power working behind them. It was the age of instinct whose truth was later obstructed by reason of the rational age, though only to find a higher and transformed expression in future spiritual age. God, for the vedic seers, was not made in the image of man, but rather man was conceived as an inferior image of God. The marriage hymn, the Purusa Sukta and various other hymns, did not represent practical or conventional institutions. In the Symbolic Age, the material factors were subordinated to religious and psychological factors. The ritualistic interpretation of Bloomfield and the allegorical interpretation of Bergaine have missed the inner meanings of the symbols of Vedic hymns. Sri Aurobindo's interpretation here is even deeper than that of Roth, Swami Dayanand and Raja Ram Mohan Roy, etc., though fundamentally he agrees with them.

The Spiral Process

Thus, according to Sri Aurobindo, the earliest stage of human history was a stage of naive truth and the later sophistications are a fall from that stage. This, however, does not deny progress as some reactionary and conservative philosophers might suggest. The fall is a sign of more integral growth. In Sri Aurobindo's Philosophy of History, social development of mankind is a fact but it is not a linear process. It is much more complex and many-sided. It is a spiral, a zigzag process, in which there is often regression to make the progress more integrated.

Instinct and Reason

The failure of rationalism in the present stage of human knowledge makes some go back to romanticism, existentialism, anti-intellectualism and even irrationalism. This however, is an ignorant attempt to stop the current. Man has fallen from his pristine unity of instinct, in the dualism of Reason. But he cannot go back, because his fall has a purpose behind it. This purpose is to make instinct more balanced, more controlled and more refined. But the apotheosis of man, the rational being, is also a wilful deception. The peace of ignorance is no alternative to facing the dangers. For that, man must transcend himself. It is only in the evolution to the Spirit that man can regain what he has lost and also can realize the possibilities of the instinct, reason and will.

The Typal Stage

The second stage after Symbolic is Typal. This "is predominantly psychological and ethical."[1] Here religion and spirituality is subordinated to Dharma, the ethical discipline. Its main contributions are the social ideals, the ideal of social honour, though these tend to become more and more fixed and traditional.

The Conventional Stage

Thus, the typal stage naturally passes into the conventional stage.[2] The types now become conventions. As the symbols become fossilized in conventions, the psychological ideas behind them are easily forgotten. Once the type is fixed, the ethical idea becomes a mere fiction, The division of society becomes a purely economic division of labour. But when even the economic basis gives way, the system becomes rather a source of degeneration and falsehood. According to Sri Aurobindo, forms of institutions must change with the purpose of the spirit behind them, otherwise they cease to serve their function and disorganize the individual as well as the social life.

Psychological Stages

Strictly speaking, these stages of development, as pointed out by Sri Aurobindo, are psychological rather than chronological. It is not a temporal division of the history of mankind, as these psychological forces work simultaneously as well as successively at different places in different times. The conventional stage, the individualistic and other stages, can be witnessed in the contemporary society at various places. They fix the stage of psychological development of society, which serves in the assessment of the value of the present stage as well as in predicting the future course of progress. The interpretations of history (apart from Sri Aurobindo's interpretation) are useful from different perspectives. But Sri Aurobindo's interpretation of history, howsoever one might disagree with its value from other points of view, is particularly valuable from the standpoint of Social Philosophy. It serves to interpret the inner psychological meaning of the past history, the ideal of social development and finally to visualize the future of mankind. It supplies a firm foundation for an integral Social Philosophy.

The So-called Satya Yuga

Thus, the ideal stage of mankind, according to Sri Aurobindo, is not a return to the glorious past, but an ascent into a more glorious future. The golden age

---

1. *Ibid.*, p. 9.
2. *Ibid.*, p. 10.

of the conventional stage, an Age in which spirit is confined but not yet dead, is often misinterpreted as the ideal stage of human society. This so-called medieval satya-yuga is the ideal of some reactionary social philosophers in the East as well as in the West. According to Sri Aurobindo, on the other hand, neither the individual nor the society can regain the true original Spirit, while keeping the conventional forms, however they may attempt to reform them. The insistence on the external form is against the nisus of time. To regain the spirit, the old forms should be broken and thrown away. Sri Aurobindo supports a revolution in the individual as well as in the social fields. This revolution in its deeper meaning is always psychological.

The Individualistic Stage

Thus, when the gulf between the conventions and the inner truth becomes intolerable, reason rejects the old form and human society passes from the conventional to the individualistic stage. The bankruptcy of the old forms leaves the individual alone to decide his course. Individualism becomes inevitable and justified when the social standards, norms and institutions are petrified and stultify the free growth of the individual soul.

European Birth of Individualism

Individualism, as is admitted by Sri Aurobindo, was first born in Europe. It spread over the world, as the rest of the mankind was still in the torpor of the conventional stage. It spread in the East not because the East had no truth of its own but because it had lost its vitality in the stereotyped conventionalism. The truths, which the individualistic Europe discovered were tme to its peculiar analytic and pragmatic reason. Individualism spread because of the West's passion for seeking the truth and realizing it in life at all cost. It began in the revolt of reason and culminated in the triumph of physical science. In the Conventional Age, religion was dogmatic and persecuted science in its name. In politics, it sanctioned tyranny. The social order was based on stereotyped conventions. Gradually, when this burden became intolerable, reason in man revolted and questioned the authority of society, state, religion and even of the moral laws and overthrew those that were found bankrupt.

The Psychology of Revolution

The spirit in the individual and society always revolts when its growth is hampered. This revolt is expressed through the best possible medium available at the time. The movement of religious freedom in Europe questioned the Scriptures, asserted the right of the individual experience and culminated in nothing less than atheism and secularism. The development in Europe, according to Sri Aurobindo, was determined more by Renaissance than by Reformation. This return of the ancient 'Greeco-Roman mentality,' coupled with 'Judas-Christian discipline' gave Europe its naturalism, science and utilitarianism.

The Triumph of Science

The imperfect human race, however, was not psychologically mature to assimilate these gifts. The unrestrained individual judgments led to a chaos in opinions. The absolute assertion of individual or class rights or desires, led to social disorganization. Thus, the search of some general standard of truth and some common principle of social justice became imperative. Both these psychological needs were satisfied in science. The truths of science were universal and veridical. They supplied a rational basis for social life. Science was the culmination as well as the end of individualistic age.

The Scientific Society

According to Sri Aurobindo, with science, the individual evolved a system which ushered mankind into a new era and at the same time gave a death-blow to individualism. This led to the expression of various types of tendencies. It led to a recoil to a new typal order, the economic or state socialism. The truths of science are not that of the individual but of the masses. They are applicable to the man not as an individual, but as a speck in collectivity, as a cog in the machine, as a member of a species. Thus, in a society based on science, all the institutions will be fixed by the scientific stage, in the naturalistic motives, with its scientific, economic and administrative experts, who will know the individuals more than the individuals themselves. This shall far surpass the old Asian or Indian order of society in its rigidity. A rigorously scientific society shall be unitarian, based upon purely economic function and capacity. The scientific society, according to Sri Aurobindo, is a mere passing phase.

Russell's Conditions for the Stability of Scientific Society

It would be interesting here, to examine the views of Bertrand Russell, who maintains that a scientific society can be stable. He admits that, "In the development of science, the power-impulse has increasingly prevailed over the love impulse."[1] He also admits that, "The sphere of value lies outside science, except in so far as science consists in the pursuit of knowledge."[2] And yet he holds that, given certain conditions, a scientific society can be stable. "My conclusion is," says Russell, "that a scientific society can be stable, given certain conditions. The first of these is a single government of the whole world, possessing a monopoly of armed forces and therefore able to enforce peace. The second condition is a general diffusion of prosperity, so that there is no occasion of envy of one part of the world by another. The third condition (which supposes the second fulfilled) is a low birth-rate everywhere, so that the population of the world becomes stationary or nearly so. The fourth condition is the provision for individual initiative both in work

1. Russell, B., *The Scientific Outlook*, p. 270.
2. *Ibid.*

and play, and the greatest diffusion of power, compatible with maintaining the necessary political and economic framework."[1] Elsewhere, Russell maintains that ethics, education, philosophy, religion and social order, all should be based on science.

Criticism of Russell's Views

But when science is dominated by power-impulse and when the sphere of value is outside it, then would even world government be not guided by power motive? Actually, Russell himself admits this in holding that the world governments would "enforce peace". But is enforcement even if it be of peace, by an external authority, even if it be a world government, compatible with the ideal of the freedom of creativity which Russell cherished so much? Would the general diffusion of prosperity abolish the envy and hatred between man and between nations. Like Freud, Russell recognizes that the impulse of aggression is the greatest threat to civilization and hence pleads for the monopoly of armed forces by the world government. But unless human nature is transformed, what is the guarantee that the world government will not utilize its force for exploitation and aggression. This possibility is inevitable, unless the world government is a totalitarian one. And Russell, certainly, would never like a totalitarian world government as he favours diffusion of power. But if the world government is democratic and if the power is thus decentralized in small units, then is it not possible that the majority party in the world government may oppress the minority party or the groups or the individuals? If the individual is given the initiative in work and play, is it certain that he would not misuse it or that the government would never curb this freedom? This is more so in the absence of religion and by the secularization of ethics. Thus, so long as human nature remains what it is and secular education cannot transform human nature, the scientific society cannot be stable. It is not difficult to imagine disastrous condition of "love, beauty, knowledge and joy of life"[2] in a scientific society, the ideals which Russell rightly cherishes so much.

Two Idea-Forces

To come to the original theme, in the East, one witnesses struggle between Western individualism and old conventionalism, in which the former is winning, though also assuming a changed form. This should have an enormous influence over the world. As against the suggestion that the Western material and rational individualism may spread over India, Sri Aurobindo categorically states, "The influence of the East is likely to be rather in the direction of subjectivism and practical spirituality, a greater opening of our physical existence to the realisation of ideals other than the strong but

1. Russell, B., *The Impact of Science on Society*, p. 139.
2. Russell, B., *An Outline of Philosophy*, p. 312.

limited aims suggested by the life and the body in their own gross nature."[1] The individualistic age of Europe, however, has fixed two idea-forces of master potency, *viz.*, the conception of democratic equality of the individuals as well as the liberty of individual growth. The former is generally accepted and is the basis of the present socialism. The latter, however, has not been accepted in practice by the Fascists, Communists and many others, though it is precisely this idea which carries the profoundest rationalism of the West and the highest spiritualism of the East; and the greatest possibilities of the future.

Not Revival but Revolution

History, according to Sri Aurobindo, does not repeat itself, though it often appears to do so. Not revival but transcendence, not modification but transformation, is the law of the human cycle. Destruction is necessary for construction. Till the dawn of the European influence, the Indian reformers and political leaders tried to rediscover the truth of the soul through a wide and tolerant spiritual reason. Such again was the nationalism in China and the half-hearted awakening in other Eastern countries. It was the influence of the Western knowledge and their way of life that awakened a radical and effective revaluation of ideas and things in Eastern countries. This trend will not stop half way. "A revolutionary reconstruction of religion, philosophy, science, art and society is the last inevitable outcome,"[2] says Sri Aurobindo. The truth of the individual should become the truth of the universal.

THE SUBJECTIVE AGE

There are, however, some tendencies which seek to modify the trend towards strict rationalism and the new typal order. The development of physical and psychological knowledge is opening a new horizon. Dynamic ideas, as Nietzsche's will to live, Bergson's Intuitionism, the Existentialism of Sartre and Heidegger are sweeping over the world. This is the dawn of what Sri Aurobindo calls the 'Subjective Age' which opens a new chapter in man's history. After the discovery of the physical, economic and the sociological laws, it becomes clear to man that this knowledge is a mere part of the whole. Hence, he tries to go deeper within him. As reason stumbles in this search, man seeks after other instruments such as intuitional knowledge and the deeper self-awareness. Thus, the rationalistic ideal is substituted by the intuitional knowledge, the utilitarian standard by self-realization, the life through physical laws by the life through cosmic laws, will and power. All this can be noticed in the present vitalistic theories, pluralism, pragmatism, instrumentalism and existentialism, etc. The subjective trend is obviously more visible in art, music and literature. This was at first exhibited in

---

1. Sri Aurobindo, *The Human Cycle, American* Edition, p. 25.
2. *Ibid.*, p. 29.

psychological vitalism and more and more concentration on pathological aspects. This, however, was succeeded by a truly psychological, mental, intuitive and psychical art, music and literature, which was more subjective, though still infirm in grasp and rudimentary in form. The will-to-power and the will-to-live, seizing upon the material and intellectual forces, led the world to the catastrophies of the great wars. The hope of humanity lies in the still hidden subjective principle. As Sri Aurobindo points out, "A unifying and harmonizing knowledge can alone find the way, but that knowledge belongs to a deeper principle of our being to which oneness and integrality are native. It is only by finding that in ourselves that we can solve the problem of our existence and with it the problem of the true way of individual and communal living."[1]

INDIVIDUAL AND SOCIETY

The goal of a society, community or nation, like that of the individual, is to seek its own self, to know the inner law and power and to realize all its potentialities. Both individual and society have a body, an organic life, moral or aesthetic temperament, mind and a soul. Strictly speaking, they do not "possess" soul, Soul is rather their very essence. Nation, according to Sri Aurobindo, is a 'group-soul' which realizes itself in corporate life. In his Social Philosophy, the society is similar to man, not only in essence but also in organisation. "The parallel is just at every turn because it is more than a parallel, it is a real identity of nature."[2] The only difference between them is that whereas the individual is an organization of vital sub-conscious self, the group-soul is more complex, since it is constituted of partly self-conscious mental individuals. The group-soul is more artificial, fluid and less organic. Even in its developed stage, it is only vaguely subjective. The nation is wrongly conceived in the objective form of geographical country. The subjective communal consciousness can be developed only after the realization that the geographical land is only an outer shell, while the real body is composed of the men and women who form a nation.[3] This body of the group soul, like that of the individual, is ever changing, though always the same.

The Objective View of Nation

In contrast to this subjective view of Nation, the objective view has been largely prevalent both in the East and the West. National existence has been understood in terms of the political status, extent of borders, economic

---

1. Sri Aurobindo, *The Life Divine*, Vol. II, p. 929.
2. Sri Aurobindo, *The Human Cycle*, p. 38.
3. Cf. "Besides geographical and climatic factors, with all those that belong to the material universe, the only causes that need to be considered by the historian are those indwelling the consciousness of man."
   — Wright, Dr. J.C., *The Humanization of History*, Hibbert Journal, Vol. XLI, 1942-43, pp. 145-46.

prosperity and development, laws and institutions, etc. History has been conceived as a record of the operation of political and economic motives which have dominated in the national life. According to Christopher Caudwell, "Man's consciousness is a real determining factor in history, but it is not man's consciousness that produces each stage of social organization for economic production but social organisation for economic production which produces man's consciousness."[1] Some other philosophers conceived history as a mass of individual biographies. Both these explanations of the historical processes are inadequate and characteristic of the imperfect self-conscious period in the national development. The subjective force had begun to work but had not yet come to the surface.

The Subjective Trend

Thus, the subjective tendency in nationalism is a very recent trend. Nations are gradually feeling their souls and trying to find them. This trend is obviously more powerful in new and slave nations, partly because their need of individuality is stronger and partly because their objective life is less satisfying. Sri Aurobindo has seen in the uprisings in India, Ireland, and other places, the tendencies of self-finding, mainly expressed in the swadeshi movements. To be itself is the law of the individual as well as of the community. This subjective trend, according to Sri Aurobindo, is more dominant in the East than in the West. The political movements in India, China, Persia and Japan, are symptoms of the advent of the Subjective Age in humanity. The imitation of other nations is deplored and each nation wants to realize its own self. It is the very demand of the time spirit. With Marx, Sri Aurobindo admits that man cannot stop the time process, but, whereas Marx arrives at a social law which does not fulfil the individual, for Sri Aurobindo, if chaos is not the law of things, the law of the time process should fulfil the demands of the individual as well as of the social self. Faith in system and harmony is a postulate on which the entire working of reason is based. The oneness of the deeper self of man and society is rather a postulate than an empirical generalization. This, however, is certified by mystic and yogic experience.

German Subjectivism

Thus, according to Sri Aurobindo, even the rise of Germany into a militant and teutonic collectivity, is an expression of the soul of the Nation, though in a very crude and barbarous form. The dangers, which such a movement has for the world, are inherent in the very concept of the Nation-soul which, if too narrow, may seek to grow alone, and at the cost of others. At the instance of the dangerous nationalism of Germany and Italy, some reject the very conception of Nation-soul as wrong. But if individualism of man and nation

1. Caudwell, C., *Further Studies in a Dying Culture*, p. 139.

has often been a source of danger to larger collectivity, that only means that the particular form of individualism is erroneous. The deeper truth is the same everywhere. Man as well as Nations should not only realize their own selves but also feel the selves in others and learn to respect, help, and profit by each other in spiritual growth. This is necessary, if Subjective Age has to help in the growth of humanity. In Germany, Traitschke wrongly applied the subjective teaching of Nietzsche to objective conditions in national and international field. The failure of Germany was not total. It was a failure in some particular directions, which unfortunately were so central that, in spite of all the efforts of more than fifty years of subjective introspection and an equal effort in scientific research, Germany missed the goal.

TRUE AND FALSE SUBJECTIVISM

According to Sri Aurobindo, there is a false as well as a true subjectivism. The dangers of the Subjective Age are as great in comparison with the symbolic, typal and conventional ages as its gains. And yet if man has not to remain confined to self-ignorance, the game is worth the candle. The knowledge of the constitution of man which has been elaborately discussed in the preceding chapter, makes it clear that while the real self is one, there is the ego, the outer and the inner mind, vital and physical and the five sheaths which can be easily confused with the real self. So also is the case with the social constitution. Egoism is contrary to the principle of life and its growth. Humanity should aim at the fulfilment of the real self. This is what true subjectivism seeks to achieve.

The Error of German Subjectivism

The ideal of self-realization was generally recognized in Germany though not so much practised in the case of the individual, but it was not recognized that these laws are equally applicable to the nations. This was the fundamental error of German subjectivism. It did look upon life from the standpoint of the Absolute, the Individual and the Universal, but it missed the real relation between these three. Hegel exalted the State as the Absolute. The humanity outside was not denied, but Germany was hailed as the best, the most advanced, self-realized, efficient and cultured nation. The essential truth of subjectivity that the same being expressed equally in all the nations, was forgotten and the biological principle of the survival of the fittest was put in its place. Nietzsche's theory of the superman's rule over others was misapplied to the relations of nations and it was concluded that the rule of Germany, the supreme Teutonic race over all other nations, is in the interest of the supreme good of humanity, justified by the law of reason as well as by that of vision.

This egoistic self-vision of Germany, according to Sri Aurobindo, was the cause of so many subjective errors. First, the individual was developed, educated, trained and disciplined as a cell of collectivity, as the instrument for the execution of the initiative of the collectivity, which was expressed through the state. Germany founded the cult of the state, perfect, dominant, all-pervading, all-seeing, all-effective. The individual was more and more subordinated till he was finally effaced in the state machinery, with the result that though Germany gained economic, scientific, social and intellectual efficiency and power, the deeper life vision, intuitive power, force of personality and psychical sweetness and largeness, were lost. This is a necessary outcome of the totalitarianism. Again, since the State represents the Absolute, service to the State is the absolute principle of morality. But while obedience was the law within the state, success was the determining factor of inter-state relations. They were based on the principle of the survival of the fittest and the struggle for survival, the struggle being economic, physical, intellectual and even cultural. Science taught that man is nothing more than life and body. Hence, these were emphasized as the highest. War became the means of success, though generally under the pretence of peace. Means were justified by the ends. All methods, which might lead to success in war and preparation for it in peace time, were morally justified.

With the survival of the fittest as the aim, which is secured by the elimination of the unfit and assimilation of the less fit, the conquest of the world by German culture was held as leading to the highest good of mankind. The culture was interpreted as the life governed by ideas, based on vital truth and organized for the highest efficiency. The capacity to adopt this culture depends on the race. Hence, it was decided that the Nordic race should assimilate the less capable and eliminate the incapable races. This was not the idea of the majority, still less of the whole of Germany but of a few personalities dominating national life. But this minority was of sufficient strength to be able to impose it on the collective mind.

The Value of German Subjectivism

All these errors have led to an absolute condemnation of German subjectivism by some thinkers. Sri Aurobindo, however, has passed a very different judgment on it. German subjectivism, according to him, was an attempt in the right direction, though with a wrong approach. Its example should be followed by all, though in a different way. As Sri Aurobindo prophetically remarks, "To go back is impossible; the attempt is always, indeed, an illusion; we have all to do the same thing which Germany has attempted, but to take care not to do it likewise."[1] To hate or abhor this phenomenon is easier than to understand the secret of its force, its tremendous sincerity and honesty of conduct and speech, which are precisely the requisites needed to defeat this phenomena in the minds of men and in the life of the human race. With his deep insight into the paradoxes of human history, Sri Aurobindo indicates how the physical defeat of Germany has not deterred its influence in national and international field.

1. Sri Aurobindo, *The Human Cycle*, p. 45.

Two Aspects of German Gospel

In the internal sphere, the compulsion of the individual by the state is prevalent everywhere, in Socialism, in Bolshevic communism, Fascism and even in many so-called democracies. In the international field, the signs were there, even before the war. Germany's defeat in the war led to the post-war victory of its gospel, in practically the whole of the continent. The rise of Germany was only a symptom of the disease of sacred egoism, inherent in the whole body of the then international relations. What Germany thought and did more systematically and rigorously was proclaimed and practised by many others in a less organized and limited manner. Germany has shown in all its nakedness the evil which was already working in the human race and thus forced the human race to choose rather than waver between good and evil. The German error of the confusion of the self with the body and life, according to Sri Aurobindo, was not a reversion to barbarism. It was a new bastard creed, an objective subjectivism, both of the application of the logic of the Absolutistic metaphysics to the conclusions of materialistic science, of a philosophical subjectivism to a pragmatic positivism.

The Two Conflicting Ideals

Modern science has created two opposite ideals, the exaggerated individualism and collectivism. The biological principles of the struggle for existence and survival of the fittest, applied to human life, gave rise to philosophies like those of Nietzsche and to certain forms of anarchism and strengthened certain forms of imperialism. On the other hand, the biological principle that Nature seeks to preserve the type and not the individual, and that the individual life is impossible without its subjection to the laws of the communal self-development, strengthened the modern collectivist theories. As has been already shown above, Germany expressed both these ideals, one in the egoistic self-assertion of the individual nation, and other in the total subordination of the individual to the collectivity.

The Ideal of Larger Collectivity

But behind the conflict of these two ideals, there is growing a new idea of human universalism or collectivism for the race which may overcome the Ideal of national separatism. Thus, one finds imperialistic, ideological or cultural international groups, *e.g.*, the U.N.O., the group of Soviet Russia and its satellites, the British Commonwealth, the Afro-Asian brotherhood, the Arab League, etc., which demand the sacrifice of the independent separateness of the nations of a larger collectivity.

The Objective View of Life

Both objective and subjective views of life have the individual and nation as data, but they differ in viewpoint, motive power and character of life. Objectivism proceeds from analytic reason. Its view is external and mechanical. In it reason looks from outside and observes the world as a process to be studied, as the given. It discovers laws which are mechanically acting upon the individuals and the groups. These laws are organized and applied as scientific laws. They are imposed upon the individual by reason or will, as an authority external to the other parts of his being, or by the reason and will of other individuals or of the group. They are imposed on the group by its own collective reason and will, embodied in the state which is external to the group life, or by the reason and will of some other external group of which it is in some way a part. Thus, the laws of the individual and collective life, social as well as international, are enforced by some external authority. The State is not an organic part of the society. It is considered as an entity in itself which imposed its own idea of right on the individuals of the community. The aim which the society seeks to find is not its inherent law. It is imposed on it by the state machinery through external laws. Nations do not aim at something essential to their nature but at something imposed by international laws. Life is not to grow from within, it has to be perfected by a machinery which shapes it from outside. As Sri Aurobindo concludes "A law outside oneself, — outside even when it is discovered or determined by the individual reason and accepted or enforced by the individual will, — this is the governing idea of subjectivism; a mechanical process of management, ordering, perfection, this is its conception of practice."[1]

The Subjective View of Life

As against this objective view, the subjective view proceeds from within. It considers everything from the standpoint of a containing self-consciousness. The law here is not imposed from outside. Its principle of progress is more and more recognition, realization and hence shaping of the self-life, self-life in this view, is a self-creating process. This process develops at first sub-consciously, then half-consciously and finally, fully conscious of the inner self. In this view, reason is a process in self-recognition, will is a force for self-affirmation. Both are only parts of the means of self-realization. The subjective view is a complex view of man's nature and recognizes many powers of knowledge and forces of effectuation. It even sometimes belittles the importance of reason and asserts the supremacy of life-impulse, the will-to-be or intuition, which is conscious feeling, perceiving and grasping of its own truth, nature and powers rather than their analysis. Thus, the subjective view aims at reaching the self and living in its truth.

Meeting of the Extremes

These two extreme views of life are based on two different views about the nature of self. If the self is individual, then the aim of life is the power, freedom and satisfaction of the individual, and one arrives at a subjective point of view. On the other hand, if the emphasis is laid on the collective

1. Sri Aurobindo, *The Human Cycle*, p. 63.

self, then the life of the individual is subordinated to that of the collectivity. These two extremes can meet only in the realization of the universal Being or existence, which fulfils itself in the individual as well as in the collectivity, by enlarging the idea of the self. The idea here is the highest at once from the subjective as well as the objective views of the life. In this ideal, individual and collectivity develop by mutual fulfilment. This is the true subjectivism, which transcends both subjective materialism and subjective idealism and discovers the real self of which the mind, life and body are mere instruments, unequal in hierarchy, but equal in necessity for integral perfection.

PSYCHOLOGY OF SOCIAL DEVELOPMENT

The Three Stages

In Sri Aurobindo's Philosophy of History there is a parallelism in the evolution of the individual and the society, since they are the two facets of the same Consciousness-Force. The same parallelism may be noticed in his interpretation of the psychology of social development. Thus, human evolution starts from an infra-rational stage in which man's actions and institutions are guided by instincts, impulses, spontaneous ideas, vital intuition or conventional responses, the stimuli of desires, need and circumstances. From this infra-rational stage, man evolves to the rational stage in which an intelligent will is the arbiter of his cognitions, conations, and affections and governs his ideas, aims and institutions. If evolution is the principle of the process in Nature, this rational stage should also pass into a third stage which is spiritual, intuitive and gnostic.

Not a rigid scheme

This three-fold classification of the stages of the psychology of social development is not a rigid, exclusive and absolute division. Often, they exist simultaneously at different places. They arise of each other and partially develop in each other. So far as a man is concerned, he is neither of these exclusively but has all these in his complex being. Even the most primitive savage has some reason as well as some spirituality in him, rational man has infra-rational urges and supra-rational inspirations. Similarly, a spiritual man also has his reason as well as infra-rational urges, though transformed and divinized. Social Philosophy does not seek to construct utopias. Its vision is not wholly transcendent of the present as it is based on human psychology and acknowledges its limitations. As Sri Aurobindo admits, "Not God, but at His highest a human being touched with a ray of divine influences, man's very spirituality, however dominant, must have, while he is still this imperfectly evolved human, its rational and infra-rational tendencies and elements."[1] And as with individual, so also in society, the tendencies of a

1. Sri Aurobindo, *The Human Cycle*, American Edition, p. 207

particular stage may overpower others, transform them or compromise with them, but their exclusive play is not the intention of the Nature. Spiritualism, in Sri Aurobindo's Social Philosophy, neither compromises nor negates nor suppresses the rational and infra-rational elements but includes, integrates and transforms them.

Two Tendencies

Thus, in the psychology of social development, according to Sri Aurobindo, the infra-rational stage should pass through the rational stage. In this growth of reason, either the spiritual tendency is done away with for some time or accepted but surrounded with a vast web of the workings of the intelligence. The first tendency was seen for the first time in the age of the Sophists in Greece, with its large number of poets, thinkers, rhetoricians and scientific enquirers, who stimulated a generalized activity of intelligence even in the masses. The second tendency can be seen in India where the early mystic seers of the Vedas and Upanishads were replaced by the philosopher-mystics, religious thinkers and even intellectual philosophers.

The Principle of Integral Growth

This new growth, for some time, seemed to possess the whole community as in Athens or old Aryan India, but societies cannot be changed so abruptly, unless the whole race is prepared. Hence, the first impetus was soon overpowered and sometimes even crushed by the new growth of the infra-rational forms. The tradition of living knowledge and lofty ideals of life remains in higher classes or the highest class as the Brahmins in India, and the masses remain in the infra-rational habits of mind, though not without some gain from the past. Only an integral growth is lasting development. Whenever a particular element in man or society overgrows the other parts, there follows a regression to make the basis firm and integral, as that is the principle of evolution in Nature. Social Philosophy should be based on the inherent principles of Nature itself, so that it may guide towards permanent evolution of man and society. Whenever these are missed or subordinated to some other principle, political, sociological, moral or even religious, there is always a danger of relapse and regression.

The Rational Stage

The present psychological stage of humanity can be generally characterized as the rational stage. It is attempting to discover and work out the right principle and a secure foundation for a rational system of society. Its progress is either adaptive or radical. Radical progressions are characteristic of this age, as reason has the nature of quick response to new ideas, needs and possibilities, though the conservative forces in man may restrain it for some time. Thus, several methods of social development have been put forward, accepted, practised, reformed, when they faltered, but opposed when they failed, and finally dethroned by some new principle which also rapidly undergoes the same process. This process will go on, till reason finds some principle or combination of principles satisfying its needs.

EVALUATION OF THE POLITICAL PHILOSOPHIES

Individualism

It has been observed in the preceding chapter that the age of reason begins with individualism, which follows after an age of dominant conventionalism. Describing individualism, Sri Aurobindo says, "In this view society is there only as a field of activity and growth for the individual man and serves best its function when it gives as far as possible a wide room, ample means, a sufficient freedom or guidance of development to his thought, his action, his growth, his possibility of fulness of being."[1] As the symbols, types and institution became conventional, the old methods of mentalizing life ceased to serve their purpose and the aid of reason became imperative to think out the way of life. The age of reason is an age of constant progress, since reason always looks for new possibilities. It questions the facts to improve them by the ideas and questions ideas to see if they square with the facts or need improvement to suit some new facts. Reeson questions every convention and institution, however universally accepted or useful, to find out new possibilities to serve higher purposes. With this universal questioning, dawns the idea that only a universal application of reason can make the society perfect. This is the idea behind the ideal of scientific society which has been discussed in the preceding chapter.

Individualism and Democracy

This reason, universally applied, can be neither that of a ruling class nor of a few eminent thinkers, as in the former case, it becomes a mere slave to power and in the latter disfigured and conventionalized in practice. This must be the reason in each individual searching for some common basis. Thus, with the principle that every individual has equal reason and will in the determination of the government and the order of the society, rationalism arrives at individualistic democracy. "For democracy means a society in which everyone has a chance to count as an individual, and to do something that is distinctively his own."[2] This is not because reason is equal in all the individuals but because, if some are given preference, reason becomes a servant to the infra-rational elements, the power motive of that class.

Equality

Thus, individualistic reason advocated equality which Aristotle declared the basis of justice. All men are by nature free and equal. As Hobbes said, "Nature

1. Sri Aurobindo, *The Life Divine*, American Edition, p. 927.
2. Cole, G.D.H., *Essays in Social Theory*, p. 99.

hath made men so equal, in the faculties of body, and mind; as that though there be found one man sometimes manifestly stronger in body, or of quicker mind than another; yet when all is reckoned together, the difference between man and man is not so considerable as that one man can thereupon claim to himself any benefit, to which another may not pretend as well as he."[1]

Liberty

Apart from equality, liberty is the most important principle of individualistic democracy. Every person should have the liberty to govern his life by his own reason and will, unless he impinges on such a right of others. Liberty is a necessary corollary of equality. Individual judgment is insignificant yet indispensable to the whole society. Everyone has liberty of reason, opinion, discussion and forming judgements. These individual judgments together make for the common judgment of the society. Thus, democracy is a government by popular vote. These judgments are organized only in the case of the ends common to all, otherwise the individual is left free to adjust, according to his own reason and will. By this practice of free use of reason, men learn to grow into rational beings and have a common agreement for a liberal, vigorous, natural and rationalized life.

FAILURES OF INDIVIDUALISM

According to Sri Aurobindo, these individualistic ideals, however, do not hold good for a long time on account of some practical difficulties. The present age is not yet ready for these ideals, as the common man is still far from being a rational person. Coming from an infra-rational past, he is generally guided in his thought by selfish interests, impulses and prejudices or suggestions from others, but not his own reason. Secondly, man uses his reason not to agree with others but to enforce his own egoism on others. Finally, man does not use his freedom to adjust his life with that of others but to enforce his aims of life in competition with that of the life of others. As Joseph A. Schumpeter puts it, "The democratic freedom is that institutional arrangement for arriving at political decisions in which individuals acquire the power to decide by means of competitive struggle for the people's vote."[2] Owing to all these difficulties, the individualistic ideals do not square with the fundamental facts and this gulf leads to ultimate disillusionment and failure.

FAILURE OF INDIVIDUALISTIC DEMOCRACY

Thus, in the individualistic democracy, not all individuals but only a dominant class of politicians rule, while the majority is ignorant. "Politics for the politicians", says G. D. H. Cole, "that is the last corruption of a

1. Hobbes, T., *Leviathan,* Edited by Ernest Rhys, p. 63.
2. Schumpeter, J.A., *Capitalism, Socialism and Democracy* (1947), p. 269.

democracy that has knocked the foundations from under its own feet."[1] But since the equality and liberty can be no longer stifled, the failure of parliamentary democracy leads to a war of classes. It was this inherent defect of individualistic democracy which led Marx to proclaim the need of class conflict. Again, individualistic democratic freedom leads to increase in competition resulting in ordered conflict. In this conflict it is not the spiritual or rational which survives but it is the most vitally successful which does so. This is not what individualistic reason intended with the democratic principles of equality and liberty. This is not the rational order of society nor is it even the least perfection of the individual.

The Contribution of Democratic Ideals

According to Sri Aurobindo, the democratic ideals have done much good to the human race in spite of all failures of democracy. In the first place, it is for the first time in human history that man is active, alive and self-confident. Secondly, more men, if not all, know, think, judge and decide all sorts of issues. Democracy trains men to use their minds and apply their intelligence to life, though not yet soundly, clearly and rightly. Equality in education and opportunities of life, have not yet been realized but equality brought about by democracy is certainly far greater than it was in the older states.

Results of Democracy

The infra-rational being in man, according to Sri Aurobindo, seeks three things, *viz.*, satisfaction, power or use and reward of his faculties and the enjoyment of his desires. In the old societies, these things were secured by each according to his birth, status and the use of his capacities within his hereditary status. In the modern society, wealth has become the sole power which can harness all other powers and provide satisfaction, use and reward of faculties and enjoyment of desires, as all other bases have been removed. This has led to disorganisation of society. A plutocratic tendency is increasing under the garb of democracy. A huge organized competitive system, and a lopsided development of industrialism, has been substituted for the old order of society. "These," Sri Aurobindo concludes, "have been the last results of the individualistic ideal and its democratic machinery, the initial bankruptcies of the rational age."[2]

A PSYCHOLOGICAL DIAGNOSIS

The fundamental defect here, according to Sri Aurobindo, is, not in the democratic principles, education and individualism, but in making reason their basis. The inner meaning of the history of social development is psychological, in which the different principles, first infra-rational than

1. Cole, G.D.H., *Essays on Social Theory,* p. 101.
2. Sri Aurobindo, *The Human Cycle,* American Edition, p. 223.

rational, have been given chance to govern life, tested for a long time and doubted with difficulty. A great crisis was resolved by man's transition from infra-rational principles to rational ones, though this was not through a linear development but after many progressions and regressions in the spiral process of development. A still greater crisis is present before mankind today, as reason has led man to control Nature but has failed to gain the inner mastery. "Our present predicament, says Bertrand Russell, "is due, more than anything else, to the fact that we have learnt to understand and control, to a terrifying extent, the forces of Nature outside us, but not those that are embodied in ourselves."[1] But Russell and other rationalist social philosophers fail to note that the inner forces cannot be transformed and integrated or even fully controlled by reason. As Sri Aurobindo points out, "Reason and science can only help by standardizing, by fixing everything into an artificially arranged and mechanized unity of material life. A greater whole-being, whole-knowledge, whole-power, is needed to weld all into a greater unity of whole-life."[2]

The Value of the Individual

This higher principle will dawn on human life only through the individuals. The individual, in the philosophy of Sri Aurobindo, is continuous with the Community and Humanity and yet he transcends these also, as he is more than a mere part of the whole. "The individual as spirit or being is not confined within his humanity; he has been less than human, he can become more than human."[3] Man depends on the universe for the development of his personality but his future possibilities are not so much due to social influences as due to his own self, the Absolute within him who transcends the universe.

Spiritual Individualism

Thus, the Social Philosophy of Sri Aurobindo sets a very high premium on the value of the individual. He is the key of the evolutionary movement as it is he who becomes conscious of the Reality. "Only the people are immortal," says the Collectivist, "everything else is transient."[4] The people' however, are the sub-conscious mass, always less developed than the developed individual who alone is the conscious vanguard of progress. The people's progress depends on accepting what the individuals have developed. So long as the individual is undeveloped, he might follow the dictates of society, state or whatever is greater than himself. But as he grows in spiritual freedom, he need not conform to the state or community, though ultimately his own perfection leads to the perfection of society. According to Sri Aurobindo,

---

1. Russell, B., *Authority and the Individual,* p. 125.
2. Sri Aurobindo, *Mother India,* p. 929.
3. Sri Aurobindo, *The Life Divine,* American Edition, p. 929.
4. Stalin, Quoted by Plekhanov, *The Role of Individual in History,* p. 8.

"The individual does not owe his ultimate allegiance either to the State which is a machine or to the community which is a part of life and not the whole of life : his allegiance must be to the Truth, the Self, the Spirit, the Divine which is in him and in all; not to subordinate or lose himself in the mass, but to find and express that truth of being in himself, and help the community and humanity in its seeking for its own truth and fulness of being must be his real object of existence."[1] Thus, in the Social Philosophy of Sri Aurobindo, the individual asserts his liberty only to realize the spiritual liberty of the society and mankind. Spiritual liberty is correlated with spiritual unity. Individual perfection is a prelude to social perfection. This spiritual individualism of Sri Aurobindo is quite different from the rational individualism and anarchism. It is the same as spiritual socialism, spiritual communism and spiritual humanism, as the Spirit is the same everywhere.

DEMOCRATIC SOCIALISM

But since this reality of the individual was not realized in the rational individualism, it could not serve to maintain the harmony of the society. The replacement of the old order by an organized competitive system and the increasing plutocratic tendency, led to the transition of the rational mind from democratic individualism. In this ideal, the collective life was given the sole importance. The existence and growth of the race is the supreme end. Individual is a mere means to that end. He is a cell of the social organism. His life should be cast in the mould of rational culture. He is a mere instrument for the maintenance and efficiency of the collective existence.

MARXIST SOCIALISM

This ideology was again the basis of Marxist Socialism which was unfortunately, based on the principle of class war, as it was born as a revolt against capitalism. "The history of all hitherto existing society," declared Marx and Engels, "is the history of class struggles."[2] Marxist socialism aims at the establishment of a classless society in which the free development of each is the condition for the free development of all. It seeks a government of the proletariat, the people. But "the people" is a vague term and the government of the socialist states is in the hands of a few individuals who constitute a dominant class or party. The class war which led to the abolition of Czardom in Russia again led to the revolution against the personality cult of Stalin, though in a different form. So long as man moves by power-motive of the vital and physical ego, there is no reason to suppose that revolution against Stalinism is the final phase of class war. So long as human nature remains what it is, the classes will always precipitate out of the vague mass of people and class war will never cease.

1. Sri Aurobindo, *The Life Divine,* American Edition, p. 930.
2. Marx, K., and Engels, F., *Selected Works*, Vol. I. Foreign Language Publishing House (Moscow), 1955, p. 34.

MARXISM

Again, true nature of socialism is also disfigured from its start by an industrial social system and its economic form. It was a direct corollary of the materialistic interpretation of history. Marx turned Hegel upside down to find the rational kernal out of the mystic cell.[1] What he found, however, was not the kernel but only the crust and he accepted it for the real essence. He had the vision to see the inevitable death of the capitalist system and the importance of the material basis of man's social life. But by making matter the whole of Spirit, economic development the sole panacea and class war the final solution, he missed the real crux of the problem. Marxist doctrines, however suitable they may have been in their own time, require a revision, nay a transformation, according to the changed conditions of today and the inherent purpose of Nature.

Contribution of Marxism

By its timely emphasis on the physical and economic aspects of social life Marxism has its value, but as an analysis of the total disease, it is far from being sufficient. "Its true nature, its real justification", according to Sri Aurobindo, "is the attempt of human reason to carry on the rational ordering of society to its fulfilment, its will to get rid of this great parasitical excrescence of unbridled competition, this giant obstacle to any decent ideal or practice of human living."[2] Socialism wants to establish peace and order in place of an organized economic battle. In the old society, this peace and order was established on the basis of artificial or inherited inequality, brought about by the denial of equal opportunity and justified on the basis of the law of Karman, or destiny or theological sanctions. Modern man cannot tolerate this injustice. The experiment to base the social order on individual liberty has failed. Socialism is a dialectical antithesis. "Socialism therefore" according to Sri Aurobindo, "must do away with the democratic basis of individual liberty, even if it professes to respect it or to be marching towards a more rational freedom."[3]

COMMUNISM

According to Sri Aurobindo, rational socialism passes into communism by its very inherent dialectic. In socialism, the democratic emphasis on liberty is shifted to emphasize equality. This change in stress leads to a radical change

---

1. "To Hegel, the life process of the human brain, *i.e.*, the process of thinking, which under the name of "the idea", he even transforms into an independent subject, is the demiurgos of the real world, and the real world is only the external, phenomenal form of 'the idea'. With me, on the contrary the ideal is nothing else than the material world reflected by the human mind, and translated into forms of thought." Marx, K., *Capital*, Vol. I. Foreign Languages Publishing House, Moscow (1958), p. 19.
2. Sri Aurobindo, *The Human Cycle*, p. 223.
3. *Ibid.*

in the basic principles of a rational society. In democracy, there is only equality of opportunity. Socialism, in addition, pleads for equality of status, as the latter is the true basis for the former. Equality of status is opposed to the personal or inherited right of property. Hence, socialism abolishes personal property. Not individuals, but community as a whole possesses and administers property. As Marx and Engels said, "This transformation of scattered private property, arising from individual labour, into capitalist private property is, naturally, a process, incomparably more protracted, violent, and difficult, than the transformation of capitalistic private property, already practically resting on socialized production into socialized property. In the former case, we had the expropriation of the mass of the people by a few usurpers; in the later, we have the expropriation of a few usurpers by the mass of the people."[1] Thus, democracy passes into capitalism unless it is socialist, and capitalism leads to its antithesis in the communism of property. But in justifying this abolition of private property, a proposition not itself unjustified, communism went so far as to deny the very existence of the individual, except as a member and instrument of society. Not only the property, but the labour, capacities, education and its achievements, the mind, the knowledge and the life of man and even the life of his wife and children, belong to society. Reason and will of the individual is no more trusted for a right and rational adjustment of man in the society. Hence, the collective reasoning mind and will determine not only all the details of the economic and political order but also that of the social order and even the ordering of the vital, ethical and intelligent concerns of the individual. Man is thus reduced to a mere working, thinking and feeling cell of the social organism. This was thought to be the only way to overcome the egoism of the individualistic life and to realize a perfect rational order of society in a harmonious world.

SOCIALIST DEMOCRACY

This extreme has been undoubtedly avoided by the more democratic socialists, because of the influence of the old democratic ideas. This approach tries to secure some sort of compromise between a limited yet rational individual freedom and the rigours of the collectivist idea. "But", as Sri Aurobindo points out, "it is evidently these rigours to which things must tend if the collectivist idea is to prevail and not to stop short and falter in the middle of its course."[2] This hesitation of the democratic socialists or socialistic democrats between the opposing principles of socialistic regimentation and democratic liberty, is the cause of the failure of socialism in so many countries. The collectivistic idea like the individualistic democracy has, even at its best, certain elements inconsistent with the real facts of human life and nature. Man cannot tolerate

1. Marx, K., and Engels, F., *Capital*, Vol. I. Foreign Languages Publishing House, Moscow (1958), p. 764.

2. Sri Aurobindo, *The Human Cycle*, American Edition, p. 225.

for long any scheme imposed on his life which is foreign to his real nature. Individualistic democracy attempted to secure political liberty protected by the state. Socialistic democracy tries to enforce a social and political equality through the state. The failure of the former led to the latter and the failure of the latter, according to Sri Aurobindo, will lead the rational and democratic idea to make yet another experiment of a third form of society, the intellectual or spiritual anarchism. An intellectual anarchism was the idea which Karl Marx himself cherished, though it is difficult to understand how it could be realized through state socialism.

The Opposition of Democracy and Socialism

Socialism, according to Sri Aurobindo, is opposed to the democratic principles of liberty, equality and fraternity. These are the demands of the individual and not inherent in the collective ideal. The individual demands liberty of mind, life and will of action, the state is more and more compelled by its nature to control these till personal liberty is pressed out of existence. This was done by social reason, only to concede another demand of the individual, equality, which was given priority in socialistic systems. Democracy granted liberty but it granted equality only in legal and political aspects. Socialism granted equality but only that much liberty which does not abolish equality. But ultimately, even this equality was found to be no less an obstacle to social good than the ideal of liberty. What still had a chance of survival is the third member of the democratic trinity *i.e.,* Fraternity. This is very much emphasized by the socialists and the communists at least in theory if not in practice, even after the abolition of liberty and equality. "But", as Sri Aurobindo points out, "comradeship without liberty and equality can be nothing more than the like association of all individuals, functional classes, guilds, syndicates, soviets or any other units — in common service to the life of the nation under the absolute control of the collectivist State."[1] Thus, in the socialist states, liberty is the freedom to serve the community under state guidance, equality is the theoretical equality of functions, fraternity is the sense of comradeship in the service of the state. This is nothing more than a negation of these principles, which, in fact, though essential to democracy, are not so essential to the collectivist ideal.

TOTALITARIANISM

Totalitarianism, according to Sri Aurobindo, is the inevitable destiny, the extreme and fullest outcome of socialism or the collectivist idea. The essence of socialism is the governance and organization of the total life of society as a whole and in detail, by the collective reason and will. This eliminates all internal competition, exploitation, confusion and waste, this also enforces

1. Sri Aurobindo, *Ibid.*, p. 227.

and perfects co-ordination and assures sufficient life for all. Sri Aurobindo is not ignorant of the fact that in certain states an attempt is being made to realize socialism through democratic principles, and he hopes that perhaps this may be successful. "But", he warns that "if a non-democratic polity and machinery are found to serve the purpose better, then there is nothing inherently sacrosanct for the collectivist mind in the democratic ideal; it can be thrown in the rubbish heap where so many other exploded sanctities have gone."[1] This warning is timely in the face of so many states leaving democracy in favour of dictatorship. Russian Communism has preserved the ideal of a proletarian equality for all in a classless society but its spirit is a rigorous totalitarianism on the basis of the dictatorship of the proletariat which in fact means the dictatorship of the communist party. The dictatorship of the proletariat abolishes even democratic equality.

A New Trend

The Socialism of Karl Marx was a rational system worked out by a logical and systematic thinking. Russians have, however, transformed it into a social religion, a collectivistic mystique. This new trend, breaking away from rationalism, has the symptoms of the death of the rational age. This swing is more marked in fascist countries, in their totalitarian mystique in the name of the national soul. Both communists and fascists have led to a crystallization of the social, economic and political life of the people into a perfectly rigid organization, the casting of thought, education, expression and action into a set iron mould with a repression of all that differs. If this denial of freedom to individual reason becomes universal, it shall be the end of the age of reason. Recent movements in Russia against the cult of Stalin, and the defeat of the fascists of Germany and Italy in the last Great War, have restored a more natural line of progress and led to prolongation of the curve of the age of reason. It has also given subjectivism a chance and freedom to evolve so that it may take up the spiral of the human social evolution where the curve of the age of reason naturally ends.

The Value of the Collectivist Idea

Sri Aurobindo, though he assigns a great value to the individual is not unaware of the value of the collectivist idea. The central idea, working behind all his criticism of democracy and socialism, is the inadequacy of reason as the guiding principle of social life. So long as reason is the basis of the cherished harmony, it is bound to stumble here and there, no matter what type of social system is adopted. According to Sri Aurobindo, "The evolutionary nisus is pushing towards a development of the cosmic force in terrestrial life which needs a larger mental and vital being to support it, a wider mind, a greater, wider, more conscious unanimised Life-Soul, Anima, and that again needs an

---

1. *Ibid.*, p. 228.

unveiling of the supporting Soul and spiritual self within it to maintain it."[1] It is only on the basis of this principle that a true harmony of the individuals, nations, and humanity can be realised.

The collectivistic idea of society is based on the fundamental fact that the individual can use and develop his powers only in a certain relation with society and that the organization of the individuals leads to much efficiency and improvement in common good. The obedience of the collective reason and will is certainly better than the life of narrow egoism. And up to a certain point, man must follow the dictates of the society and the state.

The Central Fallacy

But the central fallacy underlying both the collectivist ideal and the individualist theory is that "it ignores the complexity of man's being and all that complexity means."[2] Man is not only the body, life and mind but also a self whose supreme need is freedom. The control of the lower members, that of the body, life and mind, is the very necessity of this freedom but that control is self-control. The community again has not only a body, life and mind but also soul. But there is no common reason or will. The concepts of Group-Mind and General Will in the sense of common reason and will have been rejected by contemporary social psychologists. The group soul, according to Sri Aurobindo, "works out its tendencies by a diversity of opinions, a diversity of wills, a diversity of life."[3] Hence, the government by the people is always a government by a number of individuals, whether that number is in theory the majority or the minority. It is never the common reason or the General Will which governs in a democratic, socialist or communist state but always the reason and will of a few dominant men. In the government of the state there is bound to be the suppression of minority by the majority or *vice versa.* Democratic liberty restricted the state and gave freedom to the individual. Collectivism restricted the individual and gave freedom to the state, the supposed representative of the collectivity. As the individual reason develops, the needs of freedom and variation are felt though these need not be harmful to others. Freedom of thought, devoid of the freedom of action, leads to an intolerable contradiction and falsity, which though temporarily restrained on account of some immediate gains, will ultimately lead to a revolt in the clearest and most vigorous minds and finally in the masses. This may lead to anarchistic thought which is subversive of the socialistic order. The state may combat this movement by its educational machinery and by suppression of the freedom of speech and thought. This suppression, however, will be either ineffective in a rational society or else the remedy may prove worse than the evil it seeks to combat, as it means the end of the age of reason and of the ideal of a rational society. This is the central defect of the collectivism which

1. Sri Aurobindo, *The Life Divine,* American Edition, p. 935.
2. Sri Aurobindo, *The Human Cycle,* American Edition, p. 234.
3. *Ibid.*

aims at a thorough-going mechanization of life. From the point of view of the psychology of social development, this is the inherent defect of reason. The principles of reason can deal with physical nature but they miserably fail in the sphere of life which is a mobile, progressive and evolving force. The unifying principle of life can be found only by the transformation of the life values into those of the Spirit, for it is there alone that its contradictions can be reconciled. The rational order of society is undoubtedly an advance upon the infra-rational orders of societies, but it can never arrive at perfection by its own methods.

INTELLECTUAL ANARCHISM

According to Sri Aurobindo, as the pressure of society upon the individual increases, the anarchist thought finds its way. Besides, the unimportant, gross, vitalistic anarchism, the intellectual anarchistic thought condemns all types of government and blames the social principle for the fall of the man from a natural to an unnatural and artificial principle of life. Anarchism, according to Sri Aurobindo, has laid an exclusive emphasis on the individual and ignored the contribution of the society in man's development. Anarchists base their theory on the old dogma that man was originally innocent and perfect. But all the philosophers who advocate this original perfection have admitted a later lapse leading to the need of state control. Thus, man's fall was not due to the social principle, rather the social principle and state were introduced as a remedy for man's fall. On the other hand, if one admits, with Sri Aurobindo and other contemporary philosophers, that man's evolution is a gradual ascent, the social principle should play an important role in man's growth from infra-rational to rational stage. Man can be ready for the anarchistic principle of life, only when his infra-rational nature is governed by some higher principle. It is undeniable that this growth itself requires abolition of governmental compulsion in favour of the inner law of man. But the inner law is not the principle on which intellectual anarchism relies. It relies on the enlightened reason and human sympathy, the former producing liberty and equality, the latter fraternity and cooperation. Anarchist thinkers have not sufficiently realized the power of infra-rational elements in man, the vital egoism which defeats all calculations of the idealizing reason. Like individualism and collectivism, anarchism has also missed the complex nature of man. So long as reason is the basis, it is mere utopian thinking that the state will "wither away."[1] It is difficult to understand how the Marxist system can avoid slipping into rigorous collectivism or anarchy.

SPIRITUAL ANARCHISM

A spiritual anarchism may be suggested as an alternative but the term anarchism smells too much of indeterminism and even lack of control. Again, spiritualism has also been generally identified with asceticism and the

[1] Engels, F., *Anti Duhring*, p. 315.

suppression of the infra-rational elements, which is contrary to the principle of inner integral freedom, the very acme of spiritual growth. This theory of spiritual anarchism has not been consistently developed as a theory of social order. It has been only casually expressed by saints and religious persons including Gandhi and others. It is what religion has everywhere and always demanded.

Conclusion

Thus, the solution of the problem is psychological. As Sri Aurobindo points out, "It is a spiritual, an inner freedom that can alone create a perfect human order."[1] Spiritual freedom is the sound foundation of the principles of democracy; liberty, equality and fraternity. That being given, all other problems discussed so far, will be spontaneously solved. Spiritual comradeship can alone lead to a perfect harmony in human society, Man's present crisis is evolutionary. His whole problem is psychological. The real solution is the spiritual growth of his consciousness, though physical and mental growth is a necessary prelude to spiritual evolution, as its ascent is integral. The Spirit is the inmost essence of all. Its very nature of diverse oneness is to realize the perfection of the individual, not in isolation from society but in universal nature. It is on this principle that true communism and individualism can be harmonized. This is Sri Aurobindo's conclusion in his psychological analysis of social development. The preceding discussion in this chapter, shows the inevitability of this solution, however difficult it may be to realize it. As Sri Aurobindo points out, "This is not certain; but in any case, if this is not the solution, then there is no solution, if this is not the way, then there is no way for the human kind."[2] And there is no reason to suppose that this is not possible. As a matter of fact, the beginning is already there. The subjective turn in the present day society, the growing acceptance of the spiritual solution, at least in theory, and the appearance of the spiritual individuals here and there are sure signs. To quote Sri Aurobindo, "If the light that is being born increases, if the number of individuals who seek to realise the possibility in themselves and in the world grows large and they get nearer the right way, then the Spirit who is here in man, now a concealed divinity, a developing light and power, will descend more fully as the avatar of a yet unseen and unguessed Godhead from above into the soul of mankind and into the great individualities in whom the light and power are the strongest."[3]

NATIONALISM

Among the contemporary Indian philosophers, Sri Aurobindo has presented the most elaborate discussion on Nation. While, on the one hand, he was a staunch advocate of human unity, on the other hand, he conceived nationalism

1. Sri Aurobindo, *The Human Cycle*, American Edition, p. 245.
2. *Ibid.*, p. 246.
3. *Ibid.*, pp. 299-300.

as a help and not a hindrance to it. In his social and political philosophy, everywhere one finds wholes within wholes. An individual is complete within himself and yet he is also a constituent of the nation. A Nation is complete in itself and yet each nation is a part of humanity. Humanity again is complete in itself and yet it is part of Nature. Thus, one finds wider and wider wholes from individual to cosmic reality. The search after any one of these does not lessen the importance of lower integers. Though an individual is a part of a nation, yet his individuality, *Swadharma* and perfection cannot be delimited by the nation. The nation should be such in which all the individual members may freely evolve themselves maintaining their individual characteristics. Similarly, human society or world state should be such in which each nation may contribute to the evolution of humanity by maintaining its own characteristics, culture and individual freedom. And finally, humanity should grow not independent of Nature but very much as a part of it. Thus, according to Sri Aurobindo, nationalism does not retard the growth of human unity. His ideas here appear to be more balanced than that of the other humanists and internationalists who overlook the truth of self-realization in the individual and the nation. As it is wrong to make a state all powerful by overlooking the freedom of the individual, similarly the concept of an all powerful world state, abolishing the free existence of nations, is alien to Nature. From the spiritual point of view the higher and wider integer does not eliminate but fulfils the perfection and freedom of its parts.

The Concept of nation

According to Sri Aurobindo. "The perfection of the individual in a perfected society eventually in a perfected humanity — understanding perfection always in a relative and progressive sense — is the inevitable aim of Nature."[1] Under British rule in India, Sri Aurobindo played an important role in the Indian freedom movement from 1893 to 1910. His idea of nationalism follows from he gospel of *Bande Mataram.* For him, Nation was not a geographical area, physical territory or mental idea. He worshipped India as the Mother or Mother power who has sustained Indians for thousands of years. He planned a *Bhawani Mandir* scheme for the youth of Bengal on the pattern of Bankim Chandra Chatterjee's scheme outlined in his famous novel *Anand Math.* His speeches and writings of that period show that he raised patriotism to the pedestal of religion. In his essay entitled *Bhawani Mandir* he wrote, "For what is a nation? What is our mother country? It is not a piece of earth, nor a figure of speech, nor a fiction of the mind. It is a mighty *Shakti,* composed of all the *Shakties* of all the millions of gods assembled in one mass of force and welded into unity. The shakti we call in India, *Bhawani Bharati,* is the living unity of the Shakties of three hundred million people...".[2] In his article on Bankim

1. Sri Aurobindo, *The Ideal of Human Unity,* Sri Aurobindo Ashram, Pondicherry, 1950, p. 10.
2. Sri Aurobindo, *Bhawani Mandir,* Sri Aurobindo Mandir Annual, Jayanti Number 15, August 15, 1956.

Chandra, Sri Aurobindo made it clear that so long as the members of a nation see it only as a piece of land, it does not take the form of a divine mother power; so long as it does not cover their heart and mind, a nation is not born. Thus, according to Sri Aurobindo, the formation of nation requires not only love of country among its members but a sentiment of worship towards it. A merely physical, vital or mental approach towards a nation is insufficient, it requires a spiritual attitude.

Importance of Patriotism

Thus, Sri Aurobindo's speeches and writings were full of high patriotism. Addressing the students of Bengal National College he once said, "There are times in nation's history when Providence places before it one work, one aim, to which everything else, however high and noble in itself, has to be sacrificed. Such a time has how arrived for our Motherland when nothing is dearer than her service, when everything else is to be directed to that end. If you will study, study for her sake; train yourselves body and mind and soul for her service. You will earn your living that you may live for her sake. You will go abroad to foreign lands that you may bring back knowledge with which you may do service to her. Work that she may prosper. Suffer that she may rejoice. All is contained in that one single advice."[1] Through the medium of the newspaper *Bande Mataram*, Sri Aurobindo introduced the youth of the country to patriotism and nationalism. To patriotism, he gave the highest place among human sentiments. In his own words, "Love has a place in politics, it is the love of one's country, for one's countrymen, for the glory, greatness and happiness of the race, the divine ananda of self-immolation for one's fellows, the ecstasy of relieving their sufferings, the joy of seeing one's blood flow for country and freedom, the bliss of union in death with the fathers of the race."[2] A person devoted to his country feels almost physical delight in the touch of its earth. He loves the seas, rivers, hills, music, poetry, literature and culture of the country. This love is the basis of patriotism. It is due to patriotism that we have a pride in the past of our country, suffer for it in the present, and undergo all sort of sacrifices to build up its fulure. This sacrifice, service and endurance results from patriotism. The worship of the motherland, its constant contemplation and perpetual service, keeps patriotism alive. The articles and lectures of Sri Aurobindo were so full of patriotic spirit that they caused a wave of awakening in the country.

Concept of Nationalism

It is a characteristic of Indian culture that it has never separated the mundane from the spiritual and the former has been always interpreted as an expression of the latter. Sri Aurobindo's patriotism and nationalism were never mundane; rather they were full of religious fervour. Service of the nation was his highest

1. Sri Aurobindo, *Speeches,* Sri Aurobindo Ashram, Pondicherry, Third Edition, 1952, p. 4.
2. Sri Aurobindo, *The Doctrine of Passive Resistance,* p. 83.

religion. As he wrote. "The work of national emancipation is a great and holy Yajna of which Boycott, Swadeshi, National Education and every other activity, great and small, are only major or minor parts. Liberty is the fruit we seek from the sacrifice and the Motherland the goddess to whom we offer it; into the seven leaping tongues of the fire of the Yajna we must offer all that we are and all that we have, feeding the fire even with our blood and lives and happiness of our nearest and dearest for the Motherland is a goddess who loves not a maimed and imperfect sacrifice, and freedom was never won from the gods by a grudging giver."[1] Sri Aurobindo exhorted his countrymen to sacrifice everything for the nation. He considered devotion not someone aspect of life but the whole of it. For him service of the nation was a religious practice. In one of his lectures he said, "What is Nationalism? Nationalism is not a mere political programme; nationalism is a religion that has come from God; Nationalism is a creed which you shall have to live...If you are going to be a nationalist, if you are going to assent to this religion of nationalism, you must do it in the religious spirit. You must remember that you are the instruments of God."[2] Thus, Sri Aurobindo presented a religion of nationalism. He worshipped motherland as the Mother and the goddess and exhorted everyone to sacrifice everything for her. He demanded complete Swarajya and sanctioned every means for its achievement. In *Bande Mataram* he wrote, "We recognize no political object of worship except the divinity in our Motherland, no present object of political endeavour except liberty, and no method or action as politically good or evil except as it truly helps or hinders our progress towards national emancipation."[3] Here Sri Aurobindo has admitted liberty as the one single goal of political movement. In his moral philosophy the excellence of end decides the excellence of means and any means can be adopted to fulfil a spiritual end. Therefore, he commanded his countrymen to adopt any political method and political action considered necessary for achieving complete freedom.

Considering nationalism as a Dharma, Sri Aurobindo declared that the Indian national movement is being guided by divine inspiration. It is an effort to realize God in the country. Therefore, not even the mightiest can suppress it and it must win in the end. Sri Aurobindo's indomitable faith in the future of the country was rooted in his religion of nationalism. As he said, Nationalism is a religion that has come from God...It has not been crushed. It is not going to be crushed. Nationalism survives in the strength of God and it is not possible to crush it, whatever weapons are brought against it. Nationalism is immortal, Nationalism cannot die, because it is no human thing, it is God who is working in Bengal."[4]

1. *Ibid.*, pp. 71-78.
2. Sri Aurobindo, *Speeches*, p. 6.
3. Sri Aurobindo, *The Doctrine of Passive Resistance*, pp. 67-68.
4. Quoted By S.K. Maitra, *Sri Aurobindo and Indian Freedom*, Sri Aurobindo Library, Madras, 1948.

While speaking before his countrymen at different places Sri Aurobindo asked them to remember Rama, Krishna, Buddha, Shivaji and Guru Gobind singh and posed the question as to whether this country of great men will prostrate at the feet of the foreigners or whether they are prepared to sacrifice everything to get it liberated. Thus, Sri Aurobindo considered national movement as a divine command and spiritual rule. This love of nation, however, was never egoistic. In his many speeches he made it absolutely clear that India's freedom and evolution was not merely for India but for humanity itself, for the establishment of the kingdom of God on earth. He called upon every class of Indian society, specially the backward classes, while he was working for national awakening.

Concept of Nation Soul

The individual, the nation and the humanity are the three manifestations of the divine, ultimate Reality. Self evolution is the aim of life in the individual and in the nation. Nature at all levels is working towards self-expression. Everywhere there is a soul behind the body, life and the mind. The aim of each individual, group, race, society or nation is self-expression. Besides the development of the individuals, the goal of the family is its total perfection. The same can be said about other human groups. Everywhere the perfection of the individuals is complementary to the perfection of the collectivity.

Sri Aurobindo has conceived the Nation-soul on the basis of individual soul. In his own words, "The nation or society, like the individual, has a body, an organic life, a moral and aesthetic temperament, a developing mind and a soul behind all these signs and powers for the sake of which they exist. One may see even that, like the individual, it essentially is a soul rather than has one; it is a group soul that, once having attained to a separate distinctness, must become more and more self-conscious and find itself more and more fully as it develops its corporate action and mentality and its organic self expressive life."[1] Thus, according to Sri Aurobindo, just as each individual has a body, vital and mind, and a soul behind all these, similarly in every nation there is a vast territory, emotional unity, mental life and behind all these a nation-soul. Just as the individual is not body, vital or mind but soul, similarly the nation is not body, vital or mind but nation-soul. Just as physical, vital and mental development is necessary for the self-development of the individual, similarly for the evolution of nation-soul, defence of the motherland, physical development of the countly, increase of emotional unity and the artistic, philosophical, literary and scientific developments are indispensible. If any one of these is lacking neither the development of the individual soul nor that of the nation-soul is possible. Hence, each nation should defend its land against foreign invasion. Each nation should grow culturally along with its physical, industrial and economic growth. Just as self-realisation is the *dharma* of the individual, similarly realisation of the

---

1. Sri Aurobindo, *The Human Cycle* (1950), pp. 37-38.

nation-soul is the *dharma* of the nation. Just as individual self-realisation is not selfishness but divine command, similarly realisation of nation-soul is not national selfishness but divine command. Just as sometimes man wrongly identifies his self with the ego, similarly in different times of human history, national self has been confused with national ego in the process of national self-realisation. Just as ego in the individual leads to his own and also to the harm of others, similarly the growth of national ego in any nation leads it and other nations to trouble and suffering. An example of this phenomenon is a rise of national ego in Germany before the Second World War. Just as self-realisation is a gradual and difficult process in the life of the individual, similarly the self in the nation can be realised gradually and with much difficulty. Just as increasing freedom, harmony and unity are the symptoms of self-realisation in the individual, similarly the growth of nation-soul manifests in the growing freedom, harmony and unity among the various classes. Just as self-realisation in the individual leads to his having harmonious relations with others, similarly evolution of nation-self leads to its having harmonious relations with other nations. Finally, just as self-realisation is the *summum bonum* of the individual, similarly realisation of the nation-soul is the ultimate end of the nation.

The above mentioned parallelism between the structure of individual and nation does not mean that Sri Aurobindo has missed the distinction between them or that he has forgotten that while the parts of an individual soul have no independent existence, the human beings constituting a nation have their own individual existence as well. Pointing out the distinction between individual and nation-soul Sri Aurobindo has maintained, "There is only this difference that the group soul is much more complex because it has a great number of partly self-conscious mental individuals for the constituents of its physical being instead of an association of merely vital sub-conscious cells."[1] It is due to this very distinction between individual soul and collective soul that most of the people are not prepared to admit that there is anything like nation-soul. It is for this reason again that some scholars consider individual-soul subjective and nation-soul objective. Citing examples from collective consciousness, Sri Aurobindo has proved that nation-soul is not just a figment of his imagination.

Consciousness of Nation-Soul

Just as for a person living on ordinary physical, vital and mental level it is difficult to experience that he has a soul, similarly it is difficult for him to appreciatethe concept of Nation-soul. Again, just as individual soul is subject to spiritual experience, Nation-soul can be experienced by collective consciousness. Just as soul in the individual is not objective similarly the Nation-soul is not subject to demonstration, perception or testimony. Finally, just as one who has experienced individual soul insists on its existence

1. *Ibid.*, p. 38.

similarly a patriot directly experiences Nation-soul. To quote Sri Aurobindo, "When we realise that the land is only the shell of the body, though a very living shell indeed and potent in its influences on the nation, when we begin to feel that its more real body is the men and women who compose the nation-unit, a body ever changing, yet always the same like that of the individual man, we are on the way to a truly subjective communal consciousness. For then we have some chance of realising that even the physical being of the society is a subjective power, not a mere objective existence. Much more is it in its inner self, a great corporate soul with all the possibilities and dangers of the soul life."[1]

In many of his works Sri Aurobindo has shown that in the present times one may witness increasing consciousness of nation-soul in most of the newly awakened nations. Most of the nations today are making efforts towards self-realisation in every aspect of life. *Swadeshi* and *swadharma* are the bases of this process. Evolution according to one's own nature is the goal of each object, living being and collectivity. To fulfil this mission is self-realisation. *Swadeshi* is very important in this process. Without it a nation cannot fulfil its *swadharma*. Therefore, today most of the nations are trying to enrich their culture, language, literature, philosophy, art, religion, economic and industrial life. If a harmony in all this evolution is maintained, it will lead to the progress of all humanity. But this is possible only when everywhere a realisation of nation-soul and not national ego is the aim. From this point of view Sri Aurobindo's nationalism can be called spiritual nationalism.

Spiritual Nationalism

In different countries many thinkers have presented various types of nationalism. Some have confused national evolution with territorial expansion. This has led to imperialism and colonialism which have been very harmful to the smaller less developed nations. Others have confused nationalism with racism, religionism etc. By presenting the idea of spiritual nationalism Sri Aurobindo has, on the one hand, presented a philosophical basis for an integral evolution of the nation and, on the other hand, a political concept on the basis of which different nations may contribute to the progress of humanity while also progressing individually. Spiritual nationalism, implies that each human society, nation or other group is a sub-soul of that supreme, ultimate soul. The concept of spiritual nationalism is absolutely against any type of repression whether it may be the repression of the individual in the nation or the repression of some nation under colonialism or imperialism. According to it no section of the nation can be treated as diseased, negligible and so to be ignored or neglected. The concept implies that all the individuals gain in freedom, unity and harmony because these are the symptoms of spiritual national life. For it all types of progress is necessary — physical, economic, aesthetic, religious, moral and intellectual.

---

1. *Ibid.*, pp. 37-38.

It aims at an integral evolution of the nation. It advocates the principle that in the collectivity each constituent should fulfil its own *swadharma*. In it alone lies the welfare of the individual and the nation.

Sri Aurobindo was aware of the fact that in a society one class cannot dominate another for a long time, however superior it may be. In spiritual nationalism priority will have to be given to the progress of all backward classes, even if this involves some hindrance to the progress of others. All these principles are equally applicable to the life of the individual. In it each constituent also has its own *swadharma* and it should follow it. Body, vital or mind, none has a right to rule the others by repressing them. For the integral development of the individual all these should be given opportunity for free, harmonious and perfect development. In spiritual nationalism, not the national ego but the nation-soul is the reality. Like the spiritual individual, the spiritual nationalism rests not in the collective ego but in the collective soul. In it no individual, from saint to criminal, will be reformed by force of law or police, but would be changed internally. In the economic field, it does not aim at a gigantic machine of production, but at a system in which each individual will have an opportunity to grow freely according to its own nature. In the political field, the citizen will not be a slave or instrument of the state but a harmony will be maintained between the evolution of the individual and the nation. In the international field, the spiritual nation does not wage war against other nations but helps them in the realisation of their self without seeking their own selfish interest in this process. It is based on the principle of freedom in internal and external affairs. In a fully developed spiritual society, as the spiritual anarchist views it, all human beings will be free. And this will be possible because the primary conditions for it have been already fulfilled. In that stage, each individual will be a divine law unto himself because it will not be an ego living for its own selfish ends but a soul established in the Divine. His life will be guided by his divine nature free from ego. For the establishment of such a spiritual nation, it is necessary that first some persons and then the entire group in the nation should evolve spiritually. Spiritual individuals alone constitute a spiritual nation. To be such a spiritual collectivity is the ideal of each nation. In it lies its own welfare as well as the welfare of its constituent parts. In it again also lies the welfare of humanity. From this point of view, Sri Aurobindo has emphasised the need of spiritual transformation of human societies. He has indicated the symptoms of the advent of a spiritual age and declared that these symptoms are slowly coming up at present. Thus, Sri Aurobindo has full faith in a bright future for humanity. This faith is not based on some intellectual philosophy or logic but on the spiritual experience of an ultimate force behind the individual and collective life everywhere. It is based on the conviction that everything will happen according to the principles of this spiritual force. Therefore, the evolution of spiritual nations and ultimately of a spiritual humanity is bound to come.

Nationalism and Human Unity

The evolution of nations and the growth of human unity are based on identical principle. Sri Aurobindo tried to find out the possibility of human unity and the method for achieving it. He analysed the process of the evolution of human societies to become nations and explored its conditions, difficulties, stages and methods. This is the subject of discussion in the first part of his famous work *The Ideal of Human Unity.* According to him, the principles which have been working behind the formation of nations will also lead to human unity. As the individual and the collectivity are two aspects of the same reality, their harmony is necessary and fundamental. This again is the basis of nations and bigger collectivities. In the words of Sri Aurobindo, "The whole process of Nature depends on a balancing and a constant tendency to harmony between two poles of life, the individual whom the whole or aggregate nourishes and whole or aggregate which the individual helps to constitute. Human life forms no exception to the rule. Therefore, the perfection of human life must involve the elaboration of an as yet unaccomplished harmony between these two poles of our existence, the individual and the social aggregate. The perfect society will be that which most entirely favours the perfection of the individual; the perfection of the individual will be incomplete if it does not help towards the perfect state of the social aggregate to which he belongs and eventually to that of the largest possible human aggregate, the whole of a united humanity."[1]

Thus, while the individual's development is necessary for the development of the nation, the development of the nation and finally of the whole humanity is necessary for the development of the individual. Experiments in Nature's realm are never destroyed completely but are preserved to maintain the variety and richness of its expression. Thus, the individual need not be eliminated for the development of the family, nor the families be discarded for the development of the nation. Similarly, the free development of the nations is no hindrance to the growth of human unity. On the other hand, it may be said that just as the development of the individual members is necessary for the growth of the family and that of the families for the development of a nation, similarly the evolution of nations is necessary for the growth of humanity. This is so because families and nations are natural units of human society. Groups, associations or unities organised artificially to achieve some specific purposes may continue to live even after that purpose has been achieved or they may dissolve automatically in due course. But this is not applicable to the human unities which are natural, such as the family or the nation. Most of the thinkers accept family as a natural unit of human beings but some do not accept nation as a natural unit. According

1. Sri Aurobindo, *The Ideal of Human Unity,* Sri Aurobindo Ashram, Pondicherry, 1950, p. 8.

to Sri Aurobindo, however, the nation is the biggest unit of human beings which Nature has developed so far. This unit has not been fully organised as yet. One finds conflict in its constituent parts.

Nation and the Dominant Class

As a general rule, in each nation some particular class is dominant; it may be the elite, the business class or the labour class. The nature of a nation is determined by the nature of the dominant class and it also determines the dominant ideal. For example, in ancient India, the intelligent and spiritual Brahmin class was dominant and therefore the ideal of the ancient Indian nation was philosophical and spiritual. In United States today the business class is dominant and, therefore, their national politics is determined by the rules of trade and commerce. But no single class can always dominate a nation and no class can be kept subordinate for ever. This leads to constant conflict among different classes. The exploited and depressed classes revolt and overpower the so far dominant class. If the new class understands the needs of other classes and accommodates them, it may stay in power but since this is not normally the case, the depressed classes rise against the dominant class. Like Karl Marx, Sri Aurobindo also is of the view that the modern industrial societies are constituted by two important classes, the capitalists and the labourers. Of these, the former is generally dominant in most of the industrial societies and the more numerous labourer class is exploited and depressed. The future of the capitalists is dark, if they do not change, agrees Sri Aurobindo with Karl Marx. To quote his own words, "Therefore, the perfect counsel for a dominant minority is always to recognise in good time the right hour for its abdication and for the imparting of its ideals, qualities, culture, experience to the rest of the aggregate or to as much of it as is prepared for that progress. Where this is done, the social aggregate advances normally and without disruption or serious wound or malady; otherwise a disordered progress is imposed upon it, for Nature will not suffer human egoism to baffle for even her fixed intention and necessity."[1] In most of the nations, the dominant minority group is not prepared to relinquish its rights and this leads to civil war, class conflict and finally to the overthrow of the dominant class by the depressed class through revolution.

The above analysis of the national society is equally applicable to international society. Time has arrived today when the dominant nations should understand that they must take care of the welfare of other nations. If this is not done in time, the numerous backward nations will revolt against the domination of some few powerful nations. Human beings aspire for self-perfection, on the one hand, and self-expansion, on the other. Therefore, on the one hand, they should be allowed to organise themselves into families, classes and nations and to rise to universal human consciousness on the other.

1. *Ibid.*, p. 12.

Individual and Collectivity

According to Sri Aurobindo, "It is a constant method of Nature, when she has two elements of a harmony to reconcile, to proceed at first by a long continued balancing in which she sometimes seems to lean entirely on the one side, sometimes entirely to the others, at others to correct both excesses by a more or less successful temporary adjustment and moderating compromise."[1] Thus, sometimes the individualist and sometimes the collectivist tendency has been growing and only a temporary compromise between them has been made so far. In the gradual evolution of human communities first the family, kinship, race and class developed and then evolved the nation which may now lead to human unity. But since so far a reconciliation even between the individual and the community has not been possible the rise of collectivists bigger than the nation does not seem possible in the near future. A study of History and Sociology tells us that man has always been living in communities small or big. One finds three types of relationship between the individual and the collectivity *viz.* individualistic, collectivistic and thirdly a community in which the individual has maximum freedom. This third type of community has generally remained an ideal and has not become actuality so far. Most of the states are examples of this fact.

State and Nation

While Sri Aurobindo has appreciated the nation, the state, according to him, is inadequate as a human community. Prior to being a political unit, the nation is a psychological unit since it has internal unity while the unity of the state is based on one or the other external factor. At present, the states have created external impediments in the path of human unity because for each state the satisfaction of its limited interests is the *summum bonum* and falsehood is being practised everywhere in the name of politics. Ideally the state is based on the collective power and reason organised for the common good while in practice it is not more than an instrument for the realisation of the interests of few persons. To quote Sri Aurobindo, "The organised State is neither the best mind of the nation nor is it even the sum of the communal energies. It leaves out of its organised action and suppresses or unduly depresses the working force and thinking mind of important minorities, often of those which represent that which is best in the present and that which is developing for the future."[2]

Dual Principles

The greatest fallacy in politics today is the fact that there are dual principles operative, one for matters within the state and another for international affairs. Whereas in internal affairs one or the other civilized principle is

---

1. *Ibid.*, p. 14.
2. *Ibid.*, p. 24.

followed, there is no such rule in international affairs. If a state does not attack the other it is because it does not see any advantage in it. Besides this, there is no control of international law, morality or ideals. One finds ego everywhere in the state. It is due to this ego that the state commits atrocities on weak individuals and classes within the nation and on weak nations outside it. In recent times the repression within the state has been considerably lessened but this is not true of international affairs. Sri Aurobindo has vehemently condemned the totalitarian attitude of the state. Neither he allows all powers to the state in relation with the individual nor does he consider it the best means of human evolution. According to him whereas national culture, religion and education are useful, state control over these is unnatural tyranny. Therefore, while he considers a nation to be an important unit of human community, he seeks constantly to diminish the power of the state.

There are two impediments in the way of human unity. First, human unity requires elimination of the national ego. Secondly, the human organisation should be such as does not repress individual freedom. Empires of different kinds have been units bigger than the state, but they have failed to protect the self-respect of nations and freedom of the individuals. That is the reason why modern thinkers are against imperialism. Nationalism is different from imperialism of every kind. Whereas empire is an artificial unit, the state is a natural unit. It is a psychological unit which Nature has herself developed. Therefore, according to Sri Aurobindo, "The nation in modern times is practically indestructible, unless it dies from within."[1] While the empire is perishable, the nation is immortal and it will stay till some higher sentiment does not replace nationalism. At that time also the nations shall stay within human organisation just as families are maintained within the nations.

Constituents of a Nation

Sri Aurobindo has dwelt at length over the question of the constituents of a nation. According to him, Nationalism is based upon a common idea, a psychological unity based upon a common interest, common language and common culture, expressed in the sentiment of nationality. A nation first of all requires a land or country. It cannot exist without a geographical unity. That is the reason why a nation defends its country with all its might. Another constituent element of a nation is the economic unity because the members of a nation require some means of livlihood. Hence, the nation guards its economic interests. To quote Sri Aurobindo, "In human life economic interests are those which are, ordinarily, violated with the least impunity for they are bound up with the life itself and the persistent violation of them, if it does not destroy the oppressed organism, provokes necessarily the bitterest revolt and ends in one of Nature's inexorable retaliations."[2]

---

1. *Ibid.*, p. 39.
2. *Ibid.*, pp. 62-63.

Another constituent element of a nation is political unity. Many a times the stronger nations have tried to destroy the political freedom of the weaker nations and merge them in their own political organisation but this effort could never succeed, because, while the political unity of the nation is natural, that of the empire is artificial. Therefore, a nation can be formed only when natural political unity is found among the groups constituting it.

Yet another important constituent of a nation is a powerful organisation for the protection of life, division of labour and general progress. Without such an organisation national unity is not possible. It is because of the absence of these constituent elements that experiments with the organisation of multinational empires, world empires and confederation states in Europe have failed. These experiments, however, have lead to the formation of modern nations.

Stages in the Formation of Nation Unit

In the history of man the formation of a nation has passed through several stages. In ancient times there were small and big states in East and West which had internal unity but not all the constituent factors described so far. Hence, empires were established on the ruins of these states. The process of the formation of states proceeded further after the fall of these empires. But this time it had some special characteristics. Firstly, it had a centre in the form of state capital and secondly, it had a sovereign authority, imposing legal, administrative, political and linguistic uniformity and centrality. Thirdly, in it the administrators were appointed by the central authority. Thus, these new states were more organised than the older states. After the evolution of states in medieval times the process of state formation, according to Sri Aurobindo, passed through three stages. To quote Sri Aurobindo, "In such a process there must be in the nature of things, first, some kind of loose yet sufficiently compelling order of society and common type of civilization to serve as a framework or scaffolding within which the new edifice shall arise. Next, there must come naturally a period of stringent organisation directed towards unity and centrality of control and perhaps a general levelling and uniformity under that central direction. Last, if the new organism is not to fossilise stereotype life, if it is to be still a living and vigorous creation of Nature, there must come a period of free internal development as soon as the formation is assured and unity has become a mental and vital habit."[1] In the process of state formation most of the states have already crossed two of the above-mentioned three stages. The third stage has not yet arrived anywhere. This stage must be reached before the ideal of human unity is achieved. At present, most of the states are in the second stage mentioned above. Centralization, uniformity and rigid control are also necessary in state formation but once these lead to national unity, this external control must be replaced by internal freedom and variety because ultimately the nation unit

1. *Ibid.*, p. 118.

is not for itself. Either it is for the individual or for human community. The Nation is a link between the individual and the humanity. In the words of Sri Aurobindo, "The nation unit is not formed and does not exist merely for the sake of existing; its purpose is to provide a larger mould of human aggregation in which the race, and not only classes and individuals, may move towards its full human development."[1] The nation unit has to achieve the ideals of liberty, equality and fraternity in human society. In internal matters the ideal of equality has been achieved in democratic states but complete liberty and fraternity have not been achieved. In international relations, liberty and fraternity are mere words while without their realisation human unity is not possible.

THE IDEAL OF HUMAN UNITY

Though a staunch nationalist, Sri Aurobindo has maintained that the states should ultimately evolve towards human unity. There are grave impediments in the path of the realisation of human unity though one step in this direction has already been taken in the general feeling that human unity, must be established. In the evolution towards the goal of human unity Sri Aurobindo visualises the same stages as have to be passed for the making of a nation. The nation, as has been already pointed out, was born as an indefinite structure in which were present several elements of unification. Organisation and unity in this unit were increased by means of centralisation and pressure. In the third stage, the nation arrived at the step where not external pressure but sentiment of nationality became the basis of national unity. According to Sri Aurobindo, "If the unity of the human race is to be brought about by the same means and agents and in a similar fashion to that of the nation, we should expect it to follow a similar course."[2]

Here one can see the impediments arising in the way of human unity. Before the sentiment for human unity can grow, humanity will have to pass through the stages of centralisation and international pressure. Not much has been done towards this end by the international organisations meant for this purpose. These organisations cannot save the world from a future war since, according to Sri Aurobindo, "National egoism remaining, the means of strife remaining, its causes, opportunities, excuses will never be wanting."[3]

The ceiling on the armies and war material of the nations by international organisations is not the proper way to check war because if there is an intention to war, a nation can amass war material in no time and without much difficulty. The greatest impediment in the way of the success of international organisations is the fact that while the human beings who are members of families, clans and nations are to some extent developed and civilized, most of the nations are in the animal stage of evolution and no high

1. *Ibid.*, p. 128.
2. *Ibid.*, p. 131.
3. *Ibid.*, p. 139.

sentiment or self-control can be expected from them. Hence, Sri Aurobindo has advised that national egoism must be put to an end for the realization of human unity. Just as families and nations cannot be developed so long as individual egoism is intact, similarly true humm unity cannot be realised so long as national egoism persists and there will always remain a constant danger of war. Because, as Sri Aurobindo has said, "The law is always the same, that wherever egoism is the root of action it must bear its own proper results and reactions and, however minimised and kept down they may be by an external machinery, their eventual outburst is sure and can be delayed but not prevented for ever."[1] Therefore, human unity cannot be established without eliminating national egoism. But this ego is not the self: As has already been pointed out, the evolution of individual soul is not a bar but an aid to the evolution of nation-soul. Similarly, the evolution of nation-soul is advantageous to the evolution of human unity. Therefore, each nation should grow fully and freely. And if each nation will be based on true nation-soul then not conflict but harmony will be the basis of international relations and the ideal of human unity will be achieved.

According to Sri Aurobindo, "The ideal society or state is that in which respect for individual liberty and free growth of the personal being to his perfection is harmonised with respect for the needs, efficiency, solidarity, natural growth and organic perfection of the corporate being, the society or nation. In an ideal aggregate of all humanity, in the international society or state, national liberty and free national growth and self-realisation ought in the same way to be progressively harmonised with the solidarity and unified growth and perfection of the human race."[2] Sri Aurobindo has harmonised different communities on the basis of the principle which is the basis for the harmony of individual and society. But, according to him, this is not possible through international organisations or laws because not moral principles, reason and justice but psychological forces determine the relations among nations. Even when some nation appears to be working on some moral principle, then also either it does not make any special sacrifice for it or if it does then it is under some compulsion. So far as fraternity between various nations is concerned, Sri Aurobindo calls it a mere theory. According to him, "The war brought into relief the fact that it is only the great powers that really count in the international scale; all others merely exist by sufferance or by protection or by alliance."[3] Years after these words were written U.N.O. is still in the same state. Thus, the principle of equality has not become operative in international relations. Similarly, democratic ideals have not been achieved anywhere in the world. The states which are called democratic are actually being ruled by some capitalists, political leaders and other individuals.

And yet Sri Aurobindo had an irrepressible faith in the ideal of human unity. He wrote, "The political and administrative unification of mankind is

---

1. *Ibid.*, p. 144.
2. *Ibid.*, p. 146.
3. *Ibid.*, p. 150.

not only possible but foreshadowed by our present evolution; the collective national egoism which resists it, may be overborne by an increasing flood of the present unifying tendency to which the anguish of the European war gave a lovely and an articulate voice."[1] It is true that seeing the present circumstances the realization of human unity appears to be rather difficult but just as bigger nations have been formed in the world by the combination of smaller nations, similarly the ideal of human unity may be attained in the future. This requires tremendous efforts in the fields of political, social, economic, educational and other types of unification. This unity finds a due place for diversity, it will not only admit but even encourage small distinctions. For this mankind will have to develop relationships between the individuals, societies and mankind. All these three are natural units. None of these can be eliminated. In the beginning Nature develops the individuals, then the communities are developed and finally mankind will be developed in this very sequence. To quote Sri Aurobindo, "The united progress of mankind would thus be realised by a general principle of interchange and assimilation between individual and individual and again between individual and community, between community and community and again between the smaller commonality and the totality of mankind, between the common life and consciousness of mankind and its freely developing communal and individual constituents."[2]

IDEA OF WORLD STATE

In the development of human unity the principle of liberty and diversity is as much important as that of unity because the ultimate reality is both one and many. The general scheme of Nature is based on infinite diversity. Hence, an ideal society will have all types of freedom *viz.*, individual, national, religious, social and moral. Clarifying the concept of liberty Sri Aurobindo wrote, "By liberty we mean the freedom to obey the law of our being, to grow to our natural self fulfilment, to find out naturally and freely our harmony with our environment."[3] Unity does not hinder but help this liberty. Even after achieving spiritual and psychological unity the individual seeks complete and free development and this is only realised when others also develop freely. Hence, in the ideal unification of mankind the human beings will be allowed freedom to form communities based on social, cultural and economic convenience and there will be no external compulsion upon them. It is essential for human unity that there should be such an organisation of free and natural communities that there may be no place for internal conflict, opposition, repression and revolt. Thus, it is clear that no human unity can be established by the use of force, whether that of a nation or of some world organisation. Sri Aurobindo, therefore, is against the idea of

1. *Ibid.*, p. 159.
2. *Ibid.*, p. 180.
3. *Ibid.*, p. 184.

a world state because the power of the state always acts through external pressure, law, police and army. This again cannot be achieved through any type of international law. Its only basis will be the *dharma,* reason, will and conscious principles of various nations. Those who imagine a world state for the establishment of human unity, forget that it involves the same difficulties that arise due to state authority in a particular society. Like Karl Marx and Prince Kropotkin Sri Aurobindo also ultimately envisages a stateless society. Thus, there appears to be hardly any advantage in the establishment of a world state.

Diversity in Unity

Those who imagine a world state or a world nation in which the individuality of the nations will be abolished, forget that uniformity is nowhere the principle of life. In Nature there is diversity in unity and this principle is particularly important in the biological world. It is for this reason that too much centralisation is considered to be unnatural in human society and, on the other hand, most of the political thinkers support decentralisation. Underlying this diversity is the principle that each individual and each group has to grow according to its own *Swadharma* and nature. Therefore, according to Sri Aurobindo, "The unity of human race to be entirely sound and in consonance with the deepest laws of life must be founded on free groupings, and the groupings again must be the natural associations of free individuals."[1] This diversity among human groups or the freedom of different nations should be realised in the different aspects of culture such as language, literature and art etc.

Hence, Sri Aurobindo has supported the grow th of a national language in each nation. He agrees that the English language has helped us in maintaining our contact with other societies but insists that it can never be a substitute for the national language. This is equally true of other constituents of culture.

World Federation of Nations

Ever since man pondered over the ideal of human unity, the idea of federation of nations of some type or the other has been in his mind. After the First World War, the League of Nations was established. The idea of the League was in tune with the principle of unity in diversity but due to several causes it could not save the world from the Second World War. In his treatise *The Ideal of Human Unity,* Sri Aurobindo has analysed these causes in detail. The United Nations Organisation was established after Second World War. As to how far this world organisation will be able to save human society is a matter of discussion but since a future world war would be fatal to the very existence of mankind, Sri Aurobindo has tried to suggest ways by which

---

1. *Ibid.,* p. 297.

the aims and objectives of U. N. O. can be achieved. So far as the question of principles of human unity is concerned, these are eternal. If the U.N.O. fails to achieve these principles it will meet the fate of League of Nations. Clarifying the conditions of a free world organisation, Sri Aurobindo has written, "A free world-union must in its very nature be a complex unity based on a diversity and that diversity must be based on free self-determination."[1] No mechanical unity can be established in a world organisation. Each nation should join it by its own free will. For this no pressure should be exercised on any one since such pressure is against the ideal of self-determination. Man's aim is to establish a world culture in which each national culture gets fullest opportunity for development. This is possible only when no nation is under the pressure of any other nation and each enjoys local, territorial and regional freedom.

According to Sri Aurobindo, "Internationalism is the attempt of the human mind and life to grow out of the national idea and form and even in a way to destory it in the interest of the larger synthesis of mankind."[2] Sri Aurobindo is against this type of internationalism. It is not the true ideal of human unity. In true internationalism, nationalism will not be eliminated but fulfilled. The idea of internationalism was born in 18th century and since then political thinkers have presented several alternatives to it. With the increase in international contacts due to the progress of science, opinion has grown in the favour of internationalism. Today many consider themselves as citizens of one world along with their membership of a particular nation. It is generally thought that the idea of internationalism is the result of the fear of war. "But", as Sri Aurobindo has rightly pointed out, "we cannot rely too greatly on ideas and resolutions formed in a moment of abnormal crisis under the violent stress of exceptional circumstances."[3] True human unity, therefore, should be based upon the ideals of liberty, equality and fraternity. The basic idea behind it is the fundamental unity of all men. The geographical distance between different nations is no hindrance to it since the distance has been very much reduced by modern scientific inventions.

THE RELIGION OF HUMANITY

Hence, if the ideal of human unity has to be realised, it should not be based on external pressures, laws and mechanical principles but on the religion of humanity. This religion of humanity will perform the same function in the formation of a world-nation as has been always done by the sentiment of nationality in the formation of nations. It will raise men up from narrow egoism and establish their unity with others. Underlying the religion of humanity is the idea that humanity is the greatest god and the family, state or nation cannot replace it. On the other hand family, state or nation are

1. *Ibid.*, p. 331.
2. *Ibid.*, p. 341.
3. *Ibid.*, p. 341.

valuable only to the extent they are helpful in the realisation of human unity. The basic principle underlying the religion of humanity is, "Man must be sacred to man regardless of all distinctions of race, creed, colour, nationality, status, political or social advancement."[1] The principle of non-violence is included in the idea of human sanctity. The sanctity of man means sanctity of human body, life, heart, mind etc., all of which must be respected and each should get opportunity for free development. Fraternity is the basis of the religion of humanity. Without its growth, the ideal of human unity cannot be achieved. This fraternity among human beings is based on the fact that liberty, equality and unity are the eternal traits of the human soul.

Sri Aurobindo has said, "In other words — and this is the conclusion at which we arrive — while it is possible to construct a precarious and quite mechanical unity by political and administrative means, the unity of human race, even if achieved, can only be secured and can only be made real if the religion of humanity, which is at present the highest active ideal of mankind, spiritualises itself and becomes the general inner law of human life."[2] In the path of the achievement of the ideal of human unity, there will be difficulties greater than those faced in the evolution of nations. But just as nations evolved to fulfil the purpose of Nature similarly a world nation will also evolve overcoming all these difficulties. If man fails to find out a way to achieve this purpose, Nature may take some other step to achieve it. But the establishment of human unity on this earth is faith sufficiently grounded in the very nisus of Nature. U.N.O. has failed to achieve this ideal due to several causes. In fact, all the nations have not succeeded so far in securing a place in it. It recent years a lacuna has been removed by giving communist China a seat in the U.N.O. This world organisation has become an aristocracy because of the power of veto vested in the five permanent members of the Security Council. Another big impedient in the way of humun unity is the division of the nations of the world into two big blocks, fundamentally opposed to each other. Without the resolution of this chasm, the sentiment for international unity cannot develop in the true sense.

Sri Aurobindo's faith in the ideal of human unity is based upon his theory of evolution. If man is an evolving being, he will gradually evolve to world nation as he has evolved upto nation because nation is not the ultimate and final unit. The affiliations among different nations may fulfil only some temporary needs but these groups cannot be considered to be ultimate and final units. The very process of evolution in Nature will take us towards the ideal of human unity. To quote Sri Aurobindo, "We may rely, if on the evolutionary urge and, if on no other greater hidden power, on the manifest working and drift or intention in the world-energy we call Nature to carry mankind at least as far as the necessary next step to be taken, a self preserving next step: for the necessity is there, at least some general recognition of it has

1. *Ibid.*, p. 364.
2. *Ibid.*, p. 370.

been achieved and of the thing to which it must eventually lead the idea has been born and the body of it is already calling for its creation."[1]

In consonance with this faith in the evolution of human unity as the purpose of Nature, Sri Aurobindo has made some practical suggestions for making the U.N.O. a success. In the beginning, the U.N.O. should satisfy the following conditions:[2]

1. All the nations should voluntarily join it.
2. Justice and truth should be its bases.
3. Its constitution should be such as is likely to resolve international problems.
4. A permanent central powerful authority should be organised by it which should be sanctioned by all the nations.

By fulfilling the above mentioned conditions the U.N.O. may help in making human unity a reality. But in the end this ideal can be realised only after the establishment of a true soul in place of the disintegrating ego in mankind. In other words, only in a spiritual human society can the ideal of human unity be realised. And so long as we live isolated from true spirituality, this ideal will not be permanently realised.

Thus, while discussing the various aspects of the ideal of human unity, Sri Aurobindo has always kept his eyes fixed on the inner purpose of Nature behind the human social and political problems. Whatever happens in the world is due to the forces of the cosmic Nature working behind man. These forces can be discovered by an analysis of our past and present and on their basis we can form an idea of the future of man.

SRI AUROBINDO AND KARL MARX

Points of distinctions

On account of their entirely different background and influence, Karl Marx and Sri Aurobindo started their political philosophies from totally different premises. While Marx was influenced by materialism, dialectical evolution and economic interpretation of history, Sri Aurobindo was under the influence of the ancient Indian Vedanta philosophy. While for Marx the most important problems of human society were economic, for Sri Aurobindo man's problems were mainly psychological. While Marx presented an economic interpretation of history with economic stages of evolution, Sri Aurobindo gave a psychological interpretation of history with psychological stages. Thus, while Marx suggested economic emancipation of man as a solution to the present enigma, Sri Aurobindo suggested psychological transformation of man as the cure for all evils. Thus, Marx emphasized technology and sciences, Sri Aurobindo laid emphasis upon Religion and

---

1. *Ibid.*, p. 399.
2. *Ibid.*, Postscript Chapter 1.

Yoga. In the social field while Marx emphasized class struggle as a means of evolution, Sri Aurobindo sought for a spiritual regeneration.

Different social ideals

Karl Marx and Sri Aurobindo were both against alienation, capitalism and exploitation. Both were humanist in their hearts and wanted to make the world better. But their different social philosophies led to different conclusions and solutions. Marx cherished a classless society free from all types of exploitation including that by the state, Sri Aurobindo dreamt of a future society of gnostic beings which is certainly more glorious and awe inspiring than that of Marx.

Difference in Mass Appeal

There is some utopian element in the social philosophies of both Marx and Sri Aurobindo, but from the point of view of influence upon the masses Sri Aurobindo does not stand comparison with Marx. This is due to the fact that in the history of the human race upon the earth, in spite of all the progress of science, the means of subsistence, flora and fauna, food and cloth, have lagged behind in supply as compared to demand. Undoubtedly, the supply will be available for millions of years to come but, due to unprecedented growth in population, without any corresponding pace of economic development, nearly one-third of the world population today is groaning under the pressure of poverty, and for it the economic problems are the most important. This was realized by Marx and, therefore, he concentrated on their solution. This in its turn led to the wide popularity of his social philosophy. Sri Aurobindo, on the other hand, neglected this important aspect of human life and did not say much about it.

Sri Aurobindo's neglect of Social Institutions

Another important field of social philosophy neglected by Sri Aurobindo is that of social institutions. Here also Marx has an edge over Sri Aurobindo. While Marx has thoroughly discussed the institutions of family, marriage, social classes, etc., Sri Aurobindo hardly says anything about them. Keeping in view the fact that social institutions carry an immense influence upon the moulding of human beings, Sri Aurobindo's social philosophy here appears to be poorer than that of Karl Marx and M. K. Gandhi. Without a discussion of the role of family, marriage and social stratification, all talks of transformation of human individual and collectivity in Sri Aurobindo's social philosophy becomes very much one-sided and unrealistic. If man's problem is mainly psychological, if what we need today is spiritual evolution, how does Sri Aurobindo propose to realise it without outlining the role of family, marriage and social classes, the social institutions which have always been most influential in moulding man's outlook, attitudes, personality, etc. In his speculation about the future gnostic society also, while Sri Aurobindo has emphasized the role of integral knowledge and Yoga he has not written much about these social institutions without which no future society, gnostic or agnostic, can be developed. Marx, on the other hand, has discussed social institutions thoroughly, though his discussion has been mainly economic and moral. Spiritual evolution through integral yoga is possible in the case of human adults but what about the children and adolescents? It is they who are going to build up the future of man. And integral yoga is certainly not meant for them. They are undoubtedly more influenced by educational, social, political, moral and religious institutions. Admitted that without yoga they will not evolve in the realm of spirituality but before that ascent, their physical, emotional, social, moral and aesthetic development is necessary and this will not be realised by yoga, but by family and educational institutions. In his educational philosophy also, while Sri Aurobindo has shown immense insight in the fields of curriculum, methods of teaching, physical, moral and religious institutions, but he has not given sufficient attention to the role of the family in education, to the parent-teacher cooperation in moulding the educand's personality.

SRI AUROBINDO AND M. K. GANDHI

Mass Appeal of Gandhi's Social Philosophy

If we may compare any contemporary Indian social philosopher with Karl Marx, from the point of view of his influence on the life of the masses, he is not Sri Aurobindo but M. K. Gandhi. In our country Gandhi occupies the same place as is occupied by Marx, through his disciple Lenin, in Russia, His views about social, economic and political institutions have influenced not only thoughtful men and women in this country but throughout the world. With all his emphasis on integral approach, Sri Aurobindo's social philosophy has not been as mass appealing as that of Marx or Gandhi, though none of these is, in its turn, sufficiently integral to meet the requirements. Though by nature a religious man, Gandhi discussed in minute details the problems of social institutions, emancipation of women, removal of untouchability development of backward classes, removal of poverty, solution of the problem of the sick and old, mass education for India's illiterate millions etc. As a true follower of Gita, in faith and action, Gandhi elaborately discussed the duties of everyone, leaders and the followers, men and women, parents and children, educator and educand, government and the public, Hindus and Muslims. Realising that the most pressing problem for a slave country is to attain freedom, Gandhi devoted himself heart and soul to the task of removing the yoke of foreign rule. He successfully led the masses through the struggle. He lived the life of an ordinary Indian, dressed like him, and hence he could understand his difficulty and search for the solution. This first hand and direct touch with social milieu was lacking in the case of Sri Aurobindo. Cut off from the everyday life with his family and countrymen, no social philosopher can hope to know their problems and to solve them. Living amidst the masses, the sick, the poor, and the backward and illiterate people of the rural areas. Gandhi observed their problems, realised the urgency of their solution and devoted himself to it. His social philosophy, therefore is more realistic and down to earth, and this accounts for its widespread influence.

Sri Aurobindo's Neglect of Backward Classes

In our comparison of Sri Aurobindo and Karl Marx, we have already pointed out how Sri Aurobindo did not give sufficient attention to economic and social institutions. Here the social philosophy of Gandhi is more comprehensive than that of Sri Aurobindo. Gandhi discussed the economic and social institutions in Indian context in details, analysed their problems and suggested solution which though they may not satisfy many thinkers, certainly make his social philosophy more integral. The most important tendency in contemporary Indian social scene is the awakening of the hitherto weaker and backward sections, the so-called untouchables, the farmers and the labourers, the women and children. Sri Aurobindo did not take sufficient notice of these classes. He hardly says much about their exploitation in the past. He does not analyse their difficulties and so does not present any solutions for them. Gandhi, on the other hand, devoted almost all his life and a large portion of his thought to these sections, suggested solutions and fought for reforms. It was under his inspiration and guidance that these sections in our country awakened, realised their humble condition and started on the path of attaining equality with the other sections of society. The social philosophy of Sri Aurobindo, on the other hand, does not give much guidance in this direction. Though strong and high at the apex, it appears to be weak in its foundations. Scholars of Sri Aurbindo's thought, like late Prof. S. K. Maitra, consider Sri Aurobindo's speculation about the future of man as the most important aspect of his philosophy. This, however, is not the near future but a distant for off time, so far indeed that an average man finds it hard to believe in its possibility. And as his gaze was turned towards the distant future of man, Sri Aurobindo could not do sufficient justice to the present, its problems and their solution. *Among the philosophers of the future of man Sri Aurobindo will definitely hold a place higher than that of Gandhi and Marx but among the social philosophers of our time Marx and Gandhi will carry more influence as they concentrated on the exploited classes and the solution of every day human problems.*

Sri Aurobindo's Negligence of Rural Institutions

Sri Aurobindo has devoted his books *The Ideal of Human Unity* and also *The Human Cycle* to detailed discussion of political institutions like the state and political issues like international relations, human unity, war and peace, etc. References to these can be found in many of his other books and in dozens of his letters. But here again due to his wide gaze fixed on the whole world and Humanity, Sri Aurobindo has missed the political institutions working in the smaller units of human society, the soviets or the panchayats, units of decentralization of polity and administration. Here Marx and Gandhi show more love for details than is exhibited by Sri Aurobindo. Gandhi has written at length about the Indian villages and their conditions, analysed their problems, suggested solutions and even taken part in practical experiments for this improvement. India is a country of villages and naturally Gandhi's social philosophy with its characteristic discussions of basic education, rural and small-scale industries, emancipation of women, removal of poverty, village uplift, removal of untouchability, removal of disease and squalor etc., appears to be more suitable to guide this country. Sri Aurobindo's social philosophy lacks this local and indigenous appeal. This point can be easily understood by a comparison of Sri Aurobindo's scheme of education, as practised at Pondicherry Ashram, with Gandhi's scheme of basic education. Without going into details, a task outside the limited scope of the present thesis, we can say that while Sri Aurobindo's scheme of education may give us some glimpse in the truest meaning of education, it cannot be a model scheme of education to make India's teeming illiterate millions educated. Gandhi's scheme of basic education, on the other hand, with all its limitations, can be a more suitable and practical model to educate the Indian masses.

Lack of Humanistic Appeal

Thus, from the humanistic point of view both Gandhi and Marx have given more appealing social philosophies than that of Sri Aurobindo. This is also clear by their style of writing. The writings of Gandhi and Marx are easily understandable to any average, intelligent and educated person. Gandhi's writings can be followed even by an ordinary Indian villager. The concepts and language used by him are quite commonplace. Sri Aurobindo, on the other hand, has used a language which cannot be followed by an average man. From the literary viewpoint this may be something creditable but from the humanist viewpoint it has its obvious disadvantages. Sri Aurobindo had a love for coining new terms which has further increased the difficulty of his writings. It is thus no wonder that even some highly educated persons find his writings difficult to understand. This is specially disadvantageous in social philosophy, which aims not only at a mere theoretical discussion but also seeks to guide the social regeneration of man.

In his political ethics, as we have already pointed out in the third chapter of this thesis, Sri Aurobindo has shown a more realistic approach. While Gandhi does not approve of violence under any circumstances, Sri Aurobindo, in the spirit of Gita, approves of violence if required for the cause of righteousness. Similarly, Sri Aurobindo shows more originality in his thought as compared with that of Gandhi. In fact both Gandhi and Sri Aurobindo excel in different realms of thought but from the point of view of social philosophy, as we have already shown, Gandhi wields a wider influence than Sri Aurobindo.

The above comparison of the philosophies of Sri Aurobindo and Gandhi clarifies the salient points of Aurobindo's philosophy which merit comparison with many other philosophies. Thus, J. S. Mackenzie, Bertrand Russell and other academic social philosophers discuss the role of family, marriage, economic institutions like property, industrial institutions, political, cultural and religious institutions. Sri Aurobindo, as we have already shown, neglects the discussion of social, economic and industrial institutions. This makes his social philosophy less thorough and practical and more one-sided and inadequate from the academic point of view. This again makes it inadequate for solving the problems of our time whatever may be its claims to usher Humanity into a new evolutionary stage by means of integral yoga.

SRI AUROBINDO AND RABINDRA NATH

Humanist Approach in Religion

Almost all the contemporary Indian social philosophers, including Sri Aurobindo, Gandhi, Vivekanand and Rabindra Nath, exhibit humanist trend in their religion and social philosophies. Both Sri Aurobindo and Rabindra Nath have envisaged a humanist religion as necessary for the realisation of the ideal of human unity. Sri Aurobindo calls it 'religion of humanity', Tagore calls it 'Religion of man'. The basic principles underlying the religion of humanity, according to Sri Aurobindo, is, "Man must be sacred to man regardless of all distinctions of race, creed, colour, nationality, status, political and social advancement."[1] Tagore's Religion of man is also based on the dignity of man. In it, as its name indicates, man occupies a central place. "Religion concentrates itself on humanity, which illumines our reason, inspires our wisdom, stimulates our love, claims our intelligent service."[2] Both Sri Aurobindo and Tagore, like Gandhi and Vivekanand, were against ritualism in religion. All these contemporary Indian social philosophers have a synthetic approach towards religion. They have admitted the value and importance of every religion in making the human world better. All of them have condemned religious bigotry and orthodoxy.

Sri Aurobindo's Indirect Contact with the Masses

As Tagore always lived amidst common man, his social philosophy is full of suggestions for the social, economic and moral reform of the common man. Like Gandhi he pleaded for the abolition of Zamindari and suggested that the rich should consider themselves trustees of the nation's wealth. He pleaded for the eradication of casteism, untouchability and disabilities of women and backward classes. Like Gandhi he insisted upon small scale industries, rural

---

1. Sri Aurobindo, *The Ideal of Human Unity*, p. 363.
2. Tagore, R.N., *The Religion of Man*, p. 144.

cooperatives, local self-government and other schemes of rural development. He suggested new techniques for the education of adult rural masses. He criticised the contemporary prevalent system of education and suggested many reforms.

Sri Aurobindo did not have contact with the ordinary men and women, as Gandhi or Tagore did. Closed in the four walls of his Ashram and devoting all his energies to writing and yoga, he had only indirect contact with the outer world. While this extreme concentration has made his social philosophy full of deeper insights and wider implications, he has totally neglected the above mentioned problems of the lay man. At least he has not dealt with them in the form in which they are found in our day-to-day life.

Sri Aurobindo : The Prophet of Nationalism

Both Sri Aurobindo and Tagore have expressed intensive love for the nation and exalted nationalism. Both have condemned national egoism and pleaded for the unity of men. But then, while Tagore has shown leanings towards internationalism, Sri Aurobindo has called internationalism too shallow to achieve the ideal of human unity. While Tagore has praised cosmopolitanism, Sri Aurobindo has emphasised more on unity through diversity. While Gandhi and Tagore wanted to build up cosmpolitanism by compromise and eclectic blend of different religions and cultures, Sri Aurobindo has maintained that everyone should be true and sincere to his own religion and culture and this will enable him play his due role in the human fraternity. Hence, while in Sri Aurobindo's thought nationalism is more dominant than cosmopolitanism, Tagore pleaded so much for internationalism that the nationalist current in his thought is overshadowed by it. This difference again can be observed in the educational institutions established by Sri Aurobindo and Tagore : a map of undivided India in Sri Aurobindo's university, and departments of Chinese and other such foreign studies at Vishwa Bharati. In the political field, Tagore was a firm believer in democracy in its commonsense meaning. Sri Aurobindo's analysis of the various forms of polity goes deeper. He has analysed democracy, assessed its advantages and disadvantages, and suggested that without an inner transformation of man the ideals of democracy cannot be achieved. This was so since Sri Aurobindo's experience in the political field was deeper and wider than that of Tagore. His ardent nationalism was expressed through his public speeches before he retired to Pondicherry. This fiery nationalism is not visible in Gandhi or Tagore. It is observed only sometimes in the utterances of Vivekanand. Consistent with his insistence on cosmopolitanism, Tagore believed in the synthesis of the East and the West, of spiritualism and materialism, of religion and science. Sri Aurobindo, though an ardent believer in the ideal of human unity, is against such artificial formulae as Tagore's emphasis on the teaching of various cultures at Shanti Niketan or as Gandhi's reading of the Koran, the Gita and the Bible at his prayer meetings. Sri Aurobindo based his search for human unity on a deeper level. According to him, to follow one's *swadharma* is the only duty of a member of kingdom of ends. Whoever follows his own religion sincerely finds that spirituality which underlies all religions. Whoever follows his own culture reaches the essence underlying all cultures. Unity with others cannot be achieved by external give and take, but by reaching within ourselves to that spiritual essence which is the same everywhere.

19
Mohandas Karamchand Gandhi
(1869 — 1948)

Gandhiji was born at Porebunder in Kathiawar on October 2, 1869. His father was very honest and his mother a devoted religious lady. He was married at the age of 12. He joined school at the early age of 7. After completing his school education he went to Bhavnagar where he could not adjust himself. After some time he was allowed to go to England with a pledge that he would not touch wine and woman there. In England he lived as a simple Indian.

On his return from England Gandhiji went to South Africa and established himself as a lawyer. There he experienced shocking discrimination against Indians, which tempted him to struggle for their legitimate rights.

Gandhiji aroused Indians frustrated South African Government's attempt to disfranchise Indians. In 1896 he left South Africa for India and tried to arouse the sympathies of Indian National Congress leaders in favour of Indian settlers. Hardly had he stayed in India when he had to go back to South Africa. In 1889 he organised an Indian Ambulance Corps to help the wounded of Boer War. In 1901 Gandhiji again came back to India but was called back in 1902. On his return Gandhiji found that Transvaal Government had set up an Asiatic Department where all Asiatics were to register themselves and always carry a certificate with them. As a protest Gandhiji decided to launch Satyagraha. The Indians refused to get themselves registered and hundreds of Indian settlers including Gandhiji were arrested. Government of General Smuts compromised with Gandhiji and the Asiatics were to voluntarily register themselves. The advice was not accepted by a Pathan Indian settler who threatened to take Gandhiji's life and actually attacked him. The culprit was arrested but was released on Gandhiji's suggestion.

As General Smuts refused to withdraw the Act Gandhiji started struggle again. Though Government took rigorous steps to suppress the agitation yet thousands of certificates were burnt. To the surprise of all Indian settlers women also started participating in satyagraha. The labourers in the coal mines went on strike and there were incidents of firing there. The Indians, under the guidance of Gandhiji decided to cross the borders of Transvaal and enter there without any permit. The response to Gandhiji's call was so effective that on Junuary 21, 1914 an interim agreement was signed between Gandhiji and Government of General Smuts, under which the main demands of Indian settlers in South Africa were accepted.

After his 20 years stay in South Africa Gandhiji came back to India. He found the conditions of Indians equally miserable. In the initial stages he believed in the British sense of justice, though subsequently his faith was lost. In 1915 he founded Satyagraha Ashram where the disciples were required to follow Gandhian ideals of non-violence and Ahimsa. They were also required to wear Khaddar. In 1917 he went to Bihar where he successfully negotiated for the rights of workers with the Indigo-owners. In 1918 Gandhiji successfully settled a dispute between the owners and the workers of Textile Mills of Ahmedabad. He also underwent three days' fast before the owners agreed to his point.

In 1920 his faith in British sense of justice was rudely shaken due to the passing of the Rowlatt Act, ghastly tragedy at Jallianwala Bagh and allowing General Dwyer to go free. In 1920 at a special meeting of the Congress workers a policy of non-cooperation was accepted and subsequently launched. The movement had to be withdrawn due to Chauri Chaura incident. In 1930 Gandhiji started his famous Dandi March to violate the unwanted Salt Law. In 1931 was executed the Gandhi-Irwin Pact. In 1932 Gandhiji was again arrested along with other Congress leaders. He very successfully foiled Government attempts to separate the Harijans from Caste Hindus.

In 1931 Gandhiji also went to England as the sole representative of Congress to negotiate with the British Government for solving the question of our constitutional advancement. In 1942 Gandhiji started his famous Quit India Movement. Subsequently he was associated with the talks which the Congress had with the British Government.

In 1947 India became free but there was hatred between the two major communities namely Hindus and Muslims. There was also mass migration. Facing all odds Gandhiji pledged for payment of Rs. 55 crores to Pakistan due to that country. This brought ill-will among orthodox Hindus and on 30th January, 1948 he was shot dead. On his death glowing tributes were paid to him and even U.N.O. lowered its flags.

RELIGION AND POLITICS

Fundamental Unity of Life

"If I seem to take part in politics, it is only because politics today encircles us like the coils of a snake from which one cannot get out no matter how one tries. I wish to wrestle with the snake," said Gandhiji, "I am trying to introduce religion into politics." To Gandhi even the struggle of Indians in South Africa was "a struggle for religious liberty". "By religion I do not mean formal religion, or customary religion," he explained, addressing a meeting of

Indians, "but that religion which underlies all religions, which brings us face to face with our Maker."

Years later, Gandhi said to an audience in South India : "The whole of my life is saturated with the religious spirit. I could not live for a single second without religion. Many of my political friends despair of me, because they say that even my politics are derived from my religion. And they are right. My politics, and all other activities of mine, are derived from my religion. I go further and say that every activity of a man of religion must be derived from his religion, because religion means being bound to God, that is to say, God rules your every breath. If you recognize that truth, naturally God regulates every activity of yours." An Englishman wrote of him : "When I first saw Mahatma Gandhi at the Round Table Conference in 1931, I asked how far he was saint and how far an astute politician. I later realized that the question was unanswerable : the two aspects were inextricably blended in a singularly complex character. In India saints can be politicians as they could in Medieval Europe."[1]

Gandhi firmly believed in the "fundamental unity of life", to quote his own words. He wrote to Mr. Horace Alexander in 1926 : "In my own humble opinion, we needlessly divide life into watertight compartments, religious and other; whereas if a man has true religion in him, it must show itself in the smallest details of life. To me sanitation in a community like ours is based upon common spiritual effort. The slightest irregularity in sanitary, social and political life is a sign of spiritual poverty."[2]

While some critics, in Indian National Congress and outside, took Gandhiji to task for introducing religion into the Congress politics which they wished to be confined to real politic (as the Germans put it), some others rated him, a man of religion, for having strayed into politics and consequently degraded himself. To them Gandhiji explained, "There has been no really religious movement in the world, without its social, economic and political consequences."[3]

Gandhiji's life and thought had been shaped under the impact of special circumstances which could not but influence his outlook and determine his line of action. His public life began in South Africa with events which challenged his spirit of manhood, his fellow-feeling for his contrymen, and his sense of justice, as also his religious susceptibilities. If politics are unclean, it is partly because religious men — *i.e.* God-fearing, truthful, selfless men — have generally kept away from politics; and it is this very consideration that demands of them that they should participate in political affairs and purify these from inside. It was the aim of Gandhiji's political guru, Gopal Krishna Gokhale. As far back as in 1909 Gokhle said, "I can tell you that a purer, a nobler and a more exalted spirit has never moved on this earth...He is a man

---

1. Kingsley Martin's article *in Mahatma Gandhi* (ed.) by Radhakrishnan, p. 414.
2. H.G. Alexander : *The Indian Ferment,* p. 227.
3. Shukla, C.S., *Conversations of Gandhiji,* p. 53.

who may be well described as a man among men, a hero among heroes, a patriot among patriots, and we may well say that in him Indian humanity at the present time has reached its high water mark."[1]

"What did this religious spirit of his lead to, in action? world and its opinion nothing," observed Henry Polak, one of his earliest co-workers in South Africa. "He does not know how to distinguish Hindu from Muslim, Christian from infidel. To him all alike are brothers, fragments of the Divine, fellow-spirits struggling for expression. All he has, he gives. With him self-surrender and absolute sacrifice are demands of his very nature. His deep spirituality influences all round so that no man dares to commit evil in his presence."[2]

George Slocombe, an English journalist, wrote of him years later, "I have never met any man more utterly honest, more transparently sincere, less given to egotism, self-conscious of pride, opportunism, and ambition which are found in greater or lesser degree in all the other great political figures of the world."[3]

Thus, no arguments from any quarters could possibly move Gandhiji to eschew politics. To his mind it was a God-given mission to work for the liberation of subject India and for the propagation of non-violence in the world through India.

Results of Chasm between Religion and Politics

"Religion," in the opinion of Radhakrishnan, "has weakened man's social conscience and moral sensitivity by separating the things of God from those of Caesar."[4] As a result, the State has been declared to be above all moral obligations. Believing as he did in the supremacy of the moral law Gandhi declared, "loyalty to the country" to be "always subordinate to loyalty to God."[5]

Explaining to his own attitude to politics Gandhi wrote: "I have no secret methods. I know no diplomacy save that of truth. I have no weapon but non-violence."[6]

Implication of Gandhian Religion in Politics

The following are some of the main implications, according to Gandhiji, of the introduction of religion into politics: (i) Cling to truth at all costs; (ii) 'Do or die,' but never 'do or kill,' invite suffering on yourselves, but never impose it on the opponent; (iii) Give the opponent due notice in advance of your intention to adopt a certain course of action against him; (iv) Criticise the

1. G.K. Gokhale's speech at the I.N. Congress, 1909, p. 14.
2. Shukla C.S., *Gandhiji as we know him*, p. 43.
3. *Ibid.*, p. 118.
4. *An Idealist View of Life*, p. 46.
5. *Young India*, 21.10.1921.
6. *Ibid*, 11.12.1924.

opponent's thoughts and policies but not the opponent himself; under no circumstances revile him; (v) Don't take unfair advantage of his difficulties; (vi) Hanker after a chance to make peace with him at the earliest moment possible, so that you can again cooperate with him on honourable terms; (vii) Try to appeal to and awaken the better part of his nature, and never wish his intransigence to be prolonged so that you may win the glory of martyrdom at his hands and he may be condemned in the public eye; rather pray to God constantly to grant him the capacity to see the Right; (viii) Own up your errors and evil deeds — big and small; (ix) Don't assume an air of self-righteousness; (x) Adopt none but the cleanest methods in elections, and don't scramble for the loaves and fishes of office: (xi) Walk in the fear of God and be afraid of no man; (xii) Have the unshakable faith that, in the end, the Right alone will triumph and never the Wrong; (xiii) In the midst of an encircling gloom, pray to the Kindly Light to lead you on; (xiv) Let "one step be enough" for you; don't long to see into the distant future; (xv) Let you and your country have the moral courage to stand for the Right against the whole world, if necessary; (xvi) Let your effort be mainly directed to the increase of your own internal cleanliness and strength.

ETHICS AND POLITICS

Swadeshi and Swarajya

God-realisation is the ultimate end of life. God can be comprehended in every object. Thus, the attainment of God means self-realisation or swarajya. In a social context this means economic, political and social self-dependence. It was on the basis of this social philosophy that Gandhi initiated the swadeshi campaign. "Swadeshi is the spirit of our immediate surroundings to the exclusion of the more remote."[1] The use of swadeshi introduces self-dependence in the individual and society and also generates love for one's country. Although Gandhi was an internationalist, he was, at the same time, a patriot to his country. He had said, "I want cultures of all lands to be blown about my house as freely as possible.. But I refuse to be blown off my feet by any one of them."[2]

Sarvodaya

Public service is a means to attainment of God, because God is infused in every one. In the opinion of Mahatma Gandhi swadeshi, swarajya and sarvodaya are steps in the attainment of God. Swarajya comes from swadeshi and sarvodaya from swarajya. The ideal of sarvodaya is the ideal of Ramarajya. Sarvodaya means the all round development of every individual. Its aim is the establishment of a society in which every individual, religion, language and literature is to get an unhindered opportunity.

---

1. Quoted by C.F. Andrews in *Mahatma Gandhi's Ideas*, p. 140.
2. Quoted by Romain Rolland in *Mahatma Gandhi*, Indian Edition, p. 117.

Synthesis of Ethics and Religion

In this way, Gandhi has synthesized religion and ethics, as he opines that ethics does not preclude religion. A seed in the form of ethics does not give out a sapling until it is watered by water in the form of religion. "As soon as we leave the moral basis we cease to be religious."[1]

Importance and Nature of Morality

Ethics directs one to discuss truth and falsity and to act without attachment in order to achieve good. It is the science of ideals. It formulates laws both for the society and the individual. It is universal. "Another feature of the moral law is that it is eternal and immutable."[2] "The highest morality is universal."[3] In Gandhiji's opinion, how is justice to be done in every situation and how this policy is to be pursued — only the government or state which learns this science can be happy, everything else being inefficacious effort. "No individual and no nation can ever violate the moral law with impunity."[4]

Synthesis of Ethics and Politics

And in this way, Mahatma Gandhi synthesized ethics and politics too. Both politics and economics should be grounded in morality. The principle of might is right belongs to antiquity and has not protruded into the present. Non-violence and benevolence are the principal moral laws. "The highest moral law is, as we have seen, that we should unremittingly work for the good of mankind."[5]

Signs of Moral Laws

The following are the signs of moral laws, according to Gandhi : (1) Moral laws are static. (2) Moral laws are not relative to individual or circumstance and are universally comprehensible. (3) Moral laws are divine. (4) The result, too, of moral laws is ultimately good. (5) The history of moral laws means the history of the evolutionary deliberation of everlasting, comprehensive and immutable moral laws. As civilization progresses so does the understanding of these laws. (6) The conscience is a divine spark. It is, thus, also the preceptor of moral laws.

Judgment of Good and Bad

Mechanical or intuitive activities are not the object of moral judgement. Like rationalist and purposivist ethicists Gandhi too regards only voluntary actions as the objects of moral judgement. "No action which is not voluntary can be

1. Gandhi, M.K, *Young India*. Nov. 24, 1921, p. 365.
2. Gandhi, M.K, *Ethical Religion*. Trans. by A.R. Ayar, S Ganesan Publisher, Madras (1922), p. 46.
3. *Ibid*, p. 59.
4. *Ibid.*, p. 48.
5. *Ibid.*, p. 49.

called moral"[1] These also include activities originating in habit. According to Gandhiji, while contemplating upon morality it is to be attended to that the work is good and done with a good intention. Its result is not in our control, the only one who rewards is God.

Relation between Means and Ends

At this point the question of means and ends, as a relation, crops up. Generally, Gandhi believes that the means does not become good merely upon the pretence that the end is good. "Thus end cannot justify the means."[2] But Gandhi has also conceded exceptions to this rule. For example, it was Gandhi himself who originated and implemented the campaign against the notorious salt law. The exception has two aspects, the first where both the means and the end are related to the same individual and the second comes into action when all the superior means have failed. Under such circumstances the use of even bad means may be right. But it is essential that the aim be good under every circumstance.

Criticism of the Ethics of Gandhi

1. **Lack of Originality** Mahatma Gandhi was a religious person whose ethics is grounded in his religious faith. Although not systematic, his ethics voices the spirit of the age. But notwithstanding this redeeming feature from the scholarly viewpoint his ethics or moral thoughts are unorganised and unbalanced. Thus, he has been subjected to severe criticism. His thoughts lack any originality. According to B.G. Ray, "Gandhiji starts from Hindu religion, and the metaphysical solution of eternal problems from a Hindu angle of vision form the basis of his philosophy. He has not sought to answer or solve the problem from an independent perspective of experience or reason."[3] It is not too incorrect to say that Gandhiji did not present any novel moral laws but he cannot be said to be completely without originality. He gave to the old moral laws a completely new form. Gandhiji was the first one to introduce non-violence into the political field and he also made successful use of it. He declared punishment immoral. Gandhiji was the precursor of non-violent revolution.
2. **Extremism** According to Miller, "Gandhiji belongs to the type of sanyasis who repress the flesh consciously, reject all the colour and warmth of life, denounce everything which is not necessary for mere livelihood, hasten the dissolution of the body, so that the spirit imprisoned in it may more quickly ae united with the divine."[4] Gandhiji is called an extremist, an allegation of undeniable veracity,

1. *Ibid.*, p. 39.
2. *Ibid.*, p. 42.
3. Ray, B.G., *Gandhian Ethics*, p. 34.
4. Rene Fullop Miller, *Gandhi, the Holy Man*, p. 157.

but it should not be forgotten that he made the utmost effort to make his vows practicable and proved their practicability by following them himself. Excessive emphasis upon repression of senses has led to his ethics becoming permeated with stringency. Probably his assumption regarding celibacy may strike one as untenable and even harmful to happy matrimonial life but a balancing stress upon qualities like non-violence, love, equanimity etc., have prevented his sermons from becoming utterly heartless. Actually, Gandhiji himself was an experimenter and did not recognise any means as final. He had hoped that there would be new experiments in the application of non-violence and looked at attentively, this hope does not impress one as a false hope.

3. **Doubts about non-violence** Many critics express grave doubts regarding the probabilities of experimentation in non-violence but in order to comprehend Gandhi's thought it will be essential to set aside the general pragmatic idea and approach the hub of the problem whence the utility of non-violence, for purposes of all kinds of healthy and permanent improvements, will become transparent. There can, of course, be some practical doubts about the possibility of trusteeship. Progress is imminent in the attempts of making practical Vinobaji's campaign of Gandhism. Only the future can tell the extent of its practicability. Gandhiji endeavoured to discover the fundamental solution of all problems. Another major reason why his solution of existing problems and his sketches of man's future seem impractical is that human society has not achieved that level and man also lacks the necessary moral strength to successfully use those means. But the only conclusion which can be drawn from this is that society will have to acquire moral strength to proceed upon his path. Non-violence is a means in moral behaviour. The means contradicting it are violence and use of brutal strength. In order to conclude which of these two means is superior and to the extent to and reason for which it is so, it is necessary to precede it by analysing right and wrong. From the ethical viewpoint, right is that which is good and conversely, bad is wrong. Now, the result of any moral action can consist of two aspects — individual and social, upon the object. If any activity favours the perpetrator but harms the object, or if the result of an action benefits the individual and harms society, or it is favourable immediately but detrimental in the long run, then the activity cannot be said to be good because in order to be so, the result of an activity must be good for the individual and society, at present and in future. Here, this question arises only when the reason and the result differ. In the preceding example the result implies the reason.

Judging violence from this criterion, we realise that it can benefit either the individual or the society, never for the two together — a wealthy person exploits the poor and lives in luxury but he causes misery to innumerable more who subsist in misery and poverty. In a hierarchical society, there is of course general progress but in the absence of a state of independent thought the person's personality remains dwarfed. Besides only the more immediate results of violence can be good. Over a long period it benefits neither the individual nor society. The tendencies of a violent person become degenerate and his character devolves. People fear him but also hate him unostentatiously. Then he is always conscious of misgivings about his opponent's seeking after revenge. Violence gives rise only to further violence.

On the contrary, non-violence results in just the converse way. It may lead to some delay in the maturation of the result but the results are permanent as well as good. It is possible, too, that the one who pursues non-violence may even have to sacrifice his life and bear pain without being rewarded. But even this suffering produces a result calculated to aggrandise the spiritual pleasure of both himself and his opponent. The patience of man is dependent upon his character. A non-violent person is conscious of intrinsic happiness although he may be undergoing extrinsic pain infliction. Even though the opponent does ostensibly resist any such overtures, he internally becomes addicted to this and finally submits himself.

The next question to be considered is whether the use of force is admissible under any circumstances or not? The answer is that in some exceptions it is both necessary and possible. Violence or resorting to force is objected to only when it is used either indiscriminately or for the interests of this or that class or individual. If a particular individual class refuses to abandon, by any means, his incorrect and deplorable path and does immense harm to others then use of force also becomes necessary. At this stage it can be objected as to how is it possible to make use of one person or class as a means to the benefit of another class or individual? Its solution is that the person conducting himself in an objectionable manner does the greatest extent of damage to himself. *Gita* goes to the extent of saying that although apparently alive, he is in reality dead. In this way, if it becomes irrefutably clear that use of force is in the interests of the offending person or class and all others concerned and also that peaceful means are not going to yield any desirable result then the use of force is both unavoidable and moral. Yudhisthira's lying and Sri Krishna's urging Arjuna to war claim the sanction of identical argument. Pandavas had made unsuccessful and fruitless use of all peaceful means. The misconduct on the part of the Kauravas had assumed such proportions as to have caused the degeneration of society. Both in the interests of society and the fulfilment of duty it had become indispensable for Arjuna to fight, it being absolutely non-violent to have engaged in war, both from the mental and spiritual viewpoints, as it was qualified by lack of yearning and done with the intention of offering to God. Thus, it was also moral.

In the present age, Gandhiji too has licenced resort to use of force in exceptional cases. But it is a necessary condition that all other means should have proved ineffective and use of force should be in positive interests of both, the one using it and the one upon whom it is used. Even Gandhiji himself behaved in a similar way sometimes. The infringement of the salt law was both an evidence of use of force and unconstitutional but it was violating the law of India in the interests of India. There was no other alternative at hand. At the same time it also caused moral improvement of the English people because having reduced India to dependence they were acting in an extremely immoral way. It is also worth-noting that this action was purely for the sake of duty and done without attachment. In the war against the English Gandhiji invariably advanced love and not hatred for them. He declared himself the best friend of the Briton.

In this way, the morality or immorality of resorting to force can be judged only with reference to the entire situation and in some cases it becomes inevitable.

SOCIAL PHILOSOPHY

Cult of Non-Violence

If anyone were asked to give the essence of the social philosophy of M.K. Gandhi in one word, he should call it Non-Violence. Gandhi so much emphasized this principle that this almost sums up his approach in social, political and economic fields. Everywhere his ideal was non-violence, so much so that we can call his ideal cult of non-violence. Explaining this importance of non-violence Gandhi said, "Without Ahimsa it is not possible to seek and find Truth. Ahimsa and Truth are so inter-twined that it is practically impossible to disentangle and separate them. They are like the two sides of a coin, or rather of a smooth unstamped metallic disc. Who can say which is the reverse?"[1] In the tradition of ancient Indian thinkers Gandhi believed in non-dualism. Reality according to him is one. He, however, laid emphasis on the manifestation of the reality even more than the reality itself. Thus, his metaphysics was pluralist. In epistemology he was a relativist having firm faith in Syadwad or relativism. The basic condition for the reconstruction of the society, according to him, is the realisation of God upon earth. He believed in Indian doctrine of rebirth and his social thought aimed at ultimate ideals for which immediate ideals were mere means. He delved into politics in spite of being a religious person simply because man's world, according to him, is a continuous whole. In his own words, "The whole gamut of man's activities today constitutes an indivisible whole, you cannot divide social, economic, political and purely religious work into watertight compartments."[2] He was an internationalist like Vivekananda and Tagore and yet he was a great patriot and a nationalist. He said, "He who does not know

1. Gandhi, M.K., *From Yervada Mandir*, pp. 8-9.
2. Gandhi, M.K., *Harijan*, December 24, 1938.

what patriotism of feeling for one's country is, does not know his true duty or religion."[1]

Gandhian cult of non-violence was based upon his interpretation of human nature. Declaring the importance of non-violence in his social philosophy he said, "Non-violence is the first article of my faith. It is also the last article of my creed."[2] Hence, "Its (non-violence) spread is my life-mission. I have no interest except for the prosecution of that mission."[3] Violence, according to him, is the law of brutes while non-violence is the rule of human beings. Here he absolutely differs with Darwinian principles of struggle for existence and survival of the fittest. Non-violence, according to him, is not merely an ideal, it is a fact. Replying to his critics who called his philosophy utopian and visionary, he said, "I am not a visionary, I claim to be a practical idealist. The religion of non-violence is not meant for the Risis and Saints. It is meant for the common people as well. Non-violence is the law of our species, as violence is the law of the brute. The spirit lies dormant in the brute, and he knows no law but that of physical might. The dignity of man requires obedience to a higher law of the strength of the spirit."[4]

Advancing argument in support of his cult of non-violence Gandhi said, "The fact that there are so many men still alive in the world shows that it is based not on the force of arms but on the force of truth and love. Therefore, the greatest and most unimpeachable evidence of the success of this force is to be found in the fact that in spite of wars of the world, it lives on."[5]

The Ideals of Satyagraha

Due to his emphasis on truth and the aim of life as truth realisation, Gandhi called his techniques of social reconstruction by the name *Satyagraha* and urged everyone to be a *Satyagrahi.* He prescribed seven vows for a *Satyagrahi viz.* truth, non-violence, *brahmacharya,* control of palate, fearlessness, non-stealing (or non-possession). All these ideals he explained in great details. In each case his insistence was on perfection so much so that his critics have criticised him as an extremist and as ascetic. Most of the vows have been accepted by ancient Indian scriptures. Gandhi knew that every one cannot practise these ideals in the absolute sense and he agreed, "The taking of vow does not mean that we are able to observe it completely from the very beginning, it does mean constant and honest effort in thought, word and deed with a view to fulfil it."[6] A detailed description of these vows will clarify further Gandhian social philosophy.

---

1. Holmes, J., *Mahatma Gandhi : The World Significance,* p. 83.
2. Gandhi, M.K., *Young India, March* 23, 1922, p. 185.
3. Gandhi, M.K., *Harijan,* July 6, 1940, p. 185.
4. Bose, *Selections from Gandhi,* p. 22.
5. Gandhi, M.K., *Ibid.,* p. 27.
6. Gandhi, M.K., *Ibid.,* p. 2.

1. **Truth** As we have already said, truth is the highest ideal in Gandhian social philosophy. He has, however, taken it in the most comprehensive sense. He said, "There should be truth in thought, truth in speech and truth in action."[1] Thus, truth should be practised in all walks of life — social, economic, political etc.
2. **Non-Violence** As has been already pointed out, Gandhian social thought was the cult of non-violence. He said, "Non-violence is the law of our species as violence is the law of brutes."[2] Explaining his principle of non-violence, Gandhi said elsewhere, "The basic principle of non-violence rests on that what holds good in respect of oneself equally applies to the whole universe."[3] This is in agreement with the famous Kantian principle that act upon the principle which you want to make a universal law and exceptions are always wrong. Anyone who objected to non-violence as the creed of the coward was reproached by Gandhi. He clarified, "Ahimsa is not the way of the timid and cowardly. It is the way of brave ready to face death. He who perishes with sword in hand is no doubt brave but he who faces death without raising his little finger and without flinching is braver."[4] Western thinkers, including Prof. Arnold Toynbee, have hailed Gandhian application of non-violence to human society. Gandhi firmly believed that no real democracy can be established by violent means. Unlike Marx who prescribed violent means for the realisation of Classless society, Gandhi insisted on non-violence as the only means for the achievement of the same ideal. Gandhi did not accept any chasm between ends and means. For him no high ends can be achieved without equally high means. He said, "True democracy or the Swaraj of the masses can never come through untruthful and violent means, for the simple reason that the natural corollary to their use would be to remove all opposition through the suspension or extermination of the antagonists. That does not make for individual freedom. Individual freedom can have the fullest play only under a regime of unadulterated Ahimsa."
3. **Brahmacharya** Literally speaking, Brahmacharya means conduct adapted to the search of Brahma *i.e.* Truth. In the practical sense however, it means primarily chastity and ultimately control of all the senses. Gandhi's emphasis on Brahmacharya has always been a subject of controversy, as it clearly condemns marriage as a necessary evil. He said, "Hence, one who would obey the law of ahimsa cannot marry, not to speak of gratification outside the marital bond."[5] Naturally, this principle cannot be acceptable to contemporary thinkers. Gandhi

1. Gandhi, M.K., *Young India*, March, 9, 1922.
2. Gandhi, M.K., *Harijan*, November, 12, 1938.
3. Gandhi, M.K., *Young India*, August 11, 1928.
4. Gandhi, M.K., *Harijan*, May 27, 1938, p. 143.
5. Gandhi, M.K., *Yervada Mandir*, p. 11.

however, permitted marriage to those who cannot live without it. He said, "Marriage is the most natural and desirable state when one finds oneself, even against his will, living the married life in his daily thought."[1] India has cherished the ideal of Brahmacharya since ancient times and some of the famous Indian great men and women never married. Some examples are Shankara, Vivekananda and Ramkrishna etc. They have undoubtedly made a significant contribution to our society. Then there was an ideal of Brahmacharya in married state. According to this ideal a person performing sexual intercourse only for getting progeny is a Brahmachari though married. This ideal has always been held in high esteem in India. Gandhi being perfectly in tradition with ancient Indian thought naturally hailed the ideal of Brahmacharya, and his insistence is not without its merit though something can be said about its being an impractical ideal. Medical testimony has been both in favour and against absolute continence and yet no conclusive evidence has been available either in favour or against this ideal. On the other hand, it must be accepted that for a pure religious life, as Gandhi cherished, Brahmacharya is a must.

4. **Control of Palate** According to Gandhi, "Control of the palate is very closely connected with the observance of Brahmacharya. I have found from experience that the observance of celibacy becomes comparatively easy."[2] Also, "For the seeker who would live in fear of God, and would see him face to face, restraint in diet both as to quantity and quality is as essential as restraint in thought and speech."[3]
5. **Non-Stealing and Non-Possession** Both these ideals have been cherished in India since ancient times. Non-possession has been considered a virtue by every great religion including Hindu, Muslim, Christian, Jain and Buddhism. Gandhi has, however, taken both these in absolute sense. Explaining his ideal of non-stealing he said, "I suggest that we are thieves in a way. If I take anything that I do not need for my own immediate use and keep it, I thieve it from somebody else. I venture to suggest that it is the fundamental law of nature, without exception that nature produces enough for our wants from day to day, and if only everybody took enough for himself and nothing more, there would be no pauperism in this world."[4]
6. **Bread-Labour** Bread Labour is the principle that in order to live man must work and this work should be not mental but physical. Gandhi, like Adam Smith, called it productive labour. Explaining his ideal of Bread Labour, Gandhi said, "This labour (bread labour) can truly be related to agriculture alone. But it present at any rate, everybody is

1. Gandhi, M.K., *Young India,* Vol. II, p. 123.
2. Gandhi, M.K., *Yervada Mandir,* p. 15.
3. Gandhi, M.K., *My Experiments with* Truth, p. 334.
4. Gandhi, M.K., *Speeches,* p. 384.

not in a position to take it. A person can therefore, spin or weave or take up carpentry or smithy, instead of tilling the soil, always regarding agriculture however to be ideal."[1]

7. **Fearlessness** Ever since Indian masses waged a war against British domination of this country, Indian leaders preached fearlessness, as it was very necessary to face the atrocities of a foreign rule. Besides, the spiritual leaders have always advocated fearlessness as a necessary condition for spiritual progress. Explaining the ideal of fearlessness Gandhi said, "Fearlessness connotes freedom front all external fear — fear of disease, bodily injury and death, or dispossession of losing ones nearest and dearest, or losing reputation or giving offence, and so on."[2]
8. **Swadeshi** While previous moral principles were mainly developed in jail, Gandhi wrote about the idea of Swadeshi from outside the jail. Explaining he meaning of Swadeshi he said, "Swadeshi is that spirit within us which restricts us to use any service of our immediate surroundings to the exclusion of the more remote."
9. **Swadharma** Thus (i) In the matter of Religion I must restrict myself to my ancestral religion *i.e.* the use of my immediate surrounding in religion. If I find my religion defective I should serve it by purging it of its defects, (ii) In the domain of politics I should make use of the indigenous institutions and serve them by curing them of their proved defects. (iii) In the field of economics I should use only those things that are produced by immediate neighbours and serve those industries by making them efficient and complete where they might be found wanting."[3] The ideal of *Swadeshi* was derived from the ideal of *Swadharma* as given in *Bhagwadgita.* In spite of being an internationalist Gandhi laid emphasis upon following one's own religion, worshipping one's own God and relishing one's own culture. Explaining his stand in this connection Gandhi said, "I do not want my house to be walled in on all sides and my windows to be stuffed. I want culture of all lands to be blown about my house as freely as possible...But I refuse to be blown off my feet by any one of them."[4]

Ideal of Social Reconstruction

In consistency with his principles of truth and non-violence M.K. Gandhi considered decentralization the fundamental principle of social organisation. He was against the Communist's overcentralisation by the State. Explaining his attitude towards centralisation in socialism Gandhi said, "I do not share the socialist belief that centralization of the necessaries of life will conduce to the common welfare when the centralized industries are planned and owned

---

1. Gandhi, M.K., *Yervada Mandir,* p. 37.
2. *Ibid.,* p. 27.
3. Andrews, C.F., *Mahatma Gandhi's Ideas,* p. 140.
4. Quoted by Romain Rolland, *Mahatma Gandhi,* p. 117.

by the State. The socialist conception of the West was born in an environment reeking with violence. The motive lying behind the Western type and the Eastern is the same — the hideous welfare of the whole society and the abolition of the hideous inequalities resulting in the existence of millions of have not and a handful of haves. I believe that this end can be achieved only when non-violence is accepted by the best minds of the world as the basis on which a just social order is to be constructed. I hold that the coming in power of the proletariat through violence is bound to fail in the end. What is gained by violence must be lost before superior violence."[1] Thus, Gandhi was clearly against socialist type of revolution. And yet he was a revolutionary no less than Karl Marx. As against the scientific materialism of Karl Marx Gandhian revolutionary technique can be called scientific non-violencism. Like Karl Marx Gandhi was against capitalism and considered it an evil which should be immediately abolished. But against Marx he felt that a violent revolution cannot lead to a non-violent social order ultimately. On the other hand, violence leads to violence, whether it may be violence of the capitalist as it is in the capitalist society or violence of the state as it is in the Communist society. Gandhi, on the other hand, wanted a permanent elimination of violence against any one. Therefore, he clearly said, "I have always held that social justice, even to the least and the lowliest, is impossible of attainment by force."[2] Also, "Violence on the part of the masses will never remove the disease. Any way upto new experience shows that success of violence has been short-lived. What has been tried hitherto has been a variety of violence and artificial checks dependent mainly upon the will of the violent. At the crucial moment these checks have naturally broken down."[3]

As we have already pointed out, Gandhi was a non-violent revolutionary. His techniques of social revolution, therefore, are based on non-violence. Since the practice of non-violence requires love, goodwill, cooperation and fellow feeling, Gandhian techniques include all these virtues.

PHILOSOPHY OF HISTORY

Gandhiji was not in agreement with what in Marxian terminology is known as the economic interpretation of history. "I do not believe," said Gandhiji, "that it is Prakriti which originates and governs the thought-processes of Purusha."[4] He believed in the power of the spirit of man to shape its environment to some extent and thus affect the course of history. "I do not consider economic factors to be the source of all the evils in the world," he added, "Nor is it correct to trace the origin of all wars to economic causes. What were the causes of the last War? Insignificant ones. When the present war started, Chamberlain, who had till then bent all his energies on averting

---

1. Gandhi, M.K., *Harijan*, April 20, 1940, p. 97.
2. *Ibid.*
3. Gandhi, M.K., *Young India*, September, 3, 1925.
4. Sushila Nayyar, *Bapu Ki Karavas Kahani.*

a war, changed his opinion overnight, because presumably he was afraid of losing the support of his party if at that stage he sought to keep England out of the war. A better statesman in his place, I believe, would have succeeded in averting the war even then. Was not Helen the cause of the Trojan War? But why go so far? The Rajput wars which belong to modern history, had never their origin in economic causes."[1] As S. Radhakrishnan remarks, "History, however, is not a mere record of class struggles. Wars between nations have been more frequent and violent than domestic struggles, and in the earlier history of mankind tribes and towns fought with one another. The feeling of nationality is stronger than consciousness in the present war. All through history the ruler and the ruled, the rich and the poor, fought side by side against the enemies of the country. We hate foreign workers more than we do our own capitalist employers. There are wars for and against the Reformation which went on in Europe for two centuries... Marxists, with a few exceptions, are fighting today for the capitalist states to which they happen to belong... The conflicts between the Hindus and the Muslims in India, or between the Protestants and Catholics in Ireland, are not manifestations of class struggles. There are class struggles and civil wars, but there are wars of religions and nations also. The latter have been more decisive for human evolution. Again, it is not historically correct to agree that war is the inevitable consequence of capitalism... To represent history as a series of internal struggles, to ignore the forces of race, religion and patriotism, is to oversimplify the complex problem of human evolution."[2]

Interpretation of History

Gandhian interpretation of history interpreted the world as a progress of Divine. The world is a Field of the Victory of soul-force over matter. It is hence that Gandhi hoped that in spite of the last two great wars that we have witnessed in the world, mankind is heading towards an era where violence as a technique will be out of date. To quote Gandhiji, "The present war is the saturation point in violence. It spells to my mind also its doom. Daily I have testimony of the fact that Ahimsa was never before appreciated by mankind as it is today."[3] "I am sure", he said, "that out of this orgy of violence the people will learn the lesson of non-violence."[4] Thus, Gandhiji has not only eulogised the ideal of non-violence but advanced historical evidence in its support. Marx has also admitted historical evidence but the difference between the two is the difference in the interpretation of the history. Marx believed that individuals changed only if the society changed. According to Gandhi and other Indian thinkers including Sri Aurobindo, Vivekananda and Tagore, society changes due to the efforts of some great individuals.

---

1. *Ibid., p.* 55.
2. *Religion and Society.* pp. 38-9.
3. Gandhi, M.K., *Harijan,* August 11, 1940.
4. *Ibid.,* March, 10, 1946.

It is not the economic circumstances which create the individual but the individual creates the economic circumstances. In tradition with Indian social philosophy since Vedas to present day Gandhi has laid maximum stress upon the freedom of the individual. His objection to socialism and the Bolshevik revolution rests upon the objection that it takes away the freedom of the state with greatest fear because although while apparently doing good by minimising exploitation, it docs the greatest harm to mankind by destroying individuality, which lies at the root of all progress."[1]

SOCIO-POLITICAL TECHNIQUES OF REVOLUTION

Charkha

The difference between Gandhian technique of social revolution and that of the French or Russian pattern is clear by the symbol of spinning wheel which Gandhi considered to represent the new social order. He invented it since it gives an occasion of physical labour and abolishes the difference between rich and poor. It removes class distinctions and establishes dignity of labour. On the question of the antithetical relationship of the poor and the rich as presented by Karl Marx, Gandhi thought in a different way. Explaining his standpoint on this question, he said, "Exploitation of the poor can be extinguished not by effecting the destruction of a few millionaires, but by removing the ignorance of the poor and teaching them to non-cooperate with their exploiters. That will convert the exploiters also."[2]

Self-Purification

Gandhi introduced the spiritual practice of self-purification as one of the methods in political action. This marks the synthesis of spiritualism with politics. Pointing out the importance of self-purification as a method he said, "Because the rulers, if they are bad, are so not necessarily or wholly by reason of birth, but largely because of the environment, that I have hopes of altering their course. It is perfectly true that rulers cannot alter their course themselves. If they are dominated by their environment, they do not surely deserve to be killed, but should be changed by a change of environment. But the environment are we, the people who make the rulers what they are. They are thus an exaggerated edition of what we are in aggregate. If my argument is sound, any violence done to the rulers should be done to ourselves. And since I do not want to commit suicide, nor encourage my neighbours to do so, I become non-violent myself and invite my neighbours to do likewise."[3]

---

1. Gandhi, M.K., *Modern Review,* October 1935.
2. Gandhi, M.K., *Harijan. July* 28, 1940, p. 219.
3. *Ibid.*, September, 21, 1914, p. 250.

Soul-Force

Satyagraha, the chief weapon of Gandhian political action has been defined as soul-force by him. He said, "Its (Satyagraha's) equivalent in the vernacular rendered into English, means truth force. I think Tolstoy called it also soul-force or love-force, and so it is."[1] Satyagraha is bound to be non-violent, otherwise it turns into duragraha. Satyagraha is different from passive resistance also, it is active resistance, acting on the path of truth. Distinguishing Satyagraha from passive resistance, Gandhi pointed out, "The Satyagraha differs from passive resistance as the north pole from the south. The latter has been conceived as a weapon of the weak and does not exclude the use of physical force or violence whereas the former has been conceived as a weapon of the strongest and excludes the use of violence in any shape or form. Its root meaning is holding on to truth, hence truth-force, I have also called it soul-force or love-force. In the application of satyagraha discovered in the earliest stages the pursuit of truth did not admit of violence being inflicted on one's opponent but that must be weaned from error by patience and sympathy. For what appears to be truth to the one may appear to be error to the other. And patience means self-suffering. So the doctrine came to mean vindication of truth not by infliction of suffering on the opponent, but on one's self."[2] The most important characteristic of satyagraha is that it can be used most successfully even by one individual and that too in every sphere of life. It is an ideal weapon of war of righteousness. It is latent in every one of us, we have to make it active. It is a universal course. In essence it is the introduction of truth in political life.

Technique of Stayagraha

Explaining the working of satyagraha as a political weapon Gandhi has insisted that it is based on truth and non-violence. Besides, it includes such techniques as involve mutual dialogue such as arbitration, negotiation etc. Besides, it also includes non-violent pressure tactics such as agitation, demonstration, picketing, dharna, economic boycott, non-payment of taxes, emigration, non-cooperation, ostracism, civil disobedience and formation of parallel government. These steps were taken in the national movement under the guidance of M.K. Gandhi.

Civil Disobedience

The idea of civil disobedience was taken front Thoreau. It is a protest against unjust law. Explaining the validity of civil disobedience as a political instrument, Gandhi said "When you have failed to bring the error home to the lawgiver by way of petition and the like, the only remedies open to you if you do not wish to submit to error, are to compel him to yield to you either

1. Gandhi, M.K., *Golden Indian Number of Indian Opinion*, p. 9.
2. Gandhi, M.K., *Young India*, January 11, 1920.

by physical force or by suffering in your person, by inviting the penalty for the breach of his laws. Hence, satyagraha largely appears to the public as civil disobedience or civil resistance."[1] Gandhi distinguish between forced and wilful disobedience of the laws while the latter is involuntary and reluctant disobedience of the laws.

Non-Cooperation

Another instrument in the armoury of Satyagraha is non-cooperation. This technique was widely used by Gandhi in India's political struggle against the British. Explaining non-cooperation as a method of political action Gandhi said, "Non-violent non-cooperation is the method whereby we cultivate the fresh public opinion and get it enforced when there is complete freedom of opinion, that of the majority must prevail."[2] When non-cooperation alone does not work, Satyagraha becomes assertive and takes recourse to direct action. This may be sometimes embarrassing to his standpoint. He said, "The Satyagraha movement is not started with the intention of embarrassing a government while ordinary political agitation is often started with that object. And yet, if a satyagrahi finds his activities resulting in embarrassing the government, he will not hesitate to face it."[3]

No Destruction

In spite of gradual application of more and more pressure and even non-violent direct action, Gandhi was against any violent agitation or destruction of public property. He spoke against the sabotage and destruction of bridges, roads etc., in clear words. He was also against any secret movement or plan of action, since according to him secrecy is violence. In his own words, "Secrecy aims at building a wall of protection around you. Ahimsa disdains all such protection. It functions in the open and in the face of odds, the heaviest conceivable."[4] He was also against seizure of power by force. He did not accept forced establishment of *Jatiya Sarkar.*

Fast

Another significant and novel instrument of political action developed by Gandhi is fast. This is a weapon which very much depends upon the soul-force of the person wielding it. Gandhi himself used this weapon in the political field very successfully.

Qualifications of Satyagrahi

Gandhi wanted to organize a whole army of revolutionaries on non-violent ground. He prescribed qualifications for the soldiers of independence movement which he called Satyagrahis.

---

1. *Ibid.*, January 14, 1940.
2. *Ibid.*, November 24, 1921.
3. *Ibid.*, February 4, 1920.
4. Gandhi, M.K., *Harijan*, February 10, 1946.

These qualifications were as follows :

1. Living faith in God.
2. Faith in truth and non-violence as their creed and therefore faith in the inherent goodness of human nature.
3. Chaste life and readiness for sacrifice.
4. Absolute abstinence of intoxicants.
5. Habitual wearing of Khadi.
6. Desire to follow discipline.
7. Following jail rules unless they are against self-respect.

Gandhi himself followed these principles and asked others to follow his example. Though amenable to discussion his method was very much based upon faith and discipline. It was based upon dedication and selfishness. It required a lot of sacrifice on the part of the individual. In order to create a revolution in the country Gandhi demanded 7 lakh workers so that each village may get at least one revolutionary as base for the programme of revolution. This, however, could never be achieved and therefore, his great vision could never be realised.

POLITICAL PHILOSOPHY

Criticism of Western Socialism

Gandhian political philosophy has been lightly called sarvodaya. Thus, it was different from socialism and communism. He has explained his own position and also pointed out the difference between his own ideology and other popular ideologies. He was well conversant with socialist and communist literature. He had occasion to see how they worked and yet in the tradition of Indian thought and culture he developed an ideology which was entirely indigenous. Pointing out his objection against Russian brand of socialism he said, "From what I know of Bolshevism, it not only does not preclude use of force, but freely sanctions it for the expropriation of property and maintaining the collective ownership of the same. And, if so, I have no hesitation in saying that the Bolshevik regime in its present form, cannot last for long. For, it is my firm conviction that nothing enduring can be built on violence."[1] And yet he agreed with the fundamental principles of socialism such as abolition of private property, elimination of capitalism etc. Socialism, according to him, was prevalent in India right from ancient times and Gandhi borrowed his socialism not from Karl Marx but from the Upanishads. He said, "Socialism was not born with the discovery of the misuse of the capital by capitalists. As I have contended, socialism even communism, is explicit in the first verse of Ishopanishad. What is true is that when some reformers lost faith in the method of conversion, the technique of what is known as scientific socialism was born. I am engaged in solving the same problem that faces scientific socialists "[2]

1. Gandhi, M.K., *Young India*, November 15, 1928.
2. Gandhi, M.K., *Harijan, February* 20, 1937, p. 12.

Neo-Vedanta Socialism

Gandhi belonged to the class of Neo-Vedanta thinkers that India produced in contemporary century, including Aurobindo, Vivekananda, Tagore and others. His socio-political ideology is based upon Vedanta philosophy. The essential of Vedanta philosophy is that there is one universal essence underlying all human beings and therefore a law applicable to one person should be applied to all and *vice versa*. Gandhian socialism was religious and spiritual in the tradition of Vedanta philosophy. Explaining his socialism in details he said, "Real socialism has been handed down to us by our ancestors who taught 'All land belongs to Gopal, where then is the boundary line? Man is the maker of that line and he can, therefore, unmake it.' Gopal literally means shepherd, it also means God. In modern language it means the state *i.e.*, the people. That the land today does not belong to the people is true. But the fault is not in the teaching. It is in us who have not lived upto it. I have no doubt, that we can make as good an approach to it as is possible... And this ideal can be universally realised only if the means of production of the elementary necessaries of life remain in the control of the masses. These should be freely available to all as God's air and water are or ought to be; they should not be made a vehicle of traffic for the exploitation of others. This monopolization by any country, nation or groups of persons would be unjust. The neglect of this simple principle is the cause of distinction that we witness today not only in this unhappy land but in other parts of the world too."[1]

Classless Society without Class War

Gandhi studied communism and liked its essential principles. According to him communism basically means a classless society. He himself wanted to establish a classless society and the end of capitalism but through non-violent means. He was against the class-war theory of Karl Marx. He wanted to create a revolution without recourse to class war. He said, "I can, most decidedly, avoid class war if only the people will follow the non-violent method. By the non-violent method we seek not to destroy the capitalist, we seek to destroy capitalism. We invite the capitalist to regard himself as a trustee for those on whom he depends for making the retention of and the increase of his capital."[2]

The Individual and the State

The most important distinction between the Western brand of socialism and Gandhian socialism is based upon the relation of the individual and the state. While the former seeks to subordinate individual to the state, the latter favoured absolute freedom for the individual and limited the function of the state to bare minimum. This was so because Gandhi considered state

---

1. Gandhi, M.K., *Young India*, November 15, 1928, p. 381.
2. *Ibid.*, March 26, 1931.

as violence personified. He was against violence in any form and therefore he cherished a stateless society. Explaining his estimation of the state he said, "The state represents violence in a concentrated and organized form. The individual has a soul, but the state is a soul-less machine, it can never be weaned from violence to which it owes its very existence."[1] Thus, there is an inverse correlation between the rise of the power of the state and the spiritual progress of society. As more and more power is concentrated in the hands of the state the opportunity for spiritual progress becomes less and less. Therefore, Gandhi was against any increase in the power of the state. He wanted to keep it subservient to the spiritual individuals. Pointing out his approach in this connection he said, "I look upon an increase in the power of the state with the greatest fear, because although while apparently doing good by minimising exploitation, it does the greatest harm to mankind by destroying individuality, which lies at the root of all progress."[2] The best rule, according to Gandhi, was self rule. Everything great comes from within. The spiritual progress of a society depends on individuals. Therefore, the individual should be given maximum freedom for evolving without interference.

Decentralisation

As against concentrating power in the hands of the state, Gandhi pleaded for decentralization. He wanted to establish political organization of the country on non-violent basis through village communities. He wanted to make every village a unit, free and active for the total good. On the eve of Indian independence in 1946, he said, "Independence must begin at the bottom. Thus, every village will be a republic or panchayat having full powers. It follows, therefore, that every village has to be self-sustained and capable of managing its affairs even to the extent of defending itself against the whole world."[3] In the scheme it was not an ascending order but a horizontal circle whose circumference is ever widening, from individual to community, nation, and ultimately including the entire humanity. Explaining his vision of the future India of his dreams Gandhi said, "In this structure composed of innumerable villages, there will be ever widening never ascending circles. Life will not be a pyramid with the apex sustained by the bottom. But it will be an oceanic circle whose centre will be the individual, always ready to perish for the village, the latter ready to perish for the circle of villages, till at last the whole becomes one life composed of individuals never aggressive in their arrogance but ever humble, sharing the majority of the oceanic circle of which they are integral units. Therefore, the outermost circumference will not wield power to crush the inner circle but will give strength to all within and derive its own strength from it."[4]

1. Gandhi, M.K., *Modern Review,* October, 1935.
2. Quoted by Francis, W. Coker in *Recent Political Thought (1934),* p. 198.
3. Gandhi, M.K., *Harijan,* July 28, 1946.
4. Gandhi, M.K., *Ibid.*

Self-Government

Thus, as opposed to state government Gandhi was more in favour of self-government and self-revolution. In fact his swarajya meant self-government. This idea is based upon the spiritual thinking that anything genuine and real can come only from within. Morally speaking all good comes from within, nothing can be imposed from outside. Anything imposed from outside is foreign to human nature and cannot be called moral. Explaining his idea of self- government Gandhi said. "Self-government means continuous efforts to be independent of the government control whether it is foreign or whether it is national. Swaraj government will be a sorry affair if people look up for the regulation of every detail of life."[1]

Gandhi however knew that in practice it is not possible to abolish the state altogether nor is it possible to eliminate all use of force. Therefore, he concedes that the state and the government may exist and yet their powers should be reduced to minimum. He said, "I admit that there are certain things which cannot be done without political power, but there are numerous other things which do not at all depend upon the political power. That is why a thinker like Thoreau said that, 'that government is best which governs the least.' This means that when people come into possession of political power the interference with the freedom of the people is reduced to a minimum. In other words, a nation that runs its affairs smoothly and effectively without much state interference is truly democratic. Where such condition is absent the form of Government is democratic in name."[2]

Liberty, Equality, Fraternity

The ideal government, according to Gandhi, as according to most of the political thinkers of our age, is democracy. Gandhi, however, wanted to emphasise the principle of non-violence in the actual working of the democracy. He wanted to decentralise the whole political structure. He emphasised equality between human beings and was against too much difference in economic or political field. He wanted to run the government by reducing violence to the minimum. He prescribed social reform of criminals and opposed retributive punishment. He wanted to turn policemen into social reformers. He was against having a large army or military organisation. In nutshell his social organisation gives maximum freedom to the individual. This, however, does not mean that he gives less importance to the society. Pointing out the importance of social obligations in a society Gandhi said, "I value the individual freedom but you must not forget that man is essentially a social being. He has risen to the present status by learning to adjust his individualism. Individualism is the law of the beast of the jungle. We have

---

1. Gandhi, M.K., *Young India,* Vol. I, p. 290.
2. *Ibid.,* Vol. II, p. 491.

learnt to strike the mean between individual freedom and social restraint for the sake of the well being of the whole society of which one is a member."[1]

The Society and the Individual

Gandhian concept of the relation between the society and the individual is based upon the ancient Indian Varna system. In the Varna system different individuals were classified according to their innate tendencies and were given social roles corresponding to them. This, according to Gandhi, created conditions both for the individual development and social welfare. Explaining the law of Varna in Indian social system Gandhi said, "The law of Varna means that every one shall follow, as a matter of dharma-duty, the hereditary calling of his forefathers is so far as it is not inconsistent with fundamental ethics. He will earn his livelihood by following that good of the people."[2] Gandhi's appreciation of Varna system was based on his faith in *Bhagwadgita* which he considered to be his guide in every field of life. He did not think that caste system is a necessary corollary of Varna system. He was also against fixing rigidly the occupations of different Varnas. His was an integral approach to life. This is very much clear from his insistence that every one, howsoever scholarly he may be, must earn his bread by physical labour. Pointing out his ideal in this connection he said, "Brahmin is not only a teacher, he is predominantly that. But a Brahmin who refuses to labour will be voted down as an idiot, because the rishis of the old who lived in forests cut and fetched wood, tended cattle and even fought, but their pursuit in life was predominantly search after truth. Similarly, a Rajput without learning was good for nothing no matter how well he wields the sword. And Vaishya without divine knowledge sufficient for his own growth will be a veritable monster eating into the vitals of society as many modern Vaishyas whether of the East or the West have become. They are, according to the *Gita*, incarnations of sin who live only for themselves."[3]

Defence of Varna System

In spite of praising Varna system in very clear terms, Gandhi was against casteism and untouchability. As has been already pointed out, he did not trace caste system to Varna system. In fact he joined in the controversy on this issue and defended Varna system against the onslaught of Dr. B.R. Ambedkar. Replying him he said, "Varnas and Ashramas are institutions which have nothing to do with castes. The law of Varna teaches us that we have each one of us to earn our bread by following the ancestral calling. It defines not our rights but our duties. It necessarily has reference to callings that are conducive to the welfare of humanity and to no other. It also follows that there is no calling too low and none too high."[4]

---

1. Gandhi, M.K., *Harijan,* May 27, 1939, p. 144.
2. *Ibid.,* September, 28, 1934, p. 560.
3. *Vide* Dr. Bhagwandas : *Sanatan Vaidika Dharma* (1928), p. 104.
4. Gandhi, M.K., *Harijan,* July 18, 1936.

Anti-Untouchability

Thus, according to Gandhi, Varna system, far from being the source of untouchability, was against it. Equality demands that we should not distinguish among human beings on the basis of social occupations. Therefore, Gandhi, throughout his life, waged a war against the evil of untouchability. Elimination of untouchability was an important aspect of his programme. As he said, "Removal of untouchability means love for, and service of, the whole world, and thus merges into *ahimsa*,"[1]

ECONOMIC PHILOSOPHY

Synthesis of Economics and Ethics

Gandhi was not an economist in the academic sense of the term. He was however very much conversant with the economic problems of the country and he thought over them with his characteristic basic approach. He himself said, "I am not an economist, but India may become a self-sustained country, growing all the produce she needs. This may be an utterly ridiculous proposition and perhaps the best proof that it cannot be true is that England is one of the largest importers in the world."[2] Thus, Gandhian economic programme was based upon the ideal of self-sufficiency. Man, for him, was the ultimate consideration. Therefore, he never compromised ethical principles with economic progress. The ideal of man, according to him, is spiritual progress first and last and no economic progress can violate this principle. He however, did not sharply distinguish between economics and ethics any more than the distinction between religion and politics. Thus, Khaddar economics was based upon ethics.

Indigenous Approach

The basic ideas of M.K. Gandhi, in economics as well as in politics were drawn from ancient Indian philosophy of life. Traditional Indian thinking is against giving an important place to consumption in life. It lays emphasis on minimising the wants rather than maximising them. It is against too many desires and sanctions only the minimum desires. Thus, it is against production of such things which are classed among luxuries. Indian philosophy has always preached that man's life is for spiritual evolution and not for physical satisfaction. Born and brought up in the tradition of Indian philosophy and spiritualism, Gandhi, an ardent follower of Gita, developed an economic theory which was in tune with Indian spiritualism. His ideas, besides being based on Indian philosophy of life, were also equally derived from his experience of Indian social life of his time. He was very

---

1. Gandhi, M.K., *Yervada Mandir*, p. 13.
2. An Address delivered before the Missionary Conference, Madras on 14 February, 1939, on *Economics of Khadi.*

much perturbed by the abject poverty of his countrymen. He was moved by it and he scratched his brain to the maximum to find out the solution. But he wanted a solution which may lead to spiritual progress and not an opposite retrogression. Thus, he wanted economic progress but not at the cost of spiritual values. Therefore, he was against mechanisation though he permitted small machines necessary for every day life. The production of these machines obviously should be in public sector.

Mass Control of Necessities

Therefore, Gandhi pleaded for decentralization of industries and that of all the economic functions including production, consumption and distribution. As early as in 1928 he declared, "According to me the economic constitution of India and, for the matter of that the world should be such that no one under it should suffer from wants of food and clothing. In other words, everybody should be able to get sufficient work to enable him to make the two ends meet. And this ideal can be universally realised only if the means of production of the elementary necessaries of life remain in the control of the masses. These should be freely available to all as God's air and water are or ought to be, they should not be made a vehicle of traffic for the exploitation of others. This monopolization by any country, nation or group of persons would be unjust. The neglect of this simple principle is the cause of destitution that we witness today not only in this unhappy land but other parts of the world too."[1]

The Economic Ideology

We may conclude this discussion by reproducing the relevant portion of an article by Gandhiji which gives us an idea of his economic ideology. He said, "The political and economic organization of the state shall be based on principles of social justice and economic freedom. While this organization shall conduce to the satisfaction of the national requirements of every member of society, material satisfaction shall not be its sole objective. It shall aim at healthy living and the moral and intellectual development of the individual. To this end to secure social justice, the state shall endeavour to promote small scale production carried on by individual or cooperative effort for the equal benefit of all concerned. All large scale collective production shall be eventually brought under collective ownership and control, and in this behalf the state shall begin by nationalizing heavy transport, shipping, mining and the heavy industries. The textile industry shall be progressively decentralised."[2] About state industries Gandhi remarked, "In all state-owned and state-managed enterprizes, the workers shall be represented in the management through their elected representatives and shall have an equal share in it with the representatives of the Government."[3]

1. Gandhi, M.K., *Young India,* November 1928. p. 381.
2. Gandhi, M.K., *Harijan,* April 20, 1940.
3. *Ibid.*

Trusteeship Theory

The most important and yet the most controversial point in the economic philosophy of Gandhi is the theory of trusteeship. He was against capitalism and yet he was not against capitalists. He wanted to use their genius as managers of industries. He was against destruction of anything including the capitalist class. His non-violent means were all pervasive including the economic field. Therefore, he said, "In reality the toiler is the owner of what he produced. If the toilers intelligently combine, they will become an irresistible power. That is how I do not see the necessity of class conflict. If I thought it inevitable I shall not hesitate to preach it and teach it."[1]

Explaining the mechanism to bring about trusteeship Gandhi said in answer to a question at the Round Table Conference in England, "Not merely by verbal persuasion, I will concentrate on means. Some have called me the greatest revolutionary of my time. It may be false, but I believe myself to be a revolutionary — a non-violent revolutionary. My means are non-cooperation. No person can amass wealth without the cooperation, willing or forced, of the people concerned."[2] The socialist thinkers within the country and also outside, doubted the possibility of trusteeship. Gandhi, however, wanted to give it a fair trial though in his life time none except Jamna Lal Bajaj came somewhere near his ideal. He was against accumulation of wealth by violence but he was also against mass production or large scale nationalistion. In fact, he was against all mad race after wealth. He was aware of the dangers of state capitalism and therefore prescribed decentralisation of industries. His ideal was equitable distribution if not equal distribution. Labour, according to him, is the master of the means of production and never a slave of it. Capital is the servant of labour and not its master. He, therefore, like Karl Marx advised the labourers to get united, for a non-violent struggle. Like Karl Marx again he aimed at a stateless society, but this stage has to be achieved through non-violent revolution as anything secured through violence, according to Gandhi, is bound to fail in the end.

The above discussion of the political philosophy of M.K. Gandhi makes it clear that essentially it was based on spiritual interpretation of human nature and human society. The integral approach to life, characteristic of Indian philosophy, is explicit in every principle propounded by Gandhi. Like other Indian thinkers he was a religious man and had firm faith in God. The ultimate aim of the life according to him was liberation or Moksha as most of the Indian philosophers have called it. All the aspects of life are inter-related. His solutions of the problems of social, economic and political fields were basically the same, those based upon the principles of harmony, synthesis, cooperation, liberty, equality and fraternity, spiritual evolution and ultimately leading to God realisation and the establishment of kingdom of

---

1. *Ibid.*, September 4, 1919, p. 466.
2. Gandhi, M.K., *National Voice*, p. 212.

God on earth. In the understanding of the philosophy of M.K. Gandhi it is crucial to remember his religious and spiritual background and his link with traditional Indian thought. He was well versed with Western thinking of his time and he referred to the ideas of Western thinkers here and there but everywhere his approach was Indian and Hindu, his vision based upon the vision of *Bhagwadgita.*

20
Jawahar Lal Nehru (1889 — 1964)

Jawahar Lal Nehru was born on November 14, 1889 and got his early education at home. He was sent to Harrow at the early age of 15 and then to Cambridge and graduated therefrom. During his stay at home he was under the influence of his father which he continued to get for a considerably long time. In 1912, he came back to India and joined the Bar, but he could not temperamentally adjust himself to the new profession. In 1913 he joined U.P. Congress Organisation. In 1920 for the first time he came in contact with the workers which proved very useful in his subsequent life. In 1921, he jumped into Mahatma Gandhi's Civil Disobedience Movement. In 1922, he was arrested on account of his participating in Congress-sponsored boycott of foreign cloth.

In 1923, Nehru had the honour of becoming the Chairman of Allahabad municipality. During the same period his wife fell seriously ill and he was obliged to go to Europe for her treatment.

In 1926, Nehru sailed for Switzerland and managed to steal time to attend the Congress of Oppressed Nationalities at Brussels in 1927. In the same year he could persuade his father to accept an invitation from Moscow to attend the 10th anniversary celebrations of Bolshevik Revolution. He was much influenced by Communist progress in the Soviet Union.

In 1929, Nehru got prominence by presiding over the Lahore session of the Congress where he got the historic resolution about independence passed.

After 1929, the nation listened to Nehru with care and attention. In 1931, he got the resolution on fundamental rights passed by Karachi Session of the Congress. In 1932, he was arrested and sentenced to a 2-year term. In 1933, he was released from jail and plunged himself in political activities. It was during this period that he was again arrested for speeches in Calcutta. His mother as well as wife also fell seriously ill and in 1936 his wife passed away. He guided the elections conduced by the Government under the provisions of Government of India Act, 1937. It was due to his efforts that Congress candidates were returned with comfortable majority to the legislatures. In 1938 he visited Europe and in 1939 he went to China.

Since the British Government was not coming to terms, Congress, under the leadership of Nehru, decided not to cooperate with the Government in war efforts. In 1942 when Quit India Movement was started, Jawahar Lal was again arrested and remained in jail for three years. He also actively participated in Cripps Mission Plan, Simla Conferences, Cabinet Mission Plan and Mountbatten Mission Plan. In 1946, he became the first Prime Minister of India and formed interim Government. After 15th of August, 1947, he became the first Prime Minister of independent India and continued to hold that post throughout his life.

As Prime Minister of India he made India a sovereign democratic republic and was responsible for introduction of universal adult franchise. He also gave the policy of non-alignment in international affairs. In the economic field he introduced the system of planned economy.

Nehru wrote much while in jail as that was the only time which he could spare for the purpose. His speeches and letters are now available in book form. His significant works include *Discovery of India* and *Autobiography.*

INFLUENCE ON POLITICAL THOUGHT

Jawahar Lal Nehru's thought is influenced, on the one side by such a western thinker as Karl Marx and on the other, by the ideas of Gandhi, though he never became a blind devotee of either. His relationship with Gandhi may be compared with the relationship between Plato and Aristotle. Aristotle, Plato's disciple, gave full respect to Plato and accepted his teacher's ideas, but he also differed from his on many essential points. In the same way, Nehru often criticized Gandhi very vehemently. In 1922, when Gandhi suspended the non-cooperation movement after the Chauri-Chaura incident, Nehru was deeply chagrined. In the same way, Nehru did not owe the same allegiance to or have faith in, the principle of non-violence as Gandhi. He considered violence as a necessary tool both for maintaining peace in the country and ensuring its security.

DIFFERENCE BETWEEN NEHRU AND GANDHI

Before examining Nehru's social and political ideas in detail, it is desirable to understand clearly the difference between his ideas and that of M.K. Gandhi. The following is a brief account of their fundamental variance:

1. **Religion and Religious faith** Gandhi was, by nature, a very religious person whereas Nehru was very much an atheist. Gandhi openly praised Hindu religion, while Nehru has rarely indulged in such encomiums. Gandhi repeatedly stressed the virtues of religion but practically overlooked its vices, while Nehru did the exact opposite. Despite this, the two thinkers appear to have common views regarding the fundamental elements of religion.
2. **Non-violence** Gandhi believed that non-violence is the highest religion but Nehru did not have such abiding faith in it. He favoured

non-violence because he saw it as the most appropriate means available to India in the existing circumstances. He was also attracted towards non-violence by the spectacularly successful use made of it by Gandhi. He also came to realize that non-violence is an active force. He agreed with Gandhi's arguments favouring non-violence, but on the other hand, he also believed that violence or the use of force was necessary both for maintaining internal peace within the country and also for securing it against external invasion. He consistently refuted the Gandhian thesis that non-violence is truth because he saw the non-violent state as contrary to both logic (or rational thought) and science. In this way, Nehru visualized the use of force as unavoidable in the life of society and the state.

3. **Humanism** Both Gandhi and Nehru were humanists but their views were rooted in different substrata. Gandhi's humanism had its roots in his religious sentiment and faith in God while Nehru's conception was based on his implicit faith in man's innate power and potential. He had the deepest sentimental faith in mankind and believed in the ideal of a single, united world. He had profound faith in man's innate greatness. Thus, while Gandhi's humanism is essentially religious, Nehru's humanism may be considered scientific and ethical.
4. **Welfare State** The Gandhian concept of the welfare state differed considerably from Nehru's. Nehru did not conceive of it as a non-violent state, which Gandhiji did. Besides, he wanted to base it on secularism, not on religion. His viewpoint was more realistic.
5. **Industrial Policy** Gandhi was a staunch opponent of big industry, because of which he wished to establish small and cottage industries in the country. In contrast, Nehru favoured modern socience, and believed that the importance of large-scale industry in eliminating poverty, could not be denied. In his famous work, *Discovery of India,* he wrote, "What I object is the craze for machinery and not machinery as such. If we could have electricity in every village home, I shall not mind villages playing their implements and tools with electricity."[1]
6. **Mean and Ends** Although both Gandhi and Jawahar Lal Nehru subscribed to the view that both means and ends must possess identical moral probity, Nehru admitted that exceptions to the rule were also important. Gandhi in contrast could not countenance any such violation of the principle. His thoughts having been influenced by Gandhi on the one side and Karl Marx on the other, Nehru has spoken in favour of revolution at certain places.
7. **Ideal State** Gandhi entitled his ideal state 'Ram Rajya', but Nehru objected to the view because it carried clear overtones of a profound faith in Hindu religion, though he did not lay any great stress on this objection. Apart from this, their respective conceptions of the ideal

1. Nehru, J.L., *Discovery of India,* p. 356.

state can be seen differing in respect of the importance of non-violence, the use of force, small and large industries and many other elements.

8. **Effect of the East and the West** Gandhi was devoted to Eastern thought whereas Nehru's mind was more profoundly coloured by Western ideas because of his education at Cambridge University which had understandably formed and shaped his mind. Because of this, Nehru wanted the nation to move ahead according to the ideas of progress imbibed from the West. On the other hand, Gandhi gave his allegiance to traditional Indian values, and wanted to prevent the nation from going the Western way.
9. **Social Ideas** Elaborating on the differences between the social ideas of Nehru and Gandhi, Abid Hussain has explained that on comparing the social ideas of Nehru and Gandhi one finds that in spite of many common elements, there are notable differences in structure and force, and as a result, their conceptions appear to be very much different. Both had profound faith in freedom and equality. However, Gandhi laid greater emphasis on freedom while Nehru stressed equality. In the final analysis, these differences stem from the basic difference between the religious and the secular viewpoints.

Gandhi's thinking started from the individual whereas Nehru gave primacy to the welfare state. In his concept of Trusteeship, Gandhi visualized a change of heart among capitalists but Nehru rejected any possibility of this and so his economic views could not accommodate the theory of trusteeship.

Despite the wide range of differences between the ideas of Gandhi and Nehru explained above, a close similarity between their thoughts on non-violence, democracy, welfare state, opposition to communalism, eradication of untouchability, nationalism and internationalism may be seen.

PHILOSOPHICAL FOUNDATIONS

Naturalistic Humanism

Although Jawahar Lal Nehru may be considered primarily a social and political thinker who did not take much interest in philosophy, it is an admitted fact that every thinker does formulate some philosophy of life. Nehru invariably had his own conception of the sources and means of knowledge, validity of knowledge, the limits of knowledge, spiritual philosophy, soul, God and the universe. Nehru also had his own philosophy of life. The philosophical basis of his political thought may be characterized as naturalistic humanism which assumes Nature to be everything in place of God, and even in Nature gives to man the central place, thus aiming at human welfare as the supreme end.

The humanist thinker is rational, empirical and positivist. Nehru's theory of knowledge is a blend of all these three tendencies. Being a rationalist, Nehru wanted to submit every fact of life to the test of intelligence and reason. As a result, he had greater faith in science than in religion. He was an empiricist who wanted to establish the validity of every truth. Nehru tested philosophical assumptions on the basis of reason and experience, and like the positivists arrived at the conclusion that it is useless to cogitate upon philosophical problems. He was also opposed to religion, in the accepted sense of the word. The sole focus of his faith was man, and so he formulated the religion of humanity, substituting humanity for God.

The naturalistic bias of Nehru's humanism is made explicit by his attitude towards religion. He argued that any religion which was founded on blind faith, superstition, reaction, exploitation and vested interests was an impediment to national unity. And, in fact, most of the religious sects in the world of religion possess these characteristics. That is why Nehru has consistently criticized organized religion of every kind. He also disliked mysticism because in his view it was mysterious, concerned with the other world and inclined to demand a complete suspension of rational thought. He favoured a scientific viewpoint towards religion and so he was compelled to criticize it. It is clear that Nehru's hatred for religion originated in some personal factor. His thoughts constantly reiterate the impression that some experiences in his life destroyed his faith in religion. It is reported that once, when he went to Sevagram to meet Gandhi, Smt. Kasturba Gandhi invoked divine blessings on him, praying that God may bless him with happiness. Nehru is reported to have retorted with an enquiry about where did God live. He also humourously remarked that if God really existed, then he must be living in the profoundest sleep. Such anecdotes indicate that his personal experience made him see religion as based on superstition and exploitation.

In view of these facts and ideas, Nehru was a proponent of secularism. Clarifying his views, he declared that fundamentally, he believed in the present life, the present world, not in an imaginary future world. Whether there is such a thing as the world, or whether there was a life after death or not bothered him not at all. Nehru had come to believe that the world of today had no need of religion. In fact, he felt religion had more harm than good to offer, and so the world could progress faster and further by abandoning it. Here, Nehru's views may be said to manifest naturalistic humanism. Though he is an opponent of religion, his views repeatedly manifest humanist leanings on the basis of which some scholars have tried to establish that Nehru was religious, though in his own individual and uncommon way.

In his later works, Nehru does not appear such a vehement critic of religion or God. In fact, at certain places he gives the impression of being a supporter of religion, and also of advocating a concept of a new kind of religion. In fact, Nehru did not basically oppose religion; his opposition was directed mainly at superstition and blind faith. He wanted to maintain a rational and scientific outlook on life, and consequently, he could not accept any mysterious viewpoint. So, Nehru should be seen as an opponent of blind faith or of a superstitious religion. However, Nehru felt that by supporting or instilling superstitions, religion has only obstructed human progress. In his

Autobiography, Nehru admitted that religion is unquestionably an invaluable tool which has immeasurably benefited human society. His thoughts bore the influence of the teachings of the *Gita,* one copy of which almost never left his side. Many of his intimate companions regarded him as a deeply religious man. According to Dr. Radhakrishnan, Nehru was not a religious man in the sectarian sense but he had the deepest faith in spiritual values. He was hostile to ritualism and adherence to religious dogmas, but he accepted truth and sympathy as supreme human values. If religion was regarded as a deeply faithful quest for truth in which the individual is willing to sacrifice his all, he was willing to list himself as one of the soldiers in the glorious army of religion.

Jawahar Lal Nehru did not evince any faith in any God with form, who possessed, or was, a mysterious power. However, he accepted the consciousness of the Infinite. He also admitted that human knowledge is finite. But, in spite of this, he could not bring himself to subscribe to many of the traditional beliefs of Hindu religion, such as the concept of the soul, the identity of the soul and God, etc. Yet, he was catholic enough to accept that religion does satisfy one of man's basic urges, without which it could not have been such a mighty force as it has through the ages, nor could it have granted solace to countless disturbed, agitated and restless souls, which also undoubtedly it has done. Nehru has accepted that some form of faith is essential for maintaining enthusiasm and a sense of purpose in human life. Under the influence of F.T. Brooks, he even came to have faith in Hindu religion, *Upanishads* and the *Gita.* This development was further strengthened by Gandhi's influence. Consequently, Nehru came to state that in 1921 he came nearer to religious attitude than even in his childhood. He had a very close relationship with Mata Anandmayi. All that he has stated in the tenth chapter of his *The Discovery of India* can easily be placed alongside the most intimate revelations of any deeply religious man.

INDIVIDUAL, COLLECTIVITY AND STATE

Similar to other contemporary Indian social thinkers, Jawahar Lal Nehru, too, has refuted the principles of individualism on the one hand and collectivism on the other in his conception of the relations between the individual and the collectivity. He was humanist, rationalist, empiricist and positivist thinker. He regarded man as the supreme being in Nature, and believed that man's most important trait was his reason. Most of his difference of opinion with Gandhi arose from the question of the relative importance of faith and reason. Because of his nurture in the Western traditions of thought, it was natural for Nehru to propagate the importance of the individual, because modern individualism is unquestionably a contribution of Western philosophy. According to him, the main problem facing the world was to secure a place for human individuality without endangering the existence of the state. In most modern states, centralization of authority is growing apace. In fact, the problem of the relationship between the individual and the collective whole, or between the individual and the state is, essentially, a problem of the relationship between certain rights and responsibilities. Jawahar Lal Nehru was one of the leading proponents of human rights in the modern age. In his opinion, the human individual must be given his fundamental human rights to ensure the development of his personality. He himself struggled throughout his life to secure these rights for the citizens of India and ensured the acceptance of his proposal on human rights during the Karachi convention of the Indian National Congress. However, in conformity to the ancient Indian tradition, he also believed that duties were no less important than rights. In his opinion, citizens should attach the highest possible significance to duties in modern democracies. Through his talks at various places, he tried to arouse Indian citizens to their duties.

It is clear from the foregoing analysis that, in his political thought, Jawahar Lal Nehru has attempted a synthesis of the interests of the individual and the collectivity, and the individual and the state. He has also rejected any attempt to consider any one of them as more important than the others. In this context, his ideas bear close resemblance to those of other contemporary Indian socio-political thinkers, such as Sri Aurobindo, Rabindranath, Mahatma Gandhi and M.N. Roy.

FREEDOM, LAW AND JUSTICE

Concept of Freedom

The foregoing analysis further helps in the comprehension of Nehru's views on the mutual relationship between freedom, law and justice. In any state, the question of the freedom of the citizen is of supreme importance. A state which cannot provide for the freedom of the citizen forfeits its right to their allegiance and subjection. He implied that if the government wished to establish order in the country it would have to grant constitutional freedom to the citizens.

Importance of Civic Freedom

Even after assuming office as India's first Prime Minister, Nehru remained as staunch a supporter of civil rights and civic freedom as he had been during the movement against the British government. But, as elucidated earlier, he placed equal stress on duties as natural concomitants of rights, and the importance of the rights and freedoms of others. It is clear from this that, according to Jawahar Lal Nehru, freedom is not unconditional. It also does not mean that any individual can possess the freedom to act as he wishes or chooses. Freedom does not mean that an individual can do whatever he choses, it is not an infinite or unlimited right.

The Importance of Law

In the complex social organization prevailing in all societies today, it becomes necessary to place restraints upon individual freedom through laws. To put it differently, if we want to maintain our right to civic freedom, it is necessary that we respect the identical rights of our brother citizens. If, then, the state enacts laws to ensure this respect and to harmonize the interests and freedoms of all citizens, it does not lead to a curtailment of individual freedom; instead it works to secure and safeguard such freedom. The modern welfare society makes provisions to overcome the evils resulting from society. One way of solving social problems is to obey the laws formulated by the state. However, despite the importance attached to law, Nehru has argued that laws should not be imposed on the people through the use of force. Instead, it is far better to win the faith and confidence of the people so that they may be persuaded to accept the rule of law volunatarily. In Nehru's opinion, in the absence of an adequate social awareness generated through education and suitable propaganda, permanent social reforms cannot be brought about only by making social laws and implementing them. It follows, therefore, that before enacting laws in any sphere, the people should be informed about them so that they may offer their full cooperation in their implementation. In this way, political education is of great value in a democracy. As long as adequate education cannot be provided, social laws should not be made. However, it may be necessary to enact laws to ensure the spread of education itself. Nevertheless, before implementing a social reform, the state should subject it to a constitutional study and analysis. For example, the formulation of laws pertaining to the economic sphere should be preceded by a study of the economic structure.

Punishment and Justice

The close relationship between freedom, law and justice is best seen through instances of the punishment imposed by the state for various kinds of crimes. As a humanist, Nehru believed that a criminal is evil, to a great extent because of his environment. He opines that the causes of crime involve both subjective and objective factors. It is conceivable that crime may not be completely eradicated despite social, economic and political or any other kind of reforms, because there are certain individuals who lack self-discipline and therefore inherently tend towards crime. It is dangerous in every way to allow such anti-social elements to roam unrestrained, because they threaten the peace of an organized society. Anarchy must result if such persons are not punished and restrained. Consequently, despite his humanism, Nehru accepted the utility of punishment because he admitted that society had necessarily to prevent anti-social individuals from injuring and torturing peace-loving citizens. But Nehru did not accept the retributive doctrine of justice. He appealed to have punishment made as humane as possible. Thus, in imposing punishment, the state should be motivated neither by the desire for retribution nor as a reaction, because these motives hurt both society as well as the socializing tendency of the criminal. In keeping with the contemporary level of human awareness, Nehru favoured the reformative theory of justice. He was averse to capital punishment. He considered it a form of punishment which encouraged the bestial element in human nature and society. On the other hand, he regarded life imprisonment as even more vicious than the death sentence. He does not deny the necessity of the death penalty but he wishes it to be implemented in as humane and painless a manner as possible. Being a humanist, he favours a rational and humane attitude towards the criminal. A system of stern punishment does not raise the criminals moral level, and so the criminal ought to be reformed through punishment which does not undermine his self-respect or cause him excessive torture. Because of his views, Nehru discussed at length the need for reform in prisons.

He emphatically supported the view that prisons should be, in effect, converted into hospitals, colleges or reformatory institutions. As Nehru had long, intimate and comprehensive experience of prison conditions during the British rule, his views on this question are very important.

Support to Social Justice

Jawahar Lal Nehru's concept of justice is not limited to justice in the legal sense alone. He was a vigorous supporter of social justice. He regarded untouchability as a blot on society, and declared that any nation which treats a certain section of its citizens as untouchables, necessarily suffers moral degradation and deterioration. He was a convinced proponent of human equality. He felt that all men were children of the same God, made of the same clay. So, it was wrong to erect barriers between man and man. Because of the disabilities associated with untouchability, the persons branded untouchables developed a sense of inferiority which hindered their spiritual development. That is why Nehru was opposed to disabilities of all kinds. Throughout his writings and speeches, he expressed his repulsion at the throught of untouchability. He also raised his powerful voice against economic and political inequality. He hinted that untouchability converts the Harijans into landless laboureres, and it is through an economic solution alone that the social obstacles created by tradition and customs may be obliterated.

In addition to his strong advocacy of the cause of the untouchables, Nehru also took up the cause of women and sought to ensure their emancipation. He ridiculed the purdah system and pointed out that it was evolved during the Mughal period to segregate the women. He considered it a barbaric practice. He considered its eradication a necessary precondition for bringing reform and progress to Indian social life. Apart from eradication of the purdah system, he placed great emphasis upon the education of women also. He opposed child marriage and favoured the methods of family planning.

Like the other contemporary leaders, Nehru also opposed the caste system. He spoke in favour of inter-caste marriages and elaborated the view that these should be a common system of marriage for the whole country, along with suitable provisions for divorce. He wanted women to attain a position of equality with men in all spheres of life so that, like the men, they should be able to fashion their own destiny and contribute equally to the emancipation of mankind. In this way, Nehru wanted social justice to embrace every section and every individual in society.

THE IDEAL STATE

The foregoing account of Nehru's ideas on social justice helps in a comprehension of his conception of the ideal state. He favoured state socialism, and his ideal state was a socialistic one. In a socialistic state, there is no discrimination on the basis of religion, caste, tribe, sex, economic level, education, colour, class, or on any other basis. All are given equal rights and facilities. The state treats all its citizens as equal. No activity is considered superior or interior to others. Every profession is evaluated in terms of its contribution to the social system. The prime function of the ideal state is to provide justice to all classes, therefore ensuring equality and freedom. For this, it imposes restraints on private property only to the extent that it becomes an instrument of exploitation. Consequently, it does not refute the idea of private property, it only imposes certain restraints upon it. However, the state does prevent the concentration of capital. Social change is brought about by peaceful means. The state provides for social, economic and political justices, while ensuring the least possible interference in the life of the citizens and the maintenance of the highest possible degree of freedom. In this way, Nehru's idea of an ideal state is the concept of a well-organized, socialistic welfare state.

NATURE OF GOVERNMENT

Fabianism

Because of his intimate knowledge of the various forms of government in many Eastern and Western countries, Jawahar Lal Nehru has expressed valuable opinions about the forms of government. Initially, he was influenced by Fabian socialism, and he regarded Sidney Webb's book on Russian socialism as almost a sacred text. But he gradually realised that the Fabians did not wish to transfer property to the workers, and consequently he came to call them progressive liberal rationalists.

Anarchism

Anarchism is one form of socialism according to which the state is an unnecessary evil or obstruction. It should be eradicated and its various functions performed through the medium of autonomous institutions. Jawahar Lal Nehru accepts the view that basically the anarchists propagate a philosophy that often appeals to many superior people, but because of his practical and utilitarian leaning, he cannot accept the idea of eliminating the state altogether.

Syndicalism

Like the anarchists, the proponents of Syndicalism also aim at the eradication of the state, though there is much difference between the two theories. Though both seek the eradication of the state, anarchism transfers the functions of the state to autonomous committees, whereas Syndicalism advocates that the functions and responsibilities of the state should be put into the hands of syndicates or organizations of various professions and trades. Jawahar Lal Nehru accepts the importance of the functioning of both autonomous committees as well as business syndicates, but he does not accept the view that the state should be eradicated.

Marxism

Like the other political thinkers of his age, Nehru was profoundly impressed by Marxist thought and its practical implementation in Soviet Russia. He spoke of Karl Marx as the messiah of the backward, the exploited and the deprived classes. In his philosophy of History, Nehru has broadly supported the Marxist interpretation of history, and has accepted that a historical analysis must take into account economic and material factors. Despite this, Nehru was not a Marxist. He was not prepared to accept every idea of Marx and Lenin verbatim. Neither did he favour everything that occurred in Russia, despite the profound impression that the Russian experiment made upon him. He also favoured social reform through the sublimation of the profit motive, but he adopted an impartially critical view towards Marxism, just as he did towards other philosophies. Besides, his close contact with Gandhi also made him turn away from the Marxian concept of means and ends. He was aware that Soviet Russia was a fine example of the advantages and disadvantages of a socialistic state but he did not accept that its successes and failures could be identified with those of Marxist principles. He often said that we must accept the fact that Russia had often made mistakes, and that it has often embraced violence, opportunism and autocratic methods. He favoured friendship with Russia but wished not to be associated with the violence used by that state.

Socialism

Among the various political philosophies, Nehru has distinctly praised socialism and identified himself as a socialist. Delivering an address from the chair in the convention of the Indian National Congress at Lahore in 1929, he declared that he must accept his being a socialist and democrat, that he did not believe in kings, princes or systems which gave birth to modern kings of industry, who possess far greater power to determine the destinies of common men than even erstwhile autocrats or kings possessed. When he spoke from the chair at the Lucknow convention, he declared that socialism was not merely a facile economic principle for him but a living faith which he supported with his whole heart and head. On July 8, 1945, Jawahar Lal Nehru once again prescribed socialism as the sole solution to the many economic problems facing India. Speaking at a meeting of students at Varanasi on July 17, 1950, he explicitly identified himself as a socialist. It is clear from this that Nehru saw socialism as the one possible solution to India's economic problems. He regarded socialism as the solution, not only to India's problems, but to the problems of the whole world. He made a scientific analysis of the problems facing India, and after studying concrete events, he formulated his views on means and ends. His viewpoint towards socialism was essentially scientific, but he regarded socialism, not merely as an economic theory but living philosophy of life, a new frontier of culture. In this way, he provided a comprehensive and integral analysis of socialism in which he comprehended its ethical, social, economic and other aspects. In his address to the Lahore convention of the Congress in 1929, he maintained that we should be aware that the philosophy of socialism had gradually reaped into the entire social structure throughout the world and the sole focus of controversy was the speed and the mode of its actualization.

In this way, according to Jawahar Lal Nehru, socialism has numerous aspects, but its objective is one, and that is, the establishment of a socialistic state. He wanted to adopt the techniques of Gandhi for achieving this end.

DEMOCRACY

As already stated, Nehru, in addition to being a socialist, was also a profound democrat. In his address to the students of Hindu University, he elucidated upon the qualities necessary for democracy, and said that democracy demands discipline, tolerance and mutual respect. Democracy should mean that every individual should have equality of opportunity, that is, equal opportunities for advancing in life. His attitude towards socialism and democracy was analytical and scientific. He wished to make democracy the administration of wise men rather than a government of fools. He was not willing to accept, even for a minute, that democracy implies wilfulness on the part of citizens. Thus, he has not only supported democracy, but sought to make people aware of its follies and shortcomings. He hated foolishness, and that is why he was often both saddened and angered by useless criticisms and objections often raised in the Parliament. He visualized democracy as the government of wise individuals, an administration characterized by discipline, tolerance and mutual respect, a system of working in which matters of public interest should be dealt with through persuasion and consensus of opinion. It was his opinion that a democracy was better fitted than other forms of government for protecting the interests and rights of citizens. He engaged in a profound and subtle analysis of equality, freedom and justice, and the rights relating to these, and then laid stress on their importance. His views on freedom have already been considered in detail in an earlier section.

In addition to freedom, democracy also requires equality. In Nehru's view, equality does not admit of any kind of discrimination, because exploitation, injustice, evil and falsehood are the inevitable corollaries of inequality and discrimination. It was because of his veneration of equality that he was a strong opponent of casteism and communalism. He also favoured the cause of the minorities. It was his view that it was the duty of every democracy to secure the opinion of minorities because democracy implies that steps should be taken to safeguard the rights and interests of the minorities. Finally, clarifying his views on equality in his famous document on history, *The Discovery of India,* he has used words which make it perfectly clear that his conception of equality forms the basis of his humanistic philosophy.

ETHICS AND POLITICS

Nehru disagreed with Gandhi's view that religion and politics should not be inter-linked. He favoured a worldly political theory rather than a religious one. He favoured a dissociation of religion and politics. He was also opposed to communal politics. It is clear from his views on communalism that he accepted a humanistic ethic and believed that discrimination of any kind on a religious basis was unjustified. He strongly opposed the two-nation theory. It was his considered opinion that it were the people of different religions who together composed the Indian nation. Like Gandhi he accepted the principle of non-violence, though he was less emphatic about it than Gandhi. On certain occasions, he conceded that violence used with the positive motive of eradicating an evil was justified, because he generally favoured the view that violent means should not be employed in Indian politics. It was on the issue of violence that he criticized the communistic doctrine though he regarded himself as a socialist. While the communists believe that any means which promote the cause of the revolution are justified, Nehru has lent his support to the Gandhian ethical principle that the goodness of the end alone is not enough, the means employed must also be good. It is because of this that Nehru made every conceivable effort to keep violence and hatred from permeating the national struggle in India against the British government. Even while considering means to the solution of such social evils as untouchability, crime, child marriage, the purdah system, etc., he consistently laid emphasis upon the purity of the means employed. He was profoundly antagonistic to injustice and exploitation in any form, and he had the prodoundest faith in human freedom and equality.

PRINCIPLES OF SOCIAL CHANGE

The most significant differences between Gandhi and Nehru are to be found in their respective ideas on the principles of social change. In the broadest terms, it can be said that while Gandhi was a deeply religious person, Nehru was essentially a materialist. While Gandhi's ideal was the Ram Rajya, Nehru favoured socialism, and particularly the socialism advocated by Karl Marx. Gandhi's humanism is religious while Nehru's is naturalistic. However, in Indian politics, Nehru followed in the footsteps of Gandhi, and, like him, he believed that no permanent benefit could accrue either from the use of violence of the incitement of a class conflict. In the long run, violence necessarily culminates in injustice, and such manifestations of it as world wars cause incalculable harm. A violent revolution can succeed only where the government is disorganized. Thus, like Gandhi, Nehru also abhorred the use of violent means for the establishment of a classless society, Nehru differed from Gandhi in that he, at certain places, has supported the use of violence as part of the class struggle.

On the subject of principles of social change, Nehru has been critical of Collectivism, but he has not denied its significance. He has favoured the use of constitutional means for the reform or eradication of capitalism. In collectivistic states, the collectivist government can generate public opinion favourable to its schemes for the establishment of a new social order and bring about the desired changes through peaceful means. Collectivism is a stage lying between complete bureaucratization and perfect individualism. It does not envisage the elimination of private property nor does it give licence to its acquisition. Nehru favoured peaceful change in the social system. He admitted the relevance and significance of law in political change. In the sphere of a revolution within the state, his thoughts were influenced by those of Karl Marx on one hand and those of Gandhi on the other. He has both praised and criticised these two divergent viewpoints, and adopted a utilitarian path lying between the two extremes. In addition to political change, he has laid great stress on accompanying social and economic change, and for this purpose he has suggested the use of peaceful propaganda and government provisions. Though he admired Karl Marx, Nehru wanted to attain the socialist ideal through democratic means. The objective of socialist was even with him, the establishment of a socialistic society, but the means were democratic. Thus, Nehru could not support or justify many of the happenings in Russia, though, on the whole, he was profoundly impressed by Russia's progress because, in Russia, the profit motive had been eliminated and social reconstruction achieved without it. Nehru criticized many socialist thinkers. He refused to be a blind follower of socialism. Because of his intimate contact with Gandhi he had come to believe that there could be no dichotomy between means and ends. Believing that violence cannot solve social problems despite the need for it on certain occasions, he was an opponent of violent revolution. Nevertheless, Nehru's idea, in the main, was that every objective should be achieved through peaceful means. In the particular case of India, he was convinced of the dangers of the use of violence. Marxist philosophy had deepened Nehru's insight into history but it did not convert him to Marxism.

It was his considered opinion that though Soviet Russia could provide for us an example of the advantages of a communist welfare state, other nations should seek to attain the socialistic ideal in their own individual way because, at many critical points, Russia had made dangerous errors. Means never become ends, irrespective of their importance for the goal. In their mutual relationship, it is the means which should be guided by the ends, and both should be equally pure, as far as possible.

SECULARISM

It has been stated earlier that Nehru was opposed to the intervention of religion in the sphere of politics because he upheld the concept of a material, worldly or physical nation, and believed that secularism was the correct policy. Without believing in any concrete God, he felt that faith in some invisible, omniscient entity was necessary for life. In fact, Nehru's concept of secularism did not mean negation of religion. He observed that religious functionaries often obstructed the path of national progress, and that communal leaders fanned the flames of hatred between Hindus and Muslims in the name of religion. He had himself witnessed the horrifying scenes of communal riots. Consequently, he thought that the religion that could be the cause of such violence and bloodshed should be restricted to individual faith and kept strictly away from the state and society.

EDUCATIONAL SYSTEM

Jawahar Lal Nehru has accepted education as the most important means to social change. His attitude towards education was scientific and pragmatic.

Importance of Education

Political thinkers and educational philosophers the world over admit that it is not possible to establish a democratic society successfully without an adequate and suitable system of education. Jawahar Lal Nehru was of the same opinion. In consequence, he stressed the fact that, "It is only through right education that a better order of society be built up."[1] Being a socialist, Nehru attached particular significance to the social objectives of education. According to him, "Education is the most important requisite to open up the individual."[2] "Freedom from ignorance is as essential as freedom from hunger."[3]

NATIONALISM

Indicating the significance of nationalism as a political force, which has manifested itself throughout the course of human history, Nehru has written, "In nationalism there is a virtue upto a certain stage: till then it is a progressive force adding to human freedom. But even then it is a natural that a nation

1. Nehru, J.L., *Soviet Russia*, p. 85.
2. Nehru, *Speeches*, Vol. IV.
3. *Ibid.*, p. 183.

seeking freedom like a person who is sick can think of little besides its own struggle and its own misery. And so nationalism precedes internationalism."[1]

In this way, Nehru regards nationalism as of special significance in the struggle against colonialism. In Nehru's opinion, there is an intimate relationship between colonialism and fascism; in fact, he regards the two as very nearly synonymous. In his view, fascism and colonialism are the two new forces of a degenerative capitalism. In different countries, due to national differences, they assume different forms and according to the political and economic condition, they represent the different forces of reaction. They assist each other and give rise to conflict because conflict is inherent in their very nature.

Thus, in Nehru's opinion, both colonialism and fascism are opposed to freedom and democracy. Fascism destroys all progressive elements, brings about a decline in the moral level, and thus proves as destructive as capitalism. The same is true of colonialism also. Consequently, Nehru regarded nationalism as an important weapon in the fight against both.

Criticism of Narrow Nationalism

Jawahar Lal Nehru's humanism was more profound than his nationalism, the dangers of the latter being obvious to him. Consequently, he sternly criticised narrow nationalism. He said, "Nationalism is a reactionary force to imperialism and a step which cannot be avoided in the march to real internationalism. We must be prepared to discard a narrow nationalism in favour of world cooperation and real internationalism."[2]

Despite this, Nehru felt that parochial nationalism should be checked. He argued that we should be ready to abandon our nationalism in the interests of world cooperation and true internationalism. In one of his lectures in 1938, he declared, "Lord Cecil has pointed out the dangers of intense nationalism. May I say, I entirely agree with him and though I stand for Indian Nationalism I do so on the basis of true internationalism. We in India will gladly cooperate in a world order and even agree to give up a measure of national sovereignty, in common with others, in favour of a system of collective security. But that can come only when nations associated on a basis of peace and freedom. Freedom like peace and war is indivisible. If the aggressors of today have to be checked, aggressors of yesterday have also to be called to account."[3]

Need for a Healthy Nationalism

The foregoing elaboration does not imply that Nehru was less nationalistic than the contemporary political thinkers. Like Gandhi, he clarified the significance of nationalism by arguing. "In a contest between nationalism and inter-nationalism, nationalism is bound to win. That had happened in

1. Nehru, J.L., *Discovery of India*, p. 277.
2. Nehru, J.L., *Speeches*, 23 July, 1938.
3. *Ibid.*

every country and every crisis, in a country under foreign domination, with bitter memories of continuous struggle and sufferings that was an inevitable and unavoidable consequence."[1]

He has also written in a different context, "Whenever a crisis has occurred, national considerations or what were considered to be such, have been paramount and all others which did not fit in with them have been swept away."[2]

In this way, in the opinion of Jawahar Lal Nehru, nationalism is the most powerful force for obtaining release from the slavery imposed by foreign nationals. For a nation which is the slave of another, no sentiment is higher than that of nationalism. It is also futile to talk of or expect any support for internationalism as long as a nation is in slavery. Internationalism can be thought of only after slavery has been brought to an end. Consequently, development of nationalism in the world must precede the development of internationalism, but if the latter development is to become a reality, then the faults of nationalism must be kept in mind. In a recent address he said, "We want national unity and outlook, we have to be national and we have to be proud of our nationality. At the same time, remember that this nationalism taken to excess is a dangerous thing. It is dangerous in two ways. It may take the type of nationalism which in the past had become imperialism and had dominated over other countries or it might lead to Hitlerism. Hitlerism was intense nationalism, nationalism gone wrong and becoming a danger to the world. Another case of nationalism going wrong is that people begin to look at themselves complacently and develop a kind of selfish attitude to life, thinking that they are the best in the world and have nothing to learn from others who are second or third rate countries."[3]

As has already been shown, Sri Aurobindo's views on German nationalism were almost the same.

Humanist Nationalism

The foregoing analysis makes it clear that Jawahar Lal Nehru distinguished between real nationalism and narrow nationalism, and supported the former while criticising the latter. As he argues, narrow nationalism often leads to such aberrations as colonialism, conflicts, competition and universal conflagarations such as wars. Its selfishness knows no end. In contrast the true nationalism is a stepping stone to internationalism. This was the nationalism he favoured. As he explained, "Be national, the sons and daughters of your ancient motherland working for her liberation, and be international members of the republic of youth which knows no boundaries or nationalities and work for the liberation of the world."[4]

---

1. Nehru, J.L., *Discovery of India*, p. 366.
2. *Ibid.*, p. 367.
3. Nehru, J.L., *Speeches*, July 17, 1950.
4. Nehru, J.L., *Speech*, December 12, 1928.

Addressing a meeting of students in Bengal, he declared, "Are you going, young men and women of Bengal, to dare to think and dare to act? Are you prepared to stand shoulder to shoulder with the youth of the world not only to free your own country from an insolent and alien rule but also to establish in this unhappy world a better and happier society? That is the problem before you and if you wish to face it sincerely and fearlessly, you will have to make up your mind to lean yourselves and your country of every obstacle in your path."[1] This makes it obvious that Nehru's humanism was stronger than his nationalism. Clarifying his ideas on this point he said, "You and I are Indians and to India we owe much, but we are human beings and to humanity we also owe a debt, let us be citizens of the commonwealth or Empire of youth. This is the only Empire to which we can owe allegiance for that is the dream of the future federation of the world."[2]

Uniting this humanism with the Indian national tradition, he explained, "It was India's way in the past to welcome and honour other cultures. That is much more necessary today, for we march to the one world of tomorrow where national cultures will be mingled with the international culture of the human race. We are therefore, to seek wisdom and knowledge and friendship and comradeship wherever we can find them and cooperate with others in common tasks, we are not to aspire for others favours or patronage. Thus, we shall remain true Indians and Asiatics and become at the same time good internationalists and good citizens."[3]

In his status as one of the enlightened commentators on the history of the world, Nehru demonstrated that the emergence of nationalism throughout the world in the twentieth century is a very significant event, which forms an important step to the growth of world unity. Nationalism emerged in almost each country as a result of the two world wars. This fact should not be treated as now belonging to antiquity. Its significance should be respected.

Fundamental Elements of a Nation

As a political thinker, Nehru cogitated upon the elements that constitute a nation. He admitted the significance of national unity, and considered the factors that contribute to its growth. But he wanted national unity to be an internal growth rather than a sentiment thrust upon individuals by force. The basis of the sentiment of nationality is the national culture in which language and religion play a very important part. Consequently, Jawahar Lal Nehru favoured the development of a national language which should be the language of the common man, but he did not deny the importance of the regional languages. Along with the growth of the national language, the languages of the various regions should be protected just as the culture of the minorities is to be safeguarded. He was in favour of developing Hindustani, a combination of Hindi and Urdu as the national language.

1. *Ibid.*, p. 40.
2. *Ibid.*
3. Nehru., J.L., *Discovery of India*, p. 500.

Rejection of Dual Nationalism

While Nehru argued that a common culture is necessary for national unity, he did not accept that a common religion is also important. In the sphere of religion, he adopted a scientific, practical and mundane approach. Because of this, he was severely critical of the concept of a Hindu nation propagated by the Hindu Maha Sabha on the one side, and Muslim nationalism advocated by the Muslim League on the other. He was the severest critic of the political theory of dual nationalism. He said, "Real disunity seeps in from the communal side and we must recognise that there is an ideology fostered for the principal communal organizations which cut at the root of national unity. Yet I do not think that this ideology has affected to any large extent even the members of the organizations. As soon as there is an improvement in the communal atmosphere, this way of thinking will probably fade out."

Nehru was convinced that the religious differences between Hindus and Muslims would not have serious consequences for national unity. He reputed the idea that there were two nations in India. He clearly said that not only did he have firm faith in the possibility of establishing an integrated nation, but also that in a fundamental form, from the cultural viewpoint, such a nation already existed. Jawahar Lal Nehru saw economic factors as being the root cause of communal riots.

Criticism of Communalism

It can be said that, in this communal conflict, Nehru held the Hindus more to blame than the Muslims because he believed that Hindus were in a majority and more progressive than Muslims, and consequently it was their responsibility to do away with communalism. This is correct, but Nehru also forgot that any less civilized or backward community cannot progress and attain a higher level unless it has the will to do so. This explains why the intensity of communalism in the country did not decline despite the vigorous efforts of both Nehru and Gandhi. In fact, the lowest level from which Nehru wanted to eradicate communalism was the level at which the Muslims were in a majority and they did not regard communalism as an economic problem, a fact that Nehru was himself compelled to admit. Despite the unceasing efforts of Gandhi and Nehru, communalism continued to grow in this country, and this proves that Nehru's interpretation of communalism and the solutions he suggested were both ineffective. In his letter of October 18, 1939 addressed to Mohammed Ali Jinnah, Nehru was constrained to admit that he had failed to understand the problem of communalism, and so he had no concrete solution to offer. Consequently, the country was divided, as a result of which very large number of Muslims left India for Pakistan while Hindus in even larger number migrated from Pakistan to India. Although Nehru admitted his failure to comprehend the problem of communalism, he misguidedly assumed later on, when he became the country's Prime Minister, that he had finally come to comprehend it. But now, after the departure of Nehru, the

Muslim League has once again fomented Muslim communalism with great vigour. This makes it clear that the solutions that Gandhi and Nehru had suggested for communalism were not sufficient.

INTERNATIONALISM

The preceding analysis makes it apparent that Nehru regarded nationalism not as an end in itself, but as just a step towards the goal of internationalism. Thus, he harmonized the two concepts. Nationalism grows into internationalism. Nehru rejected the view that internationalism hinders the growth of a nationalist sentiment. The truth of Jawahar Lal Nehru's views can be seen in the history of the twentieth century. Today, not merely the slave nations but even independent nations consider nationalisms as the final criterion because of which the stronger nations are engaged in arms race. The world is split into two contending blocs. Hence, it is not appropriate to say that the era of nationalism is over, but as Nehru made clear, this same nationalism will ultimately lead to internationalism.

Foreign Policy

In order to understand Nehru's views on internationalism, it is necessary to analyse his foreign policy also. As in the case of the nation, in the sphere of internationalism, too, Nehru laid great stress on synthesis, harmony, cooperation and peace. For this, conflict and struggle must be replaced by harmony in the sphere of international relations. Nations should abandon their colonialist aims and substitute democratic goals for them instead.

Nehru was no less critical of capitalism than he was of colonialism. It is for this reason that he did not want India to take the help of any capitalist, fascist or colonialist nation in its struggle for freedom. It is on this point that he disagreed with Subhas Bose.

Emphasis on the Development of Backward Nations

If internationalism is to develop, then political cooperation must be accompanied by the development of backward and poor countries, because, prosperity, like peace, must be established everywhere if it is to exist anywhere. On October 27, 1949, in Chicago, Nehru declared, that even the supremely powerful nation must remember that if it leaves the poor nations to wallow in their poverty and suffer, these nations can become the cause of its ultimate downfall. Consequently, the prosperous nations should extend their best help to the economically backward nations.

Efforts for World Peace

In addition to his profound nationalism, Nehru maintained as unshakable faith in the glorious future of the human race and in internationalism. He advised all the nations of the world to strive for the establishment of world peace. The theory thereby expounded was the Gandhian lesson of moral struggle, which inspired Nehru throughout the period that he led the Indian National Congress.

Non-Alignment

Jawahar Lal Nehru maintained that the world could escape another world war only by following Gandhi's principle of non-violence. The same principle formed the backbone of Nehru's policy of non-alignment, which thought in terms of harmony and peaceful cooperation between nations. On the basis of this policy, every effort was made to avoid being aligned with any power bloc and to act as a mediator between the two major power blocs. Even when the nation had to pay a price for remaining non-aligned from any power bloc by sacrificing some vital national interest, Nehru favoured this rather than sacrificing the principle of non-alignment, so as to maintain the thrust towards true internationalism. However, this non-alignment was not intended to imply alienation. Thus, in Nehru's opinion, if there is a danger to a nation's independence, it may be desirable to enter into some kind of agreement or pact, but otherwise a nation should remain non-aligned and make every effort to create harmony between the different power blocs. Nehru's ingrained internationalism is most clearly manifested in his concept of Panchsheel. Most of the non-aligned nations of Asia welcomed this policy, although it could not be implemented to the extent desirable. Nehru's internationalism was founded on his humanistic philosophy. He stressed that peace and happiness should be promoted everywhere in the world through mutual cooperation, goodwill, liberty, equality and fraternity. He was a rationalist democratic thinker who had implicit faith in science. Like the positivists he believed that science can help us to make this world better. Consequently, he insisted on the establishment of large industries along with small industries as a means to eradicating India's age-old poverty. His secular, naturalistic humanism, which can also be labelled scientific humanism, was the basis of his entire political thinking.

21
M.N. Roy (1887 — 1954)

Born in West Bengal in 1887, M.N. Roy joined Bengal Revolutionary Movement in his teens. He delved deep into the philosophy of Karl Marx and rubbed shoulders with some of the greatest Marxists of contemporary history. He founded the Communist Party in Mexico in 1918. He remained a member of the presidium and secretariat of the Communist International. He also remained in-charge, training and organisation of Asiatic communists in Eastern University of Moscow. For some time he was Chief Adviser of the Communist Party of China. In 1928, he developed serious differences with communist International and returned to India.

Lenin described M.N. Roy as "the symbol of revolution in the East." In view of the existing conditions in the world, the future of humanity appeared to be gloomy. But Roy made a call to all lovers of peace and human values not to develop feelings of helplessness but to fight with unity and determination for human freedom. In his personality and ideas, Roy combined the value of freedom with firmness of commitment. With a remarkable open-mindedness and capacity to absorb new ideas Roy tried to learn from the record of human experiences.

Among the modern Indian thinkers, Manabendra Nath Roy was more a philosopher than a mass leader. He was, essentially, one of the greatest thinkers of the twentieth century and truly a citizen of the world. His philosophy may be described as a mid-twentieth century version of the Renaissance modified and enriched by the experience of the intervening centuries. He was least concerned about himself and most of his life suffered due to an honest and straightforward approach to different national and international problems. His chief concern was to realise freedom for himself and for others.

INFLUENCES

As already discussed, Roy was a born revolutionary. His revolutionary career started when he was hardly 14 years of age. On him was the most significant influence of Marxian philosophy, which he studied very thoroughly and which remained virtually the basis of his subsequent ideology though he differed from it in detail. In addition to this he was inspired by social and political leaders of Indian life. He was educated in the national schools and as such the movements started by Swami Ram Tirth and Swami Vivekanand reminding Indians of their supremacy and past cultural glory very much influenced him. Similarly, Roy was inspired by those national leaders who worked through the forum of Indian National Congress and devoted themselves to this national struggle. Great on him, was the influence of Bankim Chandra Chatterji who wrote his famous *Ananda Math*. Then we find that Roy was absolutely dissatisfied with the methods through which the Britishers tried to exploit the Indians and denied individual rights and liberties. From his very early age the growing poverty of India was an eye-sore for him and freedom, both national and individual, was the only solution to the problem. He was very much influenced by the revolutionaries who devoted themselves thoroughly in undoing the evils of partition of Bengal and were determined to revoke the action. He found that Swadeshi and boycott programmes were active and a realistic approach to Indian political problems. On the international field the victory of Japan over mighty Russia in 1905 was a great moulding and motivating factor on him. He gained confidence that colonial subjects in Asia, including India, could also win their freedom if they had determination and proper organization.

WORKS

Roy wrote sufficient to leave back his political philosophy. Some of his significant works are : 1. *India in Transition;* 2. *Revolution and Counter-Revolution in China;* 3. *Our Differences;* 4. *Materialism;* 5. *Science and Philosophy;* 6. *On the Congress Constitution;* 7. *People's Plan;* 8. *National Government People's Government;* 9. *Rise, Romanticism and Revolution.* In addition to this Roy contributed very many articles in various papers and was responsible for establishing his own journals through which he tried to propagate his ideas and philosophy.

M.N. Roy was sufficiently under the influence of Communism and basically adhered to that philosophy though he differed from Marx in details. As the time passed his faith in individual freedom increased and he also came to the conclusion that Communism provided no solution to individual liberty. He developed his own philosophy which he called Radical Humanism and for which he wanted everyone to have an independent nature and character.

PHILOSOPHICAL BACKGROUND

According to M.N. Roy, individual was an end in itself and every other organization in the society was simply means to an end. He pleaded that everything was below individual freedom which should not be subordinated to anything else. He was not ready to subordinate individual freedom even to religion or morality or to any other supernatural power. He believed that man had always been struggling for freedom and his joining the civil state and society was only on the condition that his freedom would be protected. In his opinion it was an evolutionary process and history was a witness that man always struggled to preserve his freedom. If at any stage there was threat to his freedom man faced that very boldly and tried to preserve that. He went on saying that those institutions and organizations which had been set up to safeguard individual freedom often have tried to master him and that was quite unhealthy. In his opinion, state was primarily brought into being to check all impediments and hindrances which checked the growth of man but today the state was trying to subordinate individuals and wanted to become an end in itself instead of being means to an end. Similarly religion had become the master of man's mind and tried to check individual freedom though gradually its grip was weakening.

According to M.N. Roy by nature man loves freedom. With regard to human nature he was rather close to Rousseau who said that man was born free and everywhere he was in chains. In his opinion man was governed by the same principle as physical sciences and in fact there was no basic difference between the two. He, however, distinguished between the two on the basis of rationalism. In his philosophy man was rational and as such above all the other living beings. Rationalism was the most essential and basic standard of human development. He also believed that as against man in the physical beings there was no option of making choice. In his own words, "*It is the reason in man which harmonizes the people of human will with the law governess of physical universe.*"

CONTEMPORARY MORAL CRISIS

In twentieth century most of the philosophers of history in East and West drew attention to the moral crisis in human society and warned of the danger. This danger was clearly seen in the 2nd World War which occurred in spite of all the attempts of the League of Nations. Thoughtful persons everywhere realised that the development of atomic power has led humanity to a stage where even its existence is at stake. From Sri Aurobindo to Sorokin, the philosophers of history pointed out that human race is passing through a critical stage whose problems require an urgent solution. Thus, the consciousness of crisis was almost universal. However, different thinkers analysed its causes differently and suggested different remedies. As has been already pointed out, Sri Aurobindo considered the rational dualism as the main cause of the present crisis and advised to evolve to suprarational level. Admitting the crisis, M.N. Roy explained it differently. In contrast to Sri Aurobindo, the present crisis according to him, is not due to rationality but because of its absence. Therefore, the solution of the crisis is not to rise above reason but to be rational. This solution has been supported by most of the contemporary Western social thinkers including Bertrand Russell and Karl Marx. According to Roy, our present crisis is moral in nature and due to crisis of values. The civilised human society today faces unprecedented social problems. Just as Buddhism in India criticised traditional religion and presented a scientific attitude which was later on over-shadowed by the *Mayavada* of Samkara, similarly the rational consciousness started due to progress of science in twentieth century was soon overpowered by Neo-mysticism characteristic of so many contemporary social theories. This Neo-mysticism has led to man's forgetting of his real nature, the nature of the physical world and man's status in cosmos. According to Roy the contemporary crisis is due to the confusion of intellectual methods. The sensitive persons may feel this crisis everywhere. Though most of the people want liberty one nowhere witnesses real freedom. Though most of the people want peace yet the clouds of wars are hovering everywhere. At this juncture, "What is needed is a restatement of Materialism so as to recognise explicitly the decisive importance of the dynamics of ideas in all the processes of human evolution — historical, social, political and cultural."[1]

M.N. Roy analysed the present crisis and tried to unravel its reasons. His analysis is based upon reason and experience of the entire human race. He pointed out defects and inadequacies of ancient Indian solutions of the present difficulties.[2] According to the old philosophy it is not potent enough to save us in the present crisis. The crisis itself exhibits the facts the traditional social, political and economic thinking is no more capable to guide us. All these interpretations were dualistic, unscientific and traditional, confined to some specialists. Therefore, Roy concluded that "Philosophy can answer this question only in the light of scientific knowledge."[3]

Pointing out the failures of past philosophies M.N. Roy arrived at what he calls Radical Humanism, which, according to him, is the only solution of the present day difficulties being faced by human society. This avowed social thought of M.N. Roy will be critically examined in this chapter. This is a whole system including epistemology, metaphysics and exiology. The epistemological and the metaphysical background of M.N. Roy's social thought should be understood in order to understand it more fully.

EPISTEMOLOGICAL FOUNDATIONS

M.N. Roy calls his theory of knowledge scientific. He starts with a critical evaluation of the traditional empiricist and rationalist theories of knowledge in the west and concludes like Immanual Kant, "Knowledge is possible because there is a causal connection between mind and matter."'[4] Ideas, according to him, are representative of realities only if they are based upon experience. Thus, knowledge is the result of perception. "We know things, not ideas."[5] The validity of any idea may be examined by putting it to practical test. The epistemology of the British empiricist philosophers is a one-sided

---

1. Roy, M.N., *Reason, Romanticism and Revolution,* Vol. I. Renaissance Publishers Ltd., Cal., 1952, p. 11.
2. Roy, M.N., *Politics, Power and Parties,* Renaissance Publishers Ltd., Cal., 1960, p. 6.
3. *Ibid.*
4. *Ibid.*
5. *Ibid.*

theory. Further, the ideas must change according to the knowledge of the world. Roy distinguishes between things and objects and concludes, "Ideas correspond not with things, but with objects."[1]

RADICAL HUMANISM

Thus, according to Roy, as according to the Greek philosopher Protagoras man is measure of all things. He agrees with Karl Marx that the individual is the basic unit of human society. Therefore, he aims at the foundation of a corporate society of free individuals. Distinguishing this humanism from other brands of humanism, Roy has called it scientific humanism, new humanism or radical humanism. His humanism is different by being radical. This radicalism however, is different from the ealier Western radicalism which was collectivist. Radical humanism of M.N. Roy is individualist. According to Roy, "Radical Humanism says nothing new when it demands that man must be the measure of everything. Protagoras made the declaration more than 2500 years ago. Yet, mankind seems to have forgotten its soul. The same liberating principle was repeated by Karl Marx, who is today honoured as the prophet of proletarian dictatorship, the advocates of which fanatically demand sacrifice of the individual at the altar of an imaginery collective ego."[2] Suggesting a new constitution for free India Roy declared that in it political power will directly belong to the public which will include every adult individual. He accepted the contribution of M.K. Gandhi to Indian politics though he very much differed from Gandhian thought. Explaining his philosophical and scientific attitude concerning other social theories Roy laid down, "I am not a blind follower of anybody. I do not take anything for granted. Before I accept any doctrine, I submit it to a critical analysis, which is to test the consistency of its internal logic. If I find it self-contradictory, I have no hesitation in rejecting it however exalted may be the authority. But in the process of the analytical examination, the behaviour of certain persons, or a certain doctrine may reveal certain positive features which must be retained and admired even when the claims of the person and the doctrine as a whole, are to be rejected."[3]

As has been already pointed out, Radical humanism gives special status to science. The philosophy of Roy however, may be called integral. Laying down the principle twentyone of radical humanism, Roy said, "Radicalism integrates science into social organisation and reconciles individuality with collective life; it gives to freedom a moral intellectual as well as a social content; it offers a comprehensive theory of social progress in which both the dialectics of economic determinism and dynamics of ideas find their due recognition; and it deduces from the same a method and a programme

---

1. *Ibid.*
2. Roy, M.N., *Radical Humanism,* Eastern Economic Pamphelets, No. 14, pp. 5-6.
3. Roy, M.N., *Men I Met,* Lalwani Publishing House, Delhi, 1968, pp. 26-27.

of social revolution in our time."[1] Against Marxism, Roy rejects economic determinism and dictatorship though he accepts materialism.

THE HUMAN NATURE

Roy has explained human nature with reference to anthropology, biology, psychology and epistemology. He accepts unlimited possibility of change in human nature though it is determined by biological laws. According to Roy, "To change is human nature." There is a causal spiritual evolution manifested. Therefore, the first purpose of a social organisation is to provide means of the satisfaction of physical needs to each of its members. After it one needs the cultural and educational institutions. The political institutions also aim at the satisfaction of the individuals urge to liberty since in the absence of state power no individual can himself protect his liberty. Therefore, political organisation is necessary though its sole purpose is to protect every citizen against the onslaughts of other individuals, communities and nations. The functions of state however are not unlimited. The greatest significance of human being in nature is due to his rationality. Reason has led to the birth of both the society and the state. Therefore the society and the state must preserve this rationality, this liberty of judgement. This requires peaceful conditions of physical existence. Therefore, the state should leave its citizens free to pursue the possibilities of their physical welfare as well as rational evolution. In fact whenever the origin of the state has been explained with reference to Divine and its laws held as divine rules it has led to the negation of all human liberty. If every human being is capable of rational judgement and the purpose of society is to help him in so doing, there is hardly any difficulty in cooperation between the individual and the group. This, however, requires negation of the habit to interpret human problems with reference to superhuman agencies. Therefore, M.N. Roy has rejected religious solutions of social problems and advised adoption of a scientific attitude.

SOCIAL ETHICS

Radical humanism is chiefly a moral system. According to M.N. Roy the only criterion of social ethics is the human being himself. Moral problems may be solved with reference to humanism. This social organisation aims at the moral development of each of the individual. On the other hand, only good individuals may form a good society. Only rational individuals constitute a rational society. Free individuals alone can build up a free society. Physical or economic process is no scale of the superiority of an individual. The only criterion of excellence is the moral development. Therefore, social reformation requires moral regeneration of the individuals.

---

1. Roy, M.N., *New Humanism*, p. 59.

Liberty as the *summum-bonum*

The *summum-bonum* of radical humanist ethics is the liberty. As has been already pointed out, the only purpose of the society and the state, according to Roy, is the provision of maximum liberty to the individual. In the last week of December 1946, M.N. Roy presented the fundamental principles of *New Humanism* in the Bombay session of Radical Democratic Party. These principles were presented in the form of a Manifesto including 22 principles. These principles distinguish the new humanism from communism on the one hand and nationalism on the other. Roy has presented different aspects of the central principle of human liberty in these principles of humanism. According to the principle Two, "The quest for freedom is the continuation, on a higher level, of intelligence and emotion, of the biological struggle for existence."[1] According to Roy theories of moral standard are based upon the false idea that man's aim may be outside him. Radical humanism bases ethics on its roots *i.e.*, human reason.

M.N. Roy is against relativism in ethics, whether it may be Utilitarian or Marxist. He said, "While the ethical relativism of the Utilitarians was rational, Marxian relativism, notwithstanding its appearance, is dogmatic, being a projection in the future of the Hegelian moral positivism."[2] The Marxist makes the survival of the fittest the basis of ethics. According to Karl Marx there is no ultimate standard of ethics since ethics is relative to class. This takes us to a moral vacuum. Here Marx does not advance upon Hegel. This fact may be seen in the behaviour of the rulers of communist countries where communist revolution has degenerated into communist dictatorship. Therefore, Marxist solution of moral questions is far from being adequate. It may be remembered here that M.N. Roy has mostly criticised the Russian version of Marxism. Elsewhere he has accepted Marxism as a humanist philosophy supporting reason and liberty and trying to establish individual freedom on earth. Therefore, Roy admits the value of liberal application of Marxist philosophy.

POLITICAL THOUGHT

As has been already pointed out, Roy does not authorise the state to curb human liberty. He does not accept the theory of divine origin of the state or the social contract theory. Both these theories undermine the liberty of the individual. On the other hand if we believe that every human being is capable of rational judgement there will be hardly any difficulty in the establishment of a democratic state. The democratic state is the ideal state in the political thought of M.N. Roy. It should aim at providing maximum liberty to each of the citizen and minimising all checks and impediments in it. Therefore, an ideal state requires more and more decentralization of power. Authority

---

1. Roy M. N., *New Humanism*, p. 51.
2. *Ibid.*, p. 20.

from the state should be delegated to the public bodies. The citizens should directly participate in the functions of the state through the organisation of public bodies. Elections are held directly. The political, economic and social rights are safeguarded. Citizens are provided proper and sufficient education. The formation of the state is based upon the public reason. The ideal state has been called radical democratic state. In it no one tries to grab power. It is a government of the public for the public. The rulers are free men and women who perform the functions of state on cooperative basis as the friend and guide of the public. Describing his ideal state Roy said, "The Radical Democratic State will be the school for the political and civic education of the citizen. Its structure and function will enable detached individuals to come to the forefront of public affairs. Manned with such individuals, the State will no longer be the Leviathan, always to be dreaded and distrusted."[1]

Liberty and Law

According to M.N. Roy, "The function of a revolutionary and liberating social philosophy is to lay emphasis on the basic fact of history that man is the maker of his world man as a thinking being, and he can be so only as an individual."[2] Thus, in place of parliamentary democracy Roy proposes an organised democracy in which every citizen may directly participate in the government. That is the only way to maintain the liberty of the citizens. It is then alone that a real democracy may be established. In the words of Roy, "To make democracy effective, power must always remain vested in the people, and there must be ways and means for the people to wield the sovereign power effectively, not periodically, but from day-to-day."[3] Thus, according to Roy, laws of the state should be formulated in such a way as to create minimum restriction in human liberties. He did not agree with the Marxist ideal of a stateless society. The state according to him is a means of public welfare selected by human beings themsleves. Therefore, the question of its withering away does not arise. The state has to perform those functions for which it has been created. Its most important function is to guarantee maximum freedom to the citizen. This requires establishment of democratic administration. A totalitarian state is no state in the real sense of the term. Like capitalist state it is an instrument of exploitation. These forms of the state are not rational. Organised democracy or radical democracy is the only alternative. Clarifying its nature in the eighteenth principle of radical humanism Roy said, "The new society, being founded on reason and science, will necessarily be planned. But it will be planning with the freedom of the individual as its main purpose."[4] In a planned nation the citizens should be first of all liberated from economic needs. After it they may be trained

1. *Ibid.*, p. 36.
2. *Ibid.*, p. 53.
3. *Ibid.*, p. 55.
4. *Ibid.*, p. 58.

to live free cooperative life. This is the meaning of the rennaissance. In the words of Roy, "A social renaissance can come only through determined and widespread endeavour to educate the people as regards the principles of freedom and rational co operative living."[1]

Concept of social justice

As in society so in state the standard of justice is liberty. The amount of liberty determines the amount of social justice. This may be provided by those administrators who are themselves free human beings. According to the twentieth principle of radical humanism, "Only spiritually free individuals in power can smash all chains of slavery and usher in freedom for all."[2] The other condition of provision of social justice is maximum decentralisation. In the words of Roy, "Realising that freedom is inconsistent with concentration of power, Radical Democrats will aim at the widest diffusion of power."[3] Thus the aim of social justice may be achieved by providing opportunity to fulfil his role to every individual citizen in the state. Roy calls it scientific concept of society. Thus, the final aim is the establishment of an ideal human world based upon freternity of free human beings pursuing spiritual and moral development through mutual cooperation.

Secular State

M.N. Roy agrees with Karl Marx in the condemnation of religion and religious institutions as increasing superstitions and backwardness. Therefore, he has supported secular state and secular politics. He calls synthetic approach to religion as irrelevant. His views about religion are similar to that of J.L. Nehru. In fact secularism in India has been interpreted in two different senses. On the one hand Nehru and Roy interpreted it as the negation of religion. On the other hand, Vivekanand, Sri Aurobindo, Rabindra Nath and M.K. Gandhi along with other contemporary Indian social thinkers talked of synthetic attitude to religion in order to maintain religious harmony in the multi-religious Indian society. While the former standpoint has been borrowed from the West, the latter represents the traditional Indian view. It is hence that the latter has been given general acceptance.

Forms of Government

During the period of M.N. Roy the world was mostly governed by two forms of government, socialist of communist state or the parliamentary democracy. Parlimentary democracy was generally found in capitalist nations following the policy of *laissez faire*. On the other hand in the communist nations the government was in the hands of the representatives of proletariate dictatorship. Most of the new free nations opted for parliamentary democracy. Some other

1. *Ibid.*, pp. 56-57.
2. *Ibid.*, p. 59.
3. *Ibid.*, p. 58.

nations are governed by fascist type of government. M.N. Roy discussed and evaluated all these forms of government on the basis of the standard of provision of maximum liberty to the citizen.

Criticism of Dictatorship

Arguing against dictatorship Roy said, "Dictatorship of any form, however plausible may be the pretext for it, is excluded by the Radical Humanist perspective of social evolution."[1] The means should be as much pure as the end in the politics. Therefore, Roy was a bitter critic of U.S.S.R. where means have become irrelevant in themselves. The state according to Roy, is a means for providing liberty of the citizen, it is never end in itself. It has been created to defend freedom. Marx hoped that the state will ultimately whither away, but this did not happen in communist nations. In U.S.S.R. there is no other political party except the communist party. Therefore, there is no possibility of achievement of freedom or diminition of the state power.

Evaluation of Parliamentary Democracy

In West, particularly in U.S.A., parlimentary democracy rules. This is also not humanist since the majority forming the government does not act rationally. According to Roy the value of a political party does not lie in its success in vote catching but in its principles and programmes. The public should not vote a political party simply on the basis of promises made by it. In a so-called democracy where the government is elected by counting of heads, there is no role of the individual and the reason. Ultimately it degenerates into collectivity. On the other hand a nation in which reason, ability and moral excellence are not given any importance cannot arrive at an ideal state. Both dictatorship and parliamentary democracy do not find place for human values. Therefore, Roy suggests that a proper form of government can be established only on the basis of achievement of human freedom as the aim. This aim cannot be achieved by dictatorship or formal democracy. In the words of M.N. Roy, "Thus, Between formal democracy and dictatorship, humanity is deprived of the benefit of having its affairs conducted by spiritually free individuals, and it consequently debarred from advancing towards the goal of freedom."[2] Therefore, Roy suggests, "Man must again be the measure of all things. Intelligence, integrity, wisdom, moral excellence, should be the test of leadership."[3]

Political and Economic Democracy

It is not easy to establish a real democracy. It aims at all types of freedom not only political. In the words of Roy, "In modern society, an individual, to be free, must not only be able to enjoy economic sufficiency and security, but

1. *Ibid.*, p. 40.
2. *Ibid.*, p. 41.
3. *Ibid.*

live in a social psychological atmosphere free from cultural regimentation and helpful to the development of his intellectual and other human potentialities."[1] Thus, integral freedom can be achieved in a real democracy. Clarifying this ideal Roy said, "The function of social relationships should be to secure for individuals, as individuals, the maximum measure of freedom."[2] The standard of excellence of a state is the amount of liberty given to the citizen. A society which does not give sufficient value to individual liberty cannot do any good to him. According to Roy, "The purpose of all rational human endeavour, collective as well as individual, should be the attainment of freedom in ever larger measure, and freedom is real only as individual freedom."[3] Thus, political freedom is insufficient without economic freedom since the two are interdependent. In the words of Roy, "Economic democracy is no more possible in the absence of political democracy than the latter is in the absence of the former."[4] It is hence that modern democracies aim at economic development. Here Roy supports industrialisation but like M.K. Gandhi, warns against man's subordination to machines.

Conditions of Success of Democracy

According to Roy, "The fundamental democratic principle — the greatest good to the greatest number — can be realised only when the conduct of public affairs will be in-charge of spiritually free individuals who represent their own conscience before anybody or anything else."[5] Ideal democracy is based upon real human values. Its sanction is not the support of majority but the administration of spiritually free individuals. In the words of Roy, "Values operate through individuals. Therefore, a government composed of spiritually free individuals, accountable, in the first place, to their respective conscience, is the only possible guarantee for securing the greatest good to the greatest number."[6] This does not mean that the government should be run by intellectuals. It only means that there should be unlimited opportunity of the expression of genius in society and this is possible only when the administrators are rational and free. A true democracy cannot be established by elections. Parliamentary democracy is generally a formal government. According to Roy, "Government for the people can never be fully a government of the people and by the people."[7] This requires organisation of local democracies so that the public may be aware of the democratic values. These local democracies should be authorised to call back their representatives. They may be allowed to nominate candidates for elections.

1. *Ibid.*, p. 37.
2. *Ibid.*, 38.
3. *Ibid.*, p. 39.
4. *Ibid.*
5. *Ibid.*, p. 52.
6. *Ibid.*
7. *Ibid.*, p. 43.

Thus, democracy should be above political party. Individuals should be identified by their own genius and not by their political parties. Therefore, Roy advises for decentralisation of power. This proportionately increases the possibility of freedom. Decentralisation however, does not eliminate cooperation, however difficult it may be M.N. Roy has presented his theory of Radical Democratic State as a constitution proposed for free India.

Criticism of Party Politics

M.N. Roy advocates politics without power. He criticises party politics. The true aim of democratic politics is not grabing of power but providing maximum freedom to the individuals. Born in fifteenth and sixteenth century democratic political ideology prospered in several countries in 18th and 19th centuries. In 20th century modern democracy was born out of the ideal of individual freedom. This, according to Roy, is the real democracy. It cannot be established by a king, a group of aristocrats or some political leaders. It is born out of the public itself. In it the power resides in the citizen and he does not delegate it to anyone else. This humanist politics is politics without power which aims not only at power but on freedom. Roy was a bitter critic of party politics. Politics, according to him, is a social need since no society can run without a political organisation. Thus, if ancient politics has failed, a new politics will have to be born. The political ideologies presented so far are basically totalitarian and give not much liberty to the individual. According to Roy, a good society cannot be established without the member's discretion of right and wrong. Roy has postulated an ideal state free from all types of corruption which is the biggest bane of modern democracy. He presented the idea of radical democracy in the form of a manifesto including 22 principles. These principles are the foundations of ideal democracy, different from dictatorship on the one hand and parliamentary democracy on the other.

Value of Fundamental Human Rights

India was given a new constitution after achievement of freedom. Indian Constitution is almost the biggest in the world. Criticising it Roy has maintained that it has given very little place to fundamental human rights. Roy was not very hopeful about the future of democracy in India since the Indian public opinion is still basically dictatorial or collectivist. According to Roy, the first and foremost condition of the success of democracy is to create faith in democratic values. Democratic attitude is against spiritual slavery which is found in abundance in India in the form of traditionalism. Explaining his radical democracy, Roy maintained that it starts from the ideal of human life which is always an end and never a means. Parliamentary democracy is a formal democracy. Formality is its biggest evil. The value of freedom is considerably undermined by party system in a democracy. While counting the heads the contents of the heads are forgotten. If the heads have no purpose in them, the majority vote will ultimately mean major quantity of ignorance. Roy pointed out the widespread superstitions, traditionalism and spiritual slavery in Indian masses.

Politics and Ethics

Roy has explained his idea of the relationship of politics and ethics in *The Radical Humanist* journal dated 2nd March, 1952. He analysed right and left, traditional and liberal, reactionary and revolutionary political ideologies and demonstrated that these different political ideologies do not differ in practice since all aim at access to power. This blind race to power has resulted in the degeneration of social life. A cause of this degeneration is the absence of a proper political theory. Such a political theory has been claimed to be presented by Roy in the form of radical democracy. According to it moral individuals alone constitute a moral society. The principle of economic determinism of the socialist has led to elimination of individual liberty in collectivist state. Socialism and communism equally negate individual freedom. Liberal social philosophy failed in the absence of proper moral basis. It rightly admitted that man is fundamentally moral and the origin of all power but it limited moral sense to religious faith which meant subordination of man to a superhuman power. Roy is equally against traditional religious ethics of West and East. This spiritual slavery is an impediment in liberty. The struggle against determinism is not possible by spiritual slavery. Liberalism was a result of this conflict. French revolution opposed liberalism. Natural religion was against materialism and deduced morality from a supramoral system. The ethics of nineteenth century was transcendental. The liberal social thinkers proposed the principle of utilitarianism in ethics. According to Roy, both these have created confusion in human values. Collectivist politics finds no place for man. Ethics itself should be based on sound foundation to provide a basis for social theory and political practice.

It has been wrongly believed that man cannot be self-dependent and cannot be moral without external sanctions. The revolutionary social philosophy however, believes that man is essentially free. The scientific materialism of eighteenth century was a step in right direction since it rejected creation of the earth by God. Man, according to naturalism, is a product of nature. Many of the researches in biology in nineteenth century supported rationality in man. Many researches in physical sciences in 19th century proved against many concepts of scientific naturalism. This has led to a mysticism laying emphasis upon epistemology. Psychology propagated irrationalism by condemning reason. Therefore one finds everywhere a spate of irrational tendencies. This moral crisis can be solved only by a moral philosophy based upon reason in man. Modern science accepts the proposition that man has evolved reason in the biological process. Modern age is in need of a social philosophy which bases public life on ethics. So far as opposition of authoritarianism is concerned, it is found in almost every society. Most of the political parties talk of a classless society even though based upon capitalist support. Even the industrialists have started swearing by socialism. This at least shows that morality is the demand from all corners. It has been accepted that means and ends both must be humanised. On the question of relationship of means and end, Roy supports M.K. Gandhi in place of Karl Marx. According to him a lower means cannot help in reaching a high end. Therefore, like M.K. Gandhi he supported coordination of ethics and politics. The world is a moral order following definite rules. In this background ethics should be based on human principles and solid metaphysics. Humanist ethics is based on naturalistic rationalism. It is supported by mechanistic cosmology and realistic metaphysics. Truth is not a metaphysical concept but a trait of knowledge. Similarly other human values may also be rationally explained.

Principles of Socio-Political Revolution

M.N. Roy criticised the principles of political revolution advocated by Karl Marx. He presented his own principles of political revolution in the form of 22 fundamental principles propounded as New Humanism in the Bombay Session of Radical Democratic Party in December 1946. He was equally critical of capitalism and socialism. He said, "Polarised into two camps, not of revolution and counter-revolution, but of conflicting self-interests of the two types of national states, the world is threatened by another universal total war, which may put an end to civilisation."[1] Human race cannot face the present crisis by the means of either of these two camps. Roy has rejected economic determinism of Karl Marx. He has accepted the principle of unity of ends and means advocated by M.K. Gandhi. He called his theory moral radicalism or rational ethics. He made individual liberty the basis of human relationships. Maximum liberty of the individual is the ideal of all social and political revolutions. In the words of M.N. Roy, "The function of a revolutionary and liberating social philosophy is to lay emphasis on the basic fact of history that man is the maker of his world-man as a thinking being, and he can be so only as an individual."[2]

Revolution requires breaking of all traditions. This is possible only if the individual is given unlimited freedom. Social revolution should be based upon the fundamental principle of social progress and the most fundamental principle is the freedom of man. Every big social change is initiated by great men. They are spiritually free persons. They initiate revolution and the masses follow them. This process is based upon the faith that man can make the world better and his capacity is not limited to few persons only but found in most of the persons. This change involves not only the economic field but also social, political and cultural areas. Among revolutions the most important revolution according to M.N. Roy, is spiritual revolution. According to his interpretation of history spiritual revolutions have always

---

1. *Ibid.*, p. 15.
2. *Ibid.*, p. 56.

preceded widespread social changes. The demand of political and economic freedom follows from mental freedom. In spite of all economic and political drawbacks if the human beings have a will to change, they can definitely make progress. The will to freedom and also its capacity is not limited to few persons alone. It is found everywhere. In the words of M.N. Roy, "A movement for freedom as visualised in philosophy of New Humanism must be broader than a political movement, nor can it be organised and led by a political party of the traditional type."[1] It is necessary to educate the people before incorporating any political change.

According to M.N. Roy, political change cannot be limited to itself. It brings change in every aspect of human life. Roy lays down the following rules in this connection:

1. **Propagation of political education** Before any political change may be introduced, its aim should be propagated so that the people may adopt a new attitude.
2. **Decentralisation of power** Real political change requires decentralisation of power. Therefore, the political institutions should be changed to make political power more and more decentralised.
3. **Rise of spiritual men and women** Political changes do not occur in the field of institutions alone. At their root are men who guide them. These men and woman lead intellectual, social, economic and political fields.
4. **Scientific politics** Political changes occur by politics but it is not traditional in nature. M.N. Roy condemned traditional party politics whose only aim is the grabing of power. According to his radical political thought, traditional politics is not democratic. Democratic politics does not aim at grabing of power. We require a new politics which does not aim at power. However dirty politics may be, one cannot avoid it. M.N. Roy presents the concept of scientific politics in which politics will not be run by political parties but by active spiritually free persons. According to him movement is more important than party in political change. Being individual-centred this politics may be called humanist politics. The humanist politics thinks upon political and economic problems from the humanist standpoint. In humanist politics every human being may directly participate in formulating political decisions without any representative. It is a politics of freedom because it aims not at making more and more persons servile but giving them more and more freedom. The radical party established by M.N. Roy tried to propagate such a politics. In the beginning they gave political education to the masses and propagated democratic ideas. Feeling that true freedom is the individual freedom authority must be vested in spiritually free persons, they did not aim at power but started a social movement by the name of radical humanist movement. Roy

1. *Ibid.*, p. 66.

believed that some day this movement will cover the entire world but this dream was not realised any more than other utopion dreams.

5. **Cooperative economics** According to Roy, real economics is cooperative economics in which universal social services are used for proper distribution of means with the help of modern science and technology. It is not the function of the state to control scientific and artistic trends. But its function is to create circumstances leading to more and more free expression of these tendencies. Cooperative economics as is clear by the title, is not based on competition but on cooperation in which on the one hand the producer and the consumer cooperate and on the other hand the relationships of producers are not determined by competition but by cooperation. Thus, cooperative economics reduces national waste to minimum. It is the only economics on the basis of which coordination may be achieved among various producing units, and the economic transaction between different nations.
6. **Cultural revolution** Political change, according to M.N. Roy, is not an end in itself but a means for cultural revolution. This cultural revolution, on its part, involves not only political change but also economic and social changes.
7. **Continuous research** Human history demonstrates that no change can be realised by continued imitation of the traditional means. It requires a continuous research in the instruments by means of scientific inventions and actual experiences. It is hence, that M.N. Roy called his political thought scientific. He insisted upon a continuous enquiry in politics in the light of new scientific discoveries.
8. **Mass inspiration** Political changes and cultural revolutions are not realised by a minority but by mass inspiration without any external pressure.
9. **Public bodies** In order to establish change and revolution the democratic state should organise popular bodies as primary units. This will on the one hand decentralise political power and on the other hand supply a permanent foundation for continued change and progress.
10. **Radical democracy** Political change ultimately aims at radical democracy both as an aim and a means. Radical democracy may be achieved by scientific means alone. According to Roy, this is not possible by following the means laid down by Karl Marx because they are based upon some sort of pressure upon the individual, while the political process aims at providing more and more freedom to the individual.

22
Pandit Madan Mohan Malaviya
(1861 — 1946)

Pandit Madan Mohan Malaviya was born on December 25, 1861. He graduated himself in 1884. He led a pure and simple life and loved Hindi and Sanskrit languages. He had a good command over the English language. While he has still a student he helped in the formation of Hindi Samaj of Allahabad. In 1886, when Indian National Congress was hardly a year old he associated himself with its activities and continued to use this forum till the time he dissociated himself along with Annie Besant in the thirties of the present century due to his differences over civil disobedience movement of Mahatma Gandhi. In 1902 he was elected to the Provincial Legislative Council. In 1909, he was elevated to the Presidentship of Indian National Congress. A year later, in 1910, he was elected to the Imperial Legislative Council and continued to represent India there for 10 years. In 1916, he signed the Memorandum of the Nineteen. In 1918, he was again elected as the President of Indian National Congress at Delhi. In 1919, he raised a voice against Rowlatt Act passed by the Government, which he characterised as an instrument for crushing Indian nationalism. In 1920, he opposed Gandhian programme of non-cooperation. In 1922, he managed to hold All-Parties Conference to discuss Indian political problems, and to find a solution for that. In 1924, he was elected as a member of Indian Legislative Council. In 1927, he was elected as the leader of Nationalist Party in the Assembly. In 1930 he participated in the salt agitation started by Mahatma Gandhi and was arrested. In 1931, he went to England to participate in the Round Table Conference held to discuss Indian constitutional problems. In 1932, he was elected as President of All India Unity Conference. In 1946, he adivsed the Hindus of India to get themselves ready to face the threat of Muslim communalism. He died in the same year.

Madan Mohan Malaviya was an eloquent speaker and a powerful author. He had the capacity of captivating the imagination of his audience and readers. He was a prominent journalist who started his life career as a journalist. He was a successful parliamentarian. Some of his ideas are available in his book '*The Immanence of God*'. In addition to this, his speeches have been compiled in a publication entitled *'Speeches and Writings of Pandit Madan Mohan Malaviya'* which throw sufficient light on his political, social and economic ideas.

POLITICAL IDEAS

Pandit Madan Mohan Malaviya was enlightened patriot of India who believed in the superiority of ancient Indian culture and civilisation. For him educational system was most essential for producing patriots, specially in a country like India which was struggling for her freedom. Politically he believed in the use of Swadeshi as a method for achieving aims and objectives. He believed in national and individual freedom and desired that the British Government should try to adjust itself according to changing circumstances. He was opposed to violence and terrorist methods for achieving political ends.

Indianisation

According to Madan Mohan Malaviya for quite some time the Britishers had been ruling over India without associating us in our own administration. For him, it was something unhealthy and could not be justified on any ground. For smooth running of administration, it was most essential that the views of the ruled must be clearly understood and followed by the rulers. That was the only way for appreciating and understanding each other's viewpoint. Denial of these rights and the deliberate policy of non-Indianisation could not last long. Due to close contacts with the Britishers and the impact of English language and literature, the Indians were awakening and this process could not be checked for long. Malaviyaji suggested that the Britishers should learn a lesson from recent Russo-Japanese war, in which mighty Russia was defeated by tiny Japan, which was in no way more developed than India. He also quoted from history clarifying this awakening throughout the world, including British colonies. He warned that if the British Government failed to keep pace with the time the results might not be very conducive either for the rulers or for the ruled. It was essential that more Indians should be included in the executive councils of the Governors and Governor-General. More representation should be given to the Indians in the legislative bodies by liberalising representation and giving more and more rights to the people of India. Such a policy was also consistent with the Declaration of the Queen made in 1858, but which had not so far been properly implemented. Malaviyaji concluded that unless Indians were associated with their own administration, many of our problems would not be solved. In so far as the people of India were concerned, there was no harm in demanding legitimate rights, rather it was their duty to do so to prove that they were an awakened nation. Unless we demanded rights and got them we could not think of remedying many of our social, economic and political evils. A generous and benevolent foreign regime was no alternative for self-government and on that analogy, the process of Indianisation should not either be abandoned or considerably slowed down.

Liberty

Madan Mohan Malaviya believed in both individual as well as national liberty and freedom. In his opinion without freedom it was impossible to have fullest development of both national and individual faculties. Form of government or the extent of benevolence was not any reason for perpetuation of an alien rule. In this regard, he agreed with Swami Dayanand Saraswati who said that the worst self-rule was always better than the best foreign rule. The imperial governments must realise that with the passage of time the days of imperalism and colonialism were also coming to an end. They must not deny right of self-determination to their colonies. If they did so, they were bound to meet with failure. In this regard Malaviyaji was close to Tilak who used to say that 'freedom is my birth right and I should have that'. He very strongly pleaded that our people, both the Hindus and the Muslims must get themselves ready for getting their right of self-determination. In his own words, "Standing in this ancient capital of India, both for the Hindu and Mohammadan periods, it fills me with inexpressible sorrow and shame to think that we, the descendants of Hindus who ruled for four thousand years in this extensive empire, and the descendants of Musalmans who ruled here for several hundred years, should have so far fallen from our ancient State, that we should have to argue our capacity for even a limited measure of autonomy and self-rule. " Demanding of right of self-determination was not peculiar to India. People of both free as well as subjected countries always fight for their right of self-determination. England fought world wars to preserve her right of self-determination. In fact one of the reasons for her joining the war was to guarantee this right to those from whom it was being snatched by Fascist Italy or Nazi Germany. Malaviyaji also made a comparative study of various other colonies under British imperialism and came to the conclusion that all were fighting for this right and that if India fought for such a right she was most justified. The national leaders would fail India, if they failed to arouse public enthusiasm and vigour in the masses to demonstrate their determination to struggle for their right of self-determination.

Religion and Politics

Pt. Madan Mohan Malaviya was a religious man by nature. For him religion had a very significant place in the life of both the individual as well as the nation. He also laid stress on morality. He was close to Mahatma Gandhi is so far as the relation of religion with politics was concerned. For him, both were inseparable. Religion and politics must go hand in hand. Introduction of religion into politics will neither pollute nor lower the dignity of religion. Politics devoid of religion is barren and unhealthy. Religion and morality made politics healthy and fair. Introduction of religion in politics will bring stability in political life. Malaviyaji desired that there should be religious education in India's educational institutions so that the citizens of tomorrow come out from these institutions with religious outlook.

Swadeshi

Like Mahatma Gandhi, Pandit Madan Mohan Malaviya also laid stress on the desirability of the use of Swadeshi goods. It is our duty, and if we have been failing to perform our this most important duty and using foreign goods in preference to our indigenous goods, we have committed a national crime. The sooner we rectify this mistake and willingly adopt Swadeshi, the better that shall be. The false propaganda that propagation of Swadeshi was only a political weapon was bound to create ill-will between India and Britain. On the contrary, Malaviyaji agreed with Mahatma Gandhi that use of Swadeshi will end many of our economic problems. It will not only make us independent to a great extent in the economic field but shall also provide employment to millions of our people who remain fully or partially unemployed throughout the year. The Swadeshi was an alternative to the policy of non-industrialisation being followed by England in so far as India was concerned. Swadeshi shall bring dignity in work and revive our pride in handicrafts which had decayed due to British policy of mechanisation in India. However, it was wrong to believe that the Britishers shall help us in the propagation or use of Swadeshi goods. England was using India as a market for dumping her goods and as such the use of Swadeshi was bound to clash with their sales. England was an industrially advanced country whereas India was both economically and industrially backward. Hence, the interests of both the countries were bound to clash with each other. About Swadeshi Malaviyaji said, "I look upon it as a part of religious duty which we owe to our fellow men. I consider it as the religion of humanity and our particular religion...the religion of Humanity, demands that you should promote the Swadeshi movement to the utmost extent of your power."

Representative System

Malaviyaji was a true democrat and had faith in democratic institutions including the representative system. According to him, an institution run and managed on representative system was the only civilised institution. One of the reasons of the revolt of 1857 was absence of representative system in India. Indians, both Hindus and Muslims, have been running their own affairs successfully for centuries and they were even now competent to manage their own affairs. If the Britishers continued to repeat this stock argument a time might not be far away when the people of India might feel disgusted and lose faith in British sense of justice. Swaraj could not come, nor could resprestentative institutions be introduced merely by raising slogans or arranging meetings but that required patience and sacrifice. Certain pre-requisites were essential for the early bringing of representative institutions in India namely that the people of the country should be made to realise the significance of representative institutions by arranging mass meetings and arranging regular and constant propaganda.

National Language

As early as in 1919 Malaviyaji realised the need and necessity of a national language. Without it a nation could never progress nor could sense of unity develop among its citizens. Hindi was the only language which could claim the status of a national language. Hence, we should make an attempt to produce all our technical and non-technical works in Hindi and should also use this language in our day-to-day life. When suitable words are not available in Hindi, these should either be coined or borrowed from Sanskrit which was both very rich as well as the language of our literature.

Education

Madan Mohan Malaviya laid stress on proper system of education. Like many of his predecessors and contemporaries he believed that our system of education was very defective and did not respond to our present conditions. The need of the hour was to have educated Indians who should be patriots, morally high and religiously strong. They should also be self-sufficient and not a burden on the community. On the contrary, British education was producing white-collar people having no love for their motherland and hating Swadeshi goods and past Indian culture. Malavivaji therefore, suggested that national pattern of education should be developed to achieve national outlook.

Indian National Congress

According to Malaviyaji, Indian National Congress was a useful forum for expressing Indian public opinion. It was the symbol of national unity. Malaviyaji appreciated the line of action of Indian National Congress, as followed by the moderates. He continued to agree with its programmes and also kept his association with the organisation. But when Gandhiji started his civil disobedience and non-cooperation movements Malaviyaji felt that these were not in keeping with the traditions of Indian National Congress. He therefore, did not offer himself for any satyagraha. Along with Annie Besant he practically dissociated himself from the organisation.

Industrialisation

According to Malaviyaji, it was essential to have industrialisation for our national development. Unless there was a network of industries, spread all over the country, nation could not wipe out its present poverty and come out of its backwardness. He suggested total and complete reconstruction of our national economy. He believed that sufficient finances were available in the country for running our industries.

Hindu Culture

Malaviyaji was a staunch Hindu. For him Hinduism was the most dynamic religion in the world, a religion which any nation could feel proud of. The religion, according to him, did not believe in the use of force but only in persuasion. It was through Hinduism that in the past India had become the spiritual leader of the whole world. 'It was through Hinduism that India could survive throughout these ages. In spite of many invasions from outside India this religion could face all odds whereas other cultures perished and are not even known to the world of today. He had deep faith in Vedic culture and also ancient religious books like the Vedas and Upanishads. He wanted to preserve rituals and traditions. He stood for cow protection and raised a strong voice in favour of cow protection.

Line of Action

1. **Constitutional Method** Malaviyaji was a constitutional fighter. He believed that constitutional methods should be adopted for getting political advancement. He was very much opposed to terrorist methods or any other similar method for getting the right of self-determination. He did not agree with Tilak that since India had no constitution therefore, the question of using constitutional methods hardly arose. He was so much opposed to unconstitutional methods that he dissociated himself even from the Congress when Mahatma Gandhi launched his programme of non-cooperation and civil disobedience. For him, even these methods were non-constitutional and should not be adopted.
2. **Mass Appeal** Malaviyaji had full faith in the capacity of the people to struggle for and manage their own affairs. He believed that the people should be awakened and a sense of patriotism and nationalism should be aroused in them. No good was likely to come out of our struggle as long as the people were not made to realise the evils of subordination. In so far as Indian conditions were concerned, nationalism based on culture and religion could appeal to the masses. Accordingly, Malaviyaji laid stress on this aspect of our national life.

Malaviyaji boldly raised his voice against our social, economic and political evils. He was a religious man but not an orthodox or a diehard. In spite of his open support to Hinduism, even Ali Brothers accepted his broad mindedness. He said that in India only that type of nationalism could develop which had cultural foundations. He developed the philosophy of nationalism in India on very sound footing. He had great love for the type of education which suited our times and conditions. Both as a legislator as well as a journalist, he pleaded for nationalism and Hinduism. Thus, he believed that nationalism and religion could go side by side. He believed in the value of boldness in life and thereby in moral strength. He himself followed that ideal. Though he very much appreciated in Congress organisation but when he himself failed to adjust with its aggressive character, he openly declared his views without caring for the opinions of his one-time friends in the organisation. Similarly, when he found that communalism was raising its ugly head in India, he openly suggested to the Hindus that they should get themselves ready to face the challenge of Muslim communalism. Jawahar Lal Nehru said about him : "Although greatly respected and always welcome to it he was not really of new Congress. To Congress he had that sentimental attachment to an organisation with which he had been connected almost from the very beginning, partly to an emotional fall in the direction of the freedom struggle, for he saw that the Congress was the only organisation doing anything effective about it. His heart was thus often in the Congress Camp, especially in the time of struggle, his head was in other camps. Malaviyaji was a nationalist alone. He was the supporter of the old orthodox order, culturally, socially and economically."

23
Vinayak Damodar Savarkar
(1883 — 1966)

Vinayak Damodar Savarkar was born in 1883 in Ratnagiri district. During his school days he showed a visible tendency of his love for Hindu religion. He even organised student groups to check the excesses of Muslims, whenever he came to know of these. As a student he took active interest in politics and gave all possible support to Swadeshi movement. He organised a campaign for burning foreign cloth. As a result he was expelled from his college. In 1906, he got a recommendatory letter from Tilak which enabled him to get scholarship from Shyamji Verma, an Indian revolutionary in England, to study in England. It England many revolutionaries came in his contact and were inspired by him. As the time passed he became an eye-sore for the British Government and was arrested in 1910 for certain speeches alleged to have been made by him in India in 1906. However, when he was being brought to India as a captive, he jumped from the ship into the sea but was re-arrested. The Government of India found him guilty of treason and deported him to Andamans. In 1923, he was brought back to India and interned at Ratnagiri. He was released on the specific condition that he would not participate in active politics. He remained under this condition till 1937. He, however, utilised this period in consolidating the Hindus, and pointing out the evils of Hindu society. After his release from Ratnagiri he actively associated himself with Hindu Mahasabha and became its life and soul. For many years he was its President. In 1948, when Mahatma Gandhi was shot dead, Savarkar was also tried but acquitted by the trial judge. Due to over-exertion, his health began to deteriorate and ultimately on February 26, 1966, he left this world for his heavenly abode.

Sarvarkar wrote and spoke to awaken the Hindus from their deep sleep and make them ready to face the hard realities of life. Some of his significant works are : 1. *My Transportation for Life*. 2. *Hindu Pad Padshahi*. 3. *Hindutva*. 4. *The Indian War of Independence of 1857*. (This was proscribed soon after its release in 1909 and made available to public only in 1947.)

POLITICAL IDEAS

Savarkar was a revolutionary from the very start of his political career. He was a staunch and devoted Hindu with a very firm faith in the superiority of Hindu culture and civilisation which was for him above everything else. For him everything should move round the world 'Hindutva'.

Views About Hindutva

Savarkar developed and defined the term Hindutva, which according to him was different and broader than the term Hinduism. In his own words, "Therefore those who love the land that streches from Sindhu to Sindhu from Indus to sea, as their fatherland and consequently claim to inherit the blood of the race that has evolved, by incorporation and adaptation, from ancient Saptasinhus, can be said to possess two of the most esential requisites of Hindutva" Hindutva has three essential qualities namely : (1) Rashtra, (2) jati, and (3) Sanskriti.

1. **Rashtra** The person concerned should respect the territorial integrity and geographical sanctity of national borders. He should be most willing to sacrifice his everything for the sake of protecting these geographical boundaries. He should have no extra-territorial attachments.
2. **Jati** A believer of Hindutva should belong to a family which has Hindu blood, *i.e.* his ancestors should be Hindus.
3. **Sanskriti** The person concerned should have faith in the superiority of ancient Indian culture and civilisation and should take pride in it. Thus, according to him such minorities as the Muslims and the Christians which do not feel proud of our cultural heritage or in whom the blood of Indian ancestors does not flow, did not come under Hindutva.

Hinduism

Savarkar was a true Hindu and a great moving force in Hindu Mahasabha, which was primarily responsible for the consolidation of energies of Hindus of our times. For him, Hinduism was the most ancient religion in the world and that too with rich traditions. For him, it was also one of those religions which have been preserved and passed on to us with care. Our present and the coming generations are only the trustees of a sacred trust reposed in them namely preservation of these cultural traditions. Hinduism has not decayed itself on because it is a dynamic religion which can absorb all other religions. It has a homogeneous and heterogeneous outlook. It is very rational and appealing to mind and soul. Many other world religions have drawn inspiration from Hinduism. It has been tested on the standards of time and proved its worth. Modern degeneration and perversion is only due to the rulers who are deliberately disfiguring Hinduism and misinterpreting it so as to shake our faith in our religion and thus to take us spiritually poor. It was this Hinduism which made India the spiritual leader of the world.

Differentiating between Hindutva and Hinduism Savarkar said that the former was broader and more comprehensive than the latter. Hindutva was a social, economic and political concept. It was closer to nationalism than religion. On the other hand Hinduism was a religion and as such it had closer affinity to morality than politics. Thus, Hindutva was political whereas Hinduism was a religious concept.

Like Madan Mohan Malaviya, Sarvarkar had great faith in the capacity of Hindus to run and manage their own affairs. The present political degeneration of Hindus was only due to circumstances beyond their control. The Hindus had great capacity to run and manage their own affairs and for centuries they had very well managed their own affairs. The very fact that Hindus were on the forefront of India's national struggle bore an ample testimony to the logic that they had capacity and strong desire to achieve their independence, that capacity shall further develop after the alien rule had come to an end.

Non-violence

For Savarkar, it was not desirable to accept non-violence as a creed. It was equally undesirable to adopt violence as a method for solving our social as well as political problems. It was partially desirable and as such it should be treated only as a relative and not as an absolute term. To adopt it as a method of life and mode of struggle was impracticable under present conditions and circumstances. It could be adopted only where the opponent also believed in similar methods and understood the same language. In so far as India was concerned the imperialists were not at all willing to listen to this language. They are not supposed to leave India with the use of moral force. Therefore, violent means should be adopted, if necessary, to achieve our objects. In so far as the National Congress was concerned, that was a useful forum to express national opinion and viewpoint, but radical changes were needed to reform the way in which the leadership was handling the situation. Sarvarkar was opposed to Quit India movement of Mahatma Gandhi, on the plea that India was as yet not ready for such a national struggle, though such an attitude cost the Hindu Mahasabha very much and the organisation went in the background in the years that followed.

The Partition of India

Savarkar believed in the idea of a united India. The partition of the country was suicidal and against national interests. He was very bitter when C.R. formula for the partition of the country was made public. He was pained to see that the National Congress was drifting towards partition of the country by following a policy of appeasement of the Muslims and giving them concessions one after the other which were prejudicial to our national and collective interests.

Participation in World War

In 1939, when 2nd World War broke out and Congress Ministers resigned from offices in the provinces in which they were in power, Indian National Congress proposed that India should boycott war efforts and that nothing — men, money or material — should be offered to the British Government unless it came forward with an assurance that India would be granted independence after the war was over. On the other hand Savarkar extended his hand of cooperation to the Government as he thought that association and participation of Hindus in war efforts, shall provide them an opportunity to get military training. They shall be in a position to get acquainted with latest war equipments and methods of struggle. It was, therefore, in the collective interests of Hindu community to participate in war efforts. With this viewpoint Sarvarkar could convince Hindu Mahasabha to pass a resolution to that effect.

Minorities

For Sarvarkar India was a homogeneous country in which various communities and persons belonging to all religions were living together since ages. He was pained to see that some of the minority communities were not contributing in the national progress and on the contrary were standing in the way of national progress. He made it amply clear to them that irrespective of the consideration whether they cooperated with the majority community or not, India shall go ahead with its ambitious programme of attaining independence. It was in the interest of minorities themselves that they should cooperate with the majority and thus get its goodwill. Sarvarkar said, "All that the National State can mean it that the Muslim minority in India will have the right to be treated as equal citizens, enjoying equal protection and civic rights in proportion to their population. — The Hindu majority will not encroach on the legitimate rights of any non-Hindu minority. But in no case can Hindu majority resign its rights which as a majority community it is entitled to exercise under any democratic or legitimate constitution."

Hindu Rashtra

Veer Savarkar had unshakable and undisputed faith in the superiority of Hindu culture. He did not conceal his feeling that India was primarily the land of Hindus. He wanted to see India a Hindu Rashtra. He clearly said that the Hindus had a priority right to live in India. Hindus have their gods and goddnesses who are Indian. The Hindus have also considered India their motherland. They love Indian cultural heritage and take pride in that. They respect eveything that is Indian. They have no extra-territorial attachments. They have sentimental attachments, with everything that is Indian. On the other hand the Muslims, who form a vast minority in India, have extra-territorial affiliations. They go out for Haj. They have no sentimental attachment with our gods and goddesses. They have more respect and regard for Hazrat Muhammad Sahib and the land of his birth, than India. Sarvarkar said, "A Hindu patriot worth the name cannot but be an Indian patriot as well. To the Hindu, Hindusthan being the fatherland and Holyland, the love they bear to Hindusthan is boundless. That is why they predominate in the national struggle that is going on for the overthrow of the British yoke. Even buried bones in Andamans would assert this fact." While delivering his Presidential address from Hindu Mahasabha platform, he expressed more or less similar views. In 1936 he said, "While the Hindus love those affinities which bind a Hindu to Hindu and to dwell on them with pride, the Muslims hate the very mention of them and are trying to eradicate the very memory of it all. Some of them fabricate histories and geneologies to connect their origin with the Arabians and Turks; they are trying to carve out a separate language for themselves and graft it as best as they can on the Arabian stock." Savarkar said that India was a Hindu Rashtra. But this should not lead one to the conclusion that in this country religious minorities could not live or develop. In his arrangement all shall have the right of growth, prosperity and development but clearly understanding that they were a minority and that a numerical majority in every country had certain special rights. They will also have to realise that minority cannot be a hindrance to the growth and development of the majority.

Nationality

Savarkar could not reconcile himself to the idea that residence of a person for a particular length of time within the geographical limits of a country should be the deciding factor for conferring nationality on a particular individual or community. According to him, this was absolutely a wrong standard for such an important matter. For him, nationality should be conferred after great care and consideration. The measuring rod should be that the person or community should believe in cultural heritage of the land and should as well have sentimental and emotional attachments. For him Hindus in India are entitled to such a right. He said, "But so far as materialistic and secular aspect is concerned, the Hindus are a nation bound by a common culture, a common language, a common country and a common religion."

Social Ideas

Though a very devout Hindu and a person having unshakable faith in the superiority of Hindu culture and civilization, Sarvarkar was not blind to the evils of Hindu society, which had considerably degenerated in our modern times. He found an opportunity to consolidate Hindus both by infusing new spirit and pointing out the evils. This opportunity he got when he was interned at Ratnagiri. It was at this stage that he raised his voice against untouchability and very strongly pleaded that it should be ended. For him it was a curse on the fair name of Hinduism and that in its present form it was very much unwanted. He suggested the establishment of mixed schools in which boys of all castes, both high and low, were required to study together in a spirit of oneness and brotherhood. The untouchables should be allowed to enter the temples. Sarvarkar even helped in the erection of a Patit Pavan temple in which the low castes and down-trodden were to be permitted entry without any hesitation. He suggested was that dinners should be arranged in which the persons belonging to all communities should dine together? There should be inter-caste marriages so that the myth of caste superiority was exploded. The Hindu society should be reformed in a fashion that it got rid of all evils of obscurnatism, which were curse on its fair name.

Savarkar was a revolutionary by birth. He was a top ranking patriot. He suffered all odds so that the nation was elevated. All his actions and activities were motivated by the sole object of honouring India. Both in methods and outlook he differed from the Indian National Congress. He consolidated Hindu nation and gave it a concrete programme and policy to follow. His concept of Hindu Rashtra was a suitable reply to the cry of Pakistan. His association with Hindu Mahasabha made that an All India body. The very fact that glowing tributes were paid to him at the time of his death even by Congress leaders who differed from him in his approach to political problems is sufficient evidence of the respect which he commanded among the masses.

24
Acharya Vinoba Bhave (1895 — 1982)

Vinayak Narhari Bhave was born on 11th September, 1895 in a village named Gagode, in Colaba District, in the present Maharashtra State. He was the eldest son of his family. His father, Narhari Shambhu Rao was a textile technologist. The family had a religious but unorthodox bent of mind. It believed in religious toleration. His father commanded sufficient social respect. It has been rightly said, "Vinoba was brought up in an atmosphere of a natural conscience and voluntary observance of social obligations even in small matters."

Vinoba received his early education at home. He joined a regular school at Baroda when he was 15. As a student he cared more for extra-curricular studies reading the biographies and autobiographies of national heroes and saints rather than studying his text-books. He did not very much care for decorum. His behaviour was also sometimes objectionable to the teachers with the result that he was not in their good books. He passed his Matriculation examination in November, 1913, and joined college for higher education. However, from the very start he disliked the Indian university system of education which was not based on practical life but on bookish knowledge. Ultimately Vinoba decided to discontinue his university education. He even burnt his Matriculation certificate.

In 1916, when he was about 20 years of age he left Baroda for Banaras to get real knowledge and to study scriptures of Hindu religion. At Banaras he heard Gandhiji's thrilling and inspiring speech delivered in Banaras Hindu University. He was so much inspired by the speech that he gave up his plans of joining the terrorists of Bengal or seeking shelter in the Himalayas. For some time he corresponded with Gandhiji. Ultimately both met for the first time on 7th June, 1916. In the words of Lanza-Delvasto, "During the whole of discourse the youngman had felt his heart burning within him. The question which had gnawed at him even since his adolescence had hollowed out a void into which these new words flowed, exactly filling in." Accordingly Vinoba decided to stay with Gandhiji in his Ashram. Gandhiji found in him great qualities of mind and heart. He wrote to his father, "Your son Vinoba is with me. At a tender age he has acquired a degree of spirituality and asceticism that took me years of patient labour to attain." While in the Ashram, Vinoba devoted himself to cooking and subsequently joined the scavenging team. He applied himself to the spinning wheel. In due course of time Gandhiji began to lay more and more faith in him. He was so much devoted to his work that his health broke down and he was obliged to leave the Ashram with a promise to come back after one year. On the expiry of exactly one year Vinoba returned to the Ashram. Some time later he got the news that his whole family was in hospital down with influenza. Though he was not inclined to go to see his ailing family members on the plea that he had renunciated the world, yet Gandhiji prevailed upon him and he went there. In 1921, Shri Jamna Lal Bajaj proposed to open a branch of Sabarmati Ashram at Wardha. He wanted to have a devoted disciple of Gandhiji who could preach Gandhian ideals and philosophy in the Ashram in true sense and spirit. Gandhiji selected Vinoba for the purpose. Vinoba reached the new Ashram on 8th April, 1921. There he created still more faith in Gandhiji who said that Vinoba was the jewel of his disciples.

Vinoba Bhave, came to limelight in 1940, Gandhiji introduced Vinoba to the nation in the following words : "He has abolished every trace of untouchability from his heart. He believes in communal unity with the same passion that I have. In order to know the best mind of Islam, he gave one year to the study of Koran in original. He has, therefore, learnt Arabic. He found this study necessary to cultivating a contact with the Muslims living in his neighbourhood. He is responsible for producing the youngmen who had dedicated themselves to the service of lepers."

How Vinoba was brought to great prominence throughout the world. His name struck headlines on the front pages of many newspapers though he himself was not at all interested in getting publicity and advertisement. After coming out from jail, Vinoba again devoted himself to the service of the nation.

In 1948, when Gandhiji was shot dead in Delhi, the responsibility fell on the shoulders of Vinoba to carry out his unfinished task in the social and economic fields. He carried on his task through his Bhoodan philosophy. He travelled throughout the country to have first-hand knowledge of the living conditions and problems of people of India and gradually commanded more and more respect. In 1958, Shri Jawaharlal Nehru said about him, "In the troubled but dynamic scene that is India today, the frail figure of Vinobaji stands like a rock of strength, modest and gentle, yet culled something of the vision of the future in his eyes. It is not for us smaller folk to judge him whether we agreed with him or disagreed in some matter, for he is above these minor judgments. He represents, as none else does, the spirit and tradition of Gandhiji and of India."

At the age of 87 Vinoba Bhave breathed his last in the year 1982 after voluntarily rejecting food for several days.

Writings

Acharya Vinoba Bhave has written quite a few important and interesting books which indicate the principles of his Bhoodan philosophy. Some of his publications are collections of his articles published in various journals from time to time whereas the others are collections of the stray ideas which occurred to him occasionally and have been collected by his disciples. Some are of course translations. His significant writings are:

1. Madhukar
2. Thoughts on Education
3. Geetai
4. Talks on Geeta
5. Stchitaprajna Darshan
6. Geetai Chintanika
7. Upanishadacha Abhyas
8. Ishavasyavritti
9. Vicharpothi
10. Swarajya Sastra
11. Jeevan Drishti
12. Simhavalokna
13. Philosophy of man of steadfast to wisdom.

In addition to these publications there are certain pamphlets which also give his ideas.

Basic Principles of Vinoba's Philosophy

Acharya Vinoba Bhave sought to bring about a social and economic revolution not by violent but by peaceful methods. His basic principle was that the people should themselves be willing to give up sense of ownership and should realise the need and necessity of sharing their surplus wealth, both movable and immovable, with those who are landless or moneyless. Though this could easily be done by the Government by passing an act depriving the owners of their property and compelling them to distribute that among the propertyless but, in his opinion, such a step would not achieve the basic end of voluntarily withdrawing ownership rights and thereby giving up the sense of ownership. This he has tried to implement through his philosophy of Sarvodya. He was a firm believer in man's power to change mind provided the person concerned was determined and possessed a high sterling character. A change of mind could not be brought about only when the preacher touches the inner core of his audience. With this end in view Vinoba wanted to change the very agrarian economy of India. He travelled from one corner of the country to the other.

CHARACTERISTICS OF SARVODAYA

According to M. K. Gandhi, Vinoba Bhave, Jayaprakash Narain and other leaders the following are the important characteristics of the ideal of Sarvodaya:

1. **Evolution of all** On 25th December 1975, replying to a question "What is Sarvodaya"?, Vinoba Bhave replied that the following are the five basis of Sarvodaya:
   1. Establishment of a castless and classless society.
   2. Clear and efficient administration in public sector.
   3. Decentralisation as the bases of social system.
   4. The people will achieve all power.
   5. The administrators will not consider themselves masters of the people but their servants. Thus, Sarvodaya aims at providing happiness to all and not only to the majority as aimed by other ideologies. According to Vinoba Bhave, under a good political system all the people are happy. While the utilitarianism aims at physical welfare, Sarvodaya aims at total welfare. Sarvodaya does not aim at the evolution of some, the majority or the maximum. "We are not satisfied with the maximum happiness of the maximum people," said Vinoba Bhave, "We may be satisfied with the welfare of one and all, higher and lower, powerful and the weak, intelligent and unintelligent. The term Sarvodaya expresses this superior and all pervading sentiment." At another place, pointing out the two laws of Sarvodaya, Vinoba Bhave said, "If we understand a simple thing we may achieve welfare of all. Everyone should worry about the other and not worry about anything which brings suffering to others. This is called Sarvodaya." Thus, the follower of Sarvodaya should not live on other's earning. He should himself earn his bread.
2. **Truth and Non-violence** According to Shankar Rao Deo, the ideal of a Sarvodaya society is a society based upon non-violence and truth, casteless and classless, without any exploitation and in which every individual and every group may have opportunity and means for total development. Sarvodaya ideal is absolutely tolerant, even tolerant of the enemy. It preaches Christ's message of love in exchange of enmity.
3. **Harmony** Sarvodaya aims at harmony of all. According to Dada Dharmadhikari. the ideal of Sarvodaya is non-dualism and its policy is harmony. It seeks to establish a classless, casteless and egalitarian society in which every individual and group will have opportunity of total development. This is possible by revolution, non-violence and truth. Therefore, Sarvodaya supports all these. Writing about the aims of Sarvodaya, J. C. Kumarappa has pointed out that the ideal of Sarvodaya represents an ideal social system based upon love. It has place for everyone without exception, may be a prince or a peasant, Hindu or Muslim, caste Hindu or untouchable, white or black, saint or sinner. It has no place for repression or exploitation of any individual or community. All will participate in this social system, everyone will

utilise his labour, the powerful will protect the weak and act as their Guardian and everyone will work for everybody's welfare.

4. **Stateless society** Politically speaking Sarvodaya is a developed version of Gandhism. M. K. Gandhi was a bitter critic of the state. According to him the greatest evil of the state is that it is based upon violence. Therefore, M. K. Gandhi considered the best society as stateless. Deriving inspiration from Gandhian philosophy, Vinoba Bhave aimed at establishment of a society free from all repression and exploitation. Sarvodaya ideal is against the present form of the state based upon the repressive tendency. In an ideal society there will be no distinction between the ruler and the ruled. Jayaprakash Narain and others have even criticised a welfare state since it increases the powers and functions of the government. In practice, this criticism appears to be valid since with the advent of the concept of the welfare state, the powers of states have constantly increased. Sarvodaya aims at a society absolutely free from all authority and government. This society will not be based upon Danda or the power to punish. It will be ruled by the popular opinion, though in the interim period, some sort of authority may continue.
5. **Opposed to representative democracy and party system** At present in most of the countries of the world, including India, Britain and U.S.A. there is a democratic state. Sarvodaya is opposed to this democracy. According to it this democracy is not the rule of the people but the rule of the powerful political party. Therefore, democracy consists of cut throat competition for power among political parties and no political party is controlled by the people themselves. The party system has given totalitarian forms to democracies. After the First World War, the totalitarian government established in Italy and Germany were the result of the so-called democracy and the party system. Modern democratic system is only an external show since all the issues are first decided in the meetings of the political party itself. Their presentation in the parliament and discussion upon them is merely a formality. Therefore, in modern democracy parliament and legislation are a mere show. Party system leads to moral degeneration of the members of the party. They utilise all sorts of good and evil means to make their party powerful and to win the general elections. Even the majority party is always busy in concentrating more and more power. The single point programme of the opposition parties is to oppose the party in power without caring the least for the good of the people. Therefore, Dada Dharmadhikari, a spokesman of Sarvodaya, has clearly pointed out three evils of democracy: misuse of power, fear of strong men and corruption. Besides this the Indian democracy suffers from communalism and casteism. The politics based upon party system is full of struggle for power. Democracy is limited to ballot and vote.

Therefore, Sarvodaya ideology opposes the party system. So long as it is not eliminated, it should be made more and more liberal.

6. **Decentralisation of political power** Sarvodaya stands for decentralisation of political power. This will be done by establishment of what Vinoba Bhave called basic democracy. This will be established in every village in which the village panchayat will be elected through direct election and everybody will participate in its functioning. To achieve this purpose the election of members of panchayat should be free from the party system. It should be an open election. The village should be made the primary unit of society. The citizens should know each other. According to Sarvodaya scheme, the village panchayat will elect members of Tehsil panchayats who in their turn, will elect members of district panchayat. The district panchayats will elect panchayat of the state and the state panchayats will elect the central government. This will require a total revolution in the present system. In this system the elections above the village panchayat will be indirect. Every voter and every representative will have to devote some hours everyday to physical labour. M. K. Gandhi maintained that in order to have the right to vote, the qualification will not be wealth or post but physical labour. The condition of literacy or property has proved to be useless. The physical labour gives opportunity to all those who wish to participate in administration in the interest of the state. According to Vinoba Bhave, this provision of physical labour will help in removing corruption from the political field.
7. **Economic decentralisation and equality** The decentralisation suggested by Sarvodaya is not merely political but also economic. This is contradictory to the communist proposal. M. K. Gandhi was against heavy industries. The Sarvodaya leaders argue that industrialisation leads to centralisation of wealth and political power which increases exploitation. Machines take the place of human beings and increase unemployment. The creative and artistic capacities are destroyed and human values degenerate. Therefore, Sarvodaya is against mechanisation. Economic decentralisation not only means small industries or cottage industries but its necessary condition is the right of the producers. For example, the land should belong to him who actually cultivates it. The property right should be vested in the actual user of the land or the factory. The Sarvodaya ideology seeks to bring about equality of property but not by repression. It is against the law of the forest. It does not utilise even the law of the legislature. It is based upon the law of love and love is higher than law. It has no place for profiteering, earning interest or rent. Everything will be done with the sentiment of the general good. Each will act according to his capacity and needs.

8. **Faith in people's power** As against Rajniti, Sarvodaya believes in Lokniti. Pointing out the distinction between these two concepts, K.D. Bhatt has maintained that while administration is the main element of politics, discipline is important in Lokniti. Power is the centre of politics and freedom is the locus of Lokniti. Control is rampant in politics and it becomes self-control in Lokniti. While politics involves competition of power and right, Lokniti is based upon performing the duties. Thus, in the Sarvodaya, the sequence of progress is from administration to discipline, from power to liberty, from control to self-restraint and from competition of rights to performance of duties. Lokniti is based upon people's power. The government cannot do anything about it. While the people constitute the well, the government is only a bucket. If the well has no water, from where will the bucket get it? Therefore, Sarvodaya goes direct to the people. What the government cannot do is done by the people.
9. **Internationalism and world brotherhood** Sarvodaya ideology is not limited to any state or nation. It is cosmopolitan. It aims at internationalism and world brotherhood. It is based upon the ancient Indian ideal that the whole world is like a family. The Sarvodaya society will not have national state. It has a world-wide vision and every individual is a citizen of the whole world. The boundaries of the national state will be broken and the whole world will become one family. In this process the leaders of Sarvodya have rejected the Varna system which was appreciated by M.K. Gandhi. Dada Dharmadhikari and Kaka Kalelkar have asked for elimination of Varna system since it is based upon class distinction. Sarvodaya, however, supports the ashram system for spiritual development. In the social life, the competition should be substituted by an urge for constant progress. Sarvodaya programme aims at making every village self-sufficient, developing cottage industries and establishing the superiority of labour and the equality of male and female. In its humanitarian ideology, virtues occupy the highest place. It seeks to establish the human values through change of heart.

CRITICISM OF SARVODAYA IDEOLOGY

All those arguments which are applicable to the philosophy of M.K. Gandhi are also applicable to the ideal of Sarvodaya. These are as follows :

1. **Lack of originality** M.K. Gandhi was a religious man whose ideology was grounded in his religious faith. Therefore, Sarvodaya ideology has been subjected to severe criticism. In fact, there is nothing new in it. As has been already pointed out, the idea is already in the Vedas and the Upanishads and the Bhagwadgita. It can be said that Sarvodaya ideology was derived from these ancient Hindu scriptures. As B. G. Ray has pointed out, "Gandhiji starts from Hindu religion,

and metaphysical solution of eternal problems from a Hindu angle of vision form the basis of his philosophy. He has not sought to answer or solve the problem from an independent perspective of experience or reason." It is not too correct to say that Gandhiji did not present any novel moral laws but he cannot be said to be completely novel. Gandhiji was the first one to introduce non-violence into the political field and he also made successful use of it. He declared punishment immoral. Gandhiji was the precursor of non-violent revolution.

2. **Extremism** According to Miller, "Gandhiji belongs to the type of sanyasis who repress the flesh consciously, reject all the colour and warmth of life, denounce everything which is not necessary for mere livehood, hasten the dissolution of the body, so that the spirit imprisoned in it may more quickly be united with the divine." Gandhiji is called an extremist, an allegation of undeniable veracity, but it should not be forgotten that he made the utmost effort to make his vows practicable and proved their practicability by following them himself. Excessive emphasis upon repression of senses has led to his ethics becoming permeated with stringency. Probably his assumption regarding celibacy may strike one as untalented and even harmful to happy matrimonial life but a balancing stress upon qualities like non-violence, love, equanimity etc., have prevented his sermons from becoming utterly heartless. Actually, Gandhiji himself was an experimenter and did not recognise any means as final. He had hoped that there would be new experiments in the application of non-violence and looked at attentively this hope does not impress one as false.
3. **Impractical ideal** The Sarvodaya ideal is too sufficiently high and which theoretically speaking, it may be logically consistent, yet seeing the present condition of human nature, society and international relationships, Sarvodaya ideology cannot be hoped to be realised. Like *The Republic* of Plato the Sarvodaya ideal is a mere utopia. It is impossible to understand as to how a society may be based purely on cooperation and selflessness. The ideal of trusteeship is not supported by facts of human psychology. Even if it is sought for in Indian society, it does not appear to be possible.
4. **Doubts about non-violence** Many critics express grave doubts regarding the probabilities of experimentation in non-violence but in order to comprehend Gandhiji's thought it will be essential to set aside the general pragmatic idea and approach the hub of the problem whence the utility of non-violence, for purposes of all kinds of healthy and permanent improvements, will become transparent. There can, of course, be some practical doubts about the possibility of trusteeship. Progress is imminent in the attempts of making practical Vinobaji's campaign of Gandhism. Only the future can tell the extent of its practicability. Gandhiji endeavoured to discover the fundamental

solution of all problems. Another major reason why his solution of existing problems and his sketches of man's future seem impractical is that human society has not achieved that level and man also lacks the necessary moral strength to successfully use those means. But the only conclusion which can be drawn from this is that society will have to acquire moral strength to proceed upon his path.

5. **Not possible in one country alone** It is a common place proverb today that peace and prosperity anywhere requires peace and prosperity everywhere. At present most of the countries do not cherish ideal of society agreeing with Sarvodaya ideal in any way. So long as they do not agree with Sarvodaya ideal it is not practical to realise it in one country alone. If the past history is any indicator a non-violent society cannot exist in the midst of violent societies.
6. **Impossibility of change of heart** Both Gandhi and Vinoba have talked of achieving social, political and economic changes through change of heart. This however, appears to be contradictory to facts of human psychology.
7. **Partyless Democracy not possible** So many criticisms of democracy have been advanced by M. K. Gandhi, Vinoba Bhave and others but democracy is not accepted as the perfect ideal but a lesser evil. In fact perfectionism is utopian and not based on facts of human nature. It is easy to talk of partyless democracy but it cannot be so easily understood as to how it will be achieved. Without an opposition party, the party in power will have absolute power which will corrupt it absolutely. People's power is a mere word. In fact, the power has been everywhere in the hands of those, who get themselves elected as representatives of the people. Even in panchayat elections cut throat politics is generally found in the villages. In such a situation, it does not appear to be sensible to condemn democratic state, electoral system and the system of political parties.
8. **Defects of Bhoodan** Bhoodan movement has not been a success due to the following reasoning:
   (i) Though the intentions of donors of land cannot be doubted as a general rule, however, there have been many cases when the land donated was useless for the purpose of cultivation. In so many other cases the donor was not authorised to donate the land, since the ownership was controversial. In so many cases the donor wanted to take back their donated land.
   (ii) It is said that those who donated land for the movement did so due to their fear of the communism and the belief that this movement will save them from violent reactions of the exploited people.
   (iii) Even if the movement has been a success, land would have led to fragmentation not useful to national economy.
   (iv) The pace of change through Bhoodan movement is very slow.

In spite of the statistics presented by supporters of the movement the results have not been very optimistic. Even Jayaprakash Narayana accepted, "Vinobaji did something miraculous for some years. It appeared as though a new Gandhian process of social change and reconstruction had emerged. But after his stormy Bhoodan experiment not even a mild breeze blew, not to speak of mighty "storm" of Gramdan, Gram-Swarajya or any other constructive experiment. Later, he withdrew into his inner self, and started the experiment of 'action' in the form of 'inaction'. To date this does not seem to have borne fruit. But what is a period of 10 to 20 years in history? Meanwhile, the country is heading for a downfall, not only moral but also the economic, social and cultural degradation of at least 40 per cent of the Indian people who live below the poverty line. One is reminded here of a statement of Bapu who while defining democracy, had said that it did not only mean a government established by the people's vote; it also meant that the people had the power to oust their rulers when found unworthy to rule. Democracy has also ceased to exist in India today. The pyramid of the political structure still stands on its apex. The same is true of the educational and almost all other spheres of public activity. It is a tragic story that begs description." Ram Manohar Lohia used to say that Bhoodan movement is undoubtedly useful but it may not succeed before three centuries to come.

Thus, in spite of the high expectations of M.K. Gandhi, Vinoba Bhave, Jayaprakash Narayana and so many other supporters of Sarvodaya ideology, the history of the movement since its beginning to the present day does not present an optimistic picture. May be it was presented before its time.

SARVODAYA *Vs.* COMMUNISM : GANDHI *Vs.* MARX

M. K. Gandhi maintained that basically the problem of human beings is a moral problem. If a man becomes a human being in the true sense of the term there may not be anything like conflict among human beings. Therefore, every thoughtful person must follow the still small voice of reason everywhere though it is often suppressed by selfishness and the animal element in man. Long back Swami Vivekananda explained this ideal as the ideal of man-making. Therefore, Sarvodaya insists upon moral character as a solution of all evils — economic, social and political.

M. K. Gandhi and after him Vinoba Bhave, Jaiprakash Narain and Kaka Kalelkar have the credit of conceptual formulation of the ideal, its development and its taking shape into a popular movement. Today, Sarvodaya ideology is considered as an alternative to communism, and a better alternative since it is against violence, war and class struggle. As against communism it lays emphasis upon love, humanism, peace and harmony.

Thus, Sarvodaya means welfare of all and not of any particular class. This makes for the difference between Sarvodaya and communism or utilitarianism. Sarvodaya differs from Marxism though to some extent there is some agreement on some points so much so that Gandhism has been said to be communism minus violence.

Similarities between Sarvodaya and Communism

The following are some overt similarities between Sarvodaya and communism:

1. **Opposition of social injustice** Both these ideologies are dissatisfied with the present economic, social and political injustice and inequality. They oppose social injustice and wish to eliminate all sort of inequalities between human beings.
2. **Stateless society** Both Gandhi and Marx considered state as a mere means and not an end. Both called it a necessary evil which sometimes becomes an instrument of repression. M. K. Gandhi was against the violent means of the state. Therefore, both Marx and Gandhi were anarchist. However, they differed in details in their idea about state. While Karl Marx maintained that the state will wither away with the establishment of a proletarian society, M.K. Gandhi asks for decentralisation of power for the purpose. Of these two the latter idea appears to be more practical. In fact in communist countries the states have become more and more powerful.
3. **Classless society** Both Sarvodaya and communism aim at a classless society in different ways. Communism seeks to achieve the ideal by eliminating the capitalist class and even the middle class. Sarvodaya, on the other hand, seeks to achieve the ideal by realising perfect cooperation and harmony between all the classes so that there may be no class conflict.
4. **Support to depressed class** Both the ideologies support the weaker sections or the depressed classes in society. Both insist upon provision of minimum necessities to the backward classes so that everyone should achieve opportunities for the development of his capacities. As Kishori Lal Mashruwala has pointed out, Gandhi and Marx both are worried about the repressed, meanless and ignorant, dumb and hungary sections of society.
5. **Humanism** Both Marx and Gandhi were humanist. However, while Karl Marx explained human nature through his materialist principle of economic determinism, Sarvodaya defined human nature as divine and spiritual. Therefore, while Marx presented the ideal of economic man, Gandhi's man is a moral being, first and last.
6. **Emphasis upon labour** Both communism and Sarvodaya lay emphasis upon labour. According to M. K. Gandhi everyone should earn his living and physical labour is no less valuable than the mental labour. Similarly, communism has everywhere eulogized the labour which is the factor increasing the value of the raw material and creating surplus value which is the share of the labour. Both are against the idle middle

man and the capitalist who earns without any labour on his parts. Both call him an exploiter and both are against exploitation.

7. **International peace** Communism and Sarvodaya both declare elimination of war and establishment of world peace as their aim. However, it is difficult to understand how there may be a compromise between encouragement to violent revolution and realisation of world peace, both advocated by the communists.

Dissimilarities between Sarvodaya and Communism

The above discussion shows that there is only overt similarity between communism and Sarvodaya and in fact they have more dissimilarities than similarities. Vinoba Bhave has pointed out that to say that Sarvodaya and communism differ only with reference to violence is to forget that this very difference makes the two entirely different. In fact there cannot be any compromise between the two. The following are the important distinctions.

1. **Philosophical bases** Philosophically speaking, Sarvodaya and communism are based upon totally different metaphysical background as well as epistemology and axiology. While communism is materialism, Sarvodaya is based upon a spiritual world view. While Communism is empiricism Sarvodaya is idealism. While communism is hedonism Sarvodaya is spiritualism and even asceticism. M. K. Gandhi considered self-control and non-covetousness as necessary qualities of an aspirant after Sarvodaya. He insisted upon minimisation of needs and desires. This is in tradition with Indian philosophy and Indian psychology according to which mental control is a *sine qua non* of liberation.
2. **Means-end relationship** As has been already pointed out, in our discussion of the philosophy of M. K. Gandhi, Sarvodaya believes that the means should be as good as the end. On the other hand, communists do not believe in the purity of means. For a communist revolution any means, however inhuman it may be, may be adopted to achieve the end. Therefore, while Sarvodaya insisted upon moral means, communism makes no distinction between moral and immoral means.
3. **Methodology** The above two distinctions make an absolute difference between the methodology of Sarvodaya and communism. Sarvodaya permits only non-violent, human and spiritual means to achieve any social change. Evolution and not revolution is its techniques. Even where it accepts revolution, it is absolutely non-violent. M. K. Gandhi was so much against violence that he maintained that if India adopts violence he will not like to live in this country. Communism, on the other hand, directly supports encouragement to class hatred, conflict and violence. The Russian leaders since Lenin to present day, have backed violent means to encourage communism everywhere. Communism does not believe in evolution but only in revolution.

4. **Social Classes** Sarvodaya and communism are poles apart so far as the question of class conflict is concerned. Karl Marx maintained that the history of different societies is the history of conflicting classes. According to Saravodaya world view, society is based upon cooperation rather than conflict. The communists seek to intensify class conflict, the Sarvodaya workers seek to reduce it to their minimum. Class conflict has no place in Sarvodaya. In place of conflict which emphasises love, sacrifice and satyagraha for bringing about cooperation and harmony between classes, M. K. Gandhi was against capitalism but not the capitalist. He maintained that the capitalists may remain if they think themselves as trustees of the public wealth and utilise it for general welfare. Communist, on the other hand, insists upon not only the elimination of capitalism but even the elimination of the capitalist and their stooges, the petty bourgeois.
5. **Role of Religion** M. K. Gandhi was a religious man and so were all the famous advocates of the Sarvodaya ideal. Karl Marx, on the other hand, was absolutely against religion in every form and so were all the other spokesmen of communism. Communism does not believe in the existence of God. For M.K. Gandhi, as has been already pointed out, the political leader should remember God 24 hours in a day. Thus, Sarvodaya ideology believes in God and religion and also seeks to encourage it. The structure of Sarvodaya is based upon religious and spiritual foundation. The edifice of communism is based upon materialism which is against all religion as such.
6. **Private property** Karl Marx declared elimination of private property as the communist aim in his *The Communist Manifesto.* In communism the state is the sole owner of all property and the individual is not allowed any personal property to retain with himself. This has been questioned by the psychologists and sociologists alike. It has been pointed out that elimination of property is against human nature. It takes away all incentives and inspiration to work. It hits at the liberty of the individual. It retards the total development of personality. Sarvodaya is against a life of luxury. However, M. K. Gandhi did not see any evil in a person having wealth and property so far as he is prepared to use his assets for public welfare and leads a life of self-control. For communist the capitalist can never change his heart, for M. K. Gandhi such change of heart was an important economic programme of Sarvodaya. Therefore, the Sarvodaya Movement asks for voluntary donation of land and money for the people's cause. It supported compensation to the capitalist and the land owner if his wealth and land has to be taken by the state. On this issue, thinkers have taken sides with both Sarvodaya and communism. Both the theories have their advantages and disadvantages.
7. **Democracy** While Sarvodaya supports democracy, communism is against it. Here communism is with fascism and nazism who

considered parliament a talking shop and democracy a joke upon the people. The communist thinkers have rejected democracy in favour of totalitarianism though it may be the totalitarianism of the proletariat.

8. **Centralisation *versus* decentralisation** Communism believes in centralisation in economic and political field. In the economic field it favours establishment of huge industries and centralisation of production through more and more mechanisation. In the political field it believes in centralisation of all political power in the hands of the state machinery or the communist party and finally in the hands of one person who is chief of the state or head of the communist party. Sarvodaya, on the other hand, is against economic and political centralisation. In the economic field M. K. Gandhi asked for encouragement to cottage and rural industries. He was against mechanisation and monopoly. In place of monopoly he supported cooperation movement. In the political field Sarvodaya seeks to decentralise political power in every village. M. K. Gandhi asked for giving all the economic, social and political powers to the village panchayat. Sarvodaya ideology aspires for making every village self-sufficient both economically and politically. It is against centralisation of political power anywhere. It cherishes the establishment of most liberal democracy in every field of life.

From the above mentioned dissimilarities between Sarvodaya and communism, Acharya Vinoba Bhave, the foremost spokesman of Sarvodaya in our time, said, "The two ideologies are face to face, each bent upon swallowing up the other." According to Vinoba Bhave the rich are degenerates and poor are fallen people. Therefore, the Sarvodaya ideal is to uplift both the rich and poor. Thus, the Sarvodaya aims at economic welfare in the capitalist class, it requires the encouragement of the spirit of sacrifice and non-covetousness among the rich people so that they may be led to spiritual welfare. In the poor section of society, the sarvodaya ideal preaches for more and more labour in cooperation with the middle and the capitalist class. Nowhere immoral or violent means are permitted for any class.

BHOODAN

On 15th April, 1951 Vinoba finished his meeting at Shivaramapalli and entered into Telangana as a Shanti Sainik to find a solution to the problem of landless peasants of the area. On 18th April, 1951 he addressed a meeting at Ponchampalli, a place in Telangana, where he demanded some land from landowners on behalf of the starving untouchables, so that these people could cultivate and save themselves from starvation. A big landlord Ramachandra Reddi stood up to offer 100 acres of land for the landless people and thus started the movement. Hereafter Vinobaji started his *Padyatra* and went from place to place collecting land from the landlords for distribution to the landless. His normal line of argument was that land belongs to all. Just like air and water, land is also the property of the community as a whole. Those who part with their land do not give that as a matter of concession but one who accepts the land shows the courtesy and the giver should be grateful to the one who accepts. This is just like a *Dan,* in which the person accepting the *Dan* is gratifying the person who gives that. A person who accepts land is equally discharging his debt which otherwise would have remained on him throughout his life. Similarly he would say that 'you think me one of your sons and distribute your land in a way that I too get my share'. In this way Vinoba preached that Bhoodan means perpetual love and affection for those to whom you have given your land. He argued that even morally it is our duty to see that our neighbours do not suffer in any way and they are happy and live a decent life. Such a step will end the division that exists between the haves and have-nots and the conflicts or exploitation will virtually come to an end.

GRAMDAN

Acharya Vinoba Bhave's next move was from Bhoodan to Gramdan. By Gramdan meant that the whole village should be given as a gift to the community. It does mean not donating this or that piece of land but donating of the village as a whole. Vinoba started it on 24th May, 1952 in Mengrath village, in Hamirpur District of U.P. between Jhansi and Kanpur. In the words of Vasant Nargolkar, "It meant voluntary abolition of private property and land and investing it in the community as a whole as represented by the village." In actual practice the land within the village boundaries was distributed on the basis of the number of persons in each family irrespective of the fact whether or not the family held any land previously. Henceforward the land was not to stand in the name of each individual landholder, it was decided that the assessment to be paid to Government would be paid collectively in the name of the village. Thus, came into being the first Gramdan in India which was virtually a pioneering enterprise and which set a revolutionary example for other villages to follow. In Gramdan there will be no individual ownership of land. Each family shall till the soil with the help of other families and the produce will go to the community and not to any individual. A portion of the produce will be kept for annual use and village will give each and the every individual a share from its production. There will be a few shops which run and managed by the community as a whole to meet all their requirements. Each one will be required to do sufficient labour. Many cottage industries will also start and develop.

In order to manage village affairs there will be a General Village Council consisting of representatives elected by the people but each family having at least one representative. The Council will meet at least once in a month to look after day-to-day affairs. There will also be a sub-committee of 15 persons to meet frequently to discuss and decide about the immediate village problems. There will be no political purpose and no power politics. In other words of Vinoba Bhave there will be Lokniti or people's politics instead of Rajniti or state politics. One of the advantages of such an arrangement will be that the cities shall not be in a position to exploit the villagers. In the words of Vinoba, "Let it be understood clearly that increasing agricultural production is not the aim and object of Bhoodan and Gramdan. That would be only incidental. Its main object is to widen man's loyalty to entire society. It helps to create a climate where man will have the same solicitude for the least and society as he feels for his own children. Gramdan will end duality between individual and social life."

SAMPATIDAN

In the initial stages Vinoba was not in favour of accepting any money from the people as collecting money shall essentially mean giving birth to frictions and disputes. He also felt that money was the main cause of mutual distrust and suspicion. As Vasant Nargolkar has said, "Accumulation of wealth not only within individual persons but also within an institution does not, according to him, lead to economic or social health. He holds firmly to an old doctrine that miserliness breeds covetousness." But gradually Vinoba felt the necessity of money for accomplishing his mission. According to him those who had no landed property to donate could also participate in his movement by way of donating a definite fraction of their net annual income for rehabilitating the landless labourers on land or for maintaining a body of selfless Bhoodan workers. Such an arrangement he called Sampatidan. In his opinion miserliness should be as much an offence as theft. To quote him, "Today public opinion has no respect for a thief. The same should be its attitude to the miser or the holder. That is, just as a thief is liable to be brought under law, so public opinion should regard a miser as actionable under the law. Just as cultured parents teach their children even from childhood that to take anything without asking is a great wrong, educational science should help that not to give to one who asks it in need is a moral wrong. This idea is not new but it has not yet been given effect to as a general principle."

BUDHIDAN

According to Vinoba those who are engaged in liberal professions and cannot devote whole of their time in the movement can also participate in it. This could be done by delivering lectures and contributing articles or by way of conducting study circles for the youth. This is Budhidan or partial dedication of their intellectual capacity to the promotion of this sacred cause. All intelligent people can very liberally and rightly participate in the movement. It is a very useful contribution, whose importance and significance cannot be underestimated.

SHRAMDAN

Vinoba wanted the people not to be satisfied by donating only Bhumi or Sampati but they should also participate in the movement by giving free labour for projects of public utility. The money wasted or spent in giving wages can be saved and better quality of work done if the people themselves devote their time and labour in the completion of projects in which they are most interested. That will not only mean early completion of work but a real devotion, mental charm and happiness to all people. It will also help in Gramdan and in the establishment of Gram Swarajya. Vinoba therefore, suggested to his workers that they should not depend on finances from outside for running Bhoodan Movement but instead they should depend upon the dignity of labour and its proper utilisation. In his opinion this will also help in establishing a close relation between those for whom the work is done and those who volunteer themselves to labour for their cause. He felt that this is the lasting and permanent method of establishing Gram Raj. In the words of Vasant Nargolkar, "Gram Raj coming as it does alter the laying of the foundation in the form of Gramdan emphasises the economic reconstruction of the villages. It includes measures to improve agricultural production such as bunding of fields, use of better seeds, better implements and local organic manures in preference to costly inorganic manures, preservation of forests, if any, or constructing small dams or irrigation channels collectively for the irrigation of villages. Gram Raj also means encouragement to the principle of Swadeshi and, therefore, residents of a Gramdan village would do everything in their power to revive or promote as many village and cottage industries as possible with a view to dealing with the problem of local unemployment."

DEMOCRACY

Vinoba was not very much inclined to accept democracy in its present form. According to him, in so far as the democratic principles are concerned, they are better than any other known form of Government for running the administration, but according to him, there are many unhealthy institutions which have been introduced in running modern democracy. In the very first place, the Government in a democracy tries to take upon itself to do everything and to decide about social, educational, economic and political policies for the nation. This is basically a wrong idea. The Government of the people, for the people, by the people is today being actually controlled by a few people in the name alone of people. In theory it is being controlled by the representatives of the people who in turn are being over-shadowed by only the party leaders. About the role of the representatives in national affairs Vinoba said that normally they have failed to truly represent their voters. He was opposed to the concept of welfare state saying, "Normally I do not strongly raise my voice against the Government but on proper occasions I do speak to persons in authority. Today in the name of welfare state, power and authority resides in the hands of Central Government. I would not be prepared to call such a state a welfare state but an ill-fare state. It is no welfare whatsoever to let the political power concentrate in the hands of a few persons. The ideology of non-violence will gain currency only when political power is distributed in each and every village. Does it mean that power and authority should be conferred on every single village? No, power and authority are not acquired through some one bestowing it. It has to be deserved and exercised."

Vinoba criticised democracy on the ground that it has become more or less a game which is too rough for conscientious and simple minded gentlemen. He felt that many deserving persons are reluctant to stand as candidates for elected bodies mainly because they consider that elections are not for honourable people. In a free society there should be no such impression. There should be room for dignified and honourable persons which is somewhat missing from modern democracy. The present system of elections is so defective that money is playing a very vital role in influencing the voters and that the poor are gradually being eliminated from elected bodies. All sorts of propaganda, whether healthy or unhealthy, is usually going on in elections. Even the principles which are otherwise not acceptable to the society, for example, communalism, casteisms, regionalism, linguism etc., are usually exploited in the elections. Vinoba condemned parliamentary democracy by saying that it is not a majority but minority Government. In this form of Government a minority rules over the vast majority and as such the so-called people's Government is only a sham. There is virtually no difference between monarchy of the olden times and democracy of the present days. A Chief Minister or Prime Minister who rules in the name of the people is virtually a monarch. Vinoba's severest criticism was against the role of political parties in parliamentary democracy who usually try to make their members tongue-tied and dictate terms to tow them on particular lines. This is something undesirable and unwanted. It crushes freedom and liberty which is the basic and pivotal point of democracy. Thus, the present system of democracy or Rajniti is no solution to the problem and in its stead there should be Lokniti.

LOKNITI

Thus, Vinoba wanted to replace the present Rajniti by Lokniti. In Lokniti the real power and authority will be in the hands of the people who will themselves take unanimous decisions to do everything. Thus, there will be no hand of political parties or political leaders in the elections. In Lokniti there will be tolerance and accommodation. All the political parties will come together and agree to a code of conduct to be honoured both during and after the elections. This is a vital difference between Lokniti and Rajniti. For example, whereas in Rajniti political power is the sole aim and object and even false propaganda is used for acquiring power. In Lokniti there is a guarantee that each and every individual shall be responsible and shall not use unhealthy or underhand means for acquiring power. In Rajniti there is always a sense of compulsion and control from above. The authority of the state is needed to enforce the laws enacted by the state but violated by the people as these do not suit them. In Lokniti there will be no question of flagrant violation of rules and the people will be supposed to be disciplined. In the present Rajniti there is a regular struggle going on between the rival groups each trying to capture power even through bloodshed. But in Lokniti there shall be no such craze for power. The elected persons will not try to capture power for the sake of becoming more and more powerful. They shall be ready to serve the society most selflessly and as disciplined citizens. In Lokniti there shall not be any problem of mutual or unhealthy rivalry. Whereas the people in Rajniti are required to be vigilant to defend and demand their rights, in Lokniti there is no question of being vigilant because the rights will flow and everybody will be anxious for upkeeping the rights of others rather than his own rights. Thus, in Lokniti there will be more stress on the performance of duties rather than on demanding rights.

IDEAL FORM OF GOVERNMENT

According to Vinoba a common man was not concerned with the form of Government but whether the Government delivered the goods and helped in raising social, economic, political and moral standard of the people. An ideal Government is one which is not based on violence and which allowed the common people to participate in its activities. The people should show complete self-reliance and mutual cooperation among themselves. It should be the principle of equality in respect of rights of every citizen who receives protection from the State and renders service to the community. The Government should be an instrument of removing disparity in wages as far as possible. There should be homogeneity and uniformity in laws passed by the State.

COMMUNISM

Vinoba Bhave was against Communism. He subjected it to a very critical analysis. In his *Introduction to Gandhi and Marx* he pointed the weaknesses of Communism. He said "Within the short space of 20 years the Russian Revolution has become so colourless that it has almost lost its original attraction. The reason for the same is that of the four aspects of capitalism namely, centralisation, worship of large-scale machinery, faith in violence and exploitation, scientific socialism seeks to retain the first three and avoid the last but this is impossible. It is a delusive labyrinth. It should not be difficult to see that in spite of all efforts to do away with force, it will be necessary to accompany the other three. The infatuation for efficiency resulting from centralisation, for the leisure and comfort securable through worship of large scale industries and for the promise of defence and security held out by faith in arms, is so great that people lost it in a labyrinth of delusions and accustomed to save life are unable to do without even one of these three in order to put an end to exploitation." Vinoba criticised Communism because it believes in the use of force. He rejected the concept of historical materialism and condemned rigid schooling as regimentation of thought. In the words of Vasant Nargolkar, "He shows scant respect for one of the doctrines of historical materialism, of the inevitability of the socialist revolution as expounded by Marx, Engles and Lenin. He therefore, condemns rigid schooling, regimentation of thought or indoctrination of both the young and the old. Again, Vinobaji makes a decisive reference to another famous doctrine of Maxism of struggle or conflict being a fundamental element in nature and a necessary part of any progress. Dialectics, according to Lenin, is a study of contradictions within the essence of things while development is the struggle of opposites. Vinobaji, however disagrees."

Vinoba was not blind to good points of Communism. He appreciated Communism in so far as it pleads the cause of the poor and the down-trodden. He also praised the system for bringing awakening in the minds of the people and preparing them for a scientific approach to every problem with which they are faced.

Bhoodan and Communism

There is a fundamental difference between Bhoodan and Communism though both the systems seek to bring a revolution in the life of a nation. Both seek to change the present system of administration. Both condemn democracy in its present form. Both are opposed to concentration of wealth in capitalism. Both believe in the idea of distribution of wealth and seek to distribute the property of haves among the have-nots.

But beyond this there are vital differences in Bhoodan and Communism. In Bhoodan, there is no question of snatching property by forceful methods. A law can be passed by the Government obliging the landlords to part with their lands and to give that to the landless but this is unwarranted. It would result in bitterness and the basic purpose of distribution will be defeated. The haves should denounce the idea of ownership and possession willingly and part with Bhumi or Sampati which they have. On the contrary, according to Communism, the haves cannot be convinced to part with their property or wealth and as such the State should intervene by passing legislation and using force for depriving them of their land and property. In Bhoodan there is no place for violence. Acharya Vinoba Bhave sought a society based on the principle of non-violence without use of authority or force. With this end in view Vinoba enunciated the principle of Sarvasammati. With this end in view he gave the idea of village autonomy and decentralisation and that of Lokniti rather than that of Rajniti. On the other hand Communism believes in the use of force. The communists neither denounce nor condemn force or violence. Again, in Bhoodan there is no question of party system. It is a social revolution whereas Communism believes in rigid party system with complete regimentation and subordination of individual to the party bosses. Whereas Bhoodan movement lays stress on the use of proper means for achieving lasting ends and lays stress on means rather than ends, in Communism ends justify the means. In Communist philosophy any means are justified for achieving a particular end suited to time and circumstances. Thus, basically Communism and Bhoodan do not go hand in hand. While one believes in centralisation, the other believes in decentralisation. Similarly while one believes in violence, the other believes in non-violence.

VILLAGE AUTONOMY

Vinoba Bhave saw the poverty of India with his own eyes. He travelled on feet throughout the length and breadth of the country and very closely saw the problems of Indian villages. In his opinion India cannot go ahead as long as the villages are backward and villagers poor. The development and advancement visible in the cities, is no indication of India's social, economic and political advancement. If India is to rise it is only by way of Gram Swarajya or village autonomy. Vinoba said, "Rajya or Government is one thing, Swarajya or self-government is another. Government can be had through violence. Self-government is impossible without non-violence. So the thoughtful gentlemen desire Government. They urge people to strive for self-government." Vasant Nargolkar has defined Vinoba's concept of Gram Swarajya by saying that it means, "Direct government of the local community, by the whole community itself, without, as far as possible, any unwarranted outside interference in the affairs of the village. The concept of Gram Swarajya emphasises the political ideal under Sarvodaya." In Vinoba's philosophy there should be perfect village autonomy, each village having sufficient resources to produce for its own consumption. Each village should have its own economic and political system suited to its own conditions. Each village should have a council consisting of at least one representative from each family. This council should meet at least once in a month. It should have a smaller body to attend to day-to-day problems of the village. Village autonomy, however, does not mean adoption of a policy of isolation from neighbouring villages or areas. There is always some interdependence and that is also healthy to some extent. On the whole there should be internal autonomy and the village people should believe in simple living and clean habits. Vinoba believed in the idea of cottage industries and development of small scale industries. He was, however, not opposed to introduction of machinery or large scale industry. He only opposed the craze for machinery. Neither there should by any overanxiety for the machinery nor machinery should result in unemployment. With regard to the relation of a village society with other societies, Vinoba said, 'That which brings together self-governing village units is the nominal provincial political organisation. That which brings together such provinces normally is the national organisation and that which brings about mutual cooperation between such self-governing nations is the nominal political organisation of all humanity. In this political organisation there will be a parliament of individuals, wise representatives and impartials, drawn from all over the world. This Parliament will have no power of punishment of physical force, but it will have obtained power or restraint or moral force."

GANDHISM

Vinoba was a staunch follower and serious student of Gandhian philosophy. He sought solution of his problems in Gandhian philosophy. Gandhian ideology attracted him and saved him from joining the terrorists or going deep into the jungles or peaks of the mountains. Under Gandhiji, Vinoba learnt the basic principles of his ideology. Under Gandhiji, he learnt the lesson of equality of mankind and Universal brotherhood. Gandhiji taught him dignity of labour to realise that no job was high or low or dignified or undignified but all were high and respectable. From Gandhiji, he learnt non-violence and the significance of spiritual power over physical force. Under Gandhiji, he appreciated the principle of decentralisation and village autonomy over centralisation and interdependence. From Gandhiji he learnt the lesson of serving the poor and the down-trodden in the society and also that of loving every one and hating none. Thus, he was a Gandhian in thought, speech and action. Gandhiji selected him as the first Satyagrahi in individual non-cooperation movement launched by him at a critical time of independence struggle.

Vinoba appreciated Gandhian method of Satyagraha as a weapon to be used for achieving independence. Both agreed that Satyagraha is an inherent right of a citizen and that it cannot be taken away from him even under a democratic Government. Vinoba however, felt Satyagraha is not suited to post-independence era though in the pre-independence era that was a very useful and proper method and weapon. In his own words, "Under those circumstances the nature of work was negative and yet Gandhiji associated with it many items of positive, constructive work. Now when we hold that the right of satyagraha is fundamental even when a popular rule has been established, we have to understand that its nature would also become somewhat different. It is not that there is altogether no scope for satyagraha in a democracy. Such a belief is totally wrong. But the belief that the type of satyagraha resorted to by people in pre-independence days has much scope and that it will be more effective under democratic conditions is equally wrong. Only that kind of satyagraha which is positively constructive will be more effective in a democracy. It is from this standpoint that we have to look at our Bhoodan Movement." At another place Vinoba has said that the concept of satyagraha as preached by Gandhiji was not very effective in so far as international conditions were concerned. We would have to change the nature and character of satyagraha to make it more effective and suited to our present conditions. To quote him again, "Of what use could satyagraha be in the field of international affairs. Satyagraha represents a spiritual power. It is not physical, neither it is mental. Science by its nature subordinates the human mind. We have to ascend to the level of super mind, if we are to get to know this power of satyagraha and not through popular opinion or governmental agencies then we would have to raise ourselves to the super mental level." Thus, though Vinoba and Gandhiji were very closely associated to each other yet Vinoba was bold enough to point out the necessity of a change in the satyagraha ideology with a view to making that more realistic and practicable. However, he was not in a position to give any better alternative to satyagraha. In the words of Vasant Nargolkar, "Though Vinobaji for a time seemed to be thinking very hard, he has not been able to evolve another more effective type of Satyagraha than Bhoodan itself. In his search for more direct and powerful non-violent methods of influencing people with a view to induce them to accept higher values of life, he many a time, came very near to Sri Aurobindo's famous analysis of the psychological and spiritual powers of man."

INTERNATIONAL PROBLEMS

Vinoba was much farsighted in saying that it is the most essential duty of a country that it should defend its national borders. A country which fails to defend its national borders is not only criminal before the people but greatest culprit for posterity. It was a painful shock to him when Vinoba came to know that China invaded India. For him all international disputes should be settled by peaceful methods. To quote him, "If necessary the matter should be referred to an arbitration and a settlement reached. When even such a proposal is not accepted it affects a neutral person like me and one is bound to believe that this war is being thirst on India — it is not an age of wars — this is likely to lead to very dangerous consequences. I would, therefore, pray to God He should induce wisdom in them to accept this proposal that has been put forward. If there is any alternative plan, it may also be suggested and considered." Vinoba believed that we should always be ready for negotiations. Territorial expansion is a curse and those nations which believe in imperialism and colonialism are inflamming war. Vinoba always stood for an atmosphere in which peace can be brought about and therefore no danger of war. Thus, Vinoba counselled patience even against provocation. In his philosophy counter-provocation can provide no lasting solution to the problem.

CRITICAL EVALUATION

Vinoba wants to bring about an agrarian revolution through Gramdan and Bhoodan Movements. No one can underestimate the significance of a peaceful revolution that he planned and for which he strived. It has appealed to the people who have donated him lakhs of acres of land for distribution to the landless is in itself an indication of success of his philosophy. With the spiritual power of Vinoba and his appeal which touched the souls of the audience, the Sarvodaya movement made rapid progress. But at the same time it was put to severe criticism mainly from the point of view of expediency and practicability.

1. **The problem of fragmentation of land into small pieces** It is unfortunate that in India there is already much fragmentation of land and each division after the death of the family head leads to further fragmentation. Vinoba accepted land even from a person who has a very small tract of land and this led to further fragmentation and sub-division of land. Such was a policy not suited to Indian economy. Indian national policy and programme is to encourage consolidation of land and to run cooperative system in agriculture. The sub-division of land, which Vinoba encouraged was bound to lead to many complications. It was not conducive to our economic policies.
2. **There is no system of proper distribution of the land** It has been estimated that about 75% of the land still remains to be distributed. The donor of the land loses interest as soon as he donates the land and as such he does not cultivate that piece of land with interest and zeal. Since the land has not been further distributed, no one takes interest in having excess yield from that tract of land. This results in low production and a nation like India cannot afford to neglect thousands of acres of land donated to Vinobaji.
3. **Accepting land from small landowners and distributing that to the landless is of no practical utility** On the contrary it lowers down the living standard of the donor and does not raise that of the recipient of the land. It is of no advantage to either.
4. **The land donated to Vinobaji is otherwise not cultivable** It is a burden on the donor who finds a beautiful way out of his difficulty by donating it to the landless. The landless on the other hand puts his labour in that but does not get reward for years. In most of the cases the landless cannot have the patience to wait for getting reward through such a piece of land and in fact has not the means to wait.
5. **Unpsychological** Vinobaji felt that donating of land is not a matter of gratitude. Similarly he believed that those who receive the land are under no obligation but the donor should feel grateful to the recipient because of the latter's discharging him from a social obligation. This is against human psychology. The donor at least expects a sense of gratitude from the recipient while he is parting with his legally earned property and in many cases of his ancestors. If this least courtesy is not shown, his sense of vanity will not be satisfied. Thus, on psychological grounds there is room for improvement in the movement.

6. **Vinobaji has not been in a position to touch the conscience of big landlords and propertied people** In Vinoba's movement mostly the people belonging to middle class have come forward. The land donated to him is mostly by the persons who have already little or little more than very basic needs. The very purpose of bringing about a revolution has not been achieved because the citadels of aristocracy or the great landlords have not responded to the movement.

25
Jaya Prakash Narayan (1903 — 1979)

Jaya Prakash Narayan, was born in 1903 and educated in U.S.A. Here he came in contact with many socialists and practially overwhelmed by the influence of Marxism. He studied M.N. Roy, another revolutionary of India, who had escaped to the U.S.A. to save himself from arrest and was influenced by his philosophy. For quite some time Jaya Prakash remained under the influence of Marxism but as the time passed he began to lose faith in Marxian creed, mainly because it denied individual freedom and its party regimentation was very severe. In 1934 he founded Indian Socialist Party in which subsequently he also admitted the Communists. However, finding them not very sincere to the socialist doctrines, he turned them out and thus saved his party from infiltration. In 1940, Jaya Prakash openly denounced Popular Front of the Communists. In 1942, he actively participated in the revolutionary movement. He got name and fame in 1942 during Quit India Movement. He remained in jail for four years and once he even managed to escape from Hazari Bagh Central Jail. In 1946, he planned along with other socialists for a mass revolution. In 1953, he initiated talks with Jawahar Lal Nehru for increased cooperation between the Congress and the Socialists. In 1954, he, however, resigned from the Socialist Party then known as P.S.P. and became *Jeewan Dani* for Sarvodaya Movement. Since then he was devoted to the cause of bringing about a new society in India in which there will be no exploitation and decentralization of authority will be the basic principle. He was very closely associated with Vinoba Bhave in his Bhoodan Movement. He wanted to have a new society which he termed as Sarvodaya. In 1979, Jaya Prakash passed away after a prolonged illness.

POLITICAL IDEAS

Basic Principles of Sarvodaya

The idea of Sarvodaya was taken by Mahatma Gandhi from Ruskin's *Unto The Last.* In Gandhian philosophy Sarvodaya meant collective welfare in which also was individual's own welfare and that there was always respect for work and that all types of jobs were respectable. Simple living and high thinking was true life and there should be universal development for all sections of society. Both Jay Prakash Narayan as well as Vinoba Bhave believed that Sarvodaya is a moral programme and a line of action for collective welfare. Sarvodaya is an indication of a political revolution by peaceful means through free and frank expression of ideas. It has been said, "Ideally such a structure would replace completely the compulsion of the State of individual initiative and voluntary organisation, it is a sort of enlightened anarchy." In the economic field, Sarvodaya stands for decentralization of authority. The means of production as well as distribution shall be controlled and managed by the society. In Sarvodaya society, there will be cooperative system of production both in the industry as well as agriculture. There will also be village autonomy.

Traits of a Sarvodaya Worker

A Sarvodaya worker is required to spin daily and use the cloth spun by himself. He should use goods produced by cottage and small scale industries. He should try to use cow milk. He should clean latrines or do other work relating to cleanliness of the village at least once a month. He should try to introduce basic system of education. He should try to learn at least one of the regional languages of India. He should be an ideal non-violent person with a sense of self-confidence and belief in the power of the masses. He should try to promote unity among various religions and sections of the society. He should boycott caste system and discourage the use of intoxicating goods. He should promote female education and try to spread the idea that both men and women were equal. He should try to spread regional language and provincial culture so that none of them is neglected. He should aim at bringing about economic equality and growth of agriculture. He should help in the unity of labourers and uplifting of the poor. He should serve the lepers and protect the cows.

Sarvodaya Society

The Society under Sarvodaya samaj will be free from coercive centralized authority. It shall be more or less a loose federation consisting of self-governing autonomous villages. Every village or unit shall be self-sufficient and believe in the system of economic decentralization. There should be no parliament of the type which we at present have. Those who come to power shall not be the rulers but servants of the society. The State will be unnecessary in Sarvodaya Society, and as far as possible its authority will be considerably reduced. The State does not help in the development of individual faculties. On the contrary, it is an unhealthy check even on individual's healthy activities. There is no need to load government with so many punitive weapons as such authorities in actual practice hamper individual progress. In Sarvodaya society there will be no party system and the people shall sit together to decide their own affairs. They will not require representatives to speak and talk on their behalf but on the contrary shall get opportunity to experess their own ideas themselves. In Sarvodaya society there should be real *Lok Neeti* instead of *Raj Neeti*. There shall not be party or power politics but authority shall flow from the people themselves who will work in a sense and spirit of serving the people rather than of governing over them. Conflicts are not peculiar to mankind alone but these are also seen even among the animals. Such conflicts among human beings can be due to various reasons. Such as conflict of interests or ignorance of irrational and intolerable inequalities created by the deliberate politics of those who have managed to come to power. But the solution to such problems does not lie in equipping the Government with more punitive powers but in creating awakening and consciousness among the masses so that they can adjust themselves in a better and reasonable way.

Socialism to Sarvodaya

According to Jaya Prakash Marxism was neither easy nor the appropriate solution for many of our political problems. It did not guarantee individual liberty and freedom which it claimed to give, with the result that he changed his ideology. In 1929 Indian National Congress declared complete independence as the goal of its national struggle. Jaya Prakash bade farewell to his Marxist ideology and actively participated in the civil disobedience movement launched by Mahatma Gandhi. He kept aloof from the Communist Party of India and did not subscribe to its philosophies. He, however, wanted to introduce socialism in Congress. He founded the Congress Socialist Party which was subsequently responsible for giving socio-economic programme to the Congress. He was not in favour of the philosophy of materialism because he felt that is no solution for a lasting peace. As the time passed, he seriously studied the philosophy and political ideas of Mahatma Gandhi. He was convinced that spiritual foundation was required for a lasting peace. He began to realise the value of individual freedom, equality and brotherhood which were in practice missing from Communism.

Vinoba's starting of the Bhoodan Movement and getting a donation of 100 acres of land from Shri Ram Chandra Reddy changed the very course of J.P.'s philosophy. He found in Bhoodan Movement a fair, better and effective alternative to communist revolution which provided for snatching of land by forceful methods. According to him Gandhism taught us the method of *Satyagraha* which brought freedom to India and that Bhoodan and Gramdan Movements were bound to bring economic revolution and make our political freedom a reality. He was inspired by the idea of *Lok Neeti* instead of *Raj Neeti* as expounded by Vinobaji. He was also convinced about the desirability of cottage industries and the system of democratic decentralization. He wanted to change the face of India by introducing village autonomy and raising the downtrodden and the poor who form a vast majority of Indian population. He believed that Bhoodan and Gramdan movements are constructive techniques and easy as well as practicable solution to India's problems. Hence, he subsequently decided to leave P.S.P. and join Bhoodan Movement. He found them far better than Marxism because the movement not only aimed at achieving what Communism aimed, but with the additional advantage that freedom is preserved and every individual remains true to his conscience. Jaya Prakash became a *Jeewan Dani* meaning thereby that he devoted his whole life to the cause of Bhoodan and Gramdan. In his own words, "I was, and am, not sure if the State will ever wither away completely. But I am sure that it is one of the noblest goals of social endeavour to ensure that the power and the function and spheres of the State are reduced as far as possible. I became at this time, and still am, an ardent believer, like Gandhiji, in the maxim that Government was the best that governed the least."

Significant Political Ideas

Faith in Democracy Jaya Prakash Narayan was very staunch supporter of democracy and favoured democratic institutions. For him, democracy was both a creed and a way of life. He believed in individual freedom which could best be achieved only in democracy and through democratic system. He was however, not satisfied with the present democratic system which he felt is highly defective. In his opinion the present system was highly centralized with the result that the people could take any active role in the proper functioning of democratic institutions. But control of party bosses is so rigid that individual is practically ignored and even he cannot express himself. The parliamentary system, in its present form, has a very narrow base where the authority starts from above rather from down below. It has thus an inverted structure which cannot last long. Jaya Prakash condemned democracy by saying that our present legislative bodies which govern in the name of majority are in fact minority Governments. Practical experience shows that a constituency is called upon to elect one member out of so many who wish to be returned, and the person who is actually returned might not be getting majority of total votes polled in the constituency though he might have got the maximum votes. Similarly the majority party in the legislature might not have got majority of votes polled during the polls. The decisions arrived at the majority party are not unanimous. Even in the Cabinet, decisions are not arrived at unanimously and only a few powerful persons carry others with them. This clearly shows that the majority is ruled by the minority.

Jaya Prakash felt that in our present parliamentary democracy the institution of party system is very unhealthy. It has practically denied liberty to the individuals. Party bosses try to dominate their members. There is struggle for superemacy which divides the rank and file and also promotes insincerity. There is unnecessary wastage of national money. Those who can speak well irrespective of the consideration whether they are sincere or not, dominate the show and manage to come to power. In order to win the elections all healthy and unhealthy practices are used. Even casteism and communalism are used to win the election. Therefore, Jaya Prakash strongly condemned the present system of parliamentary democracy.

But he was a democrat and wanted to see democracy running in its true sense and spirit. A democracy in its true sense must have spiritual basis and that can only be possible when the people practising democracy should believe in truth. They should also follow non-violence. They should be ready to face all oppression and high-handedness with courage and boldness. They should love liberty and believe in the spirit of toleration willing to extend their hand of cooperation. A true democrat should be ready to discharge his duties and responsibilities with willing happiness. He should be a believer in human equality. There should be decentralization of authority. The power should go from down to above and not flow from above to down below. In a true democracy there should be the system of decentralization of authority.

Partyless Democracy

Thus, Jaya Prakash felt that the introduction of party system in our present political set-up has degenerated democracy. It has made the institution of government of the people, for the people, by the people a mere farce. It encouraged party politics and divided the nation. Hence, the whole system should be changed. There should be a partyless democracy. There should be in each village a Gram Mandal or a Conference consisting of elected representatives of the village, one at least from each family. Such a Mandal shall meet monthly to decide all pending issues of the village. There will be no need and necessity of electing representatives to speak on behalf of the people but the people themselves will express their feelings and viewpoint. Each Mandal will in turn become an electoral college to send representatives to the legislatures. The authority will go down from villages to the legislatures and thus the real democracy will emerge. He has suggested that the cabinet should not be formed on the basis of party system but on the contrary there should be partyless cabinets which should enlist capable and intelligent persons from all political parties.

Panchayati Raj

According to Jaya Prakash Narayan real solution to India's political problems lies in the introduction of system of Panchayati Raj in our body politic. As long as authority is not decentralized among the millions in our villages, nothing concrete can come out. Hence, in each village there should be a Gram Sabha which shall be the basis of the entire scheme. The Sabha shall consist of all adult men and women living in that village and shall have the power to discuss about the life and difficulties of village. Gram Panchayat shall be the executive organ of this Sabha. Subsequently there shall be Zila Parishads and Block Samitis at the higher level. Block Samitis shall cover the villages falling in one block and a few blocks combined together shall form Zilas and these Zilas in turn shall constitute the State and country. Jaya Prakash

Narayan fully realized the difficulties which can arise in the establishment of Gram Sabha or Gram Conference. Such difficulties can possibly be due to family feuds that are common in our villages. The caste system can also be one of the reasons for its not very successful working. However, if proper and effective steps are taken, there is no reason to think that all difficulties and complications which come in the way of proper and successful working of Panchayati Raj cannot be overcome. He suggested, that people should be given proper education. Family feuds and party system should not be allowed to interfere in the Gram Panchayats and Gram Sabhas. These Sabhas should be given some effective powers and real authority should be given to the Sabhas so that they can effectively exert themselves. The Sabhas should be given sufficient economic resources and authority to control civil servants working under their jurisdiction. The Sabhas and Panchayats should have a non-political character. There should be no intervention from the high ups in the sphere of their jurisdiction. If this system is introduced in the villages a new life is bound to come in the country. Such a system is bound to bring consciousness among the people and they shall refuse to be exploited by the city people. In other words, indirectly cities shall also be suitably improved.

Economic Ideas

Jaya Prakash Narayan believed in the socialisation of means of production and distribution. Our present system is not healthy in which means of production and distribution are not being utilized for collective welfare. There should be nationalization of industries. Economic resources should be placed at the disposal of the nation rather than any individual. There should be reduction of land revenue and also limitations on expenditure. Economically there should be collective ownership and control of all large scale industries. Such heavy industries, as transport, mining or shipping should forthwith be nationalized. However, cooperative effort alone can bring about the balance between agriculture and industry. There should be economic rehabilitation of the poor and the down-trodden. There should be collective farming and agrarian reconstruction. There is very close relationship between culture and economics because the culture of a nation is reflected by economic conditions of its people. Economic conditions of the country should be such that every individual gets equality of opportunity and is given some minimum economic standard.

In our modern society Jaya Prakash Narayan was a socialist of the first order. He tried to awaken the youth of India by telling them to remember the role which they played during 'Quit India Movement'. He gave them a call to re-unite themselves to perform that constructive duty. He tried to shake the present democracy from its very foundations. His system of decentralization, Panchayati Raj and democracy in its new form, if properly adopted, can bring a new outlook in India.

26
Dr. Shyama Prasad Mookerjee
(1901 — 1953)

Dr. Shyama Prasad Mookerjee was born on 7th July, 1901 in Calcutta. After getting his early education at Mitter Institute, he joined Presidency College, Calcutta, from where he passed his B.A. in 1919 with Honours in English and was placed in the First Division. He did his M.A. in Bengali. In 1924, he passed his B.L. and was placed in the First Division.

Dr. Mookerjee started his life career as a lawyer in Calcutta High Court. Soon he became popular in his profession. He was hardly 33 years of age when in 1934 he was elevated to the high post of Vice-Chancellor of Calcutta University — a very rare distinction conferred at this young age. He was elected to the Bengal Legislative Assembly in 1937. In 1938, he was conferred the Degree of Doctor of Laws by Calcutta University. In the same year Banaras University also honoured him with the same distinction. In 1939, he became a member of Hindu Mahasabha and continued to remain its member till 1948, when its activities were suspended. In 1941, Dr. Mookerjee became a member of Bengal Cabinet headed by Fazlul Huq. He left Cabinet in 1943 as a protest against undue official interference in day-do-day working of Ministers. In 1943, he was elected as the President of Hindu Mahasabha. In 1946 he became a member of Indian Constituent Assembly which was responsible for enacting a Constitution for India. During this period he also negotiated with the British Government on behalf of Hindu Mahasabha. In 1948, he resigned from Hindu Mahasabha and suggested the organisation to suspend its political activities.

In 1947, he was appointed as a Cabinet Minister in Nehru Cabinet and continued there for three years when he resigned from his post in 1950, as a protest against the Delhi Pact between India and Pakistan. In 1951, he founded Bhartiya Jan Sangh, which under his leadership, became a national party. He died in 1953 in Kashmir in mysterious circumstances.

Dr. Mookerjee was a powerful and eloquent orator as well as author. Some of his important works include : *Integrate Kashmire* and *Why Jan Sangh*?

Political Ideas

Shyama Prasad Mookerjee was a staunch believer in national unity. He believed that India was a great nation and that all those living in India must accept this basic fact. The pepole belonging to various communities must be faithful to India alone. As such he very strongly repudiated 'Two-Nation Theory' as expounded by Mr. Jinnah. He was against the policy of appeasement followed by the Indian National Congress for winning over Indian Muslims. He suggested to the National Congress to take a tough and bold stand and make the Muslims of India realise that India was their homeland and they should extend their unqualified support and loyalty to India.

Indian Culture

Dr. Shyama Prasad Mookerjee was of the opinion that India was the land which predominantly belonged to Hindus. It was the land which had preserved ancient Indian culture and civilisation. It was a historical fact which no nation in the world could deny. Any political institution and organisation which tried to refute this historical fact was doing immense harm both to the present India and its past traditions. Congress was one such organisation which in the name of secularism was giving undue importance to the minorities and was also disfiguring the image of India which was built after prolonged, consistent and persistent efforts made by our ancestors. Every political institution and organisation in India must be bold enough to declare that it stood for preserving ancient Indian culture which was most dynamic and had proved its adjustability with the passage of time. Our Constitution and all our subsequent laws should be in tune with, and in the spirit of, preserving our past cultural heritage. As President of Hindu Mahasabha, Mookerjee was bitterly opposed to the idea of partition of the country. For him, C.R. Formula or Cripps Mission Plan or for that matter any subsequent plans *e.g.*, Wavell Plan or Mountbatten Mission plan which provided for the partition of the country was suicidal and against our national interests and must be rejected without any lamentation. For him, it was the most honoured duty of each citizen and more so for the leaders of a national organisation to preserve our territorial integrity and our national borders at all costs.

Mookerjee believed that no amount of sacrifice or bloodshed should deter us from performing this most pious duty. He suggested that threat of Muslim communalism to dislocate our life by violent means, if their demand for the creation of Pakistan was not met, should not, in any way deter us from our honoured task of maintaining the unity of our country. The nation must be prepared to sacrifice its everything for seeing a united and prosperous India. Even after the partition of India he suggested that the Government should take a very rigid and firm stand towards Pakistan, otherwise that might be on our heads. He said that our weak policy has resulted in the creation of

Pakistan and continuance of the same policy might be a permanent headache for India. He even resigned from the Cabinet when Delhi Pact between India and Pakistan was signed. He suggested to his countrymen that they should try to revoke the wrong act of British Government namely that of the partition of the country. Pakistan could have been avoided had the Indian National Congress not adopted the policy of appeasement, thereby encouraging the British Government to give encouragement to Muslim communalism.

Foreign Policy

As regards foreign policy of India Mookerjee was of the opinion that at this stage India could not align itself with any of the power blocs. The policy of non-alignment and neutrality was wise at this stage. It should be a vigorous policy of pursuing our ideals and political objectives. It should be followed in a fashion that it created friends for India in the world and did not leave an impression that neutrality meant weakness or shirking our international responsibilities. This could be accomplished when our policies were framed on principles and dynamic in approach and outlook. Foreign policy should be swift and adjustable. In our diplomatic relations proper image of India should be portrayed and that such an image should be based on ancient Indian culture and civilisation.

National Policy

Dr. Mookerjee believed that India was essentially a land of the Hindus and as such Hindu culture and civilisation must get pride and priority in all our arrangements. No Government should feel shy in following a policy on those lines. It, however, did not mean that other cultures had no right to develop but free flow, growth and development of Hindu culture should not be hampered and state patronage or protection should be available to it. All religious minorities have a right to live and demand state protection in India. It was the foremost duty of State to extend that to the minorities living in it. They had also a right to live according to their ancient cultural traditions and religious ideas. But all this is conditional. These minorities should treat India as their motherland and should also be willing to sacrifice their life, liberty and property for India. Mookerjee was pained to see that some of the minorities had extra-territorial affiliations and did not consider India as their motherland. Such minorities must be made to realise their duties towards the country in which they lived. The activities of such minorities should be very carefully watched. In each and every country activities of suspicious minorities were being carefully watched and if the state failed in doing that, it was failing in the performance of its legal as well as moral duties. Our secularism should neither be misinterpreted nor misunderstood. Secularism nowhere provided permission for extra-territorial loyalties. It was meant to be understood as toleration of viewpoints of other religious communities.

As India is a democracy based on the principle of adult franchise, each and every person residing in India for a specific period of time may be elected as the representative of the people. The people having extra-territorial loyalties could neither claim to represent the people nor could they act in the best interests of the nation.

The State policy in the country should be followed in such a way that minority did not stand in the way of majority. The interests of a vast majority should not be sacrificed simply because a minority was not agreeable to that or that it did not suit its convenience. It should be left to the good sense of the majority to respect minority opinion.

Economic Ideas

According to Dr. Mookerjee, present system of over-mechanisation and too much dependence on machines was not suited to Indian conditions. There was need and necessity for revision of whole economic policy. Industries should be developed both in the private and public sectors, as without industrialisation country was bound to remain backward socially as well as economically. There was dire need and necesity for developing large and small scale industries. It is most essential that public and private sectors must go hand in hand and should be complementary rather than contradictory to each other. At this stage of development India need not be over-zealous for placing industry in the public sector. In the whole universe private sector has always been given due share and place for development and has also played a very significant part. Hence, private sector should be given due place and position in our economic set-up as well.

To conclude, Dr. Mookerjee was the most dynamic personality of our modern times. It was due to his efforts and personal character that Bhartiya Jan Sangh became an All India party in no time. His approach to minority question might appear a bit bitter, but was very realistic and time itself is proving the truth of his ideas.

27
Dr. Ram Manohar Lohia (1910 — 1968)

Dr. Ram Manohar Lohia was a prominent Indian leader who propagated socialism in India. He was a good orator and always supported his arguments with figures and statistics. He was opposed to the policies and programmes of the ruling party particularly the thesis of Ashok Mehta that the Socialists should cooperate with the Congress in some respects. He however, felt that many good ideas of Gandhian philosophy could be incorporated in Socialist philosophy in India. He accepted the significance of decentralised economy. He made it clear that the socialists were equi-distant from the Congress and the Communists and as such the question of making alliance with the Congress did not arise.

PHILOSOPHY OF HISTORY

Lohia said that history is moving in a cyclical way. A stage comes in the history of the country when it attains glory, height and power. Then it falls down to the depth and makes an attempt to rise again. After struggle the nation again rises to see a fall and thus struggle and circle goes on. In this way history is not static and it is a continuous process, which is going on.

Dr. Lohia, in principle, accepted Marxian concept of dialectical materialism, but laid emphasis on 'Consciousness' which had been ignored by Marxians. He suggested that intellect and economic aims should be combined to make the whole concept more reasonable and rational.

CASTE AND CLASS

Dr. Lohia clearly distinguished between class and caste. According to him castes represent conservative forces in India whereas on the other hand classes represent dynamic force and social mobilization. He said that in human history a struggle has been going on between caste and class, the former representing stagnation and latter dynamism. In the words of Prof. V.P. Verma, "Thus Lohia's concept of the struggle between classes and castes is only a popular form of Pareto's theory of the struggle between the landed interests of the rentiers who represent residues of persistence of aggregates and the monied interests who represent residues of combination."

Asian Politics

Asian Politics, according to Lohia, has some special problems. The first problem is that in politics, religious dogmaticism is introduced which results in communal problems. Thus, in Asian politics religion and politics are closely linked, which pose a serious problem. Democratic traditions are not fully well established. Accordingly terror and political assassinations became a part of Asian politics. In Asian politics, the bureaucrats and the technocrats play a very important role. Once a class of persons comes into power, it tries to maintain its hold and control over the offices which such people once manage to get.

Four Pillar State

Dr. Ram Manohar Lohia expounded the concept of Four Pillar State. In this State there will be a system of functional federalism at four levels namely the village, the Mandals (District), the Province and the Central Government. There will be no concentration of powers and district magistracy will be abolished. There will be Panchyats at village, city and district levels and these will be responsible for policy formulation and undertaking welfare activities.

National Language

Lohia supported Hindi as the national language of India. It should be introduced in the offices as quickly as possible. It should take the place of English, if democracy is to become a success in the country. English, which could not be followed by a vast population of the country, should no longer be allowed to linger on as the language for running administration.

Small Scale Industries

Lohia believed that India was a country where man-power was available in abundance. Therefore, heavy and large scale industries was bound to create many serious problems including that of unemployment. Hence, small scale industries should be encouraged and cooperative unions should be set up. Lohia favoured the idea of setting up powerful village governments.

Socialism

Lohia felt that old orthodox socialist system was out-dated. He therefore, gave the concept of new socialist system. In the new system an attempt will be made to have equalitarian standards in so far as income and expenditure pattern was concerned. Lohia suggested that it was essential to have nationalisation of industries. However, nationalisation was no solution to all the problems. Natural resources and human energies should be harnessed to raise the living standard of the people.

Civil Disobedience

Lohia felt that Gandhian weapons of Civil Disobedience and non-cooperation were useful for winning independence. More ideas of Gandhian philosophy could be introduced in Socialist thoughts. He also accepted Gandhian ideology about decentralisation of authority. He said, "When injustice and oppression go beyond bearable bounds, when constitutional methods have proved incapable of achieving redress, it should be open to the people to violate unjust laws and wrongs and injustices that are inflicted upon them."

Equal Irrelevance

Dr. Lohia propounded the concept of Equal Irrelevance. According to him today the world is divided into two power blocs namely the Russian and the American. Both these blocs are trying to establish their supremacy. He, however, was of the view that victory of any power bloc will not lead to the emancipation of mankind. In his own words, "......the ideal of a world parliament elected on adult franchise with weightage or a senate, the notion of co-existence with approximation, the desire for irreducible equality of reasonable margins within the nation and for an absolute equality among nations and the overall method of individual and civil resistance are all ingredients of this doctrine."

Foreign Policy

Dr. Lohia was critical of Nehru's policy of non-alignment. He felt that the nation should have dependable friends. He accordingly suggested that foreign policy of the country should be re-oriented. Main principles of India's foreign policy should be as follows:

1. Involvement in power blocs disputes should be avoided.
2. UNO should be assured that aggression will never be assisted.
3. UNO and its specialised agencies should be strengthened.
4. Collective security arrangements for the region stretching from Indonesia to Egypt should be made.
5. Friendly relations with all the world Governments and the people be developed.
6. The people struggling for their freedom should be extended all help.
7. Principle of equality of all nations should be propagated by suggesting revision of all existing treaties, agreements and charters.
8. Every human being should be assured of decent living standard.
9. There should be a World Parliament.
10. Support should be extended to all socialist movements.

Lohia suggested that socialist foreign policy will be based on the principles enunciated above.

Individual Freedom

Lohia supported the idea of freedom of the individual. He felt that the people should be given freedom of association and speech. He suggested that private life of the individuals should remain untouched to the extent possible and that the state should not try to pierce through the private life of the people, as far as possible.

Method of Political Struggle

Lohia did not agree with those who suggest that violence should be used as a method for achieving political objectives. He favoured non-violence, including Gandhian technique of Civil Disobedience and Non-cooperation. He very much appreciated Satyagrah as a weapon and method for struggle. In his *Marx, Gandhi and Socialism* he said, "It is not necessary for a people suffering from starvation or large scale dismissals to depend on Parliament or to wait expectantly for another general election. They have this priceless, matchless weopon of Civil Disobedience in their hands."

Like many other Indian Socialists, Dr. Lohia could not completely shed the influence of Congress in Socialism. He was also under the influence of Gandhism. Though opposed to Nehru's foreign policy, he was indebted to Gandhiji for ideas about non-violent struggle and use of weapons like Non-cooperation and Civil Disobedience for achieving the objectives.

28
Concluding Remarks

While Karl Marx, and some Indian thinkers influenced by him, considered economic sources as determining the history, contemporary Indian philosophers have interpreted history as a divine process. This is in keeping with ancient Indian philosophy of history. But on the other hand, in tune with the modern consciousness, they pointed out that all history must be re-written from the point of view of the role of the masses rather than the kings. History so far has been considered as a narration of the deeds of the kings and war lords. These thinkers pointed out that the role of the masses is no less important in any political or social event. In fact, they considered masses as the true determiners of history. Their interpretation may be called divine determinism as against economic determinism. In this divine determinism, however, as has been pointed out by the *Bhagwadgita,* man is not merely a passive instrument. Though ultimately the Divine determines the historical events, man can participate effectively in this process and in this lies his manhood. Thus, social evolution and social change need not wait for divine interference. God determinism is not fatalism. Moreover, God is always on the side of man. Therefore, history is proceeding towards progress in human values. These thinkers were optimist in the sense that they thought that humanity is gradually progressing towards more and more expression of divinity. Therefore, they had a deep faith in the spiritual future of man.

RELIGIOUS BASIS OF POLITICS

None of our contemporary philosophers was a politician or political scientist in the academic sense of the term. They were primarily religious persons and their political activity was a direct result of their spiritual leanings. Gandhi considered political activity a religious duty. Vivekananda and Sri Aurobindo pleaded for social and political regeneration in the name of Vedanta. Tagore placed man at the centre of his philosophy and considered politics a part of religion of man. Thus, the political philosophy of Vivekananda, Sri Aurobindo, Tagore and Gandhi is based on their metaphysical beliefs and philosophy of religion.

THE STATE AND THE INDIVIDUAL

In consonance with Indian philosophy, contemporary Indian philosophers considered individual freedom as absolutely necessary for any spiritual growth. Therefore, they wanted to limit the state power to the extent of arranging physical goods and managing inter-relationships of the individuals. The state has no right to interfere in the mental and spiritual activities of the individual. This however, does not mean that they thought of a stateless society. In tradition with ancient Indian political thought they believed that the state has a useful function to perform. In fact, Indian political philosophers never thought that the conflict of the state and the individual is inevitable. Harmony has been the central principle of Indian thought, in social as well as political matters. Therefore, there should be a harmony between the rights and duties of the state and the individual.

LIMITATION OF STATE POWER

According to Gandhi, the laws of the state must be obeyed by every citizen but when the state becomes an oppressor the individual has a moral right to oppose the state. This opposition should be however, by non-violent means such as non-cooperation or *Satyagraha,* etc. It should never be by violent means. The thinking of Vivekananda, Sri Aurobindo and Tagore is almost similar to that of Gandhi. They have however, not thought sufficiently over this problem because while Gandhi was in the forefront of Indian political activity, Tagore, Sri Aurobindo, and Vivekananda were not so much immersed in it. Gandhian concept of limitation and opposition of state power is important because it guided the Indian National movement against the British people. In this movement, Gandhi pleaded for giving more and more rights to the citizens and limiting the state power purely to administrative and economic functions. Even the judiciary functions could be done by the agencies of local self-government such as panchayats etc.

DECENTRALIZATION

India is a vast country. Agriculture is the main profession here. Both these factors are important in political philosophy. Such a vast country cannot be governed by an overcentralized political authority. Therefore, Indian political thinkers, since ancient times, always pleaded for decentralization of political power. This decentralization was mainly in the form of giving almost all the rights to the village panchayats. In his scheme of ideal democracy in India, Gandhi envisaged that every village should have a panchayat, which should be given all the economic, social and political rights about the administration of the unit. Whatever the government has to do should be done through panchayat. Only the police work requires government interference. Even the economic and judicial matters may be decided by the panchayat. This idea was accepted by Tagore as well as who established panchayat in every village of his big Zamindari and himself looked after their efficient working. Vivekananda and Sri Aurobindo have praised the ancient Indian system of decentralization through village panchayats. All these thinkers were against centralization in the economic field as well. Therefore, they pleaded for small scale and cottage industries. This is also due to their emphasis on the virtue of self-reliance. Self-reliance can be developed only through decentralization.

INTENSE PATRIOTISM

Vivekananda and Sri Aurobindo were great patriots of India. Through their fiery lectures they diffused a sentimental patriotism in the masses which almost amounted to the worship of the motherland. To them patriotism was the greatest virtue and therefore they asked their countrymen to awake and arise so that India may find its proper place in the community of nations. Tagore, though not so much sentimental in his patriotism, was no less a patriot than any other. As a protest against British firing in Jalianwala bagh, he returned all the certificates and honours conferred by the British Government upon him. Whenever there was any serious occasion in national movement, Tagore always raised his voice and expressed his views to his countrymen. Gandhi was the greatest leader of the patriots in national movement. It was under his able guidance that the Indian masses could overthrow the British rule and achieved independence.

STAUNCH NATIONALISM

All these thinkers were staunch nationalists. They accepted that each nation in the world has a right to develop its individuality and others should not interfere in it. Sovereignty is essential for a nation. Besides sovereignty a nation also requires a common national language. Vivekananda, Tagore, Sri Aurobindo and Gandhi, therefore, pleaded for complete independence of the country from British rule. They advocated the teaching of Sanskrit. Here Vivekananda was extreme in his emphasis upon making Sanskrit a national language. This was not acceptable to M.K. Gandhi, a man of the masses who wanted this place to be given to Hindustani in Devanagri script. Tagore and Sri Aurobindo also accepted this formula though they themselves were also in favour of retaining the teaching of English in India. All of these however agreed that propagation of national language will help in constituting a nation. Another constituent of a nation, according to Vivekananda, is religion. This religion, according to Vivekananda, was Hindu. Tagore, on the other hand, was more cosmopolitan in his approach. He did not consider religion as essential for a nation and if at all a religion was required that should be a religion of humanity. Gandhi, the political leader of all the sections of Indian masses, could not ignore the religion of any section. Therefore, he pleaded for religious tolerance. In his evening prayer Koran and Bible were recited alongwith *Bhagwadgita*.

SYNTHETIC APPROACH TO RELIGION

Vivekananda, Sri Aurobindo, Tagore and Gandhi advocated a synthetic approach to religion. This synthetic approach to religion was the essence of the teachings of Ramakrishna, the spiritual Guru of Vivekananda. Vivekananda and Sri Aurobindo preached for unity of world religion. M.K. Gandhi suggested that we can develop national religion by synthesis of all the important religions. This synthetic approach to religion, advocated by these thinkers was essentially based upon their faith in Vedanta philosophy.

INTERNATIONALISM

Vivekananda, Sri Aurobindo, Tagore and Gandhi were born in a time when the Indian people were feeling the oppression of British rule in India and opposing it tooth and nail. It was an ideal atmosphere for the awakening of national consciousness. This was done by all of the contemporary Indian philosophers. They were however, against national chauvinism and national egoism. They, on the other hand, presented a concept of spiritual nationalism. Spiritual nationalism is not opposed to internationalism. Therefore, all these thinkers were internationalists in spite of being nationalists. Nationalism was exhibited in sentimental form by Vivekananda and Sri Aurobindo and in a lesser tone by M.K. Gandhi. Tagore even sometimes condemned it as a narrow mentality, a hindrance to internationalism.

EAST AND WEST

At the time when these thinkers were active, the West was gradually coming to know the East. In this process of introducing the East to the West Tagore, Sri Aurobindo, Gandhi and Vivekananda performed a service unparalleled by any other thinkers of the East. Tagore was the first Indian to be awarded nobel prize for literature, the highest award for excellence in a field in the West. Vivekananda, through his lectures on Vedanta, introduced Indian philosophy and religion and also ideas about social and political thinking to the West. His lectures were widely attended and intensely praised. Books by Sri Aurobindo and Dr. S. Radhakrishnan, concerning Indian philosophy, find thousands of interested readers in the West. M.K. Gandhi was a political leader in Africa even before coming to India. His introduction of non-violent means in politics made him an international political thinker. Ever since he introduced them they were discussed by eminent political thinkers of the West. Thus, these thinkers could manage to arouse a sense of admiration of the East in the West. They were also conscious of the contribution of the West to the East and they did acknowledge it. On the other hand they pleaded upon the Western elite to know the East and to follow it particularly in spiritual matters. Thus, Tagore, Gandhi and Vivekananda, Sri Aurobindo and Radhakrishnan stood for a synthesis of East and West, spirituality and science, peace and activity.

FORMS OF GOVERNMENT

As these thinkers were very much concerned with the regeneration of masses in India, they naturally pondered over various forms of Government, advanced their criticism and suggested for the ideal form of government. They were critical of monarchy, oligarchy, and aristocracy or any such form of government which did not accept the principles of equality and liberty. Therefore, the ideal form of government according to them can be such in which all the citizens enjoy equality and liberty. The ideal government again is self-government. As absolute self-government is not possible, there may be some minimum form of governing in a country. But self-government should be encouraged more and more. It is hence that these thinkers advocated the panchayat rule in the villages.

SPIRITUAL DEMOCRACY

Thus, Vivekananda, Sri Aurobindo, Radhakrishnan, Tagore and Gandhi considered democracy as the ideal form of Government. They, however, advanced a spiritual interpretation of liberty, equality and fraternity, the three chief values of democracy. A special characteristics of this spiritual interpretation was realization of harmony between the three ideals. Thus, they pleaded for the establishment of spiritual democracy, a form of government in which maximum number of people may secure maximum liberty and equality and achieve spiritual fraternity between them. As against the British rule in India they pleaded for self-rule that is *Swarajya*. The reason for this however, was religious and spiritual. *Swarajya* is closely linked with the idea of *Swadharma* and it is absolutely necessary for any spiritual progress.

ECONOMIC REGENERATION OF MASSES

Vivekananda, Sri Aurobindo, Tagore and Gandhi were equally concerned with the pitiable condition of the poor masses in India. They were pained to see the wide gulf between the rich and the poor in this country. They pleaded for providing bread and home to everyone. They had an intimate knowledge of the problems of the labourers and they had great respect for them. They were convinced that the future of the country depended not so much upon those who worked through the mind but upon those who worked by hand. The future of the country depends upon those and the labourers and less upon the so-called elite. All these were worshippers of the masses. Therefore, they presented an economic philosophy in which an economic regeneration of Indian masses may be possible. India is an agricultural country. Therefore, they suggested improvements in agriculture. Vivekananda, Tagore and Gandhi were against the establishment of big industries in private or public sectors. Big industries in public sector may be established to manufacture only those machines which are required for cottage industries. Since manpower in India is very cheap, the country hardly requires machine power. Introduction of machine power, on the other hand, throws man-power out of employment.

Therefore, these thinkers were against the mechanisation and introduction of large scale industries. Another reason for this opposition is their faith in the traditional economic philosophy of minimising needs. Indian thinkers have always insisted upon minimising needs, rather than the enjoyment of comforts and needs. *Aparigraha* has always been considered a great virtue in this country. Indian philosophers believed that where wealth accumulates man degenerates. Therefore, they have always been against accumulation of wealth and even if wealth is acquired, it should be used not for selfish ends but for social good. It was with this background that Gandhi presented the ideal of trusteeship of the rich man. The rich man is a trustee of his wealth and he should use it for the good of the people.

Thus, in spite of issuing severe warning to the hoarders, the capitalists and the mill owners against exploitation of the masses, Vivekananda, Tagore and Gandhi did not consider class struggle and class hatred as necessary for the economic regeneration of the country. They hoped that the capitalists and the rich men may be persuaded to provide for welfare of the labourers. They thought that encouraging hatred and violence in any section will ultimately diffuse them in society. Therefore, they were against the Marxist idea of waging a violent war against capitalism. They wanted a revolution but insisted that this revolution should be absolutely non-violent, as a violent revolution is bound to have its reactions to the opposite direction in future.

SWADESHI AND BOYCOTT

The economic philosophy of these thinkers was very much linked with the practical programmes of economic regeneration of the country which they suggested from time to time. An important idea in this programme was their insistence on *Swadeshi* and Boycott of the foreign goods. The idea of *Swadeshi* is closely linked with the ideals of *Swadharma* and *Swarajya*. M.K. Gandhi chalked out a whole programme for economic regeneration of the country. This programme included spinning and weaving of cloth, small scale industries, cooperative farming, improving the stock of animals and so on.

THE IDEAL OF *SARVODAYA*

The Ideal of social reconstruction according to Vivekananda, Sri Aurobindo and Gandhi may be summed up in the Gandhian concept of *sarvodaya*. This ideal was not the welfare of a particular section or even of that of the maximum number but the welfare of all. Therefore, the schemes of reconstruction particularly insisted upon the progress of backward classes such as women, poor, and the scheduled caste etc. This is so because these thinkers were convinced that unless the backward classes are brought forward society cannot progress. About the means of social reconstruction these thinkers generally emphasised non-violence and *Swadeshi*. Non-violence in social and economic field means abstaining from injuring others' social and economic rights. It means elimination of all exploitation. This, however, does not require expropriation of the expropriators. It could be done by creating awakening in the masses and by persuading the exploiters to desist from this immoral activity and to realise their real selves.

MEANS OF SOCIAL RECONSTRUCTION

All of our contemporary Indian philosophers were intimately aware of the backwardness prevailing in the country. According to Vivekananda, the chief causes responsible for India's degeneration are absence of *Sraddha,* Anglicised spirit, dishonesty, disregard for physical well-being etc., Fall of *Kshatra* spirit. Fear-complex, lack of originality and enterprise, laziness, narrowness, neglect of religion, etc. He suggested three important remedies to these evils — emancipation of women, uplift of the masses and positive education. The position of Tagore and Gandhi is almost similar to that of Vivekananda here. They were also conscious of the above mentioned defects and they also laid emphasis upon uplift of women and backward classes, uplift of the masses and provision of positive education. Both Tagore and Gandhi suggested several important means of social reconstruction.

The education ideals advocated by these thinkers were very much similar and in tune with ancient Indian philosophy of education. The ideal of education was the all-round evolution of the child. They laid emphasis upon the moral and religious education particularly so that spiritual qualities may be developed. They considered for a separate syllabi for human education. They insisted upon the need of compulsory and free primary education through mother tongue.

CAPITALISM, SOCIALISM AND COMMUNISM

During the period when Vivekananda, Sri Aurobindo, Radhakrishnan, Tagore and Gandhi were active, the most prevalent social philosophies were represented by capitalism, socialism and communism. Being highly educated and also having occasion to come in direct contact of the West where these were being practised, these philosophers fully realised the advantages and disadvantages of these systems. In their opposition to capitalism they were with Karl Marx and other anti-capitalist thinkers. They admired socialism, particularly its creed of equality and liberty. They, however, did not agree with the Western type of socialism which was brought about primarily by means of class war. They presented a spiritual or vedantic interpretation of socialism. They condemned the ideology of communism as it involved violence and dictatorship of a section over the other. They agreed with anarchism so far as minimising the functions of the state is concerned but they knew that the state cannot be absolutely eliminated. They, on the other hand, wanted to maintain it as an agency of social welfare in subordination to the people.

SPIRITUAL HUMANISM

The alternative to socialism and communism, as suggested by contemporary Indian philosophers, may be called spiritual humanism. As has been already pointed out, they gave a spiritual interpretation to democracy and socialism. They wanted to establish a spiritual society leading to spiritual progress of the individual and ultimately of all humanity. They were humanist since they placed man in the centre of their philosophies — social, economic and political. In spiritual humanism the lower unit is not subordinate to the higher nor is it eliminated in its progress to the higher. The higher, on the other hand, integrates the lower and achieves its total evolution. Thus, in a spiritual society the individual achieves maximum liberty and equality. Inter-personal relationships are guided by the spiritual ideal of fraternity. Nationalism progresses towards spiritual level in which all the constituents of the nation achieve spiritual progress. Elimination of national egoism and its substitution by spirituality is a permanent safeguard against future universal catastrophies. Thus, peace and prosperity may be established on the earth. International relations may be based upon the principle of harmony and tolerance so that the whole humanity may develop as one community. Religions need not conflict as in a synthetic approach they all appear as different approaches to the same one spirit.

Characteristics of Contemporary Humanism

This humanism expresses itself most clearly in contemporary Indian socio-political thought through the following characteristic features:

1. These thinkers have granted a focal place to man even in their philosophy of history. Since man is converted into a mere tool of material forces in the materialism of Karl Marx, these thinkers have refuted the notion of economic determinism. All of them have accepted the importance of human individuals in history, and they have given a noteworthy place to great men. On the other hand, all these philosophers also regard the common man as important and believe that the true process of history is the evolution in the consciousness of this common man. The humanist viewpoint in the philosophy of history is not clearly manifested in the psychological explanation of history provided by Sri Aurobindo. It should be remembered that psychology is essentially a human science which studies human beings. Thus, it is better to accept psychological forces as the determiners of history. From this point of view, Sri Aurobindo, among the contemporary Indian political thinkers, made the most notable contribution to the philosophy of history. Humanism is also the basis of M.K. Gandhi's non-violent philosophy of history because, as he says, while violence is the characteristic of the animal, non-violence is man's typical trait. In their analysis of the evolution of world cultures, Rabindranath and Jawahar Lal Nehru have also demonstrated the growth towards human values.

2. Because of their humanistic explanation of the philosophy of history, these thinkers advocated a humanistic concept of social progress. According to this concept the criterion of the progress of a society is the degree or extent to which that society gives importance to human values. In other words, the greater the importance attached to human values in a society, the greater is the degree of social progress in it.
3. Since these thinkers accept synthesis as their philosophical base, they believe that the individual and the collective group, the citizen and the state are mutually complementary entities. None of them has advocated anarchism. They are neither individualists nor collectivists, they believe that one is impossible without the other. According to them, individual and collective welfare are mutually complementary, between which there is no difference. Though some of these thinkers demonstrated a parallel relationship between the individual and the group because of the intimate relationship between the two, their synthetical viewpoint makes them better fitted for solving the problems of the relationship between the individual and the group. Since the state is a man-made institution, in other words, a means or a tool, these thinkers, in keeping with the ancient Indian tradition, treat society and not the state as prominent. The state is only a means to the welfare of society. But this does not imply that it can be completely eradicated. In view of the structure of human nature, the state is necessary. However, it should be employed solely as a means to human welfare.
4. It follows, therefore, that the state does not have the right to interfere in the individual's freedom under any circumstances. Laws are made not to eradicate, destroy or undermine freedom but to ensure its safety. This alone is the basis of their acceptance and compulsion. If they fail to provide this security, they can be violated, but under all other circumstances, they must be obeyed. The purpose of the law is to bring about justice of every kind — social, economic, or of any other kind. Its ultimate basis is humanism or humanistic values. Every individual should be provided with the best opportunities for every kind of growth. This is the highest objective of law. Hence, freedom and law are mutually complementary and for justice, both are equally important.
5. Consequently, all these thinkers regard that state as the ideal which can make provision for every kind of progress, which can provide for every class and every individual in society without any discrimination, which gives the individual the maximum freedom for his integral development and where the law is the protector and not the destroyer of this freedom. M.K. Gandhi gave the name of *'Ram Rajya'* to this ideal state and while Jawahar Lal Nehru called it the socialist state, Manvendra Roy gave it the name radical democracy. Thus, there is no fundamental distinction between the various concepts of an ideal

state advanced by all contemporary Indian political thinkers from Sri Aurobindo to Manvendra Roy.

6. Hence, the supreme form of government is that which can bring about the existence of this ideal state. Because of this attitude, these thinkers were critical of anarchism on the one hand and fascism, autocracy, oligarchy, aristocracy etc. on the other. This criticism was consistently based on humanist criterion. The government is merely a tool for administering the state, and the objective of this instrument is to create the ideal state.
7. It follows from the above, therefore, that the ideal form of government is democracy. And, even in democracy, these thinkers advocate the form of spiritual democracy so that the highest worth may be attached to spiritual values. Sri Aurobindo, Rabindranath and M.K Gandhi have been specific in their advocacy of a spiritualistic democracy. Roy's radical democracy is also the same. The concept of a spiritualistic democracy is a basically humanistic concept about the form of government. Consequently, it is the one ideal for every nation.
8. From the humanist angle, these thinkers have founded politics on ethics. This characteristic undoubtedly renders their thinking contemporary in the history of political thought. It is the basis of the future development of political science. Medieval political thought was not humanist whereas modern political thought is markedly humanist. Consequently, the medieval solutions posited by medieval political thought cannot be adequate guides for the present age.
9. It is for this reason that in national movements or political revolutions it is necessary to pay attention to both ends and means. These thinkers have emphasized that even in the principles of political change, the humanist bias should not be disturbed. As a result all of them favour non-violent means and seek to eradicate violent means to the extent possible. A theory of this kind unquestionably grants a humanist bias to the concept of revolution. That is why these thinkers are severe critics of the Marxist doctrine.
10. In fine, education should be a medium for the evolution of a generation which is humanistic, which regards nationalism as only one step in the growth towards internationalism. Assuming that unity in diversity is a basic element, these thinkers do not interpret humanism to mean the destruction of diversity. Instead, they want to maintain the individual identity of each nation within the framework of internationalism.

Negation of Worldly Knowledge

Ancient Indian Vedanta considered wordly knowledge as knowledge of phenomena and not knowledge of noumena and since the latter were the real knowledge, they called the knowledge of the world an ignorance. This again, was not challenged by our contemporary Indian philosophers though each one of them clearly said that the wordly knowledge is very important for individual and society. Again, though they considered social service, service of the poor and the weak as primary duties, they were always means and never ends. Now, if service of man is a mere means for God realisation no wonder that it is left aside by those who pursue other means such as prayer, penance, devotion or knowledge etc. Though in theory it appears that the Vedanta philosophy finds a place for social service, in actual practice it has never been so. This is the reason why decades after the preachings of these philosophers contemporary Indian society finds a very insignificant place for humanistic ideals or social service.

The psychological reasons for the undermining of social philosophy in ancient Indian thought have been active in our contemporary times as well. Ancient Indian thinkers and most of the religious people even now consider God realisation possible by the negation of the world. Most of the techniques of the spiritual practice even today are individualistic in character as they were in ancient India. Facts have been neglected, particularly the social facts. Indian philosophers laid more emphasis on the knowledge and devotion than on action and in spite of the protests of some activist thinkers like B.G. Tilak and M.K. Gandhi, this emphasis has continued in our own time. There is small wonder therefore that social philosophy has been neglected.

In spite of all efforts about industrial progress in India the country even today is primarily agricultural. Therefore, the sociological reasons determining the sorry state of social thinking of ancient India continue right now. Contemporary Indian society is primarily agricultural and therefore slow changing, tradition-minded, against new changes, anti-revolutionary, and narrow in outlook. Among the intelligentsia also the traditional trend of thinking being more dominant there has not been much change in the attitude of social thinkers.

The Defects of Mayavada

An analysis of the social thought of Sri Aurobindo, Rabindranath and M.K. Gandhi shows that the philosophical foundation of their thought was the Neo-Vedanta philosophy. This system of thought is Vedanta first and neo, or its novel form later. As far as the Vedanta philosophy is concerned, it assumes the *Sachchidananda Param Brahman* to be the prime substance. According to it, all individuals and all nations are the varied manifestations of the same Reality Brahman. In this way, the variety of the human race finds its ultimate identity in Brahman. However, the Vedanta philosophy, in its ancient form, did not explicitly accept the reality of the universe. As a matter of fact, of all the commentaries written on Vedanta philosophy, the most current and widely circulated has been Shankaracharya's commentary or the Advaita philosophy. Although Shankaracharya was truly the greatest social and political reformer of his age, and a symbol of unification of the nation, the principle propounded by him that the world is maya, became one of the causes of backwardness of social and political thinking in this country. Although contemporary Indian social thinkers sought rational and practical solutions to them they never really succeeded in erasing the stamp of mayavada from their thought. The sole exception to this was Sri Aurobindo. M.K. Gandhi's philosophy shows clear impress of mayavada on almost every aspect of his thought. Rabindranath's thought falls into the same class, though his humanism saves him from deteriorating into escapism. One important reason for his escaping the deep imprint of mayavada was that he was mainly a poet while M.K. Gandhi was primarily a political leader. Sri Aurobindo alone was a pure philosopher, and so he was best fitted to challenge and refute mayavada, and to provide an alternative to it in the form of Leelavada, which he established. Nevertheless, the influence of mayavada, as propounded in the ancient Vedanta, remained consistently opposed to aggressive thought and action in the social and political fields in India.

CRITICAL EVALUATION

One-Sided Interpretation of History

We have already pointed out that our contemporary Indian thinkers have interpreted history as a Divine process. While the disadvantages of the economic interpretation of history, are obvious, spiritual interpretation also has its own limitations. In spite of all the emphasis on human efforts by our social thinkers the general masses and even the elite have on the whole been depending upon providence. The ancient message of Gita that whenever the society faces a challenge, God comes in the form of a reincarnation, has only encouraged popular indolence and passivity since the people have been waiting for such an incarnation. Our religious leaders have always had faith in miracles. Therefore, there should be no wonder that the people, instead of making efforts for reform or revolution, have been waiting for miracles on the part of the God to ameliorate their condition. However sincere may be the efforts of our contemporary philosophers and whatever inner meaning they might have given to their interpretation of history, its impact on masses and even on elite has not been very healthy. Probably it is due to the reason that in their philosophy of history, facts and human planning and efforts never found sufficient place.

Contradiction in Philosophy of Religion

In the field of religion the synthetic approach, presented by our contemporary philosophers, has been definitely an improvement. It has led to religious tolerance and catholicity very much needed in this country. And yet at the same time Sri Aurobindo, Radhakrishnan, Gandhi and Vivekananda were proud of being Hindu. They undoubtedly knew the defects of Hindu religion and yet they pleaded that every one should follow his own religion. The Gandhian formula of recitation from Bible, Quran and Gita in his daily prayer appeared to be hotch-potch to many of the more serious thinkers. Besides Gandhian synthesis of religion and politics also led to mixing of religion with politics by others who misused it to the disadvantage of the country at large. M.A. Jinnah organized followers of Muslim religion and demanded a separate part of the county for them. In spite of the heroic fight of Gandhi against Jinnah the latter won the game. Whatever may be the reasons behind this disaster one academic reason may be the unsuitable marriage of politics with religion. Gandhi called himself a religious man and considered it his religious duty to delve in politics. On the other hand, some may say that politics has been generally a game of scoundrels and many will not agree that there can be a real synthesis between politics and religion. Though the religious basis of political philosophy may have its own advantages, it is certainly not without its disadvantages as well. These disadvantages have been very clear in India.

Too Much Traditionalism

In spite of being very well acquainted with the actual condition of different sections of the country and having keen minds required for analysis of these problems the traditionalism in the thinking of our contemporary philosophers led to the application of old principles to new problems. One may agree that if the problems are identical the old principles can be certainly applied to them. Distinctions, however, are more important than similarities in clear thinking. While social and political problems of our own time appear to be very much similar to those of the old, we should keep our eye particularly upon the distinctions since these distinctions will make a lot of difference in remedies. It was due to the neglect of this fact that the philosophies of Vivekananda, Sri Aurobindo, Tagore and Gandhi could not be as much influential in actually solving the problems of the country as they would have been otherwise.

Difference between individual and social development

By assuming a parallel relationship between the individual and the collectivity, these philosophers were led to the erroneous assumption that individual development inevitably leads to social development. Sri Aurobindo's theory of the future development of man is based on this assumption. Through his yoga he came to experience the supramental consciousness, from which he concluded that the supramental consciousness would soon be established at the collective level, and thus a supramental race would come into existence. Such great men as Sri Aurobindo and M.K. Gandhi have always made the mistake of assuming that whatever they achieve in their individual lives can also be achieved at the collective level. For example, in his concept of basic education, M.K. Gandhi advocated that children should make articles of daily use in the schools and hoped that these would sell at high prices in the market because people would wish to encourage the children. But, it was observed in practice that the things made in these basic schools could not even be sold. Sri Aurobindo was more practical than M.K Gandhi. For instance, while M.K. Gandhi talked of completely eliminating violence from international politics, Sri Aurobindo pointed out to the psychological fact that love and brotherhood exist between individuals, not between nations. But while elucidating his visions of man's future, Sri Aurobindo committed the same mistake of hoping that the evolution which has occurred in his own consciousness would also occur at the collective level.

The Individual and the State

Indian political thought does not distinguish between social philosophy and political philosophy. Ancient Indian philosophers did not distinguish between society and the state. In keeping with this tradition contemporary social philosophers in India also do not distinguish between society and state. Consequently, they have frequently attempted a synthesis between the individual and the state. According to M.K. Gandhi, every citizen must obey the laws of the state. According to these thinkers, the state was evolved for the welfare of individuals, and there is no inevitable conflict between the individual and state. In fact there is harmony between them. This does not imply that individuals have transferred all rights to the state. Even ancient Indian political scientists emphatically suggested that the state has the right to run the government only insofar as it brings out the welfare of its citizens. In failing to do so, the state forfeits its right to govern. In the same way M.K. Gandhi also favoured the disobedience of the laws of the state only in those circumstances in which opposition is ethically justified, since ethical laws are above judicial laws. The ideas of Rabindranath and Sri Aurobindo also correspond to M.K. Gandhi's views. All of them have emphasized the freedom of the individual. Even greater proponents of freedom were Jawahar Lal Nehru and Manvendra Roy. All these thinkers favoured the restriction of the powers of the state so as to maintain individual freedom. According to them, the state has no right to interfere in the mental or intellectual or spiritual activities of the individual. All that the state can do is to organize the distribution and possession of material goods.

Decentralization of State Authority

In the same manner, all these thinkers are also in favour of decentralization of the state's power. This concept of decentralization has been integral to Indian political thought from ancient times. In conformity with the tradition, these thinkers have supported the idea of decentralization of state authority down to the level of the village. All of the them favoured the eradication of Zamindari, development of the panchayats, community programme, development of small and cottage industries, and other schemes leading to social, economic and political decentralization. However, it is important to note at this point that while the inspiration for this concept of decentralisation was purely Indian for Sri Aurobindo, Rabindranath and M.K. Gandhi, it was purely Western for Jawahar Lal Nehru and Manvendra Roy who derived it from Western democracies. From the viewpoint of *swadeshi* or indigenous production, the former basis appears far more suitable for India, although in essence, the difference in the source of inspiration makes no difference in the view of these thinkers.

Explanation and Support of Freedom

All the contemporary Indian philosophers considered in the present work provided a spiritual elaboration of freedom. According to them, true freedom is not lack of discipline, but self-discipline. According to Jawahar Lal Nehru and Manvendra Roy, this self-discipline means the control of the reason over man, but according to Sri Aurobindo, Rabindranath and M.K. Gandhi it implies the control exercised by the soul. This latter concept conforms to ancient Indian social thought whereas the former is derived from Western thought. Despite this difference, all these thinkers have advocated the granting of the maximum possible freedom to all individuals in every sphere, and the reduction to the minimum of state authority over the individual. All these thinkers conceive of law as self-control, and so they emphasize its obedience. By calling a law a form of self-control, it is possible to point to its source. It clarifies that the law should be based on public opinion and public consciousness, which implies that if a law is not derived from these sources, it can be opposed because it is not supported by the principle of self-control. Self-control gives to law an ethical base without which the compulsion implicit in law is destroyed. In fact, the only compulsion to which man is subject is the ethical compulsion which is identical to self-compulsion. Law derives its compulsive force exclusively from this source. If laws violating this ethical basis are formulated, they should be opposed. It is because of this that contemporary Indian philosophers have attempted a synthesis of ethics and politics on the one hand and ethical rules and judicial laws on the other. However, all of them regard ethics as superior to politics, and ethical rules as superior to laws.

Explanation of Social Justice

On the question of social justice, certain differences are observed between the traditionalist social thinkers of contemporary India and those influenced by Western thought, but fundamentally they are all proponents of democratic values. From this viewpoint, M.K. Gandhi raised the concept of social justice to its idealistic limits. His concept of social justice has been elaborated in his notion of *Sarvodaya*. Jawahar Lal Nehru accepted this Gandhian concept and with this end in view, he provided forceful support to the cause of the minorities and their rights.

Manvendra Roy clarified the democratic view of justice. Sri Aurobindo adopted the integral approach towards justice, according to which justice means that every individual in society, irrespective of his class or position, should be given the opportunity to develop according to his own nature, and the circumstances should be created so that *Swadharma* can be achieved. In this way, the concept of justice adopted by these philosophers is humanistic, in which justice has been taken to mean the development of every aspect of the individual's personality, every member of a class, every class in society, and every nation in the world, each according to its own nature.

Oversimplified Psychology

It has been already pointed out these thinkers interpreted human nature in a religious and spiritual sense. Man, according to them, is a spark of the Divine. This co-called idealistic interpretation of human nature is oversimplified and far from being adequate. Gandhian principle that whatever is possible in the life of an individual is equally practicable on the mass scale only, shows his ignorance of mass psychology. He was in the habit of experimenting upon methods and techniques in his own personal life and thinking that whatever is possible for him to do should be so for any other. This thinking is fallacious and based upon wrong psychology. The fact is that something possible for a very religious person may be possible only for an exceptional person and should not be presented as a formula for mass application. This defect in the social philosophy of M.K Gandhi has been the chief reason of its failure to actually and sufficiently influence different fields of social and political life. Sri Aurobindo's speculation about gnostic individuals and gnostic race are utopian.

In conformity with ancient Indian ideal of harmony, these philosophers everywhere searched for a formula to achieve harmony in social and political fields. It is undeniable that harmony is a healthy principle and nothing is better if it can be achieved but no one can deny the role of the disintegrating processes such as conflict, competition, aggression and even violence. It can be said in favour of advocates of non-violent means that the future of humanity entirely rests upon our faith in them. But human nature as it appears in history shows that non-violence is not the best means in every circumstance and so long as human nature remains what it is, it is dangerous to propose the application of non-violent means in every situation. Sri Aurobindo, among all these philosophers, has pointed out the role of conflict and violence in delivering goods.

Disadvantages of Religious Definitions

Besides the definition of the individual on the basis of religion, society too was defined by our contemporary thinkers as an expression of the Divine. This definition, while on the one hand highlights Divine virtues and characteristics, it on the other hand, fails to pay sufficient attention to the animal characteristics. According to contemporary social psychologists masses are more governed by animal instincts rather than rational thinking and still less by spiritual incentives. It is therefore, doubtful that religious or spiritual formula may be successful in the case of mass behaviour. Religious influence on political thought is very much explicit in the Gandhian ideal of *Ramrajya*. Whatever may be its inner meaning for Gandhi himself, the historical fact is that the people generally understand Rama as a king and the term *Ramrajya* smacks of favour to monarchy. Undoubtedly, Gandhi was himself the greatest champion of democracy yet his unhappy marriage of religion with politics has been a cause of so much misunderstanding about his social and political thinking. The present Indian Constitution advocates a secular approach in the field of religion. One may wonder as to how far the religious leanings of our contemporary Indian philosophers may fit with this concept of secular society. Gandhi himself was one of the architects of Indian Constitution but he never raised his voice against secularism or found any inconsistency between secularism and religion.

Contradictory Ideals of Social Stratification

In the philosophy of society our thinkers have everywhere admired the ancient Varna system. It is undeniable that there can be no theoretical objection against the Varna system as a basis of social stratification. But who can deny that this very system itself must have something in it which led to its degeneration in caste system and finally in casteism and untouchability. To wage a war against casteism and untouchability on the one hand and to praise Varna system on the other, smacks of revivalism which is certainly a feature of contemporary Indian social philosophy. Whatever may be said about the principle of equality among different Varnas, in actual practice the followers of this system laid more emphasis upon distinctions rather than upon similarities with the result that more and more disintegration between different Varnas increased.

Compromises in Economic Philosophy

Alongwith political and social thinking the economic philosophy of our thinkers was also governed by a search for the principle of harmony among different sections. They were intimately aware of the plight of the poor and the labourers of the country and knew very well the exploitation and oppression unleashed by the capitalist and the higher classes. They even sometimes challenged this exploitation and also condemned it but ultimately they wanted to arrive at some sort of compromise between the exploiters and exploited. Whatever may be the merit of Gandhian theory of trusteeship, its inapplicability is apparent from the fact that several decades after the advocacy of this theory not even a single capitalist in the country could change his heart or come anywhere near to the ideal of trustee so much cherished by Gandhi. When social philosophy gives such an important place to ideals that it forgets the facts, followers of other disciplines have some justification in pointing out that social philosophy cannot deliver the goods and however one may philosophise about social and political problems they have hardly much practical value.

Deeper Solution for Surface Problems

The above discussion does not mean minimising the merits and advantages of the contemporary Indian philosophy. Contemporary Indian philosophers certainly presented a most comprehensive philosophy and rightly based it upon the traditional philosophy of India. They rightly tried to build up a philosophy in tradition with ancient Indian idealism and spiritualism. In the fields of social and political philosophy they rightly avoided all types of extremism and endeavoured at synthetic approach. Their analyses and suggestions, however, have not been very consistent. One reason of this inconsistency was their search for deeper solutions of the surface problems. This is particularly evident in Sri Aurobindo's remedy of all human ills through integral Yoga. Going to details and always returning to the basic issues has its advantages in thinking but if the surface view of the problems is neglected the solutions offered are far from being successful. It is characteristic of our culture that we are always in search of eternal solutions and never satisfied with temporary arrangements. But some problems in social and political field are temporary and therefore require a temporary arrangement. Moreover, overemphasis on eternity leads to negligence of social change. Social change is as much necessary for the growth of a society as social stability. In Indian social system while we have craved for stability we have not so much favoured social change. That is one reason why our society and its social thinking has not been sufficiently progressive and revolutionary.

Lack of Proper National Perspective

Another important reason for the inconsistency visible in the philosophies of our contemporary thinkers is their emphasis on mass appeal. All of them were mass leaders. They presented their thought generally in the form of public lectures and replies to questions of their followers. They were never academic thinkers. Tagore was an eminent poet but his grasp over social and political problems may be doubted. This can be seen in the inconsistency found in his concept of nationalism and internationalism. While favouring nationalism he praised it like other thinkers of his time. On the other hand while praising internationalism he sometimes condemned nationalism as narrow thinking. Vivekananda was the only contemporary philosopher besides Sri Aurobindo, who championed the cause of nationalism in social thinking, otherwise both Tagore and Gandhi were more internationalists rather than nationalists. This lack of proper perspective towards nationalism has been a cause of so much failure of our relationship with other countries, and the inadequacies of our foreign policy.

Lack of Interdisciplinary Approach

As leaders of the masses these philosophers were very well aware of the conditions of different sections of Indian society and they tried their best to suggest remedies for them. They, however, seldom cared to consult specialists in different branches of knowledge such as the economists, the political scientists, the sociologists and the social workers. While presenting their own views they seldom cared to find out the views of academic thinkers upon these problems. This has been the defect of philosophy both in East and West, and it has led to its derogation as a field of knowledge. Perhaps it has been left to future Indian philosophers to present a more rational, realistic, interdisciplinary, synthetic and balanced philosophy which may imbibe the advantages of all the different trends in contemporary Indian philosophy.

Bibliography

Ajit Bhattacharjea, *Jayaprakash Narayan,* New Delhi, Vikas Publishing House, 1971.

A. Appadorai, *Indian Political Thinking,* Oxford University Press, 1971.

A. Stanley and Walport. *Tilak and Gokhale,* California, 1962.

Annie Besant, *India : Bound or Free,* London, Theosophical Publishing Society, 1926.

——, *The Political Status of Women,* London, T.P.S., 1885.

Anthony X. Soares (Ed.) *Lectures and Addresses of Rabindranath Tagore,* London, Macmillan & Co., 1962.

A.B. Purani, *Sri Aurobindo,* Bombay, Bharatiya Vidya Bhawan, 1966.

A.R. Desai, *Social Background of Indian Nationalism,* Bombay, Popular Prakashan, 1966.

Balgangadhar Tilak, *His Speeches and Writings,* Madras, 1918.

Bhupendranath Datta, *Swami Vivekananda — Patriot Prophet,* Calcutta, Nabhabharat Publishers, 1954.

B.R. Nanda, *Gokhale,* New Delhi, Oxford University, 1977.

——, *Gokhale, Gandhi and Nehru,* Allen and Unwin, 1974.

B.R. Purohit, *Hindu Revivalism and Indian Nationalism,* Lucknow, Sethi Prakashan, 1965.

B.G. Tilak, *The Making of the Indian Nation,* Bombay, Asia Publishing House, 1960.

B.S. Sharma, *Gandhi as a Political Thinker,* Allahabad, Indian Press, 1956.

C.Y. Chintamani, *Indian Politics Since the Mutiny,* Allahabad, Kitabistan, 1947.

D.B. Mathur, *Gokhale, A Political Biography,* Bombay, Manaktalas, 1966.

Dorothea Jane Stephen, *Studies in Early Indian Thought,* Cambridge University Press, 1918.

Dayanand Swami, *Satyartha Prakash* (Translation into 'Light of Truth' by Chiranjiva Bharadwaja), Allahabad, The Star Press, 1906.

D.V. Tahmankar, *Tilak, Father of Indian Unrest and Maker of Modern India,* London, 1956.

D.V. Athalya, *The Life of Lokamanya Tilak,* Bombay, 1921.

Dwarkadas Kanji, *Indian Freedom Movement,* 1913-37, Bombay, Popular Prakashan, 1966.

F. Max Muller, *Rammohan to Ramakrishna,* Susil Gupta Ltd., Calcutta, 1952.
—— (Ed.), *Laws of Manu* (Tr. by G. Buhler), Delhi, Motilal Banarsidass, 1964.
Gopal S., *Jawaharlal, A Biography* : Vol. I, Bombay, Oxford University Press, 1976.
Hemendra Prasad Ghose, *Aurobindo, The Prophet of Patriotism.* Calcutta, A.K. Mitter.
Haridas T. Muzumdar, *Mahatma Gandhi — Peaceful Revolutionary,* London, Charles Scribner's, 1952.
Iqbal Singh, *Raja Rammohan Roy — Life, Writings and Speeches,* New Delhi, Asia Publishing House.
J. P. 's Jail Life (A collection of personal letters), Arnold Heinemann, 1977.
Jawaharlal Nehru, *Selected Works* (Edited by S. Gopal), New Delhi, Orient Longmans, Vol. 1 to 15, 1972-1982.
Kasiprasad Jaiswal, *Hindu Polity,* Bangalore, The Bangalore Printing Co., Ltd., 1955.
K.P. Karunakaran, *Religion and Political Awakening in India.* Delhi, Meenakshi Prakashan, 1955.
K. Natarajan, *Gokhale, Man and His Message,* Bombay, 1930.
Karan Singh, *Prophet of Indian Nationalism,* London, George Allen & Unwin, 1963.
K.K. Sharma, *Life and Time of Lala Lajpat Rai,* Ambala, India Book Agency, 1975.
Lala Lajpat Rai, *The Arya Samaj,* London, Longman's Green and Co., 1915.
M. A. Buck, *The Development of Contemporary Indian Political Thought,* Vol. I, Baroda, Good Companions.
M.C. Chagla, *J.P. Vindicated,* New Delhi, S. Chand and Co., 1977.
V.D. Mahajan, *The Nationalist Movement in India,* New Delhi, Sterling Publishers, 1979.
M.K. Gandhi, *The Arya Samaj,* Punjab, Arya Pratinidhi Sabha, 1910.
——, *Non-violence in Peace and War,* Vol. I and Vol. II, Ahmedabad, Navjivan Publishing House, 1948.
——, *Hind Swaraj : Indian Home Rule,* Ahmedabad, N.P.H., 1938.
——, *My Non-violence,* Ahmedabad, N.P.H., 1960.
——, *Sarvodaya,* Ahmedabad, N.P.H., 1954.
——, *Gokhale, My Political Guru,* Ahmedabad, 1953.
M.N. Roy, *New Humanism,* Calcutta, Renaissance Publishers, 1961.
——, *Reason, Romanticism and Revolution,* Vols. I and II, Calcutta, Renaissance Publishers, 1952.
Nalin Chandra Ganguli, *Raja Rammohan Roy,* Calcutta, Y.M.C.A., 1934.
N.C. Mehrotra, *Lohia : A Study,* Delhi, Atma Ram and Sons, 1975.
P. Sitaramayya, *History of Indian National Congress,* Bomaby, Padama Publications.
Radhakrishnan, S., *The Religion of Man,* London, George Allen and Unwin, 1961.

Rabindranath Tagore, *Towards Universal Man,* Bombay, Asia Publishing House, 1962.

——, *The Home and the World,* London, Macmillan and Co., 1958.

R.L. Gupta, *J.P. From Marxism to Total Revolution,* New Delhi, Sterling Publishers, 1981.

Rafiq Zakaria, *Rise of Muslims in Indian Politics,* Bombay, Somaiya Publishers, 1971.

Raja Rammohan Roy, *Life, Writings and Speeches,* Madras, G.A. Natesan and Company, 1925.

Raja Rammohan Roy Centenary Commemoration Volume, Lahore, 1934.

Ramgopal, *Lokmanya Tilak,* Bombay, 1956.

R.C. Majumdar, *History of Freedom Movement,* Calcutta, 1963.

Srinivasa Sastri, *My Master Gokhale,* Madras, 1946.

Sri Aurobindo, *The Future Evolution of Man,* London, George Allen and Unwin, 1963.

——, *The Human Cycle,* Pondicherry, 1952.

——, *The Ideal of Human Unity,* Pondicherry, 1962.

Sharma, Ram Nath, *Social Philosophy of Sri Aurobindo,* Vineet, Meerut, 1980.

——, *Sri Aurobindo's Philosophy of Social Development,* Atlantic, Delhi, 1991.

Sharma, U., *Humanism in Contemporary India Political Thought* (Hindi), Vineet, Meerut, 1980.

Tara Chand, *History of the Freedom Movement in India,* New Delhi, Publications Division, 1967.

V.C. Joshi (Ed.), *Writings and Speeches of Lala Lajpat Rai,* Delhi University Publications, 1966.

——, (Ed.), *Autobiographical Writings of Lala Lajpat Rai,* Delhi, 1965.

Vivekananda, Swami, *Complete Works,* Calcutta, Advaita Ashrama.

——, *Practical Vedanta,* Calcutta, Advaita Ashrama, 1958.

V.P. Verma, *The Political Philosophy of Sri Aurobindo,* Bombay, Asia Publishing House, 1960.

V. Nargolkar, *J.P.'s Crusade for Revolution,* New Delhi, S. Chand and Co., 1971.